THE OXFORD
ILLUSTRATED HISTORY OF
TUDOR
& STUART
BRITAIN

EDITED BY

John Morrill

Oxford   New York

OXFORD UNIVERSITY PRESS

1996

Oxford University Press, Walton Street, Oxford OX2 6DP

Oxford New York
Athens Auckland Bangkok Bombay
Calcutta Cape Town Dar es Salaam Delhi
Florence Hong Kong Istanbul Karachi
Kuala Lumpur Madras Madrid Melbourne
Mexico City Nairobi Paris Singapore
Taipei Tokyo Toronto

and associated companies in
Berlin Ibadan

Oxford is a trade mark of Oxford University Press

Published in the United States
by Oxford University Press Inc., New York

British Library Cataloguing in Publication Data

Data available

Library of Congress Cataloging in Publication Data

Data available

ISBN 0–19–820325–X

10 9 8 7 6 5 4 3 2 1

Printed in Great Britain
on acid-free paper by
Butler & Tanner Ltd.
Frome, Somerset

LIST OF CONTRIBUTORS

Simon Adams is Senior Lecturer in History at the University of Strathclyde. He is co-editor of *England, Spain and the Gran Armada* (1991) and of more than forty articles concerned with Elizabethan and early Stuart politics and foreign policy.

John Adamson is Editor of the *History of Parliament 1640–1660* for the History of Parliament Trust and is a Bye-Fellow of Peterhouse, Cambridge. He is the author of many influential essays on the role of the peerage, especially in the period 1560–1660.

Christopher Brooks is Lecturer in History at Durham University and author of many studies of early modern law and society, including *Pettyfoggers and Vipers of the Commonwealth: The 'Lower Branch' of the Legal Profession in Early Modern England* and (as co-editor) *The Middling Sort of People: Culture, Society and Politics in England, 1550–1800* (1994).

Steven G. Ellis is Professor of History at University College Galway. His many books and articles on British and Irish History include *Tudor Ireland: Crown, Community and the Conflict of Cultures 1470–1603* (1985), and *Tudor Frontiers and Noble Power: The Making of the British State* (1995).

Amy Louise Erickson is author of the award-winning *Women and Property in Early Modern England* (1983) and of several articles on the seventeenth century, and is currently engaged by the University of Sussex to study women's higher education in the twentieth century.

Mark Goldie is Lecturer in History at the University of Cambridge and Vice Master of Churchill College. He has written thirty-five articles on politics, religion, and ideas in the seventeenth and eighteenth century and is co-editor of *The Cambridge History of Political Thought, 1450–1700*.

Andrew Gurr is Professor of English at the University of Reading, and chief adviser to the Globe rebuilding project in Southwark. He is the editor of five Renaissance plays and the author of nine books, six of them about the Shakespearian stage, including *Playgoing in Shakespeare's London*, *The Shakespearian Stage, 1574–1642*, and *Shakespeare's Hats*.

John Guy is Provost of St Leonard's College and Professor of Modern History at the University of St Andrews. His ten books include *Tudor England* (1988), *The Public Career of Sir Thomas More* (1980), and an edited collection entitled *The Reign of Elizabeth I: Court and Culture in the Last Decade* (1995).

Christopher Haigh is Lecturer in Modern History at the University of Oxford and Tutor at Christ Church, Oxford. His books on religion and politics in Tudor and Stuart England include *Elizabeth I* (1988) and *English Reformations: Religion, Politics and Society under the Tudors* (1993).

Wallace MacCaffrey is Professor Emeritus of History at Harvard University. His many books include a biography of Elizabeth I and a triptych describing and evaluating the events of Elizabeth's reign.

Diarmaid MacCulloch is Lecturer in Church History at the University of Oxford and a Fellow of St Cross College, Oxford. His books include the award-wining *Tudor Suffolk* (1986) and *The Later Reformation in England 1547–1603* (1990). His study of *Thomas Cranmer: A Life* will be published in 1996.

John Morrill, FBA, is Reader in Early Modern History at the University of Cambridge and Vice Master of Selwyn College. He has written and edited seventeen books mainly about the seventeenth century, including *Oliver Cromwell and the English Revolution* (1990), and *The Nature of the English Revolution* (1992).

Rosemary O'Day is Senior Lecturer in History at the Open University. She has written and edited many books and articles on the history of early modern religion, and has recently published *The Longman Companion to the Tudor Age* (1995).

John Reeve is Senior Lecturer in History at the University of Sydney and is the author of *Charles I and the Road to Personal Rule* (1989) and of several influential essays on the relationship between the domestic and foreign policies of British Kings.

Conrad Russell, FBA, is Professor of British History at King's College, University of London and the author and editor of six books and of many essays on the Tudor and Stuart period, including *The Crisis of Parliaments 1529–1660*, one of the leading textbooks on the period, and *The Causes of the English Civil War* (1991).

Kevin Sharpe is Professor of History at the University of Southampton. He has written and edited seven books, including the award-winning *Criticism and Compliment: the Politics of Literature in the England of Charles I* (1987) and *The Personal Rule of Charles I* (1992).

John Walter is Senior Lecturer in History and Director of the Local History Centre at the University of Essex; his many articles include essays on popular political culture and on social order and social disorder in the Elizabethan and Stuart periods.

Tom Webster is a British Academy Post-Doctoral Fellow at the University of East Anglia. His interests and forthcoming publications include work both on the history of the built environment and on the history of sixtecnth- and seventeenth-century religious thought.

CONTENTS

LIST OF COLOUR PLATES

List of Maps

Editor's Foreword

The Tudor and Stuart centuries are amongst the most dynamic in the whole history of the British Isles. They were centuries above all of growth.

The population doubled causing enormous economic and social strain. A fundamental shift in food production, manufacturing, and internal and external trading patterns took place. Landscape and townscape were transformed throughout much of Britain and London emerged as by far the greatest city in Europe and perhaps in the world.

The forces released by demographic and economic change liberated large numbers of men and women. The number of freeholders, independent farmers, and small producers, and traders in raw and manufactured goods grew rapidly. Hundreds of thousands of households were freed from dependency upon the will of others.

The state grew. In place of the effectively independent kingdoms of England and Scotland, the Lordship of Ireland, and the Principality of Wales, each with control over a core area and diminishing control of its mountainous hinterlands, there was one central monarchy located in south-east England with increasing if still far from perfectly achieved control over the whole of the archipelago.

The responsibilities of the state grew too. The great schism in European Christendom in the sixteenth century allowed and required successive monarchs to define religious truth and religious practice, to set out the parameters of individual rights to freedom of conscience, and to police those parameters (a process now known as confessionalization). And the inexorable growth of population, initially far outstripping the increase of food supply and employment opportunity, enormously expanded the demand on the state to provide for the poor and destitute and to maintain order amongst the marginalized and alienated.

British monarchs dealt with this challenge to their responsibilities not by creating an army of bureaucrats who were a charge to the state and therefore to the tax-paying portion of the population, but by entering into alliances with local élites. The great thickening of the texture of government in the sixteenth century was the consequence of a conscious policy of developing landed oligarchies in the shires of England and mercantile oligarchies in the boroughs. The Tudor Parliament was the arena within which rural and urban élites shaped the growth of royal power in ways that entrusted the Crown with the responsibility for enforcing a host of new duties—poor laws, grain laws, the development of local militias, and so on.

The increasing prominence of the English Parliament—or more precisely crown-in-parliament—was inexorable. It met in less than half the years during which the Tudors were on the throne; and sessions rarely lasted more than a month. It met in more than two-thirds of the years in the century following the accession of James I, and its sessions were now considerably longer. It became less a mechanism for shaping the growth of royal power and more a mechanism for representing the subject's concerns to embattled monarchs, but it remained—except during the dramatic years of civil war and revolution—essentially a curious blend of the kings'

Great Council, teaching them the limits of their enforceable will, and a High Court, the supreme declarer of law and supreme court of appeal. The last year in English history in which no Parliament sat was 1687. It was soon to become a *British* Parliament, with the arrival of Scottish representatives, and for 120 years from 1801 a United Kingdom Parliament, with the arrival of representatives from the Kingdom of Ireland.

The Reformation coincided with (was shaped by?) the invention of printing. These centuries saw the development of a print culture which brought an information revolution to the people of Britain. From the late sixteenth century, cheap printed material—often a mixture of strong visual images and accessible text—was widely available, promoting new religious and moral values, informing the people at large of a world beyond their immediate horizons. From the 1640s onwards there were newspapers and diurnals spreading national news and instruction. As literacy spread, and as access to the printed word became available to all those who were willing to listen to the spoken word read out, minds were freed to explore new political and religious choices.

Those who had gained economic freedom thus gained increasing cultural freedom. They were increasingly literate, articulate, entrusted—as churchwardens, overseers, jurymen, managers of local charities—with power over their poorer neighbours. Some took to Protestantism in its many forms and became active in the selection of MPs and the mandating of those MPs to represent their interests in the Great Council of the land. When civil war came in the 1640s they made free political choices, and they seem to have divided as evenly as did the gentry and nobility between the King and his Parliament.

The British state grew as a force in the world. If it followed the Iberian powers by a century in establishing bases and colonies outside Europe, and if for much of the seventeenth century it played third fiddle to the Netherlands and France, by 1688 it was on the brink of establishing itself as the most far-flung, tightly organized, and well-defended of all the trading empires. There were British colonies and major trading ports in East Asia, the Indian Ocean, West Africa, the Caribbean, and no less than thirteen colonies on the eastern seaboard of North America.

This book attempts to chronicle and to explain these processes of growth. Eighteen leading scholars have written about various aspects of the dynamics of change. Each was given two particular charges: to make the best recent scholarship available to as wide a readership as possible; and to take advantage of the possibilities afforded by illustrations to reinforce their narrative. The illustrations are not to be seen as adornments to an otherwise complete text but as an intrinsic part of it.

Readers should note that in designing this book I have broken away from a traditional narrative framework that tells the story reign-by-reign. Such an approach does scant justice to the deeper processes of change that shaped the lives of all those who lived through the stirring events of these troubled centuries. However, those who want to remind themselves of the great convulsions that constantly threatened to overwhelm kings and queens—and sometimes succeeded in doing so—should begin either by reading Chapters 15–19 before they read Chapters 1–14, or more simply by browsing through the chronology on pp. 451–60.

The book therefore begins with less familiar themes than those of Henry VIII's marital difficulties or the events which brought Charles I to the scaffold and drove James II to ignominious flight. It opens with an evocation of the dramatically changing landscapes of lowland and upland England, Scotland, and Wales; and continues with chapters that look at how the texture of political and economic life was changed as government extended ever more effective tentacles into the provinces and into the borderlands that had so long separated the English state from its 'Celtic fringe'. The growth of the British state in these centuries is the story of the interaction of several different peoples who—as it has been written—'interacted so as to change the condition of one another's existence'. Chapters 5–10 then examine in different ways the social and cultural experience of those who inhabited these changing physical and mental landscapes. They look at how society was organized, at the professionalization of life (through case-studies of education, the law, and the theatre), and at how different social groups sought to make sense of the world they lived in. The following chapters look at the monarchs, their courts, and the political culture of these two centuries. How did the Tudors and Stuarts make themselves available to their subjects not just physically but emblematically? This is the great age of Reformation, when Christendom endured its greatest and most grievous schism, as Protestants and Catholics fought with words, swords, and instruments of torture to save souls. Two chapters therefore tell of how the Tudors sought with considerable success to herd all their subjects into a curious state church of their own devising—one that looked Catholic but sounded Protestant, as Conrad Russell tells us in Chapter 13—but they also tell how in the end the state was compelled to grant a grudging measure of liberty to those whose consciences compelled them to defy it and to worship in assemblies of their own devising, or who chose not to worship at all.

Then indeed the book can offer dramatic narratives of two centuries: of two troubled dynasties, in which two kings were deposed, two English archbishops executed, and two Scottish ones assassinated. The book ends with two chapters that look at the opening-out of Britain as a major power in the world, from a bit-player in the dynastic struggles of the European royal houses into a great military, naval, commercial, and colonial force, poised to outstrip even France.

Inevitably, not everything that should be in this book can be in it. Reading through the nineteen chapters on the eve of putting them into press, I regret that there has not been room for more on literature, art, music, scientific discovery. And it remains an Anglo-centric rather than a Britocentric book; a truly holistic history is still perhaps impossible. And yet, given the constraints of space, I regret nothing that the book does contain. I am gratified by the spread and richness of texture which the authors have achieved. If there is too little on what used to be called 'high culture', it is because—more than any comparable history—the book brings to light the lives of ordinary men and women as they experienced and contributed to an age of expanding opportunity. It is, I hope, a fair trade.

J.S.M.

Feast of the Assumption 1994

1

THE CHANGING LANDSCAPE

TOM WEBSTER

1. *Introduction*

The sixteenth and seventeenth centuries are a period of British history in which crucial transformations occurred. In political culture, in social and economic experience, in religious expression, and even in the fabric of the landscape, the scene at the end of our period offers important contrasts with that at the beginning. If many features remained, the changes are striking and engage our attention. Perhaps this is one of the reasons why this period saw the flowering of descriptive and topographical literature: so much seemed to be passing away that writers and artists from John Leland and William Harrison to Daniel Defoe and Celia Fiennes felt impelled to record what they saw.

From each of these writers we gain vivid insights into the societies and landscapes they knew. From Leland, Henry VIII's antiquary, we hear of the power and pride of his royal master, from Harrison, an East Anglian cleric, of the changes in housing and farming in the English countryside, from Defoe of the manufacturing and industry of the 'middling sorts', and from Fiennes of the rejuvenated urban culture of her experience. None of these descriptions is innocent and every writer has his or her own preoccupations but the impression we accumulate is of a world transformed between the arrival of the Tudors and the end of Stuart rule. When Leland visited Leicester in the 1530s he found 'the foreste of Leyrcester yoining hard to the toune'; when Celia Fiennes passed through late in the seventeenth century the country was 'a great flatt full of good enclosures'.

If change over time is one theme which emerges from these accounts, another is regional variation. Just as changing social relations and patterns of belief vary in their impact across time and space, so the patterning of each particular landscape is as rewarding a study as that achieved by the broad brush of generalization. Early modern writers accepted the primary division of Britain into highland and lowland zones. The highland zone, covering the north and west of Britain, the mountains of central Wales, the Pennines and Lake District, Northumbria and the Borders, the Scottish Highlands and Islands, and also Cornwall, Dartmoor, and Exmoor, was characterized by thin, relatively infertile soils, a wetter climate, and a fairly short growing season. The lowland zone, to the south and east, was characterized by a more gentle relief, by deep, rich soils, and by a rather milder climate. There are areas of more dramatic topography—the Downs, the Wolds, and the Chilterns—and areas of still gentler landscape—the Fens, the marshlands of Sussex and the east coast, the Somerset Levels.

Within the lowland zone we may employ a second division noted by contemporaries, between 'champion' country and 'woodland' regions. William Harrison observed

It is so, that our soile being divided into champaine ground and woodland, the houses of the first lie uniformly built in everie town togither, with streets and lanes; whereas in the woodland countries . . . they stand scattered abroad, each one dwelling in the midst of his owne occupieng.

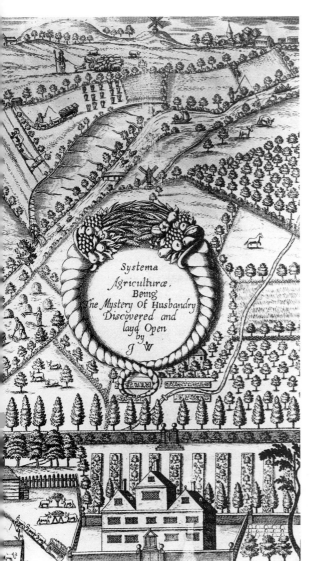

Systema
Agriculturæ,
Being
The Mystery Of Husbandry
Discovered and
layd Open
by
J W

The champion or 'fielden' country dominated the Midland plain between the Malverns, the Chilterns, and the Fens, cutting south across the country between Devon and mid-Hampshire, west into the Welsh borders and south Wales, north into the Vale of York and up into the coastal plains of Durham and Northumberland. Champion country had open arable fields, usually farmed with some degree of communal organization, and nucleated settlement.

To the south and east of this region, and in the north and west of the lowland zone, lie the areas of woodland country. Woodland dominated Sussex, Surrey, Kent, Essex, Middlesex, Hertfordshire, and much of East Anglia. To the west of the champion, woodland covered most of Herefordshire, Shropshire, Cheshire, and Devon. The term 'woodland' does not imply dense tree coverage although these regions may have been more thickly covered with trees in our period: woodland referred to the comparatively numerous hedges of these regions. The woodland tended to have smaller, more compact fields, less regular in shape. These were less often farmed communally and settlement was usually dispersed, as Harrison observed. Much of this land had been enclosed for centuries, if indeed it had ever been farmed in 'open fields'

JOHN WORLIDGE, the author of *Systema Agriculturae* (1669) was an important writer on agriculture living in Hampshire. Here he shows the active and peaceful landscape dominated by the manor house at the bottom. The eye is taken through the garden to an orchard, busy wheat fields with a floated water meadow, to sheep grazing on a common at the top. The common has a windmill, and in the distance lies the parish church and the village benefiting from all the agricultural work.

and the sinuous roads, deep banks, and complex mosaic of fields testify to the antiquity of these landscapes.

This last point reminds us that we cannot understand the early modern landscape without bearing in mind the fact that the British landscape has been intensely populated and farmed since prehistoric times. More importantly, we have to remember that the poet Cowper was wrong to claim that 'God made the country, and man made the town'. Every acre of Britain has been crucially influenced by the labours, aspirations, ideas, and activities of men and women. The idea that people change landscapes is particularly important for our period. The sixteenth and seventeenth centuries were critical years for the British landscape: they witnessed what historians have called an agricultural revolution, a process of proto-industrialization, and an urban renaissance. These claims have not been uncontested and, as we shall see, there are dangers of overstatement, in the contrast both with what preceded and with the scale of later change. The pace and impact of change varies enormously, from the transformation of the Fens or lowland Wales to the relative conservatism of Scottish agricultural landscapes. That said, the early modern period may justly be identified as years of important change.

2. *The Human Landscape*

The notion that landscapes are the product of human endeavour leads us to ask how these landscapes were peopled. The British population was slowly recovering from the ravages of the plagues of the fourteenth century. Pre-plague levels were regained during the sixteenth century and by the 1540s England may have had a population of 2.75 million, a figure rising to a little over four million by 1600. The demographics of Wales are less clear, but it has been estimated that there may have been about 278,000 inhabitants in 1536 and perhaps 380,000 by the end of the century. Figures for Scotland are still less reliable and it can be little more than an informed guess to suggest that the country had around a million people by 1700. The years of strong growth in England and Wales continued, with some loss of momentum between 1620 and 1650, with an estimated English population in 1656 of 5.3 million. There followed a period of stagnation or even decline with some little recovery in the 1680s, so that totals in 1701 were around 5 million for England, 400,000 for Wales. Declining numbers were in part due to emigration, with perhaps 300,000 people leaving Britain in the second half of the seventeenth century, but plague in England and Wales in the 1660s and bad harvests all over Britain, especially severe in Scotland, in the 1690s also contributed. Scotland may have lost 15 per cent of its population at this time.

This total, around 6.5 million for Britain as a whole by 1700 was not, of course, evenly distributed. Apart from the small level of urbanization there were considerable variations across the countryside. In Scotland highest densities were seen in the central lowlands, along both banks of the Firth of Forth, the Tay estuary, and the north-east coast. The far north and the islands were sparsely populated throughout our period although the crisis growth of the eighteenth century was just beginning when the Stuarts were succeeded by the Hanoverians. Wales was rather more uniform in population density, although Glamorgan was the most populous county and the inhospitable northern regions were below average. In England the majority lived south of the Wash. Population was not static, however, and there were local fluctuations: rapid growth, for instance, around Manchester, Leeds, Halifax, and Newcastle upon Tyne and a relative decline in parts of the west Midlands and Lincolnshire. We will return to the more dramatic demographics of the towns below.

This growth rate, representing almost a doubling of the British population, is the key to a good deal of the change in agricultural landscapes as a variety of strategies were followed to feed this growing population. It helps to account for the rising specialization of agrarian produce and also the new demands upon industrial production. However, it would be dangerous to assert that the late medieval economy was no more than a subsistence economy, or that the late seventeenth century saw a fully developed market economy. At the beginning and end of this period much production was for local consumption with a surplus for the market. Similarly, while there are important regional differences in emphasis between arable and pastoral farming, to a degree all early modern farming was mixed, whether livestock was kept for the benefit of arable or crops were grown as fodder. The basic needs of each agricultural community remained fairly constant. Each community relied upon the provision of certain requirements: the ways in which these were met varied and changed, the demands themselves less so.

Every community needed arable land, dominated by corn, especially wheat and barley, and grazing, on enclosed permanent pasture or from meadowland where hay was cultivated for winter fodder. The quality and extent of pasture determined the amount of livestock, the availability of livestock the quality of manuring and thus the productivity of the arable. Each community required wood for building and fuel, for household implements, agricultural tools, and for carts and wagons. Wood was a carefully managed resource through the Middle Ages, either as a common right from pollarded trees, where poles were allowed to grow above head height to make pasture land productive, or in private woodland. When we think of woodland, we tend to imagine a 'natural' environment, but from an early date most woodland in Britain has been managed. Enclosed with large earthworks, woodbanks, to exclude stock, trees were 'coppiced', cropped at the base to encourage an abundant growth of poles to be farmed and sold year by year. Interspersed through the woodland were longer growing 'standards' to meet more substantial demands. Wood, like other forms of agricultural produce, was cultivated and controlled by human agency.

3. *The Champion Region*

The accommodation of these basic needs varied enormously. It is here that we need our finest sense of regional variation. The farming system that every schoolchild knows, the three open fields, divided into strips and distributed among the farming community, is only part of the picture and, naturally, a partial one. The system it most nearly describes is that of the champion region, most highly developed in the counties of the Midlands plain. Here, open field husbandry was divided into between two and four great fields surrounded by a stock-proof enclosure. Within each field the land was divided into furlongs which were themselves divided into strips. An individual proprietor would hold strips scattered across the fields and ploughing, sowing, and harvesting were organized communally. When the crops were harvested, the livestock was turned out to graze on the stubble, thus providing manure. One field would be laid fallow each year to allow for recovery.

THE champion country: Long Compton, Warwickshire. The extent to which the Midlands moved from arable to pasture is evident from the ploughing remains preserved under grass. The strips and furlongs of the open fields can be traced in the ridge and furrow earthworks. Here the early modern hedges tend to follow older boundaries.

HERE we see two neglected aspects of agriculture. In the foreground is a farmer sowing seed from a small bag. To the right is another farmer preparing the ground. The horses are pulling a harrow. The harrow carries tines to break up clods of earth, to loosen and divide the surface into fine particles. The harrow depicted here is archaic; during the sixteenth century triangular harrows appeared which produced less symmetrical patterns.

This system has been much criticized as primitive, inefficient, and inflexible, mostly by historians following 'improving' contemporaries who were hostile to the system for more than practical reasons. To some degree the system was inefficient and one of the achievements of this period was radically to improve productivity. However, open field husbandry required a high degree of organization and regulation and flexibility was provided by making the furlong rather than the field the cropping unit. In addition, various strategies had been developed by the end of the fifteenth century to increase the yield of arable land, both in and beyond the champion region. The fallow was ploughed to kill weeds and a practice called 'inhoking' was followed, where the fallow was temporarily cropped with peas and legumes to provide a crop and restore heart to the land. In Scotland, soot-laden thatch and turf was spread on the arable. In a process called devonshiring, denchering, or denshiring, turf was taken off with a breast plough, burnt, and the ashes spread on the fields. Lime or marl were extracted from the subsoil and in some areas sea sand or seaweed were used in the same way. This much said, it must be admitted that the sort of husbandry exemplified in the Midlands system was never wholly successful in overcoming the central need for more manure, limited by the availability of grazing.

From archaeological remains we can reconstruct something of the appearance of these areas. Most characteristic were the earthworks that resulted from the way the soil was prepared for crops. Using a plough with share, coulter, and mouldboard required a team of six or eight oxen or horses. The mouldboard turned the sod over to one side and as the plough team followed a line round this initial ridge a bank was established. Carried out across a field this process produced the unmistakable rippling 'ridge and furrow', that can be seen preserved under grass in those fields turned over to pasture at this time.

Another characteristic which, like ridge and furrow, was a medieval practice that continued into the seventeenth century, is that the strips tended to follow a reversed 'S' profile. It has been suggested that this is a consequence of the difficulty of turning a large plough team, especially with the use of oxen. Although the first explanation carries some weight, oxen were used in some upland areas without producing the pattern, so this is not a necessary correlation. Whatever the origins of the sinuous profile, it was characteristic of much early modern arable, and is frequently fossilized in enclosures of this period, as we will see.

In summary, the landscapes of the champion region were less monotonous than is sometimes suggested. In the earthworks, in the varied cropping patterns, and in the areas of pasture, meadow, and woodland, the champion country must have been less tidy, more open, and more colourful than it is today.

4. *The Woodland Region*

If it is accepted that we are dealing with points on a spectrum rather than stark contrasts, the woodland/champion distinction is useful and does reflect differences in the landscape. The contrast between the nucleated villages and generally larger fields of the champion, and the smaller

THE woodland region: Brasted, Surrey. This view over a woodland landscape shows the complex pattern of irregular fields, winding roads, and dispersed settlement characteristic of the region. The hedges are thicker and trees more abundant than in the champion country. In the sixteenth and seventeenth centuries there was more arable than is evident here, but most of the boundaries pre-date our period.

fields, dispersed settlement, and thicker tree coverage of the woodland zone is still observable. However, the contemporary distinction implied something more. The difference was also between fields managed communally (as in the champion) or held 'in severalty' (as in the woodland), that is, whether decisions over cropping regimes, the timing of harvests, and so forth were taken by the community or by the family that farmed the individual field.

Neither should we imagine the woodland as homogenous. Further distinctions can usefully be drawn. The heavy clay regions of Norfolk and Suffolk were largely farmed in severalty in a densely wooded landscape of small, irregular closes. In contrast, the lighter soils of west Norfolk had a network of larger fields and open heathlands, following a 'sheep–corn' pattern of husbandry where the sheep were grazed on the heathlands and stubble, being 'folded' or penned at night for the manure. In the neighbouring Breckland the heath was broken up in patches for short-term arable before being allowed to revert to pasture. Here, in what is today a heavily conifered region, the landscape was relatively open, bare, and bleak.

Some of these contrasts can also be found in the woodland regions of the south-east. The Weald was mostly a landscape of dispersed settlement and amorphous enclosed fields. To make the most of poor soils a form of mixed farming was pursued which historians have called 'alternate' or 'convertible' and which contemporaries called 'up-and-down' husbandry. Fields were cultivated as arable, laid down to grass, and then ploughed again, on a cycle of four to six years. This system improved the quality and therefore the productivity of arable and pasture and allowed the farmer to keep more livestock, while allowing farmers to respond more efficiently to market conditions. This was important to Wealden farmers as 'gavelkind' partible inheritance tended to create smaller holdings and increase pressure on narrow profit margins.

Similar problems affected the diverse Scarpfoot region which surrounded the Weald. On the Kent side there were open fields, but these were farmed in severalty. These open and subdivided, but not common, fields were enclosed early. This area was one of the first to display what we will see as a general trend toward specialization: hops were grown in the 'red-hills' region of Kent before they appeared in the parts of north Kent which became more famous for the crop, and the region was in the process, from the early seventeenth century, of becoming one of Britain's leading fruit producers. The Sussex coastal plain was similarly precocious, producing leys, or areas of temporary grassland in arable fields, and legumes were adopted early. The south-east as a whole displayed great contrasts of wealth at the start of the period, from the successful coastal plain and the intense sheep–corn economy of north Kent to the heathland squatter economy of the London basin before the arrival of market gardening, and the subsistence farming of the Wealden interior.

5. *The Highland Zone*

The intense cultivation of most of the lowland zone, with its arable emphasis, is something of a contrast to the highland zone. In the south-west the open arable fields that were to be found in Cornwall were largely gone by the mid-sixteenth century and most of the region to the west of Exeter was characterized by a pastoral economy pursued in tiny, irregular fields with massive granite walls and enormous moorland commons. This pattern of pastoralism with small arable fields growing oats and coarse barley, for bread and beer, with the best valley land kept for

SCOTTISH agriculture: St Kilda, Inverness-shire. This view allows some impression of the difficulties of farming in the worst of Scottish land. The head dyke, separating infield and outfield, is clearly visible. Beyond that, a few enclosures can be seen, where farmers took 'haugh' land into temporary cultivation, but the open moorland is mostly unsuitable for arable farming.

meadow to provide precious winter fodder, was typical of the upland. This was true of Dartmoor, but also of central Wales, the Pennines, the southern uplands and the Highlands of Scotland. Cattle were often raised on the lower hillsides providing meat, hides, milk, and butter, and sheep on the fells above yielding wool, meat, and milk for cheese. The sheep provided the necessary raw material for the cloth industry and cattle were integrated in a droving network that took them to pastures nearer to markets for fattening. Thus Welsh cattle were driven to the clay vales of the West Country and to the marshlands of the south-east.

The necessity of working some arable land for fodder and household needs presented a challenge to the thin, dispersed populations of the highlands. The pattern that developed across most of Scotland, save the eastern lowlands from Berwickshire to the Firth of Forth where slightly better conditions favoured arable, had much in common with the uplands of Wales and England. The cottages of individual tenants, usually less than ten families, were loosely grouped together in a *fermtoun* or *clachan*. The arable was divided into two areas, infield and outfield. The infield was cropped every year, sown with hardy varieties of oats and barley. The infertile soil could be maintained by the not inconsiderable manure resources as cattle were stalled through the winter.

Tenants' lands 'lay in run-rig', a form of ridged strips. Unlike the open fields of the champion, it seems that run-rig strips were occasionally redistributed by lot.

The infield was supplemented by the outfield, where patches were broken up and cropped until they were exhausted, allowed to return to grass, and cultivation moved on to another patch which would have been lightly manured the previous summer. The outfield usually provided fodder. Still further from the fermtoun, additional areas of suitable land such as the flood plains of rivers were cultivated as *haugh* land, and occasionally areas of hillside were stripped, burnt, and cultivated for a short span. This most marginal land was called *brunt* land.

Despite the best endeavours of farmers, most of the land beyond the head dyke of the outfield, and much within it, was open bog and moor, entirely uninhabited during the winter months. There were, of course, variations within this scheme: in East Lothian the emphasis shifted to the arable, while on some of the bigger sheep runs arable was absent. On the most fertile and best drained soils from Berwickshire Merse to the Moray Firth cereal production could overshadow the pastoral economy.

This general emphasis on pastoralism with a little hard won arable was also the lot of Welsh farmers on the worst of the upland soils. However, Wales was (and is) a country of contrasting landscapes, subject to processes that do not equally apply elsewhere in Britain. English cultural colonization had, by the late fifteenth century, made considerable inroads into the lowlands of the north, parts of south Wales, and the Marches, bringing with it a smaller scale version of the Midland system. This was the form of most agriculture in the populous areas of the Vale of Glamorgan, the Monmouthshire coastline, the Gower peninsula, the river valleys of Breconshire, and, of course, in Pembrokeshire, the most Anglicized district. The arable was supported by hilly common pasture, the source of many of the cattle exported to English markets and cheese and butter linking into the markets of the south-west.

In central and north Wales and indeed in the more remote hills of south Wales, older legal forms persisted that determined the form of the landscape. Land held by freeholders was called *tir gwelyaug* and was divided into *tir priod*, the homestead and parcels of common arable, and *cytir*, unenclosed shares in pasture and waste. A system of partible inheritance called *cyfran* was followed where the *tir priod* was divided equally and could be enclosed. However, *cytir*, which often included some arable, remained the common property of co-heirs and could not be enclosed. The resulting landscape was a patchwork of small arable fields made economically viable by the common resources of the *cytir*. This fragile balance between equitable property settlements and the dangers of fragmentation was to be wholly disrupted in the course of the sixteenth century.

6. *Forest and Fen*

Before examining the nature of the changes in the British landscape, it is necessary to identify two other categories of landscape that do not fit easily into the classifications used above. One is the product of human, and especially royal, influence, the other a complex and ongoing struggle between communities and environments.

The term 'forest' presents difficulties for the modern reader. Rather than the primeval woods that the word conjures up, forests were legally defined areas subject, not only to the common law, but also to forest law, a code intended to protect deer and woodland for royal hunting. By the thirteenth century approximately a third of England was defined a forest, which in itself indicates that these were not uniform areas of dense woodland. In Scotland, Royal Forests covered even more ground, and while the English forests were in retreat from 1300, in Scotland they continued to be created into the sixteenth century although the law restricting practices held to be damaging to the hunt was less vigorous in Scotland. In fact villages and towns, arable cultivation and meadowland could be found within forest jurisdictions much as elsewhere.

However, some parts were densely wooded and supported distinctive cultures and ways of life. Even in the champion region, forest areas were characterized by small hamlets and small arable fields and an economy where the landless could scrape a living by grazing pigs, cattle, and sheep and from a range of small-scale manufactures. The forests of the west Midlands employed infield-outfield husbandry on the thin soils of Sherwood Forest, Charnwood in Leicestershire, and Leighfield in Rutland. The gorsy heath of Sherwood also supported large sheep walks and cony (rabbit) warrens and some convertible husbandry was practised.

THE draining of the Fens: Littleport. In the course of the early modern period an enormous area was reclaimed from the sea to provide rich arable land. However, drainage was never a completed project. As the peat was drained, it tended to shrink, leaving the silted river beds above the surrounding landscape. In 1602 Sir John Peyton embanked and drained 1,400 acres of fen at Littleport, Cambridgeshire. Here, new settlement has grown up on the 'rodden', higher land left by the former river bed.

incomodity of ye longe way to the compasture.

Our cornefieldꝰ ioyne so togeither every thrid yeare, that oꝰ heardshipꝰ go to pasture all that yeare by the outside of oꝰ parish, more than halfe to ⁱmpassinge yᵉ Lordship; so that theire iourney every day above ſyoe mileſ longe ſore-beateſ theire feete, and impoverisheth them: but oꝰ younger breede, eſpetially, iſ ſtocked by it. Beſideſ the daily tramplinge of 500, or 600 cattle in oᵘ fallow-field, and ox-pasture ſoileth, and deſtroieth the graſſe to yᵉ hindrance of oꝰ draughtꝰ, & ſheepe, and iſ no ſmall meaneſ to ripen yᵉ rotte amongſt them.

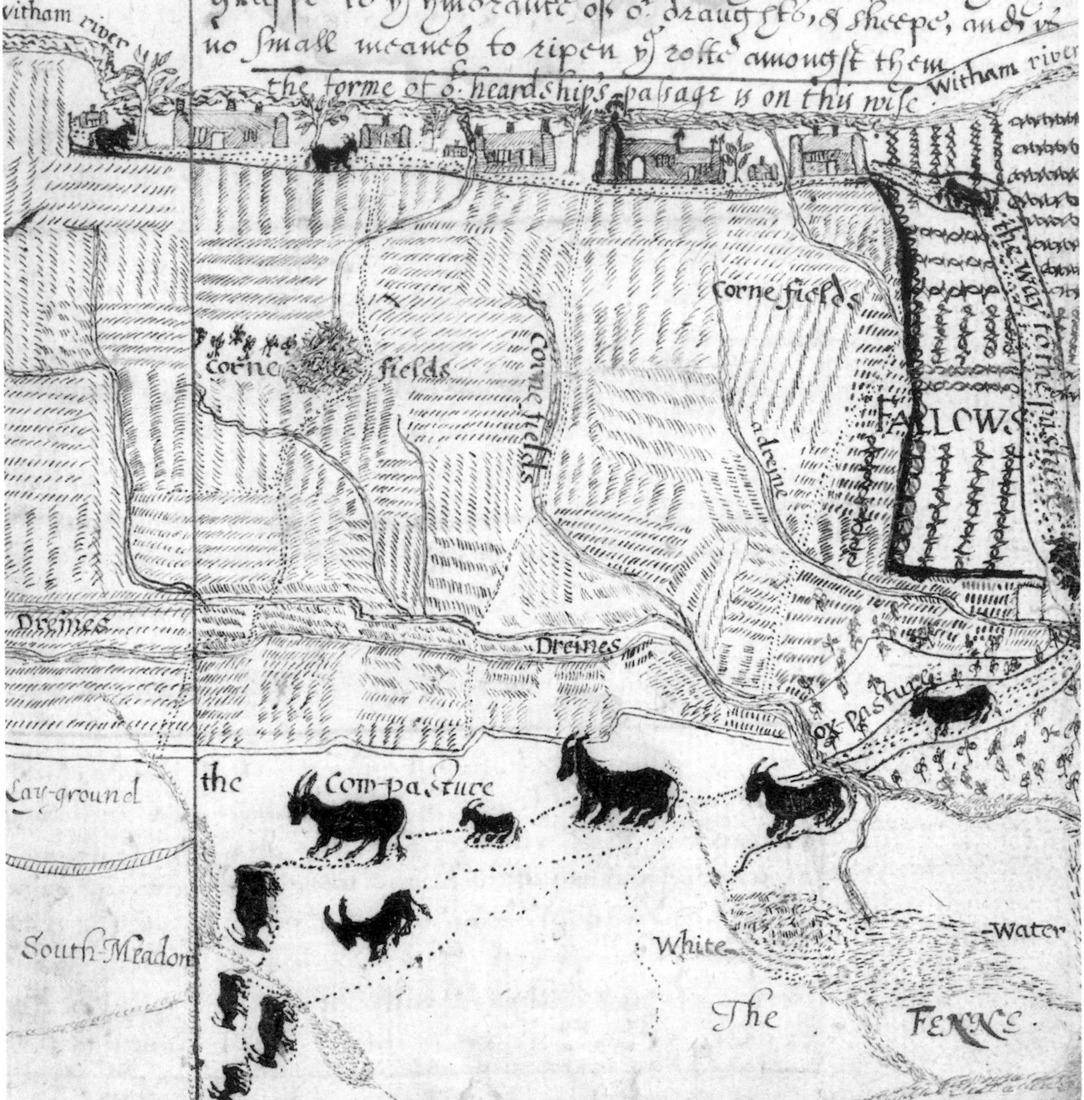

the forme of oꝰ heardshipꝰ paſſage is on this wiſe.

Witham river

Witham river

corne fields

corne fields

corne fields

a dreine

FALLOWS

the way to the bushes

Dreines

Dreines

Ox-Pasture

Lay-ground

the Com-pasture

South-Meadow

White Water

The FENNE

Brant-water

Similarly, the forests and heaths of the West Country, Selwood, Gillingham, Kingswood, Parkhurst on the Isle of Wight, Pewsham, and the New Forest, supported a dairying economy and many pigs. These were areas which made few inhabitants rich but kept many independent. The forest regions of Wessex shade into the upland moors and heaths. Similarly unproductive, the heaths could support a considerable number of pastoralists concentrating on cattle, pigs, and horses, especially the small, strong 'heathcroppers'. The fruits of this labour could be supplemented by wildfowling and furze-cutting in the bare, brown landscapes familiar from the novels of Thomas Hardy.

There are cultural similarities between the forest and some of the wetlands, but the landscapes could hardly be more different. The most widely known wetland, deservedly so, is the fenland area around the Wash stretching north into Lincolnshire, south into Norfolk, and west into Cambridgeshire. Here farmers had fought a long battle with the sea since prehistoric times with some success in creating rich summer pastures. However, there are many other parts of Britain that enjoyed a fen-like or marshland landscape. Salt marsh stretched up from the Fens along the coast to the Humber and inland to the Isle of Axholme, supporting a wealthy cattle and wheat economy on the flatlands between the Wolds and the sea. Beyond the Humber, marsh could be found in Holderness, and to the south of the Wash the coasts of Essex, Kent, and Sussex had similar landscapes. In Scotland, pastoral marshland economies could be found on the coastlines of Berwickshire, between Crieff and Perth, and around the shores of Loch Leven.

It is useful to distinguish between these marshlands and the fenland around Hatfield Chase and in the Somerset Levels in the neighbourhood of Sedgemoor and Bridgwater. In addition to the pasture, the marshland supported extensive arable farming which, in acreage at least, was unmatched by the fenland. The Isles of Thanet and Sheppey cultivated grain and also vegetables, hops, and canary seed where the seed dibbling, hoeing, and hard labour supplied some of the skills that later made Kent famous for market gardening. The Fens generally had a rich and diverse economy where small patches of arable were fertile enough to support a family and the abundant grazings and unstinted common rights, combined with fish, eels, wild fowl, osiers and willow for baskets, and reeds and peat for fuel, allowed a degree of independence that was less available in the more hierarchical marshland societies.

7. *Enclosure*

The fens and forests were transformed in the course of the sixteenth and seventeenth centuries but they were not alone in this. Although the changes in the British landscape were often piecemeal, rarely dramatic, the cumulative effect over this period was such that few areas were unaffected. The best known form of change was enclosure. We must distinguish between four types of enclosure. First, there is enclosure that leads to a change of land use from arable to pasture or vice versa. Secondly, we must separate enclosure of common arable from that of common

---

In 1629 the villagers of Bassingham on the edge of the Fens in Lincolnshire submitted this petition in favour of enclosure. They complain of the cost to their stock in the long walk forced upon them by the open fields. In this sketch, the problem is made clear by the way to the pasture to the right of the fallow field. The drains from the fields to the River Witham can all be followed.

pasture. Thirdly, we must differentiate between piecemeal enclosure, where as little as a few acres may be affected, and general enclosure, which made a much greater change in the landscape. Fourthly, we can contrast enclosure by unity of possession where one landowner had gained control over a block of land and enclosed it, and enclosure by agreement where all the interested parties, or the most powerful, agreed to abandon communal practices and enclose to farm in severalty.

In the last twenty years it has become apparent that the fifteenth to seventeenth centuries were crucial in the creation of an enclosed landscape. Our understanding of the changes has been hampered by the intense public debate on enclosure in the sixteenth century. The complaints and laws against enclosures that converted open arable fields to closed pasture, leading to depopulation and deprivation, have masked the nature of much enclosure and given too narrow a geographical focus.

It is true that the Midland counties experienced some depopulating general enclosures when meat and wool prices were holding up better than grain. In Warwickshire south of the Arden many landlords turned from mixed farming to pasture, mostly in the fifteenth century. Northamptonshire was the county that fitted best the stereotype of rapacious enclosing landlord and evicted peasant. Even here, forest areas in the county were already pastoral, and much of the outcry can be traced to high population and land hunger.

Much of the enclosure involving a change of land use took place later than expected, especially in the east Midlands, including two-thirds of Rutland and Lincolnshire and much of Nottinghamshire in the seventeenth century. It is likely that there was most enclosure in the highland zone of England, although it is less noted because it was less protested: the common arable was small and unstinted commons extensive. Much of this was piecemeal and a great deal of it by agreement or consent. Examples of sixteenth-century enclosure of this type can be identified in Lancashire and Yorkshire, Cornwall and Devon, Cheshire, Shropshire, and Derbyshire. On the Yorkshire Wolds both the sheep walks of the high wold and the huge open arable fields saw considerable enclosure by agreement. By 1600 open field arable was virtually unknown in the Dales. In these counties as much common was enclosed as arable, although it is possible to see the sinuous furrow lines fossilized in the dry stone walls of Derbyshire and the Vale of York.

Enclosure could transform the landscape. The many paths and trackways of the open fields were often rationalized. The Midlands became a more hedged landscape as a result. More importantly, those champion communities which began to farm in severalty tended to abandon the villages as the prime stimulus to nucleation, the scattered strips of the open fields were removed, leading to a pattern of hamlets and dispersed farmsteads. Many of our upland landscapes were formed in this period, or at least acquired an additional network of walls.

If anything, the landscape of Wales was more changed through enclosure than that of England. Much of the open field arable of the south coast and the Marches was enclosed in these years. Although common cultivation could be found in Glamorganshire and elsewhere into the late nineteenth century, most disappeared through enclosure by agreement much earlier. Rather more social dislocation and resistance was caused by changes to traditional tenures. There was little movement before an Act of 1542 abolished *cyfran* upon the next change of heirs. At the same time, English surveyors, working for the Crown or landowners like the Earl of Leicester on his Denbigh estates, imposed English conceptions of common upon unenclosed grazing, treating

UPLAND enclosure: Wardlow, Derbyshire. The impact of early modern enclosure was not in fact greatest in the Midlands where most concern was voiced. Further north, in Derbyshire, the effects of piecemeal enclosure are plain, as the new dry stone walls follow the line of older arable strips. Dotted across the landscape, the scars left by the pits of lead miners can be traced, running in lines as the works followed seams near the surface until they ran out.

cytir as ultimately the property of the lord although Welsh law considered the land as vested in the co-heirs who enjoyed the use rights. The insecurity engendered by these changes encouraged a good deal of *cytir* enclosure, upsetting the delicate balance of the *tir gwelyaug* system. Tiny arable holdings were unsustainable without the *cytir* and many freeholders were forced to pay composition fines for encroachment, driving the land market into hyperactivity and leading to the consolidation of large estates by enclosing English landlords.

It is less clear why the Welsh uplands were so quickly transformed in the same period. Some weight may be given to the effects of disafforestation as elsewhere. There was some very large-scale enclosure of mountainous grazing: in Cyfeiliog in Montgomeryshire, for instance, encroachments between 1561 and 1573 enclosed over 2,000 acres. Much of the woodland in the forest regions was devoted more intensively to cattle for the market and the great forests of Radnor, Brecknock, Elicottie, and Trevloch lost an enormous amount of tree cover to commercial and industrial demands.

If little has been said about Scottish enclosure, it must be noted that there was no comparable

THE varieties of agricultural work are captured in the cover to this handbook of husbandry. The maintenance of stock, ploughing, harrowing, sowing, and harvesting are all depicted. Fishing, bee-keeping, horticulture, building of fences, and the final delivery of crops to the market add to the work. The epitome of husbandry is clearly the acquisition of a number of skills and the devotion of a great deal of work.

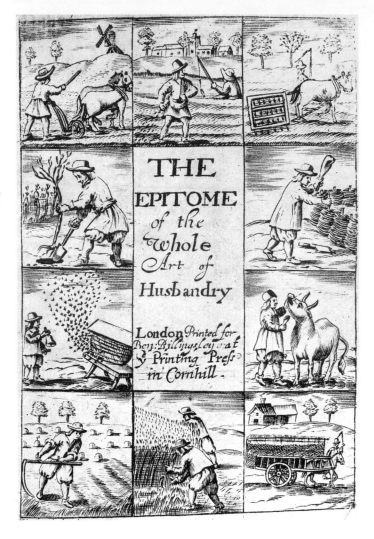

transformation during the sixteenth and seventeenth centuries. A series of Acts of Parliament removed all the legal restrictions and offered tax incentives to enclosing landlords but with little effect. Some enclosure to facilitate cattle fattening for new urban markets was seen in the south-west by the end of the seventeenth century. A little arable land was enclosed around the houses of the wealthy and there were some efforts to improve the tree cover of the lowlands by enclosure. It is possible that the relative stability of the Scottish landscape in these centuries related to low population pressure. Scotland certainly displayed little of the hunger for productive land that transformed areas of England. Stability rather than change was the keynote of Scottish agriculture before the eighteenth and nineteenth centuries.

8. *Reclamation and Colonization*

It is not always appreciated how far the drainage achievements of the Tudors and Stuarts represent a new departure. Despite the efforts of earlier generations, rising sea levels in the thirteenth century and later floods had inundated many marshlands. 6,000 acres were lost to the sea in Sussex as late as 1537 and the Pevenscy Levels were completely flooded. Work before the Union of the Crowns was a holding operation and the pace only picked up from late in the sixteenth century with varied effects. On Romney Marsh the 'improved' land went almost entirely to absentee graziers with drastic depopulating results. The only arable was tended by residents who grew corn in severalty, spreading rich mud from drainage ditches every few years, a process known as 'sleeching'. The newly reclaimed Pevensey Levels were similarly lacking in arable, exclusively devoted to cattle fattening. By contrast, the drained regions of north-west Kent and south Essex turned to wheat, barley, pulses, and vegetables, and to wheat and oats respectively. The Lincolnshire marshes underwent considerable changes after piecemeal reclamation in the sixteenth century. The coastal strip, which had supported independent cattle and corn farmers, was increasingly used by inland graziers. After a forage crisis inland around 1600, the demand for grazing drove out many of the smaller farmers leading to a relative decline in population in the seventeenth century. In Scotland, drainage schemes were late and usually on a small scale although the initiatives of individual landowners in Berwickshire and on the shores of Loch Leven should not be ignored.

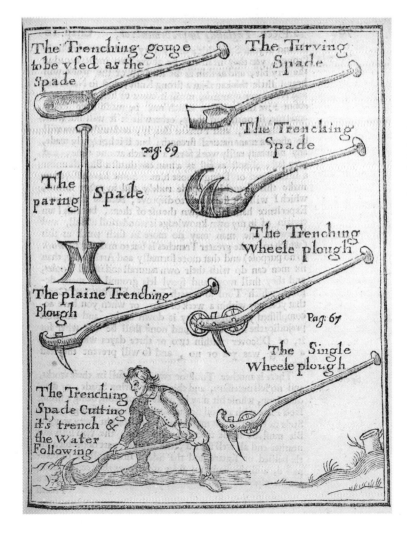

WALTER BLITH was the most prominent of a number of agricultural innovators of the mid-seventeenth century. Here, in a plate from *The English Improver* (1653), he shows a number of the tools available to make drainage more efficient and to improve crop yields.

It was, of course, the fenlands proper that experienced the greatest transformation. There were long and, in our period, fairly successful attempts to resist drainage schemes in the Somerset Levels and at Hatfield Chase. Equally dogged, though in the long run less successful, were the attempts of the various fenlanders around the Wash to preserve their landscape and way of life. In north Lincolnshire the schemes were Crown-sponsored; in the south they began as the initiative of the Earl of Bedford. The Dutch entrepreneur Cornelius Vermuyden linked the projects: he applied his engineering skills to the Isle of Axholme and Hatfield Chase in the 1620s and to the Bedford Levels in the 1630s and later. His achievement was remarkable: even before he began his major work, the New Bedford River, he had cut or recut over fifty miles of watercourse. Within thirty years some 350,000 acres of the southern fens were drained and declared fit for year-round cultivation.

His work looks less heroic from the perspective of the fenlanders. He rode roughshod over their rights and interests. The cost of the rich new arable was the loss of that distinctive lifestyle: farmers might have had to use stilts to herd their cattle, but natural resources maintained their independence. In a sense, drainage was an act of colonization, perhaps seen most vividly in the full adoption of a money economy, with the decline of rents and tithes payable in 'sticks' of eels. Moreover, it is in the nature of fenland that drainage is an ongoing process. The very success of Vermuyden's work brought its own difficulties. As the peat was drained, it shrank, making it still

THIS illustration from Holinshed's *Chronicles* (1577) gives some impression of the scale of labour involved in harvesting. The farmers, watched over by the landlord or his servant, work long hours to harvest in time. At the extreme right, one man can be seen with the 'hook' in his hand as he harvests the wheat. Below him, we can see a basket and a jug, reminding us that the labourers were fed in the field to save time in daylight.

more liable to floods, sinking below the level of the silt fens and the drainage channels themselves. The channels tended to run above the surrounding land and had to be constantly reinforced.

A similar process of 'reclamation' and colonization can be traced in the various forest regions. Here again, despite limited disafforestation in the sixteenth century, the critical drive was in the first half of the seventeenth century. Some forest areas retained their pastoral character. The heavily wooded forests of the West Country remained so beyond the seventeenth century, for instance. In the west Midlands, by contrast, enough land was brought under the plough before 1750 to end that region's traditional dependence on grain imports without unduly damaging the dairying which, on a more commercial footing, served the industrial regions around Birmingham. In the east Midlands, the forest regions lost much of their distinctive character: the Derbyshire forest lost most of its woodland feeding the demand for timber from charcoal burners, builders, and especially from miners' needs for pit props.

The total expansion of farmland in these centuries was considerable. The various attempts at drainage, reclamation, and enclosure added several million acres to Britain's farmland amounting to a gain in cultivated area in the order of 20 per cent between 1500 and 1700. This in itself is remarkable, but if we go on to examine the innovations that helped to improve productivity on new and traditional farmland, we will appreciate the scale of attempts to feed the growing population.

9. *Agricultural Innovation*

As has been noted above, perhaps the single most important limiting factor for arable production was the level of livestock that could be fed through the winter to provide extra manure. The availability of meadowland hay was crucial and despite a variety of expedients few meadows could provide more than one crop a year. The great innovation of the early seventeenth century was the floated water meadow, purportedly the invention of Rowland Vaughan of Herefordshire. A network of timber-lined channels was used to create a fast flowing sheet of water to stimulate early growth and although the water meadows needed maintenance, grazing could be provided in the early spring and again in the late summer. Used efficiently, a floated water meadow could quadruple the yield of meadowland. Remains can be identified in the river valleys of the West Country along the Frome, Piddle, Test, Itchen, Wylye, and Avon, where they were introduced by Vaughan's patron, the Earl of Pembroke, and also in Berkshire, across the Midlands, in the sheep–corn regions of Norfolk and eastern England, and along the valleys of the south Wales coastal zone.

The second major category of innovation, the improvement of cultivation by new rotations and fertilizers, shows a good deal of continuity with earlier efforts. We have noted experiments with leys and convertible husbandry and efforts in fertilization using a variety of materials. Many medieval marl pits were reopened in this period and such techniques were much more widely spread through publicity and example. For instance, liming, dependent on the burning of limestone, was an introduction to the central Scottish lowlands, spreading with the increased availability of coal and leading to the improvement of acidic pastures.

Some of these activities combined with new crops. In north Lincolnshire, enclosure, convert-

THE sophistication of orchards was a growing industry in this period. We can see how the land is fenced to exclude stock likely to damage young plants, and the equipment and labour required to produce fruit. On the left a slip is removed, on the right a young tree is planted and in the centre a mature tree is dug up. New fruits, such as pineapples, peaches, nectarines, and melons, were greeted with wonder as they arrived in the ports.

ible husbandry, and intensive manuring regimes went with an early appearance of turnips and grasses and also, on a smaller scale, industrial crops such as hemp, flax, hops, and woad. Here we must distinguish between new crops that improved fodder and soil, and the industrial crops.

The fodder crops which used to be associated with the agricultural self-publicists of the eighteenth century were already becoming widespread from 1650 onward. Some of these were new imports, especially from the Low Countries; others had been cultivated in gardens and became field crops. Turnips fall into the latter category, appearing as a field crop in the east of England on the same light soils that had been the first to grow carrots in fields fifty years earlier. Turnips flourished in diverse conditions, restored heart to the land, and provided valuable fodder. The grasses that made an impact on East Anglia, on the Cotswolds, on the Chilterns, and on the chalk downland of Kent, Sussex, and Wiltshire were imports. From the mid-sixteenth century sainfoin, clover, lucerne, trefoil, and rye-grass were all taken up by enthusiasts coming into contact with Dutch imports.

The industrial crops appeared wherever the necessary investment and labour was available. Woad was a hardy crop that could be established on newly broken up pasture, but the labour-intensive treatment, milling and balling, required experts and once the necessary investment had been made in a woad mill, the crop exhibited a certain level of inertia. Under the Tudors farms appeared in Hampshire, Essex, and Bedfordshire, spreading across the Midlands in the next century. Madder, which produced a red dye, was cultivated whenever the price of Dutch imports were high. Flax and hemp were grown in many smallholdings, to be sold on to the cloth industry, becoming established in reclaimed areas of forest and fen. Both crops provided useful by-products: paint and soap needed linseed oil from flax, hemp could be made into rope, and the seed could feed poultry.

The impact of these crops was a local phenomenon and the same is true of market gardening. Horticulture is important as the testing ground of crops with a future in the field in new areas of specialization. The influence of immigrants, the urban market, and gentle virtuosi were critical. These elements combined in the newly enclosed heathlands of the London basin, which, by the end of our period, had developed a series of micro-specializations. Battersea was a centre for asparagus, Wandsworth for watercress, Vauxhall for garden trees, Mitcham for herbs, and Fulham for parsnips. Small farmers were quick to pick up on profitable crops: the potato, for instance, moved out of the garden to appear as a field crop. Similarly, fruit-growing was taken up commercially by the third quarter of the seventeenth century after royal and aristocratic interest.

Market gardening and fruit-growing were not confined to the hinterland of London and other areas developed their own supplies with similarly productive regions appearing round Bristol, York, Edinburgh, and Glasgow. The influence of urban markets was not limited to their immediate environs: regional specialization was a broader phenomenon. Taking only the most spectacular example, the growth of a non-farming population in London affected many regions. Cheese was exported through Bristol from the Wessex clay vales, from south west Staffordshire, and the Cheshire border. Butter was exported from the Dove valley in the west Midlands, rabbits from vast warrens on the Isle of Wight, coal from Newcastle, grain by sea from the Sussex coast, cattle from Scotland and Wales. Although many localities were little changed, by the end of the seventeenth century, commercialization and regional specialization had fundamentally changed the agrarian economies of large parts of Britain.

10. *The Industrial Landscape*

A good deal of space has been quite properly given to the agricultural sector of the British landscape. Agriculture was the general experience of the vast majority of the population. However, the sixteenth and seventeenth centuries were also a period of transition for Britain's industrial landscapes, and it is to these that we may now turn our attention.

Woollen cloth manufacture was carried on almost everywhere in Britain as a by-employment. Particular concentrations developed for the manufacture of heavy English broadcloths in Devon, Wiltshire, and Gloucestershire, in the Kentish Weald, and in Suffolk, and coarser woollens in the Pennines around Leeds, Manchester, and Bradford. Most of these areas imported their wool from elsewhere in England with the geographical determinants being under-employed labour and the supply of running water and fuller's earth to keep the fulling mills going.

Although textile manufacture retained its rural and domestic base through the early modern period, the industry underwent important changes. There was a shift in the course of the sixteenth century to the 'new draperies', lighter, cheaper, more colourful, and less durable cloths. The quality of wool deteriorated as sheep became more important for meat and immigrant technology from the Netherlands influenced development of worsted production in Norwich, Colchester, and Canterbury from the 1560s. The trickle of French Protestant refugees introduced skills in silk and linen manufacture, which increased in the late seventeenth century. Each of these industries was swiftly naturalized and by the end of the period the Lancashire linen industry was starting to imitate cheap Asiatic cottons while the woollen industry of the West Riding of Yorkshire was becoming increasingly well organized, prompting one historian to claim a revolution in soft furnishings for the period.

The location of the extractive industries is, of course, more easily explained. At the start of the sixteenth century the extraction of metal ore was the main industry. Lead, copper, and tin, in that order were the most valuable non-ferrous metals. Lead was mined in Yorkshire, Derbyshire, Wales, and the south-west, copper in Cornwall, which also dominated the extraction of tin, Wales, and the Lake District. It was only in the course of this period that coal-mining emerged as pre-eminent: the figures are notoriously unreliable, but it has been estimated that production grew from 200,000 tonnes a year in the 1550s to 2,500,000 in the 1690s. Mines appeared wherever coal was to be found near the surface: on both sides of the Firth of Forth, in Lanarkshire, north and south Wales, Staffordshire, Somerset, the Midlands, Durham, and Northumberland. The impact on the landscape was considerable and areas like Whickham, near Newcastle, were blighted by the slag heaps and carriage ways. Other regions like Bentley Grange in Yorkshire and south Staffordshire bear the scars of early modern and medieval mining. Although the enterprise remained arduous and dangerous, there were technological advances. In Scotland a horse dredge was invented to gain access to seams under the sea and there were experiments with steam drainage at Raglan in the 1650s. The first steam-powered pump in the world was employed near Dudley, in Worcestershire, in 1712. By the end of the period, coal was the main fuel in salt-boiling, starch-making, sugar refining, brick, glass, and tile-making, brewing, and dyeing and had started to compete with peat and wood as a domestic fuel.

One of the industries not yet fuelled by coal was the iron industry. The needs of the industry were transformed by the invention of the blast furnace. The first one to be built in Britain appeared at Newbridge in Sussex in 1494, even at this stage more efficient than the old 'bloomeries'. Location was determined more by the availability of running water and wood to make charcoal than by the ore, some of which was imported from Sweden. Water was needed to drive

A DEPICTION of an early modern tailor at work reminds us that clothing was not produced in factories. The family would work on every stage, from cutting the cloth to the finished product. For most tailors, all this would take place in the home and most members of the family would contribute.

THE iron industry: a hammer pond at Cowden, Kent. Early modern iron works leave little trace in the landscape. An exception, however, is the water technology used to drive the bellows and hammers. All over the Weald watercourses were dammed, creating hammer ponds to provide a sufficient head of water. At Cowden Michael Weston had been making guns for six or seven years in 1574. The site produced ordnance for both sides during the Civil War. The hunting reserves of the gentry and aristocracy were perfect for conversion to such use and many made this surprising transition in the late sixteenth and seventeenth centuries.

mechanical hammers and bellows and led to the construction of artificial 'hammer ponds', another example of the sophisticated water technology of the period. The industry in the Weald boomed but was by no means confined there. In the 1560s ironworks were first established in south Wales, an area which came to specialize in smelting, with ironworks in Pembrokeshire, Glamorganshire, and the south-east, copper smelting at Aberdulais near Neath, and an ancient centre of lead smelting around Clawdd Mwyn in the Ystwyth valley. The third major region was in the west Midlands with centres in Staffordshire, Warwickshire, Worcestershire, and Shropshire. Similar concentrations appeared wherever there was wood, water, and the demand, for

MINING: Bentley Grange, Emley, S. Yorkshire. It is notoriously difficult to date early mining sites and such remains are scarce, as later activity tends to obliterate mining earthworks. This site was actively mined between the twelfth and sixteenth centuries and at least shows the remains of 'bell-pits', common throughout our period. A shaft was sunk to a depth of about six metres and excavation extended as far as was felt to be safe. The remains show a series of spoil heaps with the central shaft subsequently subsiding. We may be encouraged in considering this site to be late by the evidence of ploughing that lies under the spoil heaps.

instance in Westmorland, Lancashire, and, by 1610, on the shores of Lochmaree, in the Scottish Highlands.

It was the Black Country that became Britain's principal centre of manufactures dependent on iron. The manufacture was still on a domestic scale, but this should not blind us to the quality and variety of goods produced. The area produced scythesmiths, blacksmiths, stirrup-makers, lorimers, and especially nail-makers. The crucial innovation was the slitting mill, introduced from the Continent in the 1620s, which allowed manufacturers to produce malleable rods without the labour of splitting bar iron by hand. On a smaller scale these developments were paralleled by the steel industry, which started to grow in Elizabeth's reign with the help of Dutch immigrants. Some of the steel workers settled in the west Midlands, others near Newcastle and Sheffield. With high quality ore from Sweden, numerous manufacturers were drawn to these areas producing clocks, watches, pens, and, of course, cutlery.

It would be an overstatement to suggest that these activities amounted to an industrial revolution or even prepared the way for industrialization. Too few of the industrial regions of this period were those which industrialized later, often because supplies of labour, kept inexpensive by by-employment, were high enough to discourage the necessary technological advances. In any case, Britain lagged behind Scandinavian metallurgical skills and German mining technology. However, it would be less inaccurate to imagine, if not a revolution, then a considerable uprising of material culture. To the contribution of the metal workers, we can add the extractors of clay and the brick strikers, whose greatest achievement was the rebuilding of London. The glass industry made great gains in this period due to immigrants from Italy and France becoming established in Staffordshire, Gloucestershire, Herefordshire, and the Stour valley. Tiles, domestic pots, and clay pipes were being produced in great numbers, in greater diversity of types, in many districts, far more than the standard histories of English pottery allow. If we combine the pipkins, porringers, and condiment dishes of the potteries with the newly glazed and curtained windows, the kitchens filled with pewter, the new variety and colour of cloth, the knitted stockings, the hinges, nails, tools, the wire for pins, fishhooks, birdcages, mousetraps, buttons and buckles, the gutters and drainpipes of lead, and all the other products of domestic industry, it becomes clear that there was a substantial transformation of material culture in the early modern period.

11. *The Urban Landscape*

These manufactures, of course, were not available to all. Many of them were intended for urban markets and most passed through towns in their distribution. Indeed, it is not possible to understand either the operation of agricultural regional specialization or the changes in manufacture in this period without some reference to the towns, and the changing townscapes of Britain deserve attention in their own right. By now it will come as no surprise that Britain's towns went through a period of transition, even transformation, in the early modern period. The nature of that transition is, however, more complex than might be expected. In fact it is more accurate to think of transitions in the plural, for townscapes were no exception to the variety that we have seen characterize the rural landscape.

The very object of inquiry for urban historians has been a real difficulty. First, at what point does a settlement become 'urban'? Can economic, social, demographic, or cultural criteria be identified that mark out towns from large villages? The search for the urban variable has yielded a great deal of information without producing an uncontested cluster of factors to identify urban environments. Secondly, to what extent can a society be said to be urban at all when the population of the British town, especially at the beginning of the sixteenth century, rarely exceeded five thousand souls? This contrast of scale applies not only to our twentieth-century idea of towns, but also to a great deal of contemporary Europe. Even London was not a great city at the start of the reign of the Tudors.

The question of scale is perhaps the most important of our preconceptions that must be

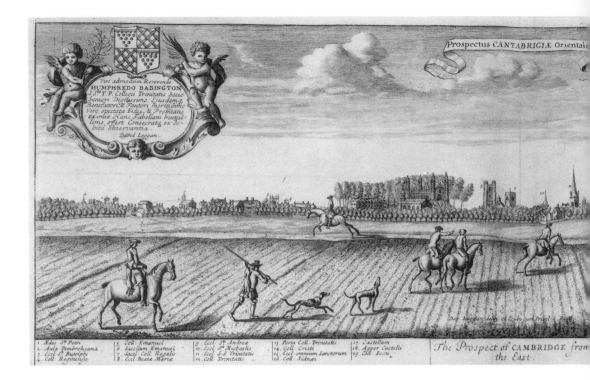

Viro admodum Reverendo
HUMPHREDO BABINGTON
SSæ T.P. Colleâii Trinitatis Socio
Seniori Dioitissimo Eiusdemæ
Benefactori & Fautori bærifsimo
Viro spectate Fidei, & Probitatis
eximiæ Hanc Tabellam humili
lime, offert Consecratæ ex de
bita Observantia.
David Loggan

1. Ædes Stæ Petri
2. Aula Pembrokiana
3. Eccl Stæ Butolphi
4. Coll Reginensis
5. Coll Emanuel
6. Sacellum Emanuel
7. Sacel Coll Regalis
8. Eccl Beatæ Mariæ
9. Eccl Stæ Andreæ
10. Eccl Stæ Michaelis
11. Eccl S.S Trinitatis
12. Coll Trinitatis
13. Porta Coll Trinitatis
14. Coll Christi
15. Eccl omnium Sanctorum
16. Coll Sidnæi
17. Castellum
18. Agger Castelli
19. Coll Iesu

The Prospect of CAMBRIDGE *from the East.*

overcome before we understand the early modern town. Norwich, which began the period as Britain's second city and ended as its third, grew from a population of 15,000 in 1550 to 30,000 in 1700. Norwich was approached by a handful of regional capitals like Bristol, York, and Exeter but the majority of towns were much smaller. The county towns may have had several thousand inhabitants, few of the market towns more than a thousand. Scotland was, and remained, less urbanized than England. The earliest date for which we have reliable statistics, 1755, has Edinburgh with a population of 40,000 after a long period of growth. This figure was equalled by the cumulative total of the next tier of Scotland's towns, Glasgow, Aberdeen, Perth, and Dundee, so Scotland's towns were never quite so dwarfed as English towns were by London. The situation in Wales has added complications as many of its towns were English plantations of the thirteenth century and remained a fairly alien presence, dominated by the colonial military presence in the castles. In terms of scale, though, the same concerns apply if anything to a greater extent. Even in 1670 the greatest Welsh towns, Brecon and Carmarthen, had only about 2,000 inhabitants.

The second assumption to overcome is that towns are wholly removed from farming. This is rarely the case. Many towns were surrounded by town fields and many townspeople farmed in addition to following a recognizably urban occupation. This caveat links to the third preconception: we are accustomed to towns being densely populated with houses closely packed together. Although some towns and some areas within towns were like this, in general the early modern town had much more open space. Exeter was described as being half orchards and many other towns had their spaces that were not built up. This blurring of the distinction between town and country was actually increasing in the early modern era as the city walls that sharply defined the division for medieval towns were often in decay by the sixteenth century. Although some towns of strategic importance such as Hull, Berwick, and Portsmouth refurbished their walls in these

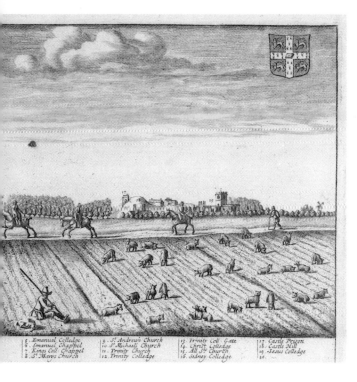

DAVID LOGGAN'S view of Cambridge (1688) is a little idealized. The town is dominated by churches and the university. The surrounding fields are filled with working people. This prospect from the east is drawn after harvest, for livestock are grazing and providing manure on arable fields.

1. *Emanuel Colledge* 9. *S.t Andrew's Church* 13. *Trinity Coll. Gate* 17. *Castle Prison*
5. *Emanuel Chappel* 10. *S.t Michaels Church* 14. *Christ Colledge* 18. *Castle Hill*
7. *Kings Coll. Chappel* 11. *Trinity Church* 15. *All S.ts Church* 19. *Iesus Colledge*
8. *S.t Maries Church* 12. *Trinity Colledge* 16. *Sidney Colledge* 20.

years, and there was a flurry of re-fortification in the 1640s, few towns were as sharply divided from the surrounding countryside as they had been.

The early modern period has been seen as one of urban crisis. It was suggested that the period before 1570 saw a demographic and economic crisis in towns, with many thriving medieval centres falling into decay before something of a revival from 1650. Coventry and York were seen as prime examples, although many other towns fitted this model. More recent study has suggested that while some towns were in a state of crisis, others were prospering, often at the expense of decaying towns, and that specific local contexts are more appropriate to explain urban decay than a general crisis. Great Grimsby, for instance, was clearly a town in decline in the sixteenth century with a shrinking population and diminishing trade but a good deal of this can be explained by the silting of the town's harbour. Boston was similarly afflicted and lost its principal trade in wool due to the new draperies. Furthermore, the two Lincolnshire ports were in decline while competitors were thriving, Hull becoming, for a time, the main port of the Humber and King's Lynn dominating the Wash.

The loss of the wool trade affected Leicester, described by Evelyn in 1654 as an 'old and ragged city' and another commonly cited town by proponents of the decay thesis. Although the migration of industry can be overstated, the loss of this role can be seen as precipitating something of a crisis of identity in the late medieval town. This crisis was exacerbated by the Reformation, for three reasons. On a topographic level, the Dissolution of the Monasteries left still more open spaces within towns. In Bury St Edmunds, for instance, the abbey precincts were left as a quarry for local builders directly in front of the market-place. On a political level, the acquisition of monastic property by the gentry gave them an influence in the towns that had been denied them by stubbornly independent borough authorities in medieval towns. On a cultural level, much of the rich civic ritual and ceremonial, the processions, plays, and pageants through which late medieval urban society had defined and remade itself, was lost when the chantries, fraternities, and guilds were abolished. In the early years of Elizabeth's reign in England, Protestants made some attempt to appropriate this culture, but from around 1580 the consensus view was that such activities were an inappropriate medium for the Word of God and civic ritual lost much of its inclusive, festive side.

12. *A New Urban Identity*

While it might be inaccurate to identify an urban crisis in some terms, it seems less so to suggest that the early modern town was in the process of having its physical and cultural identity remade, of searching for a role within a changed urban–rural relationship. The recasting of that identity had its economic, religious, and broadly cultural elements, and each of these is reflected in the townscapes produced.

Economically, the role that became pre-eminent was the market. The towns retained some of the finishing operations of manufacture and, as we have noted, became centres of consumption, but their greatest importance was as distributive centres. This role grew in importance with the growth in manufacture but was also critical in relation to growing agricultural specialization. Indeed, it has been suggested that some of the market towns that were thriving in this period benefited from their location on the borders of increasingly interdependent agricultural regions. A widespread network of 'cardinal' markets developed, acting as inland entrepôts for the regions' specialisms.

Towns had, of course, always been centres of exchange and distribution and many medieval towns owed their foundations to market grants, but the early modern town has exchange and distribution as its central role. This can be seen in the attention lavished upon the market-places, which came to be the focus of towns in the way that castles and ecclesiastical buildings dominated the medieval town. By the middle of the sixteenth century it was common to find several specialized market areas in a town, each devoted to a different product. In Scotland, Edinburgh, Stirling, and Glasgow shared markets for linen and woollen cloth, meat, meal, horses, shoes, timber, fruit and vegetables, and fish; but Leicester had separate markets for meat, wood, horses, sheep, hay, and grain. At the next level, larger markets could specialize on a regional or even a national level. In the south-east, Canterbury and Godalming concentrated on cloth, Ashford, Chichester, Maidstone, Lenham, and Rye on cattle, Dartford and Dorking on malt, and so forth. Ripon was nationally renowned for its horse market, Leeds and Wakefield for wool imported from as far away as Buckinghamshire, Oxfordshire, and Rutland. Many of these trades were accommodated in annual fairs which might be held on open land on the edge of the town, like Cambridge's Stourbridge fair. Clearly these products were not all for consumption within the market town itself, but were passing through these nodal points in a diversifying economy.

These roles gained expression in the townscapes in three ways. First, many towns gained or maintained large open areas in their centres to accommodate market stalls. During the sixteenth and seventeenth centuries much of this business was transferred to permanent shops erected on the site of the market, fossilizing the shape of the open area in the modern town centre. Secondly, the roads leading into the town centre were lined with coaching inns providing accommodation, sustenance, and hospitality for visitors. The inns took on vital roles within the marketing process, often housing the sale of goods, advertising their specialities, offering credit facilities, and providing the social space for deals to be struck. Thirdly, many towns marked their markets architecturally. Many medieval market crosses survived the Reformation although perhaps the most famous, at Banbury, was removed by reformers late in Elizabeth's reign. Increasingly, these crosses were replaced by market houses or town halls, regarded, as at Banbury, as 'far more

Market architecture: Leominster, Herefordshire. The town acquired a town hall in 1634, designed by John Abel, something of a specialist in the genre. The building is characteristic of its type: a pillared open floor providing market-space (now walled in) and a magnificent, showy council chamber above. The government presides and watches over the market which in turn supports the town government. The shape of such buildings was not substantially changed when town halls began to adopt a Classical vocabulary after 1660.

spacious and convenient'. As one of the principal functions of many town governments was to administer the market, the functions, and the buildings, tended to elide.

There are elements of continuity: town halls and market houses continued to be built through this period but stone or brick became the materials of choice. A fine stone 'mercat cross' was acquired by Aberdeen in 1686. Newcastle upon Tyne was building a new stone hall in the late 1650s and by the end of the century such buildings had been built, or rebuilt, in Bath, Rochester, Sheffield, Faringdon, Eynsham, Abingdon, and many other towns. The buildings were rarely the timber-framed structures in vernacular style of the earlier period. They tended to adopt Renaissance forms, classical details, and a new attention to symmetry. This was the new high culture of the 'urban renaissance', a culture that placed considerable emphasis on the townscape as an agent of order, harmony, and hierarchy. By the end of our period a significant number of provincial towns had laid out squares in conscious imitation of the Italian piazza. Bristol had three such squares, and they could also be seen in Birmingham, Liverpool, Whitehaven, and Warwick. The town was coming to be a centre of cultural and social no less than economic exchange. The gentry were beginning to spend more time in urban society and towns began to acquire the facilities to house and entertain them. The new urban élites demanded classical façades on their residences and many houses gained a thin brick skin on the front in an effort, often vain, to conceal timber framing. A new wave of theatre building took off, with early examples in Norwich, Bath, and Bristol. The architecture of the market hall and the theatre is echoed in the new Assembly rooms, for card-playing and balls but also to house the active urban marriage market. Some towns laid out walks, parks, and gardens for similar activities outside. By 1715, more than ever before, the town was a place to see and in which to be seen, a theatrical experience in itself.

In topographical terms, this new role for the town generated a clearer division between town and country. The best houses were almost invariably in the centre and much of the late seventeenth-century expansion was accommodated by infilling rather than suburban growth. The famous prints by Nathaniel and Samuel Buck, popular in the eighteenth century, characteristically show a densely built, compact settlement, sharply distinguished from the surrounding countryside. Where the Buck prints exaggerate, this merely makes clearer the fact that the new towns were culturally, as well as physically, distinct from the rural hinterland.

13 · *London*

London has not loomed large in this discussion of early modern towns. In part this is because the English capital is, of course, *sui generis*. However, many of the characteristics identified above apply to London, with differences of scale, and the capital went through similar transitions albeit usually earlier than the largest provincial towns. London, for instance, had its first planned square with Inigo Jones's piazza and church for Covent Garden in the 1630s; its second, west of Lincoln's Inn, was built up on two sides by 1641. Proposals to rebuild within a Renaissance plan after the Great Fire of 1666 were more grandiose than those for provincial towns and still more doomed to failure. London fulfilled the same exchange role as the provincial towns but with an immeasurably greater concentration of economic, judicial, and governmental interests. Our initial caveats about scale and density of population apply to London, at least in the sixteenth century. There was enough country in the region of present-day Oxford Street to support fox hunting, the cries of hunters giving Soho its name, and we have noted the intense market gardening to the south, from Battersea to Vauxhall and beyond.

This much granted, the population figures speak for themselves. The great expansion began in the mid-sixteenth century with around 120,000 in 1550, 200,000 in 1600, perhaps 375,000 in 1650, and 490,000 by 1700. As with other major towns, the high urban mortality rates meant that this growth was largely maintained by immigration, although it seems to have been the immigrants themselves who were most vulnerable to the diseases of the city. Perhaps more striking is London's rise in relative terms: from 2.5 per cent of the population to a full 10 per cent, a figure barely matched by the rest of England's urban population. In European terms London was the seventh or eighth largest city in 1550, the second by 1650, and competing with Paris by the end of the Stuart era.

Of course, it is somewhat inaccurate to think of London as a single entity. We must consider at least three settlements, increasingly seamless through this period. First is the ancient City of London, the principal walled square mile with its increasingly important extramural elements. In fact the population of the city itself increased less than the national average, while the suburbs expanded by 750 per cent between 1500 and 1700, with a good deal of unenforced legislation to curb the sprawling slums to the east. The heart of this element was the port of London. This was the centre of Britain's international trade and much of its internal trade, focused on the river. The port of London landed coal lighters from Newcastle and fresh fish to Billingsgate. Small craft transported goods from seagoing ships to the appropriate quays, a vital service as many of these were upstream from the port proper or from the only bridge. At Vintry wharf, for instance, wine was landed from ships from the Rhine, France, Spain, Portugal, and the Canaries. The river was full of small craft ferrying passengers and goods from one bank to the other or along the river. In the seventeenth century the docklands began to develop, with the East India Company completing Brunswick dock by 1656 and Greenwich dock under way in the last years of the century. Before these facilities were added, the port displayed a tendency to expand even further downstream.

The second pole of London life was Westminster with the Abbey, Westminster Palace, and Whitehall, a royal enclave vastly expanded by Henry VIII after the fall of Wolsey although only Inigo Jones's Banqueting House survives. For most of this period, the court was far more important than Parliament, but the region exerted a powerful attraction on upper-class settlement and professional life. Fleet Street, in the sixteenth century a district of jurists, was drawn towards the west and the Strand became an area of competing noble town houses, with the Duke of Buckingham's pre-eminent, a fact marked only by street names in the modern city. Although the Earl of Bedford's Covent Garden project was a failure with the fruit market taking over by 1654, the West End became an increasingly fashionable district after the Restoration. Late in the century Golden Square, Grosvenor Square, Berkeley Square, Red Lion Square, and Kensington Square were laid out.

The third element of London was the city south of the river. London Bridge connected the walled city with Southwark, a region of urbanization easily overlooked because of its proximity to the capital proper. By 1600 Southwark contained 10 per cent of London's population and was, in its own right, the second largest urban area in England. Difficulties of administration and

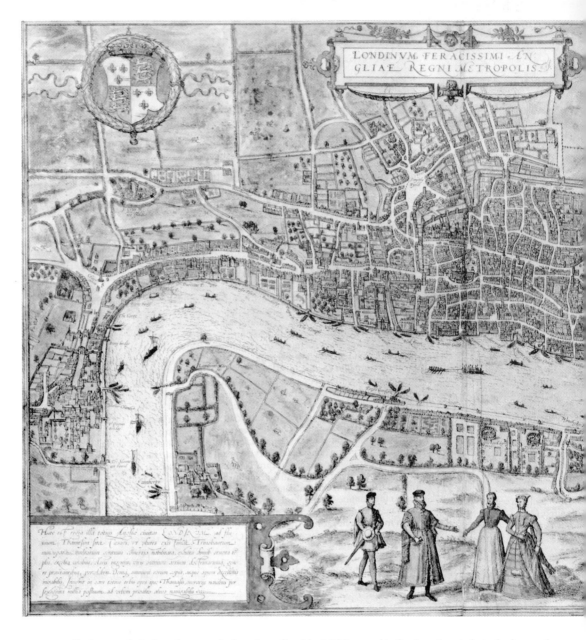

uncontrolled growth led to the area being described in 1583 as a site for 'unchaste interludes and bargains of incontinence' housing the theatres and stews and also bear gardens, bull-baiting pits, and bowling alleys. To the west, Lambeth was dominated by the archiepiscopal palace and was altogether more respectable.

By 1715 Britain could offer urban experiences of wealth, fashion, classical architecture, and high culture, as well as of crushing poverty, squalor, overcrowding, and jerry-building. However, for three-quarters of the population at least, the conditions of everyday life were rural, if not necessarily agricultural. It is clear that aspects of life in different regions of Britain had been transformed during the reigns of the Tudors and Stuarts. The impact of new farming practices and

Braun and Hogenberg's *Londinum Feracissimi Angliae Regni Metropolis* (1572) from *Civitatis Orbis Terrarum,* Volume I (1612–18). This 'picture-map' is not, of course, to be taken as a literal representation of contemporary London; it is part of a collection placing the city in the context of European urban life. However, it does illustrate aspects of London in the mid-sixteenth century. The tripartite division of the city is clear, the density of the walled city contrasting to Westminster and the south. Note the carriers on the river and the agriculture to the north. (See colour detail facing p. 160.)

agricultural innovations, of technological and economic change in the extractive, metallurgical, and manufacturing sector, and of the changing townscapes of Britain cannot be ignored. However, it would be misleading to allow this to be the dominant impression of an account of the British landscape in the period. Much continued as always. Farmers kept grain for themselves and provided themselves with bread and meat before sending the surplus to market. Many of their houses may have shown few signs of the burgeoning material culture of the period and many may have had little experience of the urban environment beyond the nearest tiny market town. Britain in 1715 was very different from Britain in 1485, but it also bore little resemblance to Britain in the late twentieth century.

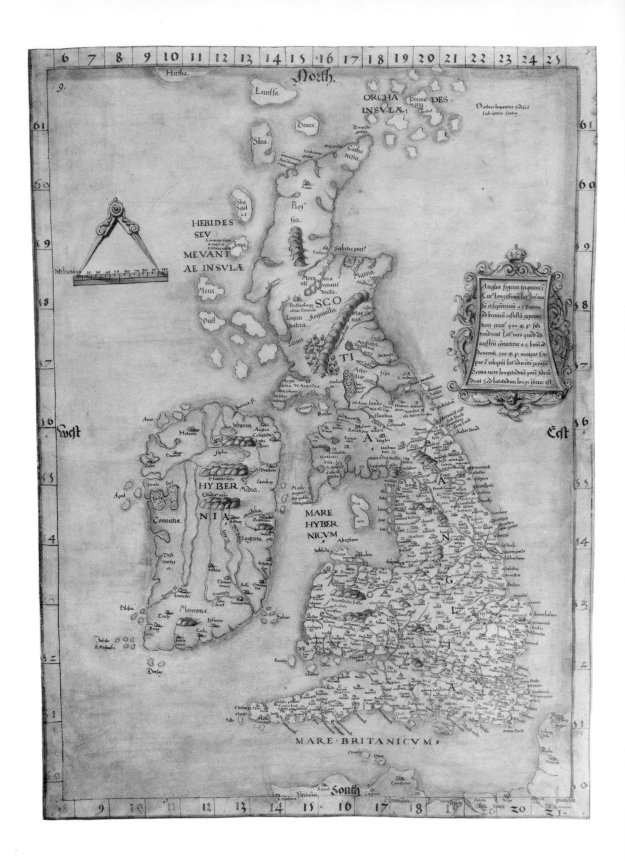

2 THE CONSOLIDATION OF ENGLAND

1485–1603

DIARMAID MacCULLOCH

1. *Introduction*

In 1399, 1461, and 1485 great noblemen seized the Crown of England and the lordship of Ireland; they brought to royal government a nobleman's attitudes to his estates. The administration of aristocratic lands was structured with a sense of heartland and outliers. Indeed a particularly grand estate, such as that revealed by the surviving archives of the Howard Dukes of Norfolk, was run in a threefold pattern: the Duke habitually toured and was keenly interested in his home territories, but in a second tier, he was a less regular visitor. In remote outlying estates, he made little investment and left active exploitation to tenants.

Henry Tudor would have recognized this pattern in the territories of his newly conquered English Crown in 1485. The heartland was the south-east, centred since the twelfth century on government institutions at Westminster beside London. Medieval England was more centralized than any other large European state, but only in this area of prosperous lowland farming country—the Thames valley, the south coast from Kent to Dorset, East Anglia, and the Midlands—did Westminster's writ fully run. This was where most medieval monarchs felt comfortable, as a scatter of well-kept royal palaces, castles, and lodges demonstrated; most city and borough representation in meetings of Parliament came from this region.

Beyond this was a more miscellaneous area—the second tier—Devon and Cornwall, along the Welsh border to Cheshire, Lancashire, the Peak District, the Yorkshire Ridings, and Lincolnshire. The hills tended to fill the horizon more menacingly above lowland prosperity, and the Crown's authority was often expressed in indirect form, through jurisdictions like the Duchies of

Map of Britain (significantly mistitled 'Angliae figura'), *c.* 1534–46. It was essential for the Tudors' strategy of centralization for monarchs to get a more accurate knowledge of their realm, and Tudor palaces contained many maps on display. This example is the earliest in England to be graduated for latitude and longitude. Notable is the fact that it marks Hampton Court.

Cornwall and Lancaster, the Earldom of Chester, or the scattered territories of the Duchy of York: former private fiefs which accidents of politics had brought back into royal hands. From these areas, fewer citizens and burgesses than in the heartland were summoned as city and borough representatives to Parliament; Cheshire returned no MPs at all until 1545. The real outliers—the third tier—were still further out, to the south, north, and west: Calais and the Channel Islands; the borders with Scotland; Wales; Ireland. Ireland was itself a three-tier territory fanning out from the English Pale around Dublin, through Anglo-Norman lordships and boroughs to Gaelic lands where the King of Westminster was a distant ghost.

The five Tudor monarchs changed the kingdom's three-tier pattern for ever. By 1603 the royal heartland had been extended to all lowland England: nearly half the dominions of the English Crown. The Tudors aimed beyond this first stage in integration. The map of the whole British Isles shown on p.34, which probably hung in one of Henry VIII's palaces, was significantly mistitled 'Angliae figura'—'the form of England'. However, the agenda would never be completed. The second stage, the integration of highland England and Wales into the heartland, was well advanced at Elizabeth I's death, but Ireland proved a harder task, and the English monarchy's medieval dream of absorbing Scotland was fulfilled only in a partial and backhanded fashion.

The uniting of the lowlands was helped by a sense of difference between northern and southern England, which had been brought home sharply to southerners when northern armies appeared in the south during the fifteenth-century civil wars. Southerners had not liked what they had seen: the anonymous Croyland chronicler spoke in 1486 of 'those ingrates in the North, whence every evil takes its rise'. The boundary of north and south was, of course, subjective, as it is today. For Greenwich-born Henry VIII, notoriously reluctant to venture north of Watford, the Croyland chronicler's Lincolnshire was 'one of the most brute and beastly [shires] of the whole realm'. Nevertheless, the south's more rapid reception of the sixteenth-century Protestant Reformation clarified the division. Even in the early 1530s Hugh Latimer, a Leicestershire man,

EXTRACT from William Tyndale's preface to his edition of a medieval Lollard pamphlet *The Examination of William Thorpe* (Antwerp, 1530), in which he promises an edition in Middle English for northerners and Scotsmen: 'This I have corrected and put forth in the English, that now is used in England, for our southern men, nothing thereto adding, not yet therefrom minishing. And I intend thereafter, with the help of God, to put it forth in his own old English, which shall well serve, I doubt not, both for the northern men, and the faithful brethren of Scotland.'

⁋ This I haue corrected and put forth in th english that now is vsed in Englãde/ for owe sothern men / nothynge therto addynge ne yet therfrom mynysshyng. And I entende hereafter with the helpe of God to put it forthe in his owne olde english/which shal well serue/ I dou te not/bothe for the northern men ãd the faythfull brothern of scot lãde.

was making contemptuous remarks about northerners and their religion, although in later years his tone mellowed to sorrow rather than anger. Gloucestershire-born William Tyndale, a gourmet of linguistics, apologized to northerners and Scotsmen for publishing a modernized version of a tract in medieval English, which he knew that they would understand better in the original. Lowland snobbery therefore fitted the progress of the English Reformation, to aid the first stage of extending direct Tudor rule.

2. *Communities in the Lowlands*

Besides the three-tier structure of the medieval English kingdom, there were rich variations within the lowlands. The main unit of lowland government since the twelfth century had been the shire or county. Modern explorations of regional history took this for granted at first: a natural myopia, because royal record-keepers in London habitually arranged their archives by county, and thus made the county unit the researcher's easiest approach. Much resulting investigation of the 'county community' provoked a healthy corrective reaction from historians who pointed out the existence of alternative forums for local life. There were regions both smaller and greater than the county. Counties contained natural divisions, and these were given semi-formal expression at parliamentary election time in some shires, where the two shire MPs were customarily chosen from different areas—in Gloucestershire, for example, from the Severn Vale and from the Cotswolds. Farming and marketing regions could straddle county boundaries; so could great aristocratic estates, some formally constituted even in parts of southern England as separate jurisdictions ('liberties' or 'franchises'), others the product of accumulation of power in one or two generations of a family. Magnates might take an interest in the areas covered by their estates rather than the shire, or they might despise the provinces which brought them wealth, and concentrate on their role at Court as the monarch's God-given counsellors.

Alongside the county community, then, were the farming community, the market community, and the community of the magnate estate. Each reflected the life and interest of particular sections of society: prosperous yeomen and merchants in farming and market areas, noblemen in their estates. The county community was distinctively the world of the gentry, who had no natural place at Court around the monarch, yet who considered themselves to have their own God-given place in local government—especially the government of the shire. Among these competing identities, it was significant that the changes brought by the Tudors strengthened the role of the gentry in lowland government. Because of this, it was county identity which benefited most from Tudor changes; in most lowland regions, it was the county or shire which developed a loyalty and personality of its own. This was a paradoxical result of Tudor centralization: a development which brought its own localism, with a strong dash of legalistic conservatism to make the task of central government more complicated.

3. *Getting to Know England*

Effective government was well-informed government: a problem for Henry of Richmond, arriving after years of exile in Brittany and France. Monarchs and ministers needed to be sensitive to contrasts of political behaviour in adjacent areas with similar landscapes and farming conditions: some contrasts were remarkably long-lived. Leicestershire was notorious for a feud between the noble families of Grey and Hastings from the Wars of the Roses to the seventeenth-century civil wars. Contrariwise in neighbouring Tudor Northamptonshire, dominance passed from wealthy monasteries to a fairly harmonious group of wealthy gentlemen, perhaps all the more determined to govern their shire effectively because of Leicestershire's unhappy example. The same contrast of quarrelsomeness and effective oligarchic rule emerged in late Elizabethan Norfolk and Suffolk, despite their common East Anglian heritage, because of the collapse of the Howard family's power in 1572. Thomas, fourth Howard Duke of Norfolk, was destroyed by his involvement in the intrigues around Mary Queen of Scots: fleeing from unbearable tensions at Court in 1569, he was arrested at his palace at Kenninghall and after prolonged delays, executed for treason three years later. The county of Norfolk found no substitute for his virtually unchallenged rule, and factions battled incessantly for mastery. In Suffolk, the Duke's gentry-following had contended before 1572 with generally more Protestant gentry who were not within his sphere of influence; after the Howard disaster, these Protestants were happy to seize the reins of government, forming a collective leadership like the gentry of Northamptonshire, which religious conservatives could do little to challenge.

Such conflicts could burst into national politics. One of the worst was a feud in 1590s Nottinghamshire between Gilbert Talbot, seventh Earl of Shrewsbury and Sir Thomas Stanhope, a county magnate with younger brothers in Court and government service. The quarrel had no deep roots; it was a pure personality clash, which ran out of steam by the end of the century, but while it lasted, almost any issue would inflame the county atmosphere. Both men tried to pull strings at Court; Stanhope had the advantage. Queen Elizabeth was fond of his two personable younger brothers in her entourage, and she was annoyed to find her time taken up with such trivia as a Nottinghamshire fishermen's petition against Stanhope's mill-weir, part of Shrewsbury's war of attrition. The 1593 Nottinghamshire county election produced Feydeau-farce-like scenes, as hopeful parliamentary candidate Stanhope and his voters chased around Nottingham looking for the election venue, which Shrewsbury had moved in order to get his own candidates elected; on this occasion there was no bloodshed, but a series of riots and duels produced agitated interventions from the Privy Council (both officially and in private letters), and lengthy lawsuits before the Council sitting in Star Chamber. Shrewsbury eventually made a dreadful mistake in incautiously choosing one of his leading estate officials to organize violence against Stanhope's properties: the man was a Roman Catholic in touch with plotters overseas. The Earl was humiliated by being put briefly under house arrest, and his national career never fully recovered. When he was finally admitted to Privy Council membership in 1601, it was pointedly done on the same day as the admission of Sir Thomas Stanhope's brother John.

Such convulsions must be confronted, reduced, or at least understood. One way was for the Crown to rely on great magnates like Shrewsbury: they knew their region intimately, and at least in theory could command its reverence, yet they were also usually familiar faces at Court, understood the monarch's wishes, and should be able to explain central government's motives to their social inferiors. Tudor government often imitated patterns laid down by the Yorkist monarchs, and in local government, Edward IV had placed much trust—indeed too much—in noblemen. Among the franchise jurisdictions which transcended shire boundaries, Henry VII would find that some were brand new and not moribund feudal survivals; for instance Edward

IV had created the Duke of Norfolk's Liberty in East Anglia, and three new lordships for the Herberts in Wales.

However, Henry hardly knew any English noblemen in 1485: noble rivalries had lain behind the recurrent instability of the Crown in the previous eighty years, and Henry generally kept his aristocracy at arm's length. Yet even he gave especial power to three aristocrats whom he could trust without question: significantly, none of them had children to whom they might feel more loyalty than to the royal family. The King's own mother, the formidable Lady Margaret Beaufort, his uncle Jasper Tudor, whom he made Duke of Bedford, and John de Vere, thirteenth Earl of Oxford (a rare long-term supporter of Henry) were all allowed to enjoy informal viceregal powers in their particular regions.

The Tudors, therefore, were not inherently opposed to noble power, despite Henry VII's self-imposed isolation and Henry VIII's outbursts of murderous paranoia about those with larger doses of Plantagenet royal blood than himself. Some great Tudor families stand out because of their ethos of Crown service in the localities and overseas. Despite three times suffering political

LADY MARGARET BEAUFORT, mother of Henry VII. Despite the appearance of pious unworldliness considered appropriate for the portrait of a Cambridge college's founder, Lady Margaret was an energetic politician and the ideal magnate to control local affairs, trusted absolutely by Henry, her personal Council became an important part of his devolved government in the Midlands. However, there were few like her on whom Henry could rely without hesitation.

Brick chimneys added *c*.1520 by Thomas Howard, second Duke of Norfolk to the towers of Framlingham Castle, Suffolk. Several of these chimneys were false, purely decorative, domesticating the grim Norman fortress of the Bigods and Mowbrays: an amusing symbol of the Tudor taming of the English aristocracy, parallel to the 1536 legislation which undermined the power of private jurisdictions like the Liberty of the Duke of Norfolk.

eclipse at the hands of the Tudors, the Howard Dukes of Norfolk and Earls of Surrey were regularly employed far from their East Anglian estates, in the north, in Ireland, Scotland, and France: they remained military leaders, like the Bigod and Mowbray houses of Norfolk before them, but they were also great administrators both in Westminster and in the regions, and their military prowess was now unambiguously at the disposal of the King. The Talbot Earls of Shrewsbury cherished the same service ethos—their motto was 'Ready to accomplish'—and showed a surer instinct for survival than the Howards. Charles Brandon was created Duke of Suffolk by Henry VIII; his career was based originally on his skill in the glamorous futilities of royal tournaments, but it continued on course because of his consistent willingness to grovel before the King.

4. *Magnates or Justices of the Peace?*

However, the Tudors found reliable regional magnates in short supply. Magnate power was ambiguous for the Crown: magnates were more likely to sympathize with central government's concerns than were localist-minded gentry, but a nobleman gone to the bad was very bad news indeed for the Crown. Moreover, Henry VII and Elizabeth I in particular were reluctant to create new peers to replenish noble stock as families died out. Where there was no powerful or trustworthy aristocrat, therefore, the monarchy increasingly relied on Justices of the Peace (JPs) to do its bidding. JPs became the most important officers in local government, a lasting success out of various twelfth-century experiments in royal administration all the more attractive because they were virtually unpaid. JPs were named for each county by a royal commission, the commission of the peace another advantage, since they could be dismissed simply by issuing another commission which did not name them. From 1363 they were ordered to hold sessions in their counties four times a year: the quarter sessions. Their formal sittings were often referred to as the 'bench'.

JPs were kept in touch with the wishes of London through the assize courts—twice-yearly visits from pairs of Westminster judges who each rode a circuit of several counties; they would arrive in state, bearing orders from the government, and primed with royal admonitions to be alert to local politics and *causes célèbres*. In the sixteenth century, JPs and quarter sessions lost some of their previously extensive legal jurisdiction, because the assize judges came to monopolize the trial of more serious breaches of the peace; however, JPs gained responsibility for a wide variety of local administration and the execution of parliamentary legislation and royal proclamations, particularly as the Tudors developed a national system of poor relief.

The JPs' new importance is attested by the rise in their numbers during the Tudor period. Under the Yorkists, between ten and twenty individuals were named for lowland county commissions of the peace; since several names were honorary, far fewer actually did the JPs' work. Numbers began rising during the latter part of Henry VII's reign; after a widespread government 'purge' on the accession of Henry VIII, they rose again under Cardinal Wolsey, particularly during the 1520s, so that by the time of Wolsey's fall in 1529, virtually all lowland county commissions contained double or treble the number of JPs in 1485. The upward trend continued through Thomas Cromwell's years of power in the 1530s, and thereafter stabilized, with occasional government efforts at reduction, until the troubled conditions of the 1590s sent numbers climbing once more.

The working membership of the justices' bench usually consisted of leading county gentry, although minor peers were also happy to be active JPs. It may seem strange that this voluntary system worked as well as it did. However, sixteenth-century gentry came to share the service ethos apparent in great magnate families; they were also increasingly anxious to become JPs to reinforce their local prestige and power. Particularly in conflict-ridden counties, even the sequence in which the commission listed the JPs could be significant, because it determined their seniority and the order of their sitting on the bench. One early Stuart Hertfordshire JP became so obsessed with this sequence numbering that he often added his number to his signature on documents! Tudor government commissioning JPs found itself a seller in a seller's market, and periodically it was able to carry out purges of JPs right across the country. These became more frequent in the later sixteenth century, when the governing class became divided in religious loyalties; Mary's government initiated the first traceable national purge on religious grounds in 1553. Lord Burghley, convinced that there were too many JPs, repeatedly tried to cut down numbers nationally, notably in 1587 and 1595, with as much long-term effect as the flattery of Canute's courtiers on the sea-tide. In any case, even Burghley realized that too frequent purges would cause more trouble and upset than they were worth.

5. *A Tudor Revolution in Government*

Henry VII began developing the role of the JP, but Henry VIII's two great ministers, Thomas Wolsey and his sometime servant Thomas Cromwell, did most to set the patterns in local government which endured down to the civil wars—indeed in many respects down to the nineteenth century. Their tightening grip on local government can be seen as continuous, but the personalities of the two men produced different strategies. Wolsey tried to control local government as much as possible in person at Westminster. Soon after being made Lord Chancellor in 1515, he insisted on gathering up the trials of important cases before a newly organized tribunal of royal councillors sitting in Star Chamber, himself presiding. Local administrators discovered what this meant when in 1519 three corrupt Surrey JPs were haled up before Star Chamber and terrified with threats of heavy fines and imprisonment; others were summoned either to the Cardinal's presence or found themselves harassed by special commissions, such as Wolsey's major investigation into enclosures in 1517–18. Wolsey ordered as many JPs as possible to come up to London annually, to renew their oath of loyalty to the Crown on the day when the new county sheriffs took their oaths, and there was at least one special summons in July 1526, with a solemn exhortation from Wolsey and lists of items for action back in the counties. Most lowland commissions of the peace reveal a cut-back in numbers of JPs after a high point in 1514–15, which no doubt also reflects this outburst of disciplining energy. Westminster had suddenly come very close to the lives of provincial rulers.

None of this was calculated to endear Wolsey to either peers or gentry: his confrontational and headmasterly style was accompanied by his ostentatious proffering of impartial justice to the poor, with the implication that they had previously received scant satisfaction from the rich. Perhaps Wolsey had no alternative: he was a jumped-up tradesman's son turned Oxford don, with none of the links of childhood friendship and shared memories which eased the administrative task of aristocratic royal ministers in dealing with the localities. Another problem was that the whole system depended on Wolsey's availability. He had much else to do: the work-load piled up in his central courts, and repeatedly he made half-hearted efforts to shift it outwards once more to the provincial councils or to the assizes.

It was in fact in his high-handed treatment of the provinces, in an attempt to solve other problems loaded on him by the King, that Wolsey first overreached himself, and felt his grip on power falter. In 1525 he sought to finance the King's proposed war with France through a non-parliamentary tax whose awkwardly novel name, the 'Amicable Grant', revealed its lack of precedent. When sorely pressed taxpayers in East Anglia rallied in thousands to a 'can't pay, won't pay' demonstration, the Dukes of Norfolk and Suffolk bluntly advised that the tax be abandoned. Wolsey had to manage the theatre of the government climb-down in Star Chamber, before a supposedly humbled delegation of taxpayers. A combination of popular anger and the opinions of two territorial magnates demonstrated to the King how badly the Cardinal had miscalculated.

After Wolsey's fall four years later, Cromwell inherited the Cardinal's concerns, aims, and difficulties. His problems were in fact worse, because he was directing a break with Rome and a religious revolution which most people did not want and which endangered the fragile web of consent on which voluntary local government rested. Both Cromwell and Wolsey encouraged the creation of a royal affinity of local men, particularly useful in recruiting military commanders for the Crown; gentlemen were only too happy to serve the King and wear his badge, as they had once worn the badges of provincial magnates. However, like Wolsey, Cromwell did not have his own personal affinity; he had no inheritance in the gentlemen's world, and his acquisition of estates was too rapid to allow him to create much of a following. The best he could do was exploit the personal contacts which he had made in his days in Wolsey's household, and rely on the eagerness of local governors to supply the King's most powerful minister with information.

Less grandiose in his personal style than Wolsey and better at rationing out his own working-time, Cromwell applied a little elementary psychology to his contacts with the localities. His characteristic device for conveying the accelerating pace of change became the circular letter, usually sent in the King's name. Cromwell's circulars were handwritten by a phalanx of secretaries, unlike the printed royal proclamations and volumes of parliamentary legislation which also issued from Westminster. Despite the extra labour involved, the advantage of this approach was that it seemed personalized: the recipient might be flattered or intimidated by receiving a handwritten letter signed by the King or his chief minister. Indeed in June 1535, Cromwell used two rival circular letters, first one to the bishops, and then one to sheriffs and JPs, telling them to keep an eye on the bishops to see that they obeyed the first letter!

This symbolized a significant shift of priorities in local government; the laity were now going to be the main agency of government enforcement. In response to his circulars, Cromwell was kept informed through reports from assize judges, JPs, and leaders of cities and boroughs; he was noticeably less reliant on churchmen for

PORTRAIT of Charles Brandon, Duke of Suffolk, in old age. Brandon—whose rise to power and wealth was entirely due to Henry VIII's friendship and his marriage to the King's sister Mary, the French Queen —could hardly complain in 1538 (a few years before this portrait was painted) when his main landholdings were transferred from East Anglia to Lincolnshire to suit the needs of government.

information, despite their anxiety to give it to him. He also began demolishing barriers to Westminster's rule. In 1536 the autonomy of franchises was abolished throughout the realm, significantly at the same time as the incorporation of Wales into the framework of English administration began. Cromwell would indeed use other means than the JPs, if it seemed appropriate. In 1538, at the height of Cromwell's power, the Duke of Suffolk was forced to surrender most of his East Anglian lands to the Crown and was given lavish compensation in Lincolnshire: an interesting redeployment of a loyal magnate, which reflected the fact that East Anglia already had an adequate great nobleman (the Duke of Norfolk), while Lincolnshire needed a strong hand in the wake of its 1536 rebellion. In 1539–41 there was a brief experiment with the setting up of a Council in the West Parts (Devon, Cornwall, Somerset, Dorset) after conservative aristocratic leadership among western gentry had been destroyed, but this was abandoned. It clearly seemed unnecessary beside what was becoming the norm in lowland government: the system of shire JPs with assize supervision.

The result was that Tudor England was run largely by volunteers: instead of the forty to fifty thousand royal officials who ran central and local government in early seventeenth-century France, late Tudor government gave salaries to only about twelve hundred, while thousands more, JPs and more humble folk, were provided by the localities at virtually no expense to Westminster. Royal officials provided expertise when necessary, especially in finance, where they could be brought in to assist the volunteer administration for special needs. The supreme achievement of this collaboration between the small royal bureaucracy and gentleman amateurs was the county-by-county financial survey planned by Cromwell and completed within nine months of a single year, 1535: the *Valor Ecclesiasticus*. This was a monumental, minutely detailed, and largely accurate investigation of church wealth, not only of immense value to Henry VIII in his outright confiscations from the Church, but a corner-stone of future royal control of church finance. The bulk of the work on the *Valor* was done by local gentlemen, mostly county JPs.

The *Valor* was a single operation under Cromwell's watchful control: by contrast, early Tudor innovations in the national tax system later suffered because of their reliance on voluntary gentry labour. From 1512, early in Wolsey's ascendancy, direct tax assessment on the wealth of individuals was revived: this had rarely been attempted since the fourteenth century, and was not tried again until the Napoleonic wars. This tax, the subsidy, was administered by county commissions of local gentry, again mostly JPs. At first they were remarkably conscientious in assessments and prompt in collections, but after Henry VIII's death, standards began to drop. By the late 1550s, the government realized how serious the shortfall was becoming, but by the late 1580s the Privy Council was moving from bitter complaints to open acceptance of chronic undervaluations. Detailed research has also shown that the decline in accuracy was much steeper for richer than for poorer taxpayers; the gentry were favouring themselves and their friends. Central government did nothing to check this; indeed Lord Treasurers Winchester and Burghley were prime offenders in producing scandalously low assessments of themselves. The gentry were allowed to get away with it.

Thus by allowing magnate power to atrophy in many areas and instead loading the JPs with responsibilities, the Tudors encouraged the growth of gentry self-confidence and self-assertion, alongside the titled nobility's traditional dominance. One can see the period 1540 to 1660 as the golden age of the English gentry: an interlude between the medieval age of aristocratic military leadership, and the late Stuart and Georgian eras, when peers gained renewed military power as Lords Lieutenant, and manipulated borough representation in Parliament. The lieutenancy originated in mid-Tudor England; it was an effort to solve local government's shortcomings, but in the golden age of the gentry, it brought its own tensions to local politics.

6. *The Later Tudors: The Coming of the Lords Lieutenant*

Later Tudor regimes built on the achievements of Wolsey and Cromwell, but no single great minister ever equalled them as a lone spider at the centre of the web. The Duke of Somerset

WILLIAM CECIL, Lord Burghley, had a keen interest in maps. Laurence Nowell, one of the tutors in his household, produced for him a pocket-map of the British Isles in 1563, and by the 1580s Burghley was eagerly using the first national atlas for any European country, compiled by the gifted mapmaker Christopher Saxton, under the patronage of another leading Elizabethan civil servant, Thomas Seckford. On his sumptuously coloured copy, Burghley personally marked the homes and names of important gentry, sometimes also the divisions within the county used for routine meetings of the JPs, and he made lists of county JPs.

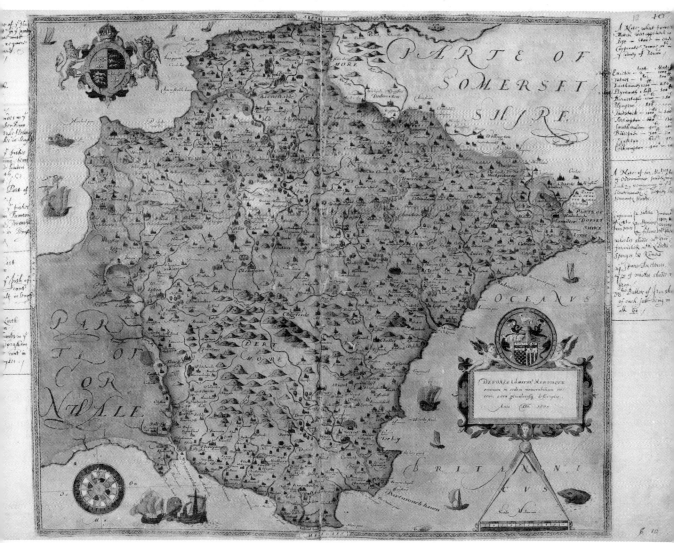

D EAL Castle, Kent. After Henry VIII's prodigious expenditure on up-to-date forts along the south coast in the 1540s, late Tudor England spent remarkably little on defensive works, apart from extensive fortifications at Berwick-on-Tweed from 1555. This did not prevent constant friction between centre and localities about the cost of paying for troops.

briefly and disastrously tried to follow suit in 1547–9, but thereafter, while William and Robert Cecil imitated Cromwell's busy attention to local detail, even they never aspired to complete dominance. Instead, there was the collective voice of the Privy Council, formalized after Cromwell's fall in 1540, probably as a deliberate attempt to make sure that no single politician would ever again monopolize power. The Council suffered eclipse under Somerset, but thereafter it recovered its leading role, and came into its own under Elizabeth I as the executive arm of government, dealing with and reacting to the relentless flow of information with a corresponding stream of outgoing letters.

The main additions to the Wolsey–Cromwell system were attempts to improve defence and security. Here the model was the administration of the borderlands, with their wardenries and noblemen acting as royal lieutenants. Lord Lieutenancies were first set up for groups of counties in 1550, to deal with widespread popular unrest which had boiled over in 1549. The system was continued patchily after 1553, but military organization in the early part of Elizabeth's reign was largely in the hands of large groups of JPs, constituted as county muster commissioners. However, the difficulties of running a system by swollen committee became apparent as England slid into war with the Spanish Empire. From the 1580s, the lieutenancies became a permanent nationwide network; usually the Lord Lieutenant was a courtier nobleman trusted by the Privy Council, although much of the work was done by a small group of deputy lieutenants, leading county gentlemen, who were reconstituted into muster commissioners if a nobleman was not available.

The full development of the lieutenancy system alongside the JPs institutionalized two different approaches to local government: one through magnate power, the other through reliance on the wider group of county gentry. JPs were liable to have less sympathy with Westminster than the magnates: their fierce pride in the 'county community' was increasing and expressing itself in their social and intellectual life. Counties consciously observed and gossiped about one another: as one Kentish gentleman remarked about a feud threatening to disrupt his own county, 'our county has hitherto carried the commendation for the unity in service, but if this takes place I fear we shall soon see it worse than Nottinghamshire'. In towns where assizes and quarter sessions were held, gentry were increasingly building houses and investing in communal leisure facilities like tennis courts. County histories were successfully published, commercial proof of local consciousness and local loyalties; heralds from the College of Arms in London regularly checked on gentry family genealogies in visitation tours, encouraging gentry pride, if perhaps also stimulating gentry rivalry. Historical consciousness bred suspicion of centraliz-

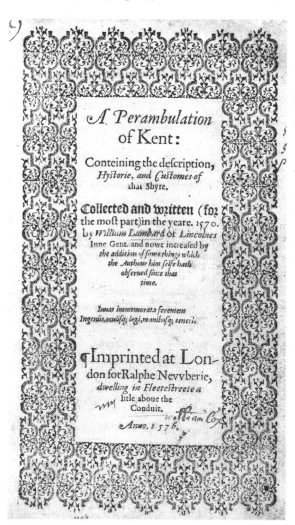

TITLE-PAGE of the first edition of William Lambarde's *Perambulation of Kent* (1576). This pioneering work of county history by a Kentish JP proved a publishing success and inspired many other county studies: an illustration of the growing emotional attachment to the county unit and interest in its past.

ing change, an outlook increasingly identified with constitutionalism and legalism. 'Precedent', in its misleading Tudor spelling as 'president', was a word much employed by county gentlemen.

7. *The Problem of Defence*

The problem was that rapid military change demanded a good many breaches of precedent. In 1573 the Privy Council implemented a scheme which it had been cherishing for some years, to improve military quality by selecting a group of men within the county levy for specialist training: the trained bands. Many counties bitterly opposed this move, partly on grounds of expense, partly because some gentlemen feared the consequences of training the lower orders in relatively advanced military techniques. As far as expense was concerned, they were penny-pinching: training for a fairly large county per year cost about £1 a head, for about 300 men. There is no evidence that the counties were not able to foot the bills; they were simply not used to doing so. Elizabethan England was a relatively undertaxed country, both by our standards, and those of its Continental neighbours. However, it never thanked the government for this, and begrudged every new exaction which Westminster tried to impose.

Arguments about defence were not eased by the Militia Act passed by Mary's government in 1558, the basis of Elizabethan military organization. This provided for two different systems of weapon provision, reflecting two methods of raising troops; the discrepancy probably resulted from compromise in the stormy passage of a very controversial bill. One system corresponded to the normal early Tudor way of financing soldiers: weapons were provided privately by individual peers and gentlemen at rates to be fixed by JPs. The second method corresponded to the Elizabethan county organization of the militia: townships provided a weapon store at rates decided by the muster commissioners. The Act left the method of assessing and raising money for the militia equally ambiguous: assessments on individuals or on townships? Conflict might not break out in a well-run shire like Hertfordshire under the thumb of the Cecil family, but in a powder-keg county like Norfolk, military administration added fuel to the flames. It was perhaps surprising in these circumstances that Elizabethan armies managed to achieve as much as they did.

The Spanish Armada's defeat led to undue local euphoria; military training slackened off, and even well-to-do yeomen became rare in the trained bands. The Privy Council could take little direct action to stop this trend, which was its own fault. During the 1580s it introduced veteran soldiers as professional muster-masters to train officers and men, and it eventually forced the counties to pay the muster-masters' salaries. The counties fiercely resented this, but it gave them an advantage. Once the Council stopped paying the muster-masters, it had little real check on

W HITEHAVEN (*facing, above*) was very much the product of three generations of the Lowther family, who owned the land and the adjacent coal mines. Sir Christopher Lowther laid out the first streets, but the project flourished under his son in the 1680s. The new port grew with the trade in coal and later tobacco. This view, by Mattias Read, is representative of a host of town and estate prospects, expressing a pleasure in increasing control over the landscape.

D ONEGAL Castle, *Dun na nGall*, 'the fort of the foreigner' (*facing, below*). Here in northwest Ulster Sir Basil Brooke, an English planter, created a Jacobean mansion on his new estates, attaching comfortable (and indefensible) modern apartments to the massive defensive tower built a century before by the O'Donnells. He thought plantation would bring an end to the endemic violence of the region.

IGHTHAM Mote, the chapel
(*above*). A thorough but careful
restoration and rebuilding in 1890–1
has brought it back to something
like its appearance when it was built
in the 1520s by Sir Richard
Clement, Gentleman of the Privy
Chamber, who had been set up as a
Kentish gentleman through a good
marriage, assisted by Henry VIII.

DETAIL of the chapel ceiling
(*right*). It shows royal badges,
rose, portcullis, and the royal livery
(green and white) in lozenges. Such
badges were a symbol of service, of
royal power stretching out into the
country; here, the actual timbers
and decorations may be reused from
temporary buildings put up for
Court ceremony, a perquisite of
Clement's royal service.

Tilting armour such as this suit commissioned for the Earl of Bedford in the 1580s was by then of no practical use in warfare, and was completely different from the up-to-date equipment and weapons which the English counties were required to provide. However, it is significant that the Earl, whose grandfather had earned his earldom by Court service and government administration, should feel the need to invest in this symbol of feudal splendour.

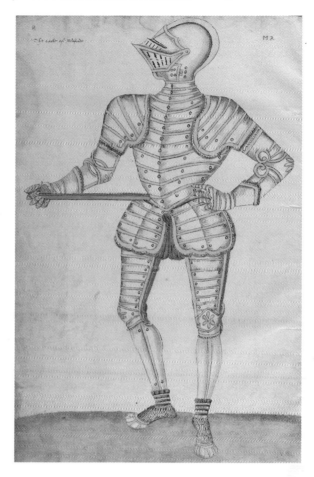

them, and hence little voice in local defence. Moreover, many counties disliked professional soldiers telling their gentleman captains what to do, and tended to appoint one of their own number to the post. The result was a steady decline in national military provision, which was to become disastrous under the early Stuarts.

In the 1590s naval provision also caused difficulties. Charles I did not invent Ship Money; the Elizabethan government first discovered how much trouble it could cause. Even in the Armada crisis there were local squabbles about who was going to pay for what, but there was a much greater fuss when the Privy Council decided to make new arrangements to pay for the very expensive naval raid on Cadiz in 1596. Not just the ports that built the ships should pay for them; the counties in which the ports were situated were told to pay half the bill. There was no 'president' for the demand! In East Anglia most county governors refused to collect the money; the deputy lieutenants in Suffolk eventually sent out angry Council orders for collection with a covering note more or less telling the local constables why they should ignore the orders. Even when faced with such astonishing insubordination, the Council was reduced to bluster and threats; it could not sack a county establishment without causing enormous damage to local government while England was still at war. In the end, it got only a fraction of its money; unlike Charles I, it was too realistic or too cowardly to push its full demand.

8. *Harmony and Tension in Local Government*

Reaction to innovation was not always mindless opposition. From 1577 the Privy Council produced printed Books of Orders to deal with various crises, and in 1586 it first published Books to regulate grain supplies to markets, in reaction to war overseas and bad harvests. The localities could see sense in this move, which reflected very traditional fears of selfish speculation disrupting food supply; they could also see the potential crisis only too clearly, close to home. There seems to be no evidence of trouble even when in 1597, the government enforced the reissued provisions of the Books of Orders in a new way, through prosecutions in Star Chamber as well as through supervision by the assize judges. Trouble would wait for the more aggressive use of Books of Orders by Charles I's government.

Another significant success of central government was over purveyance. Purveyance was the Crown's right to commandeer provisions for the royal household, using royal officials as purveyors. The purveyors' misdeeds were an ancient grievance in the shires, as was the weighting of the burden of purveyance towards areas near royal palaces. Elizabeth faced frequent parliamentary complaints, but continually told Parliament not to interfere; an unreasonable attitude, for Parliament had repeatedly passed legislation regulating purveyance as recently as Mary's reign. Instead, Burghley and Leicester turned to negotiating with each individual county to secure deals (compositions) for the main products which the Court needed. To replace the hated purveyors, leading JPs would annually choose a group of 'compounders' to negotiate with the Court to fix what the county would supply, and the fixed price which the Court would pay for these pro-

THE parish armoury store above the north porch in Mendlesham Church, Suffolk. This illustrates how motley a collection of weapons even a prosperous country parish got together in response to the government's demands for military equipment: the pieces range in date from the 1470s to the 1610s.

visions. The fixed price would be well below market values; the compounders would make up the difference with the market price that they had paid the producer by levying a county rate. By the mid-1590s most counties had come into the scheme.

Naturally, the system offered fresh opportunities for bickering over money, but overall it was a remarkable success. There was no more Elizabethan parliamentary agitation about purveyance after 1589. The vital difference between this exaction and the military ones which simultaneously caused such trouble, was that purveyance was an undeniably traditional obligation of subject to monarch. The counties did not object to purveyance as such, only to abuses; hatred of the purveyors made the idea of compounding attractive, for then the local governors could take control. Nothing could better illustrate the traditionalism of the provinces than their attitude to purveyance compared to their attitude to defence.

For central government, this traditionalism was a sore trial. Some clashes with the provinces arose from the sheer self-interest, greed, and inefficiency of local governors; however, as medieval lawlessness declined, equally troublesome was the conscientiousness and devotion to duty of many provincial magistrates. These men were developing an *esprit de corps* with their growing administrative duties; such tasks as organizing purveyance meant that they met together more and more to transact county business, and they evolved their own notions of what was best for their localities. It was often difficult for them to gauge the logic behind the government's unprecedented demands on their pockets. Moreover (and especially in lowland England), local suspicion of central government was often exacerbated by a radical Protestantism (Puritanism) which put JPs out of sympathy with the policies of the official Church; this made them all the more inclined to see their opposition to change in terms of principle, rather than mere self-interest.

Exasperated by frequent obstructionism, legalism, and inefficiency from the JPs, Elizabeth's government tended to turn to other means of getting things done. It was easy to extend the work of the Lords Lieutenant. Transport was connected with military efficiency, so if JPs refused to put the county to the expense of repairing a major road properly, the lieutenancy might use its authority to order a rate for road repair. Similarly the military officers known as provost-marshals had originally been used to catch military offenders like deserters, but since discharged or fugitive soldiers often became vagrants, it was natural for the provost-marshals to be used to control vagrants. Such invasions of spheres which the JPs now considered peculiarly their own might cause bitter resentment, particularly where there were already personal clashes between the Lord Lieutenant and his deputies or others on the justices' bench.

Just as offensive to county gentry were central government's grants of letters patent to individuals to get specific tasks done, by special methods of financing. One which aroused particular fury in East Anglia was a scheme to finance coastal defences out of the profits of fines on farmers who were not observing a statute ordering the growth of a certain acreage of flax. At least this bizarre scheme had a worthy purpose; many other grants were more suspect. Notorious were patents empowering the grantee to seek out former church lands knowingly or unknowingly concealed from the Crown at the dissolutions of monasteries and chantries, in return for a favourable lease of the properties discovered. This was a cheap way for the Crown to reward its servants at other people's expense, and it was resented accordingly. Most hated of all were patents of monopoly. Like so many other patents, they could be justified if they benefited genuine inventors in technology and manufacture, but many of them became fund-raising devices for members of the Court.

The story of the Tudor lowlands shows that central as well as local government was suffering from hardening of the arteries by 1603; a general malaise needed drastic reform. Elizabeth's administrators found a structure which needed further development after the rapid changes of the 1520s and 1530s; they worked the system with skill but little courage, and merely postponed its problems. In particular, they left unresolved the tensions between magnate rule, represented by the lieutenancy, and gentry rule by the JPs. In the less deft hands of Charles I, efforts at improvement would eventually prove disastrous.

3 THE TUDOR BORDERLANDS
1485–1603

STEVEN G. ELLIS

1. *Introduction*

On his accession in 1485, Henry Tudor assumed control not just of the realm of England but of a disparate collection of lands and lordships which had been annexed piecemeal to the Crown of the realm over the previous four centuries. Broadly, these lands may be divided into two groups. To the south there were the Channel Isles and the military outpost of Calais, which were all that remained, after the loss of Normandy and Gascony (1449–53), of the French territories claimed by English kings. In the early Tudor period the defence and recovery of the French territories remained a high priority. Henry VIII in particular made several attempts to recover the lost territories and so to add substance to traditional English claims to the Crown of France; but his efforts produced only two short-lived occupations of Continental towns—Tournai (1513–18) and Boulogne (1544–50)—and other fruitless invasions of French territory. Yet the recovery of Henry V's Continental empire was the great military objective of the reign, on which millions of pounds were spent.

To the north and west lay another group of territories, of much greater geographical extent, but traditionally much lower down the government's list of priorities. This second group was the product of intermittent attempts by medieval English kings to extend their control throughout the British Isles. Yet here the English military effort had been much more sporadic and small-scale, reflecting the region's relative lack of strategic importance, the poor quality of much of the land there, and the comparative weakness and disunity of the opposition. It comprised three regions. Wales was divided between the many marcher lordships, and the principality established by Edward I. This division reflected an earlier military frontier between the original areas of English settlement and that part still controlled by native Welsh princes before the Edwardian conquest. The far north of England formed a buffer zone between lowland England and the independent kingdom of the Scots. In Ireland, the Tudors shared a frontier with the Gaelic peoples, a politically fragmented tribal society which spanned the North Channel. The most powerful Gaelic chief, the MacDonald Lord of the Isles, threatened both English power in Ulster and

even the Scottish monarchy; but the English lordship of Ireland gave the Crown control over the more fertile and strategically more important eastern and southern parts opposite England and Wales, thus denying the island's use to any foreign prince.

2. *The Government of the Tudor Borderlands*

These English borderlands have traditionally been marginalized by historians as 'the Celtic fringe', although they actually comprised over half the geographical area of the Tudor state. Each borderland was unique, both in its characteristics and in the range of problems posed for royal government. The Celtic cultures of Wales and Ireland, for instance, differed from each other, and the north was predominantly English. Ireland was geographically separate; but in the far north the Scottish military threat (bolstered by French support) was far more formidable; and the Welsh marches were highly fragmented politically. Superficially too, the institutions of government in the three regions were also different: Ireland had a separate central administration based in Dublin, the far north had wardens of the marches, Wales had marcher lordships.

Yet these three regions also had much in common, in terms of geography, politics, and society, and therefore also in the kind of problems which their rule presented to the Tudor regime. Geographically, they were all remote from the centre of power in London; and they were predominantly pastoral regions of mountain, forest, and bog, with a harsher climate and poorer soils than the rich arable land of lowland England. Thus the settlement patterns and social structures of the borderlands were also different: the numerous towns and prosperous nucleated villages of the heavily manorialized lowlands gave place to a more desolate, sparsely populated landscape of isolated farmsteads, large parishes and manors, and few substantial gentry or major towns. The more turbulent conditions and fragmented power structures of the borderlands encouraged the maintenance of extended kinship bonds, consolidated patterns of noble landholding, and strong landlord–tenant ties.

In governmental terms too, they were areas in which the traditional English administrative system was only partially in force. Each region had its own system of march law and other regional customs operating alongside the common law. And in most of the borderlands there were no JPs or quarter sessions, but many feudal liberties, where judicial and military power rested with the local lord. The purpose of this dual system of administration was primarily military, and it was much less effective in maintaining law and order. Problems arose, for instance, over the extradition of offenders from one jurisdiction to another and over neglect by absentee lords. The last phase of medieval English expansion had seen a more consistent preference for shire government, which had been established in the principality of Wales, in parts of Ireland, and in Cumbria, but this created problems of a different sort. This system had developed in the more peaceful conditions of lowland England, where royal power was much stronger. It was too centralized for the warlike communities of the remote borderlands. Thus, assizes were frequently cancelled because of war and disorders, sheriffs required a posse to serve writs, and quarter

TRETOWER Castle, Breconshire, in the Welsh Marches. A march was a border or frontier district, usually heavily defended, which marked the boundary between territories which were politically and/or culturally distinct. Frequently, a local magnate was given special responsibility for the rule and defence of a particular area of the march—a marcher lordship, which was often very like a feudal liberty.

sessions were frequently not held because there were too few gentry to serve on the peace commissions. Overall, the basic problem was that lowland England, the political centre, was actually a quite untypical region of the Tudor state or the British Isles. Conditions demanded a devolution of power, but political experience, ideology, and administrative practice all suggested increased centralization. The Tudor response was a sporadic and only partially successful search for a solution which would balance these conflicting pressures.

Tudor officials were accustomed to think of England as an island, rather than simply the part of Britain colonized by the English before 1066. Accordingly, they believed that neither a standing army nor the normal international frontier arrangements between foreign governments in Continental Europe were really appropriate to England's relations with the rest of the British Isles. In Wales, the consequences of this misconception were not too serious. The native Celtic population had only been partially assimilated or displaced by English settlers. This had led to the existence side by side of separate communities—Englishries and Welshries—in many lordships, with different cultures, languages, and laws. Yet since there was no longer a military frontier, the chief result was a perpetuation of the existing disorders. Violence sometimes spilled over into the English border shires, but these continuing troubles did not amount to an external threat to the Tudor state.

In the far north and in Ireland, however, the consequences were more serious. The piecemeal and partial nature of English settlement in Ireland and the failure to conquer Scotland meant that the northern and western boundaries of the English state were marked by two long landed frontiers. The Anglo-Scottish border was over 110 miles long from Berwick-on-Tweed to the Solway Firth: the Anglo-Gaelic frontier in Ireland lay further still from London, and was also longer and more discrete. International frontiers were commonplace throughout Europe, but these were not normal frontiers, nor were England's relations with Scotland and Gaelic Ireland normal. Traditional English claims to overlordship throughout the British Isles meant that instead of co-operation and mutual recognition, England's relations with these polities were usually poor. Specifically, English kings claimed an overlordship over Scotland and tended to treat their Scottish counterparts as disobedient vassals: between 1333 and 1503 there was no formal peace between England and Scotland, only periodic truces and temporary abstinences from warfare. Gaelic chiefs were treated even more contemptuously, and their titles to land and property were not recognized. Power in Gaelic Ireland was so fragmented that there was no one figure with whom the King's deputy could negotiate: Ireland was indeed 'a land of many marches', in each of which the balance of power was constantly shifting. Even the comparatively stable Scottish monarchy, however, was frequently too weak to control its border subjects. Thus in both regions the English government was encouraged to secure its own ends by mischief and interference rather than by promoting peace and good neighbourliness.

The result was that large parts of the far north and English Ireland were war zones, in which the endemic insecurity of the marches led to the emergence of highly militarized forms of society like the border surnames—the semi-independent reiving clans which inhabited the Anglo-Scottish marches. The Crown's limited financial resources and the sheer length of the frontiers precluded the construction of an elaborate system of defences manned by a permanent garrison, as at Calais. Certainly, garrisons were frequently established to guard the main routes of entry, or as military staging posts. Yet frontier defence relied chiefly on the march itself—the territory

THE usual residence of a minor gentry family in the English marches in Ireland and towards Scotland was the defended tower-house or pele (here, Sizergh Castle, near Kendal, built and still owned by the Strickland family).

The Gentleman of Ireland   The Gentlewoman of Ireland

The Civill Irish Woman   The Civill Irish man

The Wilde Irish man   The Wilde Irish Woman

protected by castles and fortified towers and extending many miles inland—and its local population which was obliged like Englishmen elsewhere to do military service in defence of their country. This defensive system was sufficient to exclude petty raiders and to delay major incursions long enough for the authorities to concentrate a superior force. Yet the system relied on the co-operation of the local magnates, whose tenants made up the bulk of the forces available to the Crown. This was secured by the development of special institutions, such as the great liberties of Tipperary or Durham, or the wardenships of the marches to which the leading nobles were appointed. Thus, although the border communities had the same rights and privileges as Englishmen elsewhere, in practice they were partly excluded from the 'normal' operation of English law and government, so accentuating still further the socio-political differences between the English lowlands and the borderlands. The tensions between these claims of subjects and the constraints imposed by marcher conditions lay at the heart of the problem of the borderlands.

3. *Perspectives from London*

The government was disposed to view the border problem as essentially one of cultural degeneracy on the part of the inhabitants there. Tudor officials shared the assumption of magistrates all over Europe that civilization resided chiefly in towns, or at least in the peaceful tenant villages of the arable lowlands. Experience seemed to confirm this: public order and central control in the borderlands was invariably less secure than in the south-east. Official reports attributed these disorders not to failings in Crown policy but to the borderers' wildness and lawlessness. In all three regions, moreover, the King's loyal English lieges were surrounded by

THE difference between 'English civility' and 'Irish savagery' extended even to the individual's habit or mode of dress.

enemies and rebels. The English had long regarded the Welsh as an untamed and undisciplined people, living like animals. Likewise the Irish were consigned to the lower links of the great chain of being: in Polydore Vergil's view they were 'savage, rude and uncouth', or 'wild men of the woods'. So too the Scots: the Scots who infiltrated the English marches in large numbers were seen as beggarly rogues, reivers, and thieves, who undermined border defence. The Scots were aliens, but the mere Welsh and mere Irish were also disabled at law from holding land or office within the Englishries. And despite efforts to civilize them, they persisted in their evil ways and corrupted the King's loyal subjects living near them. In these circumstances, the King's officers felt, the proper course was to strengthen the operation of the common law so as to execute sharp justice among them, both to civilize the natives and to recover the King's subjects to their allegiance.

4. *Henry VII and Wales*

Unfortunately, 'good governance' and 'indifferent justice' cost time and money, and early Tudor priorities lay elsewhere. Henry VII was primarily concerned to secure the new dynasty against internal and external enemies. His border policies were essentially conservative, though he enjoyed some success in Wales, where his Welsh birth and descent were an advantage. Belatedly, he issued a series of charters (1504–7) offering certain communities in north Wales the status of freeborn Englishmen, allowing them to hold lands and offices reserved to Englishmen and to follow English land law, provided they paid him handsomely for the privilege. This was to anticipate a more general emancipation of the Welsh in 1536.

In other respects, Henry VII soon restored Edward IV's device of a separate council to supervise government there. The creation of the King's eldest son as Prince of Wales in 1489 prompted the establishment of a prince's council at Ludlow with jurisdiction over the principality and those marcher lordships in the King's hands, most of which were now transferred to the Prince. Initially, much of the work was organized by the King's uncle, Jasper Tudor, to whom the Earldom of Pembroke and several lordships there were regranted. After his death and that of Prince Arthur, the council continued to operate (1502–4) under a president, Bishop Smyth of Lincoln, and when Prince Henry became king and there was again no Prince of Wales, the council continued, albeit ineffectually, as the King's council in the marches of Wales. In addition, the King exacted from marcher lords an 'indenture for the marches', a bond that the lord would require his officers to exact surety from his men for good behaviour, due appearance in court, and to surrender suspects on request for trial in another jurisdiction. No doubt Henry VII's personal application to the details of government had some impact in curbing the country's lawlessness, but Henry VIII had little interest in this work. Of more importance in the longer term was the way in which many of the larger lordships came into Crown hands by inheritance or forfeiture during this period. Altogether, it has been calculated, some fifty marcher lordships were in Henry VII's hands at one time or another, and with the attainder and execution of the third Duke of Buckingham in 1521 the last of the great marcher lords disappeared. This development did at least address the underlying causes of the region's lawlessness, the fragmentation of authority there, and it also meant that Wales was increasingly bereft of great territorial magnates capable of challenging royal power.

5. *Henry VII and the North*

By contrast, the north of England presented a more intractable problem, largely because the King had also to provide for the region's defence against the Scots. Here too, Henry VII built on Yorkist initiatives, although not very successfully. On his accession large tracts of marchland lay waste following the recent Scottish war. The King's main priority, however, was to stifle any internal challenge to his position from this staunchly Yorkist region. He introduced a diffusion of power in the region by placing the chief royal castles of Berwick-on-Tweed and Carlisle, and their garrisons, under separate royal constables. Moreover, the two most powerful northern families, the Nevilles and the Percys, were now excluded from the wardenships which were traditionally theirs. Long minorities in the two families and exclusion from power thus led to a significant weakening of their regional influence.

None the less, the changes also created something of a power vacuum in the region, and this led to a virtual collapse of law and order. The Earl of Surrey, sent north to govern the east and middle marches, was largely dependent on the King's authority since he had no territorial power base there. In the west marches, a border baron, Thomas Lord Dacre, served as Lieutenant, but he was scarcely able even to defend his own estates properly, let alone maintain good rule in the region. Only five commissions of the peace were issued for Cumberland and Westmorland throughout the reign, and there were so few Justices of the Peace that quarter sessions were rarely held. Instead murders were followed by feuds or financial compositions. Things were no better across the Pennines, where extensive liberty jurisdictions hindered the work of government, rather like the Welsh marches. The King resorted to the ancient practice of farming the shrievalties, and from 1506 one of the more lawless border gentry, Nicholas Ridley of Willimoteswick, paid £100 a year to be sheriff of Northumberland. By 1526 quarter sessions had not been kept for a long time because there were so few JPs.

Only a firm truce (1500) and then peace (1503) with Scotland ensured that the situation did not get totally out of hand, although Surrey returned south with the advent of better Anglo-Scottish relations. In his place came Archbishop Savage of York, appointed president of a restored northern council in 1501. This helped to prevent disorders from spreading southwards into Yorkshire, to which its authority was restricted, but the council lapsed again with Henry VII's death. In the west, Dacre was promoted to be warden, and allowed to farm the shrievalty of Cumberland and the captaincy of Carlisle, so reducing the King's charges and concentrating power in the warden's hands again. Indeed, from 1511 until his death in 1525, Lord Thomas usually acted as warden-general of all three marches. This would have been an impossible task if Henry VIII had expected Dacre to perform effectively in all aspects of the warden's duties. In fact, the young King was primarily interested in the military aspects of Dacre's work, and his belligerent foreign policy soon breathed new life into the 'auld alliance' between France and Scotland. Although Surrey (restored to his father's title of Duke of Norfolk in reward for his victory at Flodden in 1513) and then his son were usually entrusted with any major military campaigns, Dacre otherwise had charge and was expected to intrigue against the French party, make the Scottish marches ungovernable, and defend the English marches with minimal assistance from the King. With increased estates now properly defended by new or enlarged castles and a battle-hardened tenantry, Lord Dacre had become a powerful regional magnate, able to raise 5,000 men to invade

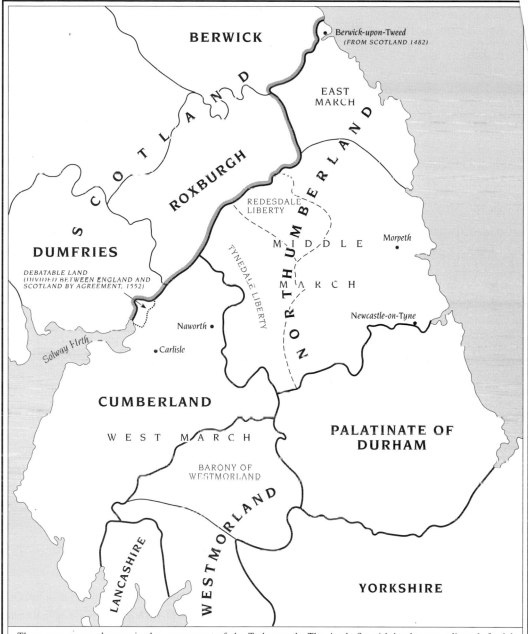

BERWICK

Berwick-upon-Tweed
(FROM SCOTLAND 1482)

EAST
MARCH

S C O T L A N D

ROXBURGH

REDESDALE
LIBERTY

N O R T H U M B E R L A N D

M I D D L E

Morpeth

DUMFRIES

M A R C H

*DEBATABLE LAND
(DIVIDED) BETWEEN ENGLAND AND
SCOTLAND BY AGREEMENT, 1552)*

TYNEDALE LIBERTY

Newcastle-on-Tyne

Naworth

Solway Firth

Carlisle

CUMBERLAND

W E S T   M A R C H

PALATINATE OF
DURHAM

BARONY OF
WESTMORLAND

LANCASHIRE

W E S T M O R L A N D

YORKSHIRE

There were many changes in the government of the Tudor north. The Anglo-Scottish border was adjusted, feudal franchises were incorporated into shires, and the Wardens of the Marches made answerable to the King's Council in the North, which provided conciliar justice and administrative oversight for the six northern counties.

Tynedale and Redesdale were annexed to Northumberland in 1495 and *c.*1542 respectively.

The West March comprised Cumberland and the Barony of Westmorland.
The Middle March comprised all of Northumberland (including Tynedale and Redesdale) except the north-east corner (the East March)

THE ANGLO-SCOTTISH BORDER REGION

NAWORTH Castle, Cumberland: a chief residence of Thomas, third Lord Dacre of the North, who was warden of the west marches towards Scotland, 1485–1525, and rebuilt and strengthened the castle.

Scotland; but he was hard put to control the east and middle marches from his territorial base around Morpeth. In consequence, the marches remained lawless and disturbed, and after Dacre's dismissal in 1525, allegedly for misconduct, bands of up to 400 thieves pillaged the countryside around Durham and Newcastle. It took a military campaign to subdue them. Thus the first forty years of Tudor rule saw a disastrous collapse of 'good governance' in the far north.

6. *Early Tudor Ireland*

In English Ireland a similar crisis of lordship had occurred rather earlier. The collapse in Ireland of the three noble connections which had dominated politics under Henry VI—Talbot, Butler, and York—the ending of the traditional financial and military subventions from England, and the lordship's important strategic and military role in the ensuing civil war, all seriously exacerbated the problems of defending the lordship in the face of a continuing Gaelic revival. Edward IV's solution had eventually been to entrust the governorship to the Fitzgeralds of Kildare, the most active of the three local earls, whose estates in the English Pale left them better placed to defend the lordship on the reduced terms now offered. Short of returning to the old subventions, Henry VII had little option but to reappoint the eighth Earl of Kildare as deputy, because the influential seventh Earl of Ormonde showed no inclination to return to Ireland. The King even overlooked Kildare's leading role in the Yorkist invasion of 1487, after Lambert Simnel was crowned King Edward VI of England in Dublin. When, however, Kildare reacted equivocally to the arrival of another Yorkist pretender, Perkin Warbeck, he was dismissed from office (1492). The King eventually appointed a military captain, Sir Edward Poynings, as governor (1494–5) with an army of 650 men. A handful of skilled administrators took charge of the Dublin government and implemented reforms aimed at increasing the Irish revenues and strengthening the King's control (notably the famous Poynings' Law, by which meetings of the Irish Parliament and legislation proposed for enactment there required the prior approval of the King and council in England). The crisis came, however, when Warbeck returned and laid siege to Waterford: he

THE siege of Enniskillen Castle, Maguire's stronghold, by government forces in February 1594 at the start of the Nine Years' War. Throughout Elizabeth's reign, the war in Ireland constituted the most regular source of employment for Tudor soldiers.

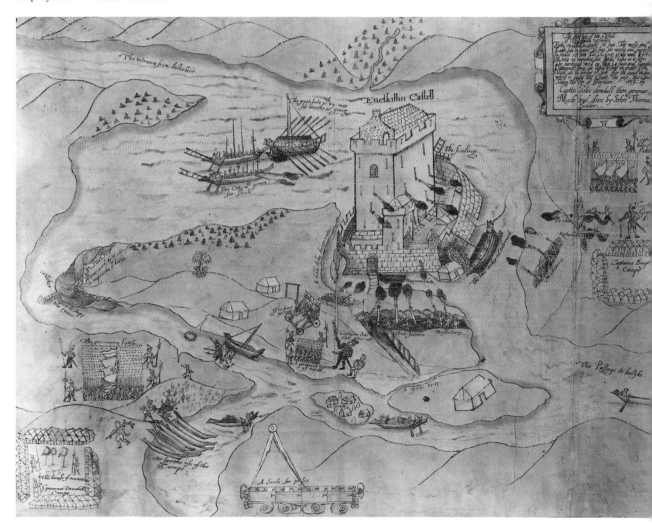

was driven off, leading to Poynings's departure, the redeployment of some captains in the Anglo-Scottish marches which Warbeck now threatened, and the gradual disbandment of the army in Ireland. By 1496 the King had established good relations with Kildare, based on the Earl's marriage to his kinswoman, a generous grant of Crown lands in England and Ireland, and guarantees for his good conduct, and he was reappointed deputy.

With the Yorkist threat now much reduced, first Henry VII and then Henry VIII were content to leave the government of Ireland to Kildare. Although the Earl was expected to govern and defend the lordship without subventions from England, the concentration of power in local hands, and the political stability which ensued from a good working relationship between King and magnate, ensured that the lordship was actually more effectively governed than under the old indenture system whereby new governors had been sent out every two or three years with fixed retinues and inflated salaries to pay them. Successive earls of Kildare exploited their position as governor to recover and rebuild ancestral estates and castles which had been reoccupied by the Gaelic Irish, to strengthen the Pale marches, and to expand into Gaelic Leinster, the midlands, and east Ulster. Although Henry VII's Irish policies were characterized by the same overriding concern for security as in the north, coupled with a preference for reducing costs over law and order, the results were less disastrous in Ireland. In part this was because the fluidity of the Anglo-Gaelic marches and the relative weakness of individual Gaelic chieftaincies gave Kildare more leverage in Gaelic Ireland. The Earl was able to build up a Gaelic clientage network, sometimes cemented by marriage alliances, in order to stabilize the defence of the marches in a way which was only partially possible in the Scottish borders. And the ninth Earl (1513–34), with an income well in excess of 2,000 marks a year, stood head and shoulders above any other noble in Ireland. Thus, as with Lord Dacre, long tenure of office helped to transform an essentially local noble of no great wealth into a great regional magnate; but the predominantly personal system of defences and alliances which each magnate built up to offset the shortcomings of royal government made it extremely difficult to find an effective replacement for them, as Henry VIII discovered to his cost in the 1520s.

7. *Reorganization under Henry VIII*

The new King showed no real interest in the borderlands until 1525. Then, with the ending of the French and Scottish wars, attention switched to problems of internal order and, increasingly under the impact of the divorce crisis and then the Tudor Reformation, of internal security. The initial response was to revive the Yorkist conciliar experiment and to replace the traditional ruling family with another noble. These quasi-bureaucratic initiatives were weakly supported, however, and in each borderland the chief result was to antagonize established local interests. In Wales, a remodelled council was established at Ludlow, with Princess Mary as figure-head, resulting in a feud between Lord Ferrers and Rhys ap Gruffydd. In the north, the King's young illegitimate son, created Duke of Richmond, was dispatched to head a new council, which in turn supervised the marches. The appointment as deputy-wardens of the Earls of Westmorland and Cumberland was resented by the Percys and Dacres, however, and the resultant disorders soon forced the King to back down. In late 1527 the council's jurisdiction was curtailed; William Lord Dacre was given charge of the west marches and the Earl of Northumberland was appointed warden of the east and middle marches on greatly improved terms. These changes strengthened the marches at a time when deteriorating relations with Scotland were leading to renewed war (1532–4), this time over disputed territory in the west marches called the Debatable Land.

Affairs were no better in Ireland, where the King's insensitive handling of the Earl of Kildare (charged, like Dacre, with maladministration) frustrated successive experiments with the Butler earl as governor (1522–4, 1528–9), and with Richmond as absentee head of an executive 'secret council' (1529–30)—a feeble imitation of the northern conciliar experiment. Kildare's obstructive attitude to all this earned him lengthy periods of detention in England (1519–23, 1526–30), interspersed with a short spell as deputy (1524–6); but as the precarious peace of the lordship degenerated into feuds, disorder, and Gaelic raids, the King was obliged to send back Kildare with the master of the ordnance, Sir William Skeffington, and 300 men to restore order. And very soon, the cost of this experiment led to Kildare's reappointment as governor (1532–4). Overall, therefore, Henry VIII's handling of the borderlands was inept. The Reformation crisis rapidly led to a breakdown in all three regions, forcing the King into administrative reform and a more interventionist strategy. In each case the new structures strengthened central control and reduced aristocratic influence, but they also cost more and did not necessarily result in stronger government.

In Ireland and the north, the charges of treason levelled simultaneously (May 1534) against Kildare and Dacre look like a pre-emptive strike by the King against potentially the most

UNTIL the 1590s, the Tudors retained military supremacy in Ireland through superior resources, weapons, and tactics. In pitched battle, English armies often defeated far larger forces of native kerne and galloglass, but Gaelic chiefs reacted by fighting guerrilla wars from their bogs and fastnesses.

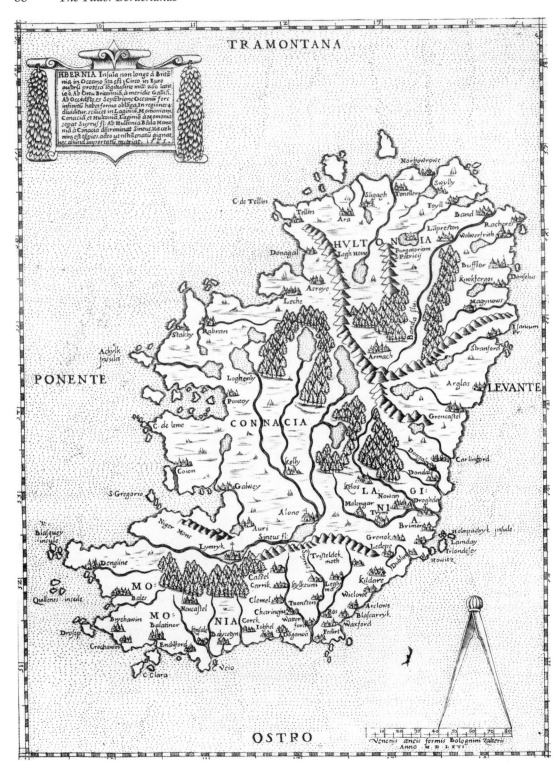

dangerous of the nobles suspected to be plotting against him. They were also the victims of man-œuvrings by Henry's chief minister, Thomas Cromwell, to advance his own clients at the expense of Norfolk's. Dacre was arrested immediately after the conclusion of peace with Scotland lessened the King's need for his military resources. Although dismissed from office and fined £10,000, his unexpected acquittal on the main charge of making private treaties with Scots enemies in wartime left the King still dependent on his co-operation to govern the west marches, but unable to use him as warden.

By contrast, Kildare's resistance to his impending dismissal rapidly led to a major rebellion which took fourteen months to suppress and cost the King £40,000. Cromwell's aim in Ireland in 1533–4 may well have been a resuscitation of Crown government, but in practice Kildare's destruction undermined the system of defences and alliances by which English rule had been consolidated and extended during the Earl's ascendancy. Royal government through an English-born deputy and remodelled council from 1534 was no substitute for a powerful resident lord enjoying royal support, and the dissolution of the monasteries further disrupted traditional power structures. Gaelic chiefs exploited the resultant crisis of lordship to encroach on the English marches. In response, the government was forced to continue as a permanent garrison (usually *c.*500 men before 1547) part of the relief army sent to suppress the rebellion. And since the wasted marchlands confiscated from Kildare and the Church yielded far less than the additional costs of an outside governor and garrison, Ireland now became an increasing drain on English finances. The Crown, however, remained generally unwilling to accept this financial deficit as the price of increased control: hence the general neglect of Ireland, interspersed with fundamental shifts of policy, which characterized Tudor rule there after 1534.

In many ways the reorganization of northern government followed a similar pattern, but there were significant differences. By 1536 the government had moved much further in its bid to strengthen royal control in response to the Reformation crisis. The royal divorce and supremacy and the curbing of noble influence had been followed by the suppression of the liberties and lesser monasteries, the Statute of Uses, and taxation in peacetime. Thus the rebel demands in the Pilgrimage of Grace, the most serious insurrection of the reign which spread throughout the north, were more specific and broadly based than those in Ireland, while reflecting a similar combination of noble, regional, and religious grievances. The great regional magnates lay low, and in Cumbria socio-economic grievances were prominent among the peasantry, but without active noble support the revived northern council proved powerless to contain the rebellion. In the ensuing reorganization of government, the King was likewise prepared initially to pay for increased control. A remodelled council and gentlemen deputy-wardens replaced the ineffectual Cumberland and the recently deceased Northumberland, but the changes again left a power vacuum in the marches, which the government attempted to fill by feeing the local gentry. While peace held with Scotland, the effects were not too disastrous, but renewed war after 1541 soon obliged the King to relieve the council of its supervision of the wardenries and to appoint a southern noble with a substantial garrison to take charge of defence. Thus the overall impact of Henry's north-

THE Tudors had really very little idea about Ireland's geography and topography until late in the century when more accurate maps were made. Irish officials observed that Dublin and the English Pale in relation to Ireland were as Dover in relation to England: visitors could get no real idea of the hinterland from what they encountered there. In this (Italian) map of 1565 not even the administrative capital was accurately plotted.

ern policy was mixed. The council performed effectively in extending royal control and good rule around Yorkshire, and containing simmering discontent there, but the Crown's acquisition of the Percy and monastic estates left the marches weak and the border surnames uncontrollable.

8. *The Welsh Act of Union*

Much the most successful of the provincial reorganizations of the 1530s was in Wales, where there was no external frontier to defend. There continuing feuding had led to ap Gruffydd's execution on another dubious charge of treason (1531), but disorders continued. In May 1534 Veysey was replaced as president of the council by the energetic Bishop Rowland Lee, and Parliament passed five statutes which, in response to earlier complaints and recommendations, aimed at tightening the administration of justice and at abolishing those Welsh customs which the government now deemed inimical to justice. Armed with these, Lee toured the marches, pursuing thieves and murderers, hanging even gentlemen. Much more fundamental in reducing Wales to order, however, were the statutes enacted and gradually enforced between 1536 and 1543, the so-called Act of Union. Effectively, they abolished the distinction between the principality and the marches and imposed English law and administrative structures throughout Wales. Five new shires were created from marcher lordships, other Welsh counties were enlarged, and some lordships were added to English shires. Sheriffs, JPs, and other officers of English local government were introduced, Welsh shires and ancient boroughs received representation in Parliament (one member each), Welsh law and custom were abolished, and the English language was made compulsory for administrative and judicial business. Lee opposed the changes, arguing that the natives were not ready for English-style self-government and that few Welsh gentry had sufficient land or discretion to serve as JPs. Wales was now united to England and the Welsh enjoyed the same rights and privileges as Englishmen. Lee's presidency (1534–43) was long remembered for his draconian rule: the imposition of English civility was a traumatic experience and certainly not the unqualified blessing which Elizabethan apologists implied. None the less the Union did lead to a gradual strengthening of law and order. More problematical was the impact of this success on English political ideas about the incorporation and assimilation of other borderlands. It strengthened official convictions that peace and civility could only be established by imposing the same administrative structures as operated so effectively in lowland England. Thus it was no accident that when affairs in Ireland deteriorated under Elizabeth, leading officials with experience of both countries, such as Sir Henry Sidney and William Gerard, urged the same treatment for Ireland, even though problems of defence were far more intractable there.

9. *The Kingdom of Ireland*

In the short term too, experience in Wales was seen as offering lessons for Ireland. The lordship's military weakness had been underlined by the unprecedented joint invasion of the Pale by O'Neill and O'Donnell in 1539. The government rushed in reinforcements and then tried a new political initiative. By erecting Ireland into a kingdom (1541) and offering the Gaelic peoples the same status as freeborn Englishmen, the government hoped to abolish the island's medieval partition between Englishry and Irishry and to extend English rule and administrative structures thoughout Ireland. The strategy devised by Lord Deputy St Leger and known as 'surrender and regrant' involved Gaelic chiefs recognizing English sovereignty in return for feudal charters confirming the lands they occupied. Thus the Gaelic population would become English subjects instead of Irish enemies, with common law titles to their land and property (and peerages for powerful chiefs like O'Neill, who was created Earl of Tyrone), and the Gaelic lordships would become English shires. Of all the Tudor initiatives for the reduction of Ireland, 'surrender and regrant', although very ambitious, most nearly matched ultimate aims with available resources, providing for a gradual extension of English rule with Gaelic co-operation. A promising start was made, reducing racial tensions and enabling the deployment of Irish troops in France and Scotland (1544–5). Yet progress was slow. Ireland was four times the size of Wales, which had taken seven years to assimilate administratively to England; Gaelic Ireland had yet to accept Henry VIII's sovereignty, and its peoples had no natural ties with the King, unlike the Welsh; and the extension of royal government in Ireland was not accompanied, as in Wales, by a corresponding increase in the size of the bureaucracy there. After Henry VIII's death, the Edwardian government quadrupled the army in a bid to force the pace. It met a rising by the O'Mores and O'Connors by confiscating their territories of Leix and Offaly to enlarge the Pale by colonization. Two forts called Governor and Protector were established to defend the colonists, and were later renamed Philipstown and Maryborough, the head towns of the new King's County and Queen's County. The natives were transplanted into Gaelic reservations nearer the Shannon. This renewed emphasis on coercion and colonization led Anglo-Gaelic relations to break down again. Moreover, hopes that colonial rents would offset additional defence costs, so that conquest would be self-financing, proved disastrously wrong. As the Irish deficit snowballed from £4,700 to £35,000 per annum, Queen Mary reappointed St Leger as deputy to restore order and reduce costs.

The Leix–Offaly plantation was apparently inspired by the Scottish policy of the late 1540s, which attempted to coerce the Scots into fulfilling the Treaty of Greenwich by garrisoning southern Scotland. A revived English Pale there aimed to protect the 'assured Scots' who supported the treaty and, as in Ireland, to reduce the risk of raids or invasion by advancing the frontier into enemy territory. Yet military costs, exceeding £140,000 a year, far outweighed these advantages, which were increasingly negated by the arrival of French troops: the garrisons were withdrawn in 1550. By contrast in Ireland, where there was no agreed frontier, it proved more difficult to extricate the army: 1,500 troops were now viewed as an effective minimum to maintain royal authority there.

10. *The Impact of the Reformation*

Of more fundamental importance to the shaping of the British Isles at this time was the advance of Protestantism. In effect, the Tudor Reformation marked the extension to the religious sphere of the existing policies of centralization and cultural imperialism. The King as Supreme Head now supervised church government and legislation in Parliament confiscated church property and enforced Protestant doctrine. In the large rural parishes of the borderlands, where few could read or write, the replacement of traditional services and colourful ceremonies by Bibles and sermons was deeply resented. In parts of Wales, Ireland, and Cornwall, moreover, the introduction of English Prayer Books and Bibles amounted to a major challenge to indigenous Celtic cultures rather than simply an intensification of existing pressures for linguistic and cultural uniformity. The Prayer Book and Bible were translated into the local vernacular, quite quickly in Wales, much more tardily in Ireland, where Gaelic was perceived as a political threat; but even so, the need to operate through two languages dissipated reforming energies.

In many ways, therefore, the impact of the Reformation exacerbated the problem of the borderlands at a time when, in Wales at least, the government had seemed to be making progress. Indeed, Elizabeth's decision on her accession in 1558 to restore Protestantism after the brief Marian Reaction seemed almost foolhardy in the light of England's military and financial weakness and the international situation. The French, with whom England was still at war, had recently captured Calais and were consolidating their ascendancy in Scotland. Mary Queen of Scots, a Catholic claimant to the English throne, had recently married the future Francis II (1559–60). In the event, the outbreak of religious unrest in Scotland and then France, and Mary's preoccupation with affairs in France gave Elizabeth her opportunity. Appeals from Scottish Protestants for military support prompted an English invasion to drive out the French and led to the treaty of Edinburgh (1560).

Thus the revolution of 1559–60 saw the establishment of a second Protestant regime in Scotland, and this was maintained even after Queen Mary's return to Scotland following her husband's death. The advance of Protestantism in Scotland in turn eased the government's difficulties in defending its northern frontier. Ideological affinities greatly improved Anglo-Scottish relations, at the expense of the 'auld alliance' between Scotland and France. Control and defence of the far north remained troublesome and costly, but the Scottish government was more co-operative and the military threat much reduced. Better relations with Scotland also reduced the government's dependence on the great territorial magnates for border defence. Northumberland and Dacre, rehabilitated after 1547, were soon eased out of

Y BEIBL CYS-
SEGR-LAN. SEF
YR HEN DESTA-
MENT, A'R NEWYDD.

2. *Timoth.* 3. 14, 15.

Eithr aros di yn y pethau a ddyfcaift, ac a ymddyried-
wyd i ti, gan wybod gan bwy y dyfcaift.
Ac i ti er yn fachgen wybod yr fcrythur lân, yr hon
fydd abl i'th wneuthur yn ddoeth i iechydwria-
eth, trwy'r ffydd yr hon fydd yng-Hrift Iefu.

Imprinted at London by the Deputies of
CHRISTOPHER BARKER,
Printer to the Queenes moft excel-
lent Maieftie.

1588.

THE Reformation in Wales was a bilingual event: both the Bible (*left*, published 1588) and the Prayer Book being made available in Welsh relatively quickly. Amazingly, although there was a New Testament in Gaelic by 1610, there was no complete Bible in either Irish or Scottish Gaelic until the later eighteenth century.

Pushed to extremity by royal policies from London which cut across dynastic or regional interests, marcher lords could turn from passive disobedience to open rebellion. In 1570 Leonard Dacre raised 3,000 Dacre tenants against the crown in the aftermath of the revolt of the northern earls; a final demonstration of Dacre power. He was attainted of treason, but fled to Scotland and exile.

the wardenships, and gradually key northern offices were transferred to their rivals or southerners. There was one hiccough: the circumstances surrounding Mary Queen of Scots' deposition and flight into England led to a court conspiracy, centring on the Duke of Norfolk, with whom the Earls of Northumberland and Westmorland were allied. The northern earls sensed the opportunity to rescue Queen Mary, restore Catholicism, and, with it, their traditional influence in northern government. Their rising (November 1569), following Norfolk's arrest, was poorly co-ordinated and quickly collapsed, however. It was followed immediately by a clash between the Queen's forces and Leonard Dacre, who, ironically, had been alienated by Norfolk's claims to the Dacre inheritance. The Earls and Dacre suffered attainder and forfeiture, and in the aftermath northern patronage was reorganized to build up a Court party: a southern noble, the Earl of Huntingdon, was appointed president of the council.

The British political system was now increasingly stable and self-contained. In the north-west, the Scottish monarchy had finally succeeded in enforcing the 1493 forfeiture of the MacDonald lordship of the Isles after a serious rising in 1545 by Donald Dubh with English support. Renewed Scottish pressure on Clan Donald had initially led to a strengthening of their power in Ireland, but the prospect of an independent third power bestriding the North Channel was fast receding. The advance of Protestantism in Scottish Gaeldom, notably in the powerful Clan Campbell, was gradually driving an ideological wedge between Scottish and Irish Gaeldom. Thus, as dynastic union looked increasingly likely to resolve the problem of the north, the nature and timing of the Tudor conquest of Irish Gaeldom seemed the one outstanding question relating to the unification of Britain.

11. *The Conquest of Ireland*

For most of Elizabeth's reign, Ireland remained a festering sore in the body politic. Unlike the north, where the government kept rivalry between the local élite and southerners in check, the gradual polarization of political opinion between the local Englishry and the post-1534 English settlers was a serious complication, with Old English and New English officials proposing different strategies and the Queen concerned above all to reduce her expenses. At different times the government's Irish policies drew on the whole range of English political ideas and administrative strategies developed for the conquest and assimilation of outlying territories during the later Middle Ages. Gaelic chiefs were made responsible for the conduct of their own clansmen and dependants through the system of booking and pledges, as with the northern surnames. 'Surrender and regrant' transformed Gaelic warlords into English nobles, lordships into shires, and tribal holdings into feudal tenures, although the terms offered to Gaelic chiefs were increasingly disadvantageous. English colonists were introduced to control strategically important districts—in east Ulster, against the Scots (1570–3); and in Munster after the Desmond rebellion (1584–9). Regional councils were established in Connaught (1569) and Munster (1570) to oversee the rule of outlying parts, although the increasing militarization of Irish society was reflected in the decision to allow presidents in Ireland a military retinue and power of martial law. And successive compositions in the Pale and Connaught aimed to pay for the increased army by turning the obligation to military service and the royal right of purveyance into an alternative system of military taxation which increasingly undermined the role of Parliament. By 1590, English rule had been gradually extended until only Ulster lay outside the system of shire government.

These measures were as much a reaction to successive crises as the result of forward planning. Ambitious but weakly supported initiatives were by turn authorized by a divided Dublin administration and countermanded by the Queen when they raised expenditure or encountered opposition. Moreover, this opposition was not confined to Gaelic Ireland because these strategies had also aimed to strengthen control over the outlying English districts. The upshot was mounting unrest and a wave of rebellions: the Butler rising and the Earl of Thomond's rebellion were Irish echoes of the intrigues surrounding Norfolk, but there were other revolts in the south and west (1568–73), in Leinster and Munster (1579–83), and in Ulster from 1593, spreading into Connaught and Munster. Although insurrections in English Ireland generally followed the mainland pattern of political demonstrations within a context of overall obedience, by contrast with the localized Gaelic 'wars of independence', political discontent increasingly coalesced with an originally distinct tradition of opposition to Protestantism, so that resistance became increasingly widespread, bitter, and ideological. Politics thus degenerated into a ruthless kind of warfare, with widespread atrocities on both sides. Yet only by attracting substantial military assistance from Spain had the most formidable of these resistance movements, the Ulster confederacy led by Hugh O'Neill, Earl of Tyrone, any real hope of matching the superior resources of the Tudor state. The confederates won occasional victories, and Elizabeth was very stretched to find money and men for the Nine Years War (1594–1603) besides her commitments in France and the Netherlands. Yet the 3,500 Spanish troops who eventually landed at Kinsale in 1601 proved insufficient to tip the scales, and Lord Mountjoy's ruthless but professional campaign gradually crushed the rebellion. With Tyrone's surrender at Mellifont six days after Elizabeth's death, the political unification of the British Isles was finally completed.

The war cost Elizabeth two million pounds, and the eventual pattern of military conquest left a bitter legacy of racial and religious animosity. The Dublin administration was now in the hands of an unrepresentative clique of New English adventurers, with little indigenous support, and dependent on the army to maintain its authority. Elsewhere too, the Union of the Crowns

Tyrones false Submission afterwards rebelling.

THE breach with Hugh O'Neill, Earl of Tyrone, might have been avoided had he received firm assurances concerning his status and authority in the new English Ulster. This scene appears to relate to his unexpected arrival and submission to Lord Deputy Russell in Dublin in 1594.

presented the new Stuart regime with major problems. The Tudors had tackled the problems of Wales, Ireland, and the north by a policy of political centralization, administrative uniformity, and cultural imperialism. By this process the values of lowland England were imposed on the other territories, thus creating an English nation-state in which the previous balance between core and peripheries was replaced by southern domination of the borderlands. 1603 removed the final obstacles to centralized control of the borderlands, with the dismantling of the traditional military frontiers. At the same time, however, it involved the Tudor state in a union with territories which were even more remote and 'uncivilized' and which, in the case of Scotland at least, could not be assimilated by the policies pursued in the borderlands.

4 THREE STUART KINGDOMS
1603–1689

JOHN MORRILL

1. *Introduction*

The accession of James VI of Scotland to the titles held by Elizabeth I brought the whole of what contemporary geographers knew as the British Isles under one sovereign prince for the first time in history. It produced a strange, hybrid, multiple monarchy, rich in unsettling ambiguity and consequent instability. To put it bluntly: there was a union of crowns but no union of kingdoms and much of the violence throughout England, Ireland, and Scotland in the century that followed was the result.

James VI and I committed himself to a rolling programme that would culminate in a true union of the kingdoms—one law, one religion, one political system—and the dog-in-manger refusal of the English Parliament in 1606/7 to go one step of the way along that road led to James's disillusionment with that institution for the rest of his reign. Charles I's less subtle attempts to impose a uniformity of religion led to a progressive collapse of his authority throughout his territories and to wars within and between each of the kingdoms. The costs of conquering and incorporating Ireland and Scotland into an enlarged English state and the holding down of these conquered kingdoms played an important part in the failure of the constitutional experiments of the Interregnum. Only after 1707, with the establishment of an Anglo-Irish stranglehold on power in Ireland and the effecting of a Union of England and Scotland that integrated the northern kingdom into a British state dominated by England but safeguarding the particular legal and religious institutions and traditions of Scotland, did the Union of the Crowns turn from a source of weakness into a source of strength.

Being King of several kingdoms was no novelty in European history. James's contemporary Philip III ruled the ancient kingdoms of Aragon (itself a federation of previously separate kingdoms), Castile, and Portugal; Henry IV was King of a France that had over the previous century or so incorporated (but messily) the ancient independent duchies of Burgundy and Brittany. Kings of Scandinavia, of Poland, of the Habsburg territories in central/southern Europe were

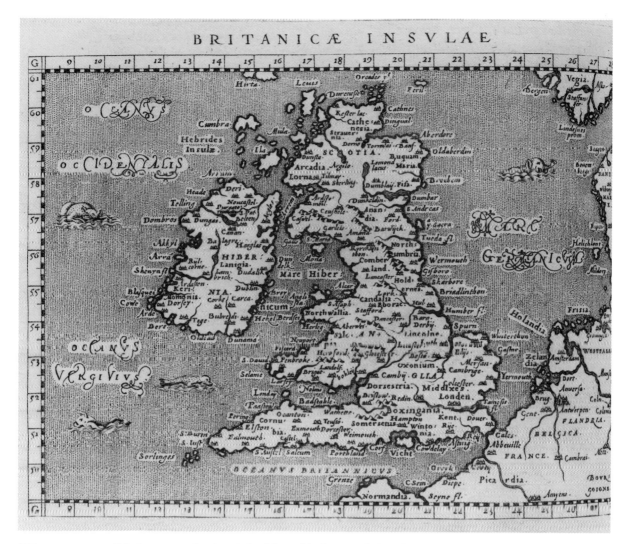

THERE was no political term covering the whole of the archipelago consisting of Britain, Ireland, and the small islands to the west and south. But geographers did regularly group them together in the late sixteenth and early seventeenth century under the title *Britanicae Insulae* or 'Britannic Isles'.

equally rulers of multiple or composite monarchies. Their powers as kings, and the rights of the peoples of each of their kingdoms, were separate and distinctive.

2. *Convergence and Divergence*

James's inheritance was none the less a complex one. There were spurs to cultural and institutional unification, but not many. The élites in all three kingdoms spoke variations of the English language, and senior officials could also (at least at the beginning of the century) communicate in Latin. By 1690 probably 90 per cent of the inhabitants of the archipelago could speak English, if not as a first language. The fact that ABCs and primers for the whole archipelago, together with all English Bibles, were produced in London greatly assisted the standardization of syntax, vocabulary, and spelling. Furthermore, the patterns of land-holding and inheritance characteristic of the areas of Norman settlement which had long dominated lowland England and Scotland, the Englishries of Wales, and the English Pale in Ireland had been imposed with a fair degree of success throughout the Celtic regions in and after 1625. Everywhere, primogeniture and the specific forms of tenure which had evolved out of feudalism now held sway.

But the component parts of the Stuart *imperium* or composite monarchy differed far more from one another than they resembled one another. Only in England (and to a lesser extent in Wales) was there a strong gentry which could collectively outmatch the peerage in land-holding, wealth, and social power. Indeed, when one compares the wealth and lifestyle of all but a handful of the English peerage with that of the greater gentry in the early seventeenth century, it is not unreasonable to speak of a gentrification of the English nobility. It was the gentry who dominated county government, who chose most parish clergy, and whose interests were most fully served by Parliament.

There was no gentry to speak of in much of Ireland, and although English families were establishing themselves as gentry families there over the course of the seventeenth century, the greatest change was the emergence of a large group of colonist freeholder farmers. Ireland was still dominated by a relatively small but changing group of very large landowners. In Scotland, the lairds were few and dependent, collectively much less wealthy than a nobility swelled during the sixteenth century by the lawyer-administrators who oversaw the Scottish Reformation and the revolution against Mary Queen of Scots, and who rewarded themselves with noble-sized estates and joined the ranks of the peerage. Nothing happened in the seventeenth century to disturb that pattern. England had a gentrified political culture, Scotland and Ireland had a baronial one. Yet they differed one from another in that the English (and also the Scots) flocked to Ireland and took over political control of it. There was virtually no English (or Irish) emigration to Scotland.

By 1689 probably one in four of all the inhabitants of Ireland were first-, second-, or third-generation British migrants; and they owned over two-thirds of the land. The greatest migrations were those made possible by the Crown's expropriation of the lands of the Earls of Tyrone and Tyrconnell in Ulster following their rebellion and flight to Spain in 1607; and the confiscations of the lands of Irish 'rebels' in the 1650s, amounting to well over a third of the island, and its transfer in roughly equal proportions to those Englishmen who had advanced ('adventured') money to pay for the army sent over to deal with the initial Irish Rebellion of 1641 (most of whom remained in England and leased out their new estates), and to those English soldiers who had taken part in the Cromwellian conquest and who were rewarded in land rather than cash. Scots continued to pour over, especially when the persecution of hardline Presbyterians was more severe in Scotland than in Ireland. Scotland's Pilgrim Fathers only got as far as Ulster. The result of this pattern of migration was that by the 1680s there were more Presbyterians in Ulster and Munster than there were Church of Ireland members; and given the numbers of Baptists, Congregationalists, and Quakers in Ireland, this meant that the Established Church there represented barely a third of the Protestant community and barely a tenth of the population.

Meanwhile, there was no English (or Irish) migration to Scotland. No Englishman married a Scottish heiress, or acquired a large Scottish estate, in the period down to 1689. When the English Army invaded and subjugated Scotland in the 1650s, the soldiers remained in garrisons; they did not become a settler community. In the early decades of the century a significant proportion of the Scottish nobility acquired English wives, English manors, and English manners. The Dukes of Hamilton and Lennox, for example, became social amphibians, as much at home on both sides of the border. James I and Charles I reserved to Scots a high proportion of the offices in their Household. As part of a campaign to improve the quality and importance of preaching within the Church of England, James I also gave a number of deaneries and other cathedral jobs to Scotsmen. But those coming south, however high their profile and however irritating to the English, were always a handful. Furthermore, no one sold up and moved permanently to England; and the number of nobles who married English women and developed interests on both sides of the border declined as the century wore on.

The economies of the three kingdoms and the two islands were not at all well integrated, and the English Parliament if not the British Crown fought against the development of fuller links. The terrain of the Anglo-Scottish borders inhibited easy links. Scotland's overseas trade was unsurprisingly with northern Europe, whereas English trade was increasingly turning to southern Europe and west and south into the Atlantic and beyond. Irish overseas trade was relatively undeveloped and naturally looked across Biscay to southern France and northern Spain.

The Union of the Crowns brought immediate disadvantages to Scotland. The English were reluctant to open English markets (domestic and overseas) to the Scots, who found that (except during the forced Cromwellian Union) they were inhibited from trade with England and barred from trade with English colonies. The situation deteriorated after 1660 when the Navigation Laws ensured that all trade to and from the colonies was carried in *English* ships. Worse still, union with England meant association with the King's foreign policy, and the King of Britain's foreign policy was always made by English ministers unconcerned with Scottish interests.

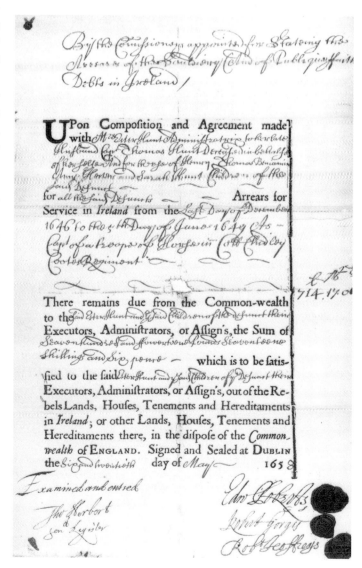

Because the English state could not raise the money to pay its troops in Ireland for their part in the conquest, each of the soldiers was given one of these debentures which they could either sell on for a proportion of its face value or cash in for land to the value stated. This one, issued to the widow and children of Captain Thomas Hunt, was in the sum of £714. 17s. 6d.

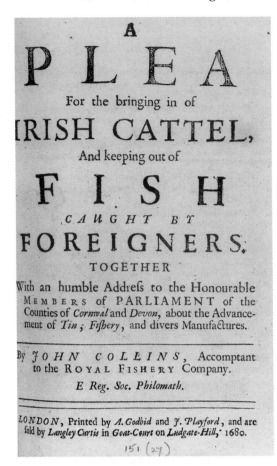

A
PLEA
For the bringing in of
IRISH CATTEL,
And keeping out of
FISH
CAUGHT BY
FOREIGNERS.
TOGETHER

With an humble Addreſs to the Honourable
MEMBERS of PARLIAMENT of the
Counties of *Cornwal* and *Devon*, about the Advance-
ment of *Tin ; Fiſhery*, and divers Manufactures.

By *JOHN COLLINS*, Accomptant
to the ROYAL FISHERY Company.

E Reg. Soc. Philomath.

LONDON, Printed by *A. Godbid* and *J. Playford*, and are
ſold by *Langley Curtis* in *Goat-Court* on *Ludgate-Hill,* 1680.

THIS was one of the responses to 'The Act Against the Importation of Cattell' of 1666 by which the English Parliament barred Irish goods from England. So determined were the West Country cattle lobby that they even added a clause describing the cattle as 'common nuisances', a phrase which prevented the King using his prerogative power to dispense (exempt) individuals from the Act. The judges had ruled that the royal prerogative did not extend to sanctioning a public nuisance!

English policy therefore closed ports to Scottish vessels yet made them fair prey to the navies of the King's enemies without bringing them under the protection of his English navy.

The Irish probably suffered less from being implicated in the King's foreign adventures and they were not debarred from trade with England's colonies. But they suffered grievously, especially in the second half of the century, from discriminatory tariffs against and even parliamentary bans on Irish goods entering England.

3. *Constitutional Relationships*

The constitutional relationship between the three kingdoms was confused in both theory and practice. Wales was by now constitutionally part of England, sending MPs to Westminster, providing Privy Councillors, major office-holders, bishops, and judges as freely as any province in England. Until 1641 the Council in the Marches of Wales exercised jurisdiction over both the twelve Welsh shires and the four English border shires of Gloucestershire, Worcestershire, Herefordshire, and Shropshire. It provided a local version of all the major Westminster courts and spared inhabitants of the region the wearisome travel and expense involved in pleading in London; it ensured that there was vigilant supervision of local order and security; and it oversaw the enforcement of 'commonwealth legislation' (Poor Laws, regulation of the grain trade, etc.) on behalf of the King's Council. There was a very similar Council based in York for the six northern counties of England. In every other *institutional* respect, Wales was part of England.

The constitutional status of Ireland was much more complicated. There was always a Lord Deputy, a Lord Lieutenant, or a Viceroy in Ireland, who was supposed to possess and to exercise the greater part of the King's natural authority on his behalf: for example, the prerogative of pardon, the right to make knights, the right to make grants under the Irish Great Seal. Some rights—such as the decision to summons a Parliament, or the right to make executive and judicial appointments—were reserved to the King, but on the understanding that he would normally take his representative's advice. There was, of course, an independent deliberative and executive Council in Dublin, an occasional Irish Parliament with its own traditions and forms, and a semi-independent judiciary (although appeals against judgements in Ireland were heard in Westminster Hall).

There was by 1600 a strong tradition within Ireland—especially amongst the Old English—which took the Act of 1541 creating the kingly title for Ireland in deadly earnest and stressed the independence, the autonomy, of that Irish Crown. Supporters of this tradition asserted the existence of an ancient Irish constitutionalism, rooted in Ireland's own version of the Great Charter—*Magna Carta Hiberniae*—and in Irish custom and statute. Such men sought during the seventeenth century to develop and extend the particular privileges of the people of Ireland. In particular they campaigned in the second quarter of the century for the Graces, a comprehensive defence of the rights (and security of title to property) of the descendants of families resident in Ireland before 1541 against the more recent settlers. But it was a constitutionalism that was constantly under threat, in part from England, but principally from the New English settlers, who wanted the Irish to be viewed as a conquered people who had no rights except those their conquerors chose newly to confer upon them.

The major problem for Irish constitutionalists was that the Irish Crown was a dependency of the English Crown. In 1649 Charles I was executed and Stuart monarchy abolished in England *and* Ireland by the English Parliament; in 1660 Stuart monarchy was restored in England *and* Ireland by the English Parliament; in 1689 James was deemed to have forfeit the thrones of England *and* Ireland by the English Parliament. On each occasion, sovereign power was transferred without consultation with any body in Ireland, and without any retrospective constitutional fig-leaf being allowed to the Irish. No member of the royal family crossed the Irish Sea in the whole of the period covered by this book. Throughout the seventeenth century—and above all from the 1640s—the English Parliament sought to make law for Ireland, and the English courts tried treasons committed within the Kingdom of Ireland. Furthermore, not only could Irish Parliaments meet only when the King in England permitted, but under Poynings' Law, they could only debate and pass laws which had been approved in advance by the King and his English Council. In practice, the authority of Lord Deputies and other royal representatives was always being undermined by the ability of their opponents to persuade the King to inhibit or countermand what had been decided in Dublin Castle. Only two men—in the 1630s Thomas Wentworth, eventually Earl of Strafford, and in the Restoration James Butler, Marquis and later Duke of Ormonde—were able for short periods to make and to enforce their own policies in Ireland, and both needed powerful allies at Court to achieve even limited success in that regard. The bottom line was that Irish policy normally had to serve English needs.

Scotland was different again. It remained a wholly separate kingdom, and the government of Scotland remained firmly in the hands of Scotsmen. There was never a Scottish Viceroy or royal deputy, except when James, Duke of York, took control in the early 1680s. The English Parliament never tried to legislate for Scotland. In 1649 the Rump of the Long Parliament abolished Stuart monarchy in England and Ireland but not in Scotland; in 1660 the monarchy was restored in Scotland by a separate declaration of a Scottish Parliament, and in 1689 James was deposed by a Scottish Parliament. (The English Parliament failed to depose him, but rather asserted that he had forfeit the English and Irish thrones by deserting the Kingdom of England.) The Scottish legal system derived from the same Norman tap-root as the English system, but was paradoxically at once both more heavily influenced by Roman law ideas than the English system and was less fully codified (at least until the herculean efforts of Viscount Stair at the end of the century). Scottish cases, unlike Irish cases, were not appealable to England; and no Scotsman was tried for treason in England—the major exception being the Marquis of Hamilton, who was tried for his part in the Second Civil War of 1648 but under his English title as Earl of Cambridge. It is of course true that Scotland was absorbed into the English Republic following the Cromwellian military occupation in 1650–1, but, as we will see, the English went to great lengths *not* to claim that they had conquered Scotland.

All this was far from satisfactory from a Scottish point of view. Renaissance monarchy remained personal monarchy, and absentee monarchy meant incomprehending and unbountiful monarchy. James VI only once returned to Scotland after he inherited the other Crowns—for a period of four months in 1617. Charles I went to his northern kingdom to be crowned and to make trouble in 1633, and to sign the agreement to hand over most of his powers to a faction of the nobility in 1641. Charles II was in Scotland for nine months in 1650–1 trying to regain his thrones and that was that. Between the Union of the Kingdoms in 1603 and the Union of the Crowns in 1707, regnant monarchs were in Scotland for barely one per cent of the time.

Initially many Scots headed south for the honey-pots of Whitehall and the flesh-pots of London, but by the later seventeenth century few found this worth while. James I made sure that there were always people around him who had arrived recently from Scotland who could keep him up to date with news and gossip that could inform his policy-making and his patronage. Charles I had rather fewer Scots around him, and most of them lived semi-permanently in the south-east of England, so although he had Scottish advisers, he did not get sound advice on Scotland. As a result, he tended to *make* policy for Scotland at the English Court without listening to the Scottish Council in Edinburgh and then treat the latter as an enforcement agency. This produced frustration in Edinburgh and led to Charles being so out of touch that he provoked a national strike against his ill-informed policies in 1637 and a national rebellion when he sought to break that strike. In the Restoration, policy in Scotland tended to be franchised out to whoever—and for almost twenty years that meant the Duke of Lauderdale—could keep Scotland quiet without it becoming a charge to the English Exchequer.

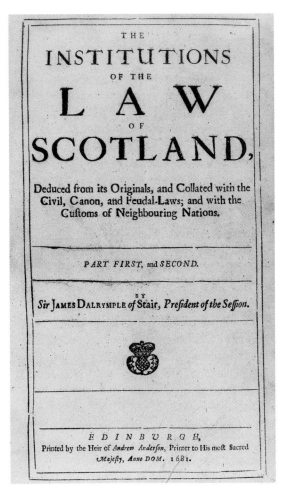

THE

INSTITUTIONS

OF THE

LAW

OF

SCOTLAND,

Deduced from its Originals, and Collated with the Civil, Canon, and Feudal-Laws; and with the Customs of Neighbouring Nations.

PART FIRST, and SECOND.

BY

Sir JAMES DALRYMPLE of Stair, *President of the Session.*

EDINBURGH,
Printed by the Heir of *Andrew Anderson*, Printer to His most Sacred Majesty, Anno DOM. 1681.

I N 1681, as an important step which confirmed the distinctiveness of the Scottish legal tradition, Sir James Dalrymple (later Viscount Stair), the President of the Court of Session in Edinburgh, published this codification of Scots law. It is striking that he emphasized the 'plain, rational and natural method' of the Scots as against the 'artificial reason' of the English common lawyers.

M ARY (*above, left*), daughter of James V of Scotland, was successively but briefly Queen of France (1559–60) and of Scotland (1560–8). She might well have been Queen of England—as the child-bride of Prince Edward (under the rapidly broken Treaty of Greenwich, 1543); or by Catholic preference instead of Elizabeth (1559), whose heir-apparent she remained until Elizabeth executed her in 1587.

E DWARD VI (*above, right*), Henry VIII's short-lived son, the boy king who reigned but never ruled. First his maternal uncle Somerset and then John Dudley, Duke of Northumberland, headed the government. Under their rule England moved decisively into the Protestant camp. Edward's death, at 16, precipitated Northumberland's desperate and unsuccessful plot to put his daughter in law, Jane Grey, on the throne.

A JUDGE on horseback (*left*). The twice-yearly travels of Westminster judges on the assize circuits were an essential part of communications between the government and the localities, and their arrival in state in an assize town was a symbol of the awesome power of royal justice.

4. *Religion in the Three Kingdoms*

There was then an Anglocentricity about royal policies that unsettled the outlying kingdoms and produced much instability throughout the archipelago during the seventeenth century. At first sight, nothing demonstrates this point so clearly as the apparent Stuart attempt to Anglicize—perhaps we should say Anglicanize—the Churches of Scotland and Ireland. And yet in the end it was the stubborn differences between the religious cultures of the three kingdoms which most obviously impeded the development of a single political culture or political consciousness.

The failure of the Reformation in Ireland—probably less than one in ten of the families resident in Ireland in 1560 came over to the Established Church—was a major source of instability in Britain itself, constantly feeding the anti-Catholic paranoia of the Puritans. Catholicism replaced the Gaelic tongue and the *brehon* law as the hallmark of Irishness. The Church of Ireland was always embattled and under-resourced. Despite the attempts of Wentworth and his ecclesiastical sidekick John Bramhall to re-endow and reinvigorate it in the 1630s, it was never anything more than a garrison Church. It always recruited clergy who preferred Ireland to England because of their dissent from the English Church, and such clergy as were trained within Ireland at Trinity College Dublin were men who wished to differentiate themselves—in their catechetics and worship—as completely as possible from the Catholic population. In English parlance, the Irish Church was dominated by Puritans.

As the century wore on, the settlement of ex-Cromwellian soldiers and disaffected Scots resulted in there being more Protestant Dissenters in Ireland than Protestant conformists. In such circumstances, the schemings of Bramhall and others to replace the (Puritanical) Irish Articles of religion approved in 1617 by the English Thirty-Nine Articles, or to introduce canons which would bring the practice of the Irish Church into line with the English Church, was ecclesiastical whistling in the wind.

The Scottish Reformation was made by men who had been in exile in England during the reign of Edward VI, and in Germany and Switzerland with the English exiles in the years 1553–8. For much of the late sixteenth century, when Scotland had a Catholic Queen and a boy King of uncertain religious alignment, there thus developed a Church that was fiercely independent of the State, with (presbyterian) structures that concentrated authority in the localities and established a fiercely iconophobic and anti-hierarchical form of government.

Such a situation did not suit the adult James VI. He needed eyes, ears, and a voice in this decentralized Scottish Church and so he set about systematically to restore bishops appointed by himself. This fitted in with his plan to build up the mutual respect of the Churches of each of his kingdoms for the Churches of the others. This lay behind his concern to raise preaching standards in England. In Scotland, he restored the office of bishop and had his new bishops consecrated in England so as to restore the link with the Apostles through the laying on of hands from generation to generation. But Scottish bishops were (and were to remain throughout the century) very different from English bishops. They did not have the same autocratic power; rather they

THIS portrait of a three-year-old boy holding a battledore and shuttlecock illustrates the convention of the early modern period for dressing boys in the same way as girls until they were 'breeched' at about five or six. It also shows how boys and girls were frequently treated as little adults rather than as children.

WHEREAS the English and Scottish service books were translated into Welsh and Scottish Gaelic early on, no attempt was made to translate the service book into Irish until 1608, when this version, with strong 'puritan' deviations from the English text, was published. It came much too late to help to convert the mass of the Irish people to the Protestant religion (the Gaelic Bible came even later—see p. 70).

were 'constant moderators' or ex-officio chairmen of diocesan boards of governors, required to enforce the majority decisions of bodies made up of representatives of the parishes and districts. Similarly, James sought to introduce a new set form of worship in Scotland, but not by a slavish following of the English model.

Charles I's ecclesiastical policies in Scotland and Ireland were far more straightforwardly authoritarian, as, of course, they were in England. There were common elements in each kingdom such as the desire to restore to each Church much of the wealth and jurisdiction wrenched from it during the Reformation. But Charles also had a far clearer sense of how God should be worshipped, and he set out to change religious observance in each kingdom. There is no evidence, however, that he strove for a narrow uniformity of practice, let alone the subordination of the Irish and Scottish Churches to the English Church.

Charles and Laud were shocked by the *laissez-faire* liturgical atmosphere in Scotland when they

Novv bleid, and bath, gif thou desire,
And purge alsua gif neid require:
Euill humouris do in monie breid,
Prouyde in time befoir thou neid.

Sone riseth				Sone setteth
3 21	d	i	S.Monanes day the firste day in .Monanes ane fair.	
	e	ii		5 39
	f	iii	The 3.day the Temple of Ierusalem was buildit againe, & confecrated with great solemnity 1.Esd.6	
	g	iiii		
	A	v		
	b	vi		
	c	vii	Befoir the byrth of Christ, 515.zears.	5 46
6 41	d	viii		
	e	ix		
	f	x		
	g	xi		
	A	xii	The Sone in Aries.	
	b	xiii		
6 0	c	xiiii		6 0
	d	xv		
	e	xvi		
	f	xvii	S.Patrikes day in Dumbertane ane Fair.	
	g	xviii		
	A	xix		6 9
	b	xx	S.Cuthbert in Langtoun in the Mers, ane Fair.	
	c	xxi		
5 51	d	xxii		
	e	xxiii		6 21
	f	xxiiii		
	g	xxv	Lady day in the Wester Weimes ane Fair.	
	A	xxvi		
5 2	b	xxvii		
	a	xxviii		6 23
	d	xxix		
	e	xxx		
	f	xxxi		

Novv helthsum Bathis thou may frequent,
Let blude alsua and not repent:
Thir ar gude meinis thee to defend,
From greifis the quhilk on thee attend.

Sone riseth	g A	i ii		Sone setteth
5 11	b	iii	The first day Rome was destroied by Alarick King of Gothis, after two zearis seige. Anno 412. Blondus.	6 49
	c	iiii		
	d	v	The tẽple of Ierusalem is purged from Idolatrie be King Ezechias. 2. Paral. 29.	
	e	vi		
	f	vii		6 68
	g	viii		
	A	ix	Palmefunday in S. Iohnstoun ane Fair.	
5	b	x		
	c	xi		
	d	xii	The fone in Taurus.	
	e	xiii		7 10
	f	xiiii		
4 50	g	xv		
	A	xvi		
	b	xvii	The 18.the people paffed fafe throw the reid fey: and Pharao with his Oift is drowned. Exod.14.15.	7 30
	c	xviii		
4 38	d	xix		
	e	xx		
	f	xxi		
	g	xxii	The 22. the people of Ifrael cummeth to Mara where the waters was fo bitter that they coulde not drink them, Exod.15.	7 41
	A	xxiii		
	b	xxiiii		
4 19	c	xxv		
	d	xxvi		
	e	xxvii		
	f	xxviii		
	g	xxix		
	A	xxx		

THE Book of Common Order, based on the service book of the English exiles in Geneva in the 1550s, was in wide use from the 1560s to the 1630s. The Calendar (*above*) ignores all the old 'festivals' and records instead the anniversaries of the great events of the Old Testament.

CHARLES I's service book for Scotland was gratuitously offensive to Scottish opinion, not only in its 'popish rubrics' and theological emphases, but even in the inclusion of pictures of angels and cherubs (*detail, left*), which were seen as idolatrous. Such images appeared regularly in the ornamented capitals introducing the gospel readings. No wonder the Scots thought this service book *worse* than the English Prayer Book on which it was based.

visited the northern kingdom in 1633, but it was a distinctive Scottish prayer book designed by Scottish bishops (albeit with fraternal 'advice' from their English friends) and not just the English Prayer Book which Charles sought to impose in 1637. It was a prayer book which the Scots immediately saw as *worse*, more popish, than the English Prayer Book and their first instinct was to believe, not that they were being Anglicized but that they were being treated as guinea-pigs for experiments which would be visited upon the English in due course.

The result of Charles's attempt to change the nature of worship in Scotland—without consulting a Parliament, a General Assembly of the Church, or even the Scottish Council—was the National Covenant of February 1638, a protest movement led by the nobility but with massive support from all social groups. Signatories swore to defend the purity of the Scottish Reformation against recent innovation and against popery; in effect to turn the clock back to the period of James VI's minority when Church and State were most strictly separated.

In the period 1639–51 the armies of the Covenant invaded England on four separate occasions in an attempt to ensure that their bleached brand of Protestantism was guaranteed for Scotland and introduced into England and Ireland. The Scots thus showed themselves to be more committed to a programme of ecclesiastical imperialism than the English had ever been. And it led to their undoing. They provoked the English into sending an army of conquest in 1650.

At the Restoration a religious compromise was reached in Scotland: the clock was put back to 1633, before Charles I's reforms as well as before the Covenants. Bishops were restored, but again as constant moderators, and the forms of worship to be used were those devised by the exiles of the mid-sixteenth century and in use since 1560. Yet Scotland remained divided, not between an English and a Scottish model of the Church, but between a 'pure' Scottish model (Presbyterianism) and a hybrid form ('Episcopacy-in-Presbytery').

5. *The Union of Britain*

Throughout the century attempts were made to redefine the relationships of the kingdoms at least of England and Scotland. Three broad possibilities were canvassed. The first was an incorporative union, of the type that seemed (to the English and to many Welsh) to have worked extremely well as far as Wales was concerned. Under such a union, the Scots would have accepted seats in an enlarged English Parliament, on an enlarged English Council, and would have embraced English law, initially expecting English judges to play a leading part in the administration of justice in Scotland though with the expectation that Scots would eventually administer justice throughout Britain. There would be comparable changes in the Scottish Church. For many Englishmen even this was unacceptable, a disagreeable dilution of Englishness that would allow floods of Scots to rush south to sponge off the English state. They said so in the debates of 1606 and 1607. But there were many other Englishmen who would accept such a union as a strengthening of Britain, and who could see the benefits that had accrued from Union with Wales. But no Scotsmen saw this as an acceptable way forward.

In a sense such a union was imposed in the 1650s. In the wake of the Cromwellian Conquest, the English Commonwealth went through an elaborate if artificial process of consultation with representatives of the Scottish boroughs and shires before bringing in an Act of Union that was consented to by a Parliament that had thirty representatives of Scottish constituencies in a body with 460 members in all. Cromwell was installed as Lord Protector of England, Scotland, and Ireland and his Council of State governed the whole archipelago, although there was an administrative body (of quasi-colonial governors) in Edinburgh. Although Scotland had thirty representatives in the Union Parliament, they were largely picked by the commanders of English garrisons in Scotland. The Scots were made to submit to English civil law (to be administered initially by English judges) although they were to retain their own criminal law (administered by a mixed bench of English and Scottish lawyers). There was to be a gradual move towards English forms of local government, with the development of the office of Justice of the Peace. Despite the pretence of consultation and consent, there is no evidence that the Scots welcomed any of these changes.

The second proposal was for a federal union, under which each kingdom would retain its characteristic institutions but work so as to co-ordinate their activities. Thus Scottish and English Parliaments would meet simultaneously with representatives of each kingdom present so as to smooth the passage of any legislative measures common to both. Similarly, there would be provision for the participation of commissioners of both kingdoms in the framing and implementation of an agreed foreign and colonial policy. There would be two national Churches but with regular meetings of commissioners to bring about, if not integration, then greater unity of belief and practice. This was always the first preference of the Scots, and it was something that the leaders of the Covenanting movement were committed to from the time of the first Scottish irruption into England in 1639 until the English Conquest of Scotland in the early 1650s. It was something that very few in England were willing to consider. In 1640 a Scottish army occupied the northeast of England and the Scots demanded a settlement with Charles I that was ratified by an English Parliament. Meanwhile the English would pay the wages of their soldiers—£800 a day. Most of the ensuing treaty was concerned with the internal history of Scotland, with the nobility reducing the King to little more than a figure-head monarch. But the Scots were also anxious to negotiate a federal union of the two kingdoms, and especially the appointment of *conservatores pacis* or parliamentary commissioners who would liaise between the free and separate executive and legislative bodies of the two kingdoms. They were reluctantly persuaded to defer detailed negotiation of that clause until after their army had returned home and disbanded. The English parliamentarians did not return to the negotiating table until they desperately needed Scottish military help with the war going badly for them in 1643. They then entered into a military, civil, and religious agreement with the Scots, known as the Solemn League and Covenant. Under this, the Scots sent 20,000 soldiers into England in exchange for cash, for an undertaking that the Churches of all three kingdoms would be brought into line (reformed 'according to the Word of God and the example of the best reformed Churches'—which the Scots assumed meant that they would be reformed in line with Scottish practice) and a civil federal union, in token of which the administration of the war effort in England was handed over to a 'Committee of Both Kingdoms', in which representatives (perhaps delegates would be a better term) of the Scottish estates sat with a strong body of English Lords and Commoners. But once more the English resisted Scottish attempts to implement the more permanent introduction of federal-union provisions and this proved one of the many issues which disaffected many Scots from the alliance with the Parliament and allowed the more loyalist nobility to seize the initiative and to commit Scotland to the King's cause at the time of the Second Civil War in 1648.

In 1603 James I set out his political aspirations on a commemorative medal for his accession. Dressed as a Roman emperor, with armour and a laurel wreath, he was no mere king but 'emperor of the whole island of Britain'. He soon dropped the title Emperor, and never sought to incorporate Ireland into a single all-embracing title in the way the term 'Spain' came to incorporate the ancient kingdoms of Castile and Aragon.

But if incorporative union was unacceptable in Scotland, and federal union was unacceptable in England, the third option had few supporters in either, except amongst dreamers and those who fawned on James VI and I. This was the scheme much beloved of James himself, a scheme for a 'perfect union', under which both countries would trade in their old and inadequate structures and participate in the creation of new and superior ones that drew on the strengths of both. James was well aware that such a perfect union could not be created overnight. Rather it would be the culmination of a process that he hailed as a programme designed to bring about 'a union of hearts and minds'. This meant essentially two things: promoting the image of Britishness and creating a greater sense of the consonance and underlying unity of the political, religious, and legal cultures of the two kingdoms.

In promoting the first, James insisted in using the style 'King of Great Britain', and issuing coins and medals promoting the term. Great care was taken in the design of a new Union flag, cunningly wrought so that the emblems of St George and St Andrew were of equal prominence. But early attempts to promote the notion that England (and Wales) were South Britain and Scotland North Britain were abandoned. James also promoted a common citizenship and rewarded courtiers who married across the old national divides, although he abandoned his original plan to have Englishmen and Scotsmen sharing the major offices in each kingdom. His (unsuccessful) promotion of free trade had the same objective. His English and Scottish subjects were to learn to mix and mingle to such an extent that they came gradually to see themselves as Britons. Then (but only then) the work of a perfect union could be more vigorously pursued.

As to the second, James moved to have 'hostile laws' previously passed by the Parliaments of the two kingdoms repealed and a joint commission of Borderers appointed to administer justice and arbitrate disputes in the 'Middle Shires', those straddling the old Anglo-Scottish border. James sought reforms of the law in both kingdoms to bring the best practice of the one to the other, to develop a greater common element in two systems which remained distinct. This was his policy too in religion, as we have seen.

James had a vision of a new Britain that escaped the frailties and inefficiencies of the composite monarchies of Continental Europe. It was a vision that accepted the need for patience and gradualism. It was enthusiastically endorsed by intellectuals and would-be placemen like Francis Bacon, but which went down like a lead balloon in the English Parliament. As far as the xenophobic English country gentry were concerned, an incorporative union along the lines of the Welsh Union might work; otherwise a union of crowns without a union of kingdoms was perfectly acceptable. They rightly perceived that English interests would dominate in such an imperfect union.

6. *Kingdoms and Nations*

Not even James had a vision of union embracing Ireland. Geographers may have formed the habit of referring to the archipelago consisting of Britain and Ireland as the Britannic Isles, but there never had been a historical myth linking the islands. Medieval historians, such as the twelfth-century Geoffrey of Monmouth, had developed the idea that Britain (i.e. England, Scotland, and Wales) had first been settled by Trojan refugees fleeing after the capture and destruction of their city by the Greeks. The founding monarch—Brutus—had then divided up the island between his three sons, the eldest (Albion) inheriting England and the younger sons Scotland and Wales. This permitted English antiquarians to claim a superiority for the English nation and the English Crown. In the fourteenth century the Scots developed their own counter-myth which acknowledged that Trojans had first occupied England and Wales, but asserted that Scotland had been occupied by colonists from Greece—the conquerors of Troy. Faced by such Scottish counter-myths and by the scepticism bred of humanist scholarship, few people took any of these historical claims seriously by 1600. English claims that kings of Scotland had regularly recognized the feudal suzerainty of the English Crown had to be abandoned in 1603 when the Scottish royal house inherited the English Crown. But the fact is that many of the inhabitants of Britain—especially intellectuals around the royal Courts—had for centuries conceptualized a relationship which bound them together into a common history. There were no such historical myths binding Ireland into the story. The term 'Britain' was widely understood and it excluded Ireland; there was no geopolitical term binding together the archipelago. All the Stuarts took the title 'King of Great Britain . . . and Ireland'. So whenever talk of union came up at any time in the seventeenth century, it was talk of a union of England and Scotland.

This did not solve all the problems. From the early years of the seventeenth century there were as many newly settled Scots as newly settled English in Ireland, and this made the people of Scotland—including the Scottish Privy Council—anxious to see the interests of Scots protected by some formal link between Scotland and Ireland. Most obviously this was true of religion, for the Kirk wished to be able to give fraternal support to the Scots of Ireland, and to protect them from churchmen and officials who wished to impose the forms and practices of the Church of Ireland.

In the 1640s the Scottish Covenanters wanted a federal union of England and Scotland that would give *both* a role in the management of the Irish Church and State. The English Parliament, however, intended to subdue the Irish, using English troops and (as far as they were concerned) mercenary troops from Scotland. Once subdued, Ireland was to revert even more firmly to being a conquered, subordinate kingdom under the English Crown.

In the course of the seventeenth century, then, there was a great confusion of identities within the archipelago. We can already find that inability to distinguish between 'England' and 'Britain' which characterizes the modern Englishman. They are used interchangeably, even when one or the other is specifically intended. Thus John Milton's *History of Britain* is exclusively concerned with the formation of pre-Norman *England*. Welshmen and Scotsmen would never make that mistake. What is clear is that over the early modern period, the sense of Englishness, Welshness, Scottishness became stronger and stronger as other loyalties—regional, tribal, patrilinear, receded. An awareness of Britishness also grew, but as often as not as something to be rejected rather than embraced.

JAMES II was willing to put the Catholic Irish (including Tyrconnel, *right*, as Lord Lieutenant) in power in Ireland—in Parliament, in the Council, in the army—and to promote the interests of the Catholic Church there, but he hesitated to overturn the land settlement of the 1650s which had given the Protestants a stranglehold on social power. The result was further instability and the bitter wars of the 1690s.

The situation in Ireland was more complicated. In 1600 there were several distinctive communities: the descendants of the Gaelic peoples (and the descendants of those Anglo-Norman settlers who had 'gone native'), with their own language, Gaelic *brehon* law, strong attachment to the Catholic religion, and the desire to achieve palatinate status under the English Crown; the Old English, the descendants of the Normans, English-speaking, committed to an independent Kingdom of Ireland that shared its monarch with England and derived its legal and political culture from England, who were largely but not exclusively Catholic; and the New English colonists and planters, who saw themselves in a conquered land, and as the purveyors of civility to an uncivilized and possibly uncivilizable native population.

By 1700 a few of the Old English families—especially those like the Butler Dukes of Ormonde who had deserted Catholicism—had Anglicized themselves. But most of the Old English had merged with the native Irish to form the New Irish. Their defining characteristic was now Catholicism (they had largely abandoned spoken Gaelic, although not reading Gaelic texts), they were politically marginalized and had a strong corporate memory of a century of persecution and expropriation. In the course of the twenty years after 1689, new penal laws were to be heaped upon them. And then there were the Anglo-Irish, or the Ascendancy, that one-quarter of the population who owned two-thirds of the land and three-thirds of political power. They were Protestant in religion, they prided themselves on their English roots, and they were developing a colonialist suspicion of metropolitan government. If there was a British consciousness in Ireland, it was probably amongst the Scots.

The story of the three Stuart kingdoms was not, then, the story of the forging of a single nation. It was a tale of two islands, of what were emerging as three kingdoms, one of which had been fabricated by the will of another, and of the relations of four emerging nations, each of which had an identity shaped or at least deeply stained by its contact with—mingling with—the others. As has been wisely said, British history denotes the historiography of no single nation but of a problematic and uncompleted experiment in the creation and interaction of several nations.

5 FAMILY, HOUSEHOLD, AND COMMUNITY

AMY LOUISE ERICKSON

1. *Introduction*

The massive carved overmantel in the Oak Drawing Room of Liverpool's Speke Hall depicts three generations of the Norris family in the sixteenth century. On the left panel are Henry, Clemence, and their five children. In the centre, their son Sir William and his two wives Ellen and Anne preside over their nineteen children. And on the right, Sir William's son Edward and his wife Margaret are shown with two children, although they eventually had seven more. The management of the extensive Norris household required careful planning. In the early modern period (approximately 1500 to 1700, roughly coterminous with the Tudor and Stuart monarchs) the word 'economy' described the running of the household, not the commercial behaviour of the nation. The basic elements in the early modern economy were therefore marriage and childbirth, in a much more obvious way than they are today, since only by marrying and having children was a family produced to undertake the labour necessary to make the household function. Domestic relationships were the model on which all early modern social hierarchy depended, and likewise the core of what we in the twentieth century call the economy.

The principal sources of evidence for the reconstruction of domestic life between the late fifteenth and the late seventeenth centuries are as follows: printed books on household management; private letters, diaries, and account books, from literate and at least moderately leisured people; and the records of numerous types of public courts, which refer to, although they were not written by, members of all levels of society. At the beginning of the period, archaeological evidence is useful; towards the end of it, the volume of written and printed documents is enormous. In addition, parish registers of births, marriages, and deaths, which survive in most parts of England from the mid-sixteenth century on, have been analysed in recent years with the help of com-

EARLY seventeenth-century portrait of the Cholmondely sisters of Cheshire, who, according to the inscription, were married on the same day, holding their swaddled babies, who were also born on the same day.

puters to produce demographic statistics on birth, marriage, and death. This cycle of raising children, marrying, raising children, and burying is the core of the domestic economy.

2. *Upbringing*

The average number of children born and christened to a family in the early modern period was between three and four, of whom two or three survived to adulthood. But this statistic covers a wide variation in family size. Upper-class families like the Norrises had more children perhaps partly because they were relatively well-nourished, but principally because brides were younger, and because the practice of sending infants out to a wet-nurse meant that wealthy women did not enjoy the contraceptive effects of suckling. In an age before artificial contraceptives, a relatively late age at marriage and the practice of breast-feeding among the majority of the population kept the birth rate low far more effectively than coitus interruptus.

Then as now, sex ratios among infants shifted as a result of biological differences: slightly more boys than girls were born, but slightly more girls survived to adulthood. The fact that these proportions are comparable to those that prevail in Britain today is significant because while in all cultures more boys are born, it is not always the case that more girls survive. In parts of Asia and North Africa today sex ratios are skewed because daughters are culturally undesirable and parents let them die, and on occasion even deliberately kill them. It has frequently been suggested (on more limited evidence than that available to twentieth-century demographers) that female infanticide was also common in ancient and early medieval Europe. Infanticide was certainly practised in early modern Britain, but it was also illegal. Court records show that boys and girls

Woodcut of a family scene from the first text to teach children Latin by the use of pictures, J. A. Comenius's *Orbis Sensualium Pictus* (first English edition 1659). The numbers refer to the accompanying lists of phrases in English and Latin. Father is shown as an artist so that his palette can provide a pun for the phrase 'The father maintaineth his children by taking pains'.

were smothered or abandoned in privies in equal numbers. Almost always the mother was unmarried and desperate, or married but with other children and in severe want.

Early modern portraits of wealthy families depict new-born infants swaddled, or wrapped tightly in strips of woollen fabric, sometimes also bound to boards. Books of advice on child-rearing recommended swaddling a baby for between one and four months, in the belief that this would encourage their limbs to grow straight. But it is not clear how far down the social scale this practice spread. The woodcut print of a family scene in *Orbis Sensualium Pictus* illustrates successive stages of childhood, starting with the swaddled infant in the cradle; another is suckling at its mother's breast; the boy standing before his mother is supposed to be learning piety at her knee; a girl spoons pap into the mouth of her younger sibling (in a standing stool, playing with a rattle); while her brother studies his book, a rod in front of him on the table, to note that the child 'is chastised if it be not dutiful'. Babies were generally suckled until the age of perhaps 3 or 4 (precise chronology in the woodcut is abandoned in the interest of cramming in as much information as possible), and were weaned onto pap or gruel. High chairs and cradles do survive from the seventeenth century, but most children slept with their parents or siblings. Children learned to walk with the help of 'leading strings' (used even by the children of husbandmen), and 'standing stools'. Neither the leading strings nor the standing stools survive, but from their pictures and descriptions they appear to have been virtually identical to the designs used for these self-same items today, made of leather and wood instead of plastic.

Small toys, like the whistles sometimes itemized in the accounts of a parent, or the hobby-horses, whirligigs, and rattles with which children are often depicted in woodcuts, have also vanished. Wealthier children received pocket money. Giles Moore, the rector of Horsted Keynes, Sussex, in the mid-seventeenth century, kept an account book in which he noted giving his niece Martha Mayhew sixpence on several occasions 'for a fairing' and 'to play and spend', and later a shilling 'to play withall' or 'to spend at dancings'. But each of Martha's occasional shillings represented a full day's wages for a labouring man, and perhaps two days' or more for a labouring widow with children to feed. Still, even these families might have parted with a penny for a hornbook to learn the alphabet, or sixpence for a chapbook story-book. Most children were set to helping their parents as soon as they were able, about age 5 or 6, sweeping the floor, minding younger children, cleaning pots and pans, scaring away birds and weeding in the garden or the fields, running errands, and gathering dung or twigs or peat for fuel and rushes to burn for light. A few years later they could do the simple sewing or knitting necessary to mend clothes and re-foot stockings, as well as spinning or knitting for wages.

It is often thought that many or even most children never made it to adulthood. Certain parts of the country did have particularly high death rates, notably the unhealthy fenland areas of East Anglia and Lincolnshire. And some groups of the population, like the orphans and foundlings sent out by charitable institutions or by parish authorities to a wet-nurse, also suffered extremely high mortality. But overall, three-quarters of children born alive lived to the age of 15. By the time they reached their early teens, most children had left their parents' house. At upper social levels they may have left even earlier, to join another household of similar or superior status, the family of destination being chosen by parents with the possibility of future marriage alliance in mind. Some households were renowned for their training of ladies and gentlemen, the boys with the master, the girls with the mistress. Among the majority of the population, some boys and a few girls were apprenticed to a trade or to housewifery; most young people worked as farm servants or domestic servants. Both apprenticeship and service contracts usually lasted for a period of at least seven years, after which successive one-year terms could be taken up. By this time in their early twenties, servants and apprentices could consider setting up their own household.

3. *Inheritance*

The most familiar aspect of inheritance prior to the twentieth century is the practice known as primogeniture, or the right of the eldest son to inherit. In fact, the law of primogeniture in early modern England applied only to certain types of land, and then only where no other provision (like a will, for example) had been made. Inheritance has been studied in considerable detail because the records for it—notably wills and settlements—are plentiful. Among the wealthy, the eldest son was markedly favoured in inheriting the family seat. He was also usually given control of his sisters' and younger brothers' cash portions, putting him in a very powerful position.

But while land was widely considered the principal form of property, the wills of ordinary people often did not mention land. It had been conveyed by some other instrument, like a deed of transfer, a child's marriage settlement, or by manorial court roll (the register of a manor's property-holders). Instead, wills focused on the inheritance of personal or 'moveable' property by younger sons and daughters and by the will-maker's 'relict', or widow. Bequests often took the form of some cash, but almost always included household furniture as well: pots, pans, and utensils (especially the fine ones of pewter or, very occasionally, silver); tables, chairs, cupboards, dish-benches, hutches, and chests. Chests for linens were extremely common, the finer ones carved with initials or a full name and brought to marriage by either bride or groom. These low chests were replaced only at the end of the seventeenth century by the chests of drawers common today. Chairs were often given as wedding presents, carved with the couple's initials. Almost every country house displays some example.

Wills reveal a great deal about the furnishings of ordinary houses which constituted a large part of children's inheritance. The look of a house can be reconstructed sometimes in wills which describe items as 'standing in the hall' or 'lying in the chamber'. Another probate document, the inventory, commonly listed all the deceased's goods by room. But the more common and the cheaper that furnishings became, the less likely they were to catch the appraisers' notice. The painted wall cloths which were a luxury to the Elizabethan yeoman, by the mid-seventeenth century had become too common to itemize in inventories. Not a single one of these cloths survives, although painting directly onto the wall does in a few domestic settings (as at Bramall Hall, Stockport, or lower down the social scale in the yeoman's house in Newark's market square, which is now a branch of a bakery chain). The final entry in each inventory was 'and other trash'

THE 'Westmoreland' bed (1525), in the Little Parlour Chamber (that is, the room above the Little Parlour) of Oakwell Hall, Birstall, West Yorkshire, bears the injunction 'Drede God, Love God, Prayes God'. Heavy curtains would have hung on all sides, providing warmth and a measure of privacy. The 'trucklebed', slid underneath, was common throughout the period, for servants or children to sleep on. The rushlight holder was ubiquitous in houses at gentry level and below. This one doubles as a candle holder. Rushes were cut in summer, stripped to the pith except for one rib of peel to hold them upright, soaked in melted animal fat, and dried. A good-sized rush of two-and-a-half feet burnt for one hour.

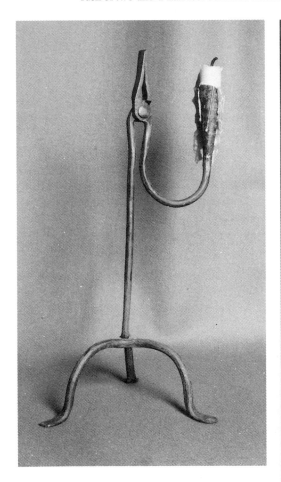

or 'etc.', which included not only the wall cloths, but all those cheap goods like spindles, wooden plates and spoons, a pair of old scissors, a battered spinning-wheel, or an old almanac, which could not individually be valued at more than a shilling.

The sixteenth- and seventeenth-century Dutch domestic interiors familiar from the paintings of the Brueghels, Jan Steen, Pieter de Hoogh, Jan Vermeer, and others give some idea of British domestic scenes, but they have no British counterpart. Dutch interiors were certainly idealized, but the patrons and buyers were merchants and the middle classes. English artists of the same period (Hans Holbein, Sir Peter Lely, or Mary Beale, for example) produced portraits of their patrons too: the wealthy, their children, pets, and houses, set against an only vaguely English landscape. Actual early modern interiors very rarely survive to look at today, since the 'improvements' of subsequent generations have altered the interiors of medieval and early modern buildings. The interior of Oakwell Hall, in West Yorkshire, the home of a prosperous yeoman who made money in the wool trade and subsequently styled himself as a gentleman, survives in extraordinarily good condition, and an inventory of its contents from the year 1611 survives, assisting reconstruction of its contents.

How could bequests of household furnishings, no matter how elaborate and extensive these had become by the later seventeenth century, ever compare with an eldest son's inheritance of land? Among ordinary people who did not own much land, the value of their moveable property was high relative to land. The importance of primogeniture was therefore limited by wealth. It was also limited by demography. Only three out of five marriages produced even one son. One in five produced no children at all, but one in five produced exclusively daughters, and unlike Continental forms of inheritance, the English system of descent preferred a daughter to a more distantly related male. In any event, these rules applied only where the property-holder did not make a will. Men of middling or modest wealth who made wills frequently pared off pieces of land for younger sons.

As is the case today, however, most men who died had not made a will. And in these cases the distribution of moveable property fell under the jurisdiction of the ecclesiastical law: two-thirds of a man's moveable property was divided equally among all his children (his wife had a right to the other third). Property was distributed among all children approximately equally both by men who made wills and in the instances where ecclesiastical courts divided the estates of men who had not made wills. In the minority of cases where the eldest son was favoured, it was not markedly so. Indeed, although the church courts were legally supposed to divide moveable property equally among all children, in practice they often used moveables to counterbalance the heir's inheritance of land, denying him any additional goods. Eldest sons were almost never granted control of their siblings' inheritance, as happened at upper social levels.

The purpose of inheritance, of course, was to set up a new household. Children who married while their parents were still alive received their inheritance early, to combine with their own saved earnings and perhaps bequests from grandparents or other kin, as a marriage portion. This was less the case for children of the upper class, particularly sons, who were dependent on their parents for maintenance until their parents', or at least until their father's, death. At the social level of yeomen farmers, the occasional surviving maintenance contract testifies to a married son or daughter providing support for their ageing parents. But this type of arrangement was unusual among the wealthy, where the reverse—a clause in a child's marriage settlement for parental support of the young couple—was far more common. A widowed mother might retire to a separate dowager house with an annuity from the heir, but a father maintained the title and the seat until his death.

4. *Marriage and Celibacy*

While marriage was the usual aim, it was by no means the only possible option. In the later fifteenth and early sixteenth centuries the religious life was still a possibility, although the monastic population was declining. Nevertheless, at the dissolution of the monasteries, there were still nearly 10,000 monks and nuns to be dispersed. This number is estimated to have accounted for less than one per cent of the population. But in the mid-sixteenth century, the earliest it is possible to estimate, about 5 per cent of people never married. This is approximately the same rate that prevails today. In the later sixteenth and first half of the seventeenth century, 15 to 20 per cent of adults remained unmarried, proportionately more people than at any time since. In the later seventeenth century the proportion remaining single fell to around 10 per cent, still a significant minority.

In the sixteenth and seventeenth centuries both men and women who never married lived in households of their own, as well as sometimes in the households of siblings. We know their family and household situation because they left wills (giving bequests to nieces and nephews and friends) and inventories (detailing a whole house, or a single room in another's house). Parish lists, or local censuses, also list single people. And in areas where relatively well-paying work was available, groups of spinsters or bachelors lived together in a precursor of the boarding-house. For some this may have been a permanent arrangement, for others only a stage in the life cycle before they moved on to marriage.

Throughout the later Middle Ages and the early modern period most people married in their mid- to late twenties. This age at first marriage is late in relation to marriages familiar from literature—Shakespeare's Romeo and Juliet, for example, were in their teens—and also in relation to developing societies in the world today. The median age at first marriage in early modern England (26–7) was the same as that in Britain in the 1980s. The relatively late age of marriage gave young people in the sixteenth and seventeenth centuries plenty of opportunity for courtship. A Lancashire mercer's apprentice, Roger Lowe, kept a diary in the 1660s in which he chronicled his own amorous endeavours, meeting his love of the moment in taverns and at fairs as well as visiting her house. The Derbyshire yeoman Leonard Wheatcroft also chronicled his 'siege' of 'the amiable mistress of my best affection', whom he married in 1657. Both Lowe and Wheatcroft also relate their negotiations as go-between in the love affairs of friends both male and female.

At aristocratic and upper gentry levels marriage occurred considerably younger than among the rest of the population. The wealthy had less time for dallying in the marriage market and their choice of partner was more restricted, sometimes limited to a power of veto over the matches proffered by their parents. Dorothy Osborne, daughter of a prominent Royalist, wrote in a letter of 1653 when the latest in a long string of potential suitors had been presented to her at her home in Bedfordshire, 'I had noe quarrell to his person, or his fortune but was in love with neither, and much out of love with a thing called marriage'. Two years later Dorothy was finally allowed to

Monument erected in 1618 by Thomas, Viscount Fauconberg, Baron of Yarm, to his wife Barbara, in the parish church of Coxwold, North Yorkshire, with a lavish inscription commemorating his love.

marry her own choice, the recipient of her letters, William Temple. There are occasional cases of parents forcing their children to marry against their will. One of the most notorious is that of the former Lord Chief Justice Sir Edward Coke tying his 14-year-old daughter Frances to a bedpost and whipping her until she consented to wed his choice. The marriage was disastrous: the groom went mad within a few years of the marriage; Frances left him the following year and went to live with Sir Robert Howard. Such awful cases were apparently rare. But choice was restricted and marriage came earlier because wealthy parents were more concerned to see their sons and daughters settled to familial advantage and producing heirs. It was commonly expected that love should be not the precursor to marriage, but its outcome. The marriage of Thomas, Viscount Fauconberg, Baron of Yarm and his wife Barbara was undoubtedly arranged by their parents. But the monument that he erected to her memory testifies to his passionate devotion:

Oh dear ashes and sweet bones of my wife, spare me if I am slow; it pleases me to make haste. . . . How I long to enter, when once dead, your bridechamber. We die, but love lives and lives on for those who are buried. The fates who once snatched you away will one day return you to me.

Everyman is a bubble: all flesh is grass.
Omnis homo bulla, omnis caro faenum.

Marriage was arranged among the wealthy because of its implications for property. At all social levels, marriage was by far the most convenient way to make a fortune. Both parties to a marriage were obliged to bring property—a 'portion', sometimes for women called a 'dowry'. This was the case for everyone from the aristocracy right down to the ballad characters 'loving Kate' and 'honest John'. These two negotiated their nuptials in a tavern: each brought £10 by inheritance plus their saved wages and household moveables. With this capital they agreed to open an alehouse together. To put this pair into financial perspective, Dorothy Osborne, a member of the upper gentry, had £4,000 in portion. Her family forbade her marriage to William Temple for so long precisely because he lacked a fortune comparable to hers. She could have chosen to elope with him, but in so doing she would have sacrificed her portion along with her family's good will. Frances Coke had £10,000, although in her case, as frequently in the realms of such wildly inflated portions, sums were promised on the basis of multiple mortgages of parental property and in the event were not forthcoming. The occasional cases of married children suing their parents for portions in the records of the Court of Chancery make sorry reading.

Women's portions are the ones most often discussed, largely because those doing the discussing are usually men. Charitable organizations were established, especially in the fifteenth and sixteenth centuries, to provide portions for poor 'maidens', in the belief that without a dowry

T HE Norman black marble font at Winchester Cathedral bears scenes from the life of St Nicholas, Bishop of Myra. Very few early modern representations of him survive. Several late medieval wall paintings were recorded in the later nineteenth century, but these have since vanished. Here, the poor father kneels in gratitude to the bishop for the dowries given to his three daughters. In another miracle, Nicholas resurrected three boys butchered in a brine-tub, earning himself the devotion of children. Nicholas's feast in December was frequently celebrated with a day of children's licence, or even the crowning of a 'boy bishop', an example of a festival of 'misrule'.

a woman would be unable to marry (or unable to marry a respectable man) and would therefore be seduced and/or forced into prostitution. Bishop Nicholas of Myra, who was said to have dropped three bags of gold through the window of a poor man's house to provide dowries for his three daughters, has 400 churches dedicated to his memory in England alone. St Nicholas's three gold balls also appear on the pawnbroker's shop sign, and he it was who later metamorphosed into Santa Claus.

Men discussed women's portions so often because it was they who invariably improved their economic status upon marriage. The laws of marital property gave all of a wife's personal property to her husband upon marriage. The common law viewed husband and wife as one person, the husband, in order 'to tye them to a perfect love, agreement and adherence', according to the anonymous author of *The Lawes Resolutions of Women's Rights* (1632). 'I know no remedy,' he added, 'though some women can shift it well enough.' A wife retained her real property in her own name, although her husband had a right to the income from it. A married woman therefore could not sign a contract, make a will, or engage in a suit of law without her husband joining her. Husbands, on the other hand, had a moral but not a legal obligation to support their wives. As a result of the risks to the wife's family—not only were they parting with comparatively large amounts of money at her marriage, but they might also have to support her again if her husband failed to do so—marriage settlements protecting the wife's property in the event of her widowhood or marital breakdown were ubiquitous among the wealthy. Even the wives of craftsmen, husbandmen, and yeomen made marriage settlements in significant numbers to guarantee themselves a modicum of property in widowhood and to protect the inheritance of their children by a previous marriage. Whether they had a marriage settlement or not, women were normally financially better off if they married, but they were also at the mercy of an unkind husband. Even the Elizabethan 'Homily on Marriage', read out regularly in every parish church, acknowledged the unequal burdens of marriage. Women

must specially feel the griefs and pains of matrimony, in that they relinquish the liberty of their own rule, in the pain of their travailing, in the bringing up of their children, in which offices they be in great perils, and be grieved with many afflictions, which they might be without, if they lived out of matrimony.

5. *Childbirth*

The view of late medieval theologians that the purpose of marriage was procreation and mutual comfort, in that order, was debated by both Puritan and Catholic pundits in the sixteenth century. Both ultimately decided that marriage was, rather, primarily about mutual comfort and secondarily about procreation. However, procreation is considerably easier to analyse in retrospect than mutual comfort. Childbirth itself occurred usually in exclusively female company: the midwife and a woman's female kin, neighbours, or servants attended her. These women were referred to as 'gossips'. But it seems likely that it was the talk during a sometimes protracted period of lying-in that aroused suspicion among the absent menfolk, and gave rise to the malicious, pejorative sense of 'gossip'. The general hostility towards women speaking was of at least biblical origins (Paul's 'Silence is the woman's glory'). Ephemeral popular prints and carvings of stone and wood in cathedrals and parish churches vividly illustrated medieval proverbs about idle tongues. The experience of childbirth formed a powerful bond among women across class

A N evil midwife accosts a woman with two infants, in the woodcut that accompanies the ballad called 'The Whisper of Wood-street' in the later seventeenth century. Woodcuts were continually reused in the sixteenth and seventeenth centuries to illustrate new publications, and the picture was not always directly relevant to the story being told. This one originated *c.*1620, and the image appeared subsequently on at least five other ballads.

boundaries, since in any village some mother would have been expecting at most times of the year, and the lady of the manor attended the births of tenant farmers' wives and poor women alike, while those women attended the wealthier women as servants.

Early modern midwives were licensed to practise by the church courts, and had to present at least six testimonials to their ability. This suggests that they may have served an apprenticeship, but very few records of formal apprenticeship survive. They swore an oath: not to exchange or hide babies (thereby wreaking havoc with inheritance); not to smother an unwanted infant and affirm it was born dead; not to extort money from women in labour; to ensure Anglican baptism; and not to use witchcraft. The injunctions clearly indicate official anxieties and suspicions surrounding midwives' power within the birth chamber. In an effort to limit the burdens on parish poor relief, midwives were further required to demand of an unmarried woman in her travail the name of the child's father so that he could be made to support it (shades of the Child Support Act of 1993).

Manuals for the physiological instruction of midwives appeared regularly from the mid-sixteenth century, written primarily by physicians. The herbalist and astrological physician Nicholas Culpeper published two midwifery manuals in the mid-seventeenth century. Jane Sharp's *Midwives Book* (1671), the only manual written by a midwife in this period, focused on anatomy, the formal study of which midwives were denied. Culpeper supported midwives against the College of Physicians, established in the early sixteenth century specifically for men with medical degrees, to exclude barber-surgeons, apothecaries, and women who 'boldly . . . take upon them great cures'. The barber-surgeons had their own organization, which from the end of the fifteenth century forbade from practice all women except the widows of surgeons; by the end of the seventeenth century these too were banned. The apothecaries company continued to include a small number of women throughout the period. But these restrictions on women's participation, like those of other professional guilds and companies, applied primarily in London and to some extent in major towns. In the countryside, restrictions were impossible to enforce, and midwives were regularly cited before the church courts for practising without a licence. Even in London the physicians proved unable to meet the need for physic, and the restrictions on women practising were eased in the mid-sixteenth century. Midwives in London attempted to organize their profession along the same lines that the men had in 1616, but were successfully opposed by the existing bodies. Elizabeth Cellier, midwife to Mary of Modena, asked James II to establish a college to train midwives, but this proposal failed at least partly because of her Catholicism.

The 'man-midwife' did not make his appearance in the birth chamber until the seventeenth century. While calling a male physician to a delivery in cases of emergency had long been common among those who could afford it, the man-midwife was still regarded with considerable suspicion on grounds of sexual impropriety as well as his presumed ignorance. Mrs Elizabeth Freke was attended by four midwives at the birth of her son in 1675. Her labour lasted four or five days, and her diary derided the man-midwife for 'affirming [the baby] had been long dead to my husband and aunt and sister Norton with my Lady Thinn, all who were with me several days in this my extremity'. But she praises God 'that never failed me or denied my reasonable request', who 'raised me up a good woman midwife of my Lady Thinn's acquaintance . . . and . . . I was safely delivered'.

Midwifery manuals advised a not unfamiliar routine of infant care, including changing the baby 'whenever he is fouled', or at least three times daily. Nappies, or 'clouts', were available ready-made from peddlars by the late seventeenth century, but any rags would have served the purpose previously. The great majority of infants were breast-fed by their mothers. Not only was it cheap, it was also known that suckling greatly reduced the chances of another conception. Even if most women did only have three or four children, they would have known of local wealthy women like Mrs Mary Green, the wife of the Recorder of London in the early seventeenth century, who died in childbed with her eleventh infant at the age of 33. The young Alice Wandesford, daughter of the late Lord Deputy of Ireland, in 1645 saw her elder sister, Lady Danby, die in the delivery of her sixteenth child. Statistically, the chance of a woman dying in childbirth was one in 100, comparable to the risk of a child dying before the age of one in England and Wales today. Nevertheless, the dangers of every birth for the mother cannot have been far from her mind, in addition to anxieties about the health and wholeness of the infant she carried, when it was widely believed that frights to the mother or unpleasant sights could cause deformity in an unborn child.

Among the well-to-do, the already high birth rate was exacerbated by the widespread practice of wet-nursing—sending a new-born infant out of the house, often into the countryside if born in a large town, to a woman paid to suckle and raise the child until weaned. Perhaps wealthy women worried that suckling would ruin the shape of their breasts. But those who advocated in print the duty of mothers to breast-feed their own children pointed to another reason that they failed to do so: William Gouge's *Of Domesticall Duties* (1622) said that 'husbands for the most part are the cause that their wives nurse not their owne children'; the Countess of Lincoln, in her *Nurserie* of the same year, regretted that she had acceded to her husband's wish that she not nurse any of her eighteen children.

Child-rearing, like labour, delivery, and nursing, was a female domain. Changing, cleaning, spoon-feeding, minding, toilet training, and early education were all undertaken by the mother, elder sisters, or servants. (In Comenius's didactic illustration, above, it is the elder sister who spoons pap into the toddler's mouth, while the elder brother sits and studies his book.) The labour involved in childbirth and child-rearing was immense, considering that not only were cleaning processes and preparing food and drink much more time-consuming, but whereas today only 12 per cent of the population is under the age of 10, fully one quarter of the early modern population was under the age of 10.

6. *Labour*

Manuals of husbandry and housewifery were published in large numbers through the sixteenth and seventeenth centuries. A major part of managing the domestic economy was keeping track of finances. Fitzherbert's *Boke of Husbandry* (1550) detailed at great length the responsibilities of the farming couple, and urged both husband and wife to keep accounts. Household account books of the aristocracy, such as the extensive accounts of the Earl of Bedford in the later seventeenth century, are not uncommon. These were clearly the husband's accounts, since lump sums were paid to the wife and many essential expenses do not appear. The wonderfully detailed seventeenth-century account books of the Berkshire yeoman Robert Loder and the Sussex clergyman Giles Moore likewise reflect only half of the domestic economy; their wives' account books do not survive. The estate management of wives appears in the historical record only in circumstances where their husbands were absent and letters between the couple survive. Husbands might be away in London on business or politics, as in the case of Margaret and John Paston in the fifteenth century or Dame Joan and Sir John Thynne in the early seventeenth. Particularly in the mid-seventeenth century husbands were away at war or in prison, as in the case of Lady Brilliana and Sir Robert Harley or Dame Anne and Sir Robert Filmer. The most complete reflections of household income and expenditure on a gentry level are, paradoxically, obtained in the account books of two unmarried women. Joyce Jeffries, of Hereford, in the 1630s and 1640s managed agricultural land and financial investments as well as feeding, clothing, and heating her immediate household. Sarah Fell, in Lancashire in the 1670s, kept accounts for the estate of her widowed mother, later the wife of the Quaker founder George Fox.

Estate management was a concern for the few. Most people were labourers in agriculture, in building or other trades, or in domestic service. Men earned an average of one shilling for a day's labour, women less. Sarah Fell paid her day labourers, especially the women, as little as a penny or tuppence, plus their food. Most people lived from quarter-day to quarter-day (Lady Day, Martinmas, Michaelmas, and Christmas), when wages were paid and rents fell due. Most people were occupied in agriculture in this period. Men's agricultural work was seasonal. Inventories list the tools of husbandry: carts, ploughs, wains, and the gears for each; harrows, forks, rakes, spades, shovels, scythes, to cultivate beans, lentils, wheat, rye, oats, barley, and hemp; guns to shoot game, perhaps a boat in the fens from which to fish and catch birds. Among the livestock, women usually tended the bees, the poultry, and the cows; men the sheep, pigs, and occasionally horses. Both men and women worked at all of the above for wages as well as for subsistence. The traditional trade names of butcher, baker, carpenter, cartwright, chandler, wheelwright, joiner, tanner, shoemaker, and so forth, were applied almost exclusively to men. But married couples must frequently have practised the trade together since in cities, where tradesmen were organized in guilds, and later companies, and so left records, a widow was not uncommonly listed as carrying on her husband's trade.

Most work, whether in town or in the countryside, was carried on within the household. Between the late fifteenth and the late seventeenth centuries this situation was changing, and the place of paid work moving out of the home. It was a very gradual shift, probably not completed until most people no longer worked in agriculture, in the later nineteenth century. In the early modern period agriculture, including selling a surplus, was combined with 'piecework' or 'outwork' for industry. Some industries were thoroughly capitalized from the fifteenth century, like the wool trade and the cloth trade. That is, they were commercially organized to produce a surplus and make a profit. The cloth merchant bought the wool, sent it out to be combed, carded, and spun by women, then on to be successively woven, fulled, sheared, and dyed by men. Most of the work was done in the homes of the workers, with the exception of some cloth merchants who specifically incorporated a large room with many windows into their own homes, to be filled with looms let out to journeymen weavers. The medieval houses of Thomas Paycocke of Coggeshall in Essex and Thomas Spring of Lavenham in Suffolk, for example, are both still standing. Weavers petitioned

THE account book of Mrs Joyce Jeffries for March 1644, when she was about 70 years old. A royalist, Jeffries was staying with her nephew at Ham Castle, her Hereford house having been plundered twice by parliamentary forces occupying the city. She never married herself, but maintained extensive links with her large family. This page of disbursements starts with tuppence for three wooden whistles to give to children, and includes expenditure on servants' wages, sewing materials, planting the garden at her Hereford house (including 400 cabbage plants), and feeding the soldiers quartered there, and ends with nearly £84 spent during the whole year at her farm near Leominster.

Parliament through the first half of the sixteenth century, protesting that this early form of factory prevented householding men from earning a living because it fixed prices for outwork at the level of wages paid to the journeymen.

Other industries, like brewing, for example, became capitalized in the seventeenth century. Silk production in London, an industry managed almost wholly by 'gentilwymmen' in the later Middle Ages on an outwork basis, employed factory-based sweated labour by the seventeenth century. In the process of becoming capitalized, industries which had not previously been so were monopolized by men. This was not simply a question of class. If it were, both men and women of the merchant classes would have organized industry. The exclusion of women was a specific policy, as with the organization of the medical trades, mentioned above. This policy limited women's ability to earn a good income, but most women like most men still worked for wages, and most work was still carried out on a 'cottage industry' or an outwork basis. In any event, these changes affected only waged labour, when all households, from the cottage to the manor to the town house, were still maintained by an enormous amount of subsistence labour.

The labour of the household was undertaken principally by women. Thomas Tusser's *Five Hundred Pointes of Good Husbandrie . . . Over and Besides the Booke of Huswiferie*, first published in 1580 but frequently reprinted, repeated a variation on the proverb common today:

> Though husbandrie seemeth, to bring in the gaines,
> Yet huswiferie labours, seem equall in paines.
> Some respit to husbands, the weather may send,
> But huswives affaires, have never an end.

The anonymous author of *The Lawes Resolutions of Women's Rights*, printed in 1632 but written in the later sixteenth century, expressed the same sentiment more pithily: 'Sweetheart going to church, and hoistbrick coming home'. As far as it is possible to tell, women did all of the cleaning, cooking, and mending, as well as the child care, inside the house. Undoubtedly fathers or elder brothers occasionally soothed fractious infants to sleep with a lullaby. But one popular ballad, of the sort that sold for a penny and must have been ubiquitous by the seventeenth century, ridiculed the man who did the household chores and washed the baby's 'shitten clouts'. A woman's domestic habits were inextricably bound up with her sexual reputation. If she were not occupied in the household what might she be doing? Surely a man who relieved his wife of domestic chores was a cuckold?

The need to avoid idleness had some wonderful results, like the beautiful decorative needlework produced in wealthy women's 'leisure hours'. But most housewives were too much occupied with the labours of subsistence to spend much time in embellishment. Housewifery at all social levels involved a very wide range of work. The subtitle of Gervase Markham's *The English Housewife* (1618), reissued more than twenty times, listed the skills required of the 'compleat' woman:

physick, chirurgery, cookery, extraction of oyls, banqueting stuff . . . ordering of wool, hemp, flax; making cloath and dying; the knowledge of dayries: office of malting; . . . of brewing, baking, and all other things belonging to an household.

It is notable that 'physick' and 'chirurgery' come first in Markham's list. Later seventeenth-

E LIZABETHAN herbal pillow edged with passement lace, in the collection of an early twentieth-century needle-woman and philanthropist, Rachel Kay-Shuttleworth. Every country house exhibits examples of ornamental needlework, and some country house owners were particularly known for their skill, like 'Bess of Hardwick', who also built Hardwick Hall in Derbyshire. Embroidery pattern books began to appear in the late sixteenth century. Styles were strongly influenced by Britain's trade in textiles with the near and far east.

century books on household management, like those by Hannah Wolley and *The Gentlewoman's Closet*, as well as the handwritten receipt books passed from mother to daughter throughout the period, also contained instructions for medical remedies as well as cookery. The receipts are usually for poultices or infusions to drink, for curing worms (a common problem where human waste readily found its way into garden soil), the stone, tumours, burns, gout, toothache, and for a perennial domestic problem, killing vermin. Remedies for animal illness were often included, as they were also in books of husbandry like the 1641 farming book of Henry Best, a yeoman of Elmswell in Yorkshire's East Riding. The late sixteenth-century *Boke of St Albans* was perhaps the earliest to offer 'medycynes' for the 'complaints of beasts and foules'.

Most human illness was in the first instance cared for by the women of the household. If specialist treatment was required, a local healer, an apothecary, a barber-surgeon, or a physician might be called in, in that order, following their availability in most parts of the country. Hospitals for the sick were confined to cities. These were run first by religious sisters and their paid employees, and after the Reformation by charitable corporations, who likewise paid women to nurse the inmates. Throughout the country, under the Elizabethan Poor Law, parish overseers paid women—often those in receipt of poor relief themselves—to nurse others in receipt of relief.

As for Markham's next category, cooking, the great majority of cooks were women, but as is the case today, higher status was represented by male cooks. The Earl of Bedford's kitchen at Woburn Abbey was staffed exclusively by men, although both women and men worked as day labourers in brewing and in the kitchen garden that supplied it. Ladies had a large kitchen staff and even yeomen's wives had a maidservant to help, perhaps in addition to a dairy maid and a scullery maid. Many parishes had communal ovens, where bread could be brought to bake or a pottage to stew. But most cooking was done at home and even poor women owned basic utensils, like the 'brasse pott' weighing more than seventeen pounds and the 'brasse pane' of nearly twelve pounds that belonged to a Dorset widow, whose goods had to be sold upon her death to maintain her three young children. The tools of housewifery itemized in inventories include meal tubs and sieves, kneading troughs, milk pails and churns, cheese presses, brewing vats, barrels, salting troughs, and fire irons, tongs, pothooks, and spits. The sheer physical labour required to prepare food is difficult to imagine today.

The textile skills demanded by Markham were probably more extensive than necessary by the seventeenth century. Inventories list only occasional spinning-wheels for linen and wool, but then they never list any smaller equipment, like carding combs, distaffs, spindles, or needles, either, which must have been ubiquitous. By the seventeenth century some bed and table linens, stockings, and underclothes could be bought ready-made from travelling peddlars or in towns from mercers or drapers. The heavier woollen clothes—waistcoats, breeches, and coats—were probably made up by local tailors or seamstresses until the later seventeenth century. Lighter shifts and shirts were commonly made at home, and the housewife, her maidservants, and her daughters also undertook all

WOOLLEN shirt and breeches, part of a complete suit of clothes belonging to a man who fell into a peat bog and died on the Isle of Shetland in the later seventeenth century. This is a very rare example of an ordinary man's clothing: peat happens to preserve cloth particularly well. Most people's clothes in the Tudor and Stuart period were repeatedly mended, handed down, re-made, and used as rags, and finally disintegrated.

mending of clothes and refooting of stockings. Washing of clothes and linens they did every few months. The quantity of textiles in an average home multiplied enormously over the period. The family of the small farmer at the end of the fifteenth century had a pair of bed sheets and a change of clothes. One hundred years later they had another pair of sheets and perhaps some napkins or a tablecloth. But two hundred years later they had a bed coverlet and curtains, window curtains, pillows and pillowslips, cushions for sitting on, towels, several sets of clothes made of Indian cotton and calico, and fabrics from the Netherlands, as well as British linen and wool, and sheets of varying fineness. These are described in wills as 'the best', 'the second best', 'the middling', 'the worst', in order to be quite clear who got which sheets.

Some aspects of housewifery remained constant. Common floors of packed earth

An English close stool of the 1630s, at Oakwell Hall. Simple toilets like this one may have been used by gentry families like the Batts. The contents were sometimes used as fertilizer, a widespread practice at all levels of society which contributed to the spread of intestinal parasites (*via* edible crops) into the nineteenth century.

or stone were swept regularly; in wealthier houses, the rush matting which covered floors soon stank and had to be strewn with sweet-smelling herbs. 'Garderobe' closets were built in to the Elizabethan Little Moreton Hall, the waste flushing directly into the moat or collected and used as fertilizer; portable close stools were used by the wealthy in the seventeenth century. But most people had resort to chamber pots, emptied into public cesspools in the countryside and public gutters in towns and cities.

The material objects to be cared for, on the other hand, changed and multiplied. Windows of glass, in small diamond-shaped panes, had initially graced only the wealthiest houses, everyone else having oiled skins, but by the end of the period glass was quite common. Windows acquired curtains. Houses which would originally have had only one chair, for the head of the household, and benches for the rest of the family acquired many more pieces of furniture: to sit on, softened with cushions; to store (and also in wealthier houses to display) eating utensils, commonly made of wood, earthenware, and pewter, and more rarely glass, silver, and china; and to store food. The massive meal chests, or arks, of the early period—airtight to prevent grain from spoiling— were joined by hutches or 'pantries', with airholes to keep cheese and other foods fresh. Those that survive have locks, to prevent servants from pilfering. A new room in which to cook, the kitchen, separated off from the hall, in which to eat. In larger houses the pantry itself was a separate room, and a dairy and a buttery might be added, as well as servants' chambers.

In addition to their indoor labours, handbooks of husbandry and housewifery make clear that women were also expected to work outside the house: to tend the vegetable garden and the

poultry, take produce to market to sell and to purchase all necessaries for the household, in addition to working in the fields at harvest time, during spring weeding, and in special types of intensive cultivation, like the saffron crops of East Anglia, for example.

7. *Dissolution of Marriage*

Marriage was generally essential for economic comfort. Then, as now, it usually required at least two people's labour and income to keep a household functioning comfortably. Nevertheless, marriage was not always for life. The only means of divorce as we know it now was by Act of Parliament, so naturally it was very rare. The only legal grounds were adultery on the part of the wife, or adultery *plus* systematic cruelty on the part of the husband. Humanist and Puritan writers advocated changing the divorce law along the lines of the German Protestant reformers, that is, with permission to remarry and on an equal basis for wives and husbands. And divorce by mutual agreement of the parties was mooted by Sir Thomas More in the sixteenth century and by John Milton in the seventeenth, but to no lasting effect.

Separation short of divorce was always possible, and, for the upper echelons of society, Parliament could decree alimony to be paid to the wife in these cases, and sequester the husband's lands if he failed to make payments. A wife had to rely on her male relatives to pursue her rights in court, as for example did Anne Bodvell, whose father, Sir William Russell, brought a case in the Court of Chancery to recover Anne's alimony of £500 and custody of her two daughters from her husband, who had allegedly given Anne the pox twice since their marriage in 1638, requiring costly but unsuccessful cures. Upper-class parents did not want to be left supporting their daughters after they had paid a marriage portion to their husbands, so marriage settlements sometimes set annual maintenance levels for the wife in the event the couple later separated. A type of divorce which did not allow either party to remarry was available in the church courts, but these cases too are rare.

Marital separation was most marked among the very rich, who could afford to live in separate houses, and the very poor, to whom another's loss of economic support meant little. A form of unoffical divorce may have been popularly accepted, and certainly many men writing in the sixteenth and seventeenth centuries were concerned over what they saw as a high rate of marital breakdown. Simple abandonment was the option for the poor, and in almost all of the examples mentioned by the Shropshire yeoman Richard Gough in his history of the parish of Myddle in the later seventeenth century, the husband abandoned the wife. It is difficult to estimate how often this happened in the early modern period; eighteenth-century estimates suggest as many as 10 per cent of all marriages ended in desertion, mainly as a result of poverty. Officially, at the end of seven years without having heard of her husband a woman was entitled to remarry.

At middle and upper social levels marital strife and separation were frequently caused by

B ooks abounded from the later sixteenth century, among them gardening how-to manuals. This illustration of caraway and potato plants—including varieties from Spain, Virginia, and Canada (also called a Jerusalem artichoke)—comes from *Paradisi in Sole. Paradisus Terrestris. Or a Garden of all sorts of pleasant Flowers which our English ayre will permit to be noursed up: With a Kitchen Garden of all manner of herbes, rootes, and fruites, for meate or sause used with us, . . . Together with the right ordering, planting, and preserving of them; and their uses and vertues* (second edition 1635) by John Parkinson, a London apothecary.

economic disagreements, in particular the unwillingness of the wife to convert land which was hers into cash which would have become her husband's property, to pay off his debts. The most infamous case of this kind was that of the Lady Anne Clifford, the greatest heiress in England at the beginning of the seventeenth century. Her husband, the Earl of Dorset, regularly banished her from the marital home (Knole, in Kent), forbade her coming to London, and deprived her of her daughter in his unsuccessful attempts to persuade her to convert her inheritance into cash. In the later seventeenth century Mrs Elizabeth Freke also kept a diary of her stormy marriage to her cousin. She blamed herself for marrying 'wholly by my affections, without the consent or knowledge of any of my friends'. For more than twenty-six years her husband tried to force her to sell land. He refused to support her, and did not see her for a year or more at a time, leaving her to move constantly back and forth with their son between her family and friends in England and his in Ireland until she inherited a house at West Bilney, near King's Lynn. At a much more modest social level, the Yorkshire yeoman and captain in the parliamentary army, Adam Eyre, very nearly separated from his wife Sarah over exactly the same financial disagreement. Eyre's diary records their stormy arguments.

Marital strife was commonly complained of by the patients of the Buckinghamshire physician and astrologer Richard Napier, who left uniquely detailed diaries in the early seventeenth century. More than four-fifths of the distressed were women, vexed by 'unthrift' or adulterous or drunken husbands. Marital disagreements which ended in violence might eventually reach church courts, local common law courts, or the central courts in London. After extended disagreements and unsuccessful attempts at mediation, the case of a Westmorland yeoman and his wife finally reached the Court of Chancery in London in 1609. Ann Layfield, trying to recover her £4 annual separation maintenance from her husband John, alleged that he was most

uncivill, not onelie in beatinge woundinge and evil intreatinge . . . that shee hath recieved three most greeveous maymes *viz* one on her eye, one other in her mouth and the third upon her hucklebone [hipbone] by the vyolence and outrageous usage of [John, who] alsoe did for the most parte followe the company of whores and lewed weemen and maynteyned and kept them in his owne house to the apparent showe of all the countrie.

Marriage more commonly ended in the death of one partner than in separation. Men who married more than once are amply represented in the visible record. Many Tudor and Stuart family portraits and parish church memorial carvings depict a patriarch with multitudinous children and two or even three wives. Occasionally plaques in church floors commemorate a man buried between his two wives. It was long assumed that women had a shorter life expectancy than men because of the risk of dying in childbirth. Demographic research suggests that in fact husbands and wives were widowed in comparable numbers. It was high child mortality that brought life expectancy at birth down to only about forty years. Once a man or woman reached the age of thirty, they could expect to live perhaps another thirty years.

The circumstances of widows and widowers differed considerably, however. Widowers remarried nearly three times more often than widows. They were in a position to do so because they could generally offer financial security, thanks to the laws of marital property, while they themselves had an economic need for labour: someone to undertake the care of their household. Widows were in a far more vulnerable position. While a widow usually received the majority of her husband's land and goods, at least to enjoy during her lifetime, this property was always liable to the debts her husband had left at his death. Widows made up the majority of those dependent on parish poor relief (in approximately the same proportion that single mothers today depend on the current welfare state). If she were in comfortable financial circumstances, she stood to lose control of that property if she remarried, threatening the future inheritance of any children by her first husband. For widows, remarriage does seem to have been based on financial need, as much as the need for household labour. It was not closely related to a widow's age or to the number of children she had or to the local economy. Wealthy widows were the least likely to remarry.

More than one quarter and perhaps as many as one third of all marriages in the early modern period were remarriages. The rate of remarriage in England today has only since 1976 regained its early modern heights, as a result of divorce, rather than widowhood. Because of higher birth rates and the fact that fathers would have been left with the care of their children, an even larger number of children then than now would have been part of step-families. The relationships between step-kin, like the conditions of single-parent families, have received little attention, despite the light these might shed on some of our current concerns. It may be that a step-parent was easier for a child to adjust to when its own parent was dead. The kin whom we today would identify as half or step-relations, as well as in-laws, were called simply 'mother' or 'father', 'sister' or 'brother', 'daughter' or 'son', with the last name appended, which reflects a more inclusive approach to family and kin connections than that which prevails today. On the other hand, family members might also be employed as household servants. Samuel Pepys hired his wife's sister Pauline as a servant, for example. But such a relationship of patronage would suggest familial antagonism in today's world.

8. Death

Death and dying were much more common sights in the early modern period than in post-Victorian times. Most children had lost at least one of their parents by the time they married; many had lost a sibling too. To attend church

THE Dance of Death, painted on the wall of the Markham chantry in the church of St Mary Magdalene in Newark. The grinning corpse warns of the certainty of death even for those most blest with worldly riches, as the man on the right certainly is, with his fashionable clothes and sword, heavy chain, and purse. The chapel was endowed in the early sixteenth century for the recitation of a daily requiem in memory of the Markham family dead.

weekly was to be physically surrounded by the long and the recently dead. And early modern representations of death on headstones and memorials were graphic: skull and cross-bones; or skeletons. Not for these people the euphemistic weeping willows and graceful urns of a later, more squeamish, age. As women ushered in and nurtured new life, so too they escorted out the dying. Poor women in particular were paid to tend and nurse the sick, to sit on 'watch' with the dying, and to strip, wash, lay forth, and wrap the dead with strips of cloth. If the plague had caused death, the house had to be 'sweetened' to remove the smell; if the goods of the dead had to be sold to pay debts, they were scoured clean first. To enter a house infected with smallpox, or the plague, which recurred in localized outbreaks throughout the period, was hazardous but earned extra money.

The omnipresence of death does not seem to have made it significantly easier to bear for the bereaved. The physician Napier treated many patients distraught upon the loss of a family member. Seventeenth-century diarists record intense grief upon the deaths of children, parents, and siblings. The anguish of Alice Thornton on the deaths of her sons, and the Essex clergyman Ralph Josselin on the death of his daughter Mary are particularly moving. The comfort of belief in a good death and a beneficent hereafter was the best consolation. The first bequest in every will was the will-maker's soul to God. The importance of funerals to the aristocracy is discussed in another chapter. Even many ordinary people were careful to arrange a dole for the poor at their burial. Most people were buried in the churchyard, with only a wooden cross to mark the spot, now long since disintegrated. Closer to the church lay the wealthier, with carved headstones, and inside the church too, status for those lying under the paving stones was associated with their proximity to the altar (just as in life the pews were arranged according to social status). The second and subsequent bequests began with the phrase, 'and as for my worldly goods . . .'. It was these bequests which consumed reams of paper in the early modern period.

Wills were proved in church courts, of which there were several in each county. Or, in remoter parts of the country, court officials visited each parish periodically to register the probates, in the same way that a parish was also expected to report, upon visitation, its unmarried mothers, its unlicensed midwives and schoolteachers, and those who failed to attend Anglican service, whether for reasons of Catholicism, sectarianism, or alcoholic stupor. Like other records of the church courts, a great number of wills survive, particularly from the early sixteenth century onwards; there are some two million of them dating from before 1700. Approximately 90 per cent of all wills were made by men. Because of the marital property laws, women were entitled to make a will only if they had never married or were widowed, or if some special exemption had been made for them by their husbands allowing them to make a will. In general, the well-to-do, both male and female, made wills more often than the poor, although a significant number of poorer people did so too. The proportions differ in the various parishes and counties that have been studied, but probably about one third of all those people eligible to make a will did so (approximately the same proportion of the population as that which makes wills today). How many early modern men and women made other types of property settlement, like deeds of transfer, will never be known because these were private transactions and did not have to be publicly registered, as probate documents did.

A man who left a surviving widow almost always named her sole executor of his estate. Where a man had not made a will, his widow was also entitled by law to administer his estate. The great majority of those proving wills, exhibiting inventories, filing accounts of estates, and defending contested inheritance in court, therefore, were women. But the court itself was entirely staffed by men: the appraisers who made the inventory; the sureties bound at the time of taking administration; the apparitors who enforced the filing of probate documents; the probate clerk; lawyers to advise on suits; the ecclesiastical judge and the overseers of the poor to whom a woman might have to turn.

9. *Social Order*

The growing number of political philosophers publishing in the sixteenth and seventeenth centuries drew constantly upon the household as a familiar and appealing microcosm of benevolent monarchy. The husband ruled his wife and children and servants just as the monarch ruled his people. At the same time, both parents ruled their children, and both masters and mistresses their servants. As the wife was the second in command in the household, so in the larger order the aristocracy and the gentry served as the monarch's deputies in an increasingly far-flung kingdom. Certainly the gentry of Leominster, in Shropshire, were confident of their importance in upholding law and order and ensuring prosperity when they erected the Market Hall in 1633 and inscribed it prominently: 'Where justice rule virtu flow; like collumnes doo upprop the fabrik of a building so noble gentri doo support the honor of a kingdom'.

Not only every person but every creature was held to have its place in the great chain of being. The classification of group creatures that remain common today appeared first in the *Boke of St Albans*, which was printed throughout the sixteenth century: a bevy of ladies or of quail; a gaggle of geese or of women; a congregation of people and an exalting of larks. Many classifications—'a noonpatiens of wyves' and 'a rascall of boyes', for example—were clearly whimsical. The Elizabethan 'Homily on Good Order and Obedience to Rulers and Magistrates' stressed the reciprocity of the hierarchy in all earnestness:

Every degree of people in their vocation, calling, and office, hath appointed to them their duty and order: some are in high degree, some in low; some Kings and Princes, some Inferiors and Subjects; Priests and Laymen, Masters and Servants, Fathers and Children, Husbands and Wives, Rich and Poor: and every one hath need of other: so that in all things is to be lauded and praised the goodly order of God, without the which no house, no city, no commonwealth, can continue and endure, or last.

Most early modern descriptions of the social order were written by gentlemen or aristocrats, and they carefully listed the aristocracy in descending order but stopped after the gentry. The titles of 'Mr' and 'Mrs' throughout this period designated merely gentry status. ('Mrs' did not designate marital status until the eighteenth century.) The appellations 'goodman' or 'goodwife' for those not of gentry status but who enjoyed some standing among their neighbours appear also occasionally, mainly in southern England.

Sir Thomas Smith in 1583 descended in his hierarchy as far as yeomen, but all men below that were members of the 'rascabilitie'. More often, less picturesque, catch-all terms like the 'middling sort' and the 'poorer sort' were employed. The 'middling sort' appears to have included yeomen, clerics, professional men, and some husbandmen, craftsmen, and tradesmen; the 'poorer sort' encompassed also husbandmen, craftsmen, and tradesmen, as well as all cottagers and labourers, and the poorest of the poor, the wandering vagabonds. There was no appropriate

TITLE-PAGE of 'The book of hunting, hawking and blasing of arms' (first edition 1486), reprinted together with 'The treatyse of fysshinge with an angle' as *The Boke of St Albans* in 1496. The book is often attributed, but probably wrongly, to Dame Juliana Berners, prioress of Sopwell Nunnery, near St Albans, whose name appears in the first edition. Two thirds of the text describes the tools and methods of hunting, hawking and fishing, including numerous medicinal recipes to treat the ills of hawks, fowl, and other beasts; one third is devoted to devising coats of arms. *The Boke of St Albans* offered 'dyvers pleasant pasttimes for noblesse', but of course for most people fishing and hunting small birds and animals were a matter of subsistence.

contemporary term to describe the settled members of the middling and poorer sorts, in the way that we would use 'ordinary' or 'common' people. Both 'ordinary' and 'common' were derogatory words. In early modern England the common man was not yet exalted as he would be in the later eighteenth century (the common woman, of course, has yet to be eulogized). One could be accused in court of being an 'ordinary railer' or a 'common hedgebreaker'. The Puritan preacher Richard Baxter did distinguish men who had incomes of £200–500 per annum, the 'better sort', from those with £40–50 per annum, who were 'very ordinary'. Yeomen had £40–50 per annum. Below that level was 'the rabble who could not read'.

While there was no name for them, these ordinary people, those neither very rich nor very poor—everyone who was not aristocratic or gentry on the one hand, nor in chronic poverty on the other—comprised the great majority of the population. The aristocracy and gentry combined, including those members of the upper gentry whose fortunes outstripped aristocrats, all

THE medieval St Mary's Hospital in Chichester became an almshouse for the aged poor in 1528, and converted its great hall (built *c*.1290) from an infirmary to individual dwellings in 1680. Eight tiny 'houses' were created within the body of the building. Each pair of houses shares a chimney stack, and the centre aisle forms a 'street'. The conversion retained the chapel, originally built so that patients could hear mass from their beds. St Mary's is still occupied, although not full. The only rent required is attendance at service in the chapel every weekday.

116 · *Family, Household, and Community*

the way down to the parish gentry whose importance extended only to the limits of their own village, comprised at the very most 10 per cent of the population. The vagrant poor amounted to not more than one per cent. Thus 'ordinary' may describe approximately 90 per cent of the total population. Within that group, the balance shifted considerably over the early modern period.

During the second half of the sixteenth and the first half of the seventeenth century the rich got richer and the poor poorer. The rich got richer as a result of, first, the redistribution of monastic lands in the mid-sixteenth century, and second, an increase in population which pushed up grain prices. Large farmers who could afford to purchased or enclosed additional land and implemented agricultural improvements (like different types of manuring or fen drainage), thereby increasing crop yields. The population was growing (despite the very high number of people who never married) precisely because there were few depopulating crises like war or famine: England was producing a surplus of grain for its needs. While large farmers were engrossing—the yeomen moving up to gentry status, some well-to-do husbandmen styling themselves yeomen—the poorer husbandmen and cottagers who lost their land got poorer, sinking into the life of wage labourers. Cottages which were legally supposed to have four acres of land attached, so that their occupants could subsist without recourse to the parish for poor relief, often did not because of the great demand for housing and landlords' interest in maximizing rents. Labourers' purchasing power in this period was the lowest for three centuries before or after. The settled poor were eligible for poor relief—assessed, collected, and distributed by their betters in the parish—under the Elizabethan Poor Laws. But vagabonds (mostly men, but a considerable minority of women) were punished, often whipped out of a parish by the settled who were frightened of having to support them. The sixteenth and seventeenth centuries are the great periods of almshouse and workhouse building.

In the second half of the seventeenth century population pressure slackened, due in part to the slaughter of men in the Civil War. The condition of labourers improved, as their real wages rose. While the previous century saw the widespread erection of substantial manor houses, urban buildings, and great country houses, many simple three-room cottages of stone were built in the later seventeenth century, reflecting a new prosperity for the poorer sort.

The population increase of the later sixteenth and early seventeenth centuries also fuelled the growth of trade and industry, an acceleration which was not affected by a subsequent slow-down in the rate of population growth. The traditional hierarchies had not accounted in their agrarian pyramid for the growing modern professions and trades whose wealth seriously encroached upon the old landed upper class: lawyers and clerks; physicians, barber-surgeons, and apothecaries; importers and exporters; brewers and coopers; milliners, mantua makers; clockmakers; calendarers; shipbuilders; merchants and middlemen of all ranks, selling wine, wool, grain, spices, fruit. To take just two examples, the trade in citrus fruit from southern Europe had grown so great since the later Middle Ages that in 1569 the German miners imported by Queen Elizabeth to the remote Westmorland town of Keswick bought oranges, four for a penny. By the early seventeenth century the trade in seeds and plants of all kinds was extensive.

Almost all professional or occupational descriptions were normally applied only to men, even where the work was carried out by a married couple, and perhaps also their children. The political philosophers assumed that women shared the social position of their menfolk. Women were generally described as the daughter of, or wife of, or widow of, someone, reflecting their subordinate position in the household. Despite an enormous proportion of women remaining unmarried, all women were assumed 'either married or to bee married' in the words of the author of *The Lawes Resolutions of Women's Rights*.

10. *Social Disorder*

Both the social order and the gender order were maintained in part by deliberate rituals of inversion—specific days of 'misrule', when the young people or the women were 'on top'. Such festival days were recorded in various towns and villages through the sixteenth century. Over the seventeenth century their number dwindled as the social hierarchy was less clear-cut and people were establishing their status in different ways. Artistic representations inverting or commenting satirically on the social order are not unusual in the medieval cathedrals of southern Europe: mosaic chickens carrying off a fox tied to a pole; rabbits carved in stone, roasting a trussed poacher; peasants bent double, supporting the weight of massive cathedral columns on their backs. They are less common in the early modern period and in northern Europe, although the image of a fox preaching to geese can be found in the misericords and roof bosses of many English churches. One unusual and very fine secular example is the wild boar hunt in which the boars are attacking the hunter, painted on the wall of the dining-hall in Bramall Hall, a Stockport manor house.

Gender inversion was more perennial, perhaps because the gender order was not undergoing any major upheaval. Images of the henpecked husband and father washing the baby's 'shitten clouts', or of witty wenches outwitting stupid swains, populated popular ballad literature in the seventeenth century, as earlier medieval images of a woman beating her husband over the head with a ladle allowed the ruled some relief in laughter at the rulers. Along with all other forms of print, the pamphlet war on the vexed question of the 'nature of women' expanded astronomically in the sixteenth and seventeenth centuries. Joseph Swetnam's *The Arraignment of Lewd, Idle,*

A FOX-WOMAN and a goose-man, turning the order of the sexes—and in the process the social order—on its head. Misericord of 1470 in St David's Cathedral, Wales. The nine daily offices in cathedral and abbey choirs involved long periods of standing for devotion and prayer. Misericords are the ledges on the undersides of the seats to allow old or sick monks or nuns to rest while still on their feet. The subjects of misericord carvings are rarely religious. The carvers preferred fantastical beasts and foliage, proverbs, fables, and depictions of everyday life, often humorous or satirical.

Froward and Unconstant Women proffered a tediously conventional misogyny ('Many women are in shape angels but in qualities devils, painted coffins with rotten bones . . .', etc.). Yet it was reprinted regularly in the hundred years following its first appearance in 1615 and provoked numerous rebuttals, like Jane Anger's *Protection for Women* and Constantia Munda's *Worming of a Mad Dogge*, among others. There was far less print expended on the 'nature of men'. For both male and the growing number of female writers, men remained the standard against which women were measured.

But the fact that the subject received so much attention in print shows that the inferiority of women was at the very least a matter of debate. Perhaps the burgeoning number of conduct and advice books for women repeated the virtues of silence, chastity, modesty, and obedience *ad nauseam* precisely because these lessons were not being absorbed by the pupils. Malicious representations of femininity—like that in the misericord at St Mary's Church, Nantwich, which shows the Devil pulling open a woman's mouth—were ubiquitous; ducking or 'cucking' stools were employed in many places to dunk 'scolds' and otherwise unruly women into the village pond. But at the same time an increasing number of urban women were objecting in print to their inferior status in the later sixteenth and seventeenth centuries. Apart from the above-mentioned pamphlet war, the best known writers were publishing in the later seventeenth century. The prolific and successful playwright, novelist, and poet Aphra Behn, buried in Westminster Abbey in 1689, created heroines who were witty, impudent, and independent. Margaret Cavendish, the Duchess of Newcastle, also published plays and poetry, as well as essays, scientific speculations, and other writings. She was notorious for her outlandish dress as well as for her unwomanly excursions into print, but vociferously defended women's need for education and their capacity for literary excellence. It is significant that Behn was widowed early and the Duchess of Newcastle was relieved of all household duties, not by her status but by the specific indulgence of her husband. Women with few domestic responsibilities are prominent among published writers.

Even as political power shifted gradually over the early modern period from an old landed élite to a new urban mercantile and professional élite, economic power remained firmly in the hands of male heads of household. As the labour of the poor sustained commercial prosperity, so the labour of women in the household underpinned not only the domestic economy, but what would, in the eighteenth century, come to be called the national economy as well.

6

AN EDUCATED SOCIETY

ROSEMARY O'DAY

In the sixteenth and seventeenth centuries there was no 'education system' clearly divided into primary, secondary, and higher stages. Continuous schooling between the ages of 5 and 18 was the exception rather than the norm for both boys and girls. When such education was provided it was class and occupation specific and it was not strictly age-related. Yet this was a period during which boys of some classes and with a specific career in prospect did attend school and, in some cases, university. For these boys, schooling was a way of defining a stage in their life cycle. The growth of educational opportunity and experience during the sixteenth and seventeenth centuries may have been such as to warrant the title of an 'educational revolution'.

1. *Vocation and Literacy*

The responsibility for 'educating' the young lay with the parents. 'Now touching children,' wrote the Elizabethan pastoral theologian William Perkins, 'it is the duty of parents to make choice of fit callings for them, before they apply them to any particular condition of life.' In a rural society and agrarian economy most children could be taught the necessary skills for a productive life by their parents and education in basic literacy and numeracy might be acquired at home as well as at an ABC school.

Only a relatively small number of vocations (callings) demanded different skills which required specialist teaching. In the early sixteenth century, most of these were those belonging to the clerical estate. Boys were needed as choristers, as chantry priests, as secular clergy (parish clergy), as regular clergy (friars and monks), as clerks, as scriveners. In order to acquire these skills boys attended elementary school and were tonsured. If they did not proceed to a religious vocation and the major orders of subdeacon, deacon, and priest they might use their basic literacy and knowledge of Latin in a career of teaching, administration, law, writing, or account keeping. At the very least they would be able to claim 'benefit of clergy' and escape the gallows if convicted of certain crimes. This privilege was restricted by Henry VIII but, even so, during

THIS woodcut of the birching of a schoolboy is full of information about the layout of the schoolroom. It is divided up, literally, into forms which cater for groups of all ages and all stages of learning. The master and the usher exercise discipline and supervision over the entire school: the usher by example (beating the unfortunate boy); the master by waving his birch. On the walls are a variety of visual aids (indicating the variety of subjects taught) as well as the hour glass by which the day is measured. The male clientele is well dressed and lively. The boys hold hornbooks (on the far left) and reading books.

Elizabeth's reign 32 per cent of capital felons in Middlesex successfully pleaded clergy. After the Reformation the clergy no longer formed an estate defined by literacy and latinity: those boys who underwent an education suited to preparation for the priesthood but who did not proceed to orders remained part of the laity.

The creation of a literate laity was partly a function, then, of redefinition of the composition of clergy and laity but it was also a role of a developing economy. Literacy was hitched firmly to social and economic roles, which varied among different social, occupational, and gender groups. Even within London the distribution of literacy was uneven and related to economic need. The printing and other skilled trades of the city had a much more obvious use for literacy than had watermen in the suburbs. In the country as a whole illiteracy was commonest amongst women (of all ranks) and husbandmen and labourers and most uncommon among the clergy and other professionals such as lawyers and attorneys and male members of the gentry. Yeomen were somewhere in between as were tradesmen and craftsmen. Yeomen quite often used the acquisition of literacy as a route to social mobility. Literacy rates were high in some crafts and low in others. There was a pronounced tendency for the populations of market towns to be much more literate than those of the villages. Overall literacy rates (by county) did not exceed 38 per cent of the male population except in London and Suffolk. The literacy rate in London—78 per cent—put the capital in a different league from the rest of the country. It drew large numbers of literate migrants from the rest of the country as well as provided a wealth of educational facilities itself.

Any suggestion that literacy was markedly and constantly improving between about 1530 and 1750 should be resisted. After a period of expansion of opportunity and achievement during Elizabeth's reign there may well have been an actual contraction of educational opportunity for the masses in the seventeenth century. Illiteracy was more common among husbandmen and less common among yeomen and tradesmen at the end of the seventeenth century than at the beginning.

2. Schooling

There was a movement for the schooling of society. Renaissance scholars saw in education on classical lines a way to improve society. John Colet was convinced that virtue could be restored to civic and religious life through the medium of a progressive Christian humanist curriculum. In 1509 he refounded St Paul's Grammar School in London: it became the model for many Tudor and Stuart endowed grammar schools and the forum for much educational experiment. It became a commonplace that the school has within it the power to counteract the evil influences of family and society upon the child. Texts designed to teach Latin grammar and enrich the vocabulary used the opportunity simultaneously to associalize and acculturate the young. A rather different imperative informed, for example, the millennialists of the Civil War period or the reformers Samuel Hartlib, John Dury, and William Petty in their bid for universal education in the mid- and late seventeenth century. Yet they too were advocating the extension of schooling as an instrument of change.

How did this advocacy of basic education as an instrument of social and moral reform marry with reality? How widespread was schooling and what did it offer? The diocese of Coventry and Lichfield was largely rural although the populous and prosperous if declining medieval city of Coventry and the up and coming towns of Birmingham, Derby, and Shrewsbury and a large number of small market towns were within its bounds. At least 200 of its 420 communities had an educational tradition if not an educational institution. Half of the 70 'schools' in Staffordshire were not institutionalized and depended upon the presence of a single teacher. The remainder had schools although not necessarily of an 'endowed' character. The schools kept at St Alkmund's and St Chad's, Shrewsbury, acted as 'feeder' schools of the endowed Shrewsbury Grammar School. Probably these small schools with grammar masters were private or supported by village subscription. The market towns were well served by endowed grammar schools. Even the smaller market towns—such as Rugby, Burton, and Southam—boasted schools which served their hinterlands as well as the towns themselves. This pattern of good geographical access to grammar education seems to have pertained elsewhere so that by the end of Henry VIII's reign almost every market town of any standing had a proper school.

It was more acceptable in those days for the young to walk considerable distances to school. The future Puritan minister and preacher Adam Martindale was sent to school in St Helen's 'almost two miles from my Father's house, a great way for a little fat, short-legged lad (as I was) to travel twice a day; yet I went it cheerfully'. But even a distance of a very few miles from the nearest school might necessitate boarding and raise problems of finance. Many schools operated a sliding scale of fees which discriminated against pupils from other towns and counties. Shrewsbury School, for instance, charged the sons of Shrewsbury burgesses 4*d.*, inhabitants of Shrewsbury 8*d.*, inhabitants of Shropshire 1*s.* and inhabitants of other counties 2*s.* Tabling or boarding out was very common. At Repton in 1622 140 of the 340 pupils were 'tablers'. Even a local school like that at Bridgnorth attracted boarders. A gentry family might expect to pay £18 per annum (plus £12 for clothing) for a son to board out while a yeoman might pay between £4 and £6 (excluding clothing). Parents might have more than one child to provide for and seek education away from home for daughters as well as sons. Ralph Josselin boarded out three of his daughters but was able to stagger the cost. The expense involved probably put many of the endowed schools out of the economic reach of husbandmen and tradesmen worth £20 a year or less. Some families circumvented the problem by boarding their children out with relatives.

Free-lance women teachers, such as Anna Hassall in Staffordshire in 1616, often serviced the demand for reading skills among the husbandman and yeoman classes. Not all restricted their curriculum. Adam Martindale was taught in the seventeenth century by a woman, 'daughter to a famous schoolteacher, that had some smattering of Latin'. This teacher used the English rules for Latin grammar and sometimes set him to read English, 'so that with her I did something better than quite lose my time, but not much'. Curates who taught a few boys in the church porch to supplement their meagre living probably offered a variety of subjects to suit their pupils—a classical education for the brighter and better off; reading and perhaps writing and basic numeracy for the rest. Some beneficed clergy also took in pupils—sometimes on a boarding basis—and possibly concentrated on preparing boys for university. A school run by Matthew Stonham of St Stephen's, Norwich, sent no fewer than thirty-eight boys to university between 1626 and 1637, during which time the endowed Norwich Grammar School sent only eleven. The endowed schools, while their foundation often represented an attempt to open up educational opportunity for a broad section of the community, frequently seem to have become the preserve of the gentle classes. Shrewsbury School served both the town itself and a hinterland which included north Wales as well as Shropshire and Herefordshire. At the start its student body of 266 had quite an aristocratic air about it—both Fulke Greville and Philip Sidney attended in the 1560s—and, although town support was high, it was essentially a school for the urban and rural élite, including the sons of clergymen and lawyers. The expenses of poor scholars at Repton were paid in accordance with the original endowment but the Sleighs, Burdetts, Harpurs, and Stanhopes all sent their sons there and boasted of its superiority to Derby Grammar School.

3. *Curriculum and Method*

What was taught? Education was regarded at this time as a tool of conversion and of control. The 1536 Injunctions ordered that the clergy should teach the youth of the parish the Lord's Prayer, the Creed, and the Ten Commandments by two methods. The clauses of the prayers should be

¶ **The Grounde of Artes:**

teaching the perfecte vvorke and
practife of Arithmetike, both in whole nū-
bers and fractions;after a moꝛe eafie and
eꝛact foꝛt, than hitherto hath bene fet foꝛth.

Made by M. ROBERT RECORDE, D. in Phyfick,
and afterwards augmented by M. IOHN DEE.

And now lately diligently coꝛrected, ⸭ beau-
tified with fome newe Rules and neceffarie Additions:
And further endowed with a thirde part, of Rules of
Pꝛactize, abꝛidged into a bꝛiefer methode than
hitherto hath bene publiſhed: with diuerfe
fuch neceffary Rules, as are incident
to the trade of Merchandize.

Wherbnto are alfo added diuers Tables ⸭ inſtructions
that will bꝛing great pꝛofite and delight bnto Merchants, Gentlemen, and others, as by the contents of this treatife ſhal appeare.

By *Iohn Mellis* of *Southwark*, Scholemafter.

Imprinted by I. Harifon, and H. Bynneman.
ANNO DOM. 1582.

THE title-page of one of the many reissues of the most famous Tudor arithmetic manual, Robert Recorde's *Grounde of Artes*, first published in 1543. It went through many editions over the next hundred years, with revisions and additions by diverse hands, the last reissue being in Charles I's reign. It reminds us of the place of the third R in the curriculum.

recited in sermons to be repeated by the congregation until they were known by heart; written versions of the same should be made available to those who could read for private study. Injunctions of 1538 stipulated that a child must be able to recite the contents of the Primer before being admitted to communion. Petty teachers were made responsible for this instruction. Apparently it was accepted that children should learn to read the prayers, creed, and commandments because primers commonly contained a prefatory alphabet. Some primers also contained a syllable table. In about 1547 an official ABC was issued which offered simple spelling exercises. Licensed catechisms were also an important part of religious instruction. In these, questions about the faith were posed and answers provided for rote learning. The first Book of Common Prayer of 1549 contained a catechism; but booksellers of Elizabeth's reign stocked large numbers of independent catechisms—in 1595 Andrew Maunsell listed no fewer than sixty versions on sale—and individual clergymen circulated their own manuscript catechisms among their parishioners for instruction. Memorization of accepted positions was fundamental to this method. Even those who could not themselves read were introduced to the world of the mind by attentive listening to

those who could and did read aloud; by memorizing long passages of books read; and by discussing what was read in a group situation. Reading was a communal activity.

Religious instruction undoubtedly provided the route to literacy for many children but others learnt to read and count at what are variously called 'ABC', 'Petty', or 'Dame' schools. Here children were taught to read as they learnt to spin and knit. It was perhaps as much a way to persuade young and fidgety children to stay still and out of harm's way as to prepare them for salvation. Writing was not taught at such schools—the modern emphasis on learning to read through learning to write was foreign to any but the progressive teacher. It was a much more passive literacy. The approach was a combination of look-and-say, familiarity with the material, and phonetics and was frequently not very considered. None the less, there were attempts to influence teaching methodology through printed manuals of instruction for teachers. The most popular manual of reading instruction was Edmund Coote's *The English Schoolmaster*, which went throught twenty-six editions between 1596 and 1656 and was still in use in the early eighteenth century. Its content was typical of late sixteenth- and seventeenth-century reading manuals. The child was first introduced to the upper- and lower-case alphabets; then the vowels and consonants; then graded vocabulary exercises (using verses to facilitate learning) which introduce words of one, two, and three syllables and which stress mechanical accuracy rather than comprehension; then syllabification using a catechistical method.

Scholar. Sir, I do not un-der-stand what you mean by a syl-la-ble?
Master. A syl-la-ble is a per-fect sound, made of so ma-ny let-ters, as we spell to-ge-ther: as in di-vi-si-on you see few-er syl-la-bles.
Scholar. How ma-ny let-ters may be in a syl-la-ble?

Then the child learnt rules of pronunciation, engaged in a spelling bee, practised reading skills via

THE first step to reading was generally through an ABC. The original ABCs were arranged in the form of a cross (Christ's Cross or Chriss-cross row) on a frame but there was soon a need for an indestructible reading aid which would include syllabic instruction and religious matter. This was met by the horn book, an embossed or incised or paper-covered slab of oak or other wood, covered with a protective sheet of horn. It was an English invention, well-known throughout the fifteenth and sixteenth centuries. By the seventeenth century increasingly ornate and complex versions were in production but this example is relatively simple, giving the alphabet in large and small letters; the vowels; the vowel sounds; the preface and the Pater Noster.

a catechism and primer, learnt rules of behaviour, and gained some understanding of number. There had been a long tradition of rhymed alphabets in England (reaching back at least to Master Bennet of Essex's *ABC of Aristotle* which exists in a manuscript of 1430) but pictorial alphabets which had been common in Germany since the late fifteenth century did not appear in England until the publication of *Alphabeticum Primum Becardi* in 1552.

Arithmetic was commonly taught after reading had been mastered. This probably meant that the very poor never learnt to do more than count. During the reign of Edward VI Robert Recorde produced a highly influential defence of the teaching of arithmetic in English schools—both penarithmetic and arithmetic using counters—demonstrating by visual aids that numeracy was accessible to the illiterate as well as the literate. Some teachers displayed a particular enthusiasm for the teaching of the third R—probably because of its commercial potential. Adam Martindale accepted that the parents of his scholars were especially concerned with the vocational aspects of their sons' education. He concentrated on the practical application of mathematics for the gentle and trading classes—surveying as well as casting accounts—and was to produce a textbook for the teaching of surveying later in his career. He taught mathematics in a peripatetic manner, travelling around and remaining in one place for six months here and three months there.

Writing was not accepted as one of the skills taught in the ABC school. More commonly it was taught by a peripatetic scrivener for a fee. None the less some teachers, including John Brinsley, argued that writing should be taught in the elementary school because it assisted in the teaching

GROUP teaching using a board and visual aids was common. Pictures, cards, diagrams, and counting frames helped the teaching of the three Rs. Educational games were available. This Elizabethan phonics aid was included in one of the increasing number of manuals addressing the teaching of reading to the young.

of reading and in memorization. He was an early advocate of teaching children to read and write by tracing letters and words and making writing patterns.

In the sixteenth century the concept of the school as a *superior* agent of socialization and acculturation was fully developed alongside its academic functions. The schoolmaster stood *in loco parentis*; but he might also perform the tasks better than the over-indulgent parent.

> First, I command thee God to serve,
> then to thy parents duty yield:
> unto all men be courteous,
> and mannerly in town and field.
>
> Your clothes unbuttoned do not use,
> let not your hose ungartered be;
> Have handkerchief in readiness,
> wash hands and face, or see not me.

Children were at school for very long hours; recesses were short and even holidays were occupied with sermons and other serious-minded activities; children outside school were expected to play their part in the work of their households. It must have been difficult to live up to John Brinsley's dictum that learning is a game. Competition between pupils was one way of channelling the aggressiveness of the young and encouraging them to learn in such an environment. Classrooms were cramped and crowded. As many as five or six separate groups of students were taught in the same room. Even under a strict regimen, noise levels must have been stressfully high in a curriculum which emphasized reading and translating aloud. Group teaching using a board and other kinds of visual aids was common. Individual visual and tactile aids—such as pictures, cards, diagrams, and counting frames—may have been used.

The curriculum at the endowed grammar schools was never rigidly classical. John Brinsley is renowned for his treatment of Lily's Latin Grammar and its central role in the curriculum of the early seventeenth-century grammar school but he advocated no less energetically the simultaneous maintenance of competence in the vernacular. In the lively dialogue between the dispirited teacher Spondeus and the progressive teacher Philoponus, Spondeus complains that once they begin work in Latin children lose their ability to read English and parents ask that he prevent this loss of skill by arranging daily Bible lessons which distract from the Latin curriculum. Philoponus urges that the vernacular is important but that learning of it can be maintained during the child's learning of Latin. The pupil should read Lily's rules, practise orthography, translate from Latin into good English prose and verse. He should write letters to his friends in both languages. Pupils should write notes on sermons, declare the best ways of expressing themselves, and read directly from Latin into English. The child will précis Latin stories in the best English possible: 'Amongst some of them, the reporting of a Fable in English, or the like matter, trying who can make the best report, doth much further them in this.' Parents and grammar school masters alike were concerned to maintain the ability of pupils to read and write good English and some (in the tradition of Erasmus) believed that a classical education led to better command of the vernacular.

It is perhaps tempting to force what we know of early modern education into the strait-jacket of our present-day system and to assume that the various levels coincided with chronological age and that the various schools followed rigidly differentiated curricula. This is mistaken. There was

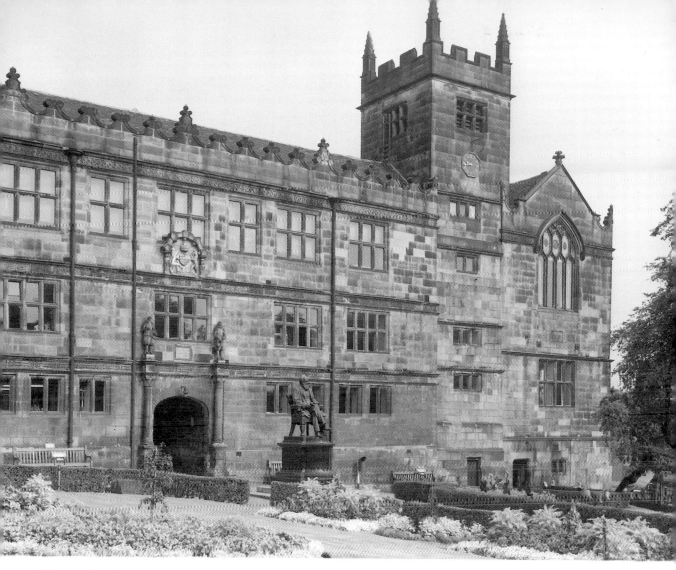

THE endowed schools, while their foundation often represented an attempt to provide for the education of poor boys in the vicinity, frequently became the preserve of the gentle classes. Shrewsbury (pictured here) and Repton early had an aristocratic complexion. Other town grammar schools, such as Wolverhampton and Derby, remained more truly local schools with a broad social catchment. The curriculum of all these schools catered for boys of a wide variety of ages (6–18), aptitudes, and vocation.

no accepted school age—even young adults attended schools in the lower forms when need dictated and it was still difficult to age-group the pupils strictly. A school list for Wolverhampton Grammar School (founded in 1515) in 1609 shows that about half the pupils who took Latin studies under the master from the ages of 9–14 left before entering the two top forms. They were not destined for university. Some children in the same age range took purely vernacular subjects.

The grammar schools were very flexible institutions. Sir Gervase Sleigh sent all three of his sons to Repton, a large endowed grammar school of considerable reputation. All remained there until their late teens but, whereas two followed a classical curriculum and went on to higher education and a learned profession, one learned reading, writing, and casting accounts in preparation for his employment as apprentice to a merchant factor. Some grammar schools made provision for such variety in their statutes. For example, the statutes of the school at Aldenham, Hertfordshire, in 1597 stipulated that the school was for the 'free instruction of 60 scholars in purity of life, manners and religion, and in Latin, English, writing, cyphering and accounts' and those of Northampton Grammar School in 1596 made similar provision. Sometimes the assumption was that the more able would follow a classical curriculum, leaving practical and vernacular subjects to the less clever. 'It shall be his care [i.e. the master's] and the Usher's charge, to teach the scholars to cypher and cast an account, especially those that are less capable of learning, and fittest to be put to trades.' Until the post-Restoration period the grammar schools of England and Wales were comprehensive institutions. They were created and run to fulfil the needs of communities which were not much in touch with the ideas of Renaissance educators.

The pre-eminence of Latin in the grammar school curriculum was largely determined by its pre-eminence within the universities. Its continued importance was ensured by the hierarchy within the schools themselves. The brighter pupils or seniors would teach the boys how to read and spell under the supervision of the usher (in some schools a second usher was hired to perform

TUDOR boys and girls from gentry and professional families might have attended a small school such as this one, run either by a local cleric or by a tutor employed by their parents. Sitting well-spaced-out on forms about a large table, they performed reading and writing tasks set by the master. To hand also were mathematical apparatus, a pointer, and reference books. A typical Tudor or early Stuart grammar school, on the other hand, would have been more crowded and noisy and children of different ages would have been taught in groups in the same classroom.

this function of teaching vernacular subjects); the usher (also known as hypodidascalus or under-master) was responsible for helping the boys to build up a Latin vocabulary, parse, and construe and make Latins; only the master would teach the true classical subjects—Latin composition and rhetoric (oral communication); Greek, and, very rarely, Hebrew. The subjects marked the stages in the hierarchy of both teachers and pupils.

It was often a deliberately Christianized and occasionally a not overly subtly Protestantized version of the Classics that was taught. From 1528 onwards Richard Cox used textbooks such as the *Paedologia* of Peter Mosellanus at Eton: this book attacked the ceremonial of the Church as pagan and showed the way to a new piety via the new learning. The colloquies and other texts of Erasmus commonly employed in English schools, while by no means Protestant, were frequently critical of the Church and certainly encouraged a Christian rather than a pagan humanism. In 1600 Richard Mulcaster published *Cato Christianus*, which was used as a textbook at St Paul's School, London, and was designed to combine the teaching of the fundamentals of Latin composition with the Christianizing of Cato according to Protestant humanist principles. Classical subjects were taught in many grammar schools less as a way to open classical texts and culture than as a way into the ministry. John Strype (during whose infancy his father had told friends 'these little fists shall thump the pulpit one day' and instructed his wife to direct John towards the ministry) learnt Latin, Greek, Hebrew, and Syriac at St Paul's in the later 1650s. When we see John Brinsley's emphasis on the translation of the New Testament into and from Latin and Greek or the detailed instructions given on note-taking from sermons or the tremendous stress on understanding the classical texts, on their importance for Christians, and on the expurgation of classical authors, then we are not surprised when contemporaries displayed an interest in religious issues and literature which was at least as evident as their interest in classical authors.

Children beginning to learn Latin were required to build up their Latin vocabulary through the making of *vulgars*—collections of Latin sentences with English meanings. Suitable collections of sentences were published. It was such a tedious approach that educationalists such as Jean Luis Vives roundly denounced it and advocated double translation as an alternative which stressed not rules but the mother tongue approach. Erasmus concurred: 'It is not by learning rules that we acquire the power of speaking a language but by daily intercourse with those accustomed to express themselves with exactness and refinement and by the copious reading of the best authors.' Roger Ascham was a keen advocate of this method of total immersion in *The Scholemaster*, first published in 1570. Texts such as Cicero's *Epistles*, the *Colloquies* of Erasmus, Mosellanus, and Corderius, and Aesop's *Fables* were used for these exercises. 'All that were presumed by their standing able to discourse in Latin', wrote Adam Martindale of his education at St Helen's Grammar School, 'were under a penalty if they either spoke English or broke Piscian's head; but barbarous language, if not incongruous for grammar [that is, strange words with correct Latin endings] had no punishing but derision.' In the more advanced forms the emphasis was upon the speaking and writing of Latin—rhetoric and composition.

Few schools taught Greek and Hebrew before the later sixteenth century, when the universities had begun to produce more teachers capable of teaching the subjects in the schools. For example, Richard Mulcaster learnt no Greek at Eton but he emerged from Cambridge with sufficient Greek to teach the subject at Merchant Taylors' School, London. Even so Greek and Hebrew were rarely taught to the same level as Latin. Even in the seventeenth century the teaching of Greek did not normally begin until the fourth form. The Greek New Testament was the basic text and *Camden's Grammar* (published in 1597) was the means whereby the language was taught. The teaching of Hebrew in schools was also a late sixteenth- and seventeenth-century development but it was probably crowded out of the curriculum at most grammar schools by the demands of Latin. Even at Westminster it was not taught until the seventh form. Whatever the counsel of progressive teachers, the evidence suggests that these subjects were taught in a dull manner. As the Puritan minister Adam Martindale put it: 'The old saying is "The soft drop wears the hard stone by frequent falling". So a long tedious method, well plied, at length brought us to somewhat.'

Teaching methods echoed those employed for instruction in vernacular subjects. Monitors were used in each form (under, Brinsley advised, careful supervision by master and usher to guard against abuse). There was a reliance upon group methods of teaching. Competition for place was encouraged among pupils. Various forms of discipline were used—sarcasm, derision, positive reinforcement, corporal punishment. Learning was encouraged by the introduction of short recesses to break up the lengthy school day, half-holidays as rewards, regularized periods of 'misrule', praise, competition between teams and different schools, drama and speechifying and so forth.

Perceptive and experienced teachers recognized that children flagged during the excessively long school day, which coincided with the working day of the average day labourer, from sunrise to sunset. Colloquies indicate that teachers were of the opinion that pupils stayed up too late at night and that their work suffered during the day as a consequence. Richard Mulcaster argued unsuccessfully for the introduction of a more leisurely school day at Merchant Taylors' School although he managed to alleviate the monotony and rigour of the course by the introduction of amateur dramatics. But in general the demands of the curriculum were set before those of the child. If it took long hours to acquire sufficient knowledge to master classical languages then long hours were required. The realization that a child was different in kind from an adult was reached only after experience of trying to teach this rigorous classical curriculum. Education was subject- and not child-centred.

4. *The Education of Women*

The absence of girls from the endowed schools is frequently presented as a gender issue but it was not. Education was regarded as directly vocational. Every individual—male or female—shared the Christian vocation and increasingly this implied some level of literacy in order to read the Scriptures and, for a few, a considerable level of learning. Beyond that, a women's vocation was realized within the domestic economy, whatever her class. The woman's domestic vocation varied according to her position within it—wife, mother, widow, daughter, sister. Sometimes it involved considerable household management skills and responsibilities; for the mother it involved teaching the children, especially the girls, a variety of skills and behaviours.

Most women learned their skills at their mother's knee. Commonly girls were educated alongside boys in the elementary school or the petty classes of the grammar schools (as at Banbury) but the proportion of the female population who received this level of formal education in school was probably small. For those who did, by the age of 9 adequate levels of literacy and numeracy

My good father. the last day I receued a letter from you. and a fore christmas. I receued forti shilinges from you. and ten from my mother : giueing you both houmble thankes : for the same. my brother is nou at soudlo, whear thare runs the grates christmas. that euer I saw. my ladi made uery much of my sister. and desiered hear. to com to hey sum times. and she should haue her chamber in the house : and told my sister she should finde her redi to plesure her. or ani frean she had : when the tearme is done. my brother. and my sister wil com to Blithfilde. to see you and my mother. which wil be shortly after candlmas : this with my houmbul duti to you. and my good mother. with the like from my sister : crauing your dely blesinges. and crauing pardin for my vntoward wryting : I houmbly take my leaue : Broughton this.19.of ienuary

Your obedient daughter
Letice Bagot

GIRLS from gentle families were taught to read and write and, when they left their home of origin, frequently maintained contact with their parents and siblings by correspondence. The very large, clear hand of Letice Bagot, which differs noticeably from the flowing, hurried, and, sometimes, difficult to read secretary hand taught to and employed by her brothers, seems to have been characteristic of many female writers of the late sixteenth and early seventeenth centuries. Spelling and punctuation were both still erratic and it helped to be conversant with the subject before reading the letter!

would have been achieved. Whether in school or at home female literacy was improved considerably, especially in the towns.

Many of the institutions which were founded to teach practical skills to girls owed their origins to provision for the orphaned and destitute. Moral training, including teaching girls to read the Scriptures, was part of a curriculum designed to protect the girl against the evil influences of poor or absent home life. Many of the earliest sixteenth-century girls' schools were in exiled communities: the normal forms of household education had been disrupted when families were separated and schools were needed to maintain the original culture in this alien environment. Girls in English noble and gentle families continued to be educated at home as they always had been. The level of their education depended in part upon their parents' and siblings' own educational experience and contemporary fashion. For example, in the seventeenth century Damaris Cudworth was educated by her father Ralph, the Cambridge Platonist; Ann Baynard was tutored by her father Edward; and Ann Elstob, Old English scholar, was tutored by her brother William. The daughters of Lord Fairfax and the daughters of George and Margaret Clifford had their own tutors. Lord North taught his own daughter. Women educated in this manner actively participated in the intellectual life of the period, circulating their writings and translations in manuscript and taking part in lively discussion and correspondence.

THE *Margarita Philosophica* (1503) shows Nicostrata with hornbook in hand opening the house of knowledge (science) to the small boy. At the lower levels the scholars study the grammars of Donatus and Priscian. They move up through logic (Aristotle), rhetoric and poetry (Cicero), and arithmetic. Eventually they study music, geometry, astronomy and physics, and ethics (Seneca). They achieve the summit of their knowledge in theology and metaphysics (Peter Lombard). The number and age of the scholars at each stage of the course is indicative.

Such activity might be justified by the responsibility borne by the women for the education of children, both boys and girls. Renaissance educationalists were bound by the common conception that a woman's family vocation dictated her educational needs. Jean Luis Vives spent more of his *Instruction of a Christian Woman* showing the way to cultivate correct social behaviour than to cultivate the mind. Sir Thomas More combined an appreciation of the abilities of his daughters with an acceptance of the traditional view of woman's domestic vocation and an admonition that his clever daughter Margaret restrict her scholarly activities to within the home. There was a direct progression to the thought of John Locke, who agreed that women should be well educated because of their family vocation, of Jonathan Swift and Daniel Defoe, who wanted women to become well-educated companions for their husbands, and others, who wanted to educate an élite of women schoolteachers. Girls with an exceptional vocation, such as those born to rule like Elizabeth, or the daughters of fathers convinced of the value of active social humanism like the Protector Somerset, received a rigorous classical education provided by a tutor within the home environs. Both James I and Charles I paid great attention to the academic education of their daughters. Such education was atypical. These women set no pattern for their sex.

The most remarkable institutional development in the seventeenth century was the rise of girls' boarding-schools. They were an extension of the medieval tradition of convent education. In 1537 Polesworth Convent, Warwickshire, had been responsible for the education of about forty daughters of gentry families. Despite the urging of Protestant reformers, the emergence of endowed schools for girls in the sixteenth century did not materialize although there are tantalizing glimpses of schools such as the boarding establishment for young ladies at Windsor which was already set in the mould of the social finishing schools which bloomed in seventeenth-century Deptford and Hackney. By the mid-seventeenth century every town of any size seems to have possessed a girls' academy. Some criticized the frivolous nature of these institutions and, like Bathsua Makin in 1673, founded more academic schools which introduced female pupils to classical and modern languages, science, and mathematics. Boarding-schools became increasingly popular with the gentry, the well-to-do middle classes, and the professional classes, who saw the education of their daughters as a sound investment for their future marriage.

5. *The Universities*

The universities of Oxford and Cambridge underwent a sea change during the period 1540 to 1640. They developed from being guilds of masters under the direct control of the Church into institutions directly under the control of the Crown. This relationship gave them a potential for secularization which had not been present previously. The colleges maintained their status as societies of scholars (fellows) but also became, as they developed their role as societies of teachers of undergraduates, seminaries for ministers and 'nurseries of the gentry'. Because of their specific vocational purpose there was never any suggestion that women should be educated within them.

In medieval times the two universities offered teaching at a variety of levels. Colleges were associations of scholars studying in the higher faculties of theology and law not in the arts. What we today would call the undergraduate body of the universities consisted of people loosely affiliated to the university by the fact of their attendance and accommodated in a variety of inns, hostels, and halls. Undergraduates then were in halls not colleges; these halls were not teaching institutions. In 1450 there may have been as many as 1,200 undergraduates in halls in Oxford alone. Exceptionally worrying to the university authorities was the fact that in the later fifteenth and early sixteenth centuries the halls themselves were in decline—undergraduates were tending instead to take private lodgings. Between 1501 and 1537 perhaps 37 per cent of known affiliates of the University of Oxford had no institutional connection through college or hall.

Both universities made attempts to revitalize their teaching system—Cambridge earlier and with more success than Oxford. At Oxford the rebuilding of the schools and the expansion of the Bodleian Library came too late to revive its role as a teaching institution. Matters were not helped by inadequate registration procedures and record-keeping. Compulsory matriculation was first introduced at Cambridge in 1544 and at Oxford in 1564/5. It enabled the universities to define an undergraduate body. By 1600 the annual undergraduate intake at *each* university stood at between 500 and 600. The total undergraduate body of *each* university was between 1,500 and 1,800.

In fact a rival teaching system was fast emerging. In the late thirteenth and early fourteenth centuries a number of colleges were founded. Peterhouse, Michaelhouse, Clare Hall, King's Hall, Pembroke Hall, Gonville Hall, Trinity Hall, and Corpus Christi were all founded at Cambridge by 1352. University, Balliol, Merton, Gloucester Hall (Monastic), and Durham College (Monastic) had all been founded in Oxford by 1300. Until the fifteenth century these colleges were not intimately involved with the teaching of arts students with a few exceptions. But the fifteenth century saw a piecemeal transfer of undergraduate students from halls to colleges. Colleges increased the numbers of undergraduates in residence and also annexed the halls which still existed. Merton, for instance, absorbed St John's, Nunn, Knyght, Colishalle, and St Alban's Halls. In general, all the halls which accommodated arts students were absorbed into colleges while the law halls remained independent. Simultaneously town-dwellers or 'chamberdakyns' were officially hounded by the university into recognized college or hall premises

THOMAS NEWMAN, a student at Exeter College, Oxford, in 1624 paid tribute in doggerel verse to his tutor's teaching efforts and the way in which he made the university curriculum comprehensible and interesting (eventually, Newman like many others concluded that over-dependence on his tutor's skills was unwise and that the remedy lay in independent study). Evidence from the notebook of a tutor, Daniel Featley, MA, of Corpus Christi College, Oxford, indicates that in the years 1604–5 he wrote numerous lectures for his students, compiled a book on 'physic' for them, and read and explained texts to them. Featley was proud and protective of his distinctive teaching style and syllabus.

in an effort to restore university discipline at a time of frequent violence between town and gown.

The teaching duties of the colleges expanded greatly. King's Hall, Cambridge, set a new trend in about 1430 by offering tuition for a fee to undergraduates who were not part of the college foundation. Some years later, in 1479/80, Magdalen College, Oxford, endowed college lectureships which attracted undergraduates away from the university's public lecture system. By the 1550s most Oxford colleges had organized full systems of undergraduate tuition. By the later sixteenth century college teaching rather than university teaching of undergraduates, on a decentralized pattern, for a university examination, was established at Oxford and Cambridge.

The English humanists did not themselves see the universities as appropriate for the function of training statesmen or gentlemen. Thomas Starkey was quite clear that they were for educating churchmen. A separate academy, located in London, was necessary for the élite. He, Thomas Elyot, and Richard Morison were all advising Henry VIII to adapt the

TACKLEY'S INN built c.1291–1300, was absorbed into Oriel College, Oxford. This drawing of about 1750 shows the hall and screens passage: to the right were the living quarters arranged in a small and simple upper and lower chamber, and a number of shops abutting on to the High Street, Oxford.

teaching offered at the Inns of Court to include the teaching of civic and Christian humanism. Thomas Cromwell was considerably influenced by their ideas, which almost bore fruit in 1539 when Thomas Denton petitioned Parliament for the use of funds from the dissolved monasteries to found a 'House of Students' to remedy the defects of upper-class education. The programme collapsed with the execution of Cromwell in 1540. It was, however, followed by several similar proposals during the century, none of which materialized. The annexation of the universities as a training ground for gentlemen occurred by default as far as the humanists were concerned. The gentry used existing institutions—the universities—which, despite their emphasis on teaching clergy, had some experience of educating members of the lay élite.

Teaching provided a welcome source of revenue for the impecunious college fellow and the more well connected the student the better. In the seventeenth century some colleges emphasized their role as nurseries of the élite. Some complained that tutors were neglecting the plebeian pupils. College discipline was said to have suffered as tutors toadied to students who were their potential patrons.

Both universities also now fulfilled the role of seminaries, educating the sons of clergy and plebeians to enter the Church's pastoral ministry. This too was new: in the Middle Ages the universities had educated the Church's élite not its resident parochial clergy.

S T JOHN'S COLLEGE, Oxford reserved 37 of its fellowships for pupils of Merchant Taylors' School, London by its statutes of 1566. Kin of the founder Thomas White, merchant, and boys from Reading, Bristol, Coventry, and Tonbridge were also favoured. The College had been founded in 1557 especially to raise the standard of the parochial clergy and had an overwhelmingly plebeian complexion because of its appeal to citizens and merchants of London and other urban areas.

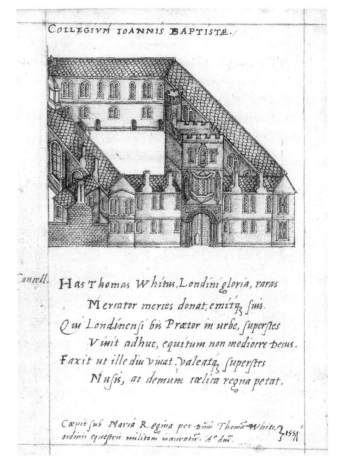

The universities became socially segregated communities. Within them the social mix varied from college to college. The sons of nobility and gentry, thrown into close proximity with students of plebeian origin, were warned by their parents and tutors of the consequences of mixing with the same. 'Consort yourself with gentlemen of your own rank and quality' counselled Henry Peacham's *The Compleat Gentleman* (1622). Fellow-Commoners enjoyed the important privilege of eating with the fellows and master rather than with the undergraduate body. They kept sizars (servants who studied at the university). Upper-class parents were determined that the university experience should not undermine the value system they held dear. The students' experience of college life reinforced local as well as class loyalties. Individual colleges favoured students from particular regions. Archbishop Parker's endowment at Corpus Christi College, Cambridge, ordered that Norfolk scholars be taught by Norfolk men. And it was the college which drew men's loyalties. Typical student unrest in the late sixteenth century was intercollegiate violence which often reflected the regional complexion of the colleges. But, if England did not become a homogeneous society because of the common experience of university education, it at least became less heterogeneous as a result. The proportion of Members of Parliament and of Justices of the Peace who had attended the university escalated during the period 1563 to 1642.

How far were the university and college authorities prepared to bend the curriculum and requirements to the needs of the new gentry and the new Church? The university statutes (Cambridge, 1570; Oxford, 1564/5) show a seven-year arts course of which the BA was but an important part of the student's total progress to become a Master of Arts. Because most students began the course at age 17 or 18 the course assumed that they had a solid grounding in grammar school subjects. None the less, the system was very flexible and permitted the very young student of 13 or 14 to make up ground with a tutor or the impecunious student to stretch the course over several years while taking employment at intervals to pay his way. At Oxford the course was clearly demarcated. For two terms the student studied grammar, for four terms rhetoric, for five terms dialectic and logic, and so on. Thus when a student left Oxford to teach in a grammar school after a year or two at university he was already as well versed in grammar and rhetoric as he would have been had he stayed the 'course'.

	University Curriculum at Oxford and Cambridge	
	Cambridge	Oxford
Years 1–4 BA course	rhetoric, logic, philosophy	grammar, rhetoric, logic, arithmetic, music
Years 5–7 MA course	natural, moral and meta-physical philosophy, Greek, drawing, astronomy	Greek, geometry, astronomy, natural philosophy, moral philosophy, metaphysics

Students appear to have voted with their feet in favour of the colleges as teaching institutions. University lectures were neglected. Students paid fines for non-attendance and went instead to the more personalized lectures offered in college in the above subjects. In 1547 Walter Haddon complained that some professors were addressing audiences of one. Similarly, college disputations were more popular than university disputations. The unique contribution of the colleges to teaching method was the one-to-one tutorial. The tutor guided the course of a student's studies, offered moral and spiritual supervision, and guaranteed the payment of his college dues. The weekly essay, which became the staple of the tutorial system, was not established at this time. The quality of a student's education came to depend upon the conscientiousness of his tutor.

Within the colleges tutors offered some of their students—probably those who planned to study for two years at the university before moving to an Inn of Court—a much more modern and individually tailored programme of studies which included history, literature, geography, travel, and divinity. When the gentry fled the universities after 1642 this generalist curriculum also withered away and it did not return. The seven-year arts course gripped the universities in the ultra-conservative atmosphere of the late seventeenth century.

6. *Education for the Professions*

The church hierarchy and Puritan activists of the middle sixteenth century sought ways to provide the Church with ministers who were well versed in the Scriptures and prepared to serve the spiritual and moral needs of their congregations. Until the later years of Elizabeth's reign, the Church attempted to control and exploit the existing educational institutions to this end while simultaneously experimenting with a variety of programmes of in-service education. Then, frightened by the spectre of nonconformity, the Crown and the hierarchy lost interest in the precise vocational content of clerical education and took refuge in the idea that the clergy should be conforming graduates. It was not until the post-Restoration period that there were significant attempts on the part of the hierarchy to wrest the responsibility for the education of clergy from the universities and to vest it in Church-controlled seminaries. As a result the clergy of the sixteenth and seventeenth centuries, a largely graduate body, shared the education offered to the gentry, with its social humanist emphasis.

7. Conclusion

For the people of Tudor and Stuart England formal, institutionalized education was neither compulsory nor normal. Whether one required schooling or education at university or Inn of Court depended entirely upon one's potential vocation in life. That more and more young people did attend school and university was a function of the changing requirements of society and economy. Education was not regarded as a luxury. 'Trickle-down' education was none the less a reality and lay men and women in some numbers were enabled to participate in a newly literate culture.

7 A LAW-ABIDING AND LITIGIOUS SOCIETY

CHRISTOPHER BROOKS

1. *The Law and the Legal Profession*

By the end of the Stuart period, 'the law' had achieved that celebrated position in British public life which it was to enjoy at least until Edmund Burke proclaimed it the touchstone of the constitution at the close of the eighteenth century. Already recognized as different from the legal codes of other European nations, the common law of England in theory protected the life, liberty, and property of the subject whilst at the same time incorporating within it the principles according to which the monarch was supposed to rule.

The reasons for the rise of the law to such an important place under the Tudors and Stuarts were complex, but most of the vital institutions had in fact long been in place when Henry VII came to the throne. The principal common law courts had been keeping their records on parchment rolls since the late twelfth century. In the provinces, the major towns had courts for hearing civil pleas, and in the countryside there were thousands of manorial jurisdictions, the courts leet and courts baron, which met at least twice a year. Criminal and administrative matters in the localities were dealt with by members of the gentry and professional lawyers who were appointed by the King to hold quarterly sessions of the peace. The entire system was bound together by twice-yearly visits to the shires by royal justices who set out on their assize circuits to supervise the trials before juries of civil as well as criminal cases. In addition to all this, there was an elaborate system of ecclesiastical courts which dealt not only with spiritual matters but also with questions of marriage, sexual morality, the payment of tithes, and the probate of wills.

By establishing and maintaining a degree of political stability and emphasizing the authority of the state, Tudor monarchs undoubtedly did much to build on these foundations so as to promote the importance of the ideal of the rule of law. At the same time Renaissance humanism contributed to an intellectual climate in which law became an all-important human science, and by opening up the possibility that the bonds of political obligation could be dissolved on the grounds of conscience, the Reformation left the protection offered by the rule of law as one of the benefits of the state which might arguably compel continuing loyalty to it. Yet, the most important factor

A view of Westminster Hall with the busy royal courts in session. By 1600 the amount of litigation per head of population which was entertained by the central courts was greater than it has been at any time before or since. The litigants came from a wide cross-section of the population and particularly from the middling sort of people such as yeoman farmers and urban merchants and artisans.

in securing the place of law and lawyers during the period was a cluster of social and economic changes—the increase in population and inflation, markedly greater activity in the land market, and the more extensive use of credit—which led to a remarkable growth in the amount of legal business which came before the courts. The increase was feeble and sporadic during the reign of Henry VII, and very seriously set back during much of the 1510s, 1520s, and 1530s, by outbreaks of epidemic disease in London, bad harvests, and civil unrest. But from the 1550s, and throughout the remainder of the sixteenth century, the number of lawsuits rose sharply. By the end of Elizabeth's reign the number of actions commenced was probably ten times greater than they had been at the end of the fifteenth century. The number doubled again in the years up to 1640, and, after the disruptions of the civil wars, returned to similar levels after the Restoration, where they remained until a precipitate drop began in the late seventeenth and eighteenth centuries.

These increases in the amount of legal business were accompanied by an equally impressive growth in the size of the legal profession so that by the time of James I, the ratio of lawyers to population was not much different from that in the early twentieth century. The most numerous of the practitioners were the attorneys, men who lived in the country but who came up to London during the four legal terms of the year. With social origins in the lesser gentry, the yeomanry, and urban middling groups, the attorneys were the lawyers most often consulted by those who had a legal problem, and they were the ancestors of the modern solicitors. Pleading in the central courts, on the other hand, was dominated by the serjeants-at-law, a select group who enjoyed a traditional monopoly right of audience in the Court of Common Pleas, and the barristers, who practised before increasingly busy jurisdictions such as King's Bench, Star Chamber, and Chancery.

The upper ranks of the church court lawyers were trained in the civil law at Oxford or Cambridge, but the common lawyers were traditionally associated with the Inns of Chancery and Inns of Court, which occupied sites in London midway between the City and the royal courts in Westminster Hall. In the later fifteenth century, the primary function of the eight Inns of Chancery was to provide preliminary training in the elements of the common law, but by the end of the sixteenth century they had come to be dominated by attorneys who lived and worked in them when they came up to London from the country. Similarly, the four Inns of Court—Gray's Inn, Lincoln's Inn, the Inner Temple, and the Middle Temple—served as the term-time residences for the barristers. However, the legal inns also attracted a large non-professional gentry membership as well as being the places where young students came to undertake the difficult task of learning the law, a course which could easily take up to seven years. The inns put on educa-

T HE Inner Temple in 1671. There was new building at all of the inns as admissions increased from around 50 p.a. in the early sixteenth century to well over 200 p.a. in the years around 1600. Although the level of the educational instruction the inns offered should not be exaggerated, their intellectual vitality during this period warranted their reputation as the 'third university of England'.

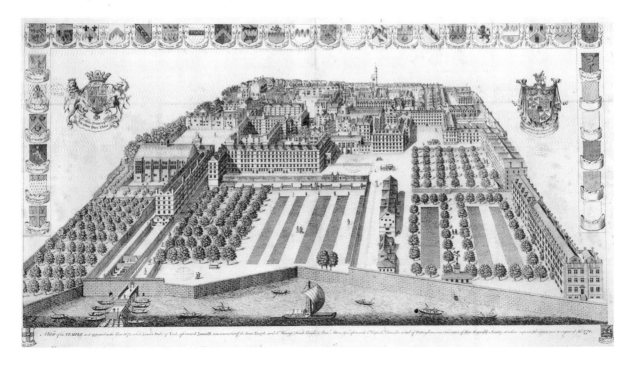

DUM VIVO THRIVO

1692

Clients Precarious Titles May Debate;   Lawyers by subtle querks, their Clients fleece,
The Lawyer only Thrives, grows Rich and Great: So when old Reynard Preaches, 'ware y Geese.
The Golden Fee alone is his Delight;   Two Purse-proud Sots y quarrel for a straw,
Gold makes y Dubious Cause go wrong or Right.   Are justly y Supporters of the Law:
Nay, rather than his Modesty hell hide,   As Fools at Cudgels, find it to their Cost,
Hell take a Private Dawb o' to'ther side: The best comes off but with dry Blows at Most:
Heraldry ne'er Devis'd a fitter Crest,   So wrangling Clients may at variance fall,
Than Sly Volpone so demurely drest: But 'tis y Lawyer Runs away with all.

tional exercises, such as moots and lectures which were given by more senior practitioners, and the 'call to the bar' at one of the Inns of Court was by the 1590s the crucial qualification for gaining the right to plead in any of the major royal courts.

2. *Law and Society in a Litigious Age*

The law was a fairly high-risk occupation in which there were in fact great variations in income, but the alleged rapacity and wealth of lawyers were legendary, and some social theorists, especially amongst the élite, viewed the increases in their number with alarm. Yet, although features of early-modern legal life such as the lack of effective means of registering titles to land and the possibility of litigants prolonging actions by dragging them through one court after another, added to contention, the vast bulk of legal business had a perfectly straightforward logic within contemporary terms. In professional and political rhetoric, moreover, the value of the rule of law was defined in terms of basic rights which protected the property of the subjects, secured the availability of the writ of habeas corpus so that they could not be imprisoned without charges being specified, and guaranteed that they should be tried before their peers. But, while these safeguards, many of which were enshrined in Magna Charta, have an honoured place in British constitutional history, they were significant precisely because so many mundane, everyday relationships were expressed in parchment and sealed with wax.

Turning first to family matters, for example, the widespread use amongst all social groups of marriage settlements in order to establish the property of the new couple provided regular employment for lawyers at the beginning of marriages, and far from simplifying matters, the doctrine of 'couverture', according to which a wife's economic and legal rights were transferred entirely to her husband, created a mass of complications. Indeed, one unintended consequence was that women, especially widows, were involved surprisingly often in litigation.

No less important, in a predominantly agricultural society, questions about rights to land were obviously paramount and hence the source of many disputes. The land law was based on the notion of 'seisin', or land-holding, rather than absolute ownership. Most parcels of land were connected in one way or another with local manorial jurisdictions and were occupied according to a bewildering array of tenures ranging from freeholds to copyholds to leaseholds for a number of years or a number of lives. In addition, many estates, both large and small, were organized into trusts by means of written documents known as 'uses'. Larger landholders from within the aristocracy and gentry frequently held anywhere from one to dozens of manors. These normally included one or more large parcels of demesne, which was either farmed directly or leased out for relatively short periods. The remainder would be held by smaller holders according to a wide variety of terms relating to length and security of tenure, including the power to alienate and to transfer the property between generations. The exact terms and conditions, as well as the regulation of rights to common, and the establishment of agricultural practices, were traditionally

A TYPICAL satire of lawyers (*facing*), with the mock motto, 'While I live, I thrive'. The conspicuous material success of some practitioners, as well as the barbarous complexity of a law which was written down in abbreviated Latin and Norman French, left both the morality and intellectual pretensions of the profession open to ridicule. Laymen also blamed lawyers for the litigiousness of the age.

determined within the manorial court, a jurisdiction which was presided over by a lawyer who was appointed by the lord to act as steward, but where the tenants, acting as a jury or homage, had a say in determining which customs governed tenurial relationships within the manor.

The latter varied significantly from place to place. Furthermore, with the acceleration in the land market which followed the dissolution of the monasteries and the pressure on the price of agricultural land which accompanied increases in population, controversies regarding the possession of land and the conditions attached to it became increasingly common. Lords of manors naturally strove to increase their income, either by raising the entry fines which were due when a new tenant took possession, or by putting up annual rents, and they also benefited when it was possible to convert land which was inheritable to leaseholds for a fixed period of years, thereby enabling them to react more quickly to changes in the market. Tenants, on the other hand, strove for security of tenure and low rents. Although they were disadvantaged by their relative lack of resources, in the legal disputes which followed some classes of tenants, particularly those who were known as copyholders, held their own with considerable success. Before the mid-sixteenth century, copyholders were largely denied access to the common law courts, and the judges held that copyhold was a form of base tenure descended directly from the bond-tenure or villeinage, which was associated in the Middle Ages with serfdom. But there were changes in the Elizabethan period when the courts began to entertain the cases of copyholders and ruled against the claims of lords of manors to exact arbitrary or excessive fines from them. Such decisions were by no means the universal salvation of small farmers, but they were probably much less at the mercy of landlords than is usually imagined. The institutional organization provided by the manor made group actions by tenants against the lord a practicable possibility, and many commentators who decried the rise of the lawyers pointed specifically to the fact that they enabled tenants to vex the lords of manors by taking them to law.

No less than that of the agricultural villages of rural England, the social and economic life of towns also had an important legal dimension. The common practice of placing boys destined for careers in business or trade into apprenticeships was accompanied by a form of contract, the indenture, which specified the responsibilities of the master as well as the duties of the apprentice, and when for one reason or another the relationship broke down, the ensuing disputes were normally taken into borough courts or before the Justices of the Peace. In most towns, furthermore, it was necessary for an adult male to obtain the 'freedom' in order to work at his trade and participate to some degree in political life, and in many towns, including London, the practice of occupations was controlled either by municipal by-laws or guild regulations. Many of the conflicts which regularly arose within this context went to court. Individuals claimed that they had been wrongly deprived of their 'freedom' either because they had broken some regulation or because they had come into disagreement with town governors. Throughout the late sixteenth and seventeenth centuries, challenges to the domination of urban oligarchs by those outside the circle of governors were often aided and abetted by local attorneys, although, once they reached Westminster, such cases had mixed fortunes because the royal judges, like the Privy Council, were generally inclined to support those in power for the sake of good order and governance. For the same reasons, the judiciary was often sympathetic to guild controls on economic activity, but prescriptive corporate powers were liable to be viewed with suspicion because they were special departures from the national common law. It was possible to argue, for example, that the free-

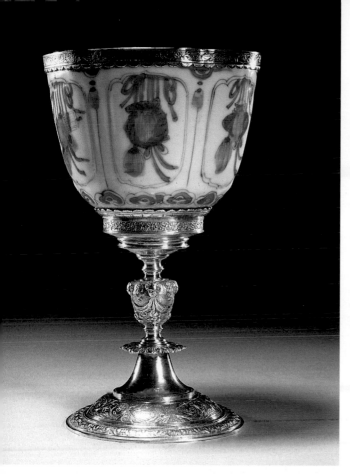

ALL three artefacts show the influence of immigrant craftsmen on the design of English gold- and silverware and pottery. The Elizabethan wine-goblet and Charles II portrait bottle are examples of 'delftware', a technique introduced to England by Dutch immigrants in the 1570s. The Charles I tobacco-box and this bottle also show how images of the monarch were proliferated by this most publicity-conscious of dynasties.

THE 'Great Picture' (*above*) shows
Lady Anne Clifford (1590–1676)
at the ages of 15 and 56 in the left-
and right-hand panels; and her
parents and brothers in the centre of
the triptych. On the wall behind the
studious and exceptionally carefully
educated 15-year-old Anne are
portraits of her tutor and her
governess, the lute upon which she
played, and her well-ordered books
and papers.

AN illumination (*right*) from a
manuscript copy of Cicero's
Orations of an idealized lawyer
addressing an idealized court. The
works of this famous Roman jurist
and philosopher were regularly
mined by lawyers for aphoristic
truths about the critical role of law in
the maintenance of civilized society.
They were also key works in the
humanist canon of the grammar
schools and the universities.

dom of a town was a valuable privilege which enabled a man to earn a living and support his family, and that, therefore, it should not be withdrawn simply because an individual criticized some decision of the mayor or showed up intoxicated at a town meeting. In a case brought by the Merchant Tailors of Ipswich in 1615, the judges declared that, within limits, the common law right of every man to earn his own living outweighed claims of corporate privilege, and it was widely held amongst the lawyers that the Elizabethan and early Stuart practice of granting patents of monopoly, which allowed favoured individuals to profit from the regulation of named trades, was an abuse.

It was a common law axiom that the public interest should always override private interests. But in practice the judges usually ruled that the determination of public nuisances should remain within the sphere of manorial or urban jurisdictions, both of which passed regulations to protect the quality of watercourses or wells and to fine those who fouled the streets or the air with manure, night-soil, or waste from industrial activities such as starch boiling, soap-making, cloth-dyeing, or the slaughter of animals. Consequently, cases which came before the royal courts were usually argued largely in terms of property rights rather than more general social needs, although so-called equitable jurisdictions, such as that of the Court of Chancery, did provide scope for the resolution of disputes on the basis of moral criteria rather than the strict letter of the law

More generally, the great majority of lawsuits in the early modern period arose either out of personal relationships or business activities. In a society in which reputations affected financial as well as social credit, many sorts of people ranging from retailers to attorneys brought cases of slander against those they thought had impugned their probity, their credit-worthiness, or their professional competence, and women in particular frequently sued in the ecclesiastical courts in order to defend themselves against defamations of their sexual honour. There was also an increase in the number of suits which claimed that someone had failed to do what they had agreed to do, or done it badly—for example, actions brought against carpenters who had not carried out building contracts to the satisfaction of their clients or medical men who had undertaken to produce a cure but in fact made the ailment worse.

What is most notable about early modern litigation, however, is the extent to which it reflects a world of financial and business dealings in which the details of agreements were left largely to individuals, liability was strictly interpreted, and draconian powers of enforcement, most notably imprisonment, might be brought to bear on those who defaulted. Many business dealings, ranging from the extension of credit by shopkeepers to the sale of wholesale goods or agricultural produce, were carried out on the basis of either informal written or verbal agreements, and, although little is known about the trials which resulted when they came to court, the decisions on the facts of the case as well as the significance of customary practices within a given trade were probably left to jurors to decide. But the most ubiquitous legal instrument of the period was the conditional bond. This was a formally written document in which one party agreed either to repay a sum of money or carry out an action by a specified date, and it was used to back up all kinds of dealings. If there was a default the aggrieved party could bring an action for debt for the penalty, which in the case of loans was normally twice the amount originally lent. Those defendants who refused or were unable to pay might find themselves stuck in gaol even if they were simply unable to find bail to guarantee that they would appear in court to answer the case against them.

M OSES PITT'S *The Cry of the Oppressed* (1691) illustrated the physical and psychological hardships of impris- onment for debt. Unless, as sometimes happened, wives and children joined the debtor in prison, his fam- ily might be broken up and his dependants thrown on to poor relief. Critics of the practice also thought it unjust to place unlucky debtors into the same category as ordinary criminals.

There can be little doubt that for ordinary householders, imprisonment for debt was the most feared of all legal scourges. Since prisoners had to pay gaolers for their room and board, and since it was nearly impossible to earn a living in gaol, a period of imprisonment frequently led to fur- ther indebtedness. Contemporaries were aware of the human and social costs of this potential vortex of misery, and there was an ongoing debate (which is touched on in Shakespeare's *Mer- chant of Venice*) about whether the need to enforce promises justified the hardships of imprison- ment, but it appears to have been uneasily accepted as a necessary social value.

3. *Crime and Moral Control*

In the Tudor and Stuart period, unlike today, it was the practice of the civil rather than the crim- inal law which dominated the lives of lawyers and contributed to their public image. Lectures on the criminal law are known to have been given at the Inns of Court, and lawyers frequently sat alongside the gentry on the commissions of the peace, where they heard matters ranging from petty theft to wife beating whilst at the same time administering the Poor Law and licensing alehouses. Equally, the royal judges at assizes conducted trials involving felonies (crimes for which the penalty could be death) such as murder and burglary. However, although it seems likely that local attorneys were by the early seventeenth century regularly acting for those brought before quarter sessions accused of misdemeanours, defendants charged with felonies were generally denied the services of legal counsel, the theory being that in such serious cases the judges themselves should see that the rights and interests of the accused were maintained.

This did not mean, of course, that problems of crime and the maintenance of social order were not matters of concern for both the magistrates, and at least at intervals, the wider public as well. As far as we can tell, the rate of murder may have been slightly higher in the early modern period than it is in present-day Britain. But, as is the case today, a very high proportion of murders took place within the domestic setting, and once it is considered that modern medical technology, and especially antibiotics, were not available to victims of assault, it may be that the difference between the two periods in terms of the incidence of violence is not all that great. What was probably most evident to contemporaries was that there were periods when threats to the social fabric and property seemed particularly acute. Most property crimes, such as petty theft or burglary, were committed by the young, the poor, and the indigent, and the incidence of such crimes fluctuated broadly in line with the overall state of the economy. Both the number of prosecutions and public anxiety reached high levels in the 1590s, and again in the 1620s, when European war, bad harvests, and domestic economic dislocation caused severe difficulties. However, from the 1630s, and particularly from the 1660s, when economic conditions were improving, the number of prosecutions entered a phase of decline which lasted until the 1690s, when there was again concern, especially in London.

One reaction to crime waves was the passage of legislation in Parliament. As was the case with the Elizabethan statute which enabled local authorities to round up 'rogues and vagabonds' who were travelling around the country (often in search of work) with no fixed place of abode, some of this legislation was aimed at controlling social groups thought, whether accurately or not, to be prone to crime, while much of the rest of it added yet more teeth to an already draconian penal code, which prescribed the death penalty for a wide range of offences starting with the theft of goods or money worth more than the very small amount of one shilling. At the local level, on the other hand, towns and counties from about the same time began to erect 'houses of correction'. Supported by parish levies, which were sometimes supplemented by charitable bequests, and reflecting the contemporary perception that there was a connection between underemployment and crime, these institutions sometimes offered training for younger inmates, but they functioned largely as places to which indigents might be removed and where petty offenders might be confined for short periods.

In the end the response to crime depended very much on individual and community initiative. There were no organized police forces; local constables were characteristically yeoman farmers, either elected at the manorial court or appointed by JPs, who had to endure the responsibilities of an unpaid office for a year. The victims of crime usually had to discover the culprits themselves and then fetch the constable to arrest them and bring them before the JPs to be bound over to appear either before quarter sessions or assize, depending on the seriousness of the allegation. The

Iames Nailor Quaker, set 2 howers on the Pillory at Westminster, whiped by the Hang-
in to the old Exchainge London, Som dayes after, Stood too howers more on the Pillor
at the Exchainge, and there had his Tongue Bored throug with a hot Iron, &
d in the Forehead with the Letter: B: Decem. 17: anno Dom. 1656:

THE religious radical James Nayler being whipped and set on the pillory. In the early modern period, custodial prison sentences were rare, but the houses of correction and transportation to the colonies, which was just beginning at the end of our period, provided new alternatives to the traditional sanctions of corporal punishment, public humiliation, and death by hanging.

next step was for the defendant to face a grand jury, who would determine whether there was a case to answer. Then, if an indictment was brought in, there was a trial before a so-called petty jury, which was most likely to be composed either of respectable citizens in towns or yeoman farmers and lesser squires in rural areas.

Little is known about what actually went on in an ordinary criminal trial, except that a comparison of the number of cases with the amount of time that was available to try them suggests that most must have been conducted in minutes rather than hours, let alone days. Although jurors did not necessarily come from the area where the crime had been committed, they must frequently have had some familiarity with one or both of the parties. There was no technical presumption that they should not use this knowledge in reaching a verdict, and it seems likely that some trials involved lively exchanges between judge, jurors, and the accused about points of law as well as matters of fact. Judges and magistrates frequently suspected juries of trying to take matters into their own hands, either by being too lenient, or, alternatively, by being biased and acting capriciously, and until the practice was declared illegal in Bushell's Case (1670), judges could punish jurors for bringing in what they considered to be manifestly false verdicts. The judiciary could also exercise control by making determinations on technical issues, such as the way an offence was classified, and there are signs by the early Stuart period that they were beginning to develop the law of evidence. For instance, although convictions for witchcraft never reached the same levels in England as they did in Scotland and continental Europe, by the second half of the seventeenth century, they were clearly on the decline, at least partly because the judiciary insisted on proof that those accused had actually caused harm to their victims.

In general, there was probably not all that much difference between judicial and magisterial attitudes towards crime and those of the propertied middling and landed classes who were likely to find themselves victims of it. Community participation in the process, and the degree of discretion which was allowed to judges and magistrates, permitted flexibility, but there was also an awareness that these could produce arbitrariness and unlawful excesses. In any case, despite the theoretical harshness of the penal code, many fewer people were indicted than were accused, many fewer convicted than indicted, and no more than half of those who could have faced the gallows actually did so. Charges were frequently downgraded so that the criminal, though punished, did not have to be executed, and the legal device known as 'benefit of clergy' allowed felons who could read, or who were said to be able to read, a verse from the Bible to escape with a branding. Thus, although the criminal law was terrifying, and genuinely dangerous, its full vigour was usually directed primarily at those who were identified either as malicious or unreformable repeat offenders. While there were occasional criticisms of the severity of the criminal code, and whilst there must sometimes have been sympathy for those who were hanged, executions were popular public spectacles at which ordinary subjects joined with the legal establishment in a macabre celebration of social solidarity through the exaction of retribution.

The hanging tree may, therefore, have been a less potent symbol of social control than it is sometimes said to be, but there were other ways in which the law could be potentially intrusive into the lives not only of the poor but of the 'respectable' middling sort and gentry as well. Apart from anything else, neighbours could present one another to the church courts for various sexual 'incontinencies' such as fornication or adultery. In addition there was a large amount of statutory legislation in the later sixteenth century which aimed to exert tighter controls on the alehouse, on swearing, on the bearing of illegitimate children, and on drinking during divine service on a Sunday. These and other attempts to enforce morality are easily identifiable with the reforming religious zeal of Puritanism, but they may not have represented a radical departure from the past. English villages had long been potentially censorious places where neighbourliness might easily verge into nosiness, where individual social and economic behaviour could be regulated to accord with 'community values' which were in fact laid down by the local 'better sort'. The new legislation, which in effect transferred the handling of offences from the manorial and ecclesiastical courts to quarter sessions, contributed to a decline of community self-control, and it provided the opportunity for zealous JPs, constables, and churchwardens to lord it over their neighbours and to subject them to their own values, including those which were inspired by religious enthusiasm. In the long run, however, the outcome was in fact more complicated than this. The jurisdictional shifts also had the effect of allowing the lawyers to become more involved and hence opened the door to litigation and judicial interpretation. Furthermore, although the common law judges were usually quick to support established authority, they were no different from many laymen in having mixed feelings about moral regulation. Some joined readily enough in campaigns against the evils of the alehouse, but others made a point of emphasizing the fact that English law, unlike that of some Continental countries, did not provide for regular moral censorship. As Attorney-General in 1601, the greatest lawyer of the age, Sir Edward Coke, drew up a set of instructions for local constables which, amongst other things, ordered them to report 'unlawful games and drunkenness in private families'. But he was also fond of the legal maxim that 'the House of every one is to him as his Castle and Fortress, as well for his Defence against Injury and Violence, as for his repose', and there were any number of cases brought to court by people who claimed that they had been unjustly arrested, that their rights had been infringed by local officials, or who took direct action against constables who tried to enter their houses. Up until the time of the Civil War, therefore, the posture of the individual subject in the face of the authority of magistrates, and a powerful religious impulse towards moral control, is best described as contentious, and the results when such disputes were aired in court may have been unpredictable. After the Restoration, once economic conditions had improved, and there was considerably more scepticism

Tᴉᴛʟᴇ-ᴘᴀɢᴇ of *The Spirituall Courts epitomized, In a Dialogue betwixt two Proctors, Busie Body, and Scrape-all . . .* (1641). Although the ecclesiastical jurisdiction over marriage and testamentary questions served a useful function, there was criticism and resentment of the meddling in sexual and other more trivial moral matters by the so-called 'bawdy courts'. The jurisdiction temporarily collapsed during the civil wars and Interregnum and then underwent a permanent decline in the later seventeenth century.

about religious certainties, the ongoing decline of manorial and ecclesiastical jurisdictions led in general to a reduction in the intrusiveness of neighbours as well as that of the state, at least amongst those who were not poor. In this respect the passage in 1650 of a statute which made adultery punishable by the death penalty was an important symbolic turning-point. Puritan Members of Parliament had unsuccessfully introduced similar measures in the 1620s, but when it finally became law it was rendered unworkable by the refusal of the public to make presentments which would subject people to such drastic penalties.

4. *Law, the Constitution, and Politics*

As the foregoing account indicates, the place of the law in early modern society was multifaceted. It was, on the one hand, a powerful expression of authority, but, on the other, one of the means most often turned to by those who felt oppressed by landlords, local authorities, or fellow subjects. Indeed, as the Duke of Newcastle reminded Charles II at the time of the Restoration, the lawyers were dangerous precisely because they had taught the subjects to wrangle about everything, including the king's prerogative. Yet, in reality, up until the end of Elizabeth's reign, the lawyers had for the most part been happy to promote the rule of law as a social and political ideal, whilst at the same time maintaining that it was one of the principal pillars which supported the monarch's throne. It was with the accession of James I that the common law and a number of its leading figures became caught up in the political and constitutional conflicts of the day.

Quite apart from the new King's tendency to make public pronouncements about the divinely ordained nature of his royal authority, James I was a Scot and his beloved plans to create a union between his kingdoms gave the Englishness of the common law a particular resonance. It was a commonplace of humanist jurisprudence that the laws of a country should be well suited to the customs and habits of the inhabitants. All over Europe, from Catalonia to the Netherlands and Lithuania, provinces which formed the constituent parts of multiple kingdoms looked to their 'ancient laws' to maintain their rights and identities. Conversely, it was equally logical for an English lawyer like Sir John Davies, who served at about this time as Attorney-General in Ireland, to explain the supposed barbarity of the native Irish in terms of the degree to which their laws diverged from those of the English. These issues were pertinent to James I's proposals because it was widely acknowledged that a 'perfect union' of the two kingdoms should involve a thorough conflation of their laws. But this was difficult because the Scottish legal system, then as today, was closer to the Continental tradition of written law which constantly referred back to the *Institutes* of Justinian, than to the common law with its pride in unwritten customs and emphasis on the trial by jury. The Scots worried that their national identity would be submerged if they were forced to submit to English laws. The English, who were in any case not generally in favour of union, appear to have been fearful of the prospect of large-scale changes which might result if the laws of a new Great Britain were put down in writing in the time of a Scottish king with absolutist tendencies.

Significantly, it was against this background in the first decade of the seventeenth century that Sir Edward Coke published his authoritative law reports, a series of professional works whose prefaces emphasized the view that the common law, and the liberties it enshrined, were the birthright of every Englishman, that it was extremely dangerous to attempt large-scale changes

From the beginning of the Tudor period, lawyers took advantage of the new availability of print to produce many works which were aimed at laymen as well as professionals. While this example of a popular work for JPs symbolizes the close relationship between the law and the monarchy, it also illustrates the development of an independent and authoritative professional tradition associated with individual legal luminaries.

in the law, and that the English common law in fact represented an essentially unaltered tradition which stretched back well before the Norman Conquest and which, therefore, evolved in a way which was uniquely suited to the nation. Furthermore, Coke's insistence on the independence of the judiciary, and his inclination to lecture the King on the true nature of the law of the land, eventually led to his dismissal as Lord Chief Justice in 1616, a disgrace which was accompanied by accusations from his bitter enemy, Lord Chancellor Ellesmere, that he showed a dangerous tendency towards becoming a populist judge. Coke then went on to become a very influential member of the House of Commons in the 1620s, a phase in his career which cast him in the unusual role of a sacked Lord Chief Justice who was regularly criticizing royal policy in the name of the liberty of the subject. In 1628, for example, he led the attack on the use by the Crown of imprisonment without charges being specified, the attempt to levy taxes without the consent of Parliament, and the billeting of soldiers on the countryside.

Coke was not a radical man. In many respects the appeal of his standpoint was that it rested simply on the premiss that if the King could take the property of his subjects, then they were reduced to little more than bondmen or slaves as opposed to freemen of England. Other lawyers had broader views, which could range from a defence of absolute authority to arguments in favour of mixed monarchy by king, lords, and commons, but in the public debates of the 1620s and 1630s, Coke's references to historical precedents and an immemorial 'ancient constitution' set the agenda even though these were, ironically, quickly taken up and put to effective use by the Crown. During the 1630s Attorney-General Noy hit on a number of financial expedients, such as distraint of knighthood and the exploitation of feudal forest laws, which were technically legal, but which ran contrary to the spirit of the law as it had been known in the recent past. In Hampden's Case, which resulted in a narrow decision in favour of the legality of Ship Money, some of the judges used the idea that the monarchy pre-dated Parliament in order to construct their arguments that the King was entitled to raise the levy.

Coke was dead when the Long Parliament met in 1640, but in its opening months a number of leading lawyers including Edward Hyde, the future Earl of Clarendon, Edward Bagshawe, and Harbottle Grimston, participated vigorously in attacks on the legal devices and legal decisions of the 1630s. Several of the Ship Money judges eventually fled into exile when the process of impeachment was begun against them. The populist side of traditional legal rhetoric, which stressed that public authority was supposed to protect the interests of the subject, and that the King, no less than ordinary men, should therefore be bound to observe the law, was brilliantly exploited by a barrister of Lincoln's Inn, Henry Parker, to produce propaganda for the parliamentary cause. Yet for the legal profession, no less than for the nation as a whole, the choice of sides was divisive. Grimston, Bagshawe, and Hyde, for example, all eventually joined Charles I at Oxford, fearful of parliamentary innovation and threats to the social order, and those who remained in the parliamentary camp, like William Lenthall, Speaker of the Long Parliament, and the legal historian John Selden, included some of its more conservative supporters.

Indeed, by the later 1640s the legal system and the legal profession became nearly as much of a target for radical calls for reform as the Established Church had been earlier in the decade. Prolific Leveller pamphleteers associated the law with the discredited monarchy and blamed the ill effects of both on the Norman enslavement of freeborn Englishmen. Most radical proposals for change were therefore less concerned with the substance of the law than with making it generally more just and accessible, returning decision-making to the localities, and ending the professional monopoly of the lawyers so that every man could become his own advocate. The Levellers' volubility and passion may exaggerate the extent to which they reflected a more deeply rooted dissatisfaction, but 'the rule of law' had been one of the principal issues at stake in the Civil War, and many people, including Oliver Cromwell, agreed that law reform was one of the benefits which might to some degree justify the bloodshed it had cost. Early in the 1650s the Rump Parliament appointed a commission to draw up proposals for law reform, and in 1651 there was legislation that legal proceedings should be recorded in English rather than Latin. Relatively limited alterations such as these were not entirely unwelcome to some sections of the legal profession, but in the event the 1650s were not propitious times for major change. As the Cromwellian regime attempted to restore stability, schemes to alter the law moved down the political agenda for fear that they might be associated with threats to property rights. At a time when communities were deeply divided along a multitude of religious and political lines, worthy proposals to reduce litigation and reliance on the legal profession by returning justice to amateur judges sitting in local courts ran into serious practical difficulties when it came to the all-important matter of establishing criteria for the selection of magistrates.

Nothing more of significance was achieved in the 1650s, and, apart from the abolition of feudal tenures and the Court of Star Chamber, which had been agreed by the Long Parliament and Charles I in 1641, all of the Civil War reforms were reversed soon after the Restoration of the monarchy. Latin and French returned as the legal languages of record until they were finally discarded in the reign of George II. More importantly, the period between 1660 and the Revolution of 1688 was one in which the judiciary once again became caught up in the rough and tumble of politics, and it emerged badly bruised. The new regime began moderately enough by appointing an able bench which included former Cromwellian appointees like Sir Matthew Hale, who was widely recognized as the ablest lawyer of the day. By the mid-1670s, however, the judiciary was profoundly compromised by the later Stuarts' attempt to use the prerogative powers to suspend or dispense with statutes in order to neutralize the penal laws against Catholics and Dissenters. Although there was no doubt that the Crown had these traditional powers, the attempt to apply them wholesale in order to evade recently passed legislation touching on the politically sensitive matter of religious conformity was deeply controversial. The failure of the bench to give full support to the legality of the Declaration of Indulgence in 1672 led Charles II to resurrect the practice of appointing judges during the pleasure of the King rather than for as long as they performed their offices satisfactorily. By subjecting the judiciary to a series of purges which resulted in the removal of no less than eleven judges between 1675 and 1683, the Crown achieved decisions which helped the Duke of York to escape conviction under the Test Acts, suppressed petitioning campaigns in favour of his exclusion from the succession to the throne, and clamped down on the press. But tampering with the bench, which continued under James II, was identified by contemporaries as the leading edge of arbitrary government, and it subverted claims of royalists that

A POPULAR print of the capture of Lord Chancellor George Jeffreys by a mob at Wapping as he tried to escape London in disguise in December 1688. Infamous for his conduct of the 'Bloody Assizes' after Monmouth's Rebellion, Jeffreys was also associated with a long list of legal abuses ranging from purges of the commissions of the peace to the trial of the Seven Bishops. He died disgraced in the Tower in 1689.

religion and property would be safe so long as the subjects continued in dutiful and loyal obedience to the Crown.

None of James II's judiciary remained in office after the Glorious Revolution, but it is likely that fifteen years of discontinuity, mediocrity, and political subservience amongst its leading figures had a damaging and long-lasting effect on the legal profession as a whole. Although it was in any case difficult for the Inns of Court to re-create the vigour of their system of learning exercises after the disruptions of the mid-century civil wars, the final collapse came in the 1670s and 1680s, when a firmer guiding hand from the judiciary might have helped to maintain them. The result was that the legal inns degenerated into little more than places where lawyers kept chambers. Formal legal education virtually ceased in England until it was born again in the mid-nineteenth century. Equally, although the causes undoubtedly extended well beyond the political machinations of the period, both the volume of litigation which entered the courts and the size of the legal profession began at about the same time to enter a phase of contraction which reached a nadir in 1750. Paradoxically, if the law had established itself as one of the great symbols of the English state, both its practitioners and its role in everyday life were probably less significant in the eighteenth century than they had been under Elizabeth and the Stuarts.

8
THE THEATRE AND SOCIETY

ANDREW GURR

1. *The Innovations*

Historians have always been uncomfortable with the implications of the idea that the hour produces the man. Determinism is reluctant to allow much scope for the individualism which finds new paths through mapless territories. Early historians delighted in celebrating the new and original. Most modern historians prefer to see innovations as broadly predetermined rather than wholly new. That shift in thinking lays special constraints on historians of culture. They have to reconcile the phenomenon of great artists like Shakespeare, renowned for his originality, with the determinism that gives the highest priority to the conditions making the artists creative. It becomes an acute problem when the artefacts for which the artists are celebrated were produced precisely in response to the demand that their work should be original.

Shakespeare was not the first nor the last artist of his time to exploit the immense possibilities that writing plays offered to ambitious literate men in the late sixteenth century. His peculiar talents greatly enlarged the scope and subject-matter of the plays of his time, and made play-going more rewarding than it had ever been. The history of that time ran in his favour. He arrived in London at the end of the 1580s, just as the playing companies began to secure a firm base and to perform regularly in what was becoming the largest city in Europe. That base allowed them to develop much bigger companies and bigger resources than ever before. Their playing was the best in Europe. They secured royal protection. But its very newness made it a hazardous career. Shakespeare did not finally commit himself to being a player and a playwright until 1594, when he was 30, six or more years after his first successes, and only then after making an attempt at a different career as a poet under the patronage of a great lord. He was the tip of an iceberg, the most successful of the many poets who wrote for the stage in these decades. His plays helped establish the respectability of play-going as part of a new pattern of growth in London life. Theatres challenged churches as places for crowds to meet and talk about the affairs of the day. The playwrights satisfied a huge appetite in the play-goers that was manifest all round the country.

Public entertainment with plays performed by travelling companies was one of the few forms of enjoyment through the Tudor and Stuart period for which records have been preserved. In that time public entertainments developed in status and in the circumstances of performance quite remarkably. There was little connection under Henry VIII between Court and country, but by the 1580s the best companies were not only used to touring the country, performing in great houses and town guild-halls, but they had large and specially built theatres in London where they were able to play before thousands of people at a time, and were offering the same plays at Court. In 1583 one pre-eminent company was set up with the Queen as its patron. In 1594 this privilege was renewed with two new companies chosen by the Lord Chamberlain to have the exclusive right to play in London at specified playhouses. When James came to the throne in 1603 he gave his family's patronage to three playing companies. From then until 1642 when Parliament closed all places of public meeting there were usually four or more theatres offering plays every day of the week. Two, following the older tradition, offered plays

A DESIGN for a hall playhouse stage and tiring-house front made by Inigo Jones, probably for the Cockpit playhouse in 1616. Note the boxes flanking the stage and the seating for spectators in the stage gallery alongside the central music room.

in the open air to large crowds. Two others, roofed and playing to a wealthier clientele, provided a new kind of venue, one that became the only kind of theatre to be built in the Restoration and after. In 1660 two new companies instantly sprang back to cater for the richer slice of society. By then play-going had become, now only for the wealthier and more literate, a valued feature of social life in England.

Building playing-places in London was the crucial step towards professional theatre. It enabled companies to build up much more substantial resources for performance than they could carry as travelling players. It also generated a new kind of audience. Once the practice of regular playing became settled in London, audiences got into the habit of seeing a fresh play every day, and the playwrights grew used to writing for an audience weaned on varied kinds of play and constantly demanding novelty. Those were the conditions that through the 1580s and 1590s stimulated an intense growth in playwriting, of which Shakespeare was both the chief promoter and the chief beneficiary.

In the earlier years there were many kinds of entertainment. Besides the small groups, usually not more than five or six players, who offered plays or 'interludes', the archives of cities such as Norwich and Bristol note regular payments made to jesters, jugglers, acrobats, different sorts of musician, bearwards, and presenters of other 'shows', few of which have left any sign of what they had to offer. The spoken word was easier to record than the skills of the performers identified in this survey of regional talents. As a Hereford pamphlet of the beginning of the seventeenth century put it,

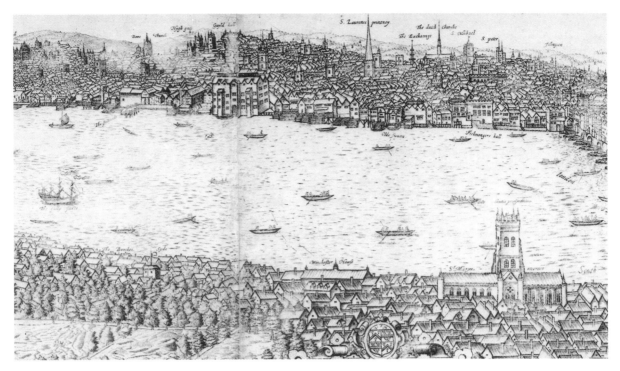

P ART of Southwark, from John Norden's *Civitas Londini* of 1593. The Rose playhouse is shown with its flag flying, to the left of the picture, near the south bank of the river. St Mary Overies, now Southwark Cathedral, is on the right of the picture.

The courts of kings for stately measures: the Citie for light-heeles, and nimble footing: the Country for shuffling dances: Westerne-men for gambouls: Middlesex-men for tricks above ground: Essex-men for the Hey: Lancashire for Horne-pypes: Worcester-shire for Bagpypes: but Hereford-shire for a Morris-daunce. (*Old Meg of Herefordshire*, 1609)

Almost no evidence about these voiceless shows survives, since the written word was the only form of record available, and only the scripts for a few of the civic presentations that incorporated speeches tell what was said at them. Spoken presentations are distinctive in the sixteenth century precisely because they were the only recordable kind. They employed the kind of skill that culminated at the end of the century in Shakespeare's plays, but the success of this form of show, the two- or three-hour play as we know it now, ought not to make us think the less of the variety of skills that may have been on offer in the less recordable kinds. Other entertainments persisted long after written drama had taken a grip on the privileged of London and had crept into the durable record of print.

Play-going was popular at all levels of society in Tudor England. The touring companies fed the appetite that helped them grow, as they came to command greater resources and greater income from the towns and houses that they visited. This helped them in the 1570s and 1580s to secure royal favour. In 1578 the Master of the Revels, organizer of Court entertainments, was given official status and a budget for the long winter season of staged shows at Court. It did not take him long to realize that the Court tradition of staging masques, set-piece shows with elaborate scenery, music, dancing, and verse, was far more expensive than importing companies of professional players with their ready-made plays. From then on the playing companies were protected by the Privy Council as necessary adjuncts to the royal pleasure, and their long-term prosperity and growth were assured.

Protection was necessary. On tour companies might be refused leave to play by the mayor and corporation of the towns they came to. A conscientious mayor might worry that large gatherings of his people would risk infections such as the plague, and might fear disruptions caused by crowds or the dubious morality of low and possibly licentious shows. The companies always ran the risk of being unwelcome, though they usually got something for their trouble. While a mayor would usually pay the players to entertain the townspeople, he might equally well pay them not to perform. Either way, they had money for their pains.

In London, though, the companies had no such expectation. Mayors of London were consistently hostile to playing, for reasons partly moral and partly commercial. When Parliament closed all theatres in September 1642 it was doing what the London authorities had been regularly pleading for over the previous seventy years. When the players' foothold in London became more secure under royal protection, successive Lord Mayors laid a complaint before the Privy Council about the trouble they caused. Sometimes, particularly in the years after the first theatres were established, 1576–84, pamphleteers were paid to attack the irreligious iniquities of play-going. The more puritanical adherents of the Church of England deplored the viewing of idle spectacles as much as they deplored the icons and rituals of the Catholic Church. Shows incited people to lechery and other kinds of sin, most notably idleness. And idleness gave the Lord Mayor a particular incentive to refuse players a place in London. Plays were necessarily performed in daylight, in the afternoons of the working week. Audiences had therefore either to be idle to start with or taking time off work to see the play. Since the Mayor and his Corporation were all citizen-employers in the great guilds that controlled the workers of London they had a vested interest in closing down shows that drew their employees away from work.

The first result of the city's opposition to play-going was that the players built their theatres in the suburbs, outside the Mayor's jurisdiction. Theatres appeared to the north of the city in Shoreditch, to the east in Stepney, and to the south across the river in Southwark. Use of the city itself was dependent on bending the rules. City innyards, and sometimes rooms inside inns, especially in winter and bad weather, were used for plays until 1594, when the Privy Council at last decided to back the Mayor and closed them to players. Companies of boy choristers did perform plays at Paul's and in the liberty of the Blackfriars inside the city from the 1570s to 1590, and from 1599 to 1608. But the Mayor's hostility was consistent and potent. Up to 1660 no player or impresario ever dared build a theatre inside the city, even in the early Stuart years when the leading companies had royal patronage. Apart from a few inns like the Bel Savage near St Paul's and the Bull and the Cross Keys in Gracechurch Street, which were never recognized officially as playhouses, and the tiny theatre built for the Paul's Boys abutting the cathedral, there was no regular playhouse within the city's bounds until 1608.

In that year, in return for a large loan, James allowed the liberties to come under city jurisdiction. The Blackfriars liberty, a prime residential neighbourhood, had a playhouse, built originally in 1596 for Shakespeare's company. They were barred from using it for the first twelve years because the residents of Blackfriars did not want a 'common playhouse' in their midst and petitioned the Privy Council to stop it from opening. In 1599 the owners leased it to a boy company, who were not so noisy and played only once a week. Shakespeare's company did not secure it for their own use for another nine years, and had to build the Globe instead. Ironically, when they did secure it in 1608 the Blackfriars had just come under the city's control. But by then Shakespeare's company was the King's Men, and their status gave them entry to this one unique playhouse now inside the city. The city continued to block all attempts to match the Blackfriars with other city theatres until the 1660s.

From 1609 until all the theatres were closed in 1642 Shakespeare's company, using the Blackfriars as their winter playhouse, was pre-eminent. In their final thirty-three years the social status of the play-goers who went to see the King's Men included the highest in the land. The Lord Chamberlain quarrelled with the Duke of Lennox over access to a box at Blackfriars in 1635. Queen Henrietta Maria went to see a play there. The company's other theatre, the Globe, which brought them to their eminence between 1599 and 1608, stayed in use through the summer for the rest of London's fast-growing population. That appropriation of theatres by the richer section of society was renewed at the Restoration.

2. *London Theatre-building*

Growth in the status of plays and playing companies in London is signalled in its most tangible form by the building of the playhouses. A few towns such as Bristol and York converted inns into playhouses, like some of the earlier London venues. Some lords built playhouses for their own entertainment on their estates in the more remote counties such as Lancashire. But only London put up the large-capacity purpose-built amphitheatres for which Shakespeare and his fellow playwrights wrote their plays. The open-air amphitheatres in London resembled the baiting arenas which provided the main competition in public entertainment. Many other towns had baiting arenas, but only London had such a huge capacity for its play-goers. Each theatre was capable of accommodating between two and three thousand people daily. That fertile resource fed the rest of the country through the travelling companies.

Amphitheatres like the Globe are unique in the history of English theatre design. Their model may have been the baiting arenas, or innyards with surrounding galleries, although they seem to have evolved in a distinctive polygonal form of their own, their ring of galleries looking like a circle, probably modelled on classical Roman theatres. Essentially they were a two or three-level scaffold of galleries built around a yard which had a stage jutting out from the galleries into mid-yard. Where the stage came out of the gallery frame it was backed by a dressing room or 'tiring house' from which the players entered. It had two or three entrance doors, one large enough to serve as a 'study' or alcove and to allow big properties to be carried on-stage. A balcony over the entrance doors in later years held a consort of musicians. You paid one penny to gain access to the yard, where you stood around the stage, and another penny for a seat in the galleries, which

A DETAIL from the panorama of London made by Braun and Hogenberg in 1572 (*facing, above*), showing the 'liberty' of Southwark on the Surrey side of the Thames, with its animal-baiting arenas.

THIS painting (*facing, below*) has been thought to represent a wedding feast. Such rites of passage with their feasting and dancing were an occasion for marking out both personal and social status. There was a transition in this period from celebrating superior status by the inclusion of social inferiors in such occasions to one of defining status by their exclusion.

of course had the extra advantage of being roofed. The yard was open to the sky, to light the scene, though the stage itself had a cover against rain.

The hall theatres were similar, although much smaller in dimensions and capacity. Their auditoria were also round, the audience sitting almost completely surrounding the stage, although otherwise they were much more like modern theatres than the unroofed amphitheatres. The most expensive seats, in the boxes, flanked the stage on each side. Some of the halls also permitted gallants to hire a stool and sit on the stage itself to watch the play. In the amphitheatres the cheapest places were in the standing-room closest to the stage, but at the all-seating halls the nearer the stage the more expensive the price became. Hall theatres provided the model for post-Restoration design.

The first of London's amphitheatres on record was a ring of scaffolding for galleries with a separate stage structure erected in Whitechapel in 1567. Known as the Red Lion, it was not an inn as the name would now suggest but a suburban property set up specifically to show plays. It was financed by a grocer, John Brayne, probably for his brother-in-law James Burbage, the chief player of the leading company of the time, Leicester's Men. What happened to the Red Lion is unknown. Burbage built the first durable amphitheatre nine years later, in 1576, calling it the Theatre. He chose to build it in Shoreditch on land with a twenty-one-year lease in which he tried to include a proviso that if need be he could pull his building down and re-erect it elsewhere. Normally buildings put up on leasehold land reverted to the owner of the land when the lease expired. Burbage was trying to save his investment in timber, probably because he knew how precarious the life of playhouses still was in the face of city opposition in the 1570s. He did not erect the Theatre until his company had the protection of a royal patent, granted to Leicester's Servants in 1574 in the wake of the restrictions laid on travelling players in the 1572 Statute of Retainers. Another amphitheatre, the Curtain, was built nearby in the following year.

At about the same time as the two Shoreditch amphitheatres, two much smaller indoor playhouses were opened for the boy chorister companies. One was a structure attached to the cathedral for the company known as Paul's Boys, the other downhill from it in Blackfriars, for the Children of the Chapel Royal. Both chorister companies seem to have been fairly commercial ventures. Their repertoire of plays, especially when John Lyly started to write for them, was aimed at courtiers, young Inns of Court lawyers, and idle gentry with enough education to enjoy the game of 'applying' the subjects of the plays to court affairs.

The concurrent opening of two large amphitheatres and two hall playhouses in 1575–7 was a milestone in the players' progress. It gave them durable venues built specially for playing. More usefully still, for the first time it generated the prospect of large profits. Custom-built theatres gave the companies much tighter control over their customers than they had in country towns and market-places. The Privy Council had granted the best companies the legal status they needed to confront the vigorous opposition of the City Fathers in London. This struggle between Court and city brought another change in the next decade, when the Privy Council, concerned to supply means of entertaining the Court through the long season of Christmas festivities, in 1583

B OLSOVER Castle, Nottinghamshire (*facing*), is a spectacular early example of Jacobean medievalism, set on a hilltop and visible from miles around. After their great symmetrical houses such as Hardwick Hall, the Smythsons built this 'cultural castle' for the Cavendish family, renovating the existing Norman keep and creating a sprawling series of state rooms and the largest riding stables outside Spain.

A BIRD'S-EYE view of the foundations of the Rose, as dug up in 1989. The photograph, which includes the surviving concrete posts from the foundations of the 1957 building over the remains and just demolished, shows spectators looking at the excavation from Park Street in Southwark. It was taken by Andrew Fulgoni from the top of a ten-storey building on the south side of the road. The remains are of two theatres and two stages. The first was made in 1587, and was a roughly symmetrical polygon. The second was an enlargement made in 1592 which stretched the original polygon northwards into a tulip-shape.

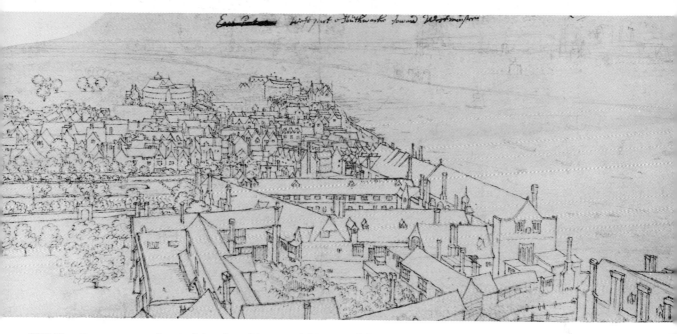

Wenceslas Hollar's pencil drawing of the second Globe, made in preparation for his engraving called 'A Long View of the City of London' in the 1630s. The drawing was done from a distance of not much more than a quarter-mile with a perspective glass, from the tower of what is now Southwark Cathedral.

set up a monopolistic company with the Queen herself as its patron. The Lord Chamberlain, the Privy Councillor responsible for those entertainments, negotiated a deal with the Lord Mayor in 1584 to give only the royal company access to the London performing venues.

That arrangement stabilized the Court's needs for a while, but the sands were shifting. The boy companies lost ground to the popular players, Paul's being closed in 1584, and the Blackfriars Boys in 1590. The adult players got a new amphitheatre in 1587, the Rose, located near the baiting arenas south of the river. Plays staged by the adult companies took over from the more learned pieces of the boys'. Marlowe's *Tamburlaine* and Kyd's *Spanish Tragedy* joined an upsurge of jingoistic and patriotic plays in the Armada years to give the amphitheatre companies an unassailably strong position through the 1590s. No hall theatres were open in that decade. The Theatre, the Curtain, the Rose, and for a while from 1595 the newly built Swan, also in Southwark, supplied all London and London's visitors with plays.

Government policy was also tightening in those years. The large number of deaths from plague in London closed the theatres for more than twelve months on end in the early 1590s, and some leading companies died as a result. In 1594 the Lord Chamberlain repeated the act of 1583, setting up two new companies whose members were drawn, as the Queen's Men had been, from all the leading companies. The Lord Mayor was appeased with a total ban on companies playing at the city inns. In the succeeding years the duopoly of these two companies was given exclusive access to the London venues, one at the Theatre, the other at the Rose. The Privy Council tried hard to have the Swan pulled down in 1597 when a new company which started playing there threatened the duopoly.

But the two protected companies did not have it all their own way. The Theatre's lease expired

THE frontispiece for Kirkman's *The Wits*, a collection of comic scenes or 'drolls' from the pre-1642 drama published after the Restoration, in 1662. It shows some of the famous figures from the plays of the period before the closure.

early in 1597, and the owner refused to renew it to players. So their financier, trying to compensate for the loss of the winter inns, and perhaps exploiting the closure of the boy companies' halls, built them a new hall theatre in the Blackfriars liberty to replace the open-air Theatre. It was an over-bold venture, running into opposition from rich locals who petitioned the Privy Council at the end of 1596 and blocked the project. As a result, the company for which Shakespeare was writing lost its theatre and had to rent the old Curtain to play in for the next few years. Their financial resources were sunk in a hall theatre they could not use. So at the end of 1598 in desperation they dismantled the old Theatre and took its timbers to Southwark to help make the Globe.

That retreat, from the proposed new hall playhouse to a new/old open-air theatre, shows how downmarket their playing was still thought to be. The Blackfriars petition specified that its residents did not want the drums and trumpets of common players and the crowds of riotous play-goers interrupting their daily business. The petition blocked progress for another decade. A subsequent tightening of the regulations about using inns for playing led to two former inns, the Boar's Head in Whitechapel and the Red Bull in Clerkenwell, being converted from inns to full-time theatres, the latter proving a durable investment. But the next step forward came from an attempt to renew the old social divide. In 1599 Paul's Boys started playing again at their small theatre in the cathedral precinct. A little later the Blackfriars Boys reopened, using the hall theatre built for Shakespeare's company. This renewed the early division of courtly audiences from popular. In the meantime, however, tastes had changed. The boys now had vastly more to compete with than there had been in the 1570s. Their appeal was exclusively to the richer end of the audience range. They learned to exploit the social divisions between their audience of literate gentry and the 'understanders' standing in the yard at the Globe and the Fortune, which replaced the Rose in 1600. The Blackfriars Boys in particular ran satirical or 'railing' plays aimed at the sophisticated courtiers and lawyers in their audience. But it was not a very durable kind of recipe, and it soon ran into trouble with government.

The Blackfriars Boys were a conspicuous part of London life through the decade from 1599 to 1608. Those years, though, also belonged to Shakespeare's Globe. His company opened its most popular plays, including *Hamlet*, *Othello*, *Lear*, *Macbeth*, and *Pericles*, during these years, besides keeping up its running favourites, *Romeo and Juliet* and the Falstaff plays. When James succeeded Elizabeth in 1603 he lost little time making them the King's Men. From then on they were the most secure and successful company in the country. In 1608 the Blackfriars Boys surrendered their lease of the hall playhouse to them, and from 1609 onwards they played a uniquely domin-ant role in London entertainment. Through the summer they continued to play at the Globe. In winter, when the Court and the lawyers and gentry were in town, they used the Blackfriars. They were attached to the Globe—when it burned down in 1613 they rebuilt it at great expense—but gradually they came to be known as the Blackfriars company. That shift reflects the rising status of plays and play-going under the Stuarts. By the 1630s men as socially elevated as the courtiers Carew and Suckling were writing for it.

Once the King's Men had the Blackfriars, all the new theatres were built to imitate it. A former fellow of Shakespeare's, Christopher Beeston, opened the Cockpit in Drury Lane in 1616. Richard Gunnell built Salisbury Court south of Fleet Street at Whitefriars in 1629. Philip Henslowe did build a new amphitheatre on Bankside in 1614, but it was meant to double as a baiting arena, and soon reverted to that function exclusively. From 1616 the theatres in regular use were the indoor Blackfriars, the Cockpit, and Salisbury Court, and the open-air Globe, For-tune, and Red Bull.

At the Restoration, with the return of the Court from France, the only theatre to reopen was the old Cockpit. It had to be adapted to meet the French tradition of picture-frame staging, now showing in England for the first time. Its boxes at the sides of the stage and its rows of seats on the balcony behind were removed to make a proscenium-arch or picture-frame stage, with all the au-dience in front of the picture. This cut the seating capacity, so it was soon replaced by two new theatres offering better provision for the new kind of staging. Pictorial scenery, with sets made from flats sliding on grooves, was introduced. Women replaced boys to play women's parts. Where five companies had played in London through the 1630s now there were only two, and they catered largely for the wealthier end of the audience range. New theatres opened in towns outside London, imitating the new London repertories. Play-going was now fully segregated from the fairground and booth entertainment that had shared plays with the city in Tudor times.

3. *Companies and their Organization*

Playing companies have a very long history in England. Up to 1642 it was a story of consistent growth. Under Henry VIII groups of four or five players travelled for their living, performing at Court or other great houses, at inns, market-places and guild-halls, taking their pay where they could. Skelton's *Magnificence*, written for five players, first played to Skelton's patron at his house and then toured the country. When the Reformation made politics a hot topic John Bale ran a company of eight men and boys touring his plays as religious and nationalistic propaganda. That heat soon brought government regulation to control and restrict playing. From the middle of the sixteenth century state censorship worked more and more rigorously to oversee every kind of published word, written or spoken. Not long after the Company of Stationers began to regulate what could appear in print, the Lord Chamberlain was assigned control of travelling entertain-ers. Progressively statute law required players to serve on licence under the authority of patrons of higher and higher rank. Under Henry VIII the patron might be as lowly-ranked as an esquire

Charitie.

youth.

A N illustration from the manuscript *An Interlude of Youth*, a play of the mid-sixteenth century, performed by one of the professional travelling companies. It shows youth in one of its manifestations as soldier. The figure on the left is an archer, that on the right a halberdier.

or a pair of Justices of the Peace. By the 1570s only barons and earls were allowed to be patrons. Fewer companies meant easier control. The Queen became a patron in 1583. In 1594 the only companies allowed to play in London were those of the Lord Chamberlain and his son-in-law the Lord Admiral. In 1603 the patrons of the only companies given access to London became the King, Prince Henry, and Queen Anne.

While fewer companies were easier to keep in order, their smaller numbers also helped raise standards, since the chosen few, being more secure, could increase their quality and the number of players as their income grew. They also grew in status at Court. The Master of the Revels, with his limited budget and the desultory payments and no allowance for inflation characteristic of Elizabethan bureaucracy, soon gave up the elaborate masques that till then had dominated the Court's festivities when he found that the outlay involved in hiring a company of players to bring their plays to Court cost the Revels Office only one-fourth the expense of setting up a masque. This promoted the best companies, and strengthened their position in London. It was their cheapness as well as their quality that first guaranteed royal support for the playing companies.

The companies that managed to play regularly in London kept the tight team organization that the travelling troupes had evolved, with additions to allow for the larger scale of urban work. The number in a group grew from Skelton's five to eight or so in the 1540s and ten or twelve, plus a dozen or more hired men by the end of the century. The eight who started Shakespeare's company in 1594 were 'sharers', taking equal parts of the profit and the expenditure that determined the company's fortunes. The shares themselves were the company's nominal capital. A player joining the best companies had to contribute as much as £100 for his share, one-eighth the cost of building the Rose in 1587. He could sell the share when he left. This system gave each sharer a vested interest in maintaining the company's quality and reputation. The Henslowe papers, records of the operation of the Rose playhouse and its successor the Fortune from 1592 until the 1620s, show that fines were imposed on players for missing a performance, turning up drunk or late, or for wearing the company's costumes outside the playhouse. Play-books and costumes were a company's chief resources.

One transformation that happened to the best companies came about as a consequence of basing themselves in the one playhouse for a season. Each year they could travel the country with no more than two or three plays in their repertoire, confident that nobody from any one town or great house the company visited would turn up to see them again. In London the opposite was the case. Because play-goers came regularly and wanted novelty, Henslowe's records show the companies at the Rose performing on six afternoons each week and offering a different play each day, more than thirty-five different plays in a full year. Some plays never got more than a single performance. Even the most popular never appeared more than five or six times a year.

Since the same eight sharers acted in every play, they needed good memories. A leading part might have up to eight hundred lines and twenty entrances, to be learned for that one afternoon's performance, with a completely new part for the next day. Travelling, for all its pains and strains, was a holiday by comparison. The demands that the London repertory system laid on the players are a striking testimony to their talents.

Such demands also guaranteed a constant process of change. These show most strongly in the plays that were written for this high-speed repertory system. The companies themselves, once they were firmly established in London after 1594, had a stable membership. As experienced troupers they evolved sophisticated means to control what they did. Highly trained as teams, working together in a home environment, their audiences probably as familiar to the players as the theatres they worked in, they shared their work more precisely than did the handicraft apprentices who made up most of the nut-cracking 'understanders' at their plays. Acting was itself a business with a long apprenticeship. Companies paid lip-service to the Statute of Retainers of 1563 which laid it down that any youth not apprenticed was a vagabond. Four or five of the leading sharers would each claim as an apprentice the boys in the company who played the women's parts. All of Shakespeare's plays could be performed, with doubling, by ten or eleven men and four boys. Only when resources permitted did the numbers grow. *Titus Andronicus*, like several plays of the early 1590s, calls for twenty-six players in its opening scene. That number marks the high tide of ambition and resource rising from the five that Skelton needed to stage *Magnificence*

A DRAWING which may have been made as early as 1595, the only surviving picture of the time showing the staging of a Shakespeare play. It illustrates characters from *Titus Andronicus*, a play set in Rome even though the attendant soldiers are dressed in Elizabethan garb, holding halberds.

in 1519. In fact the tide receded soon after 1594, to a norm of the fifteen who staged *Julius Caesar* at the Globe in 1599. The post-Restoration companies were never strong enough to match that scale of operation. Scenic staging was costly, and inhibited both the large troupes of players and the rapid changes of repertoire that had been standard in the 1590s. In the 1630s the variety available from the five companies made it possible to change the long-standing pattern of staging a different play each day into the easier pattern of longish runs of a single play. This new pattern restarted in the Restoration, and has continued with little variation down to the present.

The main changes in organization came about through government control. The statute that government used to control players was the 'Acte for the punishment of Vacabondes' of 1572. It specified that, without the right to wear the livery of a great man as patron, players were vagabonds. In May 1574 the Earl of Leicester secured a royal patent authorizing his company to play throughout the country. Subsequent companies carried similar patents with them on their travels, ready to show the mayor of each town they came to as their licence to play and their right to wear their patron's livery. It was one of the government's more effective forms of regulation. Only one town is on record as questioning the authority of a playing patent (Norwich in 1616: it turned out to be a forgery). A further tightening of this system of regulation came in 1598, when the Lord Chamberlain confirmed the rights of the duopoly established in 1594 by confining the power to be patron of a company to men of his own and his brother-in-law's status.

This narrowing of the right to run a playing company might be expected to concentrate the great actors into fewer and fewer companies, and, given the new security they enjoyed in their London theatres, to deprive the country towns and great halls of their former circuit of entertainment. This of course did not happen. Plague continued to close the London playhouses for long periods, and the long tradition which took the London companies on summer tours along a set route continued till the close-down in 1642, and was renewed in 1660.

4. *Play-goers and What they Went to Hear*

Up to the Restoration play-going was open to the whole of London society. Women thronged plays almost as much as men, although since respectable women would not walk abroad unless accompanied by a male, usually a boy or page, it can be assumed that women can never have made up more than half of any audience. Literacy was not a necessary qualification for seeing and hearing plays. In a society where literacy was relatively rare—rare enough to be a means of escaping the charge of murder, as Ben Jonson found—plays were a potent attraction at all levels of society. They were shows for the eye and the ear, in communities used to standing to hear preachers and public orators.

What has survived down to the present from this first theatrical flood in England is only the smallest tip of the iceberg of creativity it generated. The surviving written texts or play-scripts are probably fewer than one-sixth of the plays performed even on the London stages, and only the tiniest fraction of the more visual forms of entertainment. Fewer than half of Shakespeare's plays, the flag on the tip, appeared in print in his lifetime. He wrote scripts for performance, not for the reader. The other half of his work would have been lost if his fellow-players had not organized a posthumous collection of all the plays as a memorial to him, the famous First Folio of thirty-six plays issued seven years after his death, in 1623. Even that would not have happened

THE 'witches' who accosted Macbeth and Banquo, who are shown on horseback. This illustration was made for the first edition of Holinshed's *Chronicle of Scotland*, published in 1577. Shakespeare took the story for his play from the second edition published in 1587.

had not Jonson, a more pretentious writer, already prepared the way with a folio edition of his own plays. Thomas Heywood, the playwright whose career most closely matched Shakespeare's as a player and playwright, said late in his life that during his career of writing for the playing companies he had put 'a main hand, or at least a finger' into the writing of two hundred and twenty plays. Less than a dozen of these survive.

More than eight hundred play-texts from the period 1485–1688 have survived. Very few survive from before the 1560s, and most of the plays from after 1660. In the middle period, plays crept into print either because they were popular and therefore a saleable commodity, or because the author wished his work to be put on record. That happened much more often under the early Stuarts, as the quality of the written play-scripts rose to the point where, by about 1616, it was accounted creditable to have written them. Shakespeare's name did not appear on the title-pages of his plays for the first five years that they were appearing in print. Authors were only given credit once the public began to esteem plays as reading texts. Charles I was a keen reader of plays and from 1625 plays finally became respectable 'literature'. Post-Restoration plays, being written for a wealthier clientele, survive in much greater numbers than those from the Shakespearian era.

It was the last decade of the sixteenth century in which the real quality of the new profession emerged. That was the decade when play-going was an activity more truly shared across the whole society than ever before or after. In the 1590s only the common amphitheatres were open for playing, and Shakespeare's company's attempt to open a hall theatre was blocked. It was the time when, as Sir John Davies wrote in 1593, at plays 'A thousand townesmen, gentlemen, and whores, | Porters and serving-men together throng'. Before that, the educated élite like Sir Philip Sidney kept themselves aloof from common playing. After it, the hall theatres offered superior conditions at a distance from the amphitheatres. It was the first decade to produce plays that could 'please all', as a contemporary said of *Hamlet*. It was Shakespeare's decade. That unique figure did much to transform the drama of his time, and in the process he has shaped our own vision of it.

The multitude of forms of entertainment now available and the extra leisure time that modern working conditions give us to enjoy them, make it difficult to assess the phenomenon of playgoing as it grew in these two centuries. There were many choices: between country festivals and city shows, between free entertainment and what had to be paid for, between bull and bear-baiting arenas and the theatre, between standing in an amphitheatre yard for more than two hours and sitting in a roofed hall, between *Romeo and Juliet* and *Fair Em the Miller's Daughter of Manches-*

A DRAWING by Inigo Jones of the set for the second scene of Ben Jonson's *Masque of Oberon*, prepared for the court in 1610. It was a perspective set, to be viewed from in front, of a kind introduced by Jones to England in 1605 but never used on the public stages till 1660.

NATHAN FIELD as a romantic lover. He was the leading boy actor in the Children of the Chapel company which played at the Blackfriars between 1599 and 1608. As a twenty-two-year-old he played for a company patronized by the Lady Elizabeth, James's daughter, until 1616, when, possibly at Shakespeare's death, he joined the King's Men.

ter, with the Love of William the Conqueror, and most basically of all, between spending two hours in church standing to listen to a sermon and three hours standing in a playhouse. Davies has another poem in which he suggests the chief alternative for the idle man about town. His usual habit was to see a play every afternoon, 'Save that sometimes he comes not to the play, | But falls into a whorehouse by the way'. In Davies's time the theatre drew by far the largest crowds. Amongst the leisured classes in London, idle gallants, young lawyers, off-duty soldiers and seamen, sarcastically called 'afternoon's men' or drunkards because of the times it was usual to attend plays or other sports such as bear-baiting or going to brothels, play-going was standard. It provided food for thought as well as lechery. More than that, in the absence of any kind of journal or other means of propagating news, theatres ranked along with the walks at St Paul's as the best places for hearing the latest gossip, whether from other spectators or from the stage. Not infrequently the plays themselves were comments on the news and the issues of the day.

The book-plate of Simon Scroope of Danby, Yorkshire, 1698. Intended to be pasted inside the front cover of the books in his library, Simon Scroope's book-plate was turned into an occasion for celebrating in heraldry the distinction of his family's ancestry. The point is laboured by the provision of a key, listing the names of the aristocratic families represented on the shield (including seven barons, a clutch of earls, and an early-medieval Irish king).

9 THE ARISTOCRACY AND THEIR MENTAL WORLD

JOHN ADAMSON

1. *Introduction*

In 1698, when Simon Scroope devised a new book-plate for his library at Danby Hall, he could not resist the temptation to boast. Recently come into his inheritance, the young Yorkshire squire turned this conventional label of ownership into an ostentatious display of his lineage and aristocratic connections. The elaborate armorials self-consciously evoked an archaic knightly world in which military prowess was the sign of true 'nobility'. And yet beyond this harmless boastfulness, it was also a gesture heavily fraught with irony. Heraldic symbolism which had once served a practical purpose, enabling armour-clad knights to identify themselves in battle, has here become the means for a comfortable country squire to identify his books. The image neatly encapsulates a theme which runs throughout this chapter: the often uneasy relationship in sixteenth- and seventeenth-century England between lineage and learning, between military service and the civil magistracy, the arts of war and of peace, in the definition of the qualities appropriate to a gentleman.

What concerns us here is the attitudes and sense of identity of the political and social élite—those whom Sir Thomas Smith, in his famous anatomy of the English commonwealth in the 1560s, compendiously defined as 'gentlemen', meaning the titular nobility, knights, esquires, and 'mere gentlemen' who constituted the governing cadre of early modern England. (Throughout this chapter the terms 'aristocracy' and 'aristocratic' are used as a convenient shorthand to designate this group.) It was this powerful minority, no more than 5 per cent of the population, which owned between 50 and 70 per cent of the land, and through their dominant role in political, cultural, and economic life affected, to a greater or lesser degree, the lives of almost all their contemporaries.

2. *Status, Hierarchy, and Rank*

At the heart of the élite's view of the world was the concept of hierarchy, a beneficently ordered series of gradations of rank ascending from the poorest vagrant to the grandest prince. It was at

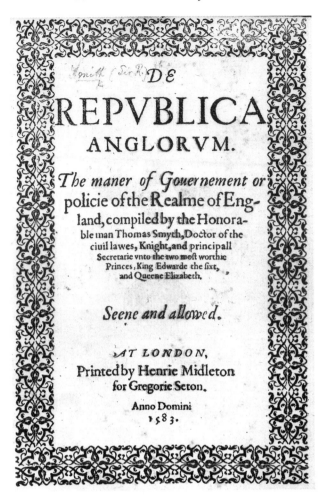

THE title-page of Sir Thomas Smith's *De Republica Anglorum*, written in the 1560s and first published in 1583, one of the earliest attempts to anatomize systematically the social structure of Tudor England.

the summit of the hierarchy, in the world of 'gentlemen', that the graduations between ranks were most carefully delineated. Its most rarefied plane was that of the titular nobility, little more than fifty families in 1600, and still well under 200 in 1700 (graduated downwards from dukes and marquesses, to earls, viscounts, and barons). Below the ranks of the nobility came knights (and, from 1611, baronets, or hereditary knights), esquires (those entitled to bear coats of arms), and so down the scale to 'mere gentlemen'—where the boundary between the world of the élite blurred with the parish élites of prosperous yeomen and successful tenant farmers. In early modern England, belief in hierarchy was as axiomatic as belief in God. Indeed the two were complementary, for inequality of rank was not merely a chance fact of human existence; it was divinely ordained. Even in heaven, God had prescribed a fixed pecking order for the serried ranks of the angelic host.

Yet at the beginning of our period, this formulation of the social order as a single continuous scale of rank was itself in the process of definition. As late as 1480, William Caxton could still regard his world as being compounded of three harmonious and complementary 'estates'—a world compartmentalized into 'knights' who defended the commonwealth, 'clerks' (priests) who prayed for it, and the 'labourers' who toiled to provide the other two estates with bread. But by the 1530s that influential pundit, Sir Thomas Elyot, could speak of a commonwealth which was no longer compartmentalized, but stratified: a commonwealth composed of 'sundry estates and degrees of men'. By 1688 Gregory King's famous treatise on social rank listed twenty-six degrees—from the lowly world of the tinker to the giddy heights of dukes. From the perspective of the élite in early modern England, the concept of hierarchy was the basis of political stability, the corner-stone of their thinking about the social order.

The demise of the language of 'the three estates' and the development of this hierarchical view of the commonwealth had been sharply accelerated by the Reformation, and the drastic change in the social standing and wealth of the clergy it had brought in its wake. By the accession of Elizabeth in 1558, roughly a quarter of the land in England had been transferred from ecclesiastical to lay hands, and with it went a profound rethinking of the relations between the laity and the once powerful clerical estate. Even though the wealth and standing of the episcopate improved under the early Stuarts, only two bishops occupied high secular office during the seventeenth century, and lay grandees remained notoriously sensitive to signs of 'pretension' on the part of bumptious high ecclesiastics.

Few sights witnessed more dramatically to this eclipse of clerical power in the decades after the 1530s than the sight of fashionable Tudor country houses rising, quite literally, amid the monastic ruins. At Leez, near Colchester, the magnificent crenellated house built for the Rich family (later Lords Rich and Earls of Warwick), the principal lodgings rose on the foundations of the monastic cloister. At Appleton House, the Fairfaxes' Yorkshire seat, the sight of the former nunnery was a perennial reminder of the material blessings of the Reformation. There, wrote Marvell in the 1650s,

> all that neighbour-ruin shows
> The quarries whence this dwelling rose.

Ecclesiastics who sought to turn back the clock and restore something of the clergy's pre-Reformation status and wealth were apt to find themselves subject to the charge of 'prelacy' or 'popery' for that fact alone, as Archbishop Laud was to find to his cost during the 1630s.

Despite the nicely defined gradations within this aristocratic club, there was nevertheless amongst its members a powerful sense of common interest and collective identity: they were 'men of rank', 'persons of honour'—usually defined in contradistinction to the vast anonymous mass of their social inferiors, the 'meaner sort' or the 'poorer sort'. For the nobility and gentry, theirs was an essentially binary view of the world. Beyond the charmed circle of the 'better sort', the custodians of order, lay the 'many-headed multitude', the forces of disorder which had to be kept in check by the stern dictates of the law. The chaplain to the Capel household in the 1620s expressed a commonplace view when he wrote of the 'common people' as 'unthankful, wayward, cruelly envious and impudent; because they are compounded of a rabble of fools, of knaves, of castaways, and desperate fellows'. 'God deliver persons of honour and gentlemen out of the mercy of clouted shoes', was the prayer of Richard Dowdeswell, the well-shod steward of the second Earl of Middlesex during the 1640s, who saw hierarchy threatened by the 'meaner sort' (those in hobnailed, 'clouted', shoes) during the turmoil of the Civil War. It was a view which had been powerfully reinforced both by the Classical stereotype of the *plebs* as the *ignobile vulgus*—the fickle, vulgar herd, familiar from Vergil, Cicero, and Seneca—and also by the essentially pessimistic message of Calvinist anthropology, that post-lapsarian man was by nature unregenerate, brutish, and lawless. This binary view of the world, divided between 'gentlemen and persons of honour' and the mass of the 'common people', extended even to the forms of recreation which men of rank deemed appropriate to themselves—and themselves alone. Pointing out to a Chester jury in the 1620s the presumption of those among the 'inferior sort' who tried their hands at such gentlemanly sports as hawking and hunting, Sir Richard Grosvenor urged that such men be punished vigorously as 'enemies to the sports and pleasures of gentlemen, to whom the law allows such recreations as are not fit for persons of a meaner condition'. It was a view that would have been endorsed as heartily by Henry VIII as by the authors of the game laws in the eighteenth century. That these satin-suited gentlemen were hunting the stag was every much an intimation of their rank as was the expensiveness of their apparel. Similarly, the mastery of the horse—essential to success in the hunt, or in that far more specialized form of aristocratic recreation, the tournament—was itself widely regarded as a metaphor for the skills requisite in government: the capacity to 'bridle' and 'harness' the power of the brute beast, to control and subdue the passions. Lifestyle was an expression of status, sport a buttress of hierarchy and a training in the exercise of power.

3. *Lineage, Virtue, and Gentility*

What was it, then, that conferred status within the ranks of 'gentlemen and persons of honour'? Most were agreed that it was the quality of 'nobility', but were anything but unanimous when it came to defining what true nobility was. Lineage, declared some, was what counted: a man might better himself by serving as a knight in war, by acquiring wealth or office, and maintaining the lifestyle of a gentleman; but several generations were required before a family acquired full 'gentility of blood'. In this context, the elaborately quartered shields of arms that festooned houses, tombs, and portraits—and Simon Scroope's book-plate—could be read as precise visual claims as to how far this process of 'ennoblement of blood' had progressed.

From the beginning of the Tudor period, however, attempts to define 'nobility' rigidly in terms of lineage and knightly service were being compromised by subtler values and nimbler minds. Influenced by such Italian handbooks of courtly manners as Castiglione's *Book of the Courtier* (first published in English translation in 1561), Tudor humanists complicated the repertory of qualities appropriate to gentility by arguing that criteria of learning, manners, and deportment were no less conferrers of 'virtue' than lineage or nobility of blood. Increasingly, 'virtue' came to be de-

ELIZABETHAN bureaucrat as medieval knight: the tomb of William Cecil, first Lord Burghley, *c.*1590, in St Martin's Church, Stamford. The style of the funeral effigy is a deliberate throwback to that of medieval tombs, stressing knightly achievements and prowess in arms as the basis for true nobility.

GENTLEMANLY recreation: stag hunting at Nonsuch, Surrey (*facing, below*), in the 1620s, a detail of *A View of Nonsuch from the North West*, by an unknown artist, *c.*1620.

fined in terms of the moral qualities and practical skills which fitted a man for the exercise of government. As Archbishop Cranmer famously argued when involved in the refounding of that 'seminary for gentlemen', the King's School, Canterbury, in 1540, it was 'through the benefit of learning and other civil knowledge, for that most part, [that] all gentle[men] ascend to their estate'. 'Civil discipline', argued Henry Peacham in his *The Compleat Gentleman* (1622)—meaning learning in the arts of government, as much as manners and demeanour—was no less an attribute of nobility than prowess in arms.

Yet for all the undoubted merits of 'civil learning', it was apparent that old ideas died hard. Even where men rose into the ranks of the upper gentry or the peerage through their pen-pushing skills in the service of the regime, it was conspicuous that these 'new men' went out of their way to affect the manners, and espouse the values, of families which had attained their social position through their 'ancient lineage' and their 'heroic ancestors'. Chivalric culture, too, went through intermittent revivals—in the 1520s, 1560s–1610s, and again during the 1630s and 1640s—in which medieval ideas of knightly virtue were adapted and reinterpreted in the light of the political and cultural priorities of the day. And although advances in military technology had been rendering the figure of the landowner-turned-knight largely redundant, the sentimental allure and emotive power of this knightly image remained strong, well into the seventeenth century. William Cecil, that Elizabethan bureaucrat *par excellence*, still affected the pose of a medieval knight in full armour for his tomb effigy in the 1590s. And even in the 1640s, many of the élite still adhered to the belief that the natural concomitant of aristocratic status was the profession of arms.

For all the ambiguities about the qualities, or combination of qualities, which conferred gentle status, there was one object, however, which witnessed unequivocally to a family's aristocratic rank: its house, the visible symbol of its position of authority within the locality, of its dynastic continuity, and its wealth.

4. *The 'Show of the House': Architecture and Identity*

In the country, observed one foreign visitor of the scale and magnificence of life in the houses of the English élite, they are 'like little kings'. Anyone approaching such ducal piles as Badminton or Chatsworth at the end of the seventeenth century could well be forgiven for mistaking them for royal residences. And if not every squire could keep up the state of a county grandee, there were still many whose houses proclaimed them to be at least the princelings of the parishes.

These houses were the kingdom's subsidiary courts. Great residences like Lacock Abbey, Wiltshire (1540), Hatfield House, Hertfordshire (1612), or Staunton Harold, Leicestershire, fulfilled a political function in the microcosm of the locality no less important than Whitehall and Westminster in the macrocosm of the realm. 'The country model', observed Roger North in the 1690s, '. . . partakes of the nature of a court, as a lord of a manor doth of regality, and should, like the court, have great rooms to contain numbers.' For it was here, in their public rooms—their halls and great chambers, their state rooms and 'rooms of parade'—that politics were discussed, local disputes adjudicated (either informally or on reference from the central courts), and visitors were entertained as befitted their rank. As Sir Henry Wotton described it in his *Elements of Architecture* (1624),

Every man's proper mansion house and home [was] the theatre of his hospitality, the seat of self-fruition, the comfortablest part of his own life, the noblest of his son's inheritance, a kind of private princedom, nay, to the possessors thereof, an epitome of the whole world.

Hospitality was demanded by the obligations of 'honour' and 'reputation', the currency of public esteem which was at the heart of the moral economy of early modern England. 'Good housekeeping [i.e. hospitality] is a thing in all gentlemen required', declared the *Institucion of a Gentleman* in the 1550s; and although seventeenth-century practice tended to relegate non-gentle ranks to charity disbursed at the gate, and reserve entertainment within the house to those of gentle rank, the dispensing of hospitality was as axiomatic to the aristocratic view of the world as the quality of a gentleman's clothes or his entitlement to a coat of arms. For the greater nobility, conspicuously expensive hospitality provided the occasion for the display of magnificence, the justification of their dominance in the social hierarchy; for gentlemen of more modest means, 'liberality' was one of the obligations of honour upon which 'reputation' depended.

The quest for 'reputation' was no less the concern of the architecture of a gentleman's house. Like his clothing, his architectural cladding was designed to impress. The façade of his house

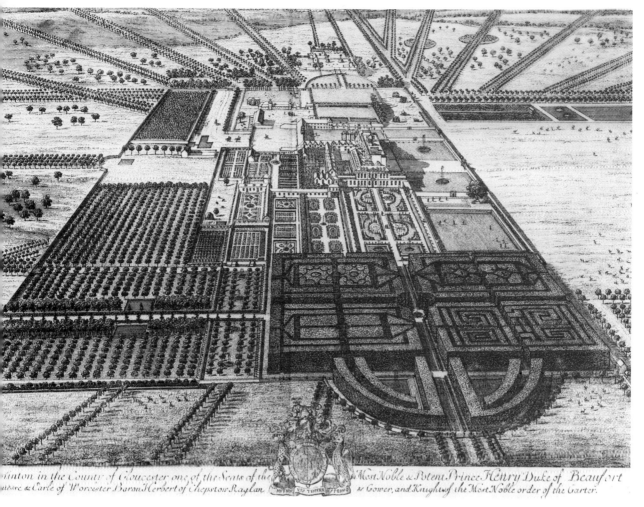

BADMINTON, Gloucestershire, here shown as it looked in 1699, is one of the most spectacular examples of the seventeenth-century aristocratic country house. Acquired by the fourth Earl of Worcester in 1608, it was substantially rebuilt and extended between the 1670s and 1690s by the Earl's descendant, the first Duke of Beaufort. Its gardens —with their extensive parterres, gigantic box garden (designed to dwarf the spectator), and alleys of trees converging on the great house—were on a scale which vied with those of the King.

(architecturally, its most important feature) was designed to arouse in equals admiration, and in inferiors a proper sense of awe. Whether it was the towering early sixteenth-century brick gate-houses as at Layer Marney in the 1520s, the elaborate frontispieces that rose over the principal entrances to so many Elizabethan and Jacobean houses of state, or the newfangled Classical porticoes that first began to appear in the 1650s, each had a common purpose: to impress from afar, and to define and dramatize the moment of entry into the ordered and elevated world of the great house. The language of the theatrical 'show' was never far from the preoccupations of builders and their patrons.

In the houses of the greater nobility, the 'show' of the façade gave entry to a world in which the life of the household was choreographed with equal theatricality. In the 1630s that upwardly

mobile lawyer, Bulstrode Whitelocke, was agog at the splendour he encountered when invited to Belvoir Castle by the seventh Earl of Rutland: 'the house with all its accommodations is a prince-like palace', and 'the state and ceremonies used by this great lord in his house, his servants, [and] hospitality, . . . fully answerable to his quality, and scarce exceeded by any subject'. Household ordinances stipulated the ceremony which was to be observed by the servants and officers of the household in the 'keeping of state'. As in a baroque church, it was the canopy (or *baldacchino*) which defined the hierachical centre of the building, usually the 'great chamber': 'that place is the chiefest and principallest state in the house', as Lord Keeper Ellesmere's household ordinances of *c*.1610 affirmed. If a peer or great officer of state dined in the great chamber ('he being an earl or upwards'), he was to have 'a cloth of estate' befitting his rank (a hanging, usually embroidered with a coat of arms, varying in length according to rank), suspended beneath the canopy. When cupbearers were required, they were to serve the lord and lady 'with taking of steps on their knee in humble and dutiful sort'. Perhaps only after the Laudian ecclesiastical innovations of the 1630s did the communion tables of the Church of England begin to approach the liturgical complexity which attended the table of a great peer when dining in state. Such was the degree of elaboration alleged to have been demanded in the household of the Earl of Essex during the 1640s ('whose servants daily offered up with bare heads and bended knees . . . doing obeisance to that idol') that one contemporary was moved to satirize it as little short of blasphemous: 'O gross foppery, and a thousand times worse than Popery!' Such ceremony was indeed invested with quasi-religious connotations, for it articulated, in language of gesture and deportment, the sacredness of hierarchy and the divinely sanctioned 'discrepancy of degrees . . . whereof proceedeth order'. While such ceremonious domestic arrangements were of course unique to the houscholds of the greater nobility, the principle that commensality provided the occasion for the entertainment of friends and neighbours in a manner appropriate to the affluence of the host and to the social standing of the guest was one honoured as much by the modest country squire, with his one or two servants, as it was in glittering interiors of Belvoir or Blenheim.

Yet beyond these public functions, the 'mansion house and home' possessed for those who occupied it a powerful significance as the symbol of dynastic continuity, the emblem of the association between name and place which gave fixity to the sequence of generations. This conjunction of family name with the house where it was seated was manifest in countless forms: in the endless bonds, deeds, and marriage settlements which recorded 'John Smith of Nibley', 'Richard Knightley of Preston Capes', or 'Sir Henry Slingsby of Scriven', and their like; and in the duality of meaning which attached to the word 'house' itself, designating both 'a family' as a dynastic succession (as in 'the house of Howard'), *and* a place of residence. (Indeed in the seventeenth century it was a common conceit that a house 'expressed' the essence of the family that lived in it—a convergence repeatedly eulogized in the literary genre to which it gave rise, the country house poem.)

The premium placed by English gentlemen on the association between the antiquity of a

CLASSICISM superimposed upon a Tudor country house: the portico of The Vyne, Hants (*facing*), erected in 1655 by the mason, Edward Carter, to designs by Inigo Jones's pupil and collaborator, John Webb. It was the first free-standing Classical portico added to any English country house, and gives the lie to the belief that the Cromwellian Protectorate was a period of cultural stagnation which saw a reaction against a Classical 'Court' style.

family seat and the antiquity (and hence the illustriousness) of its lineage had implications for its architecture and made, if not for stylistic conservatism, then at least for a vigorous interest in architectural gestures which alluded back to early Tudor or even more antiquated styles. The chequered history of 'innovatory' Classical architecture in England serves as a case in point. It was not, as often simplistically argued, that the Renaissance came late to England; for as witnessed at Somerset House, Westminster (1547), or Kirby Hall, Northamptonshire (1572), English architects already had a sophisticated, if idiomatic, understanding of advanced Classical architectural fashion. What is striking is that this mid-sixteenth-century vogue for Classicism lost momentum in the first two decades of Elizabeth's reign, to be replaced by a style more inspired by mid-fifteenth-century Perpendicular Gothic—as demonstrated by Burghley House, Northamptonshire, built in the 1560s for Sir William Cecil, and by Wardour Castle, remodelled in the 1570s for Sir William Arundell. A fashion for Gothic, castellated effects remained strong well into the seventeenth century.

Some went one better, and actually bought an ancient castle—usually the seat of some illustrious but long extinct dynasty—hoping thereby to invest their own names and titles with the glamour of historical association attaching to the place. In 1604 that successful Elizabethan office-holder, Sir Fulke Greville (1554–1628), had acquired the vast and largely ruinated fortress of Warwick Castle, former seat of Warwick the Kingmaker. There he set about spending upwards of £20,000 on building and restoration—more than the cost of building a substantial new country house—and affecting the style of an ancient grandee. But perhaps the most conspicuous example of such newly promoted men investing in old renown was Sir Henry Montagu (*c*.1563–1642), the younger son of a Northamptonshire gentry family, who had risen spectacularly under James I and Charles I from humble barrister to an earldom and a seat on the Privy Council. When he wanted to purchase an estate and set himself up as a county grandee, he did not look for a fashionably 'modern' house, but set his sights on a grand medieval fortress, Kimbolton Castle, Huntingdonshire, and, still more, on the illustrious name of its former occupants, the Mandevilles, medieval Earls of Oxford. In due course, when raised to the peerage in 1620, Montagu took the style 'Viscount Mandeville'—in the words of one contemporary satirist, thereby

> Adding the honour, as he rolled down hill,
> Of Viscount to the name of Mandeville,
> Which crowned his cadency with empty fame,
> And brought him nothing to support the same.

In the scale of the expenditure (and, in the case of Warwick Castle, of new building) which was required, these recently acquired and newly restored medieval fortresses are arguably no less characteristic of the architectural preferences of the élite in Tudor and Stuart England than such newly built houses as Longleat, Hatfield, or Audley End.

'THE chiefest and principallest state in the house': Sir Thomas More and his family in their great chamber (*facing, above*), with More's rich canopy of state, hung with gold silk and embroidered with his own and his wife's shields of arms. Rowland Lockey's copy (1593) of a lost painting by Hans Holbein.

PHILIP FRUYTIERS (after Sir Anthony Van Dyck), *The Family of the Earl of Arundel*, ?1643 (*facing, below*): the Earl and Countess sit 'enthroned' in their coronation robes. Despite the playful children, the striking feature of the composition is how closely it resembles a royal portrait.

Yet the concerns which led contemporaries to set such store by this repertory of retrospective allusion were informed by a wider series of influences than merely the veneration of antiquity and the possession of lineage (real and invented). Looking from the windows of these 'private courts', what were the points of reference by which members of the nobility and gentry fixed their bearings in the world? Four themes serve to illuminate something of the axioms by which they sought to give order and coherence to their experience, and to guide the conduct of their lives: those three corner-stones of 'civil learning' (namely, history, the classics, and rhetoric), and a fourth, apt to appear rather more curious to modern eyes: that no less dispensable means by which educated contemporaries sought to understand the influence of the cosmos on their own world, astrology.

5. *Rhetorics and Axioms*

As befitted a caste that went to such lengths to stress the linkages between the present and the past, history was regarded as the principal tutor of public life. Richard Grenewey, the translator of Tacitus, was expressing a commonplace when he suggested in the 1590s that 'History [is] the treasure of times past, as well as a guide an image of man's present estate; a true and lively pattern of things to come, [and], as some term it, the work-mistress of experience, which is the mother of prudence'. The Restoration jurist Sir Matthew Hale reflected a view that had been current at least since the advent of the Tudors when he put 'histories' at the top of his list of the 'studies of humane learning' which fitted a man for public life. But the place of history in the thinking of the élite extended beyond this didactic function. From Sir Thomas More's *Richard III* (first printed in complete English translation in 1557), if not earlier, the writing of history could provide the occasion for a sophisticated discussion of the nature of politics and rule, and accounts of the past could be made to encode reflections on present-day political concerns. The furore caused in the 1590s by Sir John Hayward's *Life of Henry IV* (in which parallels were allegedly drawn between Elizabeth's minister, Cecil, and the 'evil counsellors' of Richard II), or James I's decision to suppress the Society of Antiquaries, testified to the sensitivity of governments to the contemporary political import of historical research.

A parallel and virtually interchangeable repertory of quotation and allusion was provided by the world of classical literature and history. References to Latin (or less frequently Greek) authors were not merely an exercise in scholarly window-dressing, but a means of setting up resonances and associations which could be used to flatter, to criticize, or to suggest implications in a statement which the speaker preferred not to have directly spelt out. Latin verse provided not only the model for English lyrics, but also, more diffusely, a corpus of literary culture within which readers were expected to recognize classical cross-references and allusions. (Part of the pleasure of reading a poem such as Marvell's *Horatian Ode*, for example, lay in identifying how the resonances set up by the work's complex allusiveness affected its tone and mood.) Likewise, classical heroes and villains served as immediately recognizable archetypes for praise or blame: Tacitus' and Seneca's accounts of Tiberius' sadistic henchman, Sejanus, provided a stock-in-trade for encoding criticism of unpopular royal favourites; beneficent emperors such as Hadrian or Marcus Aurelius could be cited to represent monarchical authority in a flattering and glamorous light. What made these modes of reference effective was that, at least from the mid-sixteenth century, the literature to which they alluded formed part of the common culture of almost all educated members of the élite. Learning was perhaps more prized by the nobility and gentry during the sixteenth and seventeenth centuries than at any period before or since. And if not every gentleman matched the heroic studiousness of Sir John Newdigate—who between 1597 and 1610 scheduled no less than eight hours a day to his scholarly pursuits—some familiarity with classical learning was part of the intellectual baggage of all but the dimmest and most rustic squire.

Learning, however, was not enough. To be effectively and persuasively deployed, it had to be married with 'rhetoric': the mastery of language as a means to action; the skills of speech and writing by which to persuade, edify, and instruct. As Lord Herbert of Cherbury argued in the 1640s, it was not 'sufficient for a man to have a great understanding in all matters unless [that]

understanding be . . . well underset and illustrated with those figures, tropes, and colours which Rhetoric affords'. Given that the Renaissance view of gentility stressed the civil, magisterial role of the élite as much as (and from the seventeenth century, often more than) its military function, skill in rhetoric was essential if a man was to take his proper place in the public life of the realm. On the various stages of civic life—in Parliament, at the quarter sessions, in adjudicating disputes as a Justice of the Peace— the dexterous command of language was itself an instrument of government.

Such attitudes have an obvious coherence and rationality. Yet no less coherent and rational in the eyes of contemporaries was a range of beliefs and assumptions which, from a modern perspective, are likely to appear at best irrational, at worst crassly superstitious: beliefs in witchcraft, in ghosts and fairies, in the capacity of an

HISTORY as the tutor of politics: the frontispiece to one of the most influential historical works of the seventeenth century, Sir Walter Raleigh's *History of the World* (1614), shows History (the central figure) as 'The Instructress of Life', flanked by four columns symbolizing History's attributes: (from left to right), 'The Witness of the Times', 'The Messenger of Times Past', 'The Illumination of Truth', and as that which gives 'Life to Remembrance'.

THE vogue for astrology: William Lilly, *The Starry Messenger* (1645), title-page. Astrological beliefs reached their apogee during the 1640s and 1650s, before being assailed first by scepticism, and later by derision during the final decades of the seventeenth century.

immanent evil to inhabit particular places and times. Although the strength of such beliefs waned markedly during the last quarter of the seventeenth century, for much of our period they occupied as prominent a place in the thinking of the élite as did any of their cogitations about law, politics, or history. The hardest-nosed politicians could continue to believe in such notions as 'climacteric years' (fore-ordained turning-points in a man's health or fortune, usually thought to be multiples of the number seven), or the conviction that disastrous consequences could flow from a solar eclipse. Even so tough-minded a figure as Elizabeth I's Lord Treasurer, Burghley, did not fail to mention the phenomenon of inauspicious days in his *Advice to his Son*, noting that he had 'observed some, and no mean clerks, very cautious to forebear . . . three Mondays in the year'—namely, the first Monday in April (believed to be the anniversary of the death of Abel), the second Monday in August (the destruction of Sodom and Gomorrah), and the last Monday in December (the birthday of Judas Iscariot). But by far the most pervasive of all these beliefs within the élite (and also lower down the social scale) was astrology, a 'science' which gained currency from the middle of the sixteenth century, rising to a peak of popularity during the Civil War and Interregnum, before waning during the last quarter of the seventeenth century.

Like the belief that the study of history could provide understanding of contemporary events, the belief in astrology was founded upon a premiss which seemed no less plausible: that as the moon affected the tides, so the heavenly bodies had a direct effect on human affairs. By determining the effects which flowed from particular conjunctions of the heavenly bodies, it was possible for an expert with sufficient astronomical knowledge to calculate when those conjunctions would recur, and so predict their future influence. Nor did this necessarily conflict with belief in an omnipotent God; for as the most celebrated astrologer of the 1640s and 1650s, William Lilly, explained, 'the stars, by [God's] permission are instruments whereby many contingent events may be foreseen'. Far from being the quaint eccentricity they have since become, for much of the sixteenth and seventeenth centuries astrological beliefs were 'an essential aspect of the intellectual framework in which men were educated', and remained so at least until the Restoration.

But for all the astrologers' best endeavours, their skills in divination, their dabblings in dark and occult arts, that most important occasion in an individual's history was one they were powerless to predict: the time of death. Death and mortality had significance in early modern England not merely (or even primarily) because they were occasions of loss and grief, but because they provided the cue for a series of rituals and acts of commemoration in which members of the élite paraded their values and sense of identity before the world. For many backwoods gentlemen, there was no more glamorous moment in their lives than the hour of their leaving it. For this was an age when funeral ceremonial reached a peak of ostentation not equalled again until the Victorians, and when funerary monuments were erected on a scale not seen since the age of the long barrow. What did it mean, and what was the place of death in the mentality of the English élite?

6. *Mortality and Magnificence*

'If [the deceased] be of any great degree, or but stepped into the gentry', complained the godly Henry Barrow in the 1580s, 'then he hath accordingly his mourners—yea, his heralds peradventure—carrying his coat armour and streamers before him with solemn ado . . . as if Duke Hector, or Ajax, or Sir Launcelot were buried.' The ceremonies of an aristocratic funeral affirmed three essential elements in the value-system of the élite: honour, status, and familial continuity. Chivalric pomp obscured private grief in the welter of dynastic celebration. Originating in the distant world of 'the *comitatus*, and the war-band mourning its dead chieftain', by the mid-sixteenth century the emphasis had shifted to magnificence of display in which ceremony and decoration were contrived to proclaim both the illustriousness of the family's past and its continuity into the future. '[It] would make any man but a coward hug Death', one gentleman observed after a particularly impressive gentry funeral in the 1630s, 'to gain so stately an interment.'

What dominated these rituals were not sentiments of Christian consolation, but the symbolism of dynastic continuity. The climax of any such funeral was the 'offering', the moment of formal investiture of the heir. Here the chief mourner brought the deceased's helmet, crest, gauntlets, shield, and surcoat—those emblems of the link between gentle status and the knightly past—and presented them one by one to the heir, before placing them in turn upon the communion table. To emphasize the recipient's role as the continuator of the family's standing, he did not remain for the interment, but after the investiture departed immediately. The newly invested heir became the custodian of the family's 'name' and 'fame'.

Monuments fulfilled a similar function, and were regularly the occasion of extravagant expenditure well into the mid-seventeenth century. These, too, were intended to be mirrors of the social order, 'that by the tomb every one might be discerned of what rank he was living', as John Weever put it in 1631—though in practice during the early seventeenth century such tidy correspondences had been blurred by the ever-increasing size and elaboration of aristocratic tombs. In their various forms—as wall-mounted monuments, as altar-tombs, as life-sized effigies recumbent beneath masonry 'testers' (or canopies)—what is striking about such monuments is their preoccupation, not simply with a single individual, but with the whole network of dynastic relationships contracted by the family: the distinction of the lines into which they had married, the number of their progeny, the offices through which they had added lustre to the family's name. In this sense, the heads of the greater landed families possessed a dual identity comparable to that defined by the medieval doctrine of the 'king's two bodies'. One body was physical and transient, subject to death and decay; the other, 'the politic body', was abstract and continuous, represented by the family's name and renown. Maximilian Colt's monument to James I's Lord Treasurer, the first Earl of Salisbury (d. 1612), makes this point explicitly: the Earl's physical frame is reduced to a skeleton; but the 'body of his achievements', clearly attested by his Garter robes and his wand of office as a great officer of state, remains as a glorious reminder of the fame that sur-

vives him, and to which his family is collectively heir. Although physical corruption was rarely so starkly represented, effigies of aristocratic men and women, painted and gilded in their moment of worldly apotheosis, proliferated up and down the aisles and chancels of Tudor and early Stuart England. In parishes where the church doubled as the mausoleum of the nearby noble or gentry family, tenants and neighbours were weekly confronted by these secular advertisements of lineage, reputation, and local influence.

7. *Conclusion*

If the need to articulate rank and status was an abiding one for the nobility and gentry of early modern England, the forms in which they thought it appropriate to express such values altered over time in response to changes in social mores, the vagaries of economic fortune, and the caprices of fashion. Vast heraldic funerals had waned in popularity by the 1630s as contemporaries reacted against their cost, formality, and their inability to provide for the expression of private grief (they were now 'a fruitless vanity . . . altogether laid aside', reported John Weever in 1631). Similarly, the gargantuan public monuments of late Elizabethan and early Stuart families were rarely emulated by their post-Restoration successors, for whom expenditure on grandiose cenotaphs often seemed a less effective investment in 'reputation' than keeping up a fashionable London town house, maintaining a stable of pampered race horses, or Palladianizing the south front of their country seat. Moreover, from the 1620s, and still more so after the 1650s, connoisseurship of painting, sculpture, and architecture came to be regarded as more sophisticated forms of aristocratic magnificence than the orgies of conspicuous consumption that had attended those 'stately interments' of the Tudor élite.

Attitudes towards public hospitality followed a similar trajectory. Old ideas of 'open' hospitality yielded place to a more systematized analysis of the recipients of largess. The memorial tablet erected in the 1660s to the Countess of Bridgwater recorded what was by then a common segregation: 'the rich at her table daily tasted her hospitality, the poor at her gate her charity'. The openness of the early Tudor household gave way to increasingly private notions of who constituted the family; the tendency to view the world in terms of opposed 'better and meaner

Ragedragon. *Mr Dallender and Mr Laurence Staughton* *Esquires*

THE funeral procession of Jane (née Fitzalan), wife of the sixth Lord Lumley. Under the vigilant eye of the heralds, funeral ceremonial such as this was contrived to register gradations of social rank and the antiquity of the deceased's lineage: each 'quartering' on the banners represented the series of noble and gentry families to which the Lumleys and Fitzalans were related or from which they claimed descent. Compare the still more elaborate heraldic ceremonial which attended Elizabeth I's funeral cortège, reproduced opposite p. 225.

sorts' called into question the continued utility of an honour code which demanded purchasing the good opinion of the masses, since there was nothing to be gained in terms of reputation from 'the plaudits of the multitude'.

How many of these attitudinal changes may be attributed to, or were accelerated by, the buffetings of the Civil War and the traumas of Interregnum remains a matter for debate. Political turmoil was, however, clearly not their only cause. Advances in experimental science, in particular the discoveries of Boyle and Newton, left such explanatory systems as astrology open, first, to scepticism, and, later, to derision. While the President of the Royal Society, Lord Brounker, was still toying with horoscopes in the 1660s, by the late seventeenth century the profession of astrology was 'much despised and . . . slightly looked on'. And while the changes in élite attitudes and values after 1660 are easily exaggerated, there was nevertheless general agreement that the character of the Restoration world differed markedly from that which had preceded the conflagration of 1642—a difference which was manifest in a variety of spheres. The post-Civil War rhetoric of political and social discourse, for example, became distinctly more pragmatic and hard-edged. Or, to take another subtle barometer of social mores, the literature of parental advice to sons: from the mid-1650s, the old emphasis on munificence and honour had been supplanted by a 'cool and calculative tone', clearly distanced from the aristocratic values of the late sixteenth and early seventeenth centuries.

In the plastic arts, too, the lines between aesthetic styles became, from the 1650s if not earlier, far more precisely delineated: the eclecticism which had characterized English architecture up until the mid-seventeenth century—with its sophisticated combinations of, and periodic shifts between, Classical and Gothic idioms—had given way, by the end of the century, to the overwhelming dominance of the Classical style as defined by Jones, Webb, and Wren. And if this change may be regarded as one from broad inclusiveness to clear differentiation, it may also be regarded as mirroring a comparable change in the world of politics, where the pre-Civil War emphasis on preserving the appearance of élite unity gave way to the overt recognition of parties, and the open acknowledgement of factional divisions.

From the perspective of the younger generation—of men such as Simon Scroope of Danby Hall, taking stock on the eve of the eighteenth century—the values and attitudes of pre-Civil War England were beginning to appear as ancient and as quaintly remote as the displays of heraldic flummery that in battle had once identified medieval knights; and which still served, on coach doors and library book-plates, to make faint contact with that distant and antediluvian world.

10 THE COMMONS AND THEIR MENTAL WORLDS

JOHN WALTER

1. *Introduction*

In 1648 the Essex minister Ralph Josselin, grandson of a yeoman farmer, recorded in his diary over a passage of ten days the birth and death of his son Ralph. This moving account with all its hopes and fears would be familiar to parents today. However, after his son's death Josselin wrote:

As often times before so on this day did I especially desire of god to discover and hint to my soul, what is the aim of the god of heaven more especially in this correction of his upon me; and when I had seriously considered my heart and ways, and compared them with the affliction and sought unto my god; my thoughts often fixed on these particulars:
Whereas I have given my mind to unseasonable playing at chess, now it run in my thoughts in my illness as if I had been at chess, I shall be very sparing in the use of that recreation and that at more convenient seasons.

The example of a parent attributing the death of his son to his too great a fondness for playing chess is a vivid reminder of the otherness of the early modern mental world.

This chapter seeks to re-create the otherness of that mental world for those groups below the level of the gentry. The use of a language of 'sorts of people' to describe social groups below the landed class can be shown both to reflect contemporary usage and to denote distinct clusters of occupations and statuses within early modern English society. Merchants, traders, master craftsmen, and farmers were at the core of that group contemporaries labelled the 'middling sort'; smallholders, artisans in the less prosperous trades, cottagers, and labourers made up the bulk of those called the 'poorer sort'. But boundaries between the two groups were blurred and permeable. Labelling could not arrest the social mobility, both up and down, that characterized the society of this period, nor impose precise boundaries of inclusion and exclusion. At the same time, differences of wealth and status *within* these sorts could be pronounced. For example, though both might be held to belong to the middling sort, there was a significant difference between wealthy merchant and humble master craftsman. Moreover, at any one time there were also more subtle differences based either on space (urban/rural, highland/lowland) or place (generation/gender). However, over time, social change did make differences between these groups more pronounced. This had significant consequences for the values and beliefs they held.

At the beginning of our period both middling and poorer sorts inhabited a common mental world, many of whose beliefs were shared by their social superiors. By the eighteenth century this was no longer the case. Although there continued to be areas of common belief, they were fewer and even here attitudes to these common core beliefs had begun to diverge. The re-creation of these groups' mental world over a period of some two hundred years must do justice to this history, balancing common with contrasting beliefs, continuity with change.

2. *The Natural and Supernatural World*

For middling and poorer sort alike, it was their common membership of a Christian society that most deeply informed their world-view. A belief in God and the literalness of heaven and hell was at the centre of their mental world. It gave meaning both to their individual rites of passage from baptism to burial and to their collective destiny in a period where belief in the millennium—the coming of Christ to reign in person on earth—as an impending event was widespread. The religious changes charted elsewhere in this volume altered the nature of the relationship between the individual and God, but they did nothing to challenge the central truth that this was a Christian society which inhabited a world created by their God and whose purpose it served. Moreover, at the beginning of Tudor rule, low levels of literacy meant that the role of priest and pulpit was paramount in the dissemination of knowledge. This was a role that was to continue to be of importance throughout the period.

The knowledge that God had created the world helped to determine how men and women interpreted events in the lives of themselves, their society, and the world in which they lived. The world was a mirror in which could be seen reflected God's purpose. Thus, accidents were never simply accidents. The coincidences that fascinated contemporaries did so precisely because they were not to be seen as the product of chance. Events in an individual's life could be scanned to divine (literally) God's message. Equally, natural disasters were never simply natural. For example, the plagues or poor harvests that were frequent throughout this period were to be seen as the interventions of a jealous God, quick to punish the sins of his people. Even the weather itself was an index of God's attitudes. For example, the 'Protestant wind' which helped to defeat the Spanish Armada and in the next century to speed William III to deliver England from the popery of James II was seen as a direct token of God's love.

The Christian world was a world thought also to be physically sensitive to the moral conduct of human beings. The stories told by Richard Gough, a Shropshire yeoman who lived in the second half of the seventeenth century, in the history he wrote of his parish of Myddle, offer a window onto this aspect of the mental world. For example, he retells the story of the capture of a man who had fled after killing a boy. The murderer was only apprehended by those who had tracked him from Shropshire almost to London, after they had been led to him by a pair of ravens, 'making a hideous and unusuall noyse' and pulling apart the cock of hay in which he slept. On capture, the man confessed that the ravens had followed him ever since the murder. This belief in a world in which personal behaviour might provoke direct intervention by God was to receive powerful extension in the Protestant idea of a providentialist God.

If God could work through natural causes to achieve his purpose, so too could the Devil. Belief in the immanent presence of the Devil was perhaps as widespread as a belief in God. Ralph Josselin recorded in his diary the encounters of his parishioners with the Devil in either human or animal form. This belief in the power of the Devil was most pronounced in the case of witchcraft. A convergence of beliefs at the level of both élites and people in this period helps to explain why Europe as a whole should have witnessed a witch-craze. At the level of state, Church, and intellectuals there was a belief in the witch not as an isolated individual, but as part of a wider group which drew their power from, and were allied with, the Devil. There was an uneven reception of this belief in the demonical pact in the British Isles. It commanded more general acceptance in Scotland than in England, a difference helping to explain why the witch-hunt should be a feature of Scottish history in this period but not to any great extent in England. In England

the demonization of witchcraft never received much support outside the ranks of some writers and clerics, except for a brief while during the Civil War. It does not seem to have had much importance at all in Ireland, where witchcraft prosecutions as a whole were few, with the result that historians have found it harder to reconstruct the popular beliefs surrounding witchcraft there.

Printed reports of trials of witches, like that of the Essex witches of 1589, attempted to spread the idea that witches derived their power from the Devil. But although the Essex witches were depicted with their familiars—spirits sent from the Devil—the accounts of their misdeeds stress the harm they brought to their neighbours by their ill-will. At the popular level a belief in witchcraft emphasized this ability of individuals to harness supernatural power to effect changes in the physical world. Witches were those who through the practice of *maleficia* were thought to be responsible for the sickness

PAMPHLET accounts of witch trials were an important means of disseminating élite conceptions of witchcraft. The animals depicted here—frogs and toads—were the witches' familiars, sent by the Devil (who, it was reported, had himself appeared as the ferret sitting on the woman's lap) to assist them in inflicting damage on the families and livestock of their neighbours.

and death of humans and animals. The casebooks of Richard Napier, a Buckinghamshire clergyman and astrological physician of the early seventeenth century, provide evidence of this belief in the power of the witch; more than five hundred of his patients believed themselves to be bewitched.

A belief in witchcraft which emphasized its origins in the ill-will one member of the community bore to another reflected both the social and intellectual realities of the time. Most people lived in small, face-to-face communities, and a belief that hostile thoughts alone might produce physical damage was widely held, not least by the Church. That it was women who were most commonly believed to be witches is to be explained by a range of factors. Contemporary representations of women portrayed them as a group who by their disorderly nature and weakness were likely to be attracted to witchcraft, while the threat that solitary women were thought to pose to a society in which women were expected to be subordinated to either father or husband helps to explain why they should predominate among those prosecuted.

The popular belief in witchcraft emphasized the power of the spoken word in the form of the witch's curse. This belief in the efficacy of the spoken word was also central to the other form of magic widely practised—white magic. The practitioners of white magic, known as *cunning* men and women, offered help in finding stolen objects, healing family and livestock, smoothing the path of love, and, not least, in discovering whether a witch was responsible for the client's misfortunes. To judge from the evidence of one English county—Essex—white magic was widely available in the first half of the period.

Witchcraft was but part of a set of wider beliefs in this period that historians have studied under the label of magic. As is the case with witchcraft, this wider set of beliefs can be seen to represent an attempt to master a hostile and unpredictable universe. Labelling these beliefs magic misses the point that they were seen as rational by contemporaries in that the reasons they gave for their effectiveness seemed intelligible in terms of their conception of the nature of their world. In fact, they derived their authority from ways of seeing the world that were not always complementary. Again, religion was important here. The uneasy synthesis of Christian and pagan beliefs that was to be found in the pre-Reformation Church, as well as the orthodox belief in the power of God and his saints, had made the Church 'a repository of supernatural practice'. The images of saints, the year-round rituals of the Church, even the language of its liturgy were all held popularly to offer a source of power which could be tapped to answer more material needs. For example, in London, an offering to the appropriately named St Uncumber was believed to be able to rid wives of troublesome husbands. The wafer of the communion could be carried away from the church, dried, and used when needed to heal animals or humans. The Rogationtide procession of minister and congregation around the bounds of the local community was but one of the occasions in the pre-Reformation Church's calendar when the correct repetition of ritual was believed to ensure the fertility of the fields. Even after the Reformation, the annual calendar with its popular and religious festivities was itself a marker of the uneasy tension between Christian and earlier beliefs. The rituals and symbols of these celebrations offer powerful evidence of the persistence of earlier beliefs more concerned with matters of fecundity than faith.

Beliefs and behaviour which drew their force from the Catholic Church shaded into other practices and beliefs whose relationship became more distant. The belief in ghosts as avengers of otherwise undetected crime, familiar to Shakespeare's audience, might be underwritten by a belief that the boundary between the living and the dead was not fixed. After all, it was still widely believed at the beginning of this period that on All Souls' the dead might come back to life, hence the practice of leaving food and drink out for them. But it was harder to find religious justification for the belief in fairies, like those which the wife of an early seventeenth-century Sussex artisan encountered when searching for buried treasure.

Astrology was perhaps the most important alternative source of authority. Astrology drew its authority from classical sources. It too represented the physical and personal worlds as subject to external influence, in this case the influence of the planets. Central to this was a belief that all matter, including the human body, was composed of four essential elements—earth, air, fire, and water—over which individual planets held influence. Depictions of the human anatomy in almanacs provided a visual illustration of the belief that the microcosm of the human body, and therefore its health, was subject to the influence of the planets. This explanation of the world in terms of a divide between microcosm and macrocosm helped to inform a popular view of the natural world which, for example, saw certain plants as having affinities and sympathies which could be tapped if they were collected at the right time. The predominance of such a world-view also helps to explain why the concept of correspondence was such an important part of the early modern popular mental world. Although astrology's intellectual underpinnings were to be challenged by the philosophical and scientific revolutions in this period, at the beginning of the period broader intellectual changes, notably those historians label Neoplatonism, reinforced this vision of the world as an animistic universe full of vibrant forces which could be tapped.

Since astrology seemed to offer through its various branches a science of prediction, it had obvious appeal to men and women of the middling and poorer sort in their struggle to master the hostile environment in which they lived. Both the popularity and content of almanacs in this period bear witness to the hold of astrology.

Beyond the field of astrology there stretched a penumbra of beliefs with a recognizable, if diminishing, relationship to its mental underpinnings. Predicting the weather was vital in a society whose heartbeat was the harvest. While the local proverbial weather lore of the period reflects the importance of intense observation, this was a mental world which allowed other means of prediction. In sixteenth-century Essex, farmers variously predicted the state of the coming harvest by the date of the southwards winter migration of birds, the age of the moon at the beginning of January, and by the movement of grains of corn placed on a hot hearth, one for each month of the year.

This was a society in which a sense of time and history was predominantly cyclical—the yearly round of the seasons, from birth to death, the millennium—and in which change was regarded with suspicion. Custom, what had always been done in the past, was a prime value in the popular mentality, even if we now know that contemporaries were not above changing the definition of what was 'customary' when it was to their advantage and they were able to do so. In such a society, prophecy offered another way of predicting the future and, moreover, in such a way as to allow men and women a chance to bring about that future by their own actions. Most of the rebellions of the sixteenth century were preceded by a rash of prophecies whose purpose was to validate protest.

Historians have written of this mental culture under the label 'magic'. But it is impossible to understand the force of such beliefs unless we recognize that that label is a later importation.

What may appear today as superstitious and irrational then commanded wide respect precisely because it was seen as rational and intelligible given the central beliefs about the nature of the world they inhabited. Ironically, it was in this very period that certain intellectual changes began to challenge the mental underpinnings of these beliefs and set in train the process that would end in their labelling as magic. As we will see, by the end of the period this change in attitudes had begun to find converts among the middling sort.

3. *The Social World*

The knowledge that God had created their world also provided men and women with a set of truths about the nature of their social world and of their place within it. They found themselves part of what has been called the 'great chain of being', a universe divided up into an elaborate hierarchy of superiority and subordination which began with God and the angels and stretched down through man and the animal world to the vegetative and mineral worlds. As the homily 'concernyng Good Ordre and Obedience to Rulers and Magistrates', heard annually in each English parish church, declared:

Almighty God hath created and appointed all things in heaven, earth and waters in a most excellent and perfect order. In heaven, he hath appointed distinct orders and states of archangels and angels. In earth he hath assigned kings, princes, with other governors under them, all in good and necessary order . . . Every degree of people, in their vocation, calling and office, hath appointed to them their duty and order. Some are in high degree, some in low, some kings and princes, some inferiors and subjects, priests and laymen, masters and servants, fathers and children, husbands and wives, rich and poor, and every one have need of other: so that in all thinges is to be lauded and praised the goodly order of God, without the which, no house, no city, no common wealth can continue and endure.

This stress on the naturalness of hierarchy had important consequences for how both social and gender hierarchies were constructed.

The Church played a central role in the inculcation of ideas about the social world. At the level of local society, the parish church offered a physical representation of social hierarchy. While attendance at church allowed the local community to celebrate its collective identity, the divisions of seating and standing by age, sex, and wealth found in many churches—the poor towards the back, the 'better sort' towards the front, men often sitting separate from women, servants and youth standing—provided a mental map of the local social order. When, at the end of the seventeenth century, Richard Gough came to write his *Antiquityes and Memoryes of the parish of Myddle* he structured his account around the seating plan of his parish church.

In a period in which Church and society were thought to be synonymous, it followed necessarily that society was 'a Christian commonwealth' and that behaviour should be informed by a Christian ethic. Sermons and services provided occasions for the conscious articulation of social norms and grounded them in the duty of obedience to God. The sixteenth-century *Books of Homilies*, intended to be read weekly from the pulpit, included homilies on gluttony and drunkenness, idleness and charity. That to be read for Rogation week, when the bounds of the parish were beaten, with its stress on the Christian duty to avoid personal conflict, makes it clear that this was an occasion in which the young and old not only marked out the physical, but also the moral, bounds of the local community. Running throughout the homily was an emphasis upon the importance of the ethic of neighbourliness. This was a concept nowhere fully articulated or written down in the period but it was all the more powerful for this very protean quality. For example, it was often the conflict arising from the breakdown of neighbourliness that lay at the root of witchcraft accusations.

The belief in the power of God to intervene in the world and punish human failings was, as we have seen, central to the mental world of early modern England. A literal belief in the power of God's curse played an important part in the maintenance of social norms. For example, during the Rogationtide procession the minister invoked God's curse on any who had encroached on their neighbour's land. A sermon, entitled *The Curse of Corne-hoarders*, preached at the Bodmin quarter sessions in a dearth year warned that the curses of the poor against greedy farmers who

THIS depiction of the world as 'The Great Chain of Being'—a divine creation arranged in a series of hierarchies between heaven, where the chain begins in God's hand, and hell—is a visual representation of a central concept in an early modern mental world where society was conceived as a series of static relationships between superiors and inferiors.

kept their grain from market 'will be ratified in heaven'. Similarly, a sermon preached at Kettering in 1632 pointed out how 'God's curse hath lighted upon' enclosing landlords, leading to the death of them and their family line. That this belief was part of the popular mental world can be seen in proverbial lore. 'Ill-gotten gains ne'r last three generations' or, as in Richard Gough's Shropshire, 'will not last three crops', was a common saying.

Inhabiting a common social world—at least at the beginning of our period—middling and poorer sort encountered the ideas that informed their view of the world in the same contexts. We have seen already the importance of the Church in the construction of mental worlds. Growing up within the immediate world of the household and the local community, their first contact with the beliefs and meanings by which they made sense of their world was primarily within the context of oral culture. The everyday nature of this process makes much of it difficult for the historian to recover. It has proved easier for historians to recover the normative literature of Church and State surviving in book form, which provides evidence of what people were expected to believe and how to behave, but not necessarily evidence of how they thought or acted. But there are sources which can be made to yield such evidence. Moments of conflict, either personal or communal, frozen in the archives of the courts of State and Church, provide evidence of the norms and values held in this society.

If we take gender as an example we can see how it is possible to recover evidence of how ideas were received at the level of the people. Relationships between men and women were cast in terms of authority and subordination and were grounded in a recognition of difference which could be traced back to God's creation. Inequality between the sexes was, therefore, natural. As the 'Homily of the State of Matrimony', read from the pulpit each year, declared: 'woman is a weak creature, not endued with the like strength and constancy of mind: therefore they be the sooner disquieted, and they be the more prone to all weak affections and dispositions of mind, more than men be'. But it is one thing to know that patriarchy was preached, yet another to know how it was received. Slander suits brought in increasing number to the church courts have been made to yield evidence of the way in which ideas of gender were constructed and negotiated at the level of local society. Women, dependants of the male from whom they derived public identity—as daughter, wife, or widow—were expected to be obedient and subordinate. But the evidence of women deposing in the church courts of the period has been taken to show that in court they sought to avoid or to endorse ideas about subordination, while in civil and criminal cases they might knowingly exploit representations of their vulnerability and lack of reason for their own ends. In the riots of the period women demonstrated an ability to exploit the ambiguity over their legal status to give themselves freedom to protest about the loss of land or malpractices in the marketing of grain. As one Yorkshire encloser in the early seventeenth century complained, his fences had been pulled down by women 'upon their phantasmogorical imaginations . . . that women were lawless, and not subject to the laws of this realm as men are, but might in such cases offend without dread or punishment of law'.

Such episodes of communal conflict allow us to see how ideas held central to the regulation of early modern society were at the level of everyday culture articulated, contested, and restated. We might again take gender roles as an example. Ritual shaming sanctions like the skimmington ride also allow us to see the articulation of these values. A skimmington ride was a heavily ritualized and symbolically charged procession held in the local community to criticize

THIS woodcut needs to be read as a series of scenes in a skimmington, a communal form of policing gender roles within patriarchal society. Men who allowed their wives to dominate were assumed to be at risk of being cuckolded as well, hence the depiction of the man wearing horns, a popular sign of cuckoldry. The other scenes show the man being carried on a staff and the woman dumped on a dungheap.

the usurpation of the husband's authority by his wife. Neighbours dressed to represent the offending man and wife—the wife being played by a man in woman's clothes—and often re-enacting the incident that had given offence, were ridden on a staff or horse at the centre of a hooting crowd which sought at the end to seize and dump the wife in the local pond or dung heap. We do not know how common skimmington rides were—they seem to have been more common in some areas (notably the south-west)—but the values they sought to uphold were general. The skimmington was a sufficiently common event to be captured in the woodcut to a ballad, where the depiction of the husband wearing horns expressed the more general belief that a husband who could not control his wife would end up being cuckolded by her.

The values implicit in everyday exchanges were also made explicit in the rituals and symbols of early modern festive culture. The feasts and festivities that punctuated the year were made to carry a rich cargo of meanings. While the celebrations of Christmas and Easter served to mark out the divisions between work and play, they also served to represent (and attempted to reconcile) the divisions that made up the early modern social order. The commensality that was such a mark of these festivities emphasized the importance of the values of neighbourliness and reciprocity. By contrast, the generosity demanded of the wealthier landowners, farmers, and employers in bearing a disproportionate share of the cost of the festivities pointed up the obligations that the possession of wealth was supposed to entail, as well as paradoxically marking out their superior status. Richard Gough's judgements on his fellow men and women, past and present, in his community bear out the importance of the values of hospitality and charity. Something of the purposes served by feasting and festivity in marking out the social contours and social values of early modern society is captured in the representation of an Elizabethan wedding party in the painting by Joris Hoefnagel, reproduced facing page 160.

Festive licence, while seemingly transgressing social boundaries, served in reality to underscore the underlying expectations about the appropriate behaviour demanded in everyday life from groups otherwise subordinate by virtue of age (youth) or gender (women). The role accorded young people in policing the community through violent play helped to instil in them the values their disorder defended. That young unmarried men (and, on occasion, women) were

THIS painting, van Tilborch's *The Tichborne Dole* (1670) should not be read as a straightforward depiction of gentry charity for the poorer sort. It is a representation of social hierarchy with Sir Henry Tichborne and family in the foreground and the poor waiting to kneel to receive their loaves of bread. It reflects an idealized view of the relationship between the 'respectable poor' and their betters, something the use of such charities was designed in part to achieve, after the 'fright' of the English Revolution.

allowed on days such as May Day or Plough Monday to mock and 'extort' largess from their elders and betters only served to underline the expectation that in the everyday they would be obedient and subordinate. The inversionary rituals of this festive culture were the social equivalent of those printed images of a world upside down, increasingly available within the print culture of this period, in which fish swam in air, carts pulled oxen, and children punished their parents. Their purpose, it has been argued, was similar: to reinforce in the minds of their participants the ridiculousness of the temporary inversions they depicted and the naturalness of the real structures in society.

One final way to try to reconstruct the popular mental map of the social order is to look at the symbolic representations of society that other public performances offered contemporaries. Although low levels of literacy at the beginning of the period meant that the popular world was predominantly an oral world, the people were bombarded with ideas about the social order by the many forms of public procession and performance that marked the year. Before the Reformation Corpus Christi Day, with its procession of clergy and laity and celebration of the mass, offered a model of society as a human body. This was to be an enduring model in the period, and the subject of many sermons, which by analogy—a characteristic device in early modern thought—represented society as an interdependent whole. While it acknowledged social differences through the metaphor of limbs and organs—the head was the ruler, the feet or belly the people—it emphasized that none could survive alone. Other public performances—before the Reformation the miracle plays staged by urban guilds or civic processions—were physical enactments of the interrelationships of social hierachies. The symbols they employed and the speeches they involved offered both audience and participants a rich set of ideas about their social world. In a city like Bristol urban ritual underwrote the values of virtue, industry, and charity; in London the symbolically charged processions that attended the appointment of the mayor spelt out a series of messages for both participants and onlookers. In the countryside—as the idealized picture of the Titchborne Dole makes clear—the rituals surrounding the exercise of charity could be made to celebrate a world of social difference and unity.

4. *The Political World*

The most important model of power in both society and state was provided, again by analogy, by the relationships of authority and obedience within the patriarchal family. In the contemporary phrase, the family was 'a little commonwealth'. By analogy, monarchs were fathers to their people and should enjoy the same unquestioned authority and respect. As the 1615 tract *God and the King*, published by the authority of James I and ordered by him to be bought by all householders, put it, 'as we are born sons, so we are born Subjects'. Monarchs in their proclamations represented themselves as fathers to their people. Proclamations were printed sheets designed to be cried and posted in the market-place or read from the pulpit and they were an important means of communication with their subjects in this period. The Fifth Commandment—honour thy father and mother—became a political text which could be used to justify the authority of masters and magistrates as well as monarchs. Its teaching was central to the process of catechizing which all young people after the Reformation were expected to receive from the Church. Something of the power of ideas of hierarchy and deference can be seen in the contemporary belief that the defiance of superiors and elders within the family was a self-evident symptom of madness.

Once more, the Church had an important role to play in underwriting power hierarchies. From the Reformation on, it represented the monarch as a 'godly prince', a ruler whose authority over the ruled was derived from God. A Protestant Church which showed a marked iconophobia as regards religious images nevertheless upheld icons of monarchy. The frontispiece to the Bishops' Bible of 1569 offered a powerful iconographical representation of Elizabeth I. It has been said of the Elizabethan Church that it came perilously close to devoting as much time to the worship of Elizabeth I as to the worship of God. Indeed, in this period a whole host of factors converged to produce the idea of the monarch as a semi-divine being, a 'little god' in James I's words. Again, we can turn to the *Book of Homilies* to see another representation of this idea. The 'Homily against Disobedience and Wilful Rebellion', designed to be read on successive Sundays, reiterated with a wealth of biblical stories the sinfulness of rebellion against the monarch and stressed that the primary political duty of the people was obedience. The development of print in the period made it easier to disseminate powerful iconographic images of the monarch for popular consumption, while one of the purposes of the progresses that individual monarchs made around their realm was to provide an occasion for elaborate visual spectacles stating the nature of royal power.

The law provided another important arena in which representations of the relationship betwen ruler and ruled reached out to the people. The particular nature of the Tudor–Stuart state—the absence of a professional bureaucracy and standing army—made the law of central importance in securing the consent of the subject. The theatre of the law was used to articulate ideas about the nature of the monarch's power and of its counterpart, order. The regular meetings of the king's courts in the counties were not only occasions for the exemplary prosecution of crime. The practice of opening the court with a reading of the statutes in force and the Charge, a speech whose primary purpose was to set out the government's current concerns, gave an opportunity for reflections on the nature of order, an obsessive theme in this period, and on the role of monarch and magistrate in its maintenance. Sermons at the opening of the court or at the foot of the gallows reinforced these ideas. As the meeting of the assizes in Essex was told in 1660, the year of the restoration of the monarchy, 'stocks and whips, pillories and ropes, the prison and the gallows are those engines upon which hang the garland of peace'.

Again, we need to ask the question whether this representation of the nature of the power and

THE printing revolution made it possible for images of monarchy to become increasingly widely dispersed. Here, in the frontispiece to the Bishops' Bible of 1569, the royal icon of Elizabeth, crowned by the four virtues of Justice, Mercy, Fortitude, and Prudence, is firmly linked with the Bible and godly preaching, a powerful representation of the godly prince.

the duties of the subject had a place in the mental world of middling and poorer sort. A variety of evidence suggests that it did. The widespread belief in the royal touch, the ability of the monarch to heal scrofula, a disease of the skin popularly known as the king's evil, has been taken as powerful evidence of popular acceptance of the semi-divine nature of the monarch. It was no coincidence that after the execution of Charles I, which showed subjects (as Christopher Hill reminds us) that kings had joints in the neck, Charles II and James II were assiduous touchers, despite their own distaste for the exercise, nor that the Duke of Monmouth, Charles II's illegitimate son, should try to assert his legitimate claim to the throne by claiming similar powers. To take another example, protestors in the rebellions and riots of the period were quick to yoke their demands with protestations of loyalty to the monarch. In the widespread enclosure protests of the Midlands Rising of 1607, hedges were pulled down to the beat of a drum and cries of 'God save the King'.

Legitimation for protest was found in popular beliefs about the nature of the relationship between rulers and ruled, above all Crown and commoners, beliefs derived from Tudor and Stuart attempts to ground the legitimacy of their power in authority exercised on behalf of their (especially poorer) subjects. As the author of a 1548 pamphlet put it: 'a king is anointed to be a defence unto the people that they be not oppressed or overlooked . . . [and] by all Godly and politic means to seek the common wealth of his people'. This concept of the commonwealth was another important category in early modern mentalities. Like other normative ideas we have discussed, it lacked systematic development. At its core was a model of society as a series of hierarchical, but interdependent social groups with mutual rights and obligations. Informing this model was the idea that ultimately all property was held from God, an idea reinforced after the Reformation by Protestant preaching around the theme of stewardship and the moral responsibilities of property and power.

A commonplace of government and clerical thought, this idea of the common weal did not represent a challenge to existing structures. However, in a period of change it could offer a moral critique of a society in which it was felt market relationships were coming to dominate social relationships. Defence of the common weal was a common idea within the popular protests of the period. Thus, one group of seventeenth-century Lancashire rioters as they pulled down an enclosure called out proudly to passers-by that 'they were good members of a Common wealth for that they endeavoured and sought to keep land from being enclosed'. Although this idea might challenge the position of landlords and others, it did not challenge the monarchy since the relationship between commoners and Crown was popularly seen as the bedrock of the common weal. However, the popular discontent provoked by royal enclosure on a large scale in the first half of the seventeenth century and by the fiscal and religious policies pursued by Charles I and his two sons showed that popular obedience was conditional on the king fulfilling his role as protector of the people.

5. *Continuity and Change*

A series of changes over the course of the period were to have an effect on the early modern mental world. The impact of these changes was uneven. In terms of geography, their impact was more pronounced in urban, than in rural, areas, while what contemporaries termed 'the dark corners of the land', areas unreceptive to change, clustered in the latter half of the lowland/highland divide to be found throughout the British Isles. Socially, the economic changes that brought about a sharper polarization between middling and poorer sorts meant that it was the thinking of the former group, especially the very wealthiest, that was more open to change. But even here, the impact of change was neither uniform nor complete by the end of our period. Amongst shopkeepers and farmers ideas remained whose kinship with the earlier mental world of their ancestors can still be recognized.

Though the sources of challenge to the earlier mental world were various, they derived much of their force from the interrelationships between them. However, for the sake of analytical clarity we shall treat them separately. The growth in the power of the state at the level of the local community (and, later in the period, a growing acceptance of parliamentary authority) made the law an even more important arena in which the people could encounter ideas about the nature of political authority. While both poorer and middling sort were both affected by this change, their experiences might diverge. One of the key changes of the period was the growing political role accorded the middling sort. This group had always dominated the manor court; now they came to dominate office-holding at the level of town and village and to play a role in the administration of the county. Their importance in local administration was matched by their growing role in parliamentary elections. Thus, both at the level of their country (the contemporary term for their *pays* or neighbourhood) and the country as a whole the middling sort gained in power and influence. It was therefore members of the middling sort who in the very administration of the law came into contact with the ideas about order it expressed. As property-holders and victims of crimes in a period where prosecuted crime registered a sharp increase, they had a vested interest in securing a wider acceptance of ideas stressing order and hierarchy. Faced with what they saw as the growing disorders of their poorer neighbours in a period of rising Poor Law costs, they had also an interest in the redefinitions through use of the law of customary practices as crimes or, in the case of sexual and marital behaviour, as sins. For the poorer sort, their experience of the law was necessarily different. They were less likely to take part in the law's execution, more likely to smart from its enforcement.

But such contrasts should not be overdrawn. Members of the middling sort might still recognize the value of customary forms of regulation, such as the skimmington, in enforcing communal norms. Members of the poorer sort were also victims of crime and might recognize the value of the law. Indeed, the growing problems the poor faced helped to give greater emphasis to the role of the law and the monarch as their protectors. Proclamation and pulpit were designed to convey ideas in an oral political culture, and developing literacy amongst the people gave access to print. The evidence of riot in this period suggests that at the popular level there was both a general awareness of the protection the law might afford to popular rights and an often detailed knowledge of specific pieces of legislation. For example, the so-called food riots that occurred in years of harvest failure were at some variance with the picture of collective theft with violence this labelling suggests. Those involved shaped their actions—impounding the grain and selling it at a just price, 'fining' the exporter—in a conscious mimicry of government policy regarding the regulation of the grain trade. Such shaping of protest was designed to assert that 'they were resolved to put the law in execution since the magistrates neglected it', as one group of late seventeenth-century rioters put it. Enclosure rioters too displayed a knowledge of the law, sometimes citing recent legislation against enclosure in defence of their pulling down of fences and hedges or, as in the case of Ket's Rebellion in 1549, responding to government commissions. This ability to appropriate representations of power as authority located in the consent of the subjects for their own ends suggests that the poorer sort were able to develop quite a detailed appreciation of power and the law.

The second important change was the Reformation. The Reformation ushered in a period in which religion, defined now for the individual believer in terms of beliefs rather than behaviour, became if anything more central to the lives of the local community. The Reformation offered powerful reinforcement of the picture of a world created by God, and the Protestant Church drew even more firmly the social and political consequences of this hierarchical picture. However, the Reformation also brought consequences that were more divisive. Inevitably, the attack on Catholicism challenged many of the popular beliefs that had grown up around the Church. The elevation of sermon over sacrament, the simplification of the number of sacraments, the discrediting of concepts such as purgatory, and the hostility towards the saints and the Virgin Mary had inevitable consequences for the earlier mental world.

In effect, Protestantism was redefining mental categories and redrawing mental boundaries. The abolition of what Protestants now regarded as superstition challenged much popular thinking about the nature of the relationship between men and women and the natural world, between the living and the dead, and between Man and God. The Calvinism that became the official doctrine of the Elizabethan Church with its belief in Providence and the doctrine of judgements (punishments inflicted by God on individuals or whole societies) offered a powerful extension of the image of the world as a moralized universe in which everything which happened might serve the purpose of its Creator. But Calvinism with its predestinarian view of human society divided between the saints, the minority assured salvation, and the reprobate majority facing damnation could encourage challenges to the assumed ideological and social solidarities of local society.

Middling and poorer sort shared the common inheritance of religious change. After the Reformation England became a Protestant nation, and it was Protestantism (and its important corollary, anti-popery) which informed their view of the world and their place in it, their sense of history and their expectations about the future. The diary of a wealthy member of the middling sort, William Whiteway, a merchant in early seventeenth-century Dorchester, with its knowledge of national and international events, displays this common Protestant belief that the world's history was structured around the conflict between good and evil. Woodcuts and engravings offered powerful images of the threat popery posed to the faith and fortunes of the nation. On a popular level, reactions to the Spanish Armada and the Gunpowder Plot, celebrated annually in church services, reveal a shared sense of history. Early modern men and women had available to them a whole series of images to remind them of the threat popery had posed and continued to pose in their history. Most powerful were those paintings commissioned to hang in churches, like that hung at the parish church of Gaywood in Norfolk. One of a pair commissioned in the early seventeenth century (the other depicted the Gunpowder Plot), it pictured Elizabeth I in prayer, above the scene of the destruction of the Armada, declaring, 'Blessed be the great God of my salvation'.

However, middling and poorer sort reactions to the consequences of the Reformation also reflected diverging experiences. By the later sixteenth century, an increasingly university-educated

ONE of a pair of paintings—the other depicted the Gunpowder Plot—which were hung in the seventeenth century in a Norfolk church. It depicts Elizabeth I's famous visit to Tilbury—the text paraphrases her celebrated speech—and the destruction of the Spanish Armada. Representations of the events of 1588 and 1605, celebrating the special relationship between the Protestant nation, their monarch, and God, played an important part in the developing political culture.

clergy were better able to fulfil the pastoral role of preacher and teacher to the people. But the response they met with varied. The clergy were forced to recognize that the uncompromising nature of the creed they taught meant that especially the poorer members of their flock might prefer to cling to earlier beliefs which continued to offer them an explanation of their world and some means of controlling it. Certainly, among some sections of the poor a hostility to 'men in black coats' and to what one young girl in Wiltshire contemptuously dismissed as 'bibble-babble', ran alongside the persistence of popular beliefs that the Church now labelled superstitious. At the level of the poorer sort there was still a belief in the special powers of persons, places, and plants which met the needs of a vulnerable section of society for the explanation for, and prevention of, disease and misfortune. Ironically, the resort to cunning men and women might have increased after a Reformation that either abolished or denied the efficacy of earlier ritual practices, but continued to assert the presence of the Devil and the reality of witchcraft. Change at this level was slow and its geography reflected the impermeability of more marginal areas to the forces of change. For example, even at the end of this period the Scottish Highlands and, especially, Islands retained a rich set of rituals and beliefs designed to offer the local community some control over their environment. Religious and other intellectual changes remoulded the early modern mental world in a way that denied these beliefs coherence and validity, but they did not succeed in suppressing them. Where they did succeed was in labelling them as vulgar and superstitious errors and in persuading more and more of the middling sort to abandon such beliefs.

That Protestantism, especially in its godlier variants, was a religion of the sermon and the book meant that it was religion whose appeal was more likely to be understood and accepted by the literate. That levels of literacy in this period were determined largely by levels of wealth in turn helps to explain both why the poorer sort should have been slower, and the middling sort quicker, to accept its message. Again, the contrast between middling and poorer sort should not be overdrawn, but the middling sort's godliness was something commented on by their contemporaries. Their acceptance of Calvinism brought with it consequences for how they interpreted their world. As we have seen, it might suggest a very different way of envisaging the social order. For them, whether Glasgow burgher or English farmer, the norms and values of the festive community—'little sodoms' in the words of some of the West Country godly—might be seen as increasingly inappropriate to their vision of a godly community in which the boundaries between the sacred and the profane were being redrawn through a sacralization of the everyday world. A belief in the doctrine of judgements, that the plagues of the period were God's arrows sent to punish a people for allowing sin to go unpunished, gave an added edge to their hostility towards the behaviour of their unreformed neighbours. While this hostility might help to forge closer links with the godly amongst the gentry, it could also, as during the English Revolution, call into question the authority of a gentry, labelled ungodly. John Corbet, son of a Gloucestershire shoemaker but able through a university education to join the clergy, published in 1645 an account of the Civil War, deeply critical of the gentry, but celebrating the heroic role of the middling sort. For many among the middling sort, the English Revolution represented a formal coming of age politically.

A belief in a providentialist God gave the godly cause to examine minutely events in their own and their society's life. This was to be an important motive for the development of diary-keeping in this period. Surviving diaries often written by members of the godly middling sort take us to the heart of this mental world. They bear witness to the obsessive concern with which men and women sought to interpret fortune and misfortune as evidence of God's pleasure or displeasure. The seventeenth-century Londoner Nehemiah Wallington left some fifty volumes (there may well have been more) with over twenty thousand pages of his writing devoted to an examination of the working out of God's providence in events in his own and the English nation's history. Another member of the godly, the seventeenth-century Lancashireman Roger Lowe, also left a diary. His reaction to a stumble which left mud on his breeches in the shape of the initials of his then sweetheart was to record without seeming irony that the 'smallest of God's providences should not be passed by without observation'.

That both Wallington and Lowe, wood-turner and apprentice to a Lancashire shopkeeper respectively, came from relatively humble backgrounds counsels against too sociologically deterministic a view of the acceptance of the Reformation. Over time, Protestantism became the religion of most Englishmen. Its anti-popery and its apocalyptic vision of the English as a nation especially chosen by God helped to forge a greater sense of nationhood, not least against those other subjects of the British Crown whose varying combinations of poverty and popery they despised. John Foxe's Protestant martyrology, popularly known as the *Book of Martyrs*, played an important role in the propagation of this history, not least by its woodcuts depicting the burnings of Protestant martyrs. As the experiences of radical religion in the English Revolution and subsequent Puritan Nonconformity in the later seventeenth century were to show, godly Protestantism could attract plebeian support. Although probably always a minority, supporters of groups such as the Quakers went on to develop a more radical faith with corresponding consequences for their mental map of the godly society, one in which traditional social and gender hierarchies might be up-ended. But that members of the Quakers and other radical religious groups claimed to be able to work miracles is a reminder of the otherness of this mental world and counsels against imposing too linear a view on this development.

The third major change was the growth in education and consequent increase in literacy, changes with obvious consequences for that earlier common mental world. Once again growth was uneven, reflecting contrasts between different social groups and regions. Access to education was more common in urban than rural areas, in lowland rather than highland regions. Below the level of the gentry, it was the middling sort who were the major beneficiaries of educational change. By contrast, illiteracy remained very much the experience of all but a minority within the ranks of the labouring poor. This was also the case for women (although by the later seventeenth century almost a half of women in London were literate). Thus, if there was as some historians have argued an educational revolution, its impact was blunted at the level of the poorer sort. Nevertheless over time an increase in literacy meant that even amongst those whom historians include in the poorer sort there were those who could read and thus bridge the illiteracy gap. The minister Richard Baxter said of the seventeenth-century weavers of Kidderminster, 'I have known many that weave in the long loom that can set their sermon notes or a good book before them and read and discourse together for mutual edification while they work'. The possibilities for those with more wealth and greater education is provided by the example of the later seventeenth-century Sussex merchant and Nonconformist Samuel Jeakes, who kept a detailed account of his reading in his diary. By the time he was 15 he had read some one hundred and twenty-four books.

FIRST published in 1563, John Foxe's *Actes and Monuments*, better known as the *Book of Martyrs*, offered its readers a Protestant and millenarian history of the English Church, its illustrations offering even those with poor literacy powerful images of Protestant martyrdom. It was perhaps, after the Bible, the most important Protestant book. Churches were required to provide a copy for their parishioners, and wills of the period show careful provision being made for its transmission to later generations.

The rapid development of a print culture, one of the most important cultural developments of the period, was the fourth major change. The impact of printing was double-edged. Paradoxically, this massive outpouring of the printing presses both confirmed and challenged the earlier mental world. Initially, it allowed the wider dissemination of ideas that would not have been out of place in the Middle Ages and it brought them within the range of even the poorer sort. The boom in astrology, a body of ideas whose scientific basis was to be subjected to a growing attack over the period, was in part due to the printed word. Almanacs—by the 1660s some 400,000 were being published annually—selling for one or two pence provided their humble readers with some knowledge of the rules of astrology, lists of lucky and unlucky days, and, of course, predictions about future events.

The developing print culture reflected the centrality of religion in the early modern mental world in the large number of sermons and treatises published and, above all, in the large number

Death-bed advice was a popular genre within the development of cheap print, helping in the spiritualization of even humble homes. This woodcut is from a 1624 ballad, one of the most popular, and still in print in 1712.

of Bibles, perhaps as many as half a million by the end of the seventeenth century. The spiritualization of the household, celebrated in the woodcut to the ballad *An hundred godly lessons that a mother on her death-bed gave to her children*, was made possible by the growing availablity of devotional books and religious primers, above all by the Bible, the book most frequently recorded in wills, where the careful provision for its inheritance suggests its importance.

At one level, this growth in religious literature made it possible for a literate middling sort to read for themselves about matters of doctrine in literature of varying levels of complexity. At another, the development of a print culture also made available a religious literature for the poorer sort. Cheap printed catechisms—some sixty thousand catechisms had been published by 1640— allowed learning by rote. Religious themes were important in the chapbooks (small books of at most twenty-four pages) and ballads that poured from the presses in large numbers. Ballads like *Death's loud Allarum: Or, A perfect description of the frailty of Man's life, with some admonitions to repentance* offered greater access to works of conventional piety. As this example shows, the printing revolution also made possible the wider dissemination of ideas through the use of images that frequently accompanied the written text and which could be read by those whose reading ability was limited.

Although the proportion represented by religion in this popular literature declined over the period, other popular themes were also informed by a Christian morality and upheld the image of the world as a moralized universe. News ballads about monstrous births or 'natural' calamities pointed out the hand of God to their readers or listeners. Ballads like *The Rich Farmer's Ruine* recounted episodes where covetous farmers hoarding grain in dearth or usurers exploiting widows were punished by God with the destruction of crops or house.

The emergence of cheap print—single-sheet ballads or chapbooks—did not of itself challenge existing popular beliefs. Much of this literature was taken up with common issues like courtship and marriage, a very popular theme, and its representations of gender roles were conventional. Conduct books, another popular genre, were also conventional in the way they construed gender roles and patterns of authority. This was also the case where ballads and chapbooks dealt with the social and political order. Ballads criticizing the decline in neighbourliness and hospitality between rich and poor, operated within the conventions of the politics of nostalgia. Moral, not political, reform was the proffered solution, often to be effected, as we have seen, by divine intervention. The monarch was represented within this literature as a natural ally of the people, guarding them against misgovernment and oppression. A popular theme was the story of the king who travels his country in disguise, only revealing his true identity when he has righted wrong.

Historians are divided in their interpretation of the impact of this literature on the popular mental world. Some have emphasized the strong elements of escapism and fantasy. Others have emphasized the ragtag nature of ideas and the lack of any coherent world-view. Some have seen the commercial nature of ballad production as denying any possibility of recovering popular attitudes, while others have argued that if there was a market then the producers of ballads had to respond to popular tastes. Certainly it has proved easier for historians to talk with more confidence about the production, rather than the popular reception, of printed texts. But if we accept that literature does not simply reflect social realities, but actively constructs a culture's sense of reality, then it is possible to see how this popular literature could underwrite existing representations of society. But this still leaves open the problem of how in fact such texts were read and indeed whether there was only one possible meaning. Did men and women, for example, read out the same meaning from the representations of male and female roles in the courtship ballads? Clearly, the evidence popular literature provides about the mental world needs to be confirmed by other sources. For example, it is possible to see literary representations of kingship reflected in

Death's loud Allarum:
OR,
A perfect description of the frailty of Mans life, with some admonitions to warne all men and Women to repentance.
To the tune of, Aime not too high.

RELIGIOUS themes were prevalent for much of this period in the ballads that represented the cheapest and most popular form of print. In a society where death was an ever-present threat, the nature of the after-life was as important to men and women as their fate in this life and featured prominently in popular print culture.

BALLADS like *The Rich Farmer's Ruine*, attacking the villains of popular culture, offered endorsement of popular grievances in the period, but they were careful to suggest to their readers that God, not the people, would punish these transgressors of the moral economy.

The Rich FARMERS Ruine;

VVho Murmured at the Plenty of the Seasons, because he could not Sell Corn so Dear as his Covetous heart desired.

To the Tune of, *Why are my Eyes still flowing*, As it is play'd on the *Violin*.   This may be Printed, R. P.

A Worthy Man a Farmer, who had Corn great store,
Yet he was Cruel always to the Poor;
And as the truth of him does very well appear,
He thought he ne'r sold his Corn too dear;
As to the Market one day he did go
Finding the Prices of Corn to be low;
Said he, before I will sell ought of mine,
I'le carry it home for to fatten my Swine.

In former days, as I can make it well appear,
By my own Farm, I got hundreds a Year;
I sold for Ten the Corn that will not now fetch Five,
Is this the way for a Farmer to Thrive?

Yet I will now sell no more at this Price,
But am resolv'd to stay for a Rise;
Thus he resolv'd to hoard up his store,
That he might then make a Prey of the Poor.

Another Farmer likewise then was standing by,
Who when he heard him he thus did reply;
You have a Farm and likewise Land, which is your own
With it cause have you then to make this sad moan?
I that have nothing but what I do Rent,
With Years of plenty, rejoyce in content;
Give him the praise who such plenty does send,
Lest when you murmur you highly offend.

FATALISM was a common theme in ballads aimed at a popular readership. We cannot know for certain how they were read, but their message echoed that to be found in other areas of popular culture and, it has been argued, was a strand in popular politics.

The poore man payes for all.

This is but a dreame which here shall insue:
But the Author wishes his words were not true.

To the tune of *In slumbring sleepe I lay*.

AS I lay musing all alone,
upon my resting bed,
Full many a cogitation
did come into my head:
And waking from my sleepe, I
my dreame to mind did call,
Me thought I saw before mine eyes,
how poore men payes for all.

They make them toyle and labour sore
for wages too too small:
The rich men in the Tavernes roze:
but poore men pay for all.

Me thought I saw an Usurer old,
walke in his Forr-furr'd gowne,
Whose wealth and eminence controle
the most men in the Towne:

the protestations of loyalty to the monarch that accompanied social protest. Similarly, the ballads' location of the cause of popular grievances in the moral failings of individuals—rapacious landlords or greedy corn dealers—mirrors the tendency of protesters to blame individuals, rather than the larger and impersonal forces of social change, for their plight. Proverbs, which according to one contemporary 'may not improperly be called the Philosophy of the Common People', offer another source of evidence by which to test literary representations. Their realistic reading of the poor's chances in society and their strong vein of fatalism—'look high and fall into a turd', 'better half a loaf than no bread'—mirrored a message to be found in ballads with such titles as *The Poore Man Payes For All*.

But if the culture of print offered confirmation of existing ideas, it also provided the greatest challenge to received thinking. While the development of print might extend the life of some systems of thought and conventional representations of society, it was inevitably also the spring-board for an attack on the very basis of those ideas. The collapse of censorship in the English Revolution saw thousands of cheap pamphlets published. One man, the contemporary London bookseller George Thomason, collected some thirty thousand alone. These pamphlets offered a challenge to received ideas in all spheres of thinking. The Revolution granted access to the press to authors who would have been excluded previously by virtue of their lower social status or gender. It even allowed some women to advance ideas in print that began to challenge existing representations of their nature and status, a development that survived the reaction at the Restoration. At one level, the English Revolution was fought out through an information revolution, which allowed both straight reporting of news and the use of the printing press to spread deliberate propaganda, especially about the threat posed to society's social and gender hierarchies by the radical sects.

At the same time, the collapse of censorship allowed the publication of newsbooks which

THE Parliament of VVomen. With the merrie Lawes by them newly Enacted. To live in more Ease, Pompe, Pride, and wantonnesse: but especially that they might have superiority and domineere over their husbands; with a new way found out by them to cure any old or new Cuckolds, and how both parties may recover their credit and honesty againe

London, Printed for W. Wilson and are to be sold by him in Will-yard in Little Saint Bartholomewes. 1645.

THE temporary collapse of censorship in the 1640s allowed an extraordinary challenge in print to many received ideas. This pamphlet draws on notions of inversion, common in the early modern mental world, to represent the threat to existing social and political hierarchies by focusing on gender relationships, one of the fundamental structures of the early modern mental and social worlds.

informed their readers of domestic political news, hitherto banned. The appeal of this expansion of information can be caught in the wry comment of the London artisan Nehemiah Wallington, that 'these little pamphlets of weekly news about my house . . . were so many thieves that had stolen away my money before I was aware of them'. Although the Restoration saw the temporary disappearance of these early newspapers, they had returned in force by the end of the century. From the latter half of the seventeenth century, the development of the urban coffee-house was also associated with access to this new world of printed news, as the 1705 print of a London coffee-house illustrates. By 1700 there were newsrooms in London where the papers could be read or loaned for an hour or two for a small fee. The late-seventeenth-century still life by Thomas Warrender is a celebration of the possibilities of this new world of print and literacy.

The explosion of radical ideas into print in the English Revolution was clearly exceptional, but there was throughout the seventeenth century an underlying, longer-term shift which made it possible for new ideas to gain a much wider audience through the medium of print. The development of printing made possible the wider communication of new ideas across a whole range of fields. It is impossible here to capture the vast range of books published, but the new possibilities can be seen in the experience of the Sussex merchant Samuel Jeakes. Jeakes and his father built up a large library containing works of both Puritan theology and the radical groups of the Revolution, antiquarian histories, the law, medicine, and science. Jeakes was able to read writings in both the new sciences and in an older occult tradition.

Law, astrology, philosophy, history, medicine, and science were just some of the fields in

DEVELOPING from the later seventeenth century, coffee-houses represented the increasingly easy access to be had in urban society to printed news and political information.

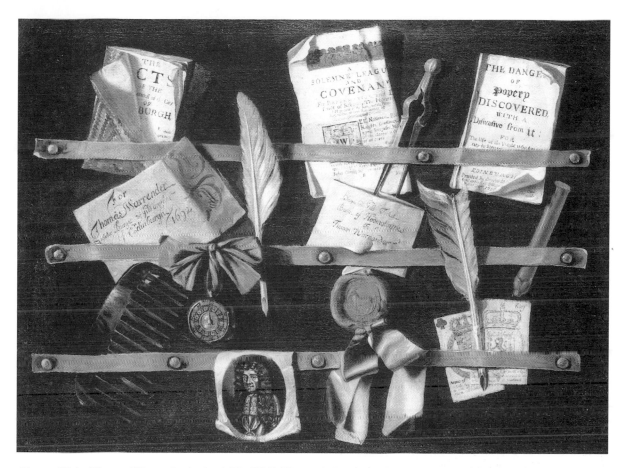

S TILL life by Thomas Warrender (active 1673–1713). Warrender's painting can be read as a celebration of the information revolution that had occurred by the late seventeenth century—with its printed tracts as a reminder of its contribution to the development of an informed popular political culture.

which printing allowed the wider dissemination of ideas. For example, the new ideas of the mechanical philosophy, with its very different view of the universe as ordered and regular, one in which God worked through natural causes, represented a radical challenge to earlier thinking. Again, change represented a shift in the conceptualization of boundaries. The world was now seen as a mechanistic universe, regulated by natural laws which denied the supernatural forces which an earlier view of the world as an animistic universe, full of vibrant forces, had accepted. Similarly, printing which had earlier in the period allowed for the wider dissemination of beliefs about witchcraft now allowed critics to pour scorn on such beliefs. Francis Hutchinson's denunciation of such beliefs in his *Historical Essay Concerning Witchcraft* (1718) was occasioned by the Jane Wenham case of 1712, the last time in England someone was found guilty of witchcraft. Levels of literacy and the cost of more substantial books—although the latter half of this period has also been called the golden age for the founding of town libraries—would suggest that it was the wealthier sections of the middling sort who would have been able to get first-hand access to these ideas.

The development of print culture also had more subtle consequences. In a predominantly oral culture the sense of the past had been confused and not fixed. Christianity had provided all of society with one model of history and time. As a consequence this was a society in which many had perhaps a better sense of the histories of the Jewish people in the Old Testament than of their own society's past. At a popular level time was still seen as cyclical, the cycle of the individual's rite of passage or the annual seasons. A sense of the past was unfixed and knowledge of history subject to what has been called 'structural amnesia'—modification by oral transmission through successive generations—as knowledge of the past was adjusted to fit the present. As the example of Robin Hood, a popular subject for balladeers and chapbook writers, suggests, the social identity and 'history' of Robin was adjusted to fit the nature of the intended audience. Custom—an important concept in this society, by which rights in manor or borough were claimed—was itself subject to this process of change, despite its common claim to an existence 'before the memory of man'. Oral culture might retain a memory of major events—the Peasants' Revolt of 1381 or past famines—but their dating was uncertain and any sense of chronology confused. Moreover, this knowledge operated at the level of local society and relied for its preservation and transmission on the mnemonics of a particular place; for example, the site of the executions of past rebels or, as in the East Anglian rebellion of 1549, the Reformation Oak outside Norwich beneath which Robert Ket, the eponymous leader of the rebellion, had held court; or, in the case of urban society, on civic ritual celebrating past benefactors.

But the development of a print culture provided readers with histories organized by past monarchs or, in the case of the antiquarians, by 'the county'. These histories were of variable quality and, in the case of the county antiquities, still contained much romantic speculation, especially about the origins of Britain. However, printed histories and chronicles rendered the past as a story of sequential change and encouraged the conception of linear time. This was a reading of the past that began to be available to even relatively humble readers; one common element in many almanacs was the reprinting of simple chronological histories. The fixing of histories in print made possible the beginnings of a critical history—the de-

---

AN
HISTORICAL ESSAY
CONCERNING
WITCHCRAFT.
WITH
OBSERVATIONS
UPON
MATTERS OF FACT;

Tending to clear the Texts of the Sacred Scriptures, and confute the vulgar Errors about that Point.

AND ALSO

Two SERMONS:

One in Proof of the Christian Religion; the other concerning Good and Evil Angels.

By FRANCIS HUTCHINSON, D.D. Chaplain in Ordinary to His Majesty, and Minister of St. *James*'s Parish in St. *Edmund's-Bury*.

PSALM xxxi. 6. *I have hated them that hold superstitious Vanities: but I trust in the Lord.*
I TIM. iv. 7. *But refuse profane and old Wives Fables, and exercise thy self rather unto Godliness.*

The SECOND EDITION, with considerable Additions.

LONDON:
Printed for R. KNAPLOCK, at the *Bishop's Head*, and D. MIDWINTER, at the *Three Crowns*, in St. *Paul's* Church-yard. MDCCXX.

FRANCIS HUTCHINSON, a clergyman, wrote his book *An Historical Essay Concerning Witchcraft* (first published in 1718) against credulous authors whose books were 'read with great eagerness . . . in Tradesmans' shops and Farmers' houses'. While print made possible powerful attacks on 'vulgar errors', at a popular level attempts to detect and punish witches continued into the eighteenth century, even though denied the support of courts and élites.

bates among plebeian radical groups like the Levellers in the English Revolution about the origins of 'kingly power' in the Norman Conquest showed the potentiality of this change even at a popular level. It also made possible the ridiculing of the fantasies of much popular oral history with its stories of giants, soon to be regarded by polite society as literally fabulous. This provides but one example of the way in which print culture began to erode the authority of orality and with it the position of those groups—women within the sphere of the household—who had held an important place in the transmission of oral knowledge. Increasingly, it was the written, rather than the spoken, word that commanded respect. Moreover, as the experience of Wales suggested print served to extend the reach of English. However, the radicals excepted, a critical popular history remained trapped in what might be termed 'the politics of nostalgia'; 'it was never a merry world since . . .' was a common idiom in cases of sedition appearing before the courts.

How far down the social scale knowledge and understanding of the new ideas to be found in print percolated in this period is difficult to say. Clearly the wealthy, especially urban, élite amongst the middling sort would have found access to these ideas relatively easy. By the very end of the period scientific societies were being established in the major provincial centres and towns could even draw on the services of itinerant lecturers. But access to did not automatically equal acceptance of the new thinking. If we return to the subject of witchcraft, we can find some evidence to suggest that the growth in education and literacy together with the explosion of the printed word was shifting the mental world of a significant proportion of the middling sort. Members of the middling sort had had an important role in the prosecution of witchcraft. It was they who had brought accusations to the court and they, as jurors, who had found those accused of witchcraft guilty. But by the latter half of the seventeenth century this was less often the case. The crime of witchcraft was not abolished until 1736, but before then jurors were increasingly sceptical of the difficulties of proof, though perhaps even then less so of the fact of witchcraft. By contrast, among the poorer sort earlier beliefs about the existence of both white and black magic remained more resilient. We cannot be certain how common episodes were in which local communities attacked suspected witches, but their existence allows us to glimpse the survival of beliefs for which the courts' growing lack of interest make it harder to find evidence. This was more so the case in areas like the Scottish Highlands or Gaelic speaking Ireland where the Calvinist and Catholic reformations respectively had failed to penetrate to any great extent.

As the evidence of witchcraft makes clear, the combined effect of these changes was to widen the gap between the mental worlds of the middling and poorer sorts. Differing levels of wealth determined that education, literacy, and print would have most impact on the mental world of the middling sort. While at the beginning of the period even wealthy farmers had most of their wealth invested in land and farm goods—in the early sixteenth century the value of the household goods of some Midlands farmers was worth less than their wood pile—by the late seventeenth century their inventories at death registered the increasing ability of the middling sort to invest in cultural consumption. Cultural differentiation between middling and poorer sorts was probably enlarged by the very fact of social change. Growing social polarization saw an increasing realignment of wealthy farmers—those who 'wade in the weedes of gentlemen' as one contemporary described them—and merchants with the gentry, with whom they now shared much in common. The abandonment of earlier beliefs, now labelled 'vulgar errors', was in part a statement of their aspirations to a new status.

The Knowledge of Things Unknown:
Shewing the Effects of the P L A N E T S,
and other Aftronomical Conftellations.
With the ftrange Events that befal Men,
Women, and Children, born under them.

Compiled by Goodridge, fuper palladium de Agricultura Anglicarum.

Together with the Husbandman's Practice: Or,
Prognoftication for Ever; as teacheth *Albert*,
Alkind, and *Ptolomy*.

With the Shepherd's Prognoftication for the Weather, and *Pythagoras* his Wheel of Fortune.

This is unknown to many Men,
Though it be known to fome Men.

Printed for H. Rhodes at the *Star* in *Fleet-ftreet*.

THIS title-page captures both the hope that scientific advance would perfect astrology and the fact that by the later seventeenth century attacks upon astrology were in the process of restricting its appeal to plebeian readers like the husbandmen and shepherds here targeted.

But this development should not be exaggerated. As we have seen, the large differences within, as well as the blurred boundaries between, the two social groups argue against too radical a contrast. Despite change, there were still points of contact with the mental world of the early Tudors. While continuity was much more a characteristic of those among the poorer sort who lacked both education and literacy, it was also to be found at the level of the middling sort. Richard Gough, our late seventeenth-century yeoman parish historian, could write dismissively of the naming of a local wood that 'monks and friars did formerly persuade ignorant people that there were fairies, (or furies,) and hob-goblins. And this wood being a thick, dark, and dismal place, was haunted by some airyall spirits, and therefore called Divlin Wood. Butt truth and knowledge have, in these dayes, dispersed such clouds of ignorance and error.' However, it is the same sceptic who later tells his readers of 'a wonderfull thing' about one of the farms in the parish. 'It is observed that if the chief person of the family that inhabits in this farm do fall sick, if his sickness be to death, there comes a pair of pigeons to the house about a fortnight or a week before the person's death, and continue there until the person's death, and then go away. This I have known them do three several times.' When his sister came into possession of the farm and fell ill, Gough tells us he went daily to see whether he could see any pigeons. He did not, and his sister recovered. Samuel Jeakes, our Sussex merchant, provides another example of the continuing strength of an earlier mental world. Jeakes cast horoscopes to determine whether his investment in the Bank of England would prosper, and the timing of his proposal to his future wife was also astrologically determined. Similarly, the time for building his storehouse in 1689 was determined by yet another horoscope, which Jeakes had built into the walls. This example of a man who lived his life through a series of revolutions—political, financial, commercial, educational, and scientific—determining his financial and emotional affairs by casting horoscopes reminds us of the otherness of the early modern mental world even at the very end of our period.

11 TUDOR MONARCHY AND POLITICAL CULTURE

JOHN GUY

1. *Renaissance Theory of Kingship*

Renaissance monarchy was personal and patrimonial. It was personal because it centred on the king and his Court. Nothing is more vivid than images of Henry VII and Henry VIII sitting in their chamber and Privy Chamber, governing their dominions with the assistance of their household servants. It was patrimonial because it was financed primarily by income received from the Crown lands. The king also received income from the profits of justice and from customs revenues, and in extraordinary circumstances he might resort to taxation. But the main thrust of early Tudor fiscal policy centred on the Crown estates.

The duties of the king were threefold: to defend the realm; to uphold the Church, especially against heresy; and to administer justice impartially. These obligations were enshrined in the coronation oath. The conventional rhetoric was that of virtue and good government. The king was the fountain of honour and justice. He was valiant in war, the champion of the tilt-yard, and was also the protector—Henry VIII by 1531 said the 'sole protector'—of the English Church and clergy.

These were standard medieval definitions, but they were given a new lease of life by early sixteenth-century humanists who took them over and refashioned them to their own ends. Throughout northern and western Europe, aspiring courtiers and intellectuals competed for employment as 'counsellors' to princes and cultivated the ideas that underpinned the monarchies of Henry VII and Henry VIII in England, Louis XII and Francis I in France, and Charles V in Spain, Italy, and the Holy Roman Empire.

Such theorists turned their attention towards the worldly objectives of rulers. High on the list were dynastic security, territorial centralization, the subordination of the nobility, increased revenues, control of local 'franchises' and feudal privileges, and the augmentation of regal power. Included were exalted theoretical claims, for the Renaissance monarchs, like their late Roman and Carolingian predecessors, governed 'by the grace of God'. These rulers claimed to rule by 'divine right', being accountable to God alone. They claimed to be autonomous and independent

H ENRY VIII dining in the Privy Chamber, drawing by an unknown sixteenth-century artist. The Privy Chamber was the innermost sanctum of the Court, whither the King retreated to confer with his intimates and advisers and enjoy his private life. Under Henry VII and Henry VIII the 'privy' apartments were in many respects the heart of national government, and Henry VIII frequently dined there, served by his gentlemen and grooms. The present scene most likely depicts the King's dining habits in the 1540s.

of external interference in the sphere of legislation. They held their power to be 'entire' and not limited or restrained. Last but not least they held that their clergy were as much an integral part of their kingdoms as the laity and that they had the right to regulate Church and clergy in the interests of policy and government.

Renaissance monarchs proclaimed their territorial 'sovereignty'. They adumbrated this principle by invoking the language of 'empire'. Since the beginning of the fourteenth century the civil lawyers in France had maintained that the king was 'emperor' in his realm (*rex in regno suo est imperator*), that he recognized no superior save God in 'temporal' matters, that the clergy's jurisdiction was confined to purely 'spiritual' affairs, and that the king might tax his clergy. The Pope had no authority to legislate for the kingdom, because the prerequisite for legislation was dominion, and the Pope had no dominion over the king's subjects. From there it was a short step to the thesis that rulers possessed secular and ecclesiastical *imperium*. Their power was likened to that of David, Solomon, and Hezekiah in Israel, and Constantine and Justinian in Rome. Such regal prototypes became fundamental to Renaissance theory. Also important as sources were the 'ancient histories and chronicles' and 'laws' and 'constitutions' of the kingdom which provided salient examples of 'imperial' kingship in action.

Not every humanist aspired to be a courtier, and many disliked the 'divine right' theory which was appropriated to underpin the 'imperial' cult. In Scotland, where the Crown was weaker and conciliarism stronger than in England, John Mair laid the foundations later cemented by John Knox and George Buchanan when he argued that the authority of rulers rested on the consent of the community, and that the community might withdraw their consent if the ruler abused his power. These were 'populist' ideas which Mair had learned while teaching at the University of Paris. They influenced a variety of English humanists.

In his Latin *Epigrams*, begun in 1500 and published in 1518, Thomas More contended provocatively that republicanism was the best form of government. In book I of *Utopia* (1516) he parodied as vicious the appetites and 'inclinations' of kings and their courtiers, while in book II he preferred the values of the monastery to those of worldly policy and invoked biting satire to suggest that the pagan Utopians were more 'Christian' than anything found in England. Again, Thomas Starkey in his *Dialogue between Pole and Lupset*, written between 1529 and 1535, stressed the limits of monarchy. His point of departure was public authority as enshrined in Parliament, and he endowed a Council of Fourteen with the 'authority of the whole parliament' when Parliament was not in session. His purpose was to impose such severe restraints on the king's exercise of patronage and *imperium* that he remodelled the English constitution in the image of that of Venice and transmuted the power of the king of England into that of no more than a doge. The Venetian republic was consistently upheld as the model for 'mixed' or limited government in the Renaissance, and Starkey's scheme, by virtue of its detail, was the most complete of its kind before the later years of Elizabeth I.

2. *The Renaissance Court*

The most spectacular assets of Renaissance monarchy were the person and image of the ruler. The printing press was still in its infancy at the beginning of the sixteenth century. In an age of widespread illiteracy, the political significance of royal buildings, heraldry, and iconography potentially outweighed that of written instruments in disseminating the 'presence' and authority of the monarch throughout the realm. Beginning with the Yorkist King Edward IV, who remodelled the royal household on the pattern of the Burgundian Court, which not only in art and dress but also in household management set the bench-mark for the monarchies of northern Europe, the English Court became the centre of princely 'magnificence' and patronage, and therefore also of politics. Under Henry VII and Henry VIII elaborate rituals and spectacular ceremonial displays were devised to propagate the 'myth' of monarchy, to regulate the organization of the Court in the interests of royal power, and to maximize the reputation of the king and the Tudor dynasty. As Sir John Fortescue, writing in the 1460s and early 1470s, explained in *The Governance of England*, the Renaissance monarch was obliged to construct new palaces, furnish them lavishly, ensure that his ambassadors were sent abroad properly equipped, and that foreign

ambassadors visiting England were suitably received and entertained. If the king could not manage this, then, said Fortescue, he lived not according to his princely status, 'but rather in misery, and in more subjection than doth a private person'.

The most significant expansion and refurbishment of the stock of royal residences was undertaken by Henry VIII, who in the last years of his reign drew extensively for this purpose on the proceeds of the dissolved religious houses. When he died in January 1547 he possessed over sixty houses the furnishings of which included over two thousand pieces of tapestry, over a hundred and fifty panel paintings, and over two thousand items of plate. The number of royal houses fell by over twenty in the 1550s, but despite further losses and exchanges Elizabeth I still possessed almost forty. No new palace was constructed or acquired by Elizabeth, although minor alterations and redecorations continued. Banqueting houses were erected at Greenwich and on the terraces at Whitehall and Windsor. Otherwise few structural improvements were made. In conjunction with these activities, the propagation of the 'cult' of monarchy was systematically attempted by successive regimes, each of which reinforced the image of the ruler by the employment of artists and craftsmen commissioned to supply badges, gold and silver plate, commemorative medals, emblems for use on seals and coinage, jewels, portrait miniatures, panel paintings, and other decorative artefacts.

Related opportunities for the ceremonial and ritualistic exposition of monarchy were afforded by public processions and royal progresses. The actual or symbolic 'display' of the ruler and his or her immediate entourage to the people was essential to maintaining the prestige of the monar-

This engraving, by James Basire after S. H. Grimm, depicts Edward VI's processional entry into the City of London on 19 February 1547, the day before his coronation. The young Edward, then a minor of 9 years old, was paraded through the streets of London by Protector Somerset to publicize the apparent stability of the regime, but Somerset was ousted from political power and his position as 'protector' of the realm and governor of Edward's person by the Duke of Northumberland in October 1549.

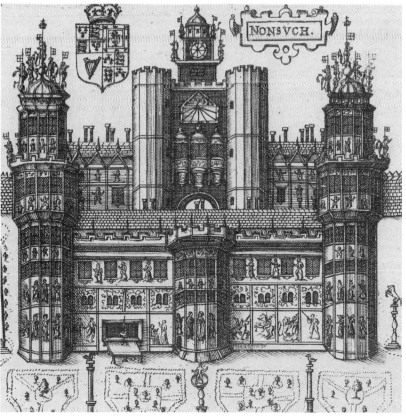

Nonsuch, Surrey, engraving of the south front, from John Speed's map of Surrey, 1610. Nonsuch was built by Henry VIII as a pleasure palace to celebrate the thirtieth anniversary of his accession. Possibly designed to imitate Chambord, Francis I's hunting palace in the Loire valley, Nonsuch was a house for the King and his riding household. It was built primarily for the King's private entertainment, which accounts for the sumptuousness of its decoration.

chy. Hence public processions on the occasions of coronations and royal funerals, and processions to Parliament, or to Westminster Abbey or St Paul's to celebrate royal weddings or births or such political events as the defeat of the Spanish Armada or the anniversary of Elizabeth I's accession day, were meticulously and lavishly stage-managed. On such occasions spectacles staged to celebrate events of primarily dynastic significance would be choreographed and packaged so that they appeared to mark events of national and religious importance. The accompanying Court festivities and pageants were imitated in the City of London and at the Inns of Court, and were repeated on a smaller scale in civic communities and in great households throughout the land. Printed programmes were sold at the Accession Day tilts in the later years of Elizabeth I's reign so that spectators might fully comprehend the meaning of the symbolic allusions and heraldic devices. Such occasions ranked among the more magnetic and potent of the various ceremonies of state.

Royal progresses, when the monarch and members of the Court left their circuit of the main cluster of royal residences in the environs of London and the Thames valley and undertook stately perambulations around the countryside, were driven partly by the demands of ceremonial display and ritualism, and partly by domestic and physical requirements. A distinction should properly be drawn between a royal 'progress' and the itinerant Court. A 'progress' was planned some months in advance, as in the case of Henry VII's first provincial tour when he set out for York 'in order to keep in obedience the folk of the North', and as in 1541 when Henry VIII made a similar journey. Again, the summer progresses of Elizabeth I were designed as occasions when tableaux vivants, aquatic pageants, allegorical speeches, triumphal arches, and civic spectacles could promote nationally the cult of Astraea and the 'imperial virgin'.

More mundanely, the availability of fresh water and of sewage facilities determined how long the Court might stay in one place. The Court was peripatetic primarily because of its needs in respect of victualling, sanitation, and recreation. The royal household comprised perhaps 1,500 people. Eighty to one hundred had access to the king's Privy Chamber and a total of 500 access to the public rooms 'above stairs', while some 1,000 served 'below stairs' in the kitchens, pantry, bakehouse, spicery, laundry, stables, falconry, etc. Feeding the Court and supplying it with the items needed for its daily life was a massive operation. In addition, the Court generated an enormous quantity of waste and effluent, which, in conjunction with the courtiers' habit of relieving themselves in chimneys and against the walls of buildings until such practices were outlawed by Elizabeth I, made mobility essential for the avoidance of disease and infection. Finally, hunting

THIS magnificent horse armour (the 'Burgundian Bard', *facing, above*) was given to Henry VIII in 1509 by the Emperor Maximilian I, on the occasion of his first marriage. The decoration includes a trailing design of pomegranates, the badge of Catherine of Aragon. In 1515, Henry made the Flemish designer of this armour, Martin van Royne, master of his own armoury.

BADGES of loyalty, *c.*1540: this stained-glass shield of the Tudor royal arms (*facing, below left*) was put up by that grateful courtier, John Russell, first Earl of Bedford, as a token of his allegiance to Henry VIII. Note the use of the 'covered' or 'imperial' crown—symbolizing the Tudors' assertion that they acknowledged no jurisdiction superior to their own.

HERALDRY as a precise visual language: the arms of Thomas Cranmer, Archbishop of Canterbury, *c.*1535 (*facing, below right*). The left-hand side depicts the arms of the see of Canterbury; the right, those of the Cranmer family. The red (or 'gules') crescent signifies Cranmer's position as a second son.

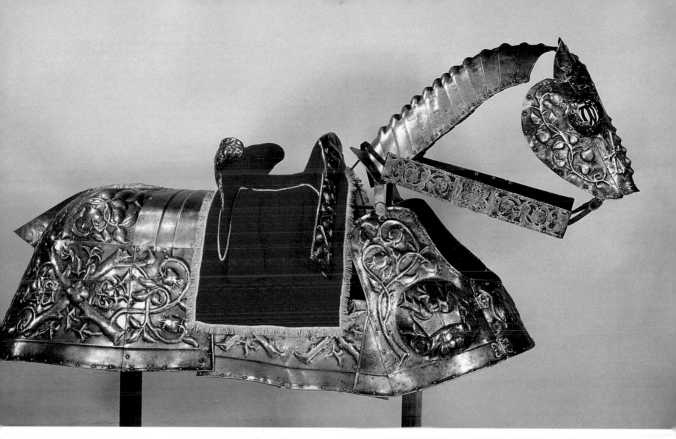

THE Great Seal of England authenticated the acts of the King or his government—such as treaties, grants of offices or Crown lands, and writs of summons to Parliament. When not in use, it was kept in a special bag (*right*) embroidered in gold and silver thread. By Elizabeth's reign, a new purse was supplied annually. It was carried solemnly before the Lord Chancellor in procession or borne on his arm on ceremonial occasions.

AT royal funerals such as this (*below*), for Elizabeth I, a robed effigy of the dead ruler, sceptre in hand, was placed in a prominent position on top of the coffin. At the moment when the ruler's body natural was removed from view, the effigy was a visible affirmation of the permanence of the usually invisible body politic of monarchy.

The Chariott drawne by foure Horses upon which Charret stood the Coffin covered with purple velvett and upon that the representation, The Canapy borne by six Knights.

and hawking ranked among the favourite pastimes of Henry VIII and Elizabeth I. They were best enjoyed in the 'grass season' after the hay was cut, and it was predominantly for this reason that the months from July to October were the conventional times of royal 'progress' while the winter months were marked by relatively random peregrinations in and around the royal residences in the Home Counties.

3. *Early Tudor Theory of Kingship*

Thomas More was *not* among the contemporaries impressed by the rhetoric and iconography of princely 'magnificence'. Like William Shakespeare, who wrote his English and Roman history plays in the last decade of the reign of Elizabeth I and the first of James VI and I, More knew that politics and dramatic representation were often two sides of the same thing. In his *History of Richard III*, compiled between the years 1513 and 1519, More dubbed politics as 'king's games: as it were stage plays, and for the more part played upon scaffolds'. Like Thomas Starkey, More loathed tyranny, and both these humanists offered ambiguous reactions to Renaissance kingship. They did so because the reign of Henry VIII increasingly saw a clash of competing values. This clash was partly between the values of humanism and chivalry, and partly a collision over the theory of kingship.

In the reigns of Henry VII and Henry VIII the leading political manuals were still the writings of Sir John Fortescue. In his *Praises of the Laws of England* and *Of the Nature of the Law of Nature* Fortescue had argued that the authority of the king of England was 'political and regal'. Unlike the kings of France, whose 'regal' power to legislate and tax had been restored by Charles VII, the kings of England could not govern without the consent of the realm expressed in Parliament. They 'do not make laws nor impose taxation on their subjects without the consent of the three estates of their kingdom'. The king 'cannot at his pleasure change the laws of his kingdom'. Statutes are established 'by the assent of the whole kingdom', and the civil law maxim 'What pleases the prince has the force of law' is unknown to English law. Henry VII was not averse to coercive fiscal measures or even to altering the rolls of Parliament on occasion to suit his purpose, but in general he followed Fortescue's advice, particularly over taxation.

Yet, if Fortescue's king of England took the advice of his counsellors and ruled 'politically', he could also act 'regally' when required. In times of emergency he might govern exactly as he saw fit. Moreover, he alone was the judge of what constituted an emergency. By the time of the debates on the Petition of Right (1628) stereotyped versions of Fortescue's theory had been annexed by common lawyers and parliamentarians to justify a thesis of limited or 'constitutional' monarchy. But Fortescue's tracts did *not* establish the paradigm which so many commentators conveniently assumed. What Fortescue erected was the model of a self-limiting, self-regulating king who chose *as a matter of honour and duty* not to exceed the bounds of reason or to act contrary to the public good. The dissonance between this interpretation and the model of 'imperial' kingship as propounded by Henry VIII in the 1530s is more apparent than real.

Henry VIII began and ended his reign with a series of ruinous military campaigns in France and Scotland: the humanists increasingly set the martial and chivalric values of the Court in opposition to the values of *bien publique* and good government. Partly the humanists were reacting against Henry VIII's rhetoric, which artlessly sought to represent as defensive and thereby to justify what were manifestly offensive invasions on the grounds that France and Scotland were part of the 'patrimony' of the English Crown by virtue of dynastic claims. Partly, too, the debate represented a split between the materialist values of royal and aristocratic culture, which stressed the importance of princely 'magnificence' and chivalric display, and the philosophical and religious values of the humanists.

The values of 'commonwealth' were also appropriated by religious reformers who, like Luther, had a social gospel to proclaim. In the sermons of Robert Crowley and Hugh Latimer in Henry VIII's reign, and in the lectures of Martin Bucer at Cambridge in the reign of Edward VI, Protestantism and the social gospel fused. The slogan, 'The kingdom of God in this world', was controversial, but it was one upon which many humanists and reformers could unite.

Again, the humanists reinvigorated the debate concerning the nature of 'true' nobility. Increasingly the claims of merit (especially of intellectual achievement) were preferred to those of high birth. Thomas Cromwell's client Richard Moryson, who secured a place in Henry VIII's Privy Chamber, went so far as to argue that it was merit, and not birth, which was the precondition of entry into the Privy Council. And such arguments—that the values of *bien publique* and 'commonwealth' were more important than aristocratic values and the traditional *cursus honorum* prevailing at Court—influenced the theory of kingship because they affected how the 'virtue' of the king was defined.

Yet the touchstone was the Royal Supremacy. A novel and comprehensive theory of monarchy was announced by the Acts of Appeals and Supremacy. The catalyst was the first divorce campaign of 1527–33, when Henry VIII annexed the language of 'imperial' kingship in order to break with Rome and declare his supremacy over the English Church. Henry's political theology was proclaimed in the preamble to the Act of Appeals (1533):

Where by divers sundry old authentic histories and chronicles it is manifestly declared and expressed that this realm of England is an empire, and so hath been accepted in the world, governed by one supreme head and king having the dignity and royal estate of the imperial crown of the same, unto whom a body politic, compact of all sorts and degrees of people divided in terms and by names of spirituality and temporalty, be bounden and owe to bear next to God a natural and humble obedience; [the King] being also institute and furnished by the goodness and sufferance of Almighty God with plenary, whole and entire power, preeminence, authority, prerogative and jurisdiction . . .

Henry VIII defined his prerogative in terms of his *imperium*. He argued, first, that the kings of England from the second century AD had enjoyed secular *imperium* and spiritual supremacy over their kingdom and national Church; and, secondly, that the English Church was an autonomous province of the Catholic Church independent from Rome and the papacy. The Act of Supremacy proclaimed the King's new style in 1534. Moreover, the role of Parliament should not be misinterpreted. The Tudor supremacy was never equivalent to a doctrine of parliamentary sovereignty. It was modelled on the prototypes of ancient Israel and the late Roman empire: the Crown assumed full responsibility for the doctrine and ordering of the Church. It was not for nothing that Henry VIII's favourite kings were David and Solomon, and that he could quote verbatim from the Old Testament and *Code* and *Institutes* of Justinian. Nor was Elizabeth I's position significantly different. Despite the purposeful ambiguity of the settlement of 1559, Elizabeth consistently held her royal supremacy to be magisterial. She might delegate the exercise of her authority to royal or statutory commissioners, but *imperium* was vested in the monarch alone. For

Elizabeth as much as for Henry VIII or the early Stuarts, the Supreme Governor was 'authorized' immediately by God; disobedience to the monarch was ultimately disobedience to God.

Henry VIII, rather than James VI and I, thus propounded the theocratic model of the divine right of kings. His *imperium* was ordained by God and embraced both 'temporal' and 'spiritual' government. The kings of England were invested with an 'imperial' sovereignty, part of which had been 'lent' to the priesthood by previous English monarchs. Moreover, royal *imperium* was antecedent to the jurisdiction of the clergy and was inalienable. Despite its partial 'loan' to the clergy, it could be resumed by the king at will. By exercising his *imperium* the king could redefine the duties of 'his' clergy, summon church councils within his dominions, revise canon law, dissolve the monasteries, and even expound the articles of faith. In particular, he could require Convocation to rule on his matrimonial affairs, and then invite Parliament to reinforce their (favourable!) verdict by statute and common law.

Henry VIII's new understanding of the theory of kingship made an immediate impact on the *mise-en-scène* of Court ceremonial. Whereas before the Act of Supremacy the emphasis was on chivalric and classical displays—'disguisings', 'maskings', interludes, dances, tournaments, and other sports staged at each of the traditional festivals—after 1534 Henry jettisoned such spectacles in favour of his anti-papal campaign. It has been said that in 1533–4 ' "the Renaissance prince" was transformed into the "Reformation patriarch" '. A new iconography of kingship was

THE miniature by Hans Holbein the Younger, *c.*1535, depicts King Solomon receiving the Queen of Sheba and her train. The figure of Solomon is a portrait of Henry VIII. The Queen of Sheba was a traditional emblem of the Church, hence the subject represents Henry VIII as supreme head receiving the homage of the Church of England. On the backcloth is an inscription taken from 2 Chronicles 9: 7–8, which implies that Henry VIII is appointed directly by, and accountable only to, God. In this extract the text of the Vulgate edition of the Bible has been altered. The word 'constitutus' is used to remove any ambiguity that Henry VIII may have been elected or acclaimed by popular consent. The scene illustrates a typical royal interior of the mid-1530s.

¶ The Byble in
Englyshe, that is to saye the con-
tēt of al the holy scrypture, both
of ý olde, and newe testamēt, with
a prologe therinto, made by
the reuerende father in
God, Thomas
archbysshop
of Cantor
bury,
¶This is the Byble apoynted
to the vse of the churches.

¶ Prynted by Edward whytchurche
Cum priuilegio ad imprimendum solum.

M.D.XL.

required for which the gold standard was set by Hans Holbein's depiction of Henry VIII as King Solomon receiving the homage of the Queen of Sheba: that is to say, of the Church of England. Holbein's engraved title-page to Coverdale's Bible in 1535 again showed Henry VIII enthroned in state, handing the scriptures to three mitred bishops, while in Cromwell's Great Bible of 1539 Henry was depicted distributing the Word of God to his subjects, who loyally cried 'Vivat rex' and 'God save the King'.

Not surprisingly the theory of the Acts of Appeals and Supremacy created tensions in the body politic: 'imperial' kingship was posited against the values of the common law and constitutional monarchy. The dissolution of the monasteries heightened this tension. For the *original* purpose of the dissolution had been to provide a permanent landed endowment for the 'imperial' Crown. It had never been Cromwell's intention that the confiscated lands should be sold. Only under the threat of a papally sponsored crusade against the 'schismatic' Henry VIII did sales of land begin, and further massive sales were required to pay for the campaigns of 1542–6 in Scotland and France. The initial plan had been to *retain* the bulk of the ex-religious lands: hence 'absolutist' or theocratic kingship was to be underpinned by patrimonial kingship. A landed estate, or patrimony, was to be constructed, so extensive and valuable that the king would 'live of his own' perpetually, and recourse to Parliament to secure taxation would only be necessary in case of war. Henry VIII proved all this to be wishful thinking, but the ambiguity remained. 'Imperial' kingship, of which the royal supremacy was an integral element, was hereafter cast in opposition to feudal notions of contractual kingship, to humanist ideals of classical republicanism, and to the common law. (When Thomas More mounted the scaffold in 1535, he believed Henry VIII to be a tyrant.)

4. *A Crisis of Mid-Tudor Monarchy?*

Was there a crisis of mid-Tudor monarchy? The answer, emphatically, has to be no! Such a view implies that the monarchy and its institutions were in serious and imminent danger of collapse in the reigns of Edward VI and Mary. This was never the case.

It is true that between 1547 and 1560 the localities suffered the effects of population pressure and the rise of the market economy in agriculture. The people became casualties of price inflation, increased rents, food shortages, currency debasements, plague, and influenza. A dip in the European trade cycle exacerbated these economic problems. National politics were dominated by unstable regimes: first those of Protector Somerset and the Duke of Northumberland under Edward VI, and thereafter that of Mary Tudor and her Spanish husband King Philip I. England under Edward VI and Mary saw regional revolts, religious strife, unsuccessful or unpopular wars, fiscal bankruptcy, and a series of attempted *coups* each with military overtones. In Edward VI's reign the royal supremacy, controversially, became the vehicle of an 'official' Protestant Reformation that began with the stripping of images and rood lofts from the parish churches.

TITLE-PAGE to the Great Bible, *The Byble in Englyshe* (first published in 1539), in the definitive edition of 1540 which contained a prologue by Cranmer. Henry VIII, seated enthroned beneath a diminutive God the Father, is depicted as supreme head of the Church of England. He distributes copies of the Bible to Cranmer, Archbishop of Canterbury, and to Cromwell, vicegerent in spirituals, who pass them in turn to the bishops and great lords. The Bible is heard, but not read, by the acclaiming crowds at the foot.

An allegory of the Reformation drawing special attention to the destruction of images ordered in February 1548. From his death-bed Henry VIII points to his successor, seated enthroned beneath a cloth of estate. To the right of Edward VI are placed Protector Somerset and members of the Privy Council. Henry VIII and his son are portrayed as having overthrown popery and superstition and substituted in their place the pure Word of God which is the true law of Scripture. Edward VI was regularly apostrophized as King Josiah, the Old Testament ruler who implemented the book of the law and oversaw the burning of the idols. In this depiction the members of the Privy Council represent the priests and elders of the Old Testament account.

Thereafter, the advance of Protestantism in London and the south-east of England led to sharp ideological divisions. A relative power vacuum after Henry VIII's death allowed censorship controls on the printing presses to dissolve. The result, which Mary was unable to reverse effectively, was that torrents of pamphlets and propaganda were unleashed by rival confessional groups seeking to create and mobilize a favourable public opinion.

The mid-Tudor era was undeniably turbulent; there were dangerous moments. Northumberland's *putsch* against Somerset in 1549 and his failed attempt to grab the throne for Lady Jane Grey in 1553 potentially threatened civil war. Wyatt's rebellion posed a fundamental challenge to Mary's regime, while the 'stirs' and revolts in East Anglia and the south-west in 1549 were the closest thing that sixteenth-century England saw to a class war. Again, the Protestant exiles on the Continent in Mary's reign fused their confessional convictions with their political frustration to produce a theory of resistance which called for civil disobedience, revolution, and the deposition of tyrants. These were interesting and exciting times!

Yet the monarchy held fast. Somerset and Northumberland maintained careful (if largely staged) deference to Edward VI's regality. Court ceremonial was left intact, and (if anything) intensified in order to preserve the appearance of normality. Northumberland's succession *coup* failed. Mary commanded instant gentry support as her brother's legitimate successor despite her known Catholicism. At Court almost as many revels, masques, plays, and 'pastimes' were staged per annum as during the reign of the young Henry VIII. The vitality of the Edwardian revels would surprise, were it not clear that their purpose was to boost morale both within and outside the Court. Mary instructed the Revels Office to keep costumes and scenery to a minimum to limit costs: materials were to be retained and recycled. But the show went on. Only full-scale tournaments were abandoned in this period, in Edward's reign to avoid injury to the boy King, and in Mary's because Philip declined to participate and because of the Spanish courtiers' preference for other forms of martial entertainment.

Government institutions were equally resilient. An important legacy of Henry VIII had been the rise of the corporate Privy Council. By 1540 the Privy Council of nineteen or so members was established as the monarchy's chief policy-making and executive arm. Under the mid- and late-Tudor system, the Privy Council governed England under the Crown and acted as a buffer between the royal household and the provinces. In theory and practice the ruler's 'imperial' sovereignty became limited by the advice of the Council (which simultaneously gave effect to humanist-classical theory on the subject of 'councils' and counselling).

Under Edward VI and Mary the Privy Council was forced to expand in order to widen the consultative process and offer seats to vital supporters of successive regimes. Its increased size reflected the relative weakness of the monarchy as compared to that of Henry VIII. Whereas there were 19 Privy Councillors between 1540 and 1547, there were 47 in the reign of Edward VI, and 50 under Mary.

But there is a difference between *notional* membership and the numbers of *working* Privy Councillors who regularly attended meetings. Under Protector Somerset (1547–9) the number of working Councillors oscillated from 13–14, to 18, to 21, rising to 23 in 1547. After Somerset's fall, 19 new Privy Councillors were admitted by the Duke of Northumberland. But the size of the working Council still stood at 22 in 1549, and rose to 32 members only in 1553.

Under Mary, the size of the Privy Council rose because Mary sought to reward and patronize loyalists and supporters of the Catholic cause in addition to experienced advisers. Yet within three months of her accession, the Privy Council numbered only 19 members who were regularly active as working Councillors.

As a result the Privy Council avoided dilution and maintained its position as an élite executive agency. It still operated as a corporate board and continued to govern efficiently: letters and warrants were signed by Councillors collectively at the board. Moreover, the elements of collective responsibility and corporate decision-making, which were the key to the Privy Council's success, were actually strengthened during the 1550s.

An increased dependence of the Crown on Parliament is discernible in Mary's reign. Mary could not legally divest herself of the title of 'supreme head' or reverse Henry VIII's Reformation statutes without the consent of Parliament, which in turn would not agree to Mary's reunion with Rome and the re-enactment of the heresy laws in November 1554 until the terms of the papal dispensation to the purchasers of ex-religious property were incorporated into a statute which stated that lay titles to secularized church lands were valid and that disputes concerning them were triable by common law alone. Again, in December 1555 the Crown's bill to seize the lands of the Protestant exiles was decisively rejected. Lastly, Mary's plans to crown Philip King of England were consistently thwarted by Parliament.

Far from 'sterility' being the keynote of this decade, however, many fertile and enduring reforms were discussed or initiated in the 1550s. Among the most significant was the switch in the theory of taxation and its focus precipitated by the Crown's insolvency. Under Northumberland, politicians like Sir William Cecil and Sir Thomas Smith moved increasingly towards definitions of national or 'state' finance. They blurred the traditional distinction between 'ordinary' and 'extraordinary' revenue, and argued that taxation was due equally in time of peace or war. They asserted that subjects had a civic duty to meet the 'necessary' costs of government, and held that the lion's share of ordinary Crown revenue should be raised from regular taxation and from increased excise duties rather than from the proceeds of Crown land.

Both Northumberland and Mary adopted this advice, levying taxation which subsumed the 'extraordinary' needs of defence within the 'ordinary' needs of government, and which justified taxation on the grounds of beneficial rule and necessity. This implied that a revised system of *public* or national finance should supersede the existing system of patrimonial or 'royal' finance. It implied that a nation of willing taxpayers should assume responsibility for a national budget indexed to match population, inflation, the costs of warfare, and the needs of an expanding bureaucracy. A product of the fiscal pressure of the 1550s, this radical theory did not find favour with Elizabeth I. On the other hand, the proposal to recoup a greater proportion of the regular costs of government from the excise revenues rather than the Crown lands became a reality when Mary revised the Book of Rates, doubling many duties and introducing new ones on cloth, 'dry' goods, wine, and beer. This increased effort to exploit customs revenues *was* sustained and developed by the Elizabethan regime, which eventually resorted to customs farming and other fiscal expedients, and which relied decreasingly on patrimonial income to meet the costs of government and the royal household.

5. *The Monarchy of Elizabeth I*

Elizabeth I was an unmarried woman. In view of her private (and sometimes public) insistence that she would 'live and die a virgin', it was inevitable that the politics of her reign would be distinctive and her monarchy potentially vulnerable. Elizabeth is rightly regarded as a strong ruler,

ELIZABETH I: the 'Sieve' portrait (*c.*1579–83) possibly by an Italian artist. The themes are similar to those of the 'Pelican' portrait (facing page 352), but the iconography is more elaborate. Elizabeth holds a sieve, a symbol of the chastity which underpins her godliness and claim to 'imperial' power. On the column on the left, medallions depict the story of Dido and Aeneas, comparing Aeneas's decision to prefer imperial power over personal love with Elizabeth's own choices. The final medallion shows the 'imperial' crown. On the globe at the right, English ships patrol the oceans, an image which links the 'imperial' monarchy to seapower and to the newly-emerging English claims to a worldwide maritime 'empire'. This link was made by John Dee's *General and rare memorials pertaining to the perfect art of navigation* (1577), and was supported in the Privy Council by Sir Christopher Hatton, one of Elizabeth's favourite courtiers, who is shown in the centre of the right background group.

but she had fundamental obstacles to overcome in dealing with her male courtiers and Privy Councillors. Many contemporaries found the prospect of female rule terrifying. In the eyes of the Protestant exiles of the 1550s in particular, the precedents of the reign of Mary Tudor in England and the Scottish Regency of Mary of Guise (widow of James V) between 1542 and 1560 were appalling and it was in response to these experiences that John Knox published his *First Blast of the Trumpet against the Monstrous Regiment of Women* (1558).

Elizabeth I carefully managed her own policy. As Sir Robert Naunton later explained, 'Though very capable of counsel, she was absolute enough in her own resolution, which was apparent even to her last'. She knew her mind; her instinct to power was infallible. When her Privy Councillors tried to manipulate her, they were rarely successful; she would lose her temper and the matter would rest in abeyance. Yet she repeatedly postponed important decisions: unless panicked, she could procrastinate for years. Her successive ditherings drove Sir William Cecil (later Lord Burghley), her chief courtier and Privy Councillor, to distraction. Thus she wavered over the intervention of 1559–60 in support of the Protestant lords in Scotland; over the safety of the realm and the succession issue in the 1560s, 1570s, and 1580s; over the trial and execution of Mary Queen of Scots in 1585–7; and over what became the most vexed issue of all, whether or not to offer military assistance to the Dutch Protestants in their heroic struggle against Philip II.

Elizabeth's attitude has to be offset against her financial position and the conservatism of her subjects, who were far from being Protestant 'converts' before the outbreak of war with Spain. It has been said that Elizabeth's greatest asset was her *lack* of preconceptions; she was not a conviction-politician like Sir Francis Walsingham or the Earl of Leicester. Her preference for *realpolitik* exceeded that of the later Burghley. Apart from her concern to redeem Mary's loss of Calais, she ignored conventional royal ambitions. Her father's territorial illusions were absent. She had no urge to conquer Scotland or France. She shirked a dynastic marriage despite constant diplomacy conducted until 1582. After a rising of the northern earls in 1569 on behalf of the Catholic Mary Queen of Scots, now in exile and in prison in England, she briefly intervened in Scotland in order to weaken the Marian party in the civil war. But she avoided fiscal and military over-extension. She found the Protestant internationalism of Leicester and Walsingham repellent. And, when war with Spain finally erupted, she acted defensively, refused to join a Protestant coalition, and assisted Henry IV and the Dutch on a purely minimalist basis.

From the vantage-point of the reign of James VI and I, Francis Bacon recalled how Elizabeth had 'allowed herself to be wooed and courted, and even to have love made to her', observing that these 'dalliances detracted but little from her fame and nothing at all from her majesty'. In these remarks Bacon put his finger on the essence of Elizabethan politics: first, that to succeed at Court politicians had to pretend to be in love with the Queen; secondly, that the conduct of the 'game' of courtship was Elizabeth's most effective tool of policy. For the dithering, prevarication, and generally dismissive behaviour which was understood to be archetypical of the conventional 'mistress' provided Elizabeth with her weapons of political manipulation and manœuvre. In order to beat her male courtiers at their own game, she changed the rules and capitalized on the power granted to her by virtue of her gender.

Yet policy-making is only a small part of the business of government. The bulk of the task is the *implementation* of policy: it was certain that under a woman ruler, and especially an unmarried one, the Privy Council would retain its place as the élite executive bureau because the inherent social assumption was that the business of government was properly conducted by men. Under Elizabeth the Privy Council advised the Queen at Court and assumed collective responsibility for the management of finance. It enforced the religious settlement of 1559. It managed national defence and fortifications. And it enforced law and order and regulated economic affairs. There were 19 members in 1559; 19 in 1586; 11 in 1597; and 13 in 1601. Privy Councillors worked harder as the reign progressed: in the 1560s they met three or four times per week, but by the 1590s they met almost every day, sometimes in both mornings and afternoons.

But if the Privy Council consolidated its position, there was a minority of strategic issues upon which Elizabeth attempted to forbid discussion or at any rate she did not take her Privy

At New Year 1576 George Gascoigne presented Elizabeth I with a lavish manuscript containing 'The Tale of Hemetes the Heremyte' translated into four languages. The frontispiece shows the kneeling poet offering his work to the Queen. The story concerns three lovers, each of whom is barred or separated from his mistress. In the miraculous presence of the Queen, each lover is satisfied and restored. The work is an allegory of 'courtship' in the reign of Elizabeth I, when in order to succeed politically it was necessary to pretend to be in love with the Queen. It is a book about 'courtship' in the sense of wooing or making love to another person, and 'courtship' in the sense of being a courtier and suing for favour and reward.

Councillors' advice when it was offered. Accordingly, her frustrated Councillors turned to Parliament, where they orchestrated debates and persuaded their clients to deliver planted speeches in attempts to mobilize public (and Protestant) opinion in their favour.

Historians have conventionally treated Elizabeth and Burghley as if they were two halves of a pantomime horse. The reality is that they were virtually different species. The issue crystallizes on the subject of 'councils' and counselling. Was the 'sovereignty' of the ruler to be limited by the advice of the Privy Council? Like her father, Elizabeth believed that her *imperium* was ordained by God alone and her prerogative unlimited by her counsellors' advice. The full implications of this dissonance did not become apparent until after the execution of Mary Queen of Scots, but the issue had been alive since the religious settlement of 1559, for on that single, but crucial, occasion, Elizabeth *was* outmanœuvred and manipulated by her Councillors. Burghley went further down the Protestant road than the Queen had either intended or preferred. In this respect the Elizabethan regime had been established on false premises.

Integral to this debate was one of the most striking developments of the sixteenth century: the rise of the classical prototype of the 'state' and doctrine of the 'mixed polity' and its incorporation into English monarchic theory—that is to say, the thesis that in England there was a 'state' and 'government' as well as a queen. The 'state' in this sense became an impersonal form of political authority: the supreme authority within a 'body politic'. This went considerably further than Starkey's *Dialogue between Pole and Lupset* with its view of 'limited' monarchy. It became possible to say that rulers *themselves* had a duty to consider 'the weal and advancement of the state which they serve'. It became possible to conceptualize the 'state', the 'interests of the state', and 'reason of state' in contexts which (certainly in the eyes of conviction-Protestants) meant more than the person or 'private interests' of the ruler. Government and sovereignty were two aspects of the same thing, but following Aristotle, Polybius, and Cicero, commentators argued with a vigour and conviction not previously possible that the best form of government was 'mixed' or consti-tutional monarchy. Where relevant they invoked the literature of late medieval conciliarism to buttress their interpretation. The working papers of Burghley and in particular of Secretary of State Sir Francis Walsingham epitomized this approach, which has not unjustly been categor-ized as 'monarchical republicanism'.

This theory accurately reflected the political roles of Burghley, Leicester, and the Privy Coun-cil in politics and Parliament before the outbreak of war with Spain. In practice, England be-tween 1558 and 1585 *was* essentially a 'mixed polity', one in which the Queen governed in partnership with the Privy Council. But increasingly after 1572 conflict arose between the views of Elizabeth and those of the supporters or sympathizers of presbyterianism, especially over Elizabeth's attachment to the thesis of 'imperial' kingship.

The rub was that the supposedly 'reformed' English Church was still the Church of Constan-tine. Elizabeth's ecclesiastical authority was modelled, like Henry VIII's, on that of the late Roman emperors. When Thomas Cartwright argued in the 1570s that the institutions of Church and State should be distinct and the government of the Church purely spiritual, he propounded the 'mixed polity' as the ideal form of government in Church and State. This touched a nerve which Elizabeth could not ignore. Even if the Elizabethan regime *was* to all intents and purposes a 'mixed polity', the link with 'popularity' made it *lèse-majesté* to declare this fact in print or to claim that there were things an 'imperial' Queen could not do without Parliament.

E LIZABETH I in the Privy Chamber, Dutch or German School, 16th century. Elizabeth is portrayed receiving two envoys from the Netherlands in her Privy Chamber shortly before the Earl of Leicester's ill fated expedition to assist the Dutch in 1585. Leicester and Walsingham are among those depicted as in attendance, and Mary Queen of Scots is in the corner seated on the floor. Although the subject is not fully explained, the Queen of Scots may have been included to signal her political significance in the European politics of the 1580s.

The result was the intensification of 'divine right' theory after Mary Stuart's execution when the Protestant succession was assured. The final round was played out in the 1590s in the contest to extirpate Puritanism and affirm beyond the bounds of any legal challenge the authority of the Court of High Commission. By 1591 the common law judges had declared that 'by the ancient laws of this realm this kingdom of England is an absolute empire and monarchy'. This was the language of Henry VIII's Act of Appeals: the judges reaffirmed the validity of the 'imperial' theory of kingship. Their decision meant that they interpreted Elizabeth's *imperium* to be as theocratic as Henry VIII's. They acknowledged that Parliament had enacted the legislation whereby the settlement of 1559 had been erected, but held that Parliament was merely the instrument whereby the ruler's prerogative was set forth. Even if Parliament had never met, Elizabeth possessed an 'imperial' prerogative which she could exercise in person in the Church or delegate to whomsoever she chose.

Ambiguity is never the best note upon which to conclude an argument. But deep ambiguity was the legacy of the Tudors to the early Stuarts in the theory and practice of kingship. Personal monarchy had been eroded by the rise of the Privy Council as the élite executive board and by the central role of Parliament in the making of the Protestant religious settlement. Whereas Edward IV and Henry VII had governed England with the assistance of their household servants, the Privy Council by 1603 managed almost the full range of government business and proclaimed the succession of James VI and I. Patrimonial kingship was dead. Although Elizabeth's ordinary revenue was on the whole sufficient until 1585 because (with minor exceptions) she avoided foreign entanglements, her fiscal policy collapsed after 1585. Increasingly she relied on excise duties, taxation, and prerogative devices: purveyance, impositions, and finally licences and monopolies. Such methods were wholly consistent with the theory of 'imperial' kingship, but they emasculated what remained of the ideal of patrimonial kingship.

Chivalry had lost its political force, and even the preoccupations of humanism were to some extent subsumed by the battle under Whitgift, Bancroft, and later William Laud for the soul of the Protestant Church of England. Personal rule was unthinkable in the first decade of the reign of James VI and I, when the Privy Council retained its role at the centre of government, even if the rise of George Villiers, Duke of Buckingham, and the instincts of the future Charles I effectively eroded the Privy Council's autonomy in the decade which followed the death in 1612 of Burghley's son and political heir, Robert Cecil, Earl of Salisbury.

Yet the debate between ideas of 'imperial' kingship and the conceptualization of the 'state' and 'mixed' constitution did not reach its climax until 1642. When in response to the feudal-baronial arguments of Parliament's *Nineteen Propositions*, Charles I's propagandists yielded to the allure of the Polybian theory of the constitution in their *Answer to the Nineteen Propositions*, the Crown itself took the crucial step whereby the 'opposition' or 'counter'-thesis to 'imperial' and 'personal' kingship became attainable as an official norm. And it was this interpretation which the authors of the Revolution Settlement attempted, if only partially successfully, to promulgate in 1688–9.

HOLLAR'S engraving (*facing*), 1647, shows the new Banqueting House by Inigo Jones which was meant to be the first step in the building of a grandiose, Classical palace. Charles I, who was still devising plans for a new palace in the late 1630s, was executed on a scaffold outside the Banqueting House.

12 STUART MONARCHY AND POLITICAL CULTURE

KEVIN SHARPE

1. *Introduction*

The sixteenth century bequeathed an ambivalent legacy to the Stuart dynasty. The development of the Privy Council and more frequent meetings of Parliaments made England a 'mixed polity'. Yet the king remained the hub of a network of clientage and patronage which was the system of government. And the Reformation made the ruler spiritual as well as secular head of the realm. Long before James VI succeeded to the English throne, Tudor propaganda had schooled his

subjects in the divine right of kings. James I inherited a system of government in which the person of the ruler was central and a political culture in which the monarchy had been exalted to its greatest height.

At the heart of the governmental system and the political culture was the Court. The Court was traditionally, and to some extent remained, less a fixed place than a body of men and women in attendance on the monarch. It is best to define the personnel of the Court loosely rather than over-precisely—as the entourage surrounding the king, from consorts and children, mistresses and ministers, attending aristocrats and foreign dignitaries, down to barbers and pastry chefs, guards and gardeners. But there can be little doubt that by the beginning of the seventeenth century, the Court had changed fundamentally from the courts of medieval monarchs. In the first place, though still peripatetic when the monarch went on progress, the Court was increasingly centred in the royal palaces—St James's and Hampton Court, most of all Whitehall, since Henry VIII's reign the monarch's principal London residence. More and more during the sixteenth and seventeenth centuries, as monarchs travelled less, attendance at Court meant coming to London. The building of aristocratic houses in the Strand, the development of Covent Garden and the West End, the fashionable squares and the theatres, the emergence of the London season, are all evidence of the mounting importance of the Court in the nation. Secondly, the Court grew considerably in size from the few hundred who attended Henry VII to the thousands who waited on Charles II and James II. This growth stemmed not only from the increased numbers of nobles and gentry who visited Whitehall, but, as the evidence of portraiture and engravings shows clearly, from a broadening of the membership of the Court. Playwrights and painters, like Jonson, Davenant, and Lely, scene designers and engravers (such as Inigo Jones and Robert White), mathematicians and virtuosi (Newton and Aubrey for example), astrologers and philosophers, like Boyle and Hobbes, joined the ranks of noblemen, ministers, judges, and personal servants to constitute a Court that became the intellectual and cultural as well as the political headquarters of the nation. Not surprisingly both the functioning of the Court and perceptions of the Court were central issues in the political debates and discourses of seventeenth-century England.

The Court's most important political function was as a centre of patronage and access to the monarch. The decline in the royal progress made the Court, increasingly Whitehall, the forum to press a suit or plead for a pension, place, or favour. Not all, however, could easily travel to London; and with the monarch increasingly distanced by changes in palace architecture and the elaboration of formal ceremony, still fewer could gain direct access to the ruler. Leading courtiers with personal access to the sovereign, therefore, emerged as brokers to advance the suits (and sometimes views and grievances) of others. Courtiers, from the well-established nobility, like the Howards or Herberts, to bedchamber servants such as Endymion Porter, became patronage managers. The role of patronage was to bind the most important governors of the localities to the king at the centre and ensure that lines of communication remained open so that none, despair-

I N this strikingly original portrait (*facing*), Prince Henry, eldest son of James VI and I, stands in a pose reminiscent of Holbein's Henry VIII, while Lord Harington of Exton kneels in adoration. The unsheathed sword, as well as the setting of the hunt, associates the young prince with martial pursuits.

ing of a hearing, pursued the politics of violence rather than petition. The authority of each monarch depended, as we shall see, on the extent to which his Court successfully fulfilled that function.

As well as the headquarters of patronage, the Court was the show-case of personal monarchy. Throughout early modern English society, from the aristocratic household to the hamlet, status and authority depended on degrees of magnificence and display. The Tudor monarchs showed the most sophisticated appreciation of the need for the royal household and Court to outshine any rival in abundance, conspicuous consumption, and magnificent display. For elaborate dress and precious jewellery, huge feasts of thirty dishes, and Hollywood-budget spectacles not only announced (as they still do today) to foreign rulers and English subjects alike the wealth and power of the sovereign; they also, through the awe they inspired, fostered the culture of obedience and deference on which the authority of early modern government rested. Those who came to Court in early modern England attended a 'theatre of monarchy' whose images and special effects represented power as a divine mystery. No less than the modern cinema, they moulded the perceptions of the age. Nor was the impact of the Court, as some argue, confined to those who attended at Whitehall. As the monarchs increasingly employed a host of impresarios—painters and engravers, pamphleteers and numismatists—the image of the ruler was disseminated more broadly to the country. Civic rituals and festivals echoed courtly spectacles; engravings of royal and courtly portraits adorned provincial town halls and homes; woodcuts and ballads relayed images and tales of the Court to the country.

Indeed as some monarchs had always hoped, the Court became a model as well as focus for the rest of the nation. Nobles and gentry began to redefine their own role less as warriors, more in terms of service at Court, and to emulate the fashions of the Court, in architecture, dress, and deportment, in their houses in the country. English advice books for young gentlemen, like Henry Peacham's bestseller *The Compleat Gentleman*, are known as 'courtesy literature'. Words for the practice of amorous pursuits —'court' for example—suggest that the influence of the royal Court on many aspects of life spread to circles beyond the propertied élites. Perhaps not surprisingly the Court and courtiers often failed to live up to the ideal image of themselves that they projected. The ideals of devotion to the interests of the commonweal, service to the monarch, chivalric conduct and gallantry were compromised at times, especially in James I's or Charles II's reign, by factional war, personal vendetta, sexual scandals (like the Overbury affair), and unseemly, even vulgar, behaviour—not least by the king himself. From the last decade of the sixteenth century, we discern a growing disenchantment with the Court in the country. There emerged—not least from within the circles of the Court itself—a body of acerbic critics and satirists who lambasted the corruption and debauchery of the Court and courtiers. Such critics began to contrast the failings of the Court in reality, with the ideal courts of romantic and chivalric literature; and as a counter to its failings they constructed an alternative idyll, the ideology of the country as a locus of traditional values—honesty and integrity, innocence and purity,

DE CRITZ's portrait of James I (*facing*) captures his sharp intelligence but lacks the iconic mystery of portraits of Elizabeth or the calm majesty of Van Dyck's portraits of Charles I. Here the Garter Badge is prominently displayed, but in general James paid little attention to his visual image.

TITLE-PAGE of Peacham, *The Compleat Gentleman*, 1626. With the developing importance of the Court and London season, *courtesy* books like Peacham's became bestsellers, each new edition reflecting changing fashions at Court.

fellowship and community. Such a rural idyll bore no more relation to the reality of local rural life than the actual Court to its ideal archetype. But the language of 'court' and 'country' was an important aspect of contemporary discourse and perception, and it bears witness to the extent to which political questions and debates in early modern England centred on the ideal and experience of courtly life.

2. *Royal Courts and Styles*

It is tempting to discuss the Stuart Court as if it were an unchanging entity. Indeed the institutions, offices, and rituals of Court life were to a large extent continuous—surprisingly even during the Protectorate and across the gulf of regicide and republic, to the years of Restoration and beyond. Yet, in many respects, the Court changed in structure and, as importantly, in style with each reign, sometimes with changing political circumstances within the span of a single reign. Most obviously, the marital status and sex of the ruler determined the most basic arrangements, with significant political consequences. Elizabeth I, having no consort or children, had a single Court. Here she was attended, in the most intimate quarters of her bedchamber, by women who could not easily, in the patriarchal structures of the age, convert their proximity to the Queen into major political influence. All of her Stuart successors were married and had children. As a consequence there was always more than one Court at Whitehall (and other royal palaces) around which servants and aspirants gathered. The disharmonies in any family make it easy for us to appreciate that the Courts of the king, queen, and royal children did not always act in concord; in James I's reign, the courts of Anne of Denmark, Prince Henry, and Prince Charles each became rival centres for the disaffected who wished to pursue policies quite different from the King's. By the early eighteenth century, indeed, the 'reversionary interest', consideration of the likely policy and patronage preferences of the heir to the throne, became an acknowledged aspect of political calculation.

Such consideration reminds us that the age and experience of the ruler were no less important for the Court—or Courts we should probably say—than the monarch's marital status. James I was well into middle age when he ascended the throne, James II in his fifties when he succeeded his brother. Both Charleses were under 30. The political consequences of such generational differences have been little studied and require research, but, at the most obvious level, age influenced the choice of personnel, the manner and style of the Court, the attitude of the monarch, and the political influence wielded, and political calculation made, by magnates, courtiers, and factions. The Duke of Buckingham for one might have been less inclined to link his fortunes to Prince Charles had James been younger and in better health. James II's age might have kept him on the throne had not the birth of his son threatened the continuation of his unpopular Catholic policies. Nationality, of course, was another factor: not only the nationality of the ruler, but of the consort and the entourage. The politics of Queen Elizabeth's reign had been dominated by considerations of the nationality, and hence religion, of any prospective consort. The prevalence and influence of his Scottish compatriots in the English Court undoubtedly soured James I's relations with his Parliaments. And the foreign Catholic wives of Charles I, Charles II, and James II fuelled the anti-popery which in all three reigns lit the fire of political crisis. In 1688 William of Orange was welcomed or accepted as king, as a counter to a detested French influence as well as to Catholicism.

Most of all, it was the personality of the ruler which shaped the arrangements and fashioned the style of the Court. The monarch's attitudes to the dispensation of patronage, to festivals and entertainments, to rituals and customs such as touching to cure the king's evil, profoundly affected the functioning of and attitudes to the Court and monarchy. Similarly, royal preferences for formality or familiarity, sexual mores and recreations determined the degree of access to the monarch, the style of counsel and debate, and the fortunes of magnates and factions—that is to say, the nature of all political life. If then we are to understand the political culture of the Stuarts and their Courts, we need to have some sense of how each royal (not just monarchical) personality reconstituted the Court and the politics of patronage, of place, and of the representation of authority.

3. *The Scottish Succession: James VI and I*

The arrival of the Scottish King James VI to be the new head, as James I, of the English Court presented a shock both to the monarch and his subjects. Queen Elizabeth, whose long reign had spanned a whole generation, had founded her authority on the exploitation of her femininity and the cultivation of a mystique behind which, especially in her later years, she retreated, remote from direct engagement with her courtiers. Her Court was large and complex, its rituals were sophisticated and elaborate, the royal show was carefully stage-managed and packaged. James came from a poor country whose Court was small and simple, and its style more open and direct. Where English political thought had developed the idea of the divinity of kings, in Scotland the Presbyterian Kirk had stressed the contractual nature of kingship and the limitations to royal powers. Scottish politics were still in part clan politics and successful royal rule depended more on agility at the cut and thrust of personal exchange with the lairds than skilful acting on the stage of majesty. The contrast between the two Courts, as contemporaries were very quick to notice, was marked. It was compounded by the personal style of the King. For all his considerable intelligence and intellectualism, James was a practical, down-to-earth character, with little sympathy for rituals and florid formalities, let alone entertainments presenting the monarch as a god of love and nature. The Scottish King could be insensitively blunt and grossly indecorous. Though his detractors exaggerated his personal failings and contributed to this bad press, James himself showed little concern with public relations. He presided over evenings of drunken debauchery and was personally slovenly and unkempt. Such lack of decorum, compounded by James's own homosexual relations and the sexual scandals of his reign, both sharpened the criticisms of the Court and diminished the authority of majesty which depended as much on style and image— ways of doing things—as on the talents and policies of the ruler. The King and Court that became the target of scatological broadsheets and pornographic ballads squandered the Tudor legacy of royal mystique and divinity.

James's personal style in some ways reorientated the Court for the better. During the last years of her reign the isolation of and difficulty of access to Elizabeth had dangerous repercussions— most obviously manifest in the rebellion of the Earl of Essex, who despaired of securing her favour. Arguably too the prevaricative style of the Queen, her reluctance to engage, had glossed over problems that needed to be confronted. James, in complete contrast, was willing to acknowledge and ready to tackle problems; and he remained open to a wide variety of influence—from Catholics and Protestants, those counselling peace and war, or men urging a variety of domestic reforms. No figure or faction during the early years of the reign needed to despair of persuading the King to advance their persons or policies; the Court functioned, as it was meant to, as the centre of all political positions and groups.

The royal family contributed to this openness, and more. Though she has been accorded insufficient attention by historians, James's Queen, Anne of Denmark, was politically astute and active. Though sexually estranged from her husband, she evidently continued to wield influence

J AMES I was, as the editor of his *Works* acknowledges, unusual in his love of debate and writing. His *Works* included religious commentaries, polemics against Jesuits, and treatises on kingship. He regarded his writings as the testament of his kingship.

upon him, and from her own Courts at Denmark House and Greenwich she manœuvred behind the scenes in conjunction with courtiers to supplant favourites and advance her own candidates—most infamously George Villiers. The King's eldest son, Prince Henry, not only provided at St James's a home and patronage for many alienated from his father's favours and by his policies, he established a Court so radically different in style from that at Whitehall that some even viewed it as a centre of opposition to the King. Unlike his father, Henry was chaste, decorous, devoted to the tilt, and a champion of belligerent intervention in Europe. The entertainments at his Court announced as well as reflected his martial values. After his early death in 1612, the Court of his younger brother Prince Charles also functioned as a centre for those frustrated by the King's foreign policy and, by 1624, as a campaign headquarters for the war party. Moreover, the influence of Anne, Henry, and Charles effected another shift in the Court. The patronage of Continental artists, architects, and gardeners and the fashion for the elaborate twice-yearly entertainments of music and dance called masques (which owed most to Anne and her sons) brought the politics of the Renaissance Court portrait and spectacle to an England still largely isolated from European fashions.

While James's personality made for healthy openness and his family offered alternative centres of patronage, the King's capriciousness and sexual infatuations with attractive young men were forces for instability. James's predilections for the young Scot Robert Carr, and his promotion of this relatively obscure figure from page to Viscount, then Earl, alienated the ancient aristocracy and upset the scales of influence the King had so shrewdly balanced during the first decade of his reign. Still worse, his obsession with George Villiers, elevated to be Duke of Buckingham, led James to allow one figure to acquire a virtual monopoly of patronage, which dangerously narrowed the Court's connections to the powerful political élites of the localities. Buckingham's dominance of the Court and King and James's public demonstrations of their sexual relationship not only offended sensibilities; sodomy was in this period a felony for which the penalty was execution. The rise of an ambitious personal favourite to political dominance drove courtiers and natural allies of the Crown into disaffection and opposition, exacerbated difficulties between the King and his Parliaments, and effectively destroyed his foreign policy. As the nexus of patronage and public-relations headquarters of monarchy, the Jacobean Court, for all the King's personal qualities, was an all too conspicuous failure.

4. *Order and Formality: Charles I*

The immediate revolution in Court life effected by Charles I might well have been a deliberate reaction to the style of his father. Charles had left Scotland as a boy of 4 and not returned before he succeeded as king in 1625. Unlike his father he was naturally withdrawn and inclined to formality and these traits, developed by his admiration for the splendidly regulated Spanish Court

CHANGES in architectural style: (*above*) Blickling Hall, Norfolk, designed by Robert Lyminge and showing almost no traces of Classical influence. It was built in 1616–27, just at the time when Inigo Jones was building the Queen's House at Greenwich, designed for Anne of Denmark (*below*). The comparison dramatically demonstrates how Jones's neoclassicism marked a radical departure from the style of Tudor and Jacobean architecture. He believed that the perfect harmonies of proportions not only reflected but disseminated ideals of order, so making architecture a branch of government.

CHARLES I as Garter Knight, by Lely after Van Dyck. Charles attached great importance to the Order of the Garter. He changed the badge to incorporate the silver rays of the French Order of the Holy Spirit, underlining the religious as well as chivalric ideals of the order.

which he visited in 1623, dictated the organization and tone of his royal household. In contrast to the easy approachability of James, Charles tightly regulated access to his person, strictly delineating and limiting the courtiers who had entrée to his privy quarters, and secured his privacy by changing locks in the privy lodgings. Under Charles the daily life of the Court was, as it had been under Elizabeth, organized around a set of elaborate rituals and ceremonies from the King's waking, dining, and going abroad to his retreat at night. In his Court, as in his Church, Charles attached great importance to such rituals because he believed them to be the essential expressions of reverence for sovereignty. The rules he devised for the governance of his household and Court are marked by their emphasis on the awe of majesty. No one was permitted to come too close to the King's person, his chair or canopy, and articles in contact with his person were treated as sacred objects to be cherished. The Court entertainments make explicit the ideas informing these practices. Where James seems to have favoured rollicking good entertainment and took pleasure most in the dancing, the Caroline Court masques enacted a philosophy and ideology known as Neoplatonism. In these entertainments, the King appeared as the force who by his very being transformed darkness to light, wilderness to harmony, vice and chaos to virtue and order. Such an ideology of kingship was promulgated no less in the paintings of himself and the royal family which Charles commissioned from Van Dyck: the virtuous king, having mastered his own passions, stands as the force who might civilize all men and lead them to self-regulation by example. Though silent in masques and on canvas, Charles articulated through the culture of his Court a philosophy of rule which he desired and expected others to emulate.

The change in organization and style at Court are central to understanding the politics of the reign. More distant, less easily influenced than his father, and, unlike James, personally very happy in his marriage, Charles did not govern through favourites. After the death of his friend Buckingham, the King himself very much led from the front, leaving his ministers to their respective responsibilities. As in James's early years, a wide variety of factions and views were again represented at Court. Moreover, the Court of Charles's Queen, Henrietta Maria, provided patronage and a centre for not only her Catholic entourage but some magnates who, critical of the King's foreign policy, sought a French alliance and war against Spain. For much of the 1630s, Charles's Court functioned politically as it should: to accommodate differences and contain conflicts.

Both within and outside the Court, however, were the seeds of future troubles, some sown by the King himself. Charles was sparing with his favours and affections and did not easily gain the love, trust, and loyalty he expected. While open to advice, his rigidity once he had made up his mind fostered the politics of inflexibility and principle rather than negotiation and compromise. When civil war came, nearly half the King's Privy Councillors and courtiers failed to support his cause. And though he won respect for the moral reforms he effected, Charles's Court became tainted by a fatal suspicion: that the Court—and perhaps the King himself—were governed by papists. Such fears, which echoed through the country, were fostered by the enhanced emphasis on religious ceremony, still more by the public worship of English Catholics at the Queen's chapel and the conversions to Rome of some prominent courtiers. The fears were misplaced; Charles was devoted to the Church of England. But in religion as in politics, he too often failed to feel the need to explain his position until it was too late. In consequence the Court which Charles constructed as his model for the whole nation was perceived by many as the headquarters of the popish Antichrist, to be destroyed, if need be by violent revolution.

5. *Commonwealth and Court*

At first we might be led to think that the revolution which decapitated the King, abolished the monarchy, and established a republic also destroyed the Court, root and branch. Certainly the Court as it was under Charles I was dismantled for all time: England's first true Renaissance Court was also its last. The personnel of the Court were divided and dispersed; some fought for Parliament, some made their peace with the new regime; some fled to exile. Royal palaces were sold off to raise money, as was much of the spectacular artwork the connoisseur King had collected as a beacon of his majesty. The Puritan tendency to iconophobia—to suspicion of sensuous imagery in state and church rituals—was accompanied by the republicans' preference for a plainer style—in speech, dress, and display. Nevertheless, in important senses, the remnants of a Court, still more the image of kingship, remained even during the earliest years of the republic, from 1649 to 1653. First, the Council of State, the successor to the Privy Council, continued to meet at Whitehall Palace, where ambassadors were received. Though we know little about the nature of the Council's entertainments, a Master of Ceremonies continued in office; and royal furniture, tapestry, some paintings, and plate—often engraved with the royal arms—were retained for the government's use. Whilst there were fewer courtiers of the old type in evidence, the Commonwealth's civil service, the larger Court, expanded and its costs surpassed that of the King's. Whatever the reality, the regime attracted the charges of corruption, incompetence, and extravagant waste that had fuelled country critiques of the royal Courts of the Stuarts.

The Council of State was even less successful than the royal Court in binding the powerful men of the localities to the centre—not least because it was less representative of the political nation. And even more than the Courts of the Stuarts, the Commonwealth failed to present an image that

T HE *Eikon Basilike* went through 35 editions in the year following its publication the day after the King's execution. It presented Charles as the exemplar of Christian kingship and as the defender of conscience over hypocrisy, deception, and politicking. Charles kneels holding a crown of thorns, contemplating a heavenly crown; in some versions, the verse from Hebrews 11:38 'of whom the world was not worthy' is added. The image powerfully kept alive the King and monarchy and did much to destabilize the republic.

THE Lord Protector's Great Seal shows how Cromwell as Protector quickly adopted the trappings of royalty. The engraver Thomas Simon's account for his work mentions the seal designed 'in imitation of Charles Stuart'. It shows Cromwell mounted with baton in imperial pose, dominating the capital, and described as Protector of England, Ireland, and Scotland. On the obverse the device is a singularly regal one with the imperial crown and arms of the nations quartered with Cromwell's family arms, the white lion, and motto.

sustained its authority. Not that it failed to try. A new Great Seal, commemorative medals struck after victories in battle, a new vocabulary of legitimation cast in the language of providence rather than divine right, indeed official organs of propaganda, were instituted to replace the image of the Court and King with the symbols of a new regime. They failed. The *Eikon Basilike*, supposedly Charles I's own account of his kingship, the person of his son, the literature of royalist nostalgia, popular memory and custom, the very palaces and artefacts deployed by the Commonwealth, sustained the memory of the King and belief in the need for government with something of the monarchical in it. And Charles II's attempts to regain his throne kept him constantly in the minds and hearts of the people of England.

When the Commonwealth government was dissolved in 1653, the first steps back to a king and Court were taken when Oliver Cromwell was appointed Lord Protector—of 'England, Scotland, Ireland etcetera'. From the beginning the change in style was more marked than historians have noticed. Cromwell was installed in 1653 with a ceremony monarchical in character; an inauguration medal was struck; his Great Seal featured an equestrian portrait of the Protector evocative of the famous portrait of Charles I by Van Dyck; the Protector's arms were topped with an imperial crown nearly exactly resembling the one used by Charles I. Not surprisingly from 1654 there was debate as to whether Cromwell should take the title as well as trappings of kingship. While many in the army, and perhaps Oliver himself, were resistant, it rapidly became clear that a quasi-king and a Court were, as the lawyers and parliamentary gentry urged, necessary institutions for the government of England.

So, even though he declined the actual title, Cromwell restored the monarchy and Court in all but name when he became hereditary Protector in 1657. The reinvestiture ceremony, with coronation oath and enthronement, followed a royal coronation in all its stages but for anointing and crowning. Not only did Cromwell move into Whitehall Palace, other former royal palaces, such as Hampton Court, were repurchased as retreats for 'His Highness'. Though smaller than that of Charles I, a royal household and entourage was re-established. Cromwell had a guard of halberdiers resembling the Yeomen of the Guard and his servants and watermen were clothed in the Protector's livery. His Court—and contemporaries began now customarily to refer to it as such—became more hierarchical and more marked by ritual and ceremony. Cromwell, a good country gentleman himself, may have seen its political value as a bridge to secure support for his regime from the local gentry who increasingly returned to govern the shires. He created peerages and restored an Upper House. He received visitors and revived something of the old Court life, entertainments, and display. More of the late King's goods were brought in to enrich his surroundings; paintings and miniatures of the Protector were distributed; the Banqueting House was used for receptions; a form of masque was even revived—by William Davenant, the deviser of Charles I's last entertainment. Soon, in panegyric, Cromwell was lauded in the traditional language of royal paeans, as the father of his people, the Sun of the cosmos, God's lieutenant on earth. His magnificent funeral was a more stately and majestic occasion than that of James I. After standing under a canopy of state flanked by 500 candles, Cromwell's effigy was led in an elaborate cortège formed by his household servants from the Strand to Westminster. The Court, albeit of a deceased substitute prince, was again visible to the crowd who thronged the way.

Both in its failure and its success, Cromwell's Protectorate and Court advanced the restoration of monarchy and royal Court. Be-

I N 1655 the Dutch struck a medallion in order to ridicule the subservience of the French and Spanish kings to the Protector Cromwell. Cromwell rests his head in Britannia's lap, with his arse sticking out, while the French and Spanish ambassadors dispute who is first to kiss it. The French texts reads 'Withdraw—the honour belongs to the king my master, Louis the Great.' The medallion was engraved the same year with verses explaining the image. Though unflattering to Cromwell, it also powerfully underlines his successes abroad and the respect he won from foreign princes.

cause of his dependence on the army, whatever his own preferences, Cromwell could not dispense all his patronage to the gentry, who were determined to end military rule. As a consequence his Court, though it restored a welcome sense of normality, never functioned politically to win the nation to indefinite Protectoral rule. For the conservative gentry, Cromwell did not go far enough, either in substance or style, to restoring the old ways. By contrast, to the stricter republicans in the army and the country, he went, by a long way, too far: his Court symbolized his betrayal of the Good Old Cause for which they had fought in 1642. Indeed Cromwell's failure is exemplified in his Court which simultaneously announced him as a traitor to republicans and a usurper to royalists. Yet in that he had succeeded during his lifetime in providing some stability, not least by a partial appropriation of old customs—and symbols, Cromwell and his Court accelerated the political flow that led to the Restoration.

6. *Restoration or Reconstitution?*

Every effort was made in 1660 to present the Restoration as a straightforward return to the old order. The rhetoric of healing in panegyrical discourse announced the body politic restored to health after eleven years of sickness. Charles II, who had of course dated his reign from the day of his father's execution, was, like Charles I, celebrated as the Father, the Solomon, the Moses, the King David of his people. The coronation ceremony, on the King's birthday and St George's Day, was regarded as the most magnificent ever. The City of London erected a series of triumphal arches and allegorical tableaux, celebrating peaceful Restoration and the defeat of rebellion, to entertain the King and his entourage and to awe the spectators with the power of majesty reinstated. In Westminster Abbey the coronation was enacted with sacred solemnity, all the nobles touching the crown as a token of their allegiance. Charles II played his part in the pageant well. *En route* to England from exile, he offered to many the magical royal 'touch' for cure of the 'king's evil' (scrofula); at his coronation he pronounced a pardon of unprecedented extent; he conducted himself with solemnity and dignity before his public. Knights of the Bath joined Knights of the Garter to enrich the ceremony and underline the restoration of a culture of kingship and courtliness as well as of the monarchy itself.

The reality was different from the spectacle. For in reality the royal regalia, Arthur's chair, Edward the Confessor's crown, orbs, and sceptres were not simply restored to Charles Stuart; melted down during the Commonwealth, they had to be remade. In important senses the same was true of the monarchy and political culture of the age. Cromwell's embalmed body was exhumed and burnt, his head was publicly displayed on a stake, and Charles I's statue restored, but the memory of regicide and republic could not be so easily erased. During the 1650s the nation had been well governed and in foreign affairs and commerce had enjoyed glory and gain under republican rule. Whatever the official cult of royalism, even some panegyrists were reluctant to condemn totally the republican regimes and even willing to draw some lessons from them.

Not least the lessons of the 1650s were also etched on the King himself. During years of exile and hardship, sheltering with and receiving help from ordinary folk, Charles had undergone the unusual royal experience of close engagement with his people, which influenced his personal style of monarchy. Though he could exhibit a strong sense of the reverence due to majesty, he was—quite unlike his father—a down-to-earth figure, witty and affable, familiar and often

vulgar. Though he continued to 'touch', Charles II never revived the masques or rituals through which his father had represented the mystique of monarchy. As the reign progressed, the Court descended into public debauchery that even shocked the French and the King's vulgarity tended to base crudery. Charles's series of young mistresses—the first since Henry VIII's reign—were paraded scandalously in public and even represented on the coin of the realm or engraved sacrilegiously as Madonnas. The vices of drink, whoring, and pox were soon seen to be symptomatic of the political ills of corruption, arbitrary government, and popery. The mystique of kingship was greatly dimmed when 'the angel clothed in flesh' began to appear altogether more fleshly than angelic.

If the Commonwealth irrevocably demystified monarchy, it left a still more important legacy: the fact of permanent divisions in the body politic. In 1660 the language may have been that of union, harmony, and public interest, one King and one Church, but between the lines echoed the fear of division, intrigue, and insurrection. For all the popularity of the Restoration, politically it was the victory of a party not the nation. Remarkably soon political debates and disagreements made it clear how far issues and divisions remained—over the prerogative and religion. An astute politician, Charles II was able not only to adapt to this new political world but even to turn it to his advantage. He recognized the need for compromise; he acknowledged the need at times to feign and disguise. With Parliaments now a regular institution, he learned the first lessons in the art of political management to win support; he played on fears of instability to strengthen his hand. Arguably though the mystique of monarchy had been damaged, in practice he was

D IRCK STOOP'S *Coronation Procession of Charles II*. On 22 April 1661, his birthday, Charles II processed in triumph from the Tower to Whitehall. The City prepared allegorical arches to express the 'inexpressible happiness which these kingdoms have received by the glorious Restoration . . . after a dismal night of usurpation and oppression . . '. Charles approached the first arch as Aeneas viewing the torments of the Titans (representing the English rebels).

stronger than any of his predecessors. But as divisions hardened into parties, the illusion of Restoration gave way to a new political order in which the monarch had to play skilfully a careful political game.

The truth of this was made painfully clear by the refusal of Charles II's successor to play that game. The open Catholicism of James, Duke of York, had been the principal force for instability during the later years of Charles's reign. When his brother skilfully defeated attempts to exclude him from the succession, James wrongly interpreted it as a victory for himself and his cause, rather than as a triumph of political management. As a monarch he displayed pride, rigidity, and a reluctance to heed counsel, failing in the essential political arts of realism and manœuvre. The new King had much going for him in 1685. Charles had discredited the Whigs and won over the Tories. James had a reputation as a fearless soldier and fine Admiral. After the profligacy of his brother's reign he presented a welcome contrast of style. He was careful with money; he reduced waste and extravagance at Court. And whilst he never entirely resisted the temptations of mistresses, James was relatively discreet and in public set a moral tone for his Court. He banished

JAMES II by Kneller, 1684–5. James had been a celebrated and successful Lord Admiral before his accession to the throne. The anchor and sea battle, however, also symbolize authority and control over the tempests of the passions.

drunkards and blasphemers; he insisted on marital fidelity; he had little time for balls and plays and worked hard with a devotion to duty.

Unfortunately his Court and kingship were to contemporaries more obvious for their Catholic than moral tone. Unlike his brother, James was not prepared to disguise his faith; like his father he was committed more to fixed principles than to politicking. James's central objective as king was to secure toleration for Catholics and to advance their faith and cause. Contrary to Whig legend, he attempted no Catholic monopoly, nor arbitrary rule. But, uninterested in the politics of explanation or representation, James failed to dispel the fears that he aspired to popish absolutism. Rather, the complexion of his Court confirmed them. Charles II had learned to stick by his friends the Tories for fear that otherwise they would not support him. James by contrast removed the Protestant nobility, surrounded himself with committed Catholics and so made his Court a narrow party enclave rather than the nexus of all politics. In 1688, when he fell to an invading force led by William of Nassau, James failed to secure the aid of the Tories as well as Whigs. Rather than earthing him to the most powerful currents of the political nation, James's Court and patronage had left him isolated at Whitehall, then cast him into exile.

The debates about the rights of James II's deposition and William and Mary's claim to the throne—debates centred on elective kingship, the contracts between rulers and subjects, the quarrels between and within parties—again suggest that, for all the attempts to put the clock back, the Civil War and Commonwealth had changed the nature of politics, and so changed the political culture and the royal Court. The King's person, personal style, household, and entourage were still the centre of government and politics, but now more obviously part of, than *above*, the political fray. The administrative changes, long wars, and absences of William III during the next reign were to throw the Court and monarchy into the maelstrom of the bitterly contested and sharply divided politics of party. Stormed by parties and factions which limited the King's room for manœuvre, the Court more reflected and promoted the new politics of division and contest than the harmonious residence of God's lieutenant on earth.

13 THE REFORMATION AND THE CREATION OF THE CHURCH OF ENGLAND

1500–1640

CONRAD RUSSELL

1. *Introduction*

The word 'religion', like the word 'Parliament', causes difficulty to historians because the word has remained the same, while the thing it describes has not remained the same. The changes which have happened to the word are a bit like peeling the layers of an onion. The belief in an omnipotent and benevolent Creator, and in a personal salvation, the core of the onion, are all that is left. Without the leaves, it does not look like the same onion.

Yet even this image understates the change which has happened in the meaning of the word 'religion' since the sixteenth century. The word itself means 'binding', and for most people, religion was what bound them together: it was the reason why a community was a community. In most villages the only public meeting-places were the church and the alehouse, and only the church could contain all the villagers: it was only when the whole village was gathered in church that its unity was formally expressed. In 1500 it was the church, more than anything else, which turned individuals into a society. This is why thinking of religion in terms of personal salvation does not tell the whole story. To many people, the Church, universal and eternal, to which Christ had promised that he would be with them even to the end of the world, was the only channel through which God's grace normally came to man, and was something far more important than the mere sum of its parts. To deny the necessity of a united Church was, in effect, to deny that there was such a thing as society. Heretical rebellion was a threat to society, as much as to salvation.

The so-called heretics did not disagree with these values: they merely thought that it was the other side which threatened them. In 1547 Thomas Cranmer, the first Protestant Archbishop of Canterbury, struck the same note in his *Homily On Obedience*:

THE statue of Henry VI in School Yard, Eton. Every charitable foundation, including every Oxford and Cambridge college, prayed for the soul of its founder and regarded the performing of this duty as part of what justified its existence. The school still sings on Founder's Day: 'Rex Henricus, sis amicus, | Nobis in angustia, | Cuius prece | Nos a nece | Salvemur perpetua,' (King Henry, be a friend to us in trouble, that by your prayers we may be saved from eternal death.)

Where there is no right order there reigneth all abuse, carnal liberty, enormity, sin and babylonical confusion. Take away kings, princes, rulers, magistrates, judges and such states of God's order, no man shall ride or go by the highway unrobbed, no man shall sleep in his own house or bed unkilled, no man shall keep his wife, children and possessions in quietness; all things shall be common, and there must needs follow all mischief and utter destruction.

It was not only the present community which was held together by religion. Edmund Burke's definition of society as a partnership between the living, the dead, and those yet unborn copied the definition of the City of God by St Augustine in the fifth century. The continuity illustrates how much the ideas of Church and of society had in common. Before the Reformation, this partnership had a very practical expression. Until Protestant reformers set out to destroy belief in purgatory, it was believed that the souls of many of the dead endured a spell in purgatory, from which they might be released by prayers said by, and masses said for, the faithful. Family tombs in parish churches carried inscriptions asking passers-by to pray for the souls of those buried

within them. It was an essential part of the tariff of salvation that masses should be said for one's soul after death. Those who could afford it tended to endow chantries, privately employing a priest whose principal duty was to say masses for the soul of the person who endowed it.

Perhaps the circumstance which made people most constantly turn to religion was the need to come to terms with death. Few parents were not predeceased by at least one of their children, and marriages broken by premature death were about as common as marriages broken by divorce today. Few people were as unfortunate as Thomas Hoyle, Alderman of York during the Civil War, who was predeceased by fourteen children and a grandson, but the experience seems to have made him and his wife steadily more devout. After the Reformation, the doctrine of predestination was often essential to filling the void left by the inability to pray for the dead: the bereaved took comfort in the certainty that the departed were assured of salvation. John Shaw, a Presbyterian clergyman during the Civil War, commented 'then did my harp hang on the willows, yet the assurance of her happiness did something mitigate my grief'. Of Lady Slingsby, dying after a long and painful illness, it was reported that:

As she lay awaken in the night, she would spend the whole time in discoursing her latter end, making a recollection of her sins, and working upon herself a hearty sorrow for them; and finding the apprehension of death terrible, she would say she desired nothing so much, as that God would give her a willingness to die when soever he should call for her; and that she might attain to it, she would make use of all the promises which confirm her faith, and cause her to see a vanity in all earthly things.

JOHN DONNE, poet and Dean of St Paul's, whose tomb portrays him standing in his shroud, tried to use religion to stare death out of countenance.

> Death, be not proud, though some have called thee
> Mighty and dreadful, for thou art not so,
> For those whom thou think'st thou dost overthrow,
> Die not, poor death, nor yet canst thou kill me.
>
> *Holy Sonnets* (1633), no. 6.

This ability to make a good end was essential to the consolation, not merely of the dying, but even more of the survivors. If the faith in which they died did not appear to the survivors to be the true faith, it offered them no consolation.

Religion was seen as the root of all morals, and its rejection as a total rejection of morality. Sir John Strangeways, a royalist MP during the Civil War, was uttering the conventional wisdom when he wrote that 'men from whom God hath withdrawn his grace, do always follow those councels, which carry them to their own destruction'. The 'motiveless malice' of Iago in *Othello* is perhaps an example of this conventional wisdom.

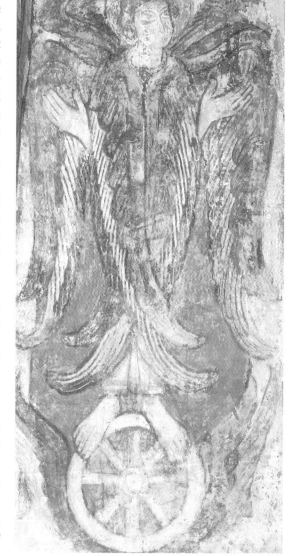

It was to religion that people turned when faced with a shock or crisis. An unhappily married couple were said to be suffering so badly from jealousy and want of affection that 'nothing but the power of religion could make them live like man and wife'. Bulstrode Whitelocke, a seventeenth-century lawyer, found on his wedding night that his wife rocketed into an attack of hysteria so acute that he feared for her life. Finding, in his own words, fortunes 'so different from that which new married men look for and enjoy', rather than calling a doctor, as someone might do now, 'he looked up to him who orders all things'. That story illustrates how religion carried a social and emotional load which is now distributed round many different systems of support.

In addition to these personal uses, religion carried many more official uses. The Church provided a large part of the country's legal system; and excommunication, its supreme penalty, was supposed to be what it said, exclusion from society. Overuse diminished, but did not destroy, its terrors. The Church dealt with failure to pay tithe to maintain the parish clergy, or to repair the parish church. It handled defamation cases, often between women accusing each other of adultery, and made sexual offenders do penance in a white sheet. It dealt with cases about wills and marriages. Official functions like assizes or meetings of Parliament began with prayers and a mass or a sermon. Before printing, which was just coming in at the beginning of this period, the Church had a near-monopoly of news and of entertainment. It was biblical stories, and, before the Reformation, lives of the saints, which filled the place in people's

WALL-PAINTING of a seraph from Canterbury Cathedral. Late-medieval religion relied on the image as much as the word.

lives now filled by television soaps, and for those who could not read, the stories were told through images and wall-paintings. Perhaps religion entered into the consciousness of ordinary people as much by this route as by any others. This involvement of the Church in every corner of life was sustained by a priest–parishioner ratio which, before the population increase of the sixteenth century, allowed priests a detailed knowledge of individual parishioners' lives. In Bristol before the Reformation, the median ratio of parish clergy to communicants was 1 to 86.

In this context, it would have been very hard to treat anyone's religion as a private matter even if people had wanted to. They usually did not want to. Tudor and Stuart England had little sense of privacy. A parish constable, suspecting adultery, once found a man in a woman's house, and reported that he found the man in one room, and his breeches in another. The churchwardens at Cannington in Somerset once presented a couple to the church courts for suspected fornication because they were seen together with suspicious frequency. This readiness to interfere was sanctioned by a doctrine of moral responsibility which held that those who saw a sin and did not correct it 'countenanced' it. Sir John Strangeways, again enunciating the conventional wisdom, said that:

a man comes to be partaker of other men's sins by countenancing, consenting and suffering without punishment, as well as by formally committing them.

The itch to interfere is at all times a strong human emotion, and such ideas made it a positive duty for those who felt this itch to indulge it. This was a society in which the idea that there was only one religion was deeply embedded in the whole social and mental fabric of the country. It was a society in which learning to live with the fact that there was no longer one religion, but several, was going to create an inexpressible series of intellectual, psychological, social, and moral difficulties. Those difficulties came in with the Reformation, and it can be argued that we have not worked our way through them yet.

2. *The Church before the Reformation*

The Church before the Reformation was a formidably well-organized machine, for conveying true doctrine from the Apostles down to all subsequent generations, for conveying the grace of God to each individual sinner who had need of it, and for providing help or consolation in each particular type of trial or misfortune. We will perhaps come nearest to understanding the functions of the pre-Reformation clergy if we think of them as like doctors. A doctor is expected by his patients, whether realistically or not, to be able to write a prescription for the relief of each condition to which the patient may be subject. There is no need for the patient to understand how or why the prescription works. It is his task to trust the doctor, and to take the prescription precisely in the manner, and at the times, prescribed. If he does this, he should have a good chance of recovery. Doctors tend to distrust patients with a little medical knowledge, who like to try to make their own judgements about the appropriate treatment. Even more, they distrust practitioners of alternative medicine, who offer prescriptions which they think may be at best useless, and at worst dangerously in conflict with their own. This is how the late medieval clergy tended to feel about their unauthorized rivals: astrologers, prophets, cunning women, fortune tellers, and *a fortiori* anyone who offered the services of a rival creed. In much the same way, those who

THE elevation of the host was the supreme moment of medieval worship. The priest faces the altar, not the congregation.

came to the late medieval clergy were not expected to understand why their clergy's prescriptions might lead to spiritual health or worldly prosperity: they were expected to take them as prescribed.

The clergy's power was not primarily their own. It had been standard doctrine since the fifth century that the power of a priest to administer the sacraments did not in any way depend on his personal merits: it depended on his office. The priest was first and foremost a pipeline, through whom the worshipper could be connected to the inexhaustible reservoir of divine grace. This power resided first and foremost in the priest's ability to say mass. By consecrating bread and wine at the altar, the priest could perform the feat of transubstantiation, transforming the bread and wine into what became, in some sense, the body and blood of Christ. He was then able, by offering up what he had consecrated, in some sense to repeat Christ's sacrifice on the Cross, thereby putting his parishioners in touch with it and making them able to benefit from it. It was not even necessary for anyone to be present at mass for it to have the desired effect. At mass in a parish church, everyone was expected to be present, and the mass symbolized the unity of the community which was put in touch with divine grace. Yet when a chantry priest, endowed to say mass for the soul of one dead person, said mass in private, the mass might still benefit those, dead or alive, for whom he said it.

The Church was also an organization for offering up prayer to God, to move him to mercy, not only to those who were praying, but to the whole Christian community, past, present, and future. The monasteries, where the monks were supposed to have withdrawn from the world and to live in prayer, were an essential part of the Catholic community. In the traditional threefold division into working, fighting, and praying men, the praying men had a specialized function, which they exercised on behalf of the other two groups as well as themselves. Even though most monks were not priests, and did not possess the crucial priestly powers to say mass and to hear confessions, their prayers, their singing, their scholarship, and their illumination of manuscripts, among other things, made a contribution to the spiritual welfare of the whole community.

Outside the monasteries, active in the world, were the friars, who travelled round from place to place, preaching and teaching. They had originally been largely concerned with combating heresy, and they often annoyed parish clergy by turning up in their parishes, preaching and hearing confessions, and proving that the newcomer was a much bigger draw than the old, familiar face. The friars, unlike the parish clergy, were supposed to prove their superior holiness by living in poverty. The Observant Franciscans were not supposed to handle money, and unkind wags started the story that they used a shovel instead.

Spiritual power was valued as a means to worldly, as well as spiritual, ends. As George Gifford, an Elizabethan clergyman, later put it, 'this is man's nature, that where he is persuaded that there is power to bring prosperity and adversity, there will he worship'. Most worshippers wanted some way of securing more prosperity, and warding off more adversity, than other worshippers, and in addition to its basic spiritual tools, the later medieval Church had built up a vast collection of spiritual aids. Contrary to later Protestant myth, these do not seem to have been mainly invented by priests to increase their own profit, but to have grown up in response to overwhelming popular demand. People had rosaries, on which they might tell the beads as they prayed. They could pay for candles to be put on the altar, or they could sprinkle holy water, which had been blessed by a priest. Many monasteries, and some churches, had some physical relic of a saint, which might enjoy special spiritual power to ward off adversity or bring prosperity. Particular shrines might endow prayers said at them with peculiar efficacy: a Londoner dying in 1521 added a postscript to his will, asking his wife to go to pray at the shrines of Our Lady of Walsingham and Our Lady of Willesden. Prayer at these places was more likely to move the Virgin Mary to intercede with God for the person concerned than prayer merely said in an ordinary church.

Behind these beliefs was the doctrine of intercessory prayer to the saints. A good saint might help a worshipper by presenting his case to God, in much the same way as a good lawyer might help him in court by presenting his case to the judge. Since pilgrimages were the main medieval form of tourism, there might be much competition about the question who had the biggest saint. Increasingly, like lawyers, these saints developed a tendency to specialize. St Margaret, for example, was a specialist in protection during childbirth, while St Barbara, who offered protection against thunder and lightning, became by a natural extension, the patron saint of gunners. Religion, among much else, discharged the functions now undertaken by insurance.

There is every sign that the late medieval Church was developing in this way because that is what its worshippers wanted. There was some shift going on in the centres of popular piety, as there has been at most other times in the Church's history. The monasteries were no longer as central in popular devotion as they had been in the eleventh and twelfth centuries. The chantries may also have peaked shortly before the Reformation. There seem to be two main growth areas shortly before the Reformation. One is the growth of shrines involving prayer to specialist saints. The other is the growth of lay fraternities, who would hire their own priest to say mass for them and perhaps preach to them, club together to pay for their funerals, dine together on set occasions, and pay for such things as lights before the altar. The fraternities indicate a trend towards growing lay control in the Church before the Reformation, but they do not indicate any decline in Catholic piety. In fact, the trends in popular piety around 1500 were mostly heading, not towards Protestantism, but well away from it.

When we go over the complaints against the late medieval clergy, they do not normally indicate any basic dissatisfaction with the religion they represented. Complaints against drunken, litigious, or avaricious clergy happen in all periods, and need not have any specific theological content. Complaints against the sexual activity of priests are found in any century. There is no reason to believe that late medieval clergy were more lascivious than clergy in other periods, and little sign of any rejection of the ideal of a celibate clergy. By far the commonest complaint against priests, especially in remote areas, was of their failure to attend sufficiently regularly to say mass, and their failure to walk long distances to hear death-bed confessions. These complaints do not indicate a rejection of the mass or confession: they indicate exactly the opposite. People wanted more of these services, not less.

There were two exceptions to this general rule. One was a strand of tough populist scepticism about many of the claims of religion. In Bristol in 1535 it was reported that there 'some women do say they be as good as Our Lady, for we have borne four or five children and know the father of them and she bore but one and knew not the father'. The preacher took these women for Protestants, but he was unlikely to have been right: this was not a characteristic Protestant belief.

The other possibility is that they might have belonged to the small and largely underground sect of the Lollards. This group had survived, in a rather tenuous way, from the time when John Wycliffe, an Oxford theologian, had denied transubstantiation in the 1380s. From this, Lollards moved on to attacks on the papacy, confession, the mass, church bells, crosses, the habit of praying in churches, and, at one time and another, almost anything which might make a Christian's salvation depend on the goodwill of a priest. Lollards, who were often ready to recant their beliefs under pressure, developed great skill in avoiding persecution. They often managed, like a certain John Birt, detected in heresy in London in 1532, to 'slip aside'.

The Lollards anticipated the Protestants in almost all their key beliefs except the central Lutheran belief in Justification by Faith, which held all the rest together. Yet there is still room for doubt, both about the nature of the connection between them and about its size. In 1526 two members of the Lollard congregation at Steeple Bumpstead (Essex) came up to London to see Friar Robert Barnes, one of the leading preachers of the new Lutheran doctrines. They produced their precious Lollard translations of parts of the New Testament. Yet Barnes 'made a twit of it',

Exodus chapter 20, the Ten Commandments, from Tyndale's translation of the *Pentateuch*, 1530. Protestants were people of the book: they wanted the word, not the image.

and gave them instead copies of William Tyndale's New Testament, 'for it is of more cleaner English'. The Lollard tradition was not sophisticated enough to impress an up-to-the-minute German-influenced Lutheran from the chattering classes.

Lollards also existed in Bristol. In 1533 William Hubberdine, the leading preacher against heresy in the area, claimed that there were twenty or thirty heretics in Bristol, not all of whom were necessarily Lollards. William Hubberdine was an excitable preacher who was not likely to understate his case. In the end, he died because he got so excited in the pulpit that he jumped up and down until it collapsed underneath him and killed him. The churchwardens, accused of negligence, replied that 'they had made their pulpit for preaching, not for dancing'. If William Hubberdine in all his fervour could find no more than twenty or thirty heretics in Bristol, their strength in a town of near 10,000 people was less than overwhelming. Lollardy helped to provide a fertile soil for the growth of Protestantism in England, but that soil needed a lot of watering from outside.

3. *The Appearance of Protestantism*

Martin Luther affixed his 95 Theses to the church door at Wittenberg in 1517, and was excommunicated in 1520. It was not at first clear that his ideas would finally be excluded from the Catholic Church, rather than being absorbed in a modified form, and the name 'Protestant' was not attached to his followers until 1529. By the middle 1520s there were clearly groups of committed adherents of the 'new learning', in London, Cambridge, and a number of other places.

These ideas caught on piecemeal, and many people adhered to some of them without necessarily accepting them all, and indeed remaining orthodox on many crucial points. As the years went by, believers were slowly sorted out into two rival and continually opposed camps, leaving a large mass of people uncommitted, uncertain, or simply careful in between. From 1530 to 1539 six per cent of wills proved in London show sympathy with these new doctrines. This is almost certainly an underestimate, since the doctrines were dangerous to profess, and one of the smaller risks was that the will might be refused probate. Yet even on the most optimistic estimate of under-counting, these were not a numerically overwhelming force. They included considerable numbers of influential people, and the strong sympathizers with the new doctrines included both Thomas Cromwell, Henry VIII's second chief minister, and Anne Boleyn, his second Queen. Such people were capable of bringing many others behind them. Yet a group with support which was, in the middle 1530s, unlikely to have been much over 10 per cent in their strongest town in the country cannot convert a country without strong support from the top. During the crucial years of Henry VIII's reign, from the meeting of the Reformation Parliament in 1529 to his death in 1547, it was an open question whether and to what extent they enjoyed this support, and if they did, for how long it would last before the wind changed again.

Even though these new believers worshipped the same Christian God, it is perhaps more accurate to classify their faith as a different religion than to classify it as a different branch of the same religion, for their answer to the crucial question, 'what must I do to be saved?' was totally different from the more popular Catholic answers of the later Middle Ages. Just as Tudor economic thinking concentrated on cutting out the middleman, so did Protestant theology, for the key theme which underlay all its different tenets was that salvation did not depend on the intercessory work of the priest, but on our faith. Luther's key doctrine was that it was our faith which justified us, and our faith was a matter between us and God. The priest did not know whether we held a justifying faith or not. According to Stephen Gardiner, Bishop of Winchester, who was a hostile witness, they thought that to enter Heaven 'needs no works at all, but only belief, only, only, nothing else'. Catholics regularly attacked this exclusive stress on faith as likely to encourage immorality by its denial that good works helped to justify. There may have been one or two occasional Protestants who took it this way, yet if we look at Protestant attacks on Justification by Works, they are not attacking the sort of moral good works which come to the mind of a modern audience, but the ritual observance undertaken to satisfy the priest. William Tyndale, biblical translator and one of the earliest English Lutherans, told the story of a pregnant woman who ate meat on a Friday 'which thing she durst not confess in the space of seventeen years, and thought all the while she had been damned, and yet sinned she not at all. Is not this a sure burden, that so weighteth down the soul unto the bottom of Hell?' This woman was the sort of person for whom the doctrine of Justification by Faith might appear as a liberation. From the fact that her story was known to Tyndale, we may deduce that it did. Tyndale extended this attitude to most of the other ritual observances of Catholicism:

if, after thou hast heard so many masses, matins, and evensongs, and after thou hast received holy bread, holy water, and the bishop's blessing, or a cardinal's, or the Pope's, if thou wilt be more kind to thy neighbour, and love him better than before, if thou be more obedient unto thy superiors, more merciful, more ready to forgive wrong done unto thee, more despisest the world, and more thirst after spiritual things… then do such things increase grace; if not, it is a lie. Whether it be so or no, I report me to experience.

This passage illustrates very clearly that when Protestants attacked Justification by Works, they were not asserting that there was no need for moral behaviour but that it was not possible to win salvation by routine ritual observance. Catholicism seen by a Protestant was a faith which could be bought out of a slot machine

Most of the ritual observances of Catholicism were attacked on the ground that they led people to worship the thing created, rather than the creator. Prayer to the saints, for example, was seen as turning the saints into gods, and was therefore a breach of the commandment: 'thou shalt have one God only'. Worship before an image of a saint was even worse: it was two removes from God, and not merely one. Desecrating and destroying images, so that people should no longer worship them, appeared to Protestants to be an essential preliminary to getting them to worship God instead. An old Lollard, in this at home with new Protestants, dismissed Our Lady of Willesden as 'a burnt arse elf and a burnt arse stock, and if she might have helpen men and women which go to her of pilgrimage she would not have suffered her tail to have been burnt'. The Lollard was being even ruder than she seems to a modern reader: to be 'burnt' meant to be infected with venereal disease.

This attitude, which was concerned with the mind of the receiver, not with any alleged intrinsic holiness in the object, was applied to much else. Above all, it was anathema to a Protestant outlook to believe that the elements in the mass turned into the body and blood of Christ simply because the priest mumbled words over them. With their continual attack on what they thought was worshipping anything other than God, Protestants accused those who worshipped at mass of worshipping a God made of bread. They had some trouble trying to arrive at an agreed doctrine of what they called the holy communion, and in the end failed. To the extremer Protestants, the Zwinglians, the whole service was commemorative, and designed only to remind worshippers of Christ's sacrifice on the Cross. To the majority, it was possible for those who approached the Communion with faith to receive Christ, but not for others. Typically, it was the faith which gave efficacy to the ceremony, not the efficacy of the ceremony which created faith.

Because they were so consistent in attacking ritual observance as useless, Protestants always had difficulty in answering the classic parishioner's question: 'what must I do to be saved?' The key experiences which justified took place in the privacy of a worshipper's own mind. The archetypal moment of Catholic worship was collective: a congregation united in veneration at the moment when the priest elevated the consecrated host. The archetypal moment of Protestant

SIR THOMAS MORE, Lord Chancellor and chief heresy hunter, 1529–32, by Hans Holbein. According to Tyndale, he recorded the heresies of Robert Forman 'as truly as his story of utopia', and would have like to prosecute him for heresy.

ANNE BOLEYN, the chief beneficiary of the break with Rome, protected Rome's other enemies, including Robert Forman, when she could.

worship was utterly lonely: the worshipper alone before God, looking into his own soul to ask whether his faith was sufficient, and hoping he knew the answer.

This is one of the reasons why, from the beginning, some Protestants were tempted to deny that man had free will, and claimed that God had predestined some to salvation and others to damnation. In 1528 Robert Forman, a young London vicar recently down from Cambridge, where he had concealed Luther's books, was examined by Sir Thomas More. He avowed a classic Lutheran belief that we were justified by our faith. He then added what was later to become the classic Calvinist belief, that some were predestined to damnation, and 'God taketh them for nought, be they never so good', but for those 'He hath chosen from the beginning and predestinate to glory, all works be good enough'. This solved all the problems of deciding why some people had saving faith and others did not, and it was only over the next century that it became apparent that it created as many problems as it solved. Forman was saved from the burning More would probably have inflicted on him by the intercession of Anne Boleyn.

This stress on faith demanded a new view of the role of the clergy. Where Catholic clergy had been akin to doctors, Protestant clergy were more akin to teachers. They could not simply write a prescription of so many Hail Marys, so many masses, or so many pilgrimages. They had to make the worshipper understand how Christ had died to save him, and understand how he owed Christ love and faith in return, and could afford to trust in his mercy however sinful he might be. The religious life of a good Protestant could be more like the lectures and reading list of a modern undergraduate than the predictable observance of the ordinary Catholic. Because the view of the clergy's job was changed, the demands placed on them changed also. A Catholic priest who could say mass was doing his job. If he could not preach, he was not doing it very well, but the basic essentials were there. By contrast, a Protestant minister who could not preach was barely doing his job at all.

Protestants had no desire to destroy the unity of the Church. They were as convinced as any Catholic that Christ had left only one true Church, and that outside it there was no salvation. They also believed that without one Church for all worshippers there was no civil order and no social peace. This meant they had to aim at 100 per cent success: Catholicism had to be wiped out as if it had never existed. Even 95 per cent success, because it would destroy the existence of a single Christian Church, would mean total failure. Yet, at the same time, because they were taking

salvation out of the control of the Church, and retreating to a faith in which the crucial moments left the believer alone with his God, and because Catholics saw them as destroying the unity of a single visible Church by 'leaping out of Peter's ship', Protestants had some difficulty in explaining their doctrine of the Church. It was a difficulty they have not yet quite overcome.

4. *Henry VIII and Religion, 1529–1547*

In 1529 the doctrines which competed before Henry were not yet fully formed or clearly distinguished, but by his death in 1547, he was facing two ideologically armed camps. Between these creeds, Henry made no final choice. It was said that Henry was like one that would throw a man from the top of a high tower, and bid him stop when he was half-way down.

In 1521, when Henry first took notice of Luther's doctrines, he rejected them outright, and the resulting book led the Pope to grant Henry the title of Defender of the Faith, which his present successor still uses. However, Henry, like other political leaders, tended to judge doctrines, not so much in terms of whether they were true or false, as in terms of whether they were loyal to him or not. Henry's ideas of loyalty were fundamentally changed between 1525 and 1529, when he set out to get a divorce (technically, an annulment) and failed. Henry needed a divorce because he had no male heir, and the lack of one threatened a revival of dynastic civil war. Unfortunately, he not merely needed one, but wanted one with the obsessive and undiplomatic urgency of a man with a mid-life crisis who has fallen desperately in love. Anne Boleyn, the woman he selected, was the sister of a former mistress, a Lutheran sympathizer surrounded by heretics, and widely disliked as a gold-digger.

If Henry was to get a generally accepted divorce, he needed the authority of the Pope to pronounce his existing marriage null and void. He argued that the dispensation the Pope had given him to marry his wife, who was his brother's widow, was *ultra vires* and automatically void. That argument was an attack on the Pope's authority from the beginning, and would have voided other marriages in Europe as well as Henry's.

Not only was Henry's argument weak: it was politically inexpedient for the Pope to grant it. Henry's Queen, Catherine of Aragon, was the aunt of Charles V, the Holy Roman Emperor, who conquered and occupied Rome in 1527, just as the negotiations were coming to a crisis. It is unlikely that the Pope wanted to grant Henry's request, but it is unlikely that he could have granted it if he had wanted to. The Emperor, literally and metaphorically, carried more guns than Henry did. Henry found this fact unbearable.

By 1529 Henry's attempts to secure a divorce from Rome had clearly failed, and for the next five years he increasingly furiously marked time, wondering what to do next. In 1529 he summoned what became known as the Reformation Parliament, but without any very clear idea of what he wanted to do with it. The idea of taking an English divorce without the Pope's consent was in Henry's mind, however vaguely, from 1527 onwards. However, the political way to such a divorce was not yet open, for the key positions were still held by people not willing to grant it.

CATHOLIC and Protestant doctrines competed before Henry VIII like the goddesses competing before Paris with the apple. The chaos caused by the goddesses lasted only the ten years of the Trojan War, but the chaos started by Henry VIII is still in progress.

WOLSEY was dismissed in 1529 but died before he could be tried and executed. In this illustration from George Cavendish's *Life of Wolsey*, the King's agents (*right*) pack up his silver, an eerie foretaste of the royal plundering of the Church that was to follow; on the left the Dukes of Suffolk and Norfolk take the seals from this overmighty prelate. Within a few years they were to be leading defenders of Catholicism against the Protestant voices who replaced the Cardinal in Henry's inner counsels.

He would need a theological judgement from the bishops in the Upper House of Convocation, among whom in 1529 Catherine had a clear majority of supporters. He would then need a judicial ruling from the Archbishop of Canterbury. William Warham, Archbishop of Canterbury, was clearly signalling that he was not prepared to grant a divorce without papal approval, but he was over 80, and Henry hoped to nominate his successor. It perhaps makes sense, then, that the key actions of the Reformation Parliament from 1529 to 1532 were meant to terrify, not the Pope, but the English clergy. On the other hand, the die was not cast, for it was clear throughout these years that if Henry were granted a papal divorce, he would take it.

Events began to move rapidly in August 1532, when Archbishop Warham died, for the first time making an English divorce a practical option. Shortly before this happened, Henry had secured the Submission of the Clergy, giving him control over the clergy's power to make laws for the Church. He had also smuggled through, in the Act in Conditional Restraint of Annates, a little-noticed but vital clause allowing him to appoint his own bishops and archbishops without papal approval.

Henry's first action on Warham's death was to arrange a summit meeting with the King of

France. At this meeting, in October 1532, he took Anne with him and had her ceremonially treated as Queen. Henry had secured the political alliance without which he could not afford to risk war with the Emperor. Anne became pregnant in the first or second week of December 1532. From then on, things moved very fast indeed. In the first week of January, in the third week of the pregnancy, Henry chose his new Archbishop. He was Thomas Cranmer, sympathizer with the new doctrines and chaplain to Anne Boleyn. Having got his clause authorizing him to choose an archbishop without papal approval, Henry used it as a nuclear deterrent instead of firing it. He got Cranmer's appointment approved by the Pope in the normal way. Then, since he knew his marriage was invalid and he was still a bachelor, he married Anne at the end of January 1533. Some time later, in April, Cranmer completed the legal process of granting his divorce from

CATHERINE of Aragon, by an unknown artist. Henry VIII *knew* his marriage to her was null and void, and could give lengthy reasons for his belief. Unfortunately, they were bad ones.

Catherine. It was then necessary to stop Catherine appealing to Rome against this 'pretended divorce'. This was done by the Act in Restraint of Appeals of 1533, which, with the echoing declaration that 'this realm of England is an empire', began with a preamble declaring independence from Rome. Yet this too was a nuclear deterrent. The preamble threatened to break all relations with Rome, but the body of the Act, the part which was legally effective, only stopped appeals about marriages, wills, and tithes. Appeals about such crucial issues as heresy were not stopped. The Pope was being told, in carefully graded diplomatic threats, that if he accepted the *fait accompli* of Henry's new marriage, his authority in England could continue, but if not, not. It was not until the Act of Supremacy of 1534, a year later, that Henry fired the nuclear missile he had been brandishing since 1527, declared himself Supreme Head of the Church, and severed relations with Rome.

5. *Henry VIII as Supreme Head, 1534–1547*

What had Henry done in 1534? It seems to have taken Henry himself some time to work this out. The policy he had eventually followed had been his second string, a result of his failure to secure his preferred option of a papal divorce. Because it was a second string, he does not seem to have made careful plans for it.

He had fundamentally altered the balance of power in English ecclesiastical politics. In 1525 Lutheran sympathizers were potentially disloyal, certainly heretical, and liable to burning if detected. Yet the central political fact of 1534 was that loyalty now meant loyalty to Henry's new marriage and to the heir whose birth was awaited. Only those who rejected the Pope's authority could give that loyalty. That meant that only those who sympathized with the 'new learning' could be fully loyal subjects. Like any political faction formerly out of favour and in danger, they seized with alacrity on the chance to prove that they were now the loyal ones. All the clergy were commanded to preach Henry's new Royal Supremacy. Sympathizers with Protestantism did so eagerly, and usually took the chance to throw in attacks on a little bit more Catholic doctrine as well. If they got into trouble for this, as they often did, they had three powerful protectors: Anne Boleyn, the new Queen, Thomas Cromwell, the new first minister, and Thomas Cranmer, the new Archbishop of Canterbury. Between them, these three enjoyed a great deal of patronage, and those they promoted were usually more open supporters of the new ideas than they were.

On the other hand, Henry did not believe he had changed his religion, and retained a firm devotion to most (not quite all) forms of theological orthodoxy, and especially to the traditional doctrine of the mass. If some of Henry's inner circle shared his gut rejection of the Pope, others, such as the Duke of Norfolk and Stephen Gardiner, Bishop of Winchester, shared his gut attachment to the mass. Both these groups had networks of allies, stretching down to the level of parish clergy, and each was rooted in Henry's favour by their agreement with him on one crucial doctrine. Henry had thus set up a sort of double-headed definition of orthodoxy. Anyone who did believe in the Pope was a traitor, and anyone who did not believe in the mass was a heretic. It was logically possible to pass both these tests at once, but the overwhelming majority of

HANS HOLBEIN's drawing of Thomas Cromwell. Unlike some others, Cromwell seems to have known what he wanted from the Royal Supremacy. In the end he took too many risks, and was executed in 1540.

Henry's subjects, his Council, his bishops, and probably even his successive Queens, probably did not. In other words, almost everyone in England, if their secret thoughts were known, was liable to prosecution either as a heretic or as a traitor.

This produced an unstable situation, in which Henry was surrounded by two groups who did not regard it as safe to coexist with each other. For that reason, they were perpetually trying to jockey each other out of Henry's favour.

They did not, in normal circumstances, dare to do this by direct attacks on each other, but instead watched carefully for the indiscretions of each other's smaller and more vulnerable clients. In 1538 Friar Forrest, a traditionalist Cromwell had been watching for six years, finally denied the Royal Supremacy when the wrong people were listening. For this, he was executed; but in burning and not hanging him, Cromwell chose to perpetrate a grotesque joke. He had just pulled down a large wooden image which was the centre-piece of a Welsh shrine. This image had been protected by a prophecy that it should set a forest on fire. Cromwell therefore chose to use the wood of the image to burn Friar Forrest. Hugh Latimer, the later Protestant martyr, preached the sermon. It was a bitter fight, and neither side was fighting for religious liberty. From beginning to end, it was kill or be killed. Numbers of deaths were usually small, but only final victory could guarantee survival, and both sides fought for it with all the political weapons they could command, while Henry played the part of vacillating umpire.

The outcome of this struggle depended on the friendships of people around Henry who had no clear religious commitment, and on the variations of foreign policy, as well as on the religious battle. There is only enough space here to mark out some of the big turns of the wheel.

In 1536 there were three events which began a reaction in favour of the traditionalists. The first, in January, was the death of Catherine of Aragon. This opened the way to the renewal of

A PAGE of the English Bible, acquired by Evesham Abbey in 1539 and annotated following its suppression, presumably by a monk of the Abbey. After recording its patron saint, he continues: 'and the year of our Lord 1539 [1540] the monastery of Evesham was suppressed by King Henry the viii, the xxxi year of his reign, the xxx day of January at evensong time, the convent being in the choir at this verse "Deposuit potentes" [He hath put down the mighty], and would not suffer them to make an end, Philip Ballard being abbot at that time, and xxxv religious men at that day alive in the said monastery . . .'.

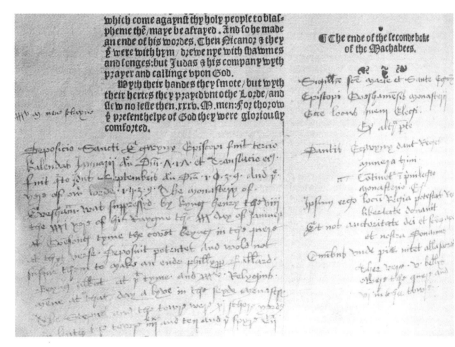

the alliance with the Emperor which many around the King believed to be essential to England's diplomatic and commercial interests. These people helped to instigate the next major event, the fall of Anne Boleyn, whose life was the other obstacle to an imperial alliance. In May she was executed on the improbable charge of adultery with her brother. The third, in October, was the outbreak of the Pilgrimage of Grace. This was the biggest rebellion of Tudor England, and was largely driven by attachment to the old ways in religion. It failed, largely because it was based in the north, too far away from London, but it enjoyed much sympathy in the south, and its strength seems to have convinced Henry that he needed to draw back.

That decision was counteracted by the King's decision to dissolve the monasteries, in two bites, in 1536 and 1539. Cromwell, who was one of the architects of this measure, is likely to have welcomed it for religious reasons, but the force he used to persuade the King is more likely to have been a plain need for money. Once again, a sharp lurch in one direction was counteracted by an equally sharp lurch in the other, and Henry expected his Councillors and subjects to be equally loyal to both.

This double lurch was repeated in 1539–40. In the parliamentary session of 1539, Henry responded to the continual pressure to put an end to doctrinal uncertainty, and induced the Parliament to pass the Act of Six Articles. That Act, titled 'An Act Abolishing Diversity in Opinions', reads as if it were meant to be the end for the growth of Protestant ideas. It upheld transubstantiation and the mass, the celibacy of the clergy, private masses and confession, and spelt out the penalty of burning for denial of the mass. In July 1540 Robert Barnes was burnt at the stake, telling the sheriff who was about to carry out the sentence that 'if saints do pray for us, I trust to pray for you within this half hour'. At the same time, Henry executed Thomas Cromwell, apparently for encouraging attacks on the mass.

These measures looked like an announcement of open season on Protestants. The Catholics of the City, led by a Catholic Lord Mayor whose nomination had been blocked for three years by Cromwell and his allies, rushed to inform against neighbours who had tried their patience for so long. Yet as the prisons filled up, the Catholics found, as Protestants had done before them, that power vanished as they reached out to grasp it. The Recorder of London took fright at the prospect of 'an uproar among the King's people'. Henry seems to have shared these fears, and the prosecutions were stopped by royal command. Each side in turn had had to face the fact that the other was too deeply entrenched to be extirpated. This was a lesson the English had to re-learn, with increasing panic, at regular intervals for the next 150 years.

6. *The Reigns of Edward and Mary*

As Henry's reign wore on, struggles between the factions increasingly resembled a game of musical chairs, with the King's death as the moment when the music would stop. As that moment approached, the faction struggles grew more bitter. When it came, it was the Protestants who found themselves sitting down. They did not sit for as long as they expected.

In other countries which were as divided by the Reformation as England, one side ended up securely on top, but the task took a long time. The parallels suggest that if the weight of orthodoxy was unambiguously on one side, backed by steady but not excessive persecution, division could be ended in some forty years. In France, which may have produced more spontaneous

S OMERSET HOUSE from the Thames. Edward Seymour, 'Protector' Somerset, built this palace with stone from the charnel house of St Paul's, which he destroyed for the purpose: it represents the close connection of this regime with greed and plunder.

conversions to Protestantism than any other European country, the task took seventy-five years. In England, first Henry's son Edward (1547–53), and then his daughter Mary (1553–8) had the chance to try. As chance would have it, they had five years each, and were trying in opposite directions. After these equal and opposite attempts at monopoly had both failed, division was more firmly entrenched than ever.

Edward, son of Henry and his third wife, Jane Seymour, inherited the throne at the age of 9, and effective power passed to his uncle, Edward Seymour, Earl of Hertford and later Duke of Somerset. The unambiguously Protestant policies he and his advisers followed seem to have given considerable offence. The abolition of the chantries gave the Crown much needed money, but it deprived many people of their only reliable means of coming to terms with death. The impression of greed was underlined when Somerset, building his grand new palace at Somerset House, dug up the charnel house at St Paul's for the stone, scattering bones of dead citizens at random. The first English-language Prayer Book was followed by the key gesture of taking down the altars on which the sacrifice of the mass had been offered, and replacing them with communion tables, more suitable to a merely commemorative service. In June 1550, when the high altar at St Paul's was taken down, there was a stand-up fight, and a man was killed. The limits of consent were being strained. In 1551 there was an epidemic of the sweating sickness, in which people dropped dead within hours of becoming ill. This was of course blamed on religious change, and taken as a sign of divine disfavour, and a London woman told her curate that 'men did die like dogs because they cannot see their maker borne about the streets as they have seen it in times past'. Edward's heir presumptive, Mary Tudor, caught the mood and swept through the City in a large procession with each retainer illegally carrying a rosary. Freedom to preach the Gospel carried other dangers, including the spread of ideas too radical for the Edwardians themselves. John Hooper, Bishop of Gloucester, one of the most radical of the Edwardian reformers, even wrote to a friend in Switzerland lamenting the spread of heresy in tones reminiscent of Stephen Gardiner. We will never understand Protestantism without remembering such letters.

So long as Edward lived, time was on the reformers' side, but Edward, in 1553, fell fatally ill, and his heir, Mary Tudor, was likely to reverse all his policies.

The Marian regime, like the Edwardian, hoped it could put an end to the explosive ambiguity. Gardiner and Norfolk came out of the Tower, while Cranmer and Northumberland (who had displaced Somerset) went into it. Yet Mary moved less hastily than Somerset had done in 1547. She came to the throne in July 1553, but the formal reconciliation with Rome did not come until November 1554. In the interim, Mary succeeded in planting in the Pope's mind a crucial doubt about whether she would be reconciled at all. As a result, she acquired negotiating power, and was able to win from the Pope the crucial guarantee for possessors of former church lands without which no reconciliation could have been effective.

Similarly, it was always likely that Mary would marry Philip II of Spain, heir of the Emperor Charles V. She succeeded, by judiciously frightening Philip about hatred of foreigners in England, in winning a series of concessions for English interests which made the treaty one of the best achievements of a century of English diplomacy. That hatred was real enough, but it did not mean that there was any better marriage available for Mary. Marriage was a political alliance, and only France and Spain were big enough for the necessary alliance. Of the two, France in 1554 was the more hated. For a woman, who was expected to do the child-bearing while her husband governed, no marriage was likely to be acceptable, and it is hard to think of a woman ruler in any country who made a success of it. Mary Tudor certainly managed it more successfully than Mary Queen of Scots north of the border.

The arrival of Philip, the reconciliation with Rome, and, as Mary and the whole country for a while believed, a pregnancy which would again have put time on the side of Rome, all promised fair; and accession rapidly made it apparent that she could ride on a tide of Catholic devotion. In September 1553 a disgusted Protestant reported that 'the mass is very rife; there is no news but candlesticks, books, bells, censers, crosses and pipes'. All this was before the official restoration of the mass, and appears to have sprung from genuine religious enthusiasm.

Yet the City Protestants appear to have hoped that, as in 1540, they would prove to be too strong to be suppressed. They could not rely, as they had done under Henry, on friends at Court, and had to rely instead on threats, not always oblique, of riot. When the City authorities commanded apprentices and servants to attend their parish churches, they also forbade them to wear daggers. It was in the face of that threat that the traditional policy of burning heretics went into force to back the new return to old orthodoxy. They were able to start work at once on four hundred cases in which London Catholics had informed against their Protestant neighbours. The policy of burning enjoyed some public support, and one London heretic, avoiding burning by penance, found that some of the crowd spat at him, and said 'it was a pity I was not burned already'. After another had bravely endured burning at St Albans, 'some superstitious old women' said that 'the devil was so strong with him as all such heretics as he was, that they could not feel pain almost'.

It was not the authorities' intention to burn people: what they wanted was recantations, which discredited those who made them and their beliefs. Sir John Cheke, the foremost scholar of

Edward's regime, gave them one. Matthew Parker, later Archbishop to Elizabeth I, who was carefully keeping his head down in Cambridge, noted on his copy of the recantation 'we are but men'. On the other hand, when a group of martyrs was escorted up Cheapside by a procession of 1,000 people, the propaganda gesture had boomeranged against those who made it.

Meanwhile, the restoration of Catholicism in the parishes and the universities was proceeding quietly and steadily. The policy of concentrating on the universities, where future clergy were trained, was a sensible way of concentrating on the long haul, and produced many high-quality Catholic clergy who were to be a thorn in the flesh of Elizabeth I. Yet Mary, like Edward, did not have the long haul. The first mistaken pregancy was followed by a second. Meanwhile in the country a massive series of epidemics produced the worst mortality in three hundred years. Mary, like Edward, went out of power in a world which looked as if the Lord had witnessed against her. Yet Mary, like Edward, had used her five years to give her creed a shot in the arm which made it far harder for her successors to abolish it. Yet, like Edward, she was succeeded by a sister who could be expected to reverse everything she stood for.

7. *The Reign of Elizabeth I, 1558–1603*

Elizabeth I, Anne Boleyn's daughter, was the first ruler since the Reformation to be granted the forty years needed to establish a policy and give it the advantage of familiarity. Yet when she came to the throne, neither she nor her supporters nor her opponents knew that she was going to enjoy this advantage. Like Edward and Mary, she had a successor of the opposite religion to her own: Mary Stuart, Queen of Scots, whose accession could be expected, however uncertainly, to bring the old religion back again. In 1562, just short of her predecessors' regulation five years, Elizabeth fell desperately ill of the smallpox, and her death was imminently expected. Had she died then, she would have left a country still preponderantly Catholic, Mary Stuart would probably have won the resulting civil war, and England today would probably be as Catholic a country as France. As Mary had gambled on marrying, Elizabeth gambled on not marrying. Therefore she, and even more so, her Councillors, who would live to see it, always feared that all her policies would be reversed by her successor. William Cecil, her Secretary of State and right-hand man, was clearly a Protestant, but to his dying day in 1598, he kept a certificate signed by the vicar of Wimbledon, that he had attended mass under Mary. He did not know when he might have need of it.

As Mary, who was only granted a short time, chose to play it long, so Elizabeth, who was granted a long time, chose to play it short. She did not use her forty-three years to convert the country to a single unambiguous line which might hope to be accepted when the majority of adults had grown up with it. Instead, she reverted to her father's tradition of a double-headed or siamese orthodoxy. In a nutshell, Elizabeth settled for churches which looked Catholic, and sounded Protestant. Since Catholics were often primarily concerned with the appeal to the eye, and Protestants with the appeal to the ear, this might have been a clever compromise. As it was, it was too clever by half, and most of the leading figures in Elizabeth's Church spent the reign itching to get rid of the half of the Church they thought did not belong.

The first tension was between the religious settlement of 1559 and the men chosen to run it. Elizabeth was a Protestant: it is hard to see how Anne Boleyn's daughter could have been anything else, since it was the duty of good Catholics to think her illegitimate, and therefore not lawfully on the throne. Yet she was a Protestant of an old-fashioned sort. Under Mary, she had been in danger, and out of touch with developments in Protestant thinking; yet most of her new bishops had been in exile in Germany or Switzerland, keeping abreast of the latest Protestant thinking.

Elizabeth required her clergy to wear vestments which made them look like a Catholic priest. She required them to continue many traditional ceremonies like the making of the sign of the cross in baptism, which advanced Protestants viewed as superstitious, or to require their parishioners to kneel for communion. On the vexed question of a communion table or an altar, she announced a policy so ambiguous she cannot have intended it to be observed. She announced that the table was to be kept in the east end of the church, where the altar had stood, but carried into the middle, where an advanced Protestant communion table went, at service time. I know of no record of churchwardens moving furniture for every quarterly communion, and the result seems to have been what Elizabeth probably intended: a policy of local option. She certainly did not follow her announced policy in her own chapel, where the table stayed permanently at the east end. She even kept a crucifix on it, and at least two of her bishops rejoiced when it was eventually smashed by a mad German undergraduate.

The object of all this ceremony seems to have been to make it possible for the milder sorts of Catholic to come to church as required by law. In this, she seems to have been reasonably successful until the Pope excommunicated and deposed her in 1570, and made it painfully clear that Catholics must not attend their parish churches. Many continued to do so after that: until

L AURENCE HUMPHREY, President of Magdalen College, Oxford, looks quite different from a Catholic priest. He holds the Word, and is wearing a layman's ruff underneath an academic gown. He was one of those who converted Oxford to Protestantism, but to an anti-ceremonial Protestantism which often annoyed Elizabeth I even more than a conforming Catholicism would have done.

churches. Many continued to do so after that: until then, it seems that most did, and the fiction of a single united Church was kept up.

It was kept up at the expense of her new bishops, who found many of these arrangements at best distasteful. John Jewel, about to become Bishop of Salisbury and the Church's most famous apologist, described the settlement as a 'leaden mediocrity'. Edwin Sandys, eventually Archbishop of York, was still protesting against the surplice in 1589. At the same time he had to defend himself against his own more enthusiastic followers, who went beyond his belief that it was distasteful, to the more uncompromising belief that it was unlawful. Sandys spent a large part of his will explaining why it was not a sin for him to enforce a policy in which he did not believe.

Where the bishops and their followers came into their own was in the defining of the doctrine of the Church. The discipline, the content of the Prayer Book, the layout of the churches, the choice of ornaments and vestments, and such organizational matters were all settled in 1559, by Queen and Council, before any of these bishops were offered office. They had to take it or leave it, and some of those who were offered office as bishops chose to leave it.

The first Elizabethan Convocation of 1563 tried to reform the ceremonial side of the Church, and, after great official pressure, failed by one vote. On the other hand, they were left a free hand in drawing up the Thirty-Nine Articles, which defined the doctrine of the Church: this was left to them because laymen were not supposed to meddle in doctrine. Since Henry's reign, Protestant theology, largely under Swiss leadership, had moved on well beyond Luther. Instead of stopping at Luther's insistence on Justification by Faith, without being able to explain why some people got faith and others did not, many had moved on to the position some had taken from the beginning, that we had no free will, and divine predestination explained why some acquired a saving faith, and others did not. As the reign progressed, the name of Calvin was increasingly associated with these ideas, but in 1563 most of the committee which drew up the first draft of the Thirty-Nine Articles had got them from Zurich.

Article X, on free will, and Article XVII, on predestination, look to the untrained eye entirely unambiguous. In fact they are not: wherever one more sentence would remove any latent ambiguity, that one sentence is not there. That ambiguity is probably the achievement of Edmund Guest, Bishop of Rochester, and was to be important for Charles I and his bishops, but for the time being, the hottest Elizabethan Protestants believed they had got what they wanted. Jewel and Grindal among the episcopate, and Perkins and Travers among their hottest Protestant critics, were equally able to worship in a Church they all thought imperfect because, as Jewel put it, 'the doctrine is everywhere most pure'. Thus, as the ceremony prevented the Church from flying apart at the Catholic end, so the doctrine prevented it from flying apart at the Protestant end. In the medium term, Elizabeth thus achieved what she wanted. Yet the fact remained that this was a Church with which no one was satisfied.

The double-headed orthodoxy meant, as it had done under Gardiner and Cromwell, that almost anyone who was sound on one point was unsound on another. This meant that those facing accusations were always tempted to bring counter-charges against their accusers, and to call in their friends in high places to help them to do so. Very few good Protestants were happy using all the forms of worship laid out in the Book of Common Prayer. When the Queen lost her

RYCOTE chapel, Oxfordshire, an Elizabethan church which 'looked Catholic', showing the rood screen and the communion table on the site of old high altar.

patience with this, and tried to insist on full conformity, a faction fight was set in motion which Henry VIII and Cromwell would have had no difficulty in recognizing. In 1575 Parkhurst, Bishop of Norwich, whose blind eye had been particularly good, died, and the Queen replaced him with Bishop Freake, who arrived with stern orders to enforce full conformity. Almost at once, he found he was in conflict with all the leading Protestant gentry of the shire, led by the son of the Lord Keeper, and even with his own diocesan Chancellor. His only effective allies were the Catholics: indeed, it almost seems to be true that the only friends of full conformity in Norfolk were the Catholics. The Council finally outmanœuvred the Queen by bringing her down to Norfolk on progress, and discovering popish relics in the houses of the gentlemen with whom she stayed. Thomas Cromwell would have been proud of them. In 1583, when there was a national drive for conformity, the Norfolk Protestant gentry pulled the same trick again, discovering the Bishop's butler and his lawyer going to secret masses, and leaving the Bishop frantically protesting his ignorance.

These were the only techniques by which a show of unity could be kept up in a deeply divided country. The only hope of an end to this situation was in the slow process of conversion. Yet under Elizabeth, that was not much help either. From about 1570 in Cambridge and 1581 in Oxford, the universities were turning out a steady stream of well-educated Protestant clergy ready to preach the Gospel according to Calvin's *Institutes*. In what the hotter Protestants liked to call 'the dark corners of the land' these graduates might be the first sign of the Reformation to reach the parish. Yet such conversions profited the Church little, for once these young graduates were converted to a vigorous Protestant faith, they were often converted away from readiness to conform to the Church's ceremonies as they were required. It is the old problem of the double-headed orthodoxy: those who were most strongly committed to the Church's doctrines were least able to worship according to the Church's ceremonies. As under Henry, each side struggled to prove that it was the other which was unorthodox. While one side denounced the other as 'Puritans', they retaliated by denouncing their tormentors as 'papists'. Each charge was a matter of definition, and neither can be taken at face value. What is clearly the case is that, in the years between 1580 and 1620, the orthodoxy of the Church practised in the parishes was a lot closer to the ideals of Elizabeth's bishops than it was to the ideals of Elizabeth I herself.

8. *The Baby and the Bath-water, 1595–1625*

In the middle 1580s Thomas Cartwright, the Cambridge Presbyterian and campaigner for the abolition of bishops, said it was the 'high noon' of the Gospel. Conversion was proceeding apace, and the generation which remembered the world before the Reformation was beginning to die out. Yet one may say of missionary movements what John Donne said of love affairs, that 'his first minute, after noon, is night'. In the 1580s the wave of conversions to a Protestantism which Calvin would recognize still had some thirty years to run. Yet at the same time, it was just beginning to be possible to recognize the first small seeds of a change of intellectual fashion. With the execution of Mary Queen of Scots in 1587 and the defeat of the Spanish Armada in 1588, the fear of popery receded a little.

That made it easier for a very few people, of whom Richard Hooker, Fellow of Corpus Christi College, Oxford, was the first to come out, to begin to question the central idea of the

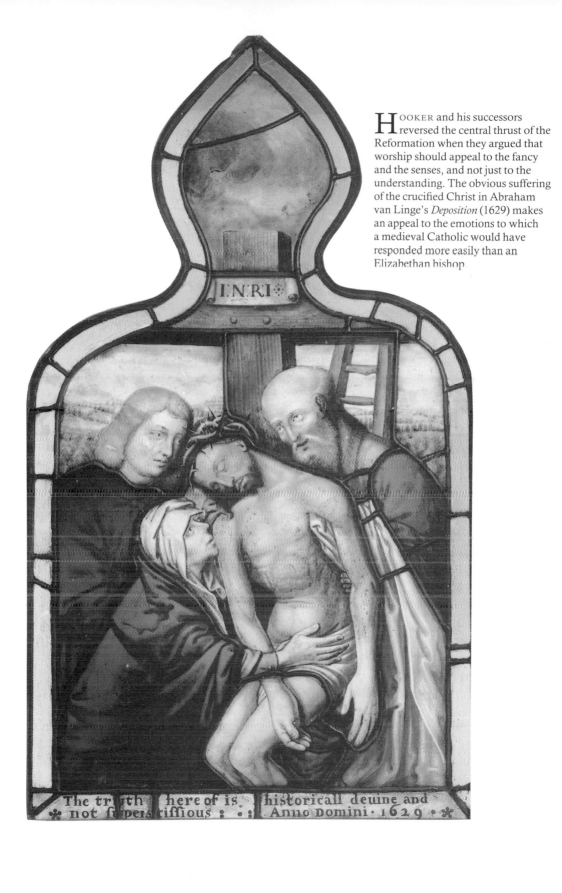

The truth here of is historicall deuine and not superstiffious : .: Anno Domini · 1629 · ❋

HOOKER and his successors reversed the central thrust of the Reformation when they argued that worship should appeal to the fancy and the senses, and not just to the understanding. The obvious suffering of the crucified Christ in Abraham van Linge's *Deposition* (1629) makes an appeal to the emotions to which a medieval Catholic would have responded more easily than an Elizabethan bishop.

Reformation, that the farther it was from popery, the purer it was. For Hooker, and for William Laud, a young Oxford theologian who took his degree as Bachelor of Divinity in 1602, the Church of England was not a fundamentally new Church: it was, in Hooker's phrase, a 're-formed continuation' of the Church of Rome. Hooker saw the Church of England as taking over not a building which needed to be pulled down and replaced but one badly in need of repair. It then made sense to retain, not to replace, as much of the original fabric as possible. As Laud later put it, 'we live in a church reformed, not one made new'. For such people, it was no longer a sufficient summary of religion to 'love God and hate popery'.

Richard Hooker has been described as the inventor of Anglicanism. All the elements were old, but they had never been put together in that form before. Two generations later, when his beliefs for the first time captured the seat of power, Richard Hooker was to be one of Charles I's favourite theologians, but in the 1580s he was a very lonely voice. What his successors were able to ride was a European-wide reaction which began to ask whether the Reformation had thrown out the baby with the bath-water. Numerous clergy began to ask whether its attack on clerical wealth had been carried too far. Some began to wonder whether the Reformation emphasis on preaching had been carried too far. The cautious ones confined themselves to the praise of prayer, but John Howson, another rising young man from Oxford, made a serious point in complaining that preachers were turning churches into schools. Hooker came near to reversing the central thrust of the Reformation when he argued that worship should appeal to the fancy and the senses, and not just to the understanding. At first, the granite edifice of Calvinist theology was not their main target, and Laud, Hooker, Andrewes, Neile, and Howson, five of the most famous of this group, seem to have all begun as Calvinists. It was to be a very different story when they had the confidence of a generation's thinking behind them.

These people were still very far from power or influence in March 1603, when Elizabeth I died, and King James VI of Scotland became James I of England, and the English Church had to adjust to the idiosyncrasies of a new leader. James never forgot that he was also King of Scotland, and it remained one of his preoccupations to prevent the Churches of his two kingdoms from diverging unmanageably. Scottish Protestants, from James downwards, were almost uniformly committed to Calvinist theology. On this, James had to draw the English Church towards Scotland. The dominance of Calvinist theology therefore grew even stronger than it had been in the last decades of Elizabeth.

Yet at the same time, there were ways in which James was equally keen to draw the Scottish Church towards that of England. He was deeply attracted to the idea of the Royal Supremacy, which he had not enjoyed in Scotland, and liked the preaching of English ceremonial conformists when they were extolling royal authority. He was allergic to people who claimed to disobey authority in the name of individual conscience, and to those who claimed for the Church independence from the State, as Scottish Presbyterians did. While he loved listening to preaching, he was also happy with a degree of ceremony which made the hotter Calvinists on his episcopal bench uncomfortable. He also knew that he had to bring to an end the war with Spain he had inherited, and could not afford another major European conflict. He was, for this reason among others, allergic to those who saw foreign policy as an ideological struggle between Protestant and Catholic. For all these reasons, James was able to patronize anti-Calvinists while having no time for their anti-Calvinism.

HENRICO ROBINSONO CARLEOLENSI, COLLEGII HVIVS ANNIS XVIII PRÆPOSITO
PROVIDISSIMO, TANDEMQ ECCLESIÆ CARLEOLENSIS TOTIDEM ANNIS EPISCOPO
VIGILANTISSIMO, XIII° CAL: IVLII ANNO A PARTV VIRGINIS M DC XVI°. ÆTAT: LXIII
PIE IN DŌIŌ OBDORMIENTI, ET IN ECCLESIA CARLEOL: SEPVLTO, HOC COLL:
IPSIVS LABORIBVS VASTITATI EREPTV, MVNIFICENTIA DEMV LOCVPLETATVM, IS-
TVD QVALECVNQ MNHMĒION GRATITVDINIS TESTIMONIVM COLLOCAVIT.
Non sibi, sed Patriæ præluxit, Lampadis instar. | In minimis fido Servo, maioribus apto,
Deperdens oleum; non operam Ille suam. | Maximâ nunc Domini gaudia adire datur.

UNDER Elizabeth, Henry Robinson as Provost of Queen's College, Oxford, made the college a leading centre for the education of godly ministers. Under James he became (in the king's words) a bishop, and therefore no Puritan. He died in 1616. In his memorial brass in Queen's College he is shown in cap, gown, and ruff, and carrying his pastoral staff.

The result was yet another double-headed orthodoxy. James, like Henry and Elizabeth, up-held a combination of doctrines such that almost no one was happy with all of them. Like Henry, he therefore employed groups of people each of whom wanted to get rid of the other. George Abbot, Archbishop of Canterbury from 1611, served uneasily with Lancelot Andrewes, Bishop of Winchester. Abbot was an unambiguous Calvinist who dreamed of the eradication of popery, while Lancelot Andrewes was an anti-Calvinist who welcomed the clarity being given to the anti-Calvinist cause by the Dutch theologian Arminius. Yet James had uses for both of them. Neither of them served easily with Henry Howard, Earl of Northampton, a Catholic born in

1540, who left a will saying that 'I die in the religion in which I was born'. When reproached for employing such a man, James is said to have replied 'that by this tame duck, he hoped to catch many wild ones'.

This need was still a high priority, for the Catholic community was showing remarkable signs of survival. All through Elizabeth's reign, the tide of conversions had flowed in favour of Protestantism. By about the beginning of James's reign, the tide had reached slack water, with conversions in one direction equalling conversions in the other. A typical story from late in Elizabeth's reign involves the two brothers Reynolds, a Catholic and a Protestant, who argued so vigorously that they converted each other. The majority of James's Catholic subjects had reached a *modus vivendi*, even if an uncomfortable and unstable one, with their Protestant neighbours. They paid fines, but these were described by zealous Protestants as a 'toleration by retail'. There were still some irreconcilables, and on 5 November 1605 a group of them, let down by the end of the war with Spain, tried to blow up Parliament at the state opening. This common threat to King, Council, judges, and Parliament for a while pulled them all together in an anti-Catholic stance, and James's reversion to his more natural stance of using a tame duck to catch wild ones seemed to many to be a betrayal. Unlike James, they had not yet faced the fact that Catholicism was not going to be abolished by the force of authority.

At the end of James's reign, the drift to renewed war with Spain, which was dominating political discussion by 1621, exposed the weaknesses in James's double-headed orthodoxy. The hotter Calvinists, like Abbot, tended to see a struggle between good and evil, in which choice was automatic, while anti-Calvinists tended to see political struggles in which English interests did not necessarily demand participation. Both sides tried, with even more determination than before, to 'manipulate James's stated fears of popery and of puritanism'. This was a type of battle whose rules had been familiar since the 1530s: each side knew what it had to tell the King about its opponents, and each side knew to which reciprocal allegations it was vulnerable. The penalty was no longer death, but since politicians tend to fear disgrace even more than death, ecclesiastical faction struggles in the last years of James were, in a more subdued way, of the same kind as those in the last years of Henry.

9. *Charles I and the Coming of Civil War, 1625–1642*

In March 1625 James was succeeded, as Henry VIII had been, by a king who took the unambiguous decision that one side should prevail. Indeed, it is arguable that Charles could only see one side. In all the ambiguities of which the Elizabethan Settlement was full, Charles saw one side of the argument, and never fully understood that there was another. He was the first King of England who could properly be described as an 'Anglican'. He classified what had been half the leadership of the Church under his father, and the dominant half at that, as 'Puritan', and therefore subversive and to be excluded.

For Charles, as for Hooker, the Church was a 'reformed continuation' of that of Rome. He saw its continuity as residing in the institution of bishops, and therefore believed that any Church which did not have bishops was not a Church at all. Under James, the Church had organized collections for the relief of its co-religionists in Geneva. Under Charles, they were not seen as co-religionists, but as protagonists of a different religion.

THE remarkable thing about this allegory of the four gospel-writers stoning the Pope (who sprawls across two women representing avarice and hypocrisy) is that it was in the possession of Henry VIII. He probably acquired it in 1542. The painter was Girolamo da Treviso, a military engineer who died in Henry's siege of Boulogne in 1544.

To many of James's bishops, denial of predestination and belief in free will were tantamount to evidence of 'popery'. To Charles, on the other hand, belief in predestination and the denial of free will were tantamount to evidence of 'puritanism'. To many survivors of James's bench of bishops, like Davenant of Salisbury, this idea was incomprehensible. For many others, who, like the first Elizabethan bishops, had put up with the Church's unfortunate ceremony for the sake of its pure doctrine, the reason why they remained in the Church of England was taken away at a stroke. After the appointment of Joseph Hall to Exeter in 1627, Charles never appointed a Calvinist to the bench of bishops again. As under Edward and Mary, some reacted by going into exile, this time in New England, but the majority, knowing kings were mortal, rallied to a rear-guard action, while praying privately at home for delivery from the new doctrines of Arminianism.

Charles, and William Laud, whom he appointed to Canterbury on Abbot's death in 1633, knew that it had been normal for many people to omit parts of the Prayer Book service, and some of the ceremonies required by the Elizabethan Settlement. To James, this had been acceptable so long as they did not make too much noise about it. To Charles and Laud, it was a sign that discipline was breaking down. In requiring full ceremonial conformity, they were doing something the law entitled them to do, but which had never been done for more than a few months at a time at any stage since 1559.

In other cases, such as making it compulsory to keep the communion table at the east end, and in some cases calling it an altar, they were trying to do things which had not been done since the Reformation. In enforcing bowing to the altar, they were doing something which provoked a member of the Long Parliament (who was 39) to say that 'I can remember, and I am not yet very old, that there was not one man that bowed in the University of Cambridge or any other place where I came'. Worship, as it had been under Rome, was again designed to appeal to the eye as much as to the ear. In fact, the justifications and explanations of worship under Charles often had more in common with pre-Reformation Catholicism than they had with anything that had been seen since. Charles was not a Catholic: he was a High Anglican. However, since this was an animal previously unknown to theology, it is not surprising that many people did not recognize it, and identified it with the species it appeared to resemble, the Roman Catholic.

For his first twelve or fifteen years, Charles provoked less disorder by these efforts than Edward or Mary had done. This does not necessarily mean that he caused less resentment. It is partly because England had become a much more demilitarized society than it had been in the 1550s. It was no longer necessary to forbid apprentices to bring daggers to Laudian churches. Ridicule was a commoner weapon. The lack of apparent disorder was partly because New England allowed the safety valve of emigration for those who became most heated, and partly because peace allowed Charles the luxury of calling no Parliament between 1629 and 1640. It was partly also because power in England had become so decentralized that Charles and Laud, in the time at their disposal, were able to achieve far less than they had hoped. As Laud wrote in his diary in the week when he was given Canterbury: 'there is more expected of me than the

H ENRY VII's chapel at Westminster Abbey, in which he and his queen were buried, is one of the most extravagant chantry chapels ever built. It is a remarkable witness to the conventional later-medieval piety of the first Tudor, and of the young Henry VIII. The only commoner ever buried there was 'King' Pym, the parliamentarian leader, in 1643.

craziness of these times will give me leave to do'. Advowsons, the right of choosing parish clergy, were private property and owned by individuals. A massive campaign of depriving clergy would only have led the owners of the advowsons to appoint others like them. Since deprivation in one diocese was not a legal bar to reappointment in another, they would have ended up taking in each other's clergy like each other's washing.

Yet the apparent calm of England in 1637 was deceptive. Many gentry knew that England could not permanently hold both Charles and them, and their apparent quiet conceals only the politician's ability to wait for his opponent to be down before he kicks him.

It was not England, but Scotland, which brought Charles down, for Scotland, unlike England, was not yet a demilitarized society. Charles's interpretation of the Church of England, instead of narrowing the gap between England and Scotland, had widened it until it was almost too wide to see across. A king could not afford to rule two kingdoms which could not recognize each other's worship, any more than a modern ruler can afford to rule two states which do not recognize each other's passports. Charles chose to force Scotland into line, imposing a new Prayer Book, not through a Scottish General Assembly and Parliament, but by Proclamation from Whitehall. He claimed to be acting in the capacity, which it was not even clear that Scottish law granted to him, of Supreme Head of the Church of Scotland. This was an assault on Scottish religion and Scottish nationhood both together. After three years of vain attempts to open a dialogue with Charles, the Scots, in August 1640, appealed for help to their English co-religionists and invaded England.

It is then that the extent of English dissatisfaction with Charles became apparent. For the first time since 1216, a large body of Englishmen allied with an invading army against their own king, colluding with and advising the Scots. Many of the rest of the English gentry, regarding it as unwise to fight a war with so deeply divided a country, stood aside and worked for peace. At Newburn, in August 1640, the Scots defeated the English army. They then occupied Newcastle, and gained control of London's coal supplies.

Charles, being financially and politically unable to rally his subjects against these invading Scots, was forced to call what became the Long Parliament, in November 1640. In that Parliament an effective working alliance between the Scottish army and the leading English politicians for a while swept all before it. Very slowly, however, it became apparent that the Scots, as the price of their support, intended to impose a Scottish Reformation on England. Like Charles himself, and like so many ecclesiastical factions from the Act of Six Articles onwards, they found that monopoly power, as they reached to grasp it, slipped out of their hands. What the Scots were demanding was too unacceptable to be enforceable. If there was in England a majority for abolishing bishops, it was a temporary and unstable one, and there was clearly no majority for abolishing the Book of Common Prayer. Large numbers of Englishmen, even if they were unwilling to use every last sentence of the Book of Common Prayer, were even more unwilling to give it up altogether. Over eighty years since, the Elizabethan Settlement had given it the sanctity of familiarity, and the English were not prepared to accept Scottish orders to give it up.

Thus the Scots, who had knocked Charles down, gave him a party to get up again. When they finally went home, in September 1641, they left a deadlock: they had given the Parliament the strength to bring Charles to his knees by taking away 60 per cent of his annual revenues. Yet at the same time they had endowed him with a party of equal strength to that of his opponents. From that situation, there was likely to be no escape except war.

THE SHEPHERDS ORACLES.

Hope   Charitie

Faith

Good workes.

Obedience

RELIGION

Written by Fran: Quarles.

London *Printed for* John Marriott *and* Richard Marriott *&c.* W. M *sculp:*

Attacks on the established church in the 1640s sometimes bore remarkable similarities to the attacks on Catholic clergy during the Reformation—the difference being that the former were without the backing of the King, and did much to create their own opposition. Indeed Charles I was seen by some as the defender of the church against those seeking to destroy it 'roots and branches'—as in this frontispiece to Francis Quarles's *The Shepherd's Oracles* (1646).

Religious war had been a recurring nightmare for the English since 1536. Its avoidance, for over a hundred years, had been a feat of some political skill, and provides some justification for the double-headed orthodoxies, balancing factions like quarrelling siamese twins, which had been undertaken by Henry, Elizabeth, and James. Yet these strategies had bought time, not solutions. They had prevented religious war, but they had not solved the problems of a country which, in every sense, had been 'but halfly reformed'. They had not settled whether the reformers or the traditionalists were going to win.

Time was on the side of peace, since, in the century after the Reformation, time tended to make religious division less terrifying, and therefore less likely to be a cause of war. In continental

292 · *The Reformation and the Creation of the Church of England*

Europe the age of religious wars ended with the Peace of Westphalia in 1648. England in 1642 may not have been much more than thirty years away from a stage at which a changing religious climate would have made religious war almost impossible. Indeed, a dim awareness of this, and the consequent urgent sense that this was a last chance to achieve total victory, may have been one of the things which drove on some of the more devout contestants. If Charles had chosen to continue his father's skills in juggling religious factions, he might have found the task had grown harder with time, but he would not have had to keep it up for very much longer. Yet Charles and his opponents, as much as Cromwell and Gardiner, still shared the illusion that total victory might be possible. It was the illusion which they shared which divided them.

The result showed that it was an illusion, for even victory in a civil war did not allow the winning side to extirpate the other. By 1660 the balance had swung yet again. This experience left people facing a terror which was even deeper than that of religious division: the fear of moral relativism. Many people seem to have been quite unable to combine firm faith in their own religion with the acceptance that the other person's might be right, and therefore did not need to be persecuted. In being asked to tolerate the other person's religion, they felt they were being asked to lose some of their faith in their own. We know Cromwell's famous exhortation to the Scottish Covenanters: 'I beseech you in the bowels of Christ, think it possible you may be mistaken.' What is not so well known is the Covenanters' reply: 'Would you have us to be sceptics in our religion?' That voice is still heard today, and attempts to find a convincing answer to it are still continuing. It is not until a convincing answer is found that the Reformation will finally cease to be politics, and become history.

14 THE SEARCH FOR RELIGIOUS LIBERTY

1640–1690

MARK GOLDIE

1. *Introduction*

In Victorian times Liberal publicists celebrated the days when England was ruled by Oliver Cromwell and the Puritans. And professors in Presbyterian, Congregational, and Baptist colleges wrote books tracing the heroic lineage of their churches back to the well-springs of the Reformation. It all belonged to the long labour of loosening the grip of the Anglican Establishment on British society. It expressed a sense that for two centuries Britain had been divided into two cultures: Anglican and Nonconformist, church and chapel, country and town, land and trade, English metropolis and Celtic provinces.

In important ways this was an accurate picture. The Restoration of 1660 marked the defeat of the Puritans, yet by the end of the Stuart age a degree of religious pluralism had been achieved. Under the Toleration Act of 1689 England became the only major European state, apart from the Netherlands, to have achieved legalized toleration. It was a lopsided settlement, in which the Church of England remained legally established and socially advantaged, while a counter-culture of Protestant Dissenters (also called Nonconformists) remained subject to civil disabilities. But the Tudor ideal of the Church as the undivided nation at prayer had begun to give way to Disraeli's notion of the Church as just the Tory party at prayer.

The political struggle for toleration in the Restoration was matched by a growing institutional debility on the part of the Church of England, so that religious diversity became entrenched in the social fabric. The parish church of St Giles, Cripplegate, in London was incapable of serving its population of 30,000. No ecclesiastical courts held sway in the teeming alley-ways. Its shop-keepers and artisans went 'gadding' to whichever sermons they liked. There John Milton, the great Puritan poet, wrote *Paradise Lost* (which the ecclesiastical censor wanted banned); and there Daniel Defoe, the iconoclastic Dissenting tradesman turned journalist and novelist, grew up. The parish harboured several Nonconformist meeting-houses or 'conventicles', as well as com-

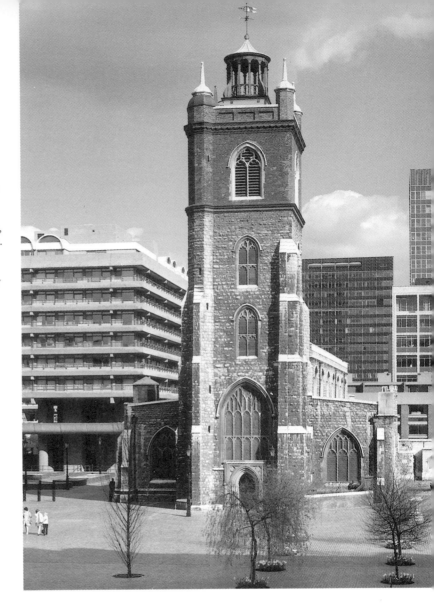

TODAY surrounded by a sea of concrete in the Barbican development, the church of St Giles Cripplegate was once at the heart of a labyrinth of narrow streets in one of London's largest parishes. The district teemed with the unchurched and with those who preferred other churches—Nonconformists, Catholics, Huguenots, Jews. Amid the urban sprawl the old ideal of a cohesive Anglican parish community was under severe strain.

munities of Huguenot (French Protestant) émigrés, Irish Catholics, and Jews (whom Cromwell had allowed to resettle). The parish was an early epitome of modern cultural pluralism.

Yet, in an important sense, the Victorians mislead us, and so does the elephantine urban parish of Cripplegate. Until the 1690s scarcely anybody wished to define themselves as belonging to distinct 'Presbyterian' or 'Congregational' churches, and true separatists were rare. Most people continued to believe that the Christian Church should be organized into national Churches, governed by godly princes at home and militant in defence of Protestantism abroad; and in turn arranged into parishes, providing godly preaching and moral discipline. 'Schism' and 'separation' were decried as sins against the unity of Christ's Church. Even the word 'toleration' was often used pejoratively. Most of those called 'Puritans' insisted that *they* were the true heirs of the Elizabethan Church. They did not readily embrace denominationalism and longed for a reunited national Church. To be tolerated as a marginalized fragment was a poor alternative.

In fact, many 'Puritans' never left the official Church. Ralph Josselin remained a 'nonconformist' in the early Stuart sense: he did not conform to those rubrics of the Book of Common Prayer that offended him, yet he continued to be vicar of his parish. Parishes remained the fundamental units of communal life, especially in rural areas. At Terling in Essex as many as one third of the churchwardens were in trouble for Nonconformity during the Restoration. Josselin and the Terling churchwardens were examples of a widespread 'partial conformity', so that the boundary between Anglicanism and Dissent remained extremely porous.

In tracing the path towards religious toleration and diversity we need, therefore, to tread between the rigid denominationalism which the Victorians assumed became permanent after the Civil War, and the opposite supposition that England remained a purely 'confessional' state, dominated by a 'Church and King' vision of religious conformity.

2. *The Godly Experiment*

Many of those who went to war against Charles I in 1642 were appalled by the Pandora's box which they unwittingly opened. They did not intend the 'anarchy of private conscience' that they let loose: the multitude of sects and heresies, the 'rude mechanick preachers', the mystical enthusiasms, the capricious and ignorant interpretations of Scripture, and the attacks on tithes and infant baptism. Moderate Puritans ('Presbyterians' as they came to be called) wanted to cleanse the English Church of 'popery' and 'prelacy', and to reinvigorate the godly discipline which they sought to inculcate in their villages and counties. Liberty, for them, meant freedom from the Devil's instruments and from those impediments to godliness spawned by the Roman Antichrist, which were infecting the Court of Charles I and the Church of Archbishop William Laud. Liberty did not mean freedom to cast aside decent uniformity in public worship, nor to ignore the sound doctrine of learned divines, still less to go to an alehouse or play football on the Sabbath.

Thomas Edwards's *Gangraena* offered a hefty catalogue of prurient horror at the supermarket of zany sects that London offered by 1644—he had even seen women preaching. Similarly, the *Catalogue of the Several Sects and Opinions in England* (1647) illustrated anabaptists, libertines, naked Adamites, divorcers, and 'anti-scripturians'. Denunciations of this sort were a hostage to fortune in Restoration times, when excluded Presbyterians themselves began to beg for toleration, and the triumphantly restored Anglican Church reminded them of their own intolerance in the 1640s. Caught between the Scylla of popery and prelacy and the Charybdis of sectarian anarchy, the Puritans spent the rest of the century trying to find firm ground on which to stand.

A crucial dilemma was the vexed question of church government by bishops. By 1641 the parliamentarian leaders were so alarmed by Laudianism that they were prepared to abolish bishops altogether—and, in 1645, to execute Laud. This 'root and branch' approach to episcopacy was soon underwritten by the need to bring in the Scots to help fight the war, for the Scottish army was purchased at the price of the Solemn League and Covenant of 1643, by which the full rigours of Scottish Presbyterianism were to be exported to England. Yet, if abolishing bishops is the simplest definition of 'Presbyterianism', there was little deep-seated conviction about it. Many moderates would have been content to accept the plan for a 'reduction' of episcopacy, from 'lordly prelacy' to 'apostolic simplicity', put forward by James Ussher, the Archbishop of Armagh, who, remarkably, was to be given a state funeral during Cromwell's Protectorate.

By the late 1640s moderates were distinctly unhappy with the proceedings of the Westminster Assembly of Divines, which planned to create a purer non-episcopal Church, and which issued a Directory for Public Worship to replace the Elizabethan Book of Common Prayer and the Thirty-Nine Articles. Few people wanted the Genevan and Scottish system of Presbyterianism, with its parish elders, synods, and assemblies, its excommunications, its harrying for heresy at the merest deviation from the doctrine of divine predestination to heaven or to hell—its sheer authoritarian clericalism. The hectoring Scots soon had good reason to denounce the English as 'Laodiceans', spiritual feet-draggers, and 'Erastians', who put secular interests above the wisdom of the best Reformed theologians.

By 1645 the unity of 1641 had collapsed. The 'Independents', who placed the freedom of individual congregations above the hierarchies of both bishops and presbyteries, had emerged. If not numerous, they soon had Cromwell's sword behind them, and the army *coup* of 1648 destroyed plans for a Presbyterian settlement. John Milton's trajectory was symptomatic: in 1641 he joined

THE Civil War spawned a multitude of sects. This Anglican-Tory print of 1680 shows the sects in league with the papacy to destroy Church and King. The bust of Charles I, the martyr-king, lies fallen at the bottom left corner. The committee comprises a Muggletonian, Ranter, Quaker, Anabaptist, Presbyterian, Independent, Fifth Monarchist, James Nayler (the Quaker), and a naked Adamite. The Pope is in the top right corner.

the common chorus of condemnation of prelacy, but by 1645 he was pronouncing that the Presbyterian alternative would amount to putting a pope in every parish. He also condemned parliamentary censorship of books as a popish tyranny, and advocated divorce as allowable by Scripture.

By the mid-1640s radicals had come to fear, in equal measure, the triple evils of 'popery, prelacy, and presbytery'. In place of clerical authority the case for religious toleration was boldly stated in the tracts of Henry Robinson and the Leveller William Walwyn. It only remained for the Whig philosopher John Locke, a generation later, to reiterate their arguments in classic form in his *Letter Concerning Toleration* (1689). Religious conviction, they argued, cannot be forced, and coercion only makes martyrs or hypocrites. The sincerity of our beliefs matters as much as being right or wrong, and, in any case, no human authority can claim to have infallible knowledge in religious matters. The State and the Church have different spheres, and the State should concern itself only with socially harmful behaviour—though it is true, they generally thought, that Catholics, atheists, and some sectaries *were* dangerous to society, and could not be tolerated. These claims were audible by the mid-1640s and tangible in the 1650s, but very far from being widely accepted.

Out of the bewildering shambles of English religion in the 1640s Cromwell forged a remarkably serviceable compromise: an established national Church, retaining its parochial structure, its trained ministry, and its tithes, but without bishops and the panoply of diocesan control, and open to a diversity of worship, which could be conducted either within the parish structure or in independent congregations. It was not dissimilar to the settlement made permanent after 1689. The clearest marker of Cromwell's commitment to toleration was his effort to protect James Nayler from the wrath of his Parliament in 1656. Nayler, a Quaker, in an act of misguided symbolism, rode into Bristol on a donkey, his followers strewing branches before him. For his blasphemy Parliament ordered his branding, tongue-boring, and flogging.

Yet, in the 1650s, diversity flourished. Presbyterians like Richard Baxter were able to create a synod-like association of like-minded ministers around Kidderminster (where Baxter's statue stands today). The Independents (who later came to be called Congregationalists) clung to Calvinist predestinarian doctrine, but rejected Presbyterian church hierarchy. The Baptists, believing that adult conversion should precede baptism, rejected infant baptism (and were often called anabaptists). The Quakers, or Society of Friends, rejected practically all outward ritual and the ordained ministry. And, beyond them, the fringe: the Fifth Monarchists, who discerned in the books of Daniel and Revelation Christ's imminent second coming, for which they must urgently prepare the world; the Muggletonians, who had their own brand of millennial prophecy; and those called 'Ranters', who were suspected of overthrowing all moral restraints because, in the words of St Paul's Epistle to Titus, 'unto the pure all things are pure'.

The fringe groups quickly faded away, but the four main strands, with the addition of the Methodists in the eighteenth century, continued to constitute the mainstream of the Nonconformist tradition. They put down deep roots in many communities, regularly revitalized by pastors capable of prodigious feats of evangelism—in the 1650s George Fox, one of the Quaker founders, traversed thousands of miles. Baxter achieved his mission through his massive correspondence, acting as adviser and 'agony uncle' among people much given to intense spiritual anxiety. Yet if these charismatic leaders loom large, the number of their followers was never

THE Cromwellian years not only gave free rein to Puritan radicalism, but also saw a tenacious loyalism among devotees of the old Anglican rites and rituals. Holy Trinity Church stands next to Staunton Harold Hall in Leicestershire. It was begun in 1653 by Sir Robert Shirley, who died in the Tower in 1656. The inscription over the entrance defiantly announces that Sir Robert did 'the best of things in the worst of times'.

great. No less tenacious during Cromwell's Protectorate was a quiet, underground loyalty to the old Prayer Book, for Anglicanism also proved itself to be an authentic mode of spirituality and worship. It was not destined to wither away after its official apparatus was dismantled in the Civil War. At Staunton Harold in Leicestershire the Cavalier gentleman Robert Shirley defiantly built a church, 'when all things sacred . . . were demolished or proscribed', as the inscription over the door reads.

3. *Anglicanism Restored*

It is striking how spontaneous was the restoration of Anglicanism in 1660. Well before Parliament passed the Act of Uniformity in 1662, those loyal to the Prayer Book, to the ministers ejected in the 1640s, and to episcopacy, were active in reconstructing the old Church. Puritan ministers intruded in the 1640s were unceremoniously thrown out. In Lincolnshire, parson John Yaxley, who had turned the baptismal font into a horse trough, was evicted by three armed Cavaliers; the Archbishop appointed a new incumbent the following week. The Norwich corporation stopped funding Puritan lectureships and bought a pair of silver candlesticks for the cathedral altar. At Christ Church in Oxford the undergraduates dumped the black 'Geneva gowns' into the River Isis. Bishops began to ordain ministers, to resurrect the machinery of the church courts, and to recover their estates. In reaction against the trauma of civil war Anglicanism acquired a self-confident and articulate identity. It came to be seen less as a Church 'halfly reformed'—a tawdry halting ground between Catholicism and Calvinism—and more as the purest expression of the 'primitive' Church of the Apostles and the Fathers of the earliest Christian ages, before episcopal brotherhood was usurped by the papal monarchy of Rome and by the priestly democracy of Geneva.

This assertiveness boded ill for those who hoped for an ecumenical church settlement, a broadly inclusive Church which would avoid dogmatic uniformity. Yet hopes were high. The King's Declaration at Breda (1660) left open the form of settlement, and offered 'liberty to tender consciences'. Charles was conscious of the power of the Presbyterians, who saw themselves as the chief instruments of his Restoration. He even offered bishoprics to their leaders: Baxter refused, and only Edward Reynolds accepted. However, at the Savoy Conference (1661) the tough-minded episcopalian Peter Gunning (later dubbed 'the hammer of the schismatics' in his diocese of Chichester) quarrelled with the cantankerous Baxter. The general election swept Cavaliers into Parliament, and their leaders forced a narrow settlement, despite the King's hopes for compromise. Later, Breda seemed the lost foundation for a broad Church, and Dissenters harped upon the broken promises of 1660.

The Act of Uniformity has been the corner-stone of Anglicanism ever since. Its version of the Prayer Book is revered by traditionalists today, and there are churches which advertise '1662' services. The attraction now is largely aesthetic, but in 1662 the Act was a

THIS frontispiece from a tract called *The Moderation of the Church of England* (1679) shows a female emblem of the Church of England, bathed in shafts of divine light, and seated between pillars surmounted by the crown and the mitre. To the left is a Papist gunpowder plotter, with a Jesuit inciting him, and to the right is a Protestant rebel, with a Puritan minister urging him on. Below are wolves in sheep's clothing, implying that Puritans are a fifth column for popery.

sword of retribution against the Puritans, and it drove from the Church a phalanx of people who dearly wished to stay within it. It demanded of ministers three commitments which snagged their consciences: re-ordination of those who had not been episcopally ordained (implying that their previous ministries counted for nothing); renunciation of the Covenant of 1643 (which thousands had solemnly sworn); and acceptance of every iota of Prayer Book rubrics, including the wearing of 'popish' surplices, and 'idolatrous' kneeling to receive the eucharistic sacrament. Between 1660 and 'Black Bartholomew Day' in 1662 some two thousand clergy left their parishes and colleges. Their later sufferings, from poverty, imprisonment, and harassment, were to be recorded in Edmund Calamy's martyrology. That John Walker responded (in 1714) by publishing the sufferings of Anglicans ejected during the Civil War served to harden the divide between 'Anglican' and 'Nonconformist'.

The intransigence of 1662 destined the Church's institutions to be immovable until shaken to their foundations by Victorian reformers. The Church was custodian of ten thousand medieval churches but had too few buildings in the growing towns, and urban evangelism increasingly fell to the Nonconformists. The Fifty Churches Act (1712) made small headway—Christ Church, Spitalfields, for example, forlornly asserting itself in a resolutely non-Anglican district in London's East End. The bishoprics and some choice deaneries remained fabulously wealthy, while many vicars were too poor to hold up their heads in gentry society. A visiting bishop could still expect to be ceremoniously greeted by several hundred gentlemen on horseback, but the excommunications delivered by his diocesan courts were increasingly ineffectual.

4. *The Great Purge*

The Act of Uniformity was the central plank in the 'Clarendon Code'. The Corporation Act drove lay Puritans from public office in the boroughs. When, during the Great Plague of 1665, ejected ministers reoccupied pulpits abandoned by fleeing churchmen, outraged Cavaliers responded with the Five Mile Act, excluding those ministers from their old stamping grounds. In North Wales Philip Henry was charged with living within five miles of his former parish church: the magistrates had the road measured, and he was acquitted by dint of sixty yards. Worst of all was the Conventicle Act of 1670, which Andrew Marvell famously called 'the quintessence of arbitrary malice'. It defined as illegal any private meeting for worship of five or more persons, and allowed informers to receive a portion of fines exacted for 'conventicling'. Nor was the legislation of the Cavalier Parliament the only resource for persecutors. The Elizabethan Recusancy Acts, designed against Catholics, could be used against anybody who failed to attend parish services. Those acts allowed for capital punishment, and Charles II was amazed to learn in 1664 of twelve Baptists at Aylesbury sentenced to death for Nonconformity: he reprieved them.

This was a formidable legal arsenal which, potentially, made possible a Puritan holocaust. But, as in every sphere of early modern government, enactment was not the same as enforcement. The 'era of the great persecution' is fixed in the annals of Nonconformist martyrology— and the image of the imprisoned John Bunyan, the Baptist tinker who spent twelve years in Bedford gaol, is still reproduced as an icon of Christian fortitude in postcards and Christmas cards today. However, the record of enforcement is patchy. First, it varied geographically, according to the willingness of local magistrates and bishops to act. Bishop Reynolds of Norwich

THE Society of Friends (Quakers) went furthest in abandoning the outward forms of traditional Christian ritual and hierarchy. Women like Margaret Fell played a major role in the formation of the Quakers. To the horror of contemporaries, Quaker women preached. During the Restoration the Quakers suffered persecution more than any other group.

turned a blind eye; so did the magistrates of Great Yarmouth. At quarter sessions zealous justices quarrelled with lenient ones.

Secondly, enforcement varied according to the degree to which different groups were held in odium: Presbyterians suffered least and Quakers suffered most. The Quakers' rejection of all ritual and priesthood seemed scarcely Christian, their refusal to take oaths seemed politically suspect, and their rejection of 'hat honour'—the doffing of hats to social superiors—was downright levelling. William Penn kept his hat on in front of the King, but the King was more tolerant than many magistrates. The Quakers also more readily allowed themselves to be arrested, rather than run away, as part of their witness for truth—they were still doing so outside nuclear air bases in the 1980s. Some 400 Quakers died in Restoration gaols, and probably 15,000 were prosecuted. In 1684 Penn, who founded the tolerationist colony of Pennsylvania, was charged with preaching, immediately after he arrived back in England. The Quaker 'books of sufferings' provide historians with the richest narratives of Dissent under the penal laws.

The last variable in enforcement was the changing exigencies of national policy. The purge was severe in the early 1660s and in 1670–1. But the Nonconformists were temporarily liberated in 1672 when the King published his Declaration of Indulgence: 1,500 licences for meetings were issued, and some began to construct the first purpose-built chapels. The same happened under James II in 1687–8, when he issued an Indulgence. There was also a tacit liberty in the late 1670s when attention was focused on the Catholic threat.

By contrast, the most savage phase occurred between 1681 and 1686—probably the worst period of religious persecution in English Protestant history, with the possible exception of the 1580s. During this 'Tory revenge' every means was used to destroy Dissent. Meeting-houses were broken up and burnt; ministers died in gaol, or fled abroad; even poor relief was restricted only to those who attended their parish church. In London the notorious Hilton gang operated. This was a team of informers who monopolized prosecutions, infiltrated secret meetings by feigning conversion, secured blank warrants from magistrates, forcibly seized goods to meet unpaid fines, and denounced constables who were soft on Dissent. Meanwhile, 'factious' boroughs were forced to surrender their charters and political independence. Anglican Tory gentry from the surrounding counties moved in to wrest control from town merchant élites. At Poole in Dorset the whole corporation was prosecuted for failing to indict Dissenters. The machinery of this purge was laid bare in 1688 when James II, in pursuit of a tolerationist alliance between Catholics and Dissenters, set up a commission of inquiry into those who had lined their pockets by prosecuting Nonconformists. The depositions offer tableaux of everyday harassment: constables and churchwardens who distrained tools and pewter dishes from artisans, egged on by avaricious lawyers and equipped with warrants signed by senior gentry or cathedral deans.

It is too easy to assume that religious persecution was the result of unthinking bigotry, and hard for the modern liberal mind to understand how devout and learned writers could offer arguments for coercing consciences. One argument was political. The Dissenters were invariably called 'fanatics'—they were the spawn of civil war, whose cry of 'conscience' was merely spiritual arrogance, and whose conventicles were 'nurseries of rebellion'. Just as conservatives in the

S COTTISH Presbyterians had little love for bishops: they thought prelates unscriptural. The remnant of the Covenanters of the 1640s continued a guerrilla warfare on behalf of King Jesus against King Charles II and his bishops. James Sharp, Archbishop of St Andrews, who had sworn the Covenant, was especially hated for his apostasy. On 3 May 1679 he was dragged from his coach on the road between St Andrews and Cupar and brutally murdered. The flight of the assassins and the subsequent rebellion is remembered in Sir Walter Scott's novel *Old Mortality*.

1990s express contempt for 1960s radicals, so Restoration Cavaliers and Tories scorned the radicals of the 1640s. A culture of anti-Puritanism developed, expressed in such plays as Sir Robert Howard's *The Committee* (1662) and in Samuel Butler's poem *Hudibras* (1663). Cavalier gentlemen memorized Butler's couplets about the Puritans who 'Call fire, and sword, and desolation | A Godly thorough Reformation'. The charge of innate rebelliousness seemed confirmed by the persistent terrorism of the Scottish Covenanters against the Restoration regime. When, in 1679, Archbishop Sharp of St Andrews was assassinated by Psalm-singing 'avengers of the Lord', the English Tory press was quick to draw propagandist lessons. Plots and rumours of plots, from Venner's Rebellion in 1661 down to the Rye House Plot of 1683 and Monmouth's Rebellion of 1685, served to damn all Dissenters.

In Tory eyes, the counterpoint to those seditious conventicles lay in Anglican teaching on the sanctity of kingship, the duty of 'passive obedience and non-resistance', and the divine right of episcopacy. The Dissenters were held to be collectively guilty of the execution of Charles I, deprecated in sermons delivered every 30 January. The cult of Charles the Martyr—the church dedicated to him at Tunbridge Wells is one of several—was the nearest thing to Anglican sainthood. Charles's *Eikon Basilike* (1649), with its frontispiece showing the Christ-like King holding a crown of thorns, was a bestseller. 'Kingship', said the divines, 'hath been crucified betwixt two thieves, the pope and the people'.

Another argument for intolerance lay in a tradition of thought called 'adiaphorist'. Whereas dogmatic Puritans tended to insist that whatever God has not prescribed he has forbidden, many Churchmen took the view that there were 'things indifferent' to salvation, neither required nor forbidden. In such matters as these the civil ruler may lay down formularies for good order and decency of worship. Writers in this tradition argued that while purely spiritual matters should be resolved by bishops and pastors, all 'externals', the outward forms of worship, ritual, and church government, were in the hands of secular governors. They reaffirmed the salient feature of the English Reformation as a 'magisterial' Reformation, executed by the State, with the Crown as 'Supreme Governor'. They said that Catholics, Presbyterians, and sectaries were all guilty of undermining the authority of the godly prince. The difficulty with this argument was that it looked like a complacent Erastianism, leaving the Church at the mercy of the State. This was not wise under the later Stuarts, and has ever since seemed unwise to those who fear what a secular State might do to the Established Church.

5. *The Shaping of Dissent*

Cast into the wilderness, and often likening themselves to Israel in captivity in Egypt, the Puritans were forced to come to terms with their status as a separated fragment. The evolution of Puritanism into Dissent was a painful one. Only a minority had earlier embraced separatism. These few were heirs to the small sectarian communities which had grown up, since Elizabethan times, in East Anglia, in exile in the Netherlands, and elsewhere. They judged that they should not 'tarry for the magistrate' in the work of completing the Reformation. But the mainstream, the Presbyterians and Independents, quite apart from their taste of power in the 1640s and 1650s, which still cast its hopeful spell after 1660, were convinced that they belonged at the heart of the English Church. As late as the 1690s the Presbyterian historian Roger Morrice plaintively

extolled the virtues of Elizabeth's Archbishop Grindal, suspended for tolerating Puritan meetings, and Archbishop Abbot, suspended under James I as an impediment to the growing Laudian movement.

For most Puritans the ejection of 1662 was an agony. They hoped it would be temporary, and tried to renegotiate the terms of the Act of Uniformity in order to be readmitted. Many continued to attend their parish churches: they held private meetings as well, but took care not to hold them at the same time as the parish services. Partial conformity was also sponsored by the realities of the social hierarchy. There were Puritan gentlemen who took in ejected ministers as household chaplains, but who also appointed ministers to local parishes. The parish church remained the arena in which the social hierarchy was represented. Despite his Puritan allegiances, Colonel John Birch's monument dominates his parish church at Weobley in Herefordshire. (It was, however, a sign of changing times that a man given to a biblical sense of godly militancy should be portrayed, after his death in 1691, in the secular dress of a Roman soldier.)

The phenomenon of partial conformity makes statistics of the size of Nonconformity somewhat spurious: 'membership' was not a distinct fact. It is commonly reckoned that perhaps 10 per cent of English people were Dissenters—maybe 20 per cent in the towns—figures somewhat greater than the contemporary estimate in the Compton Census of 1676, which was designed to play down Nonconformity. In some areas, where episcopal control was lax, Puritans continued to operate wholly within the confines of the Established Church. This was so in the chapelry of Meerbrook in the Staffordshire moorlands, where the absence of recorded 'Dissenters' should not mislead us. In that Anglican chapel today there is a monument commemorating Roger Morrice, a Presbyterian minister.

When Charles II issued his Declaration of Indulgence in 1672 the Puritans were gratified, for it lifted the bane of persecution, but they still suffered in conscience. Baxter casuistically attempted to show that his conventicling was not 'separatist', and he refused to be registered as a 'Presbyterian', as if that were an independent sect. In the terminology of the German sociologist Ernst Troeltsch, the Puritans were struggling to put aside the 'church-type' mentality and evolve into the 'sect-type'. Circumstances pushed them inexorably towards denominationalism. Vast though the gap was between Presbyterians and Independents, on the one hand, and the Quakers and Baptists, on the other, the experience of exclusion and persecution—and the vitriol of those who denounced all of them as 'fanatics'—drove them together. Gradually the institutional signs of denominational autonomy emerged: purpose-built chapels, Nonconformist academies, and the ordination of ministers to succeed the ejected of 1662.

Why did a small minority matter so much in Restoration life? Partly it was because there was a fund of sympathy for them within Anglicanism. Many ministers had teetered on the brink when confronted by the Act of Uniformity. The gap in attitudes and background between those who fell in and those who went out was small. John Tillotson, who rose (to the outrage of High-Churchmen) to become Archbishop of Canterbury in 1691, did not conform until 1664. There

Now owned by the National Trust, Loughwood Meeting House (*facing*), near Axminster in Devon, is one of the earliest Nonconformist chapels, built for the Baptists in about 1653. In order to avoid the attentions of the magistrates it was necessary to be self-effacing: it looks like a cottage, and is still hard for the visitor to find. The interior is dominated by its pulpit: this chapel is not a sanctuary for a sacramental religion, but a preaching box for a religion of the Word.

THE Protestant Nonconformists excelled as writers of popular devotional works. John Bunyan's *The Pilgrim's Progress* has been translated into over 200 languages, and during three centuries has been one of the world's best-selling books. It has gone wherever evangelical Protestantism has gone, and it was, for example, a favourite text of the Taiping rebels in nineteenth-century China.

were many within the Church who thought the 1662 settlement narrow. Their ecumenical spirit led to schemes for 'Comprehension', which would have readmitted the ejected ministers by relaxing the terms of 1662. Those who sought this compromise came to be labelled 'latitudinarians': later they would be called 'Low Churchmen'. By the 1680s another term had been coined for the hardliners who rejected such compromises: 'High Church'. The Church was thus divided within itself. There were bishops like John Wilkins, who had married Cromwell's daughter and had been a 'fellow traveller' during the 1650s, though most were hardline followers of Archbishops Sheldon and Sancroft. The latitude-men and the 'trimmers', who were seen to be lax toward Dissent, were edged out of the Anglican strongholds of Oxford and Cambridge, but made a name for themselves as fashionable preachers in London; many came into their own after the Revolution of 1688 when they became bishops.

The Dissenters were immensely influential beyond their own communities because of the books they wrote. Their devotional works became bestsellers in a society with a huge thirst for prayer books, sermons, and meditations. John Bunyan's *Pilgrim's Progress* (1678) has been a classic ever since, profoundly influencing Christians throughout the world. It tells the story of Pilgrim's conversion experience, of youthful sinfulness, of trials and temptations, of the setbacks and perseverance of a true believer in an ungodly world. It is peopled by allegorical characters, Lord Hategood, Mr Worldly-Wiseman, Mr Love-Lust, as well as Faithful, Hopeful, and Charity. Richard Baxter's *Call to the Unconverted* (1658) reached its 23rd edition by 1687. As well as the writers, a disproportionate number of London printers were Dissenters, selling tolerationist tracts and Whig pamphlets, dodging the censorship laws, and suffering fines when caught.

The Dissenters had high visibility in urban and trading communities. Immediately after the Toleration Act ninety congregations took out licences in London: this compared with the capital's 120 parishes. In the City some of the wealthiest merchants and colonial adventurers were

Dissenters. Elsewhere there was a high incidence of Dissent among textile artisans, for instance in the West Country towns which provided the Duke of Monmouth's rebel army in 1685. Baxter's 'godly men' were typically 'tradesmen, merchants, drapers, weavers, tailors'. The weaver, with a radical tract propped against his frame, envisioning a New Jerusalem, was as characteristic of a Devonshire town in the Restoration as he would be in 'the making of the English working class' a century later. The exclusion of Dissenters from professional life made the pursuit of other avocations necessary, and by the early eighteenth century, for instance, Quakers had established themselves as ironmasters in Birmingham. Meanwhile, there was a gradual decline in rural Dissent with the passing of the old Civil War Puritan gentry. Except among the urban plutocrats, it became unrespectable for a gentleman to be a Dissenter. Anglicanism was increasingly the religion of the gentry and of those anchored by deference to that class. By the close of the Stuart age England's two cultures of church and chapel were clearly visible.

6. *Heresy and Anticlericalism*

The ties of orthodoxy were loosened not only by the rejection of ecclesiastical hierarchies, but also in the growth of heresy and anticlericalism. These readily found a place within the gates of the Established Church, since the Dissenters were generally doctrinally conservative and deeply respectful of their suffering ministers. The greatest 'heresy' of the second half of the century was Arminianism: it was so universal as to become orthodoxy. Civil War Puritans had denounced the Arminianism of Laud's followers as a popish deviation from the key Calvinist doctrine of predestination. Arminians believed in the openness of God's saving grace to everybody, and the necessity of doing good works in co-operation with God's grace. The Puritans certainly lost this war: by the Restoration they were bitterly complaining that Calvinism had practically disappeared from England.

Their own ranks were not immune. Baxter engaged in a steady mitigation of predestinarianism and got embroiled in controversy. His retreat was spurred by the ogre of 'antinomianism': he feared that

R ICHARD BAXTER (1615–91) was an embodiment of Puritanism. He was an army chaplain in the Civil War, and was still living that down, when, aged seventy, he was prosecuted for seditious libel. Although the *bête noire* of high-flying Tories, he himself deplored sectarianism, and longed for a reuniting of Puritans and Anglicans in a single national church. He was one of the most prodigious preachers and writers of the century.

strict Calvinism led people to overthrow all morality and obedience, as being irrelevant to God's Elect. It is hard to find firm evidence that sectaries practised sexual promiscuity, but antinomianism was an extraordinarily potent obsession. Baxter and other Calvinists were caught between the Devil and the deep blue sea, because no less potent was the opposite fear of 'moralism'. It seems bizarre today that an emphasis on doing good should seem destructive of Christianity, but Bunyan had a point when he denounced the latitudinarian Anglican Edward Fowler. To the Christian, salvation lay only in the atonement wrought by Christ's blood: if acting morally was all that mattered then, said Bunyan, Socrates and Cicero were as good teachers as Jesus Christ, and Christianity had nothing special to offer. But Bunyan was fighting a losing battle. The general drift, at least among latitudinarian Churchmen and moderate Dissenters, was to reject 'formalism'—credal and ritual dogmatism—and to insist that what mattered was holy living. The anti-formalists paved the way for the ethical, as opposed to doctrinal, tone which dominated Christianity during the eighteenth-century Enlightenment.

A wilder shore of heresy lay in the growth of deism. This is a complex issue: like 'moralism' it came to taint mainstream Christianity during the eighteenth century. In its strictest form deism denied that biblical revelation had anything to teach beyond the simple truths of natural religion discernible by reason. It debunked miracles and providential interventions in earthly events; it rejected the doctrine of the Trinity; it replaced Christ's divinity with his humanity; and it rendered irrelevant the mediation of a sacramental priesthood. The term 'unitarian', to describe those who rejected the Trinity, was coined in the 1680s, and deism came of age when John Toland published *Christianity not Mysterious* in 1695. The Blasphemy Act of 1697 (which some people today want to extend to protect religions other than the Christian) was an attempt to put a stop to heresy.

In his *Account of the Growth of Deism* (1696) William Stephens blamed its rise on the behaviour of English clergy since the 1640s. Gentlemen, he said, went on the Grand Tour partly to learn of the depravity of popery in priest-ridden countries like Italy, but it was scarcely necessary to go abroad, for the folly of the clergy was visible enough in Protestant England. There was common complaint of the clergy's quarrelsomeness and cynical pursuit of self-interest behind their torrent of hectoring sermons. Many said the Civil War was a conspiracy by out-of-pocket Puritans to grab the bishops' wealth. Stephens was describing the growing culture of anticlericalism.

Restoration coffee-houses were rife with inventive epithets for the clergy: 'black-coats' and 'Baal's priests'. Complaints which once ran along the narrow channel of anti-popery now filled a broader channel of anti-priestcraft. The word 'priestcraft' was coined in the 1650s and became commonplace by the 1680s. The anticlericals argued that many church doctrines and rituals, though held up as being by divine right, were no more than human inventions concocted by priests to manipulate the credulous. This argument could take an anti-Christian form, but much casual anticlericalism went along with a sort of churchmanship. Restoration play-goers were regaled with images of Puritan hypocrites and ranting 'tub' preachers—but, notionally at least, this was all in the name of moderate and sober Anglicanism. When John Eachard published his *Grounds and Occasions of the Contempt of the Clergy* (1670) he had outright heresy less in mind than social contempt for underpaid clergymen, forced to become household servant chaplains or to farm their glebe.

7. *The Legacy of 1688*

The deep-seated tensions between Anglican and Dissenter were momentarily resolved in the face of James II's vigorous promotion of Catholicism. Protestant solidarity achieved its greatest consummation, and English bishops their greatest prestige, when, in 1688, James charged seven bishops with sedition and put them in the Tower. The Seven Bishops became Protestant heroes, medals were struck, and their portraits engraved. Symbolically, Presbyterian leaders visited them in gaol, and the hierarchy seemed willing at last to conciliate them. A scheme of Comprehension was offered to prevent the Dissenters from succumbing to royal edicts of toleration.

King James's commitment to toleration has aroused scepticism, then and now. But it made strategic sense to appeal to all those groups—Catholics and Protestant Dissenters—who had reason to resent the Anglican hegemony. And it tallied with the gradual evolution of English Catholics away from Counter-Reformation militancy and towards contentment with a denominational status not unlike that of the Protestant Dissenters. The King's chief Dissenting supporter, William Penn, said that the Catholics were Dissenters too.

Most Protestants, however, could detect in Catholicism only popish aggression, with French absolutism and the Roman Inquisition close behind. The advent of William of Orange seemed a providential deliverance, but it did not deliver harmony among English Protestants. Some High-Churchmen were unable in conscience to accept the forcible overthrow of the legitimate monarch, Catholic though he was. They were especially outraged when the new regime sacked several bishops for failing to take the new oath of allegiance to William and Mary. A third of the bishops and some four hundred clergy left the Established Church, forming the Nonjuror schism which lasted several decades. This High-Church separatism was to be echoed by the Oxford Movement in Victorian times, and by opponents of the ordination of women in the 1990s.

The Dissenters similarly found themselves, against expectations, cast into further separation from the Church. The Toleration Act of 1689 was originally meant to succour only those few separatists, mainly Baptists and Quakers, who could not be accommodated within a broadened national Church by a Comprehension Act. But, within months of the disappearance of the Catholic threat, and with news from Scotland of the forcible destruction of episcopacy there, the Comprehension scheme broke upon the rocks of renewed High-Church intransigence. The Toleration Act now had to serve all Dissenters. Even the most 'reconcilable' Presbyterians began to hold chapel services in competition with parish worship. It marked the final exhaustion of the ideal of a single, national, Reformed Church, and the reluctant beginning of a permanent religious pluralism.

15 POLITICS IN AN AGE OF REFORMATION

1485–1585

WALLACE MacCAFFREY

1. *The Reign of Henry VII*

Henry Tudor's victory over Richard III, at Bosworth on 23 August 1485 founded a new dynasty; his successful defence of his throne at Stoke-on-Trent on 16 June 1487 ended the Wars of the Roses. The issue between the two Houses of Lancaster and York had in fact been settled by Edward IV's victory at Tewkesbury in 1471; it was his early death (at 41), leaving a 12-year-old heir and the ensuing usurpation of Richard of Gloucester which destabilized the political order Edward IV had built and thrust Henry into a bid for the throne.

His two victories secured the throne; he would not have to fight for it again. Yet in 1487 a canny gambler might still have hesitated to stake much on his chances of survival. The past record was poor. Three English kings had lost their lives and thrones in the last thirty years. The ease with which Richard had seized power and the improbable success of Henry's expedition had rendered the throne all too vulnerable, as the attempts of two bogus claimants, Lambert Simnel in 1487 and Perkin Warbeck in the following decade, again made clear.

On the other hand, Henry was fortunate in succeeding a ruler little loved, who left behind no surviving partisans. Moreover, to Edward IV's followers Henry was the avenger of their late master and by his marriage to Elizabeth of York the restorer of the rightful royal line. Furthermore, there was no great magnate, such as the kingmaker Warwick or the Duke of Buckingham who had headed the first attempt to replace Richard with Henry Tudor.

Henry VII's policy was in part a continuance of his predecessors', the imposition of strong and unquestioned royal leadership after an interval of instability in which the authority of the Crown had been badly damaged. However, it also reflected the special circumstances of Henry's own experience. Henry Tudor was a stranger in the land when he ascended the throne he had conquered. He had left England at 14 after a childhood spent in a remote Welsh castle. For the next fourteen years he lived a lonely exile in Brittany and France. Thrust on the throne by the events

HENRY VII, by Michiel Sittow, 1505. The dark-horse candidate who won his crown on the battlefield of Bosworth, by his marriage he united the contending claims of Lancaster and York. Feared rather than loved, he survived to leave to his son a secure throne and a strengthened monarchy.

of a single afternoon, he had to master the realm he now ruled. As Shakespeare's Richard II tragically learned, mere anointment with the sacred oil did not make a king; he had to prove himself a ruler, not only in will but in deed, not only in the giving of commands but in the receiving of obedience. In the nerveless hands of a Henry VI the monarchy had fallen into deep disorder.

Edward IV, like Henry a usurper, had re-established royal authority by exploiting not only the legal powers and the formal structure of the monarchy but also the informal resources of his personal lordship. He had constructed a network of personal loyalties and dependencies which stretched across the realm. He made use of his own kin and his most trusted associates by placing them in well-endowed regional bases of power, brother Richard in the North, Lord Hastings in the Midlands, the Woodvilles on the Welsh border. Through them as intermediaries the lesser aristocracy of the shires were linked to the Court. The King also made use of his 'affinity', the clientage of lesser dependants, at once as local landowners in the southern counties and as members of the royal household, his intimates. These ties were cemented by the use of patronage, which matched loyalty with reward.

Henry had no kinsman whose services he could employ— apart from his uncle, Jasper Tudor, sent to govern Wales until his death, childless, in 1495—nor an established clientage. His personal following consisted of the small band of men who had joined him in Brittany, many of them members of Edward IV's affinity, who, bitterly hostile to Richard, had fled overseas after the abortive attempt to dethrone the usurper and replace him with Henry in 1483. Others were servants of his mother, the Lady Margaret Beaufort. These men naturally formed a nucleus of the royal council; the King also recruited a substantial number of men who had served the Yorkist kings, but it was the pre-Bosworth contingent who formed an inner core of royal confidants. The council was in any case a fluctuating body, rarely acting collegially. The King preferred to deal with individuals or with informal groups, depending upon the nature of the business.

Initially Henry won the ready response of the gentry; their backing in 1487 enabled him to deal quickly and decisively with the conspiracy on behalf of the bogus pretender, Lambert Simnel, which he crushed in battle at Stoke-on-Trent. The King found it less easy to deal with the second pretender, Perkin Warbeck. That episode dragged on for several years and led to the discovery of treachery in the royal household. The Chamberlain, Sir William Stanley, whose services at Bosworth had carried the day for Henry, was condemned for treason along with Lord Fitzwalter, another courtier on whom the King had showered favours. There was further discouragement in 1497 when the sullen indifference and underhand encouragement of the southern gentry allowed an army of Cornish rebels to march to the outskirts of London before they were defeated. These events aroused Henry's sense of vulnerability, which was heightened by the deaths of his two older sons and of his Queen; from 1503 the dynasty's future hung on a single life, Henry, Prince of Wales.

As a consequence of the events of 1495 Henry recast the organization of his household, creating the Privy Chamber, an inner corps of personal attendants, who alone had access to the royal person, thus severing the ties which had existed with the much larger body of household knights, to a merely formal relation with the monarch. This move signalled a general distancing of the King, both from the nobility and from the lesser land-holding élites.

This also signalled a shift in the royal strategy of government. With much less reliance on the informal links with the larger community of the realm, favoured by the Yorkists, there was far more use of legal and bureaucratic channels to compel the obedience of the subject. The King himself—especially after 1503—played a directly supervisory role in the business of government, working through new specialized committees of the council, staffed increasingly by lawyers. Much of their efforts went into a vigorous exploitation of the Crown's fiscal rights, many of them little used, some half-forgotten, such as wardship. This right, derived from the practice of earlier times, entitled the Crown to assume control of the lands and person of any minor heir whose property was held directly from the Crown. The royal officers were set to work examining the estates of individual landowners and exacting the fees due the Crown under such circumstances. Others sought out 'concealed lands', property in which the royal rights were illegally ignored or withheld.

One object of such enterprises was straightforwardly financial, the augmentation by every means of royal revenues. Indeed the laying up of riches became something of an obsession with the King. There was, however, a second, no less important, motive at work. The King, ever fearful of danger to his fragile dynasty, was determined to keep his subjects, great and small alike, on a tight rein. His favourite device, an ancient legal weapon, now furbished up for use, was the penal bond (or recognizance). A subject who had fallen foul of the law and was already obliged to pay a fine (by instalments) or to observe certain restrictive conditions was additionally forced to sign a second obligation. Under its terms failure to fulfil any of the precedent conditions to which he was already obliged would result in a crushing, often confiscatory, financial penalty. This threat could be kept hanging over the victim's head at the royal discretion. A high percentage of the nobility and many gentry fell under these menacing sanctions, flies caught in a legal spider web, held inert by their captor.

At the same time the King, acting through his councillors, tightened his hold on the shire élites. Appointment to local Crown office, such as constable of a castle, steward of an estate, or keeper of a park, had been at the centre of the patronage system. A reward for service, it enhanced the standing and often the income of the appointee. Now it became much more an office, a responsibility for which the holder was answerable to the Crown and duly punished for non-performance. Furthermore, the recipients of royal patronage were now denied any privileged

H ENRY VII and his queen. Unlike the late Gothic splendour of the chapel at Westminster which Henry built for the tombs of his family—see the plate facing page 289—his tomb was executed by an Italian craftsman, an early import of the contrasting Continental Renaissance style.

status *vis-à-vis* the law. Even the royal councillors or the King's kin through his mother were duly mulcted for any infraction of the law.

It was a regime of fear in which the King, acting through his corps of professional lawyers/administrators, ruled with a heavy hand and in which nobility and gentry were kept at arm's length, compelled to execute many arduous tasks for the King and to obey his laws scrupulously, but denied the customary rewards. Even the highest in favour were given the ephemeral rewards of office instead of the lasting gratification of land. Relations between King and subject were those of command and obedience, of master and servant, rather than the reciprocal link of patron and client.

Henry's aloof and bureaucratic style of government muted the usual jostling competition of political life and cooled the fever of faction. The inaccessible monarch, who chose his own servants solely on merit, could not be flattered or coaxed into the bestowal of favour. Whatever benefits he granted had to be earned and to be paid for in arduous service. This was not a recipe for popularity and some of the accumulated resentment of his subjects became evident in the reaction which followed his death. His confidential lawyers, Dudley and Empson, provided scapegoats who went to the block while the penal bonds were cancelled.

Nevertheless Henry might look about him with some satisfaction at the conclusion of his reign. From his own point of view he had secured the ends he set himself. The threats to the dynasty had faded away; he could pass on a safe inheritance to his son. The throne stood clear of the pressures of faction. The monarchy, damaged by the events of the fifteenth century, was not only restored to health but now enjoyed greater strength and firmer control over its subjects than in the past.

However, his success as a ruler had been achieved by a highly idiosyncratic style of rulership, which bypassed the élites and relied heavily on the exercise of royal power through bureaucratic channels, backed by the direct intervention of the monarch. To the governing classes it was incomprehensible or at least baffling. Henry was a king who held them, his natural counsellors and servants, at a distance. Nor did they understand a king who was obsessed with accumulating income not for the traditional purposes of war or in bounty to his servants but to establish even more fully his freedom from dependence on their goodwill. It is not surprising that they greeted his death with relief.

2. *The Age of Wolsey*

The death of Henry VII and the accession of his son in April 1509 instantly transformed English political life. In place of the dour and colourless father there now stood the ebullient 18-year-old Henry VIII. Handsome, a skilled athlete, an accomplished musician, humanistically educated, he combined the characteristics of late medieval chivalry with those of the Renaissance prince. His outgoing geniality and his rather overpowering personal charm won immediate and enthusiastic popularity in the Court and the country. Relations between monarch and aristocracy eased promptly. The latter recognized Henry as one of their own kind.

The personality of the new King was specially reflected in the style of his Court. For his father the royal *métier* had required demanding labour. The son revelled in sheer enjoyment of his inheritance. The new Court glittered as entertainment followed entertainment—masques, jousts,

DETAIL from early seventeenth-century picture of the Thames at Richmond, with the old Royal Palace. Built by Henry VII to replace an earlier structure, Richmond Palace was a favourite Tudor residence: Elizabeth spent the late summer here annually, and like Henry VII she died here. The palace was destroyed later in the seventeenth century.

hunting, dancing, music—in all of which the King was a leading participant. The drudgery of administration was left to the ministers he had inherited from his father.

And yet, if Henry mingled more freely with the aristocracy than his father, he took pains to surround himself with a style of Court life which ostentatiously asserted the unique dignity of the monarch, a dignity enhanced by ever more splendid and elaborate ceremony. The King would also provide a more splendid setting for his Court revels. He acquired two new palaces from his minister, Cardinal Wolsey, Hampton Court and Whitehall, by confiscation while he built three new ones, St James's in Westminster and Oatlands and Nonsuch in Surrey. The other royal houses numbered almost thirty by 1547 and Henry was to spend some £170,000 on his residences.

But, beyond the pursuit of pleasure, Henry had other goals in view, ambitions which cast him in the traditional mould of his royal predecesssors and which were shared by the aristocracy. He longed to emulate the martial glories of an Edward III or Henry V and for twenty years, on and off, pursued a pale revival of the Hundred Years War by fitful interventions in the see-saw struggle on the Continent between Francis I of France and the Emperor Charles V for the control of Italy, usually as an ally of the latter.

These military enterprises demanded the raising of unprecedented sums of money and required large-scale organization, which called for the great administrative talents which Henry found in Thomas Wolsey, a man admirably equipped for the job. This ambitious cleric, a chaplain of Henry VII, advanced in a few years to an unprecedented position in the political scheme of things. Lord Chancellor, Archbishop of York, and Cardinal by 1515, he had become sole minister to the Crown. Wolsey's unique position meant that the other royal councillors shrank into insignificance beside the Cardinal's towering figure, his subordinates rather than his colleagues. The royal confidence in the minister gave him a grip on power which was unchallenged and in which the normal competition for royal favour was extinguished. However much the courtiers and the nobility at large resented the ostentation and arrogance of this upstart, they had to accept the monopoly of the royal confidence as the prime fact of the political world. Once again, as in Henry VII's reign—although for different reasons—the normal competition for royal favour was damped down, this time by the looming presence of the sole minister.

The Cardinal dominated the world of business; the world of pleasure, the royal household,

FLODDEN FIELD (from Holinshed's *Chronicles*), where in 1512 James IV of Scotland tried to exploit English preoccupations with the French wars, only to lose his life (and those of half the Scottish nobility).

was less under his thumb. He had to keep a sharp look-out for rival sources of influence developing among the men who were in daily attendance on the King and who shared his amusements. As early as 1519 Wolsey, fearing the influence of the gentlemen of the Privy Chamber, daily intimates of the King, contrived to replace them with dependants of his own. The minister's fear highlighted the paradox of his position. His power, great as it was, ultimately hung on the favour of the volatile and wilful royal egotist, all too susceptible to influences in his entourage.

Wolsey's reign was brought to a close when the centre of gravity did indeed shift to the innermost sanctum of the household. By 1527 the King had determined to have an annulment of his marriage to Catherine of Aragon and her replacement by Anne Boleyn. The King now set Wolsey the greatest of his tasks, to secure a papal annulment of his first marriage. This time the Cardinal's talents were inadequate to fulfil the command of his master. As success at Rome eluded him, Wolsey, faced by the hostility of Anne Boleyn and hounded by the frustrated Henry, saw his influence fade. Anne provided a magnet for the accumulated animosities of all those who had resented the *arriviste*'s monopoly of royal favour. In 1529 the King dismissed him.

3. *The Age of Cromwell*

Wolsey's downfall proved to have a significance beyond the immediate circumstances of the case. The fault line which now appeared in the fabric of politics would endure to the end of the Tudor era. The factions which split the English Court in the 1530s would in the decades to come harden into permanent divisions. Personalities and immediate issues would fluctuate with time and circumstance, but the fundamental differences of the 1530s arose from deeper causes than mere Court rivalries.

The resolution of the King's 'great matter' had consequences far beyond the initial occasion; to secure the annulment nothing less than religious revolution would suffice—the rejection of papal authority and the establishment of a separate English Church ruled by the King. For Henry the pursuit of his newly discovered role as Supreme Head of the Church gave him a purposefulness hitherto lacking. Moreover, in spite of the King's theological conservatism, the very act of repudiating Rome's authority soon drew England into the orbit of Continental Protestantism. As a necessary corollary the political fault line which initially separated Court factions based on personalities and the immediate issue of the annulment widened into a gulf between two ideological parties, divided by the deepest religious convictions.

Religious reformers found their first patroness in Anne Boleyn, but her triumph was short-lived; it ended in a welter of blood and ruined careers. The great survivor of this shipwreck was Thomas Cromwell, once a servant to Wolsey, now his successor as chief minister. Himself an advocate of reform, he skilfully extricated himself from the Boleyn faction on Anne's fall. His invaluable services to Henry in the skilful surgery by which he stitched together a new ecclesiastical order for the realm and—an afterthought—dissolved the monasteries, ensured his monopoly of the royal counsels, but also aroused bitter opposition, which found expression in the Pilgrimage of Grace in 1536.

A regional insurrection, centred in Yorkshire, but engineered by a group of courtiers, gave voice to the rancour within the Court against the low-born minister and against his policy of religious reform. That hostility found its echoes among a provincial gentry whose religious conservatism was linked to a sense of alienation from a distant Court as well as a complex of local grievances. The rally of leading nobles to the King and the lack of response outside the northern counties defeated the rebels and ensured Cromwell's survival. But in 1540 Cromwell's enemies got the better of him when he fell victim to a palace intrigue in which the conspirators persuaded the King that the minister's religious reformism was tainted with heresy.

The years of the 1530s saw the overthrow of papal authority, the dissolution of the monasteries, and the first hesitant steps towards religious reform on the Continental model. They also saw an important shift in the role of Parliament. The fact that the religious revolution could only be implemented with parliamentary participation meant—what could not be foreseen in the 1530s—that it would play a vital part in the zigzag series of religious changes of the next three reigns. More immediately, Cromwell's skills would be called upon to pilot the necessary bills through the two Houses, a first—and significant—essay in the modern art of parliamentary management.

Cromwell's wide-ranging vision comprehended additional possibilities for parliamentary action, hardly less important than its role in passing the religious statutes. He saw that the state's power could be used to resolve or at least ameliorate some of the problems generated by the contemporary population explosion—poverty, unemployment, and social disorder. His tentative moves in this direction, added to the religious Acts, produced an unprecedented volume of parliamentary enactments, inaugurating an age in which the scope of legislation and of members' activity in Parliament would increase rapidly.

4. *Henry VIII's Last Years, 1540–1547*

There was no successor to Cromwell; the era of sole ministers was over. The King's decision to rule through a reorganized council marked a definitive shift in the character of royal government. There was now a Privy Council, a legally defined inner core of councillors, set apart as a 'cabinet', at once a supreme administrative board and a consultative committee. Equipped with its own secretariat and archives, it monopolized the great business of state. Equally important, it served to focus the political life of the realm in a single collegial body. There was now a clearly defined élite who collectively monopolized the confidence of the sovereign. The new order displaced both the anomalous array of Crown servants, great and small, who did the bidding of Henry VII, or the sole ministers of the previous thirty years. It was a long step towards a more formal and bureaucratized state structure.

At the same time the momentum which Henry's will had imparted to the religious changes faltered. Already before Cromwell's fall the Act of Six Articles had asserted a firmly conservative royal position on the principal issues dividing Catholics and Protestants. Yet though opposed to further reform, the King gave no clear sense of direction. The reformers continued to cling to a foothold in the Court; heresy remained unextinguished, and England in schism with Rome. In such an atmosphere of uncertainty, faction bred fertilely in Court and Council.

In this situation the scramble for preferment became less orderly and more dangerous; it was difficult to avoid tying one's fortunes to the fluctuating uncertainties of factional rivalry. Yet if the risks increased, so did the prizes to be won. The monastic dissolution had placed in Henry's

EARL OF ESSEX.

THOMAS CROMWELL (created Earl of Essex in 1539), after Hans Holbein. He succeeded Wolsey as Henry VIII's sole minister, 1533 to 1540, and carried through the managed revolution of the 1530s, organizing the newly separated *ecclesia anglicana* and overseeing the dissolution of the monasteries; his patronage of the more radical reformers lost him the confidence of the conservative King—and his head.

hands a princely endowment from which he could reward—by gift or sale—favoured servants. Well-placed courtiers, like Russell (future Earl of Bedford) or Paulet (soon to be Marquis of Winchester) could—and did—lay the foundation of substantial landed fortunes for themselves and their descendants.

5. *The Great Dukes*

Two factions emerged in the Council of the 1540s. One party was headed by Seymour, Earl of Hertford, brother to Henry's third wife and uncle to the young Prince Edward. The other was led by the religiously conservative Bishop Gardiner of Winchester, and included Thomas Howard, third Duke of Norfolk, premier peer of the realm. As the King's health declined, the contest took on a new and grim dimension since it was not only the favour of the existing King which was at stake but control of royal power when a boy sat on the throne. The struggle reached a bloody climax with the fall of the Howards. Norfolk's son, the Earl of Surrey, went to the block; the Duke escaped only by the chance of Henry's death. Seymour and his colleague, Dudley, Lord Lisle, son of Henry VII's disgraced minister, led the victorious faction. With Henry's death on 27 January 1547 these men, as the Privy Council of Edward VI, became the rulers of England.

To these men time and circumstance gave a uniquely favoured opportunity to advance their own fortunes. Their first act was to reward themselves with a lavish distribution of peerage creations and promotions. Material rewards followed, a wholesale plundering of the monastic lands for their benefit. The inherent instability of a regime which lacked a royal hand at the tiller forwarded the process. When Seymour, self-promoted Duke of Somerset, fell from power in 1549, his victorious rival, Dudley, now Duke of Northumberland, was able to keep his seat to the end of the reign but only by wholesale bribery of his supporters.

The political inheritance, both at home and abroad, was a less favouring one. Henry's clumsy attempt to add Scotland to his dominions by marrying his son, Edward, to the infant Mary, Queen of Scots, had entangled England in a futile military adventure aimed at bullying the northern kingdom into submission. Protector Somerset's ill-advised continuation of the Scottish war deepened the crisis and provoked French intervention in the northern realm. At home the seething discontents of the peasantry boiled over into open disorder. In Devon the imposition of a new Protestant liturgy—in Norfolk resentment against enclosing landlords—touched off rebellion. Somerset was overthrown by his conciliar colleagues. They crushed rebellion and made

---

THIS image of Henry VII (*facing, above left*) crowned and supported by the Lords Spiritual and Temporal appears on the title-page of an edition of the statutes belonging to the City of London, made in the final years of the fifteenth century.

EVEN before his schism from Rome, Henry VIII (*facing, above right*) prided himself on being a champion of Christian evangelism (which earned him the papal accolade 'defender of the faith'). Here a young and determined Henry holds a text from Mark 16—'go out into the world and preach the gospel to every creature'. The text is not in the authorized Latin of the Vulgate but one of the fashionable new Humanist retranslations.

UNTIL about 1534 the Tudor Court's culture was still based on the chivalric ideal. Tournaments (*facing, below*) involved mounted knights in full armour, each bearing a massive lance, charging towards each other in the 'lists'. In February 1511 Henry VIII ordered a two-day tournament at Westminster to celebrate the birth of a son to Catherine of Aragon. The child died shortly afterwards.

THIS manuscript (*above*) shows Mary Tudor 'touch-ing for the Queen's Evil'—curing her subjects of scrofula (a form of tuberculosis). All Tudor and Stuart rulers exercised this gift, which was believed to be unique to monarchs and a sign of their divine right to govern.

THIS is one of nine limnings presented to Elizabeth I as a New Year's gift (*right*). It depicts Elizabeth engaged in the traditional Catholic ceremony for Maundy Thursday in which, in imitation of Christ, she washed the feet of a number of poor per-sons corresponding to her age.

THOMAS HOWARD, third Duke of Norfolk, after Hans Holbein the Younger. A leading councillor for two decades, and premier noble of the realm, Howard was uncle to two of Henry's queens, and (as leader of the conservative religious faction) the engineer of Cromwell's fall in 1540. At the very end of Henry's reign he was himself overthrown by Seymour ('Protector' Somerset), and spent Edward VI's reign in the Tower. Restored by Mary, he died shortly thereafter.

a humiliating withdrawal from Scotland which left the French in control there.

However, the short-lived Somerset regime left a permanent legacy. On the Protector's urging, Parliament had set in motion the stalled train of reform and carried England into a full-blown Protestant reformation. The Books of Common Prayer of 1549 and 1552 created a confessional regime which deepened the factional division of the Court into a national rift between two ideologically polarized parties. Yet hardly was the Protestant regime in place when on the death of the 16-year-old King in 1553, the throne passed to the ardently Catholic Mary, who triumphed over Northumberland's vain attempt to substitute the Protestant Lady Jane Grey, and then promptly reversed the religious poles, restored the ancient religion, and reconciled the kingdom to Rome.

6. The Reign of Mary Tudor

The accession of Mary restored a royal presence, but the new ruler was handicapped by the mere fact of her gender, which, in the opinion of most of her subjects, disqualified her from ruling. Contemporaries, to a man, shared the views of John Knox, whose pamphlet *The First Blast of the Trumpet against the Monstrous Regiment of Women*, denouncing female rule as outside the natural and divine order, appeared in 1558. Sharing their views, Mary promptly sought a husband, Philip of Spain, an unpopular choice which sparked an abortive rebellion. In 1554 a conspiracy was hatched, aimed at halting the Spanish match and by wedding Anne Boleyn's Protestant daughter, Elizabeth, to a descendant of the Yorkist line, Courtenay, Earl of Devon, excluding a foreign ruler. The ensuing rising in Kent momentarily shook the throne before it was crushed. Mary married Philip in July; for a year after the marriage Philip remained in England, sharing responsibility with his wife. After 1555 he returned to England only once briefly, but in effect he conducted England's foreign relations, involving her in the war which led to the loss of Calais in 1558.

At home Mary struggled unhappily and not very successfully with the problem of an unwieldy and faction-ridden Council, a problem made worse when Councillors deliberately carried their

WILLIAM PAGET (*c.*1549), first Baron Paget of Beaudesert, the 'master of practices'. Of humbler origin than courtiers such as Russell or Paulet, he was also a more assertive player in the political game, particularly under Mary, when in a fierce contest with Bishop Stephen Gardiner he sought unsuccessfully to dominate the Council. He did not, however, forfeit peerage, estate, or office, and was the founder of another landed noble family.

quarrels into the House of Commons and thwarted the passage of the Queen's legislative programme. Although the restoration of the mass passed, albeit against a significant minority vote, the Queen had to yield to parliamentary insistence by guaranteeing the rights of those who had bought monastic lands.

Mary's chief preoccupation, the re-establishment of the old religion, sharpened the confessional divisions already apparent in the last reign and drove those politicians who were too closely identified with reform into retirement. Open resistance to the restored Catholic regime was largely limited to those classes which were outside the political community, but from the end of Mary's false pregnancy in 1555 English politicians, looking to an uncertain future, were aware that the putatively Protestant Princess Elizabeth would be their next sovereign and that yet another change of religion loomed.

7. *The Elizabethan Settlement*

The end of Mary's short reign in November 1558 brought to the throne another woman ruler but one whose assured self-confidence and assertive will were wholly masculine and whose grasp of power contrasted sharply with her sister's fumbling efforts to maintain her authority. Elizabeth, very much her father's daughter, was in full command of the political scene.

To the universal expectation that she would marry Elizabeth opposed an unshakeable resolve to reign a virgin queen. Her decision posed a grave problem for her subjects. Elizabeth was the last of Henry's children. Who was the next in line for the English throne? Mary, Queen of Scotland (and of France, 1559–60), was next in strict hereditary right, but Lady Jane Grey's younger sister, Catherine, could claim by virtue of Henry's will. The terrifying prospect of a contested succession chilled the blood of Englishmen who had not forgotten the Wars of the Roses. Council and Parliament, backed by popular opinion, were desperately urgent in their petitions that the

Queen marry or at least settle the succession. Elizabeth skilfully evaded their pleas, putting them off with half-promises, never fulfilled. Ultimately, in 1569, a clutch of courtiers concocted a scheme for marrying the Queen of Scots, now an exiled captive in England, to the premier peer, the fourth Duke of Norfolk. Quashed by Elizabeth, it was revived in a more dangerous intrigue, the Ridolfi Plot of 1571, which envisaged Spanish intervention to back the marriage. Its discovery brought Norfolk to the block and fatally tainted Mary's cause in the minds of patriotic Englishmen.

In spite of her resolve to rule a virgin queen, Elizabeth soon came to command the confidence and in time the passionate loyalty of her people. Her strategy of rulership was a highly personal one, which skilfully dealt with the peculiar conditions of feminine rule. To her Council and Court she displayed a truly masculine personality, as masterful as her father's, which brooked no slackness of obedience to her every command. Unlike him she was not easily manipulated. Greedy for flattery, she was yet impervious to the flatterer's solicitations. Determined to assert her unconstrained will, she was nevertheless willing to listen and to be persuaded. Steadfastly loyal to her servants once she had given her confidence, Elizabeth brought a reassuring stability and an enduring continuity to the Court world.

Outside the Court Elizabeth cultivated a very different image. She wooed her subjects assiduously. Her annual summer progresses in which she moved across the countryside, a guest in successive country houses, interspersed with visits to various towns or one of the universities, gave her the chance to use her feminine charms, to show herself a benign and smiling princess, graciously responsive to her subjects' welcome, ready with the apt phrase of praise or flattery. This was an image reinforced by the Queen's abstention from the royal extravagances of her father, by a pacific foreign policy, and by a steady propaganda which presented Elizabeth as the national protectress of her people against foreign foes and domestic violence.

In shaping her own Privy Council Elizabeth chose a judicious mix of veteran servants of her three predecessors plus an infusion of restored Edwardians like William Cecil, who returned to the secretaryship he had held in her brother's time. There was a strong element of professional administrators, like Lord Treasurer Winchester, Sir Walter Mildmay (Chancellor of the Exchequer), or Lord Keeper Nicholas Bacon. The contingent of peers was largely Court-based, experienced politicians chosen for their usefulness not for their rank. A substantial number of Privy Councillors—Cecil, Bedford, Knollys, Sidney, Dudley—were second or third-generation servants of the House of Tudor.

MARY Queen of Scots's marriage to Henry, Lord Darnley—celebrated in this medallion of 1565—and the succeeding birth of James VI (I) greatly strengthened her claims, strenuously resisted by Elizabeth, to the English succession. Fortunately for the latter, Mary's indiscretions lost her the Scottish throne and drove her into exile (and captivity) in England.

The complexion of Elizabeth's Council reflected a change in the nature of English politics which had begun in her father's time. First of all he had forged new links between the Court and the political classes, the county land-owning élites. The strategy adopted was different from that of the late medieval 'affinity', the clientage of royal dependants focused in the royal household, as in Edward IV's time. Now the network stretched across the whole country and drew in the whole body of the aristocracy, the fifty odd peers and a few thousand of the great landowners. Henry gave explicit encouragement to the process by expanding part-time, honorary Court appointments, such as esquires of the body. There were no less than 263 of the latter category in 1535, and they included men from every county in the kingdom. The élite body of Gentlemen Pensioners, the royal honour guard, offered places to some score of young aristocrats; even more desirable were posts in the King's immediate establishment, the Privy Chamber.

An important corollary of this 'nationalization' of politics was a lessening of the political role of the nobility as intermediaries between sovereign and country. The century of Tudor rule saw a marked diminution in the number of great regional magnates. The fall of the Duke of Buckingham and the dissolution of his Welsh border lordship in 1521 was followed by the similar fate of the West Country Marquis of Exeter in 1538. The Percys of Northumberland suffered shipwreck in the 1530s, enjoyed temporary rehabilitation under Mary, and then went into a long eclipse after the failed rising of 1569 while the Nevilles, Earls of Westmorland, destroyed themselves altogether by participating in that episode. The Howards of Norfolk, struck down by Henry, restored by Mary, were the authors of their own downfall when the fourth Duke's dabbling in the Ridolfi plot brought him to the block.

The role of the nobles in Council and Court under the last Tudor mirrored their diminished importance in high politics. With few exceptions the noble members of the Elizabethan Privy Council were peers of Elizabeth's own creation or of her brother's. Of those who were not, only the Earl of Sussex played a major role in affairs. This meant that county gentry, looking for patrons, either for their own advancement or for support in local rivalries, had to turn directly to the Court. It was now the Privy Councillors who were the patronage brokers for the whole kingdom.

Under the Queen both the great Councillors, Burghley and Leicester, extended their networks of patronage on a nation-wide scale with connections in every county. When a great regional magnate, like the Duke of Norfolk, fell, his clients in East Anglia turned to the Privy Councillor, Lord Hunsdon, now Lord Lieutenant of Suffolk and Norfolk, while in the West Country and the Welsh borders two other Councillors, the new-coined peers, Bedford and Pembroke, replaced the long-descended Buckingham and Exeter.

At the same time many county gentry set out to establish direct links with the Court. Families like the Gawdys or the Knyvetts of Norfolk dispatched a younger brother to Court, to advance his own career but more importantly to serve the interests of his elder brother at home. Within the counties the older vertical structure built around a noble leader was replaced by a horizontal model in which gentry families, more or less equal in wealth and status, such as the dozen or so gentry dynasties of Norfolk, managed their own relations with the great Court patronage brokers.

A second major shift in the political order had been evident since Henry VIII's time. Clerical pre-eminence in the conciliar ranks, a marked feature of Henry VII's reign, was in marked decline by the latter years of his son's. They were conspicuously absent from Edward's Council and after a brief come-back under Mary, were entirely excluded by Elizabeth. In their place there now existed a corps of high-ranking professional politician/administrators whose services were in-dispensable to any regime, regardless of their ideological predispositions. Mary had to fill her Council with men who had backed Protestant reform in her brother's time and—worse still—lent their hands to the usurpation of Lady Jane. In Elizabeth's original Council at least eight of the twenty had served under three of her predecessors.

Successful survivors of thirty years of jungle warfare, they were servants of the Crown rather than the creatures of a single monarch. Their origins were various. Paulet, successively promoted Baron, Earl, and in 1550 Marquis (of Winchester) and Russell, a Baron under Henry and Earl of Bedford under his son, came of middle-rank county families. William Paget, Baron Paget of Beaudesert in 1549, had behind him a London merchant background. Herbert, promoted Earl of Pembroke in 1555, was the son of a Welsh border family, Sir William Petre, Secretary of State, of a Devon yeoman. In every case it was a record of proved competence as royal servants which forwarded their careers. They were, in short, a meritocracy.

8. *Elizabethan Heyday*

Yet even if England was undergoing a shift from dynastic monarchy to the more bureaucratic model of the early modern state, highly personal considerations could still affect the course of politics. The harmony of Elizabeth's judiciously selected Council was ruffled when the Queen introduced an outsider, chosen by her not for his political or administrative skills, but because he found favour in her sight—Robert Dudley, second son of the late unlamented Duke of Northum-berland. Given a household office (Master of the Horse) at her accession, he was soon touted as a royal suitor, and when his wife died in 1561, consort apparent. The match did not materialize but Dudley, patronized by the Queen, given an earldom (Leicester), endowed with abundant lands, and a place on the Privy Council, advanced to the first political rank.

That a ruler so coolly politic in her judgement should have made such a blatant display of per-sonal favouritism seems paradoxical, but her action had its political as well as its personal logic. In the first years of the reign Secretary Cecil had set the pace of action, coaxing a reluctant Eliza-beth into a risky, albeit highly successful, Scottish venture, by which the French were expelled from Britain and a pro-English government established at Edinburgh. The Secretary bade fair to dominate Elizabeth's Councils as Wolsey or Cromwell had those of her father. Henry could af-ford to delegate authority without losing caste, a queen risked the imputation of dependency on the minister.

Her reaction was to promote a rival, Dudley, who could counterbalance Cecil's weight in Council. The favourite was given a stake to enable him to play but no favour in the game. Eliza-beth's role as umpire poised above the fray, for whose favourable judgement the two rivals had to contend, secured her independence. To create faction in the Council was a risky strategy but Elizabeth had full confidence in her ability to manage the rivalry. When Leicester dabbled in the conspiracy to marry Mary Stuart to the Duke of Norfolk and incidentally to shove Cecil aside, the Queen pulled in the reins sharply and he quickly submitted. Thereafter he and Cecil worked in double harness, pulling the coach of state.

The two decades from 1570 were the golden years of the reign. Good harvests and a merciful respite from epidemic disease made for greater population growth than would be seen for some

WILLIAM CECIL, Baron Burghley (*left*), by Marcus Gheeraerts. He was successively Secretary of State and Lord Treasurer under Elizabeth, her principal and most trusted minister for forty years, shaper of an irenic and defensive foreign policy, hammer of the Catholics, and administrator *par excellence*. Unlike his predecessors, Wolsey and Cromwell, he never lost the royal confidence, but died in office and founded a richly endowed noble family.

ROBERT DUDLEY, Earl of Leicester (*right*), by an unknown artist. Royal favourite and aspirant husband to Queen Elizabeth; he failed to win her hand but was generously rewarded by royal patronage enabling him to play a leading role in her Council. As patron of the evangelicals at home, his aggressive, interventionist foreign policy brought him into conflict with the more cautious Burghley.

generations to come. In 1569 the strength of the Elizabethan regime was tested when the northern Earls of Northumberland and Westmorland raised a revolt, calling for the restoration of the old faith. The rapid collapse of the movement and the failure to raise any echo of support elsewhere in the kingdom were strong evidence that the religious settlement of 1559 was putting down roots. By 1572 Elizabeth's popularity throughout the country was manifested in the spontaneous annual festivities to mark Accession Day (17 November). Confidence in her leadership was given concrete form in the willingness of Parliament (and the taxpayers) to bear heavy and sustained taxation. The one front where prospects were less fair was Ireland. There recurring revolts of major dimensions required an ever larger expenditure of English money and the maintenance of a standing army.

The events of these years do in fact reflect a profound reorientation at several levels in the conduct of the kingdom's political life. Its roots lay in a shift from a dynastic towards a national polity. The initiatives came from above, from the Crown, but they triggered off responses from below. Out of these responses grew an articulated body of public opinion and an embryonic national political community.

The moving force in these changes was the decision about the national religion made in 1559. The Queen and her ministers had set themselves the task of establishing a national Church, of recasting the broken mould of custom and weaning the English people from age-old patterns of social life, shared with the western European world, to new loyalties and habits distinctively English. The summons to these new loyalties was a national act, made by the Crown acting in Parliament; a national Church became a complement to the secular State, participation in worship a civic duty.

The effect on political life was profound. Traditional rivalries at Court and in the country were now intertwined with the new disagreements over religion, which were by their nature national. At Court factions became identified by their religious orientation. These were no longer those between Catholics and Protestants (the adherents of the old faith were driven underground); but rather between differing visions of the new faith. Parliament became a forum where discussion raged passionately around proposals for altering the established religious order or punishing those adherents of the old faith who refused to conform to the new. In many counties personal and family rivalries came to be coloured by these religious differences.

The 1559 settlement derived its character from the royal conviction that the age of reform was over. The changes made then were final and brooked no further discussion. However, for many of her most zealous Protestant subjects England was but 'halfly reformed'. There were too many 'Popish remanants' in the public worship and too little pastoral zeal among uninstructed and uninspired parish clergy. Unable to achieve further measures of reform in Convocation, the ecclesiastical parliament, these 'Puritans' turned to the House of Commons and there, session after session, pressed their cause. The Queen, determined to protect the inviolability of her ecclesiastical prerogative, attempted to halt all discussion of religion in the House and when simple command did not suffice, she took stronger measures, even dispatching persistent parliamentary agitators to the Tower to cool their heels. In this struggle Elizabeth emerged the victor; the settlement legislated in the first year of her reign remained intact in all essentials at its close; it would endure for generations to come.

However, the struggle with the Puritan agitators in the Commons raised another issue—that of parliamentary free speech. The House was not prepared to accept the royal doctrine that the sovereign could limit the agenda of parliamentary discussion by excluding what Lord Keeper Bacon termed 'matters of state', subjects which were reserved to the monarch—as distinguished from those 'commonwealth matters' which were open for their consideration. On this issue, the Commons, while yielding in detail, stubbornly insisted on defending the principle that it was their right to set their own agenda. The issue was still unresolved in 1603, but the history of the early Stuart Parliaments showed how firmly the sense that the Commons was a forum in which all matters of public concern should be aired was grounded. The halcyon years of foreign, and, after 1569, of domestic peace when the Queen's popularity was at its height drew to a close in the 1580s, when events largely beyond her control drove her—against all her instincts—into all-out war.

Had she died then, Elizabeth would have retained among her contemporaries the image of Astraea, the golden age goddess of peace and plenty. Nor was the image merely allegorical. The Queen had been unvaryingly consistent in her linked policies of peace abroad and economy at home. Her ministers had truthfully boasted of a princess who eschewed the building of palaces and other princely pleasures so that expenditure should go solely for public ends. The perception that rhetoric was matched by her deeds had won the Queen the devoted loyalty of a people potentially divided by religion and sceptical of the capacities of a woman ruler. It was a strategy of rulership which required that the sovereign be an active political manager, commanding the energies and taming the rivalries of contending politicians within the Court circle while on the national stage, in order to win the confidence of the political élites, she cultivated her popularity as eagerly as any modern elected head of government.

9. *The Tudor Sovereigns*

Of the three great Tudors it is the second Henry and his daughter who remain most vivid in our perception; both to contemporaries and to us they loom larger than life. Henry compelled obedience by an overawing mixture of charm and intimidation. Elizabeth governed her subjects by what a seventeenth-century observer called her 'love-tricks'. Henry VII, a much more opaque figure to us, inspired both respect and fear, if little love, in his subjects. In all three cases it may well be that the sheer virtuosity of the performance and their successes in realizing their immediate goals veil to us the delicate, indeed fragile, balance on which the whole political system rested.

The Tudor monarchs had largely increased both the scope and the functions of what was beginning to be called the State. The incorporation of the Church into the monarchy, extensive new measures for regulating society and the economy, a refurbished militia, the needs of government

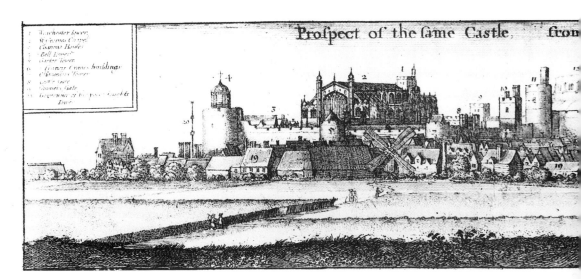

intelligence in a time of deep unrest multiplied the activities of government at an age when long-term inflation was raising costs steadily. At the centre a remodelled Privy Council provided an effective executive, but who was to execute the orders they issued? The traditional financial resources of the Crown, land revenues and customs duties, supplemented by periodic one-off parliamentary subsidies, paid the running costs of government but provided no money to pay for a civil service competent to carry out the manifold tasks of everyday government. The solution lay in recruiting the unpaid services of the county magistracies, the JPs, once primarily law officers, into omnicompetent functionaries, laden with an ever-increasing burden of duties.

What induced these men to take on such onerous—and unpaid—duties? They were already by dint of their landed wealth pre-eminent in their own localities. What appointment to the county bench did was to add to their informal authority the dignity of a royal commission and its wide-ranging legal powers, inducements which balanced the arduous labours of office. But there was in this tacit contract an unspoken clause. The policies which royal government required the élites to execute had to square with their interests and their views. This meant that the monarch must first of all win the confidence of the élites in his or her capacity to rule and secondly secure their effective co-operation in carrying out royally determined measures. It meant too a sensitive and flexible adaptation of those measures to the collective judgement of the local governors.

Each ruler at the moment of accession stepped on to a stage where he was to play the leading role in a drama in which he was both author and actor. He had to overawe and to charm, to exploit the aura of the royal office, to exert the force of irresistible will, and to deploy all the arts of persuasion, blending them in a performance which enthralled the audience. Each of the great Tudors successfully combined these ingredients in varying proportions. The system—if system it could be called—depended almost exclusively on the fine tuning of idiosyncratic royal personalities. There was a minimal cushion of bureaucracy ready to take the strain if the delicate interaction of the royal personality with the political classes went wrong. It was a mode of government capable of brilliant successes, but if the actor was not equal to the role, failure would entail heavy costs. This was a difficult act for their successors to follow.

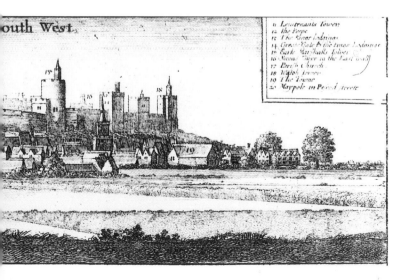

WINDSOR Castle, after an original by Hollar, 1650–60. Henry VII and his son joined in the building of St George's Chapel and in other major extensions which made this royal residence more of a palace and less of a fortress. With Richmond, Hampton Court, Whitehall, and Greenwich it was part of the chain of river palaces where the Tudor Court was most often to be found.

16 POLITICS IN AN AGE OF PEACE AND WAR

1570–1630

CHRISTOPHER HAIGH

1. *Introduction*

In January 1570 three kingdoms were in crisis. In Scotland, the Protestant regent was murdered, and there was civil war between competing nobles supporting the boy-King or his exiled mother. Ireland was under martial law, as Lord Deputy Sidney struggled to restore what might pass there for order after rebellion by Fitzgeralds and Butlers. In England, the revolt of the northern earls had collapsed, its leaders had fled, and Elizabeth's army was busy hanging, fining, and thieving. But Leonard Dacre was holding out in his border castle, the rebels had asked for aid from Spain, and the Pope was soon to announce Queen Elizabeth's deposition. Three Privy Councillors were in custody for plotting to overthrow Secretary Cecil and shift English policy: the Duke of Norfolk was in the Tower, the Earls of Arundel and Pembroke were under house arrest, and the Earl of Leicester had wept for the Queen's forgiveness. Military operations in the north and in Ireland had to be paid for by a forced loan, and old scandals about Elizabeth's sexual relations resurfaced.

But things soon improved—though in Ireland not by much. A second Scottish regent was murdered and a third died from illness, but the Earl of Morton lived and prospered. He managed to divide Queen Mary's faction, and to overcome the hardliners. In May 1573 he took Edinburgh Castle, with help from English artillery (though Elizabeth had insisted that cannon shot be collected for reuse). The appeal of Mary, locked up in England, weakened. She schemed with the Florentine banker Roberto Ridolfi to seize Elizabeth's throne, with a rebellion in England led by the freed Duke of Norfolk and an invasion by Spanish troops paid by Rome. But the plan was far-fetched, the allies unreliable, and security poor: correspondence was intercepted, agents were arrested, the Duke went back to the Tower, and Mary's plottings were widely publicized. The Parliament of 1572 clamoured for the execution of Norfolk and the exclusion of Mary from the English succession. Elizabeth agreed to the first, and side-stepped the second.

JAMES DOUGLAS, Earl of Morton (d. 1581), was Regent of Scotland for James VI from 1572–8. The inscription is translated 'Neither rashly nor nervously': his firm rule brought stability between the upheavals of the fall of Mary Queen of Scots and the factionalism of the 1580s.

Elizabeth's government was now more coherent and stable. The execution of Norfolk, the enforced retirement of Arundel and Pembroke, and the death of Lord Treasurer Winchester removed the most prominent conservatives from the Privy Council. William Cecil became Lord Burghley in 1571 and Treasurer in 1572, and Thomas Smith and Francis Walsingham served as joint Secretaries. The Earl of Warwick joined his brother Leicester on the Council in 1573, and its Protestant commitment was now much clearer. Above all, the events of 1567–72 had shown the dangers of playing politics when there was a rival claimant to the throne, an alienated Catholic opposition, and a hostile Spanish empire—and in France in 1572, the St Bartholomew's Day massacre of Protestants showed what might happen to English Protestants if they lost hold of power. Leicester abandoned his wilder ambitions, co-operated with Burghley, and became a respectable patron of Calvinist scholars and preachers.

2. *The Politics of Stability, 1572–1579*

There followed a period of order and good government, such as had not been seen in England since the 1520s and in Scotland since the 1530s. The English Privy Council met twice a week, usually with up to ten of the courtiers and bureaucrats in attendance. The formal business was dispatched briskly, and only foreign policy issues and the treatment of Mary required lengthy discussion. There were some disagreements among Councillors, but no struggles for power. The key members were related, and shared the same ambitions and assumptions. The Queen rarely saw her Council as a whole, and dealt privately with Burghley, Leicester, Walsingham, Sussex, and, later, Hatton, so their leadership was assured. The wider royal Court was dominated by the same individuals and families, and the factionalism of the 1560s had passed. The Parliaments of 1571, 1572, 1576, and 1581 were carefully managed by Councillors and their agents: they voted taxes as required, and supported the bills the Council (if not necessarily the Queen) wanted.

It was a narrow, but a coherent and effective, regime, which got on with the routine job of government without fuss or drama. Of course, there were political risks for a Council with a pronounced Protestant ideology and a restricted power base: important interests were excluded from influence and its rewards. There were risks, but internal division was not one of them. Indeed, when there was dispute within government it was often between the Queen herself and her most trusted advisers: they might press for the persecution of English Catholics (as they did in 1571), for the execution or exclusion of Mary Queen of Scots (as in 1572), and for military aid for foreign Protestants (as in 1576), but Elizabeth herself held back. Perhaps the Queen herself compensated for opinions unrepresented among Council leaders; perhaps she was more conscious of the dangers of decisive action.

The lessons of 1569–70 produced the politics and policies of the 1570s. The Queen concluded that she must conciliate her Catholic subjects: it was announced in Star Chamber in 1570 that there would be no inquisition of consciences, and Elizabeth restrained the preaching of Protestantism—hence her clash with Archbishop Grindal in 1576 over the prophesyings. But Burghley, Leicester, and others concluded that Catholics must be repressed and Protestantism preached. A bill for the punishment of those who did not receive communion in the Church of England passed the Lords and the Commons in the Parliament of 1571, with the open support of bishops and Councillors: it was vetoed by the Queen, and she blocked the proposal when it was raised again in the Parliaments of 1572, 1576, and 1581. Councillors tried to shield Grindal from Elizabeth's wrath, and managed to prevent her reducing the number of licensed preachers.

Legislation for the poor was another consequence of the fears provoked by revolt in the north. The Privy Council ordered inquiries into vagrancy, and the reports sent in by local justices were apparently alarming. In 1572 Parliament provided for a national system of poor relief: JPs were to survey the poor in each parish, assess how much was needed to support them, and determine the contributions to be made by richer parishioners. But the migrant poor, classed as vagabonds, were to be whipped and sent home—wherever that might be. The main provisions were copied in Scotland in 1574. Another English Act in 1576 sought to provide work for the unemployed: justices were to supply raw materials for the poor to work on, and build houses of correction for the punishment of those who refused to labour. But fears of riot and rebellion passed, and there was no systematic attempt to implement the legislation until the economic crisis of the 1590s. The responsibilities given to JPs may, however, have helped social cohesion, suggesting a concern for social welfare even when not very much was actually done.

For these new tasks there was an expanded body of Justices of the Peace. The Norfolk commission of the peace had 28 members in 1574, but 46 in 1579—and, after various ups and downs,

61 members in 1601. Worcestershire had 28 JPs in 1562, and 52 by 1584; and there were similar increases everywhere. Elizabeth and Burghley objected to the new appointments, and tried to cull the commissions. But the gentry of England were expanding in number and competing for prestige; they sought local office as the badge of significance. Their county patrons and Court connections lobbied for their nomination to the commission, and then for elevations in the order of precedence. Bluntly, English gentlemen did not want to be JPs to serve their counties: they wanted to be JPs to be seen to be JPs—and any necessary service was rather a nuisance. In practice, only about half the justices were active, but the burden upon the dutiful was heavy.

English government worked well in the 1570s, and so it should have done. Its tasks were easy, with peace and prosperity. There was no foreign war between 1563 and 1585, and so no war taxation or military recruitment. There was intervention in Scotland in 1572 and Ireland was a constant drain, but commitments were limited and costs kept down. Elizabeth asked Parliament for single subsidies in 1571, 1576, and 1581, and the weight of direct taxation was probably lighter than it had been since Henry VII's time. There was no harvest failure between 1562 and 1585, except for 1573, so no sustained need to regulate food supplies or put down social unrest. There was no widespread plague between 1563 and 1593, so no need to control movement or prevent panic. Each summer the Queen progressed through southern England dispensing goodwill to her subjects. She made stately visits to Warwick in 1572, Bristol in 1574, Worcester in 1575, and Norwich in 1578. Elizabeth's popularity soared, and few now doubted her devotion to her people.

Some Protestants doubted her devotion to the Gospel. She refused to reform the Prayer Book, cut off Mary's head, harass the Catholics in England, or assist the Protestant rebels in France and the Netherlands. She ordered the bishops to stop the prophesyings, and the ministers to dress up in surplices. But although Elizabeth would not act like a Protestant, she took good care to talk like one. She reminded her Parliaments that she had chosen truth over popery in 1559, and her Councillors stressed her commitment to the Protestant cause at home and abroad. There was suspicion of her caution, of her reluctance to do as the enthusiasts asked. But Sir Francis Knollys told the House of Commons in 1571:

What cause there might be to make Her Majesty not to run and join with those who seem to be in earnest, we are not to search; whether it be for that orderly and in time she hopeth to bring them all with her, or what secret cause or other scrupulosity there may be in princes, it is not for all sorts to know.

For the moment, at least, Elizabeth had the benefit of the doubt.

3. *The Origins of War and Persecution, 1579–1585*

The political stability of the 1570s came to an end at about the same time in all three kingdoms. In Scotland, dissident magnates used young James VI as a figure-head to force Morton to resign the regency in 1578—though Morton soon regained control of the King, and effective power. In 1579 Esme Stewart arrived from France, and rapidly captured the affections of the King; he was made Earl of Lennox and a Councillor, and plotted against Morton. In 1581 Morton was executed by opponents on the Council; in 1582 James was captured from Lennox by the Earl of Gowrie and the Ruthven Raiders; in 1583 he was recaptured by old Lennox supporters, and Arran became Chancellor; in 1584 the Ruthven group failed in an attempt to regain power, and

Gowrie was executed—but in 1585 they succeeded, and Arran was overthrown. The King had been a pawn, played by nobles who could not agree among themselves.

In Scotland, power changed hands with bewildering speed: in Ireland things were simpler, if more bloody. In 1579 James Fitzmaurice landed at Smerwick with a small force of Italian and Spanish troops paid for by the Pope, and with Dr Nicholas Sander as his propaganda chief. They tried to raise rebellion in the Pope's name, though the revolts they sparked in Munster and Leinster owed more to the resentments of Old English and Irish against the extensions of English power. Lord Deputy Grey and the English government concluded that there was a general Catholic conspiracy throughout Ireland, and implemented a fierce military repression. The invaders at Smerwick surrendered in 1580, but were massacred by Grey; there were widespread executions, compounded by famine in 1582. The risings were defeated, but the English analysis proved self-fulfilling: the repression fused political and religious discontents, and created the Catholic opposition which the government had feared.

THIS watercolour map of the 1580 siege of the papalist fort at Smerwick Bay shows the deployment of English ships, troops, and artillery. The map was prepared for William Winter, captain of the *Achates*.

THE title-page of John Stubbs's 1579 *The Discovery of a Gaping Gulf*, which challenged Elizabeth's image as godly queen and mother of the nation. It was part of an energetic campaign to mobilize opinion against Elizabeth I's projected marriage to the Duke of Anjou.

In England, trouble stemmed from the linked issues of religion and foreign policy, with a dash of sex. In 1578 Elizabeth began negotiations for a marriage to the French Duke of Anjou. At first her motives were political. She hoped that her flirtation would give a lever on French policy, and ensure that French aid to the Dutch rebels against Spain reduced pressure for help from England. But Elizabeth seems to have become serious about the prospect of marriage—or perhaps determined her Councillors should think she was serious, and stop pestering her for troops for the Netherlands. Whatever the truth, the Councillors believed her; some of them were horrified, and mobilized Protestant opinion. Walsingham seems to have orchestrated a campaign of sermons against the marriage, and Bedford apparently briefed the godly lawyer John Stubbs. In the autumn of 1579, timed to coincide with the Privy Council discussions of the proposal, Stubbs published *The discovery of a gaping gulf, wherein England is like to be swallowed by another French marriage, if the Lord forbid not the banns by letting Her Majesty see the sin and punishment thereof*. It was political dynamite.

THE DISCOVERIE OF A GAPING GVLF VVHEREINTO ENGLAND IS LIKE TO BE SWALLO-vved by an other French mariage, if the Lord forbid not the banes, by letting her Maieſtie ſee the ſin and puniſhment thereof.

Saue Lord, let the King here vs in the day that vve call Pſal.20.verſe.9. Menſe Auguſti. Anno.1579.

Stubbs dared to question Elizabeth's commitment to the Gospel and her care for her people, the foundations upon which her public appeal had been built. How could a responsible Protestant Queen of England countenance marriage to a Catholic Prince, 'a principal prop of the tottering house of Antichrist'? Elizabeth suppressed the book by proclamation, and Stubbs and a servant of Bedford were convicted of sedition. They were punished in London on 3 November 1579, and the event was a public relations disaster for the Queen. The two men had their right hands cut off; Stubbs took off his hat with his left, cried 'God save the Queen!', and fainted. The crowd stood in shocked silence, perhaps contrasting the godly patriotism of the two men with the Queen's apparent willingness to betray her religion and her country. The campaign against the marriage spread: Sir Philip Sidney reminded Elizabeth of her obligation to English Protestants; Bishop Cox composed a theological treatise; there were more sermons, and lampoons, ballads, and broadsheets on the streets of London. Elizabeth told Anjou that her people would never consent to the marriage.

Negotiations with the Prince continued, and in 1581 Elizabeth declared she was going ahead with the wedding—but she knew it was impossible. She tried instead to secure an alliance with

France against Spain, but the French distrusted her without the marriage. Elizabeth's strategy of using the French to support the Dutch against Spain was collapsing. At the same time, the public furore over Anjou and *The discovery of a gaping gulf* had made it more difficult for Elizabeth to resist the Protestant clamour for English intervention in the Netherlands. Why would she not save the cause of the Gospel abroad? Why, indeed, had she not done more for the cause of the Gospel in England? Why were the Catholics not crushed? Until 1579 Elizabeth had the benefit of any doubt about her Protestant commitment—but when Stubbs lost his hand, she lost the benefit. After 1579, her Protestantism had to be proved. The proofs led to persecution, political instability, and finally to war.

From 1579 Elizabeth's political position was weaker and she was forced to adopt policies she had hitherto resisted. Circumstances changed. The Queen's caution towards English Catholics had made sense when it seemed they would decline into insignificance. But in 1574 the first seminary priests arrived in England, and in 1580 they were followed by the first Jesuits: Catholicism was not going to die, it would have to be murdered. The executions of priests began in 1577, and became more frequent from 1581. The Parliament of 1581 passed a Recusancy Act, which sharply increased the penalties for absence from church services to £20 a month. More fiercely still, in 1582 a royal proclamation declared all seminary priests and Jesuits in England to be

Francis Walsingham (1530–90) was Secretary of State from 1572, and a proponent of vigour against Catholics at home and abroad. Elizabeth I called him 'The Moor', because of his dark complexion or his reputation for scheming. He was portrayed (probably by John de Critz) wearing a cameo badge of loyalty to the queen.

traitors, punishable by death. In 1585 this provision was given statutory force: priests and those who helped them were to hang, and from 1581 to 1590 103 did so.

Burghley, Leicester, and Walsingham believed that English Catholics were part of an international popish conspiracy against Protestants, so for them Catholics were fair game. But Elizabeth never shared this apocalyptic vision of ideological warfare, and the coming of the new priests did not justify such a persecution. But a weakened Queen succumbed to pressure, and there followed twenty years of rack and gibbet. As a consequence, the Protestants' conspiracy theory was fulfilled. Some Catholics did turn to plotting against Elizabeth, especially the Throckmorton group in 1583 and the Babington group in 1586. They planned to murder Elizabeth, and to put Mary on the throne with the help of foreign troops. The Throckmorton plot generated a real panic, and Londoners knelt in the streets to give thanks for the Queen's safety. Whether from genuine fear or to stiffen her anti-Catholic resolve, the Privy Council took decisive action. It organized a Protestant vigilante force, its members pledged to protect the Queen and, if they failed, to hunt down her killers.

It is likely that the 1584 Bond of Association was a ploy in the long campaign by Leicester, Walsingham, and others to take England into war against Spain, in alliance with Dutch and French Protestants. The idea certainly originated among Leicester's followers. The Dutch leader, William of Orange, had just been murdered, and Spanish forces had taken a string of Flemish towns: all Protestants were at risk and should stick together, it was argued. But the pressure for war proved extremely divisive, and Council and Court unity had crumbled. The Earl of Sussex led the opposition in the Privy Council to military action, and his old antagonism with Leicester had revived by 1581. Sir James Croft was Spanish in his sympathies, and leaked Council debates to the Spanish ambassador in return for a pension. Burghley and Walter Mildmay were increasingly nervous of the likely costs of war, which led to difficulties with enthusiasts such as Walsingham.

In August 1585 Elizabeth finally agreed to send an army to support the Dutch, and so began twenty years of crippling war. Perhaps her hand had been forced by the treaty between Philip II of Spain and the French Catholic League. Faced by the prospect of Spanish domination of France and the Low Countries, leaving England dangerously exposed, she was willing to prop up the Dutch. Protestants had argued for twenty years that foreign Calvinists were essential bulwarks against the march of international Catholicism; if they were defeated, England would be next. Such a scenario convinced those who saw Rome as the Antichrist, masterminding the forces of darkness in constant struggle to exterminate the truth. But it had not convinced Elizabeth. This world-view exaggerated the cohesiveness of Catholicism, the power of Spain, and the significance of England. Philip II was not going to invade England: he was far too busy in Italy, Portugal, the Americas, and the Low Countries—and would remain so. In 1585 Elizabeth went to war, but not in defence of essential strategic interests. The Queen had capitulated to a Protestant cause she could no longer resist.

4. *The Burdens of War, 1585–1593*

In the 1570s English government had worked well, because it was not tested: from 1585, it was. The circumstances which had brought order and stability changed, and the task of government became more demanding. Peace gave way to war, first in the Netherlands, then also at sea and on the coasts of Spain and Portugal, then in France, and finally on a large scale in Ireland as well. Between 1585 and 1603 at least 105,800 men were conscripted for military service overseas, out of a population of about 4,000,000; the wars cost about £4,500,000, when the Queen's ordinary revenue was £300,000 a year. The men and the money had to be raised, but in difficult situations. War also brought disruption of trade, and unemployment among weavers who produced for the export market. Burghley was worried in 1587 that English trade was embargoed from Spain, Portugal, North Africa, France, Flanders, and Hamburg, and concerned that the unemployed would resort to rebellion. They did not, but the tax base was eroded and revenue proved difficult to collect.

Prosperity and plenty gave way to hardship and dearth. After twenty good years, there were poor harvests in 1585, 1586, 1589, and 1590—and then again in 1594, 1595, 1596, 1597, and 1601. Elizabeth's government was unlucky: it had good harvests in peacetime and bad harvests in war, and the combination of war taxes and high food prices was disastrous for both official and private budgets. Religious persecution intensified, as Catholics were identified as a Spanish fifth column: twenty-one priests were executed in 1588, the year of the Armada. By 1591 specialist recusancy commissions were monitoring the Catholics: there were to be weekly searches through each parish, and every householder should be questioned. Under such pressure, there were real, and probably imaginary, Catholic plots. There was certainly a Babington Plot in 1586, but the Stafford Plot of 1587, the Lopez Plot of 1594, and the Squire Plot of 1598 are more doubtful: some at least were official fabrications or manipulations, to maintain vigilance against Catholics in England and enthusiasm for war against them abroad.

On 8 February 1587 Mary Queen of Scots was beheaded, a victim of wartime paranoia, Catholic conspiracies, and her own foolishness. Mary had agreed to a plan by a dozen young Catholics to murder Elizabeth and rescue herself from captivity—but her letters had been intercepted and Walsingham knew everything. Mary was brought to trial under the 1585 Act which had legitimized the Bond of Association. She denied both the competence of the commission which tried her, and her own complicity in the Babington Plot: she was convicted. But Elizabeth had refused to punish Mary for her involvement in the Ridolfi Plot: would things be different in 1586–7? At first, events followed the course of 1571–2, with the Council pushing Elizabeth against Mary, and calling a Parliament to intensify the pressure. Hatton, Croft, Knollys, and Mildmay led the Commons, Lord Chancellor Bromley and Burghley the Lords, into a joint petition for Mary's execution. Elizabeth's reply was an 'answer answerless': she would not commit herself.

It is likely, but not certain, that the Stafford Plot was Walsingham's way of making her do so. The 'plot', to blow up Elizabeth with gunpowder under her bed, was probably a ploy to convince the Queen that she would not be safe as long as Mary lived—and to neutralize the French ambassador's pleas for Mary's life, by implicating him. After Mary's death, Walsingham apologized to the ambassador, assuring him that he had never really been suspected. The tactic worked: Elizabeth duly signed the execution warrant, but she tried to escape blame by leaving Secretary Davison to dispatch it without her explicit authorization. Once Mary's head was off, Davison was the scapegoat: he escaped with his life, but his career was ruined. He was a small sop to James VI, affronted by his mother's fate. But for all James's personal distress and public

THIS drawing of Mary's execution was done by or for Robert Beale, clerk of the Privy Council, who was sent to deliver the death warrant to Fotheringay. Although Mary died with dignity, the assembled officials were extremely nervous and the executioner botched the job.

posturing, he had made it clear that his own safe succession to the English throne was more important to him than a mother he had not seen for twenty years. The pill was bitter, but it was swallowed whole.

James had matured into a subtle politician, schooled by the embarrassments of his puppet years. He began his personal rule in 1585, after the fall of Arran, determined on effective co-operation with the nobles. He appointed them to high office, persuaded them to sit on his council, and entertained and hunted with them. He managed to drive up levels of taxation, and raised £100,000 by successive debasements of the coinage. He secured a pension from Elizabeth in 1586, and married a princess of Denmark in 1589. He constructed a broad-based government, skilfully balanced the Kirk and the Catholic nobles of the Highlands, and created room for political manœuvre. When in 1589 Elizabeth produced evidence that Huntly and other Catholics had been conspiring with Spain, James was reluctant to break with them. But when they attempted a pre-emptive strike, he raised an army with the Protestant nobles and marched against them. Rather than fight against the King in person, the rebel army melted away and James was safe for the moment.

But not for very long. The maverick Earl of Bothwell plotted against Chancellor Maitland, and for a time was the darling of the Kirk for his hostility to the Catholics. He made four attempts to seize control of King and kingdom, in 1591, 1592, 1593, and 1594, but his disruptiveness forfeited support and finally he went into exile. To gain allies against Bothwell, James had to promise a campaign against the Catholic earls, and in 1594 he had to deliver. He marched into the Highlands, burned the houses of the earls, and forced them too into exile. By April 1595 James had broken his most troublesome nobles. He was entitled to brag. In 1598 he wrote *The True Law of Free Monarchies*, describing the divine origin of royal power and the subject's duty of obedience; in 1599 he wrote *Basilikon Doron*, a manual for his son on how to be a good king. Now James was *Rex Pacificus*, bringer of stability at home and peace abroad. For he had one advantage shared by few contemporary rulers: he avoided war, and did not stretch the meagre resources of his state.

At first, Elizabeth's military commitments were restricted and the difficulties were in the field rather than at home. By the treaty of Nonsuch, Elizabeth had promised to assist the Dutch with 6,400 infantry, 1,000 cavalry, and £126,000 a year for their maintenance. The Earl of Leicester commanded the force, and in two years he achieved nothing. He was an inexperienced general, relations with his own commanders and his Dutch allies were poor, and his army was too small, badly supplied, and inadequately financed. His companies were always short, through under-recruitment, desertions, and death, and his captains liked it that way: they claimed full wages, and pocketed the shares of dead men and deserters. To save money, Elizabeth held back on reinforcements and payments, and Leicester's financial controls were inadequate. Troops went unpaid, and at Deventer things got so bad that Sir William Stanley and his men handed the town over to the Duke of Parma and marched off to fight for Spain.

But by 1588 the continuing demands of even a limited war were telling in England, together with poor harvests and trade disruption. There were problems in recruiting soldiers, especially where the burdens were heaviest. County lieutenants and their deputies also found it hard to raise rates for militias, and coat and conduct money for troops going overseas. In the summer of 1588 Burghley knew of widespread refusal to pay, and feared that continual demands would alienate the poor. In 1589, when troops and sailors were demobilized from the expeditions to France and Portugal, there was some dis-

A DUTCH engraving of *c.*1585–7 celebrates Leicester as governor of the Netherlands. Elizabeth had sent him over as captain-general, but the Dutch made him their governor to bind England to their cause.

order and even more fear of trouble. Local Provost-Marshals were appointed to maintain order by force, and execute vagrants under martial law. There were local disruptions—a riot in Sussex in 1591 when, ominously, the Queen's coat of arms was torn down—but the Council faced reluctance to contribute rather than outright resistance.

The raising of men and money, the operation of the Poor Law, the persecution of Catholics, and the maintenance of public order asked a lot of the county gentry. But it did not always seem that their efforts were appreciated. The Queen and Lord Burghley believed that compact local commissions were more efficient, and the lieutenancy and subsidy commissions were severely reduced in size. There were purges of commissions of the peace. In 1587 twelve justices were dismissed from the Wiltshire commission, and nine in Norfolk. In 1595 fourteen were dismissed from Norfolk, a dozen from Wiltshire, and twenty-six from Kent. These prunings produced magisterial élites, resentment among those passed over, and factional competition to avoid dismissal or secure reappointment. It is likely that administrative efficiency suffered, with too much to be done by too few, and local politicking reducing co-operation. It was no way to run a war.

Elizabeth and her Lord Treasurer had been notoriously careful with money. But the costs of war intensified financial stringency, and reduced the stock of rewards for county service. The Elizabethan patronage system was already overstretched, with only 1,200 posts to reward roughly 1,500 local administrators. So it was necessary to shift the burden of official patronage from the Crown to the community. Increasingly, rewards were in the form of monopoly grants and administrative patents, giving sole rights to sell products or to prosecute categories of offenders. Such creations of artificial privileges and privatizations of official functions brought resentments and frictions. The enforcement of laws came to look like extortion, and the necessary demands of wartime government like oppression. In some counties there were long-running struggles between government agents and local justices who saw themselves as legitimate protectors of local interests. Again, it was no way to run a war.

5. *The Politics of Stress, 1593–1601*

The pressures generated in the early stages of war intensified as conflict escalated, new theatres were added, and invasion scares became annual. Worse, the expansion of military activity coincided with plague in 1593, years of successive harvest failure in 1594–7, and diseases associated with under-nourishment in 1596–8. Unemployment in the cloth industry continued, as trading conditions remained poor. The burden of national taxation was more crippling than at any other time in the century: allowing for inflation, Henry VIII had taken a higher annual average in 1541–7, but he had had good harvests (except in 1545) and Elizabeth's wars went on year after year. More was demanded when communities were less able to give, and the return on the efforts of officials diminished. In the counties, deputy lieutenants and subsidy commissioners had to balance their duty to the war effort against their duty to their neighbours—and their concern for public order and the safety of property.

Parliament had been asked for only six single subsidies in 1559–84, and for a subsidy for the war in 1587. But there was a double subsidy grant in 1589, triple subsidies in 1593 and 1597, and a quadruple subsidy in 1601. There were nine subsidies in 1559–89, but ten in the remainder of the reign. The Crown collected benevolences from office-holders in 1594 and 1599, and forced loans in 1588, 1590, and 1597; the last was not repaid, and was effectively a tax. But as the frequency and size of such demands increased, so their effectiveness declined. The forced loan of 1597 was supposed to produce £145,000, but only £98,000 came in. More seriously, the yield of each subsidy fell, from about £120,000 from the first subsidy of 1589 down to about £85,000 each from the third and fourth subsidies of 1601. The assessments of individuals were cut, and the numbers of taxpayers reduced. The shortages had to be met by sales of Crown lands.

There seem to have been three influences at work. The first was the general slippage of assessments since the death of Henry VIII: the average individual assessments of the peerage, who assessed themselves, fell from £921 in 1534 to £487 in 1571, and £311 in 1601. The second was the shortage of rewards from the Crown and so of opportunities for patrons to exercise their influence. So subsidy assessment became a form of inverse patronage: a commissioner could favour his friends with low assessments, with a risk to the Queen of competitive down-bidding. The third influence was the calculation by commissioners of what a county could pay in hard times without threatening social stability. The levies from gentlemen were held down to secure their ability to employ workers, and poorer taxpayers were allowed to fall out of the tax net. As tax thresholds were raised so subsidy rolls grew shorter, and yields fell. Multiple subsidies were granted and money came in, but the parliamentary taxation system was being undermined.

Burghley complained that the rich paid too little and the poor too much, and was afraid that repeated taxation would lead to rebellion. Certainly there were risks when taxation and dearth came together, as they did between 1594 and 1597. There were riots in London in 1595, in Somerset in 1596, and in Kent, Norfolk, and Suffolk in 1597. In Somerset the rioters had said 'they were as good to be slain in the marketplace, as starve in their own houses!' But an attempt to raise full-scale rebellion north of Oxford failed in 1596: there was preliminary planning and agitation, but on the day of the revolt only four men turned up. It was the fear that social order would collapse under the stress of war and poverty which prompted the Enclosure Act of 1597 and the consolidating Poor Law of 1598. But the danger passed, harvests improved, and Burghley had worried too much. Perhaps the flexibility of subsidy commissioners had helped, easing back on taxes in the years of greatest difficulty—but when conditions improved, assessments stayed down.

County governors were equally cautious in their impressment of soldiers and collection of militia rates—and with good reason. With casualty rates of about a half for each force, there was resistance to recruitment and often mutiny among those pressed. Sir John Smyth led a mutiny at Colchester in 1596, arguing that the country was being ruined by war and that the levying of men to serve abroad was illegal. The Privy Council complained to county commissioners that their allocations had not been fulfilled, but things just got worse. In 1598 there were difficulties in Oxfordshire, Norfolk, Suffolk, Rutland, and Warwickshire, and thereafter they were general—with the authorities of London, East Anglia, and Kent the most uncooperative, since they had been asked to do most. For some counties the Queen resorted to bribery to get the soldiers needed: she offered to pay for arms and coat and conduct money for men from Northamptonshire in 1600, and for arms and clothes for Kent soldiers in 1602.

The expansion of the war also brought political factionalism, so that the war effort was undermined by dispute and indecision as well as by shortages of men and money. The Council and the Court were divided into proponents of land war and advocates of a maritime strategy. After the

THIS emblematic portrait of Lord Burghley in old age proclaims his status and qualities. He wears the badge of the Order of the Garter, and his shield with Garter hangs from a tree; he is dressed in sober dignity, and the flowers, mule and tree symbolize his loyalty and steadfastness.

death of Leicester in 1588, his stepson the Earl of Essex became the acknowledged leader of the swordsmen. Essex, backed by Sir Robert Sidney and Lord Willoughby, argued for Continental land campaigns, with armies to support the Dutch and the French and defeat Spain in battle. Lord Admiral Howard and Sir Walter Raleigh pressed for a war at sea, to harry the coasts of

Spain and Portugal and intercept Spain's silver fleets from Mexico. Burghley and his son Robert Cecil supported the sailors, because theirs was the cheaper option and the prospect of spoils would generate private investment in naval operations. Burghley remained nervous of the consequences of high taxation, and tried to ensure that Essex's costly land strategy was not adopted.

This is probably the most important explanation of the Cecils' stranglehold on government and patronage—for the Queen shared their hostility to expensive military campaigning. A second reason may be Burghley's preparation for the death of Elizabeth, and a hope for political continuity through Cecil control. Essex was denied an effective power base, by keeping his allies from the Council and rejecting his candidates for office. The deaths of Leicester in 1588, Walsingham and Warwick in 1590, and Hatton in 1591 had weakened the enthusiasts for war. The new Councillors were mostly cautious administrators—John Fortescue in 1589, Robert Cecil in 1591, Sir John Puckering in 1592, and Sir Thomas Egerton in 1596. Essex himself was appointed to the Council in 1593, and the former soldiers Lord North and Sir William Knollys joined him

Robert Devereux, Earl of Essex (1566–1601), painted by Marcus Gheeraerts as he wanted to be seen: the courtier, shining in silver; the soldier, with hand on sword; and the statesman, thoughtful and severe. Gheeraerts was the fashionable Court painter of the 1590s.

in 1596. But the Council shrank in number and was dominated by Cecilians. For most of her reign Elizabeth had had nineteen Councillors: in 1597 she had eleven, attendances were low, and the Cecils took the routine decisions.

By this stage, the Elizabethan regime was dangerously narrow and out of touch. Robert Cecil joined his father on the Council; Buckhurst, Howard, Hunsdon, and Knollys followed their fathers; Essex followed his stepfather. There was no regional magnate on the Council, and no Catholic; attendances were thin and Burghley usually authorized warrants for payments himself. Rewards went to a favoured few insiders. Burghley granted wardships to the Latin Secretary, the Chancellor of the Exchequer, the Clerk of the Privy Council, and one of the Masters of Requests. In 1598 Lord Treasurer Buckhurst and Secretary Cecil took over the lucrative starch monopoly. Essex had a lease of the customs duties on sweet wines, but for his friends he could get nothing. He failed to get Francis Bacon appointed Attorney-General in 1594 and Solicitor-General in 1595: he pressed his candidate so hard that the Queen declared she would have anybody but Bacon. There was a bitter struggle over the wardenry of the Cinque Ports in 1597, with Essex backing Robert Sidney and the Cecils Lord Cobham: Cobham got the post, succeeding his father.

It was partly Essex's own fault. He was arrogant, ill-tempered, and paranoid: he blamed the world for his failures, the Queen for his slights, and Robert Cecil for everything. In July 1598 there was a dramatic dispute over the appointment of a new Lord Deputy for Ireland. Robert Cecil wanted Knollys, Essex Sir George Carew, each hoping to get a rival's supporter dispatched from Court. When Elizabeth refused his nominee, Essex turned his back on her; when she boxed his ears, he went for his sword and had to be restrained. Essex was a catalyst, but there was bound to be trouble: from those outside the charmed circle of Cecil cronies; from the swordsmen who did not get the glory they expected; above all from the nobles who were not pampered and paid for as they thought was their due. The French ambassador observed in 1597 that Elizabeth's government was 'little pleasing to the great men and nobles', and Essex put himself at the head of the malcontents.

In April 1599 Essex got his last legitimate chance, to show what he could do, and to get commands and rewards for his friends. Elizabeth decided upon a full-scale campaign to crush Tyrone's rebellion in Ireland, and Essex was given the task. He was to lead an army of 16,000 foot and 1,300 horse, with orders to defeat Tyrone in Ulster. But he did not. He first tried to quieten Leinster and Munster, marching here and there and squandering his forces in garrisons. Elizabeth complained he was costing her £1,000 a day for a summer progress, and insisted he attack Tyrone. But it was too late, his main army was too small, and in London his credibility was collapsing. He told his friends he would take the army to Wales, raise more men, and march on London to re-establish his political authority. He was persuaded out of this; instead, he made a truce with Tyrone, and dashed back to Court to rebuild his political position. Essex had lost his chance, and with it Elizabeth's trust. Now he too was an outsider.

John Hayward published *The First Part of the Life and Reign of King Henry IV*, dedicated to Essex and, it was thought, commissioned by him. It was a history of the reign of Richard II, and for Elizabeth the political parallels were dangerous: an incompetent monarch, a corrupt Council, oppressive taxation, a resentful aristocracy—followed by the deposition and murder of the King, and the installation of a successor. The first edition rapidly sold out, and the second was suppressed by the Privy Council. In 1600 the Earl of Cumberland appeared at the tilts as the 'Discontented Knight', complaining that his service had not been rewarded. On 7 February 1601 Shakespeare's *Richard II* was revived at the Globe, paid for and attended by Essex men: the play showed harsh taxation, self-seeking Councillors, and financial privileges for the monarch's cronies. On 8 February Essex staged his attempted *coup*: it flopped.

Essex did not get the support he expected, from the nobility or from London. He was an even worse conspirator than he was a general, and he paid with his life. But it was a dramatic illustration of the alienation of the aristocracy that so many had dabbled in treason—so many, indeed, that the Queen dared not punish them. The Earls of Rutland and Southampton and Lords Mounteagle and Sandys were deeply involved; the Earls of Bedford and Sussex and Lord Cromwell were implicated. Lord Mountjoy had contemplated using his Irish army to support Essex, and we do not know what other discontented nobles might have done if Essex had been less clumsy. The revolt and the attendant conspiracies cannot be dismissed as the follies of a single political misfit: the causes were structural, and arose from the difficulty of reconciling the costs of war with necessary patronage and political expenditure. Robert Cecil warned a supplicant in 1602 that 'Her Majesty's mind is not so apt to give as before her wars, they having made her sift all corners to maintain them and made her indeed value and balance every gift in more curiosity than before.' The English state could not pay for both domestic peace and foreign war.

6. *Peace and Discord, 1601–1610*

By 1601 Elizabeth I's subjects were weary of her. Only a handful of her nobles had joined Essex, but many more were discontented after years of neglect. The county gentry were tired of collecting incessant subsidies, rates, and loans, pressing men for the wars, and maintaining public order in periods of distress: all, it seemed, without reward. Taxpayers felt they had given enough, and yields fell. The poor had been told that their Queen cared for them, but, with dearth, unemployment, repeated taxation, impressment, and a crack-down on petty crime, it was hard to see how. The Earl of Northumberland reported to an impatient James VI that taxes for her wars, and monopolies and wardships to reward her cronies, had made the Queen's rule resented. Elizabeth knew he was right. She set off again on a cycle of summer progresses to try to recapture the love she had lost, and in 1601 she agreed to the suspension of offensive monopolies. 'God make us thankful, and send her long to reign amongst us', Speaker Croke told the Commons. But few can have agreed.

Elizabeth died on the night of 24 March 1603, after forty-four years as Queen. There was a shocked silence in London next morning, as people waited to see what would happen. Nothing did. Robert Cecil had been in contact with James for nearly two years, and had planned a trouble-free succession. Alternative claimants had no chance. The war with Spain effectively disqualified the Infanta, and Arabella Stuart was taken into custody. There were extra watches in London, Catholic priests were deported or imprisoned, and the fleet patrolled the coasts. By the afternoon of the 25th it was clear that all was well. There were bonfires and dancing in the streets of London; 'We have a king!', the crowds cried. James was the fortunate beneficiary of Elizabeth's unpopularity: even a Scot was an improvement. As he rode south to claim his throne, James was greeted by cheering new subjects; he later remembered them 'receiving him so joy-

JAMES VI and Robert Cecil began their coded contacts in the spring of 1601. Sometimes they corresponded directly, sometimes through intermediaries. Here James ('30') asks Lord Henry Howard ('3') to thank Cecil ('10') for 'his care and vigilance for my preservation'.

fully that all the ways betwixt Berwick and London were paved with people'. But then things got harder.

There were high hopes of James, but they could not all be fulfilled. He had promised (or was thought to have promised) English Catholics toleration and English Protestants persecution—of Catholics. When he ordered the suspension of the penal laws, recusancy increased, Protestants protested, penalties were reimposed, the Catholics had been cheated, and the Gunpowder Plot of 1605 followed. James had to deliver everything Elizabeth had failed to give: honours, offices, pensions, peace, and freedom from taxes. He had to be generous to his new people, and so he was. There were more new knights in his first four months than in the whole of Elizabeth's reign, but soon Francis Bacon was asking for 'this almost prostituted title'. There were new posts in the royal households, and annuities for men who mattered (and for a few friends who did not); soon James was said to be wasting the Crown's resources. James had to end the war with Spain, and so he did. But the peace of 1604 made him vulnerable to suspicions of being soft on popery, and brought unreasonable expectations of economy and prosperity.

The King began well, however. Mountjoy had made peace with Tyrone, and Dunbar kept Scotland content. The leading English office-holders were confirmed in their posts, and the only casualties were Raleigh and Fortescue. James expanded the Privy Council to bring in the old nobility and the Scots. The Essexians were restored to favour, two more Howards and the Earl of Northumberland joined the Council, as did the presidents of the two provincial councils and four Scots. The new regime was a broad and representative coalition of interests, as Elizabeth's had not been. But in creating a more 'British', and not simply an English, Council, James raised fears of a Scottish take-over—and when Scots surrounded the King, the fears seemed justified. A new Court entourage of Scotsmen, the Bedchamber, was imported, and the English Privy Chamber was distanced from the King. Scots dominated the royal households, controlled access to the King, and when he was—as so often—away hunting they had him almost to themselves.

The Scots became political ogres and scapegoats. James planned to create a unitary empire of Great Britain: his accession medal depicted him crowned with imperial laurels, described as 'emperor of the whole island of Britain'. The Lord Admiral set to work designing a Union flag. But if union was ever a realistic political possibility, the Scots' presence ditched it: they had almost taken over the ruling of England, and what might they do in a new Britain? James retreated from his ambition for a British state, and in 1604 the English Parliament rejected even the title of the kingdom of Great Britain: it was argued that a new name made a new kingdom, and left a Scottish King to do as he wished. James then proceeded more cautiously, and English and Scottish

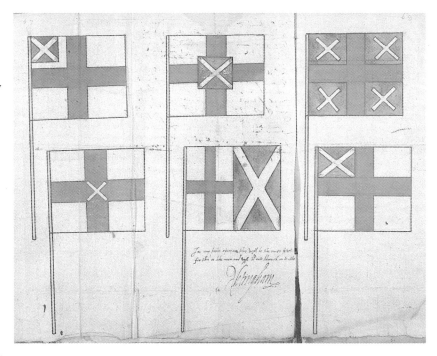

THE designs for an Anglo-Scottish union flag produced for Lord Admiral Nottingham combined the banners of St Andrew and St George. Nottingham preferred the two side by side, 'for this is like man and wife, without blemish unto other'.

SALISBURY'S prodigy house at Hatfield was built between 1607 and 1612 at a cost of £40,000 to demonstrate his wealth and grandeur. His annual income was probably £25,000, with £17,000 from the profits of office—when he was trying to reduce royal expenditure!

commissioners proposed a commercial union, cross-border co-operation, and mutual naturalization. But in the parliamentary session of 1606–7 the limited Instrument of Union was rejected, rather than give greedy Scots further access to the riches of England.

The Scots were also blamed for the King's financial difficulties. When James came to his 'land of promise', he shared his fortune with his friends, and he had to pay out for political security in Scotland. In 1603–4 James gave £2,186 in gifts from the Exchequer to English subjects, but £12,749 to Scots, and by 1610 the Scots had collected £243,087 in grants from English resources—the equivalent of three parliamentary subsidies. By 1605 the Council was warning the King that his generosity could not be afforded, and that the expedients used to fund it brought 'great distraction and scandal'. The Lord Treasurer and Council tried to trim the King's bounty in 1608, 1609, 1610, and 1611, but James always broke the rules he had agreed. The King liked giving, and indulged his friends. But some 'liberality' was essential for a new King in a foreign land: he bought loyalty by grants to the English, made a splash with Court display, and expanded the royal payroll. Of necessity, James cost more than Elizabeth: he had a wife and three children for his English subjects to support, as well as his Scottish favourites.

But the English refused the support which was needed: they had paid enough of late. The long Elizabethan wars were over, and there was no willingness to endure further regulation and taxation. In a decidedly post-war era, with expectations of comfort and cheap government, any

WHEN the bureaucrat Robert Cecil was promoted to the aristocratic Order of the Garter in 1606, he used the installation to stake his claims as a courtier and nobleman, Earl of Salisbury. John de Critz's grand portrait of him in Garter robes was to bolster his ego and impress visitors.

demands from the Crown were unwelcome. When James failed to remit the uncollected portions of the 1601 subsidies, there was disappointment; when his ministers asked Parliament for taxation in 1604, it was refused; in the Commons there was criticism of monopolies, purveyance, and wardship. In the emotional session which followed the failure of the Gunpowder Plot, subsidies were voted—but the final request for three subsidies and six fifteenths passed the Commons by one vote. So James was in a fix. By a mixture of carelessness, natural extravagance, and political necessity, his was a high-spending government. But after years of war taxation, his subjects expected him to cope on his customary revenues—with a suspicion that if they were no longer enough, it was because he had given them away to the Scots.

By 1608 the Crown's debt was £600,000, and its annual deficit £178,000. But it was difficult to cut expenditure and politically dangerous to force up revenues. Drives for economy achieved very little, and when Cecil, now Earl of Salisbury, reduced the debt by hefty land sales it was, of course, at the expense of future rents. Additional customs duties were resisted by merchants and criticized in Parliament, but when the Exchequer Court found one specific imposition lawful in 1606 this was used to justify a range of new duties. In 1610 the Commons petitioned against the impositions as unparliamentary taxes, but James replied that he could not give them up without compensation. Arguments about impositions interrupted attempts at a general settlement of the Crown's finances in 1610, and the voting of a subsidy in 1614. If Parliament would not make grants to the King, however, he had to seek pickings where he could. His officers exploited loopholes, monopolies and wardships, and the Crown's claims to cheap provisions, purveyance—those provocative sources against which the Council had warned.

Salisbury concluded that things could not go on as they were. (In fact, he was wrong: they could, and did.) He persuaded the King that reliance on prerogative revenues threatened the stability of the state, and that James must seek a composition with Parliament. Salisbury has been praised for his vision; perhaps he should be damned for his misjudgement. It was impossible to reduce royal expenditure to a level Parliament would fund, and impossible to persuade Parliament to fund a realistic level of expenditure. Salisbury asked the 1610 session for 'supply' of £600,000 to clear the debt and annual 'support' of £200,000—and the haggling began. To eliminate the deficit, the Crown needed £200,000 plus compensation for the revenues to be surrendered; the best offer the Commons made was £200,000 as compensation. Fortunately, the King was saved from a disastrous deal. In the recess, constituents made it clear that they would not pay the necessary taxes, and courtiers lobbied against the abandonment of prerogative income. The 'Great Contract' collapsed: Salisbury and Parliament had failed the King.

7. *The Instability of Politics, 1610–1618*

There followed a period of remarkable political instability. The political order of James's early years had been based on a balance between the Bedchamber dominated by the Scots and the Privy Council dominated by the Earls of Salisbury and Northampton. But the débâcle over the 'Great Contract' wrecked this cosy arrangement, and thereafter favourites and ministers were made and unmade with confusing frequency. The political leaders of Elizabethan England had held office for years on end, and died in post: Burghley served for forty years, Knollys for thirty-seven, Leicester for thirty, Walsingham for seventeen. Robert Cecil and Thomas Egerton were both Councillors to Elizabeth and James for twenty-one years, and Northampton worked with James for eleven; Egerton retired ill, and the others died in office, if not quite in favour. But when the Elizabethan dinosaurs passed on, the new Jacobean generation found politics a much less predictable business. Political casualties were again as common as they had been in Henry VIII's time, though the injuries were not fatal.

Robert Carr was Lord Privy Seal for less than two years; Suffolk was Treasurer for four years, Montagu for nine months, and Cranfield for three years. Francis Bacon was Lord Chancellor for four years, and John Williams for another four. Winwood was Secretary for three years, Lake for three, and Naunton for five. Only Winwood died in office; the rest were sacked, some were disgraced, and several were the victims of factional conspiracy. The first disruptions were caused by Robert Carr, the only Scottish favourite to play a major public role in English politics. In 1611 Carr was made Viscount Rochester, and he was soon acting as James's unofficial secretary and patronage broker. He allied with Pembroke, Southampton, Thomas Overbury, and other anti-Spanish Protestants, against Salisbury and the crypto-Catholic Howards. But the death of Salisbury in 1612 led to political realignments and a scramble for his offices. Salisbury's old ally,

FRANCES HOWARD (1592–1632) was at the centre of two Court scandals and political realignments, her divorce in 1612–13 and her trial for murder in 1615–16, which gave the Jacobean regime an aura of corruption. This portrait, attributed to William Larkin, shows her in the fashionable dress of a recognized Court beauty.

Northampton forged a new partnership with Rochester, cemented by Rochester's marriage to his niece Frances Howard—rapidly made available by a divorce from the Earl of Essex.

For two years Northampton ran the Council in London, Rochester travelled with the King, and James himself played a more active role in government. When Northampton died in 1614, his nephew Suffolk became Treasurer and Rochester, now Earl of Somerset, became Chamberlain and Lord Privy Seal. But the Howard–Carr axis was soon broken. In 1615 Somerset fell victim to his former Pembroke allies, and to his own neglect of the King. James had a liking for the young George Villiers, and Pembroke, Archbishop Abbot, and Queen Anne engineered his appointment to the Bedchamber. Somerset sulked and raged, the King grew more irritated, and in the autumn the Pembroke group struck again: Somerset and his wife were arrested for murder. Thomas Overbury, who had been sent to the Tower after trying to block Somerset's desertion to the Howards, was said to have been poisoned on their orders. The trials were great public shows, with sex, violence, and politics among the aristocracy. The Earl and Countess were convicted and imprisoned. Ben Jonson's masque *The Golden Age Restored* celebrated the return of Justice, the Earl of Essex rejoined the Court, and Pembroke took over as Lord Chamberlain.

The rise of George Villiers proved as disruptive as the rise of Robert Carr. It too was meteoric: he was made Master of the Horse, Knight of the Garter, Baron, Viscount, and, in 1617, Earl of Buckingham and Privy Councillor. James made Buckingham as he had made Somerset—to be a confidant, a manager of patronage, a buffer between the King and the world of politics. Buckingham was endowed with riches and was refused no favour—and he was much more astute than Somerset. He married into the provincial aristocracy rather than a political family, and he did not fall out with James until he was sure of Prince Charles. He broke the Scots' strangle-

NICHOLAS HILLIARD's 'Pelican' portrait of Elizabeth (*facing*). This and his 'Phoenix' portrait, both early 1570s, reveal a growing stylization in pictures of her. Over each shoulder a closed imperial crown surmounts the rose and fleur-de-lys, representing her dynastic claims, while the Pelican pendant on her breast symbolizes redemption and charity—characteristic of Elizabeth's self-sacrificial love for her subjects.

THESE representations of Charles I and his queen, Henrietta Maria (*above*), are set into the windows of the hall at Magdalen College, Oxford. Charles established his Civil War Headquarters in this university town and his cult as martyr-king was later similarly to thrive there.

ALL the portraits of Charles II—even this youthful image (*left*) painted during his exile in the Low Countries—show him as a relaxed, self-indulgent figure. There was nothing of the stiff formality that all painters reflected in their images of his father.

hold on the Bedchamber, and packed in his own relations and dependants. He claimed a monopoly of patronage, and usually got his way. Above all, he avoided dangerous political entanglements and remained independent of factions, the King's man only. As Somerset had not, he was able to help the King balance the Howard and Pembroke alliances—until the Howards crossed him in 1618.

Factionalism had made the control of royal finances impossible, as patrons rewarded their followers and bid for new friends. By 1617 the debt was £726,000 and the deficit £137,029. Buckingham espoused reform, and backed investigations by Lionel Cranfield into the Exchequer, the Household, the Ordnance Office, and the Admiralty. It was probably these inquiries which prompted the Howards to strike at Buckingham, before Cranfield laundered too much of their dirty washing. They trailed pretty young William Monson before the King, hoping to out-Villiers Villiers—but they failed and fell. Buckingham destroyed them. Lord Treasurer Suffolk was dismissed, charged with corruption (justifiably), and fined. His sons lost their Household offices, and his son-in-law the mastership of the Wards. The Earl of Nottingham was removed as Lord Steward and Lord Admiral, Sir Thomas Lake as Secretary, and Lord Wotton as Treasurer of the Household. Buckingham became Lord Admiral, and Cranfield Master of the Wards. It was the biggest political purge since 1558.

The falls of Carr and the Howards were public scandals, which sullied the images of Court and government. Ballads, broadsheets, tracts, and newsletters circulated salacious details and seedy

SAMUEL ROWLANDS's 1616? broadside 'The Poysoned Knight's Complaint' was one of the many pamphlets which publicized the scandals surrounding the death of Sir Thomas Overbury as typical of the moral decay of the age. But Time, on the left, reveals the secret poisoning, and Justice gives the knight revenge.

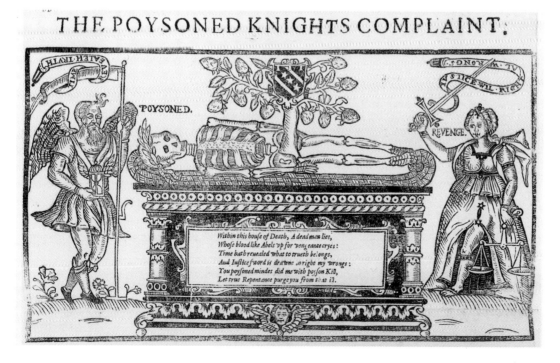

speculation about Somerset and his Countess (Suffolk's daughter). *The Bloody Downfall of Adultery, Murder, Ambition* blamed their crimes and their fate on 'the customs of this age', especially the morals induced by the life of courtiers, 'comely without, but within, nothing but rotten bones and corrupt practices'. The trial of Suffolk in 1619 revealed an elaborate system of bribery, kickbacks, extortion, and misuse of public funds. Suffolk cooked the books, and his wife and their agent Bingley made the deals. As Lord Chancellor Bacon put it, 'My lady kept the shop, Bingley was the 'prentice that cried "What do you lack?", but all went in to my lord's cash'. It was no longer possible to accuse just the Court Scots of avarice, duplicity, and exploitation; the English were at it too, and the greatest families among them. What was the King thinking of?

Not a lot, it seems. James's self-selected task in life had been to become King of England, and that had been achieved. He had worked hard to survive in Scotland and to succeed to England. He had tried and failed to achieve political Union, and he had tried, with more success, to reduce religious tensions. He liked to strut as an international statesman and a European scholar, but neither role was for him a full-time occupation. There seemed little more for even a conscientious

King to do—and James was not very conscientious. So he was free to hunt at Royston or Newmarket with his friends, Hay, Carr, Villiers. The 1610s were James's 1570s: government (if not politics) was easy once again, with peace, good order, low mortality, and religious unity, spoiled only by poor harvests in 1612, 1613, and 1615. He could take time off from England for a trip to Scotland in 1617. But his carelessness allowed royal finances to deteriorate still further, while links between central government and the county gentry were weakened.

After the failure of the 'Great Contract', the King's money-managers had to return to expedients and petty projects. The rank of baronet was invented in 1611, simply so the honour could be sold at £1,095 a knight. But the market was flooded, the price collapsed to £220 by 1622, and the early purchasers were cheated. The sale of peerages began in 1615, Irish titles were offered as a cut-price variety, and established aristocrats were outraged. It is true that the size of the English peerage had not been increased in line with popu-

CHARLES HOWARD, Earl of Nottingham (1536–1624), was lord admiral from 1585 until 1618, when he was a casualty of the demand for navy reform and Buckingham's coup against his family. In *c.*1620 the old man was portrayed by Daniel Mytens in Garter splendour, with his flagship behind in action at sea.

lation, and that there were few flagrantly inappropriate new creations. But the nobility was touchy about its dignity: in 1621 thirty-three English peers protested against the equal precedence of Scottish and Irish nobles, and the invasion of the English peerage by Scots. The trade in monopolies and patents, which had caused protests in Parliament, revived again as the Crown's needs grew and supplicants clamoured. There were direct sales of monopoly privileges, and regulatory rights were granted as royal favours.

The demands made upon local government were, by comparison with the 1590s, very light. There were no subsidies to collect between 1610 and 1621, no impressments for overseas service, no fears of rebellion or widespread rioting. There was pressure on the deputy lieutenants from 1612, to get the militia system back into working order. Routine mustering had virtually ceased after the peace of 1604, and there was some resistance to revival. But the enthusiasm of Lords Lieutenant varied, and some counties were not much troubled. In 1616 there was a minor overhaul of the commissions of the peace, and lawyers were appointed to give their proceedings more professionalism. But the government did not oppress the localities; rather, it neglected them. Salisbury had maintained a flexible network of county contacts, providing rewards for service and significance. Between the collapse of the Cecil connection and the triumph of the Villiers machine, however, factionalized Court politics fragmented patronage. So Buckingham's drive for a one-faction state brought a political earthquake.

8. *The Playboy and the Prince, 1618–1624*

Buckingham was determined to prove he was no mere playboy—and James that he was no mere plaything. As self-appointed patron of administrative reform, Buckingham was the protector of Lionel Cranfield and the public enemy of waste and corruption. Cranfield sat on the interlocking commissions which examined spending departments, and produced blueprints for savings. Buckingham supplied the political muscle that got things done. In 1618 there were new orders for the Household, which was to reuse candles and sell leftover food. The Navy commission combed the estimates, exposed fraud, and improved purchasing. In 1619 the reformers were honoured in the naming of ships, with *Happy Entrance* and *Constant Reformation*. In 1620 a report on the Ordnance revealed past peculation and promised drastic economies. Cranfield offered to run the Wardrobe at half its previous cost, and negotiated new contracts with suppliers. The Treasury commission monitored income and expenditure, revised the customs leases, and recovered funds from corrupt officials. And in 1619 and 1622 there were renewed efforts to curtail the King's generosity.

But Buckingham and Cranfield depended upon the corruption and laxity which they sought to tackle: disinterested reform would leave them politically exposed. Cranfield leased duties, sold offices, and managed the Wards to clear a large profit for himself. Buckingham established the fortunes of his family and friends by royal gifts and grants of patent rights. He was the King's patronage broker, but he manipulated appointments and rewards to secure his own political advantage. He insisted upon control of patronage, arguing that the King's favour towards him must be manifest by his trust—and that a client's loyalty towards him must be manifest by his dependence. As Buckingham's power and confidence grew, so did his expectations: disagreement was treated as disloyalty, but reliable followers were ruthlessly advanced. Salisbury had

Thomas scott was the leading pamphleteer against a marriage to the Infanta and for a war with Spain. The frontispiece of *Vox Dei* ('the voice of God', 1624) shows Christ's concern for king and kingdom, with Charles, Buckingham, and Frederick protecting James and the royal family against Spaniards and Catholics.

A time to love and a time to hate; a time of warre and a time of peace. Eccl.3.8.

been flexible in the distribution of favour, refusing to take sides in local disputes; Buckingham would promote one faction and undermine another, and thrust his own men into the government of counties. The Buckingham machine tolerated neither opponents nor neutrals.

The consequences appeared in Parliament. James called the Parliament of 1621 for money, to suggest that he could afford a war if the Habsburgs were obstructive over the Palatinate or the United Provinces. Two subsidies were voted, but soon there were covert attacks on Buckingham: in the Lords the sale of peerages and in the Commons grants of patents were rods to beat the favourite and his friends. There were allegations of corruption, and Lord Chancellor Bacon was offered as scapegoat to save the Villiers clan. Parliament was prorogued, Buckingham's enemies were arrested, and Cranfield the (comparatively) clean was made Lord Treasurer. By the second session of the Parliament, the demands of Court politics and of foreign policy were the same: war headed the agenda, to harass the Habsburgs and keep the Commons busy. Buckingham's agent, Sir George Goring, proposed a petition for war against Spain, unless her troops were withdrawn from the Palatinate. But the petition which was drawn also asked for Prince Charles to be married to a Protestant. James saw this as an attempt to tie his diplomatic hands, and after a squabble he dissolved the Parliament.

The King's diplomacy aimed to secure the restoration of his son-in-law Frederick as Elector Palatine—with the threat of war as a stick and the offer of Charles as husband for the Spanish Infanta as a carrot. But Parliament did not produce convincing sums for war, and the marriage strategy made faltering progress—so in February 1623 Buckingham and Charles dashed off in disguise to Madrid, to claim the Prince's bride. It was to be Elizabeth's Anjou marriage all over again, but with a faster denouement. Tortuous negotiations failed to settle religious and diplomatic issues securely; there was an outcry in England at the prospect of a Catholic marriage, with the pamphleteer Thomas Scott as the Stubbs of 1623; and on their return to London the newly promoted Duke and the Prince joined the 'patriot' war party to rebuild their Protestant credentials. Buckingham himself licensed the first English translation of Camden's history of Elizabeth, with its frontispiece depicting the naval dramas of her reign.

But the call back to war was made to a country deep in economic depression. Wars in Europe had disrupted cloth exports, and Baltic currency debasements prompted an outflow of silver from England. There was unemployment in the cloth industry, and disorder in a number of cloth-making counties. Shortage of coin and bad harvests made it hard to collect the subsidies of 1621 and the forced loan of 1622. In October 1621 the Lincolnshire subsidy commissioners offered to resign, after the Council complained that the yield had fallen and demanded a higher rating for officials. And there was plague in 1624–5. There were enthusiasts for war against Spain—the Earls of Pembroke, Southampton, and Warwick, for example, now joined by Charles and Buckingham. But there would be different views among the MPs who voted war taxes and were answerable to their constituents, the commissioners who made subsidy assessments, and the Justices who enforced the Poor Laws. The Prince and the patriots wanted their war, but the county gentry knew its price.

And so did the King. James asked the 1624 Parliament for six subsidies and twelve fifteenths, and refused to go to war for less. Since the largest grant hitherto made had been four subsidies and eight fifteenths in 1601, this was virtually a declaration that he would not go to war at all. MPs argued that the country could not afford such burdens, and that fifteenths weighed too heavily on the poor: they voted for three subsidies and three fifteenths. Cranfield, Lord Treasurer and now Earl of Middlesex, knew this was a tiny contribution towards the real costs and feared the impact of war on customs revenues. He tried to strengthen his arguments by bringing his pretty nephew Arthur Brett to Court, but was broken by Buckingham, who orchestrated an impeachment on charges of corruption. Charles and Buckingham got their way. They had the money to start a war, if not to carry it far. James was isolated in the Bedchamber, with Villiers guards around him. Middlesex was thrown aside, and the Privy Council was ignored: the playboy and the Prince were in command.

9. *The Burdens of War, 1624–1630*

Buckingham and Charles were not, however, in control. Their conversion to fighting Spain rather than marrying her Infanta had been welcomed, as evidence of their Protestant commitment rather than because there was a widespread wish for war. Some Protestant enthusiasts wanted total war against Spain and the Empire, props of the Romish Antichrist. But after twenty years of peace they did not know the true costs of a war, nor how they might be met. Campaigns could not now be financed from capital: Elizabeth had sold Crown lands to pay for war and Salisbury had flogged more to reduce James's debt, leaving little for the final sell-off in 1626. With the Crown already in debt and its lands gone, there was no security for heavy borrowing. And Parliament would not grant, and the counties could not collect, the taxes which might cover the King's costs. Though harvests were better in 1626 and 1627, the plague of 1624–5 shattered trade through London and war against Spain hit exports of cloth—and then there were poor harvests in 1628 and 1629, and a disaster in 1630. It was no time to be at war.

James died on 27 March 1625, and Charles was his own master. On 1 May he married Henrietta Maria, Princess of France. A war against the Habsburgs dictated an alliance with France, but the price of a French bride was concessions to English Catholics. So the French marriage frightened Protestants almost as much as a Spanish match had done—especially as Buckingham had a suspicious number of Catholic kin, and Charles lent his ships to Louis XIII for a campaign against a Huguenot rebellion. Such suspicion would not have mattered if war had gone well, but it did not, partly because it was underfunded. In 1625 one expedition was crippled by desertions

T HIS grand group portrait of the immediate Villiers family in 1628 shows the Duke and Duchess of Buckingham (holding hands), with two earls (one held by his nurse), two countesses, a viscount, and a future duchess. George had done well for them!

and disease, and another by drunkenness and disease. When the French made peace with Spain in 1626, Buckingham went to war with them to change their minds: in 1627 he led an attack which was beaten back with heavy losses, and in 1628 a fleet was sent to relieve the Huguenots of La Rochelle, but they surrendered and the expense was all for nothing. These were unnecessary campaigns, incompetently fought—but that did not reduce the bill.

It had to be paid in Scotland and Ireland, as well as in England. The Scottish Act of Revocation in 1625 cancelled all grants of royal lands since 1394, and reclaimed Kirk property in private hands. Its aim was to force landholders into financial compositions with the Crown, and the measure was deeply resented by the aristocracy. In Ireland there were attempts to buy higher taxation by major concessions to Catholics in 1626, but the Old English would not pay for a larger army to hold themselves in subjection. In 1628 there was a more modest deal, with a relaxation of economic controls and greater security of property in return for three subsidies of £40,000 a year. But the Protestant settlers were hostile to any arrangement which reduced the disabilities of the Old English; in 1629 Lord Deputy Falkland was recalled, and the persecution of Catholics began again. Thus Charles began his reign in Scotland with ill-considered aggression, and in Ireland with vacillation. In England he was equally provocative.

The English Parliament of 1625 voted only two subsidies, and refused a second grant. Perhaps some members wanted to restrain the war, perhaps others thought Buckingham would waste any more. But the burden of taxation in a time of plague was the main reason for caution. The wars had to be paid for none the less, and privy seal loans were collected. The Parliament of 1626 was told that the King needed £1,067,211 for a year of fighting: the Commons voted for three subsidies and three-fifteenths, a third of the requirement, but delayed a formal grant. Buckingham was accused of failing in war and squandering the King's resources, and Charles dissolved the Parliament to avoid an impeachment. Again, a forced loan was needed. The Privy Council and the Villiers political machine went into action, payment was made a test of loyalty, and £243,776 was collected. In 1628 Parliament voted for five subsidies, a quarter of what was then required, and held up the grant to force the King to moderate the voracious demands of the wars. Both loyalty and administrative capacity were put under strain.

The parliamentary votes of supply were inadequate, and the sums collected were small. As in the 1590s, subsidy commissioners protected their counties: fewer taxpayers were listed, and assessments were cut. A single subsidy had yielded £120,000 in 1589, £85,000 in 1601, and £70,000 in 1624; it yielded £55,000 in 1628, though the Council had asked for the same return as in 1563. And the real value of subsidies was slashed by inflation. But in hard times such burdens were heavy enough, and subsidies were only part of the pressure. In the invasion scare of 1625, Essex had to provide and pay for a garrison at Harwich, while the plague still raged and the cloth industry was depressed: the month's exercise cost £5,000, more than twice a subsidy. Across southern England men were mustered for the militia and pressed for overseas service, and they had to be billeted, paid, and kept in order. There were refusals of rates and riots against billeting. The deputy lieutenants were ground between the King's demands and their counties' resistance. In Norfolk in 1628 military administration broke down, and the deputies offered to resign for lack of local support. Once more, it was no way to run a war—but it was the only way there was.

Parliament's 1628 Petition of Right was couched as a protest against arbitrary government: in fact, it was a protest against arbitrary war. Charles had gone to war, counting on the full support of his Parliament: he did not get it. But if war could not be financed in a parliamentary way, it had to be financed in a prerogative way; if troops could not be raised in a statutory way, they had to be raised in a prerogative way; and if men who did not pay or obey could not be punished by common law, they had to be punished by prerogative power. Or the wars would have to end. But they were Buckingham's wars, and Charles stood by him against his enemies. In 1626 the Duke's coach had been wrecked by angry sailors; in March 1628 there was a mutiny in front of his house; in June his astrologer was hacked to pieces by a mob. Then, on 23 August 1628, Buckingham was murdered by an officer desperate without pay. Peace became possible. And when in 1629 the House of Commons denounced the payment of non-parliamentary taxes, peace became certain. There would be no more wars and no more Parliaments—for the present.

The years 1624–30 reproduced the problems of Elizabeth's last years. Men and money for war were demanded while harvests failed, trade and industry slumped, and epidemic disease cut down its victims. The difficulties were much the same as those of 1525–9, 1544–50, 1556–8, 1594–7, and 1638–41—the consequences of fighting a costly war on an inadequate tax base and in a harsh economic climate, generating political tensions at the centre and resistance from the localities. And, as before, peace was made, the bad times passed, and political calm was restored. As before, there was a scapegoat to take the blame, and the dead Buckingham filled the role played in turn by Wolsey, Somerset, Mary, and Burghley. Charles now had a chance to mend his political fences and show what he could do. He had not aimed for autocratic kingship: he had got into wars his subjects would not sustain, and fought on as best he could. There had been no shattering crisis of society or the constitution, simply a conjunction of misfortunes which then went away. It was up to the King what happened next.

17 POLITICS IN AN AGE OF REVOLUTION
1630–1690

JOHN MORRILL

1. *Introduction*

The six decades spanning the years 1630–90 witnessed civil war, invasion, and conquest, and the violent overthrow of two monarchs. At the heart of this time of troubles lay the 1640s, during which there were more than 600 separate military clashes in which men were killed. More than half the large pitched battles ever fought on English soil were fought in that decade, and it culminated in the abolition of the Stuart monarchy, the House of Lords, and the Established Church. And this is only a summary of the English experience. In Scotland and Ireland, the political and religious revolutions were accompanied by social revolutions, and by a greater intensity of violence that left scars that were not to heal.

It is hard to explain this massive disruption in the development of the British state. Perhaps the sheer complexity of governing three kingdoms each with its own distinctive Council, Parliament, lawcourts, and religious settlement created an instability that no one of the kingdoms had of itself. Perhaps having a sequence of kings all of whom had Catholic wives and religious convictions out of kilter with those of a majority of their English subjects was something that the political nation could no longer accommodate. Perhaps the spread of literacy and the printed word created a political culture that matured more rapidly than the political institutions through which those with enhanced wealth, social power, and cultural power sought to express their aspirations. Historians fight over such matters as fiercely with their words as seventeenth-century Englishmen fought over them with their swords. Some persist in calling it 'The English Revolution'. Others see it as the last of the great European wars of religion, a crisis deferred but not ultimately prevented by sixteenth-century compromise. Others again see the crisis as the 'War of Three Kingdoms', a crisis in the relations of a multiple monarchy, a convulsion on the way to the incomplete creation of a multinational British archipelagic state, emerging in parallel with the rise of France or Spain out of equally disparate polities. Contemporaries refer to it most often as

'England's Troubles', and in the sense that it represents England's Troubles within itself and in its relations with its neighbour kingdoms with whom it shared a head of state, that might well still be the best title of all.

2. *The Personal Rule*

Yet the 1630s were a period of deceptive calm. In England and Wales at least, it was probably the most peaceful decade in living memory. There were few riots, no rebellions, no treason trials, few if any killings of public officials. The King had a vigorous, centralist, authoritarian policy in both Church and State. In alliance with Archbishop William Laud, he set about restoring the wealth and jurisdiction of the clergy, to unpick much of the secularism that had marked the Reformation process, and he wanted to turn the piecemeal activity of recent years to repair and beautify parish churches into a national crusade. No longer would each parish be left very much to its own devices in interpreting Prayer Book rubrics and royal injunctions. Now there was to be a national standard of liturgical practice enforced by strict visitation. Jacobean ecclesiastical *laissez-faire* was to give way to a Caroline preoccupation with strict conformity, even uniformity. It drove dozens of clergy and thousands of pious laymen to depart to the 'howling wildernesses' of New England, and a well-publicized handful who spoke out too stridently were charged with libel or with sedition, and had their ears cut off, or were severely whipped at the cart's tail through the streets of London. There was much in the programme that had a populist appeal—a permissiveness that challenged Puritan views that the sabbath should be all worship and no play, that de-emphasized (without overturning) the role of the preacher, and that restored forms of worship that appealed—through 'the beauty of holiness'—to all five senses. It was a faith that welcomed all the people to kneel to receive their risen Lord at the altar rail, and which did not condemn many of them to sit around as a godly clique commemorated what God had achieved for *them*, the elect, in his death and resurrection. Yet the evidence is that it was hugely unpopular because it was expensive, because it represented outside interference and intervention, and because it reeked of popery.

This was highly damaging because there were so many other things to feed those with suspicious minds or with a neurotic obsession with the popish threat represented by the memory of the Marian martyrdoms, the Armada, and the Gunpowder Plot. Such men—looking at the way whole regions of Germany were being burnt and bludgeoned back into the Catholic fold—expected fresh popish outrages by the day. The King's strong-willed Catholic Queen took the royal children and an increasing number of courtiers with her to mass in the spacious Catholic chapel created for her in Somerset House; the King formed a close personal friendship with George Con, the papal envoy; the King openly indulged a passion for the art and culture of the Catholic Reformation; and far from confronting the international popish threat to the very survival of Continental Protestantism, he showed a willingness to assist the Spaniards against the Dutch, as by letting Spanish troops move across England *en route* to the Netherlands so as to avoid the Dutch blockade on the Channel. All this royal indifference to the threat of popery was perhaps the greatest single solvent to that trust that glued his people to him in unquestioning obedience.

That momentum of obedience was also slowed by his secular policies. Never had the Privy Council spent so much time monitoring and cajoling local magistrates, overturning local customs and intitiatives with a blind determination to enforce national norms—in respect to the relief of poverty, the maintenance of highways, the regulation of the grain and brewing trades. Overhaul of the financial system gave Charles an enhanced and adequate peacetime revenue—by the late 1630s Charles's disposable income (after allowing for inflation) was double that which his father had inherited from Elizabeth. In 1638 only one component part of that income (the £200,000 a year Charles was demanding for the maintenance of the Fleet ('Ship Money')) was proving contentious and Charles could have abandoned that and still been in credit on an annual basis. There was much grumbling at these policies, but very few men were refusing to serve as magistrates or were being dismissed for non-co-operation. The gentry still needed the King as much as he needed them.

Things must have appeared to be going smoothly enough.

The Privy Council was full of men who had been out of favour and office during the years of Buckingham's ascendancy; and many of them (including the Earls of Arundel, Pembroke, and

CHARLES I raised almost £200,000 a year in the later 1630s from Ship Money, an emergency prerogative rate on all householders, and he was able—to good effect—greatly to strengthen the Fleet with purpose-built ships such as *The Sovereign of the Seas*. The policy was a naval and financial success, but achieved at high political cost: it epitomized the 1630s.

WARWICK Castle, modernized in Elizabeth's reign, was held in 1642 by Robert, Lord Brooke, one of the few peers from families ennobled by the Stuarts to be an active Parliamentarian. After his death in 1643, it served as an administrative headquarters and as a prison for captured royalists.

Strafford and lawyers such as William Noy and Dudley Digges) had been amongst the most effective parliamentary critics of the policies of the 1620s. Demands for the recall of Parliament were muffled and incoherent; demands for a more active Protestant foreign policy were more mumbled than proclaimed. Many of those who had been outspoken in their criticism of Charles's policies in the 1630s and who were not brought into office (this is above all true of those who had been most critical of the King's religious policies) did spend much time at remote country retreats such as Richard Knightley's home at Fawsley in Northamptonshire, or at the cultural castles of Lord Brooke at Warwick or Lord Saye near Banbury to work out what was to be done. And the answer was, that there was not much that could be done. They planned ways of compelling the King to get the judges to adjudicate on the legality of his actions; they went in rather unsystematically for acts of non-compliance with financial demands; they pondered the merits of emigrating to New England.

We can be sure that they were not planning a civil war.

By 1638 Charles was financially stable in peacetime, with an itch to assist the Catholic side in the Thirty Years War in order to be rewarded with the righting of an ancient wrong—the restoration of the Palatinate to his sister's family. He did not need an active foreign policy because no one was interested in invading England. There was peace, sullen obedience, general implementation of policies designed to achieve social justice, religious uniformity. If Charles I had only been King of England, this situation could have developed in many different ways; but because he was King of Scotland and Ireland too, his position in fact was much less stable than it seemed.

3. Ireland and Scotland

In the end, it was to be the explosion in Ireland in 1641 that was to turn crisis in the British archipelago into a war of the three kingdoms. But it may be that that explosion was not the natural outcome of a decade of authoritarian and brutal government indelibly linked to the name of Thomas Wentworth, Earl of Strafford (Lord Deputy from 1633 until his execution by the English Parliament in 1641). Wentworth is the ultimate in poachers turned gamekeeper, having been one of the most outspoken critics of Buckingham and all policies associated with him in the 1620s. But once in office he showed—as Lord President of the Council of the North and as Lord Deputy in Ireland—a devotion to the King's interest that exceeded even his devotion to the interests of his own posterity. He was sent to Ireland first and foremost to make the Irish Exchequer balance the books; Charles was no longer able or willing to allow England to bear the costs of garrisoning Ireland. This meant raising revenue in Ireland but not in ways that would cause rebellion and high defence costs. The trick therefore was to mulct the New English Elizabethan and Jacobean settlers more ruthlessly than the older, Catholic communities. Those—like the Earl of Cork—who had defrauded not only the native population but also the Crown must now disgorge much of their ill-gotten gains. In the medium and long term, Strafford undoubtedly had plans for more plantations in Connaught and Munster, and few of the Old English or Gaels had much to thank him for—except the sight of their recent tormentors tormented; and the experience of as much religious freedom as any of them could remember.

Strafford's religious policy was to delay any new attack on Catholicism—which he distasted—until the Church of Ireland was equipped to undertake the task of evangelism. In the meantime he saw persecution as futile and counter-productive. Rather than drive the Catholic bishops underground, therefore, he reached an understanding in which Rome appointed bishops acceptable to him and they delivered the political acquiescence of their flocks in exchange for *de facto* toleration. Meanwhile Strafford, bypassing James Ussher, the scholarly and ineffectual Archbishop of Armagh, appointed John Bramhall, a Yorkshireman of similar bluntness to himself, as Bishop of Derry with a brief to transform the Irish Church. This meant restoring its wealth by an attack on those laymen who had gained control of tithes and church lands; bringing its articles of religion, canons, and liturgical practices much more into line with the best English practice; driving out all (especially Scots) who dissented from these changes; and strengthening the jurisdiction of church courts and ensuring that the secular courts were at the beck and call of churchmen who came up against opposition. By the late 1630s Wentworth had achieved all his short-term objectives. But he had made innumerable personal enemies and (worse) he had built up hatreds within the Protestant community against his *laissez-faire* policy towards the Catholic community that led to Protestant demands for a new reign of terror against the majority population. It was fear of this renewed terror which caused the Catholic community to seek to take advantage of the political paralysis in England in 1641 by launching a pre-emptive strike so as to disarm the Protestant communities of the Pale and of Ulster. It was a rebellion which was to have fateful consequences for all three kingdoms.

But it was the collapse of Charles's authority in Scotland which was to trigger the collapse of his authority in all three kingdoms.

Charles I had got off to a poor start in Scotland with his Act of Revocation, an attempt to renegotiate the terms on which the nobility held the land—especially former church lands—conferred upon them by the Crown. A collective act of non-compliance and non-co-operation by the Scottish nobility was largely responsible for the defeat of this policy; but distrust festered. Charles was Scots by birth and he stammered in a Scottish accent; but he never made any real attempt to understand the ways in which his powers in Scotland and Ireland differed from his powers in England.

This was made all too plain during his first visit to Scotland as its monarch in 1633, especially in a spectacularly provocative coronation ceremony which was modelled on the English ceremony and which incorporated part of the English coronation oath instead of the Scottish oath laid down by Scottish statute. The setting—not Scone or Stirling but Holyrood Palace, decked out with a railed altar and arras containing a woven golden crucifix—only added to the alarm and the gloom. This visit created a deep antipathy between Charles and many leading Scottish nobles (whose personal power as regional magnates still really mattered in Scotland); and it heightened his tendency to make policy for Scotland in England in consultation with those Scottish nobles who had Briticized themselves (like Hamilton and Lennox) and then to tell the Scottish Council to enforce it. This ensured that Charles had no way of measuring his desires against the limits of his enforceable will, which had been the essence of good counsel north and south of the border for centuries. His greatest follies came in clumsy and enforced changes in the Church of Scotland. As in England and Ireland, he continued to harrass those who had gained possession of church lands in an attempt to restore the wealth and standing of the clergy. He did not so much seek to Anglicize the Kirk as impose changes that went *beyond* what was established in England. Aspects of the new Scottish canons and the new Scottish Prayer Book—both intro-

THE Service Book introduced into Scotland in 1637 provoked riots in many places, plotting among the nobility, and paralysis in the Council. It led to a National Covenant to resist religious and constitutional innovation. Scottish tracts and popular engravings such as this one by Wenceslas Hollar, left the English with little doubt about the strength of feeling north of the border.

The Arch-Prelate of St Andrewes in Scotland reading the new Service-booke in his pontificalibus assaulted by men & women, with Crickets stooles Stickes and Stones.

duced without reference to a General Assembly or Parliament—were more offensive to the consciences of the great majority of Scottish Protestants than their English equivalents would have been. The Scottish Prayer Book, for example, contained visual representations of angels, anathema in a deeply iconophobic culture, and required the priest at the celebration of holy communion to stand at an east-end altar facing away from the people.

The response of the Scottish people (after an initial reflex of protest in the churches themselves) was a massive act of passive disobedience. By far the greater part of the nobility, lairds, ministers, and others bound themselves together in a solemn oath to disobey commands which were against the law of God and the founding documents of the Scottish Reformation. This National Covenant was a collective act of defiance by the people of Scotland against the King of Scotland, more organized because more determined than the act of defiance that had peacefully defeated the Act of Revocation; and it was a constitutionalist call for the return, by and through Parliaments and General Assemblies lawfully convened, of the Scottish Church to its purity of worship and order at the time of the Second Book of Discipline and the Golden Acts (i.e. the 1580s and early 1590s). That is all. It was not a call to arms or an invitation to war. It was Charles I who decided, as King of Great Britain and Ireland, to bring the resources of all his kingdoms (and of the Pope and King of Spain) to bear on his recalcitrant Scottish subjects. It was he who planned a campaign involving not only an English army, but also the (Protestant) security forces in Ireland (and if necessary an Irish Catholic Army), and loyal (Catholic) Highlanders (who much preferred government of benign neglect from London to government by Calvinist enthusiasts in Edinburgh). It was he who failed properly to co-ordinate that campaign; gave the Scots plenty of time to prepare for his coming; and it was he who led his English army to humiliating defeat. By late 1639 Charles I had two real choices and one false one: to make painful concessions to the Scots and to resume the Personal Rule in England; to make painful concessions to a recalled English Parliament in order to raise the monies necessary for a more effective campaign against the Scots; or to renew the war with the Scots without any new resources. Charles never considered the first real option; he toyed with the second real option; and then he opted for the third, false choice.

If in 1629 it had been up to the King what happened next, the unsurprising outcome was that he provoked a crisis. And no one was better qualified to turn a crisis into a catastrophe.

4. *The Civil Wars*

If the 1630s were years of sullen peace, the 1640s were years of controlled violence. Between the summer of 1640 and the summer of 1642, royal power collapsed in all three kingdoms; between the autumn of 1642 and the summer of 1646 there was fighting within and between all three kingdoms—in England alone men were killed in well over 600 battles and sieges, with perhaps 80,000 people killed in the fighting and perhaps 10,000 buildings damaged beyond repair—one calculation is that one in ten of those living in towns lost their homes. In 1646 and 1647 those who had won the war found themselves losing the peace, as crippling taxes, harvest failure, and a trade slump brought demands for settlement at any price the King would accept. In 1648 the war of the three kingdoms was resumed and in its aftermath the Parliament of England put Charles I of England, Scotland, and Ireland on trial. The decade ended with monarchy and Established

Church abolished in two of the kingdoms, the House of Lords in one of them, and Oliver Cromwell embarked on a brutal conquest of Ireland.

In the spring of 1640 the King called a Parliament and tried to negotiate with it a deal whereby he would settle some grievances in return for a large grant to permit him to invade Scotland more effectively than he had the previous year. MPs knew that he could dissolve the Parliament at will and many were willing to negotiate from a position of relative weakness. He then made that fatal false choice. Fearing that there would be too many strings on the twelve parliamentary subsidies (more than double any previous grant) being prepared by the 'Short' Parliament, he dissolved it only fifteen days after it first met. He then prepared to invade Scotland on a shoe-string budget. As he scrimped and saved to set forth a very unprepared army, the Scots decided to take the initiative. They invaded England, occupied the North-East as far south as Newcastle and declared they would not return home until there was a lasting peace guaranteed by the English Parliament. The Long Parliament was a unique Parliament in that the King had no power to prorogue

or dissolve it because its existence was secured by 20,000 Scottish troops. One of its first Acts prevented its dissolution without its own consent; and this was quickly followed by an Act that provided for elections every third year, elections which would take place whether or not the King issued parliamentary writs.

The Scots invasion made possible a constitutional revolution in all three kingdoms in 1641: in Scotland providing for a powerful Scottish executive over which the King had little control and a Scottish Kirk rid of bishops and of all English influences; in Ireland a restoration of the social and political authority of the Tudor and Jacobean planters and a return to sectarian anti-Catholic policies; and in England a dismantling of the instruments and institutions which had implemented the Personal Rule. Thus Star Chamber, High Commission, Requests, and the regional councils were abolished or truncated; the instruments of 'fiscal feudalism' of the 1630s were declared illegal; the greater part of the Privy Council, the judi-

T HE King presides over the Lords and the Lords appear to dominate the Commons—a harmonious image of mixed monarchy which was very much at odds with the reality of 1643 when Edward Husbands published his *Exact Collection* of all the exchanges between the King and the Houses that led into the Civil War.

THE BISHOPS LAST GOOD-NIGHT.

Where Popery and Innovations doe begin,

There Treason will by degrees come in.

108

Only Canonicall prayers

no afternoon sermons

So we desire it.

Then no Bishops

Bishops.

Citizens.

The Pope.

Jesuit, Fryer, and Papist.

Estate prostitutes
Betray
Noix-country

If they had ruld still, where had we been?

God keepe us from Prelates, Popish Prelates.

A RCHBISHOP LAUD is seen (*on the left*) as preventing extempore prayer and free preaching and as being, as one critic put it, the little thief crept in by the window, to open the door for the Pope and his cohorts (*right*).

ciary, and the episcopate resigned, were dismissed, or were impeached; and the men and the policies linked to William Laud were subject to an unremitting assault in the Parliament House, in the press, in the parishes.

By the summer of 1641, the Scots were satisfied and they signed a treaty with England and went home. They were pushing a Scottish-style church settlement on the English and proposed a closer federation of equals between England and Scotland, but were prepared to negotiate it at a distance. For two years they were at peace amongst themselves and disinclined to get involved in the deepening crisis south of the border.

Yet reform only deepened the crisis in England in two ways.

First, Charles's sullen and sulky acceptance of those reforms, set against his previous record, persuaded many that he would disown them as soon as he could, and it pushed some men to demand further reforms and specifically for the kind of parliamentary control of appointments and control of royal councillors which had been tried and which had failed so often in the fourteenth and fifteenth centuries. These desperate demands, and the reliance on mass picketing of Parliament and the Court by London apprentices that accompanied them, made many feel that there was now a parliamentary tyranny even worse than the royal tyranny that had just been laid to rest.

Secondly, although remedies for secular misgovernment had been easy to agree, remedies for religious misgovernment could not be agreed. Many—the future royalist party—wanted to get back to what they termed 'the pure religion of Queen Elizabeth and King James, without any connivance of popery or innovation'; others—the future parliamentarian party—wanted to reform the Reformation, to abandon a church settlement so incapable of tackling popery head on and so easily subverted by Laudian fellow-travellers of popery. They wanted to replace it either with a Genevan/Scottish style Presbyterianism or a New England style Congregationalism.

In this fetid atmosphere, the Irish Rebellion of October 1641 turned a chronic crisis in England into an acute one. The rebellion was a pre-emptive strike by Irish Catholics desperate to disarm

M.^r FFordes house rifled, and to. make her Confesse where her mony lay, they tooke hot tonges clapping them to the Soules of her feete & to the Palmes of her handes so tormented her that with the paine thereof shee died,

They haue set men & women on hot Grideorns to make them Confesse whe[:] re there money was

THE massacres in Ulster in 1641 and 1642 were the worst civilian massacres in the history of the British Isles and the stories of the refugees and the publication of many images such as these (*left*) ensured that anti-Catholic panics played an important part in the civil war on the British as well as the Irish side of the Irish Sea.

THE Solemn League and Covenant (*right*) bound the English and Scots to introduce common forms of religion and a federal constitution. The English consistently refused to implement it, while calling on the Scots for military support.

the Protestant community before it launched a pogrom against them. It quickly got out of hand and led to the slaughter of perhaps 3,000 Protestants, and the flight to England of many more. Whoever controlled the army that was essential to stop the slaughter would have the military force to dictate a settlement in England. The issue which compelled men to take sides was the issue of who should control the army and the militia; the issues which guided men's choice of sides were religion, trust, and honour. In January 1642 the King attempted to stage a *coup* (by seizing his leading opponents in the two Houses) and failed. He then withdrew from his capital and stumped around the Midlands and North constantly escalating the military option. Many saw him as dangerously out of control; but many others saw him as sorely provoked by a Parliament which dwindled as the more moderate and confused slipped away, provoked by increasingly arbitrary and unprecedented measures and a pandering to the whims of the London crowd and of the demands of religious extremists.

And so the country drifted into a civil war that most did not want. Most men tried to avoid choosing sides or getting involved. Some in many counties tried to organize peace movements, or at any rate tried to declare their counties 'neutral' so as to allow the war to be settled elsewhere. But enough men accepted orders from the two Houses or mobilized of their own accord to overcome the disorganized pleas for peace.

It was a war in which men and women throughout society made free political choices. This is how it differed from earlier wars. And while many opted to follow the line of least resistance and did what others ordered them to do, or made rational calculations as to how best to safeguard their families and property, many others made tough and courageous choices, abandoning for the sake of conscience their homes and neighbours, disobeying their fathers, landlords, employers. And when we look at the pattern of free choices, we find that there are as many royalist gentry as parliamentarian gentry (perhaps 4,000 on each side and perhaps 10,000 avoiding being labelled), as many royalist yeoman, lawyers, clergy, merchants, manufacturers, as parliamentarian ones. The war split the country by conscience uninformed by class.

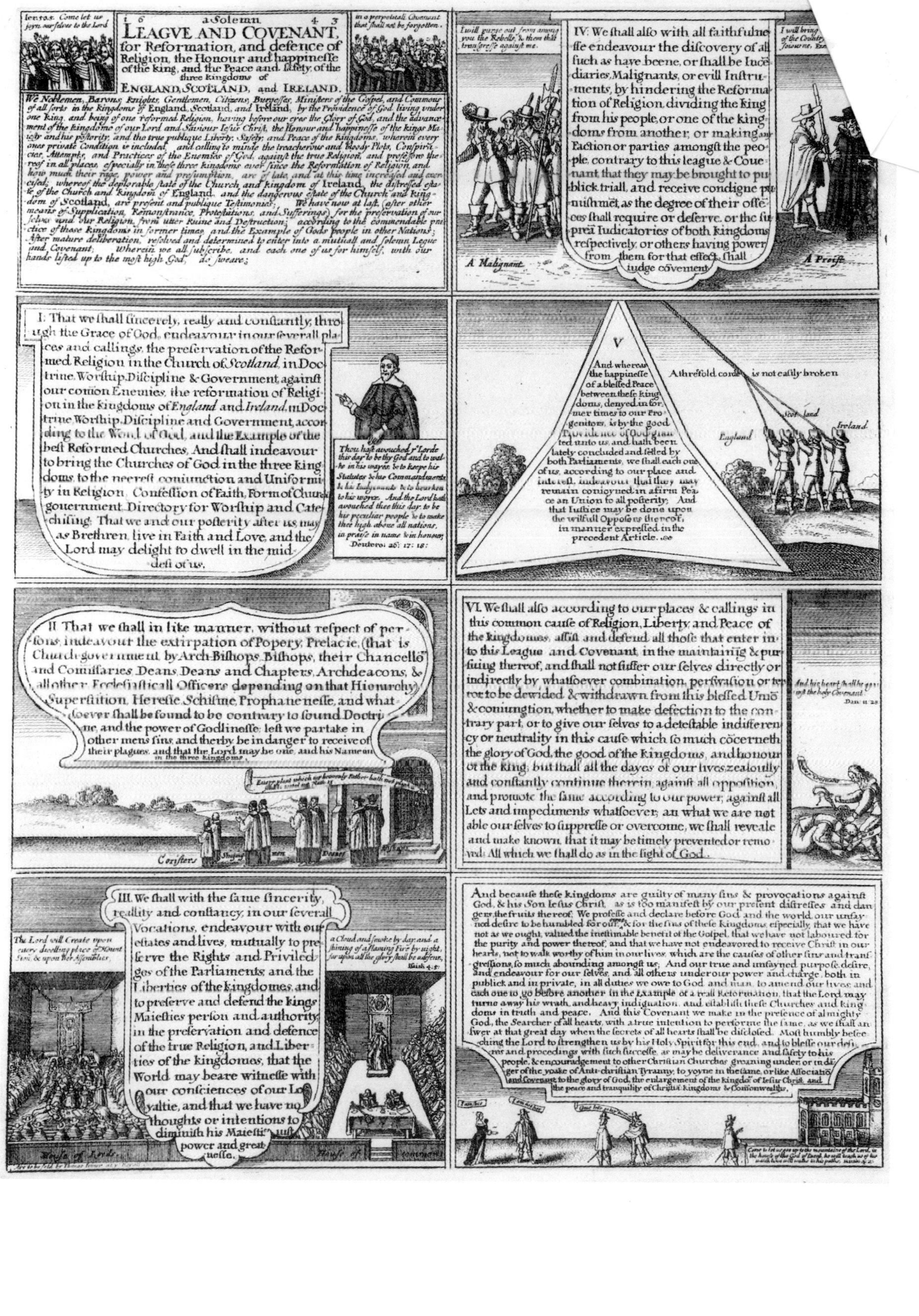

Panel 1 (top left)

Iew.10.8. Come let us joyn our selves to the Lord in a perpetuall Covenant that shall not be forgotten.

a Solemn
LEAGUE AND COVENANT,
for Reformation, and defence of
Religion, the Honour and happinesse
of the king, and the Peace and safety of the
three kingdomes of
ENGLAND, SCOTLAND, and IRELAND.

We Noblemen, Barons, Knights, Gentlemen, Citizens, Burgesses, Ministers of the Gospel, and Commons of all sorts in the Kingdomes of England, Scotland, and Ireland, by the Providence of God living under one king, and being of one reformed Religion, having before our eye the Glory of God, and the advancement of the kingdome of our Lord and Saviour Iesus Christ, the Honour and happinesse of the kings Majesty and his posterity, and the true publique Liberty, Safety and Peace of the Kingdomes, wherein every ones private Condition is included: and calling to minde the treacherous and bloody Plots, Conspiracies, Attempts, and Practices of the Enemies of God, against the true Religion, and professors thereof in all places, especially in these three kingdomes ever since the Reformation of Religion, and how much their rage, power and presumption, are of late, and at this time increased and exercised; whereof the deplorable state of the Church and kingdom of Ireland, the distressed estate of the Church and Kingdom of England, and the dangerous estate of the Church and Kingdom of Scotland, are present and publique Testimonies. We have now at last, (after other meanes of Supplication, Remonstrance, Protestations, and Sufferings) for the preservation of our selves and our Religion, from utter Ruine and Destruction: according to the commendable practice of these Kingdoms in former times, and the Example of Gods people in other Nations; After mature deliberation, resolved and determined to enter into a mutuall and solemn Legue and Covenant, wherein we all subscribe, and each one of us for himself, with our hands lifted up to the most high God, do sweare.

Panel 2 (top right)

I will purge out from among you the Rebells, & them that transgresse against me.

IV. We shall also with all faithfulnesse endeavour the discovery of all such as have beene, or shall be Incendiaries, Malignants, or evill Instruments, by hindering the Reformation of Religion, dividing the king from his people, or one of the kingdoms from another, or making any faction or parties amongst the people, contrary to this league & Covenant that they may be brought to publick triall, and receive condigne punishment, as the degree of their offences shall require or deserve, or the supreame Iudicatories of both kingdoms respectively, or others having power from them for that effect, shall judge convenient.

A Malignant   *A Preist*

I will bring the Counsell of the Oulde Iosurne, &c.

Panel 3 (second row left)

I. That we shall sincerely, really and constantly, through the Grace of God, endeavour in our severall places and callings, the preservation of the Reformed Religion in the Church of Scotland, in Doctrine, Worship, Discipline & Government against our comon Enemies, the reformation of Religion in the kingdomes of England and Ireland, in Doctrine, Worship, Discipline and Government, according to the Word of God, and the Example of the best Reformed Churches, And shall endeavour to bring the Churches of God in the three kingdoms, to the neerest conjunction and Uniformity in Religion, Confession of Faith, Form of Church government, Directory for Worship and Catechising: That we and our posterity after us may as Brethren, live in Faith and Love, and the Lord may delight to dwell in the midst of us.

Thou hast avouched y Lorde this day to be thy God and to walke in his wayes, and to keepe his Statutes & his Commandements & his Iudgements & to hearken to his voyce. And the Lord hath avouched thee this day to be his peculiar people & to make thee high above all nations, in praise in name & in honour. Deut.26: 17: 18:

Panel 4 (second row right)

V

And whereas the happinesse of a blessed Peace between these kingdoms, denyed in former times to our Progenitors, is by the good Providence of God granted unto us, and hath been lately concluded and setled by both Parliaments, we shall each one of us, according to our place and interest, endeavour that they may remain conjoyned in a firme Peace and Union to all posterity, And that Iustice may be done upon the wilfull Opposers thereof, in manner expressed in the precedent Article.

A threfold corde is not easily broken

Scotland   *England*   *Ireland*

Panel 5 (third row left)

II. That we shall in like manner, without respect of persons, indeavour the extirpation of Popery, Prelacie, (that is Church government by Arch-Bishops, Bishops, their Chancellors and Comissaries, Deans, Deans and Chapters, Archdeacons, & all other Ecclesiasticall Officers depending on that Hierarchy) Superstition, Heresie, Schisme, Prophanenesse, and whatsoever shall be found to be contrary to sound Doctrine, and the power of Godlinesse: lest we partake in other mens sins, and therby be in danger to receive of their plagues, and that the Lord may be one, and his Name one in the three kingdoms.

Euery plant which our heavenly Father hath not planted shall be rooted up.

Coristers   Singing   Dorsal

Panel 6 (third row right)

VI. We shall also according to our places & callings in this common cause of Religion, Liberty and Peace of the kingdomes, assist and defend all those that enter into this League and Covenant, in the maintaining & pursuing thereof, and shall not suffer our selves directly or indirectly by whatsoever combination, persuasion or terror to be devided & withdrawn from this blessed Union & conjunction, whether to make defection to the contrary part, or to give our selves to a detestable indifferency or neutrality in this cause which so much concerneth the glory of God, the good of the kingdoms, and honour of the king; but shall all the dayes of our lives zealously and constantly continue therein against all opposition, and promote the same according to our power, against all Lets and impediments whatsoever; an what we are not able our selves to suppresse or overcome, we shall reveale and make known, that it may be timely prevented or removed: All which we shall do as in the sight of God.

And his heart shalbe against the holy Covenant. Dan.11.28

Panel 7 (bottom left)

III. We shall with the same sincerity, reality and constancy, in our severall Vocations, endeavour with our estates and lives, mutually to preserve the Rights and Priviledges of the Parliaments, and the Liberties of the kingdomes, and to preserve and defend the kings Majesties person and authority, in the preservation and defence of the true Religion, and Liberties of the kingdomes, that the World may beare witnesse with our consciences of our Loyaltie, and that we have no thoughts or intentions to diminish his Majesties just power and greatnesse.

The Lord will Create upon every dwelling place of Mount Sion, & upon her Assemblies.

a Cloud and smoke by day and a shining of a flaming Fire by night, for upon all the glory shall be a defence, Isaiah 4. 5

House of Lords.   *House of Commons*

Panel 8 (bottom right)

And because these kingdoms are guilty of many sins & provocations against God, & his Son Iesus Christ, as is too manifest by our present distresses and dangers the fruits thereof, We professe and declare before God and the world, our unfayned desire to be humbled for our sins, & for the sins of these Kingdoms especially, that we have not as we ought, valued the inestimable benefit of the Gospel, that we have not laboured for the purity and power thereof, and that we have not endeavoured to receive Christ in our hearts, not to walk worthy of him in our lives, which are the causes of other sins and transgressions, so much abounding amongst us; And our true and unfayned purpose, desire, and endeavour for our selves and all others under our power and charge, both in publick and in private, in all duties we owe to God, and man, to amend our lives, and each one to go before another in the example of a reall Reformation, that the Lord may turne away his wrath, and heavy indignation, and establish these Churches and kingdoms in truth and peace. And this Covenant we make in the presence of almighty God, the Searcher of all hearts, with a true intention to performe the same, as we shall answer at that great day when the secrets of all hearts shall be disclosed. Most humbly beseeching the Lord to strengthen us by his Holy Spirit for this end, and to blesse our desires and proceedings with such successe, as may be deliverance and safety to his people, & encouragement to other Christian Churches groaning under or in danger of the yoake of Anti-christian Tyranny, to joyne in the same, or like Associations and Covenants, to the glory of God, the enlargement of the kingdoms of Iesus Christ, and the peace and tranquility of Christian kingdoms & Commonwealths.

I am he.   *Gone but I am he.*

Come let us joyn our selves to the Lord in the bands of the Covenant, the hands of the glory of God, he will teach us of his wayes & we will walke in his paths. Isaiah 2.3

THE CIVIL WARS IN THE THREE KINGDOMS (1642–1651)

Englishmen were at war amongst themselves. So were the Irish and as many as 20,000 English and Scots troops were soon in Ireland propping up the Protestant and settler interest there. In due course the Scots entered the English civil war in order, as they hoped, to secure a Presbyterian church settlement throughout the British archipelago and a constitutional union along federal lines. But the decision gave Charles's remaining friends in Scotland (headed by the Marquis of Montrose) the chance to open up civil war there. With Irish Catholic troops crossing to Britain to take part in that conflict and Charles seeking to negotiate a deal with the Catholic Irish Confederacy, there was indeed a war of three kingdoms.

Levels of violence and destruction differed widely from region to region; the least affected areas were East Anglia and Kent; the most affected Ulster, the Western Highlands of Scotland, and the Severn and Thames valleys of England. Almost every borough was garrisoned and defended by hastily thrown-up earthworks that involved the pulling down of suburbs. More than one hundred towns were besieged for a month or longer—some, like Newark and Chester, for many months. There were twenty battles on English soil involving more than 10,000 men and perhaps forty involving more than 5,000 men. Battles in Ireland and Scotland tended to involve fewer men and fewer prisoners but far higher casualties. For much of 1643, 1644, and 1645 there were 150,000 men in arms in England alone (about one in eight of all males between the ages of 16 and 50) and over 200,000 in arms throughout the archipelago. There was a higher proportion fighting and dying than in the Great War of 1914–18. The war was won by the parliamentarians because they won the really important battles (Marston Moor, 2 July 1644; Naseby, 14 June 1645); because they improvised more effectively, regrouped their forces more successfully (especially in the New Model Army created by the fusion of three run-down armies in the winter of 1644/5), and kept their troops paid and supplied for longer. All this meant imposing taxes at ten times pre-war levels, imposing excise duty on necessities such as beer and salt, and borrowing from London merchants on the security of the lands previously owned by the bishops and the cathedral chapters. It may be too that many more of the parliamentarian than of the royalist officers and men had a fervent belief that God was on their side and it showed in the actions undertaken by the self-made godly colonels and generals of whom Oliver Cromwell and John Lambert were a type.

By the early summer of 1646 Charles I had run out of armies and out of supplies to raise new armies. He surrendered to his enemies and settled down to play on the differences that had opened up amongst them: English versus Scots; rival slates of would-be counsellors and ministers; supporters of alternative but incompatible church settlements; civilians versus unpaid soldiers; and ultimately those who could not envisage settlement with him and those who could.

Parliamentarians had gone to war to protect the King from himself, to prevent him from surrounding himself with panders and sycophants who were indifferent to, if not admirers of, popery; and to new model the Church, to cleanse it of popish remnants—'to throw to the moles and the bats every rag that which hath not God's stamp and name upon it' as the preacher Stephen Marshall put it in 1641. They wanted a cleansed but coercive Church of which the whole nation would be voluntary or involuntary members. No one publicly and very few privately sought either the abolition of monarchy or liberty for tender consciences in matters of religion. But as the political structures disintegrated under the sheer functional radicalism of a total war, so unthinkable thoughts began to be thought.

Muskets fired by inserting smouldering cord into the breach of a matchlock may have been an advance on the bow and arrow, but it remained a very cumbersome and tricky operation.

For most parliamentarians the horrors of the late 1640s—massive debt, an unpaid army living off the land, harvest failure, trade recession—could not but induce a sense of futility and emptiness. And as they looked around, they saw evidence of a world falling apart; and they read or heard about all-too-credible stories of men (and women too) taking advantage of the collapse of authority to set up conventicles, to baptize horses, and other blasphemies. Others openly petitioned for manhood suffrage, for the return of the enclosed commons to the common people, even—it was said—for the levelling of men's estates. No wonder so many inside and outside Parliament believed that they had procured a remedy worse than the disease of mild royal tyranny. Settlement, *any* settlement, was better than continuing crisis. Put a (surely?) chastened King back in charge and hope for the best. But those who had fought and seen their colleagues die in the war of 1642–6 would not stomach a sell-out. Twice, in August 1647 and more completely in early December 1648, the army marched on London, purged the Parliament, and laid its own demands before the King. But between these two military *coups* came the second civil war, as the King, as ever too impatient to wait for things to fall naturally into his hands, once more raised three kingdoms in arms.

The first civil war had seen some bloody action—Prince Rupert's sacking of Bolton and Leicester most obviously—and much killing in hot blood. But it had been conceived as a war in which two sides both claiming divine favour awaited God's judgement on their causes. Defeated generals and garrison commanders were not court-martialled or killed in cold blood. In 1648, they were. The New Model generals treated their opponents as men who had committed sacrilege, who were seeking to overturn the judgement of God. If the royalist commanders at the sieges of Pembroke and Colchester or after the battle of Preston could be tried and shot or beheaded, then how much more could the author of the whole war, King Charles I, be tried and executed. As early as April 1648 the Army leaders branded the King as a 'Man of Blood', a chilling biblical phrase from the book of Numbers. A Man of Blood was a man against whom God sought vengeance for the slaughter of the Lord's People; the Army was appointing itself the agent of divine vengeance on a man whose sacrilegious acts demanded punishment by death. In January 1649 the Army demanded the trial of the King, packed the commission that tried him, and presided at his public execution outside the Banqueting House in Whitehall. It was an act typical

of the whole Revolution: it was accomplished by men who knew what they would not have, but not what they would have.

5. *The British Republic*

The execution of Charles I was followed by the Parliament of England abolishing Stuart monarchy in England and in Ireland (but not Scotland). It proclaimed the English right to determine the constitutional status of Ireland which presaged the extraordinarily effective and ruthless conquest of that island by Oliver Cromwell. Within two years he succeeded where English armies had so often failed, in a complete military subjugation. The Long Parliament had already pledged two million pounds worth of Irish land to those who had adventured cash to set forth the armies of the early 1640s; now an equal sum was pledged to pay the wages of the soldiers in the army of conquest. Even though the original plan to execute 100,000 of the Irish for their part in the massacres and rebellion and to herd the rest of the Catholic community into the western province of Connaught proved to be beyond the administrative capacity of the English Commonwealth, more than one-third of the land of Ireland was

CROMWELL stormed Drogheda in September 1649 and called the slaughter of the 3,500 men of a garrison 'a just judgement of God upon those barbarous wretches that have imbrued their hands in so much innocent blood'. In fact the town had never been held by the Irish Confederacy and most of the garrison were English.

confiscated and redistributed to English investors or demobilized soldiers. A new proprietorial class lorded it over a resentful native population. With the total disestablishment of the Church of Ireland and an army of occupation guaranteeing complete religious freedom, Ireland certainly experienced a revolution in the 1650s, and one that was not reversed at the Restoration.

The Rump Parliament abolished Stuart monarchy in England and Ireland, but it did not seek to abolish it in Scotland. As far as the English were concerned, the Union of the crowns of England and Scotland was severed and Scotland was freed to follow its own historical path. Only when the Scots, refusing to see any historical destiny for themselves outside a federal union of the British kingdoms, first proclaimed and then crowned Charles II as King of Britain, did the army of the English Commonwealth follow up its victories over the Irish with an invasion, conquest,

A VIVID republican account of Charles II's attempts to regain his thrones with the assistance of a motley collection of papists, presbyterians, and episcopalians.

A MAD DESIGNE: OR, A Description of the King of Scots marching in his Disguise, after the Rout at Worcester, With the Particulers where He was, and what He and his Company did, every day and night after He fled from WORCESTER.

and incorporation of Scotland into an enhanced English state. The Scottish Parliament and executive council were abolished, the power of the Scottish nobility emasculated (or at any rate suspended and deep-frozen) by the abolition of their local jurisdiction and by the conversion of their tenants into secure copyholders. English judges were sent north to assimilate Scottish law to English law. In 1654 Scotland (like Ireland) was invited to send thirty representatives to a 460-member English Parliament, but those chosen were mostly those nominated by the colonial administrators sent to run Scotland. The Scottish Church was not disestablished, but wherever English garrisons were planted, the soldiers planted and nurtured separatist religious groups. This too represents something very like a revolution; albeit one aborted in 1660 when the Scottish aristocracy clambered back to power. It was an early example of constitutional cryogenics.

So the execution of the King presaged revolutions in Ireland and in Scotland; but barely so in England. By the summer of 1649 Stuart monarchy, the House of Lords, and the Established Church were abolished; soon four million pounds worth of Crown, Church, and 'malignant' royalist lands were sold off (perhaps 10 per cent of the land of England), but much of it passed to those who had already owned or worked it or who were already substantial landowners. And there were some very radical calls for much more fundamental change: in Surrey, Berkshire, and Northamptonshire small groups occupied wastelands and established short-lived communes in which property was held in common; strident voices could be heard demanding an end to primogeniture, the conversion of copyholds into freehold, the overturn of 'illegal' enclosures. Utopians called for a host of agricultural innovations based on new scientific principles; religious fundamentalists called for the end of professional lawyers and a new law code short enough to fit into a pocket-book and based on the law of Moses. The 1650s were a decade of strong language and bold gestures; but those who controlled the Army and therefore the country were unmoved. The lawcourts changed their language but not their process; existing property rights were upheld, even the right of the clergy to tithes; Exchequer, Chancery, Assizes, Commissions of the Peace, all the institutions below the very top of government were confirmed and reinvigorated. Power within the existing structures was still possessed by many of the families who had held it before the civil wars. There was a shift of power *within* the gentry but not *from* the gentry.

The abolition of the main distinguishing features of the Church of England—bishops, church courts, Book of Common Prayer, Thirty-Nine Articles—and the expulsion of perhaps one in three of the incumbent clergy did not mean that there was a religious revolution. The parish structure was largely unaffected, and the gentry held on to most of their patronage and financial control of local churches. Successive regimes remained committed to there being *a* national Church of which all men and women were entitled to be members. They allowed each parish to determine its own form of worship and practice; as a consequence by the end of the decade at least a third and perhaps a half of the parishes were using at least parts of the old Anglican Prayer Book.

Alongside this decentralized and largely non-coercive national Church was a broad measure of toleration. All Protestants who accepted the principle that God had revealed himself and his purposes in the Bible, who accepted the creeds, and who were committed to living in peace with their Christian brethren were free to establish their own Christian communities. This allowed the Baptists and other Congregationalist groups to flourish; but those who denied the divinity of Christ were persecuted, as were the Quakers whose militant non-violent protests against tithes and against the heartless preaching by 'hireling priests' in their steeple houses brought the full

THE QVAKERS DREAM:

OR,

The Devil's Pilgrimage in England:

BEING

An infallible Relation of their several Meetings,

Shreekings, Shakings, Quakings, Roarings, Yellings, Howlings, Trembliggs in the Bodies, and Rlnngs In the Bullies; With a Narrative of their several Arguments, Tenets, Principles, and strange Doctrine: The strange and wonderful Satanical Apparitions, and the appearing of the Devil unto them in the likeness of a black Boar, a Dog with flaming eys, and a black man without a head, causing the Dogs to bark, the Swine to cry, and the Cattel to run, to the great admiration of all that shall read the same.

London, Printed for *G. Horton*, and are to be sold at the Royal Exchange in Cornhil, 1655.

THE Quakers were a populist evangelical movement which drew huge crowds by the 1650s. To their enemies amongst the orthodox Puritan godly, they were a byword not so much for self-expression as self-indulgence and indulgence of the things of the flesh.

weight of local authorities vindictively down on them. Most spectacular in probing the soft underbelly of Interregnum liberalism and provoking a vicious counter was James Nayler, who rode into Bristol in 1656 re-enacting Christ's entry into Jerusalem in order to demonstrate that Jesus is in everyone (but especially in James Nayler) and who was then hauled before Parliament to be punished for a blasphemy against which many felt there ought to have been a law. Unluckily for Nayler, the vote to have him executed narrowly failed; and the Parliament then passed a hideous series of orders for various parts of his upper body to be bored, branded, or beaten prior to his perpetual imprisonment without heat or access to paper. Unsurprisingly he died in prison a few months later. There was more liberty in the 1650s than ever before; but at a cost.

Brooding over this at best attenuated revolution was the Army and its presiding genius, Oliver Cromwell. From 1649 to 1653 the Army was too busy conquering Ireland and Scotland to put its mind to long-term political settlements. The Generals therefore indulged the fantasies of those intellectuals who had wrung their hands in disapproving but paralysed indecision at the time of the Regicide but who now drew on Roman and Renaissance Italian republican theory to plan what they hoped would be an enlightened humanist oligarchy. These men—John Milton, Algernon Sidney, Henry Vane, Oliver St John prominent amongst them—were élitists unsullied by Calvinist conversion experiences, deeply anticlerical, ready to jettison ancient constitutionalism and to embrace kinglessness. They were not democrats, and their deepest conviction was that they should be allowed to create a system that guaranteed men as enlightened as themselves perpetually to govern. In the meantime they were happy to play a dominant role in the unicameral legislature/executive formed from that fraction of the Long Parliament who had accepted Pride's Purge of December 1648 and the subsequent Regicide. Many of these 'classical republicans' admired most the merchant Regent Governors of Holland and they fantasized about creating a federal union of Britain and the Netherlands.

Not surprisingly, once the Army was free of its other commitments it fell out with these high-minded self-deceivers and in April 1653 Cromwell, as Lord General, used force to drive them from office. In its place he summoned a constituent assembly nominated by the Army Council and consisting of men whom he and his fellow officers believed had 'the root of the matter in them'. They were given eighteen months to find a more permanent form of government and—in Cromwell's anguished words—to find a way to equip the people to take up the responsibilities of freedom. Freedom from tyranny could only be turned into true freedom if the people turned from the things of the flesh to the things of the spirit. Until that time, the forms would have to be those which were 'for the people's good, not what pleases them'. Cromwell wanted each of this godly assembly to contribute the fragment of the truth he had been vouchsafed to the building of the mosaic of God's truth. It was characteristic of Cromwell that while he ached for them to follow God's will, he hectored them and then left them to their own devices. He was always uncomfortable with power and preferred to see himself as a constable to the nation, keeping the peace while others made the laws. In fact he created a political Tower of Babel and after five months the Assembly resigned, handing power back into his hands.

Immediately Major-General John Lambert proposed the adoption of a paper constitution (the Instrument of Government) based on the proposals for a limited monarchy that the Army leaders had been working on in the later 1640s, with a single person as head of state presiding over a powerful executive council and constrained to meet regularly with Parliaments from which convicted royalists were excluded and with modest adjustments to the franchise. Initially it seems that Cromwell would serve as a constitutional monarch within this framework but, constrained by his own scruples, he was finally sworn in under the title of Lord Protector.

Uneasy lies the head that wears no crown. The very title 'Lord Protector' recalled the royal dukes who ruled for their infant nephews. Ambiguities simply mounted when Cromwell agreed to a parliamentary revision of the constitution in 1657 which turned him into King in all but name: he was installed in a ceremony based on royal coronations, he created his own Upper House, his coins showed him with royal regalia. Yet he held out against taking the title.

As Protector, Cromwell was constrained to work with and through a council of state comprising his closest colleagues in the Army and a group of pragmatic lawyers and landowners. He was constrained to meet Parliament regularly (but he and his council imposed an oath that more than a quarter of the first Parliament refused, preventing them from retaining their seats; and they arbitrarily suspended more than a quarter of those elected to the second Parliament).

On the other hand, he was unconstrained by custom and precedent. Thus, in the period between his first installation and the meeting of his first Parliament, he and his council approved seventy ordinances enforceable as statute in the courts; he and his council divided the country up into eleven areas ('cantons' said his critics) over each of which he placed a senior army officer with sweeping powers to tax all former royalists, to create a more effective militia made up largely of demobbed army veterans, and to supervise the work of local magistrates; and he and his council locked up without trial those he held to be blasphemous, those he thought might be plotting against him, and those who challenged his constitutional right to collect excise tax. He once said: 'if nothing were done but what is according to law, the throat of this nation might be cut while we send for some to make a law'. It was a tyrant's plea.

Paradoxically, it was the lawyers and the civilians who tempted him to take the crown in 1657, telling him 'kingship is known to the laws'; and because he believed deep down that tying

♥ King	♥ Queen	♥ Knave	♥ I

The Saints think it meet that the Rump make a League w. Oneale	The Damnable engagement to be true and Faithfull.	Hugh Peters shews the bodkins and thimbles given by the wives of Wap. pin for the good old cause.	A Comitte of Godwin Ny & Peters and Owen discovering the marks of Grace in Ministers.

♥ II	♥ III	♥ IIII	♥ V

Onsley Father and Sonne	St Gibert Gerard and his two sonns.	The Rump roasted salt it well it stinks exceedingly.	The E. of Pem: in y H. of Com. tha nks y Speaker for his Admission.

♥ VI	♥ VII	♥ VIII	♥ IX

Worsley an Inckle Weaver a man of Personal Valor.	Nathaniel Fines whereby hangs a tale.	Lambert K. of y Golden Tulip.	Huson the Cobler entring London.

♥ X
The Rump and dregs of the house of Com remaining after the good members were purged out.

THOSE 120 or so MPs who sat on after Pride's Purge and the trial and execution of Charles I (the 'Rump') were eventually thrown out by Cromwell in April 1653, briefly restored to power at the fall of the Protectorate in 1659, and demonized by the Restoration— as on this set of playing cards.

himself down to work within the web of ancient constitutionalism would deny him the freedom to build God's new model kingdom in England, amongst God's new chosen people, he could never agree. He was a man 'not wedded and glued to forms of government'; neither was he a man who could bring himself to take up that which divine providence had destroyed and laid in the dust. A year later—on 3 September 1658—after several months of physical and mental decline, he died.

With Oliver gone, there was no one who could hold together an army once more slipping into serious arrears, let alone combine the yearnings of the radicals for a state that defended indefeasible natural rights such as the right to freedom of religious expression, with those who hoped that the change of political institutions at the top need not affect the natural social order. Throughout the 1650s the House of Stuart was unable to mobilize more than a feeble armed uprising in support of a Restoration. But time was now on their side. Richard Cromwell was forced to resign in May 1659; the army then split into factions as to what to do next. There were *coups* and counter *coups*. By December 1659 there were weeks with no government of any sort. The chaos was ended when the apolitical General in charge of the army of occupation in Scotland— George Monck—led his well-paid troops south, brushing aside opposition from the disintegrating English divisions, occupied London, recalled the surviving members of the Long Parliament as it had been on the eve of Pride's Purge in December 1648, and stood back as that assembly determined there should be fresh elections for a Convention based on the pre-war franchise. Convicted royalists were allowed to vote but not to stand as candidates (although their sons who had been too young to be implicated in the wars could be and were elected in large numbers). Monck stood inscrutably by, his true intentions irrecoverable.

The Convention met and the presumption was that it would negotiate the return of the King on terms similar to those accepted by his father just before Pride's Purge. In anticipation of this, and to sound as reassuring as possible, Charles issued his Declaration from Breda, promising that he would accept Parliament's determination of all the most contentious issues—indemnity, the rights of the dispossessed and the new purchasers of land confiscated and sold by successive regimes between 1646 and 1660, the disbandment of the army, and how best to procure 'liberty for tender consciences'.

In the event this Declaration was greeted by an almost involuntary spasm of loyalism that took the members as much as everyone else by surprise. On 8 May they voted unanimously to restore the King without prior conditions (though not, as we will see, unconditionally).

6. *The Restoration in England and Wales*

Monarchy, House of Lords, the Church of England were all restored in 1660. But stability was not restored with them.

The basic principle of the Restoration was—as the Convention Parliament proclaimed on 8 May—that 'it can no way be doubted but that His Majesty's right and title to this Crown and kingdom is and was every way completed by the death of his most royal father of blessed memory, without the ceremony or solemnity of a proclamation.' After the failure of Cromwell's political eschatology and the futility of paper constitutionalism, there was a dramatic reassertion of ancient constitutionalism, of historical-rootedness. The presumption was that the coral reef of precedent, custom, and statute that had grown up to define the powers of the Crown would protect the liberties of the subject more than any alternative solution could.

Yet Charles II could not govern like Charles I. Although all the ordinances of the Long Parliament and of the Interregnum regimes were declared null and void (as lacking royal assent), the reforming legislation of 1641 was in place. That legislation had swept away the 'prerogative' courts (such as the Star Chamber and the High Commission). It had also swept away all the prerogative forms of revenue (such as Ship Money and coat and conduct money) which Charles I had claimed the authority to raise in what *he* deemed political emergencies; and those feudal revenues his predecessors had been tempted to exploit for financial gain and political loss were abolished in return for fixed and permanent excises and a hearth tax (an acceptable form of poll tax). It did not remove the King's freedom to choose his own ministers and counsellors; nor his sole control of the armed forces of the nation. No major measure approved by Charles I in 1641 was repealed in the early Restoration and only one was significantly modified—in 1664 a new Triennial Act was passed which abandoned the 1641 principle of mandatory elections every third year and simply provided for a session of Parliament at least every third year. This allowed Charles to hold almost annual sessions of the loyalist Parliament elected in 1661 until he finally dissolved it in 1679. And the Triennial Act of 1664 was so toothless that when Charles violated it by not calling a Parliament in the last four years of his reign, there was nothing to be done.

Historical-rootedness made the men of 1660 unenthusiastic about hedging kingship with more restrictions than had been agreed in 1641. Three other developments initially contributed to this reluctance.

The first was the personality of Charles II. He appeared to be the opposite of his father. He was all things to all men; and he was determined to bring into government all but the hardline republicans. He offered positions in his Council and at his Court indiscriminately to old royalists, those parliamentarians who had fought against his father but baulked at regicide (popularly if misleadingly known as Presbyterians), and even Cromwellians (George Monck was a General and Edward Montagu an Admiral under both Cromwell and Charles). Those who did least well were those who had suffered most, especially those who had been in exile—Charles did not want men with grudges in power, and he recognized that those whom he could most afford to offend were the most fanatical royalists. Nine Regicides were executed (and as many locked up for prolonged periods); the corpses of Cromwell, Ireton, and Bradshaw were dug up and their skeletons hanged and then cast into a pit; and assassination squads periodically sought out republican exiles but usually failed in the missions. So there was a vindictive side to Charles's nature. But he did genuinely seek to accommodate all who wished to be accommodated. This was a truth reinforced by his determination to ensure that those who had gained lands from the land sales of the Interregnum should be adequately compensated. Again, it was ex-royalists, especially those compelled to honour mortgages taken out to repurchase confiscated land or to pay heavy fines to their opponents, who lost most. No wonder there was a grim and ironic joke hissed out by many of them at the time—that the Act of Indemnity and Oblivion which cancelled out the political crimes of all but a handful of the most incorrigible was, in fact, an act of indemnity for the King's enemies and of oblivion for his friends.

The great exception to this principle of power sharing was in the Church. In 1660 the King attempted a similar policy. He attempted to loosen the terms of membership of the Church of England so that most of those who had worked within the Cromwellian Church could accommodate themselves to it—a policy of 'comprehension'; and he invited many leading moderate Puritans to take up bishoprics and deaneries. In addition he proposed a broad measure of toleration outside the national Church for Roman Catholics and Protestants whose consciences were too tender for them to enter the state Church. But amidst escalating distrust on all sides, and faced by relentless pressure from the gentry in the Cavalier Parliament for a Church which restored a narrow conformity to the words and rubrics of the Elizabethan Church, Charles abandoned the search for 'comprehension' and allowed the vindictive Act of Uniformity of 1662. Altogether one in four of the clergy left the Church by the end of that year, with disastrous long-term consequences. Charles did not fight very hard for comprehension, but he did fight hard, and returned often to that fight, for toleration. But his insistence that it must include Catholics as well as Protestant Nonconformists led to defeat after defeat for his attempts.

The second development was that the established gentry families who dominated the Parliaments of the 1660s sought to achieve a very considerable decentralization of power. It was their intention to give the Crown a healthy annual revenue (well above Charles I's one million pounds per annum in the 1630s), a strong militia, and loyal and Anglican borough corporations; but they ensured that the implementation of all the new policies was firmly in gentry hands with only limited control from the political centre. The gentry used Parliament not to increase parliamentary power (the experience of the 1640s and 1650s was that Parliament was as capable of tyrannical actions as the Crown) but to increase gentry power; and the Crown went along with this programme. The greatest single demonstration of this lies in the ecclesiastical legislation of 1662–70 which allowed the gentry (not the church courts) extensive discretionary power to police religious conformity and uniformity.

What made this decentralization all the more feasible was the easing of the economic and social strains occasioned by the population growth and inflation of the century and more before 1640. Throughout the later

THIS portrait of the Duchess of Cleveland and her bastard son by Charles II, portrayed as Madonna and the infant Jesus, is a powerful statement of the amoral as well as the immoral culture of the Restoration Court.

seventeenth century population levels—aided by record levels of emigration especially of fertile young adults—stabilized, and prices with them. The massive programmes of intervention by the state to keep order and prevent widespread suffering could be stood down. There was less that the state *had* to do.

Thirdly, then, Charles turned out to be a King with very little political vision and therefore he made little use of the powers to which he was restored. He had policy preferences—he genuinely believed in religious toleration, especially for a Catholic community that had stood by and suffered with his family in the time of troubles; and he had a strong preference for a foreign policy alignment with France—but he was unwilling to push those preferences to confrontation and tended to back off when the political temperature rose. Essentially he was a man whose youth and adolescence had been taken up with a burning passion to become King; once he sat on the throne he had no passion left to *do* anything as King other than stay on the throne. He had no vision that might constitute a threat to anyone's interests.

One consequence of such a personality was that he neglected the business of government. Anxious to please as many people as possible, he doubled the size of his Privy Council to more than seventy, making it unmanageable both as a deliberative and as an enforcement body. It became more and more flabby and marginal. Day-to-day responsibility passed to the principal officers of state, especially the Secretaries of State and the Treasurer (or Treasury Commissioners). Policy was made on the hoof, by small knots of counsellors or confidants called into Charles's private quarters at all hours. In the medium term this caused great resentment and fear amongst those who began to fear a new popish plot to undermine government, but in the short term it helped to emasculate that most characteristic of all Tudor institutions, the argus-eyed Privy Council that—unlike most other royal councils—not only deliberated, but *did* things.

The problem with all this is that it left the fundamental problems that had produced the Civil War unresolved. The King headed an executive that was appointed by and answerable only to him. Amongst the responsibilities of the King and those appointed by him were the formulation of foreign policy, decisions about the making of war and peace; and the policing of a religious settlement in which the King himself had no confidence.

If the King and his ministers made foreign policy, only Parliament could fund it. The incorporation of the 1641 reforms into the Restoration package made this more true than ever; and with the Crown now reduced to an income from land representing only 5 per cent in real terms of what had been realized in the 1540s, the Crown had even run out of collateral for loans other than to anticipate future parliamentary tax income. Some mechanism for ensuring that royal foreign policy was acceptable to Parliament had to be found.

It is possible that the second major source of instability was in fact the greater: a comprehensive political settlement was yoked to a narrow, persecuting Anglican religious settlement, with the consequences spelt out in Chapter 14. The Anglican Parliament passed a whole battery of laws against those who attended religious assemblies outside the Established Church, and the King regularly tried to use his prerogative to prevent their enforcement or relied on the benign neglect of sympathetic magistrates, especially in the towns. And yet, at times when it was politically expedient, he would hunt with the Cavalier pack and run with the Anglican hounds. The inconsistency of royal policy only exacerbated divisions within local communities and created the greatest single source of political division that was to culminate in the emergence of two dis-

S IR Peter Lely's portrait of the ageing Cromwell (*left*) leaves us in no doubt about how he viewed himself—as the general, protecting the Commonwealth from internal and external foes; and as the puritan statesman, caring little for the trappings of greatness.

S IR Thomas Fairfax (*below, left*) combined decisiveness as a general (he led the New Model Army from 1645 to 1650) with indecisiveness as a politician. He opposed the trial and execution of the King, but stood by unmoving as his subordinates staged the coup that led on to that very regicide and to the abolition of monarchy.

A NTHONY Ashley Cooper (*below*), first Earl of Shaftsbury, was a man of contradictions. A royalist turned parliamentarian in the 1640s, he in turn held office under, and then opposed, both Cromwell and Charles II. The latter's Lord Chancellor (1672–5), he became the leading exclusionist (1678–81). Perhaps the most consistent thread in an inconsistent career was a passionate commitment to religious toleration.

tinctive political ideologies, and just possibly two parties, the Tories and the Whigs. For thirty years the country hung between a lingering commitment to the notion of the confessional state and a recognition of the fact that religious pluralism was a fact of life.

7. *Ireland and Scotland*

The other major unfinished business of the Restoration was the problem of Triple Monarchy, the relationship of England, Ireland, and Scotland and their peoples. The archipelagic dimension of later Stuart history arose less from the degree of interaction between the component nations and kingdoms than from the unnatural degree of isolation of each from the others. After the early Stuart push for some form of integrative union, and after the ruthless process of incorporation witnessed in the 1650s, the startling thing about the Restoration settlement from the British perspective is the dis-integration of the polity.

Charles II entrusted the government of Scotland entirely to Scotsmen—for much of the reign the formidable Duke of Lauderdale—and the government of Ireland principally to members of the Protestant communities of Ireland, most notably to the Old English Protestant Duke of Ormonde. Foreign policy continued to be made for all kingdoms by English ministers and was ratified as and when necessary by an English Privy Council with a number of Irish and Scottish Lords sitting on it. Under the renewed Navigation Acts, Scottish merchants were more rigorously excluded from English colonial markets than they were before the wars, and discriminatory tariffs were raised against the import of goods from Ireland and Scotland that would compete with English goods (e.g. Irish linens and Irish hides for the leather industry). Yet in the thirty years after 1660 there were few in any of the kingdoms who called for a change in the constitutional relationship between them.

The Scottish nobility needed time to lick their wounds, recover their fortunes, and fleece their tenants, over whom they resumed a stranglehold. They were content to make a strong collective bond with the restored monarchy in the creation of a fairly autocratic state. Never hitherto had the Council's legal power to use torture against dissidents been so widely deployed. Scotland was restless and there were major rebellions in the later 1660s, 1670s, and mid-1680s, each of which was put down brutally. There were always more English troops stationed in Scotland than in England, and the Scottish Parliament gave the Crown sweeping powers to raise troops to deal with disorder. That disorder stemmed largely from survival of many hardline Covenanters, made all the more incorrigible by persecution.

If the Restoration in England was backdated to 1641, in Scotland it was backdated to 1633 (the year of Charles I's coronation). This meant that Charles II was freed from the constraining bonds

K NOLE, originally an episcopal palace, was massively extended by the Sackvilles from the first Earl's profits in office (as James I's Lord Treasurer he was nicknamed 'Lord Fillsack'). This magnificent closet (*facing, above*) has late seventeenth-century wall-hangings made of rough textured mohair dyed green, watered and stamped to resemble silk damask.

T HIS raised-silk embroidery (*facing, below*) shows, centre, Charles II at the nadir of his fortunes, hiding in the oak tree at Boscobel after his defeat at Worcester in September 1651; fleeing (with his mistress?) on horseback; and then—front left— resplendently crowned at his Restoration in 1660.

JAMES MAITLAND, first Duke of Lauderdale, was a new phenomenon in Scottish politics—effectively Charles II's viceroy. He dominated Scottish politics for two decades and, unlike his ally Archbishop James Sharp who was assassinated, died in his bed.

of the Scottish reform process of 1638–41, but Scots were freed from the radical royal religious innovations of 1633–7. However, this restored bishops as James VI had left them in Scotland (they acted not as diocesan autocrats but as permanent moderators—i.e. chairmen—of diocesan synods and the constituent presbyteries). This, together with the ban on the use of the liturgies and other documents of the Westminster Assembly was too much for many of the clergy. Almost one-third resigned and set up in opposition to the state Church. Although periodically the authorities in Edinburgh tried to ease the terms of membership of the Church so as to lure moderates back in, the spasms of persecution were more intense and vindictive than in England. Thus in 1670 when the English Parliament enacted that repeated offenders in holding illegal conventicles were to be deported, the Scottish Parliament approved the 'clanking act' which included the death sentence for anyone preaching at a conventicle; while in 1677, Scottish landowners were made legally responsible for the religious conformity of their tenants. These extreme measures were the product of Covenanter militancy, and they only served to reinforce it. The climax was the ambush and murder of Archbishop James Sharp as he neared St Andrews in 1679. The brutal suppression of the Cameronian rebellion in the south-west of Scotland, known as the 'killing times', saw a reign of terror unparalleled on mainland Britain in the century, and preceded by a year or two the equally brutal French army suppression of the Huguenot towns in France following Louis XIV's Revocation of the Edict of Nantes. The killing times presided over by the Duke of York, the King's brother and heir to the throne, provoked no great backlash in England.

The Scottish Parliament dominated by these complaisant nobles, and rendered safe by the fact that the single-chamber assembly simply voted yea or nay to proposals put forward by a steering committee effectively chosen by the King or his representative, assisted rather than hindered the growth of royal pretension: in 1681 (as the English Commons sought to pass another Exclusion Bill), the Scottish Parliament declared the inviolability of divine, hereditary right.

The brutalization of the tenants by the lords, and the nobles' contempt for the Covenanters since oppressing them in the 1650s, led to the bitter irony that in 1685 when the Earl of Argyll opposed the accession of the Catholic James VII, neither his tenants nor his peers rose with him.

The Restoration settlement in Ireland consolidated the political power of the Protestant communities and left the Catholic communities marginalized. Its history is dominated by the first Duke of Ormonde. He had been unflinchingly loyal to Charles I, however often that King went behind his back, and he spent much of the Interregnum at the exiled Court. He had two long spells as Viceroy (a title that implied a greater devolved authority in himself as chief executive acting in the King's name), the first from 1662 to 1669, the second from 1679 to 1685. Ormonde held senior office in the English royal household, and was better able than many of his predecessors to get many of his closest friends and clients into key positions around the King, watching out for his interests while he was in Ireland.

The Protestant head of the Catholic Butler clan who had been a major family in south-east Ireland since the Norman settlements there in the twelfth century, Ormonde did not so much straddle and balance the various factions as find himself being denounced by all. Charles sought to square several circles created by the land settlement of the Interregnum, and when the dust settled almost every interest was outraged. The Cromwellian settlers had to surrender less than the one-third originally envisaged, but they resented every acre reclaimed; the Catholics thought the proposed settlement far too harsh and its administration corrupt and falling insultingly short of what was promised. The share of the land owned by Catholics dropped from 59 per cent in 1640 to 22 per cent by the mid-1660s, so there remained a substantial Catholic presence which had no place in government. The Old English, who had been an interest which could not be ignored in Parliament and regional government before 1640, were now politically dispossessed.

The other predominant issue was the religious settlement. Eighty per cent of the population was Catholic, 10 per cent belonged to the Established Church, and 10 per cent to Protestant sects—most notably the Scottish Presbyterians and the Quakers. The basis of the settlement was that only Church of Ireland services were legal and only Church of Ireland members were eligible for office. These were unenforceable laws and only spasmodic attempts were made to enforce them. Viceroys attempted to reach accommodations with the Catholic hierarchy to allow *de facto* toleration if the hierarchy could deliver a guarantee of the political loyalty of their flocks, and much time was wasted trying to draw up binding oaths of loyalty acceptable to the Viceroy and his council, to the Catholic majority, and to Rome. The inevitable result was a bitter division within the Catholic leadership that was useless to the state. But Catholics fared better than those Presbyterians and Congregationalists whom the bishops ruthlessly drove out of the Church of Ireland—Bishop Jeremy Taylor evicted thirty-six Scots from livings in his diocese in a single day. And once outside the Church, Protestant Dissenters were more likely than their Catholic neighbours to feel the weight of the law against illegal conventicles.

In a sense, the Restoration was a breathing-space in Irish history. After a century of aggression, and despite calls for further Plantation, the English rested with what they had, and did not seek to take more; indeed they discouraged those who had settled in Ireland from taking more. But they also had no interest in a closer constitutional or economic relationship with Ireland. Not quite a security threat, not quite a commercial opportunity, the English lost interest in Ireland. Denied what they saw as their just rights to restitution, denied a political voice, and denied the religious freedom they thought both Charles II and his father had promised them, the Irish Catholic community felt even greater alienation from the Anglo-Irish state. And the English-in-Ireland tended to drift from being just that, men and women whose families, property, and vistas straddled the Irish Sea, into a colonial settler community, increasingly frustrated and angered by the kid gloves that Viceroys were required to wear when they dealt with the conquered natives of Ireland. Restoration Ireland was not a happy place.

8. *The Second British Revolution, 1678–1690*

The euphoria of the Restoration did not last long. By the time of the English naval humiliations in the Second Dutch War (1665–7), coinciding with the Plague and the Great Fire of London, disenchantment had set in. There was a tremendous sense of political drift. Charles's Cavalier-Anglican Chancellor, the starchily proper and self-righteous Earl of Clarendon, was blamed for all that had gone wrong and sent on his travels again. Charles turned to a diffuse group of advisers who shared little except the very contempt for the exclusivist pretensions of the Anglican establishment which was deepening within the King himself. The policies associated with this group—especially the alliance with France and a grant of religious toleration founded on the Royal Prerogative—brought Charles into direct conflict with the Cavalier Parliament. In 1673 he was forced to jettison his policies and most of his leading ministers in a humiliating climb-down, which he made without flinching.

Charles had tried tacking against the prevailing political wind. Now he decided (at least in public) that it was easier to sail with it. He therefore gave control of day-to-day government to an Anglican loyalist, the Earl of Danby. Danby governed from the Treasury and his first task was to restore sound finances by improving tax yields, and securing more parliamentary grants. This he achieved by using secret service funds to buy the attendance of naturally loyal back-benchers, and by sweetening their humour by appointing more of them to army commissions and Household or local offices, by strengthening the hand of the bishops and magistrates in identifying and penalizing Dissenters, and by switching to an anti-French and pro-Dutch foreign policy. The keystone was the marriage of the elder daughter of James, Duke of York, to William of Orange, effective ruler of the Netherlands.

It is one of the central paradoxes of the Restoration that it was Danby's period in power (1674–9) which triggered the first great crisis of the Restoration. In 1679 Parliament sought to impeach Danby, the pillar of Cavalier-Anglicanism, on a charge of seeking to introduce popery and arbitrary government. Despite a royal pardon, he was to spend the next five years in the Tower. He took the blame for a King who had cynically used him while subverting his policies if they were too effective. The revelations of Ralph Montagu, a disaffected place-seeker, at the end of 1678, that while Danby was breathing fire against France and securing parliamentary grants to raise a large army, Charles had been assuring Louis he would not use it against him and would like a fat French pension, blew away both his only effective parliamentary manager and the fiction that the King had converted to Cavalier-Anglicanism.

There followed the great Restoration crisis, a revived crisis of those twin and interlocked menaces, 'popery and arbitrary government'. As one MP put it in 1679, 'lay popery flat and there is an end of arbitrary government'—there could be no arbitrary government where there was no

T HIS strip cartoon (*facing*) of the various stages in the investigation of the popish plot makes the Whig case most effectively.

popery. As the Restoration proceeded, the fear of popery revived. This was not only because of Charles's own policies and practices but because although Charles had seventeen children, they were all bastards. By the mid-1670s it seemed probable that Charles would be succeeded by his brother James, and James resigned all his offices in 1673, clear evidence that he had defected to the Roman Catholic Church. Charles now had a Catholic wife, a Catholic mother, a Catholic mistress, a Catholic heir, and (as it became clear in 1673) several Catholic ministers. The shadows of popery returned as they had earlier in the century. The Test Acts, designed to flush out secret papists, drove many out of office. But still the hallmarks of arbitrary government were all too evident to those who wore paranoid glasses—as in Danby's apparent interest in building up a standing army, his corruption of MPs, his persecution of those of tender conscience, his attempt to impose oaths of unconditional allegiance.

The result of all this was a sharp rise in the political humidity which in turn generated a spectacular electrical storm. Allegations of a plot by Catholics near the centre of the Court to assassinate the King and put James on the throne preceded the storm and for three years Charles's regime was rocked to its foundations. In three successive general elections, the spectre of popery and arbitrary government polarized the political nation. Charles, protected by a large Tory majority in the Lords (and gradually by a trade boom that boosted customs revenues and removed much parliamentary leverage), withstood attempts to pass a bill that would have excluded James from the succession. He was a master of political dissimulation: he offered to take his critics into his Council but not into his confidence or into power; he sacrificed more than twenty innocent men to the kangaroo court presided over by a glowering Lord Chief Justice Scroggs; and he offered restrictions on any Catholic successor which did nothing to allay the fears of his subjects that popery and arbitrary government were already knocking on the door.

Just as in 1640 everyone favoured reform but the remedies gradually came to seem to many to be worse than the disease, so in 1679 panic subsided, leaving some committed to reforms which others, inhibited by memories of the 1640s, could and would not go to extremes to achieve. A reaction thus set in and Charles was able to purge the most vociferous Whigs from local and national office, imprison and fine Dissenters of all sorts, and enjoy the financial benefits of a healthy revenue surplus boosted by a pension from Louis XIV.

By 1681 two political ideologies were beginning to crystallize. The first of these ideologies grew out of that involuntary spasm of 8 May 1660—the historical-rootedness of all that underwrote property and liberty. It was an irreducible commitment to the divine right of kings, divine right of the Church, divine right of the gentry. It was a commitment to patriarchalism and social and religious paternalism. This was Toryism.

The second was a commitment to a wide body of notions that come together under the heading of reason and conscience: that forms of government were contingent, rooted less in a prescriptive legal antiquarianism and custom than in the 'public good'; that kings derived their authority from those they governed, perhaps by a formal contract, certainly by an enforceable coronation oath; and that accordingly the people could withdraw obedience from a King who 'contradicted the ends of his own institution'. This political stance frequently accompanied a more open attitude to religious truth; an insistence on the rights of individuals to act in accordance with conscience (the light of reason) and a suspicion of priestcraft and the right of a clerical estate or state to determine matters of belief or practice. Most subscribers to this ideology were liberal Anglicans who had sympathy with the plight of the Dissenters. Many attended both Anglican and Nonconformist worship.

This was Whiggery. It was less elemental and more diffuse than Toryism. It contained a group that was strongly aristocratic: élitist, keenly Erastian, antiformalist; and another that was anti-monarchical, grounded in the populist, democratic republicanism of the 1650s.

There were thus Tory and Whig polarities; but it is by no means clear that there were parties in any recognizable modern sense. Human nature being what it is, many people—especially out in the provinces—mixed elements of these two positions (in particular many combined Whiggish political ideas with Tory religious ones). By 1681 many who had reacted strongly against the Popish Plot and the threat of present and future tyranny had rebounded in the face of their fears of a return to civil war and anarchy. After facing a severe challenge to his power in 1678–81, Charles II was able to achieve a position of relative calm in his final years, although perhaps it was little more than the calm of the 1630s.

It was the essence of Toryism that loyalties to King and Church were indivisible; and that both were seen as underpinning the divine right of the gentry to own property and to govern paternal-istically. While they had stood by James's right to be King, therefore, they had yet to work out how to behave if he turned his private religious belief into public policy. Within three short years, James was to destroy the natural loyalty of Tory Anglicans without securing any other viable power base. By the end of 1688 he was in exile.

James certainly intended to secure a full equality for the Catholics of his three kingdoms. That meant full and equal rights to worship (and therefore not to be second-class citizens, paying tithes and being subject to the jurisdiction of a Protestant Church while attending mass in out-of-the-way places). It meant sharing the buildings, educational institutions, and resources of the Established Church, and it meant having their own bishops. It also meant equal access to secular employments. To offset 150 years of persecution, Catholics were to benefit from a massive

Monmouth's precipitate rebellion in 1685 was a complete failure. Unlike William in 1688, he was unable to secure any support from the nobility and gentry, and his appeal to the Nonconformist craftsmen and traders of the West led to the deaths of 4,000 at the battle of Sedgemoor and in the 'Bloody Assize' that followed.

The Late D. of M. entring Lime with 1500 Men.

The D. of Grafton &c. fighting their way through sever⁰ of y Rebells horse in y lane leading to Philips Norton

Severall of y Kings Forces in search after Ferguson

One Pitts is to be Whipt through every Town in Dorsetshire for Seaven Years together

The Restoration brought an end to military rule but politics remained volatile. Even small electorates could become very boisterous, especially when Charles and James gerrymandered the borough charters. This mayoralty election in Oxford was a case in point.

affirmative action programme, securing positions at every level in government, including the judiciary and armed forces, far beyond their current strength in the population. And it meant that Protestant propaganda was to be silenced and Catholics allowed free rein to balance a historical imbalance. The coping-stone was to secure a parliamentary repeal of the laws that discriminated against Catholics.

James believed that such a programme would cause the scales to fall from the eyes of all but the most bigoted of Protestants. He hoped and expected to leave his throne to a successor—as like as not his Protestant daughter—who would find the Catholic community too large and too loyal for any renewed persecution to be feasible or sensible. In due course Britain would once more be an essentially Catholic country. In the meantime, there was to be a general toleration based on the prerogative. Judges who doubted his right to grant such a toleration, like that majority of judges who opposed his use of the prerogative to allow Catholic officers, would be summarily dismissed. In the whole of the seventeenth century down to 1685, kings had only sacked five judges. James sacked eighteen in just three years. The Dissenters, grateful to him for their relief, would come to prefer the benefits of liberal Catholic rule to the vindictive legalism of Tory-Anglican rule.

For twelve months he deluded himself that the Tory Anglicans whose near monopoly in local and national government—and in the Parliament of 1685—was the product of Charles's last years would go along with this programme. They were, he thought, unswervingly loyal to the Crown. But they were loyal to a package that integrated the interests of Crown, Church, and gentry. James now forced them to make a choice they did everything possible to avoid having to make—to distinguish their loyalties within that package. They continued to denounce resistance by force to him as King (encouraged in that stark fact that he could afford to keep an army of almost 30,000 men in the south of England to discourage thoughts of resistance); but they used every device of casuistry to obstruct his government. By early 1688 James had sacked all the Tory ministers he had inherited from Charles, a majority of the Lords Lieutenant, three-quarters of all JPs, and he had cancelled a majority of all borough charters and given himself the right to nominate the members of most borough corporations, while restricting the right to elect borough MPs to those same members of the corporation. James had in fact set out to pack the House of Commons with his own nominees. The unexpected birth of a son to James's second wife in June 1688 opened up the spectre of a line of Catholic monarchs. The Tories cast around for ways of paralysing his government—by a tax strike, by continuing challenges in the courts, and so on. When William of Orange arrived to challenge James's actions in packing Parliament and to question the legitimacy of the Prince of Wales, very few Tories assisted him; but even fewer assisted James against him. The doctrine of non-resistance did not involve them in lifting so much as a little finger to help a papist King.

Having realized that Tories would not help him, James sought to form an alliance with his erstwhile enemies of Whig and pro-Dissenting views. He offered their leaders office, and their rank and file full religious and civil freedom including political control of the towns. He received only patchy support. Most Dissenters agreed with the Marquis of Halifax that James was hugging them now the better to squeeze them thereafter. It is far from clear that the Dissenters whom James intended to dominate his packed House of Commons would have passed the pro-Catholic legislation he had in mind (and it is even less likely he could have forced it through a fiercely Tory-Anglican House of Lords).

The anxious English were also aware that James's policies in Scotland and (especially) Ireland showed a naked authoritarianism he was concealing in England. He stopped short of meeting Irish Catholic demands for a reversal of the Commonwealth land transfers, but in every other respect he handed power in Ireland over to a Catholic Lord Deputy, Catholic lords, the Catholic bishops, and a Catholic army.

In 1688, however, unlike 1642, England led and Scotland and Ireland followed (though, in truth, it was the Netherlands who led England). William, fearful of losing the reversion of the British crowns, determined to draw Britain into his global conflict with Louis XIV, and encouraged by appeals from a cross-section of the English political élite launched a high-risk invasion across the Channel in November 1688. James, overwrought and perhaps undergoing a nervous breakdown, fled as soon as key sections of his numerically superior army began to desert, first back to London and then to France. In the ensuing months, a political settlement emerged that

WILLIAM came to London both as conquerer and deliverer. The Dutch engravers, unlike the English, are not squeamish about portraying him in both roles.

De ko: van Vrankryk, louis de XIII. ontfangt de ko: van engelant Jacob den tot S: germain en laye daegs na de receptie van de Koningin met Zeeger Pr: van Walles s koninas bastaerden, veele Roomse Lords en Paters.

was a fudge and a compromise but one which—like the fudge and compromise that created the Church of England in 1559—was to prove remarkably enduring. And just as the 1559 settlement was a Protestant triumph with Catholic trappings, so the 1689 settlement was a Whig triumph in Tory trappings.

After James's flight, William (and his army) occupied London. An assembly of all surviving members of Charles's Parliaments and members of the London Corporation engineered the summonsing of a Convention (with the precedent of 1660 in mind). That Convention offered the crown to William and Mary so long as they were willing to listen to the recital of a declaration of rights that had no binding force. In due course the Convention distilled those parts of the declaration that prevented William and Mary from repeating the constitutional crimes of James II into a Bill of Rights. There was held to have been an interregnum from James's flight until William

HAVING secured England, William had still to secure the thrones of Scotland and Ireland, the latter involving the famous lifting of the siege of (London)Derry (Nov. 1689) and the victory at the battle of the Boyne (June 1690).

A SEMI-ALLEGORICAL celebration of the Glorious Revolution as the newly planted Orange tree of liberty withstands the tyranny of France and the Antichristian schemings of papists.

and Mary's acceptance of the offer of the Crown. The offer to both with full executive authority in William's hands—his bottom line—breached the natural order of succession. This was more of a medieval than a modern *coup*.

It changed the King without doing much to change the monarchy. James was deemed to have deserted the kingdom and thereby forfeited the throne (the Scots forthrightly deposed him as a tyrant and the Protestants in Ireland just did what the English told them). Those that wanted to, could believe this meant that he had been deposed; those that did not want to believe it, did not have to do so. No blood was shed and there was no way of showing that there had been actual resistance or a withdrawal by the people from a contract violated by the King. Those who wanted could believe that a contract now existed between Crown and people; those that did not, did not have to do so. But it was a Whig triumph. Tories believed in swearing allegiance to a rightful and lawful King until death did them part from him; when he fled they would have preferred to negotiate his return on terms, or a Regency, or to crown his daughter Mary. But the greater part of them could live with the soft-focus constitutionalism of 1689.

The compromise came about because those men who held moderately to Tory ideas and those who held moderately to Whig ideas agreed not to force their views down their friends' throats. In 1689, unlike 1642, the centre held and the fanatics on either side, the Jacobites of the future and the republicans of the past, were stymied. But (for the Tories) worse was to come. To keep James from returning, the English embarked on a quarter-century of global war with the French. This turned the executive into a parliamentary steering committee that needed to be able to command a majority in the Houses of Parliament so that the costs of the wars—and subsequently the servicing of the ineradicable National Debt created by the scale of those costs—could be met from annual parliamentary grants. It led to the emergence of Cabinet government and to the principle that ministers must be members of—and daily answerable to—the legislature. The constitutional strains that contributed to and resulted from the 'Revolution' of 1688 firmed up the two parties—Whig and Tory—which, with many mutations, came to dominate English political life for the next 200 years. The throne became for the first time in its history clearly elective, yet in the 280 years since the principle was put into practice in 1714 every succession has been the hereditary one.

The insecurities of the war years, and the further constitutional divergence of England and Scotland, created the context out of which another compromise produced in 1707 the Union of the kingdoms of England and Scotland into the British state with one Parliament, one economic system, but two legal systems and two national Churches. This has also endured—uneasily—to the present. Perhaps most centrally of all, the principle of religious pluralism was conceded, at least in England. It was a grudging and incomplete toleration, and its precise meaning and limits were long contested. But (like the Great Reform Bill of 1832) it was a great watershed. Conservative voices might seek to interpret it as narrowly and meanly as they could, but the measure and the principle it underwrote were irrevocable. The Stuarts would have been a happier dynasty if they had been able to embrace the Anglicanism of the majority of their people. Their struggle for alternative religious forms was the greatest single source of friction in all their reigns. It is a biting irony that the measure which most unequivocally marked their passing was an Act of Toleration.

18

ENGLAND AND THE WORLD UNDER THE TUDORS

1485–1603

SIMON ADAMS

1485 is not one of the more prominent dates in the wider history of England's foreign relations—let alone Britain's. It marks a midway point in the eight decades between the collapse of the Lancastrian empire in France and Henry VIII's break with Rome. The most significant trend of the period was the consolidation of the existing commercial relationship with the Burgundian Netherlands in the famous treaty of 1496, the *Intercursus Magnus*, and its various revisions. The 'Great Entercourse' gave exported English cloth access to the Netherlands market without payment of further dues or levies, while leaving in place the existing English customs duties on both imports and exports. Following the treaty a new commercial institution, the London-dominated Merchant Adventurers, was licensed to regulate the Netherlands trade.

The treaty was not universally popular, as the numerous attempts at revision make clear, but so important was the trade to both parties that neither could afford to let it lapse and it shaped English commercial policy for a century and a half. The expansion of the Antwerp market during the first half of the sixteenth century produced a boom in cloth exports, but in so doing it destroyed the Staple for the export of wool at Calais. Given that the custom on wool had paid for the garrison of Calais, the decline of the Staple meant that the fortress was ultimately untenable. The Antwerp commercial nexus thus became the subject of one of the great debates of the century: was England so economically dependent on Antwerp that she was more or less a client-state, or was the cloth trade so crucial to the prosperity of Antwerp that the Netherlands were in fact the client?

The obsession of succeeding kings in the fourteenth and fifteenth centuries with their French domains and ambitions had brought earlier English expansion in the British Isles to a temporary halt. Moreover, the sea passage to Ireland and the barrenness of the Anglo-Scottish borders made them effectively natural frontiers. As a result these centuries became the golden age of an independent Scotland and a virtually autonomous Ireland. Yet the precocious Scottish sense of

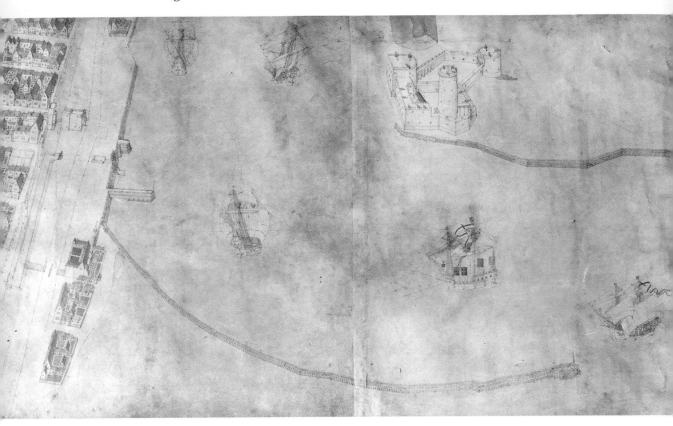

C ALAIS harbour in the 1540s, by which time silting had prevented large ships from using the port. The surrender of the Rysbank Fort (*centre*) early in the siege of 1558 sealed the fate of the town.

national independence and the introversion of Gaelic Ireland did not prevent either from dabbling in English politics during the civil wars of the fifteenth century. Henry VII attempted cautiously to restore control over Ireland and to teach James IV a lesson, but, typically, wound down operations as soon as the expense began to mount. Improved relations with Scotland culminated in 1502 in the Treaty of Perpetual Peace and the marriage of James IV and Margaret Tudor. This amounted to a diplomatic revolution for the Stuarts had carefully avoided a dynastic link in the past—now the two royal Houses were close relations in blood.

This cautious foreign policy became more difficult to maintain during the reshaping of European politics that followed the French invasion of Italy in 1494 and the ensuing wars that dominated the first half of the sixteenth century. From the consolidation of opposition to France came a series of dynastic marriages, among them Henry VIII's to Catherine of Aragon and those that created the 'empire' of Charles V. The Italian wars posed a dilemma: on the one hand, England was not directly involved; on the other, she would be affected by the wider results of the struggle and being in a position to attack either France or the Netherlands, English assistance was sought by both sides. Henry VII was content to exploit this situation to his immediate advantage, but his son's response was more complex. In foreign policy, where his knowledge and interest has never been disputed, Henry VIII displayed the same strange mixture of megalomania and common sense, brutality and sensitivity that he did in his domestic policy.

Henry's ability to conduct an active foreign policy depended ultimately on his financial resources, but the instruments at his disposal were shaped to a considerable degree by personal preference. He inherited a diplomatic 'system' consisting of a representative at the Papal Curia, an agent largely funded by the Merchant Adventurers in the Netherlands, and occasional embassies composed of clerical lawyers or courtiers. Under the Treaty of London (1518) a resident ambassador was posted to the French Court, while a second was later assigned to Charles V's, but other than to terminate the Roman representative in the early 1530s, Henry made little further change. The King's hand is seen more clearly in his armed forces. He created the largest fleet outside the Mediterranean (fifty warships at his death), but his notorious conservatism in military matters—notably his dislike of firearms other than cannon—meant that by the 1520s the weaponry of his armies was obsolescent. He dabbled only fitfully in the other two areas of military innovation: the creation of permanent units and the mass employment of mercenary troops.

Henry VIII's foreign policy falls into four distinct phases. The initial one (his first French war) was brought to an end by the election of Charles V as Holy Roman Emperor in 1519. The second phase lasted until 1528–9 when the dispute with the Papacy initiated the third. The fourth was the conflict with Scotland and France that began in 1542. Much has been written recently about Henry's chivalric interests, his ambition to be a second Henry V, and his perennial desire to add Boulogne to the Calais Pale, but this case can be overstated. He did not go to war immediately on his accession, but only in 1511 and then under pressure from Julius II, who offered him the

THE campaign of 1513 was a favourite subject for the decoration of Henry VIII's palaces. This detail from a painting at Hampton Court depicts several of the more famous episodes: Henry's meeting with Maximilian I, the 'Battle of the Spurs', and the siege of Tournai.

French crown if he would join the Holy League against France. The expensive war that followed, which left Henry with the untenable outpost of Tournai, was a chastening experience, and Henry was particularly embittered by the way in which he had been exploited by his allies, Ferdinand of Aragon and Maximilian I. Not only did he avoid further direct military involvement after 1514, but his later foreign policy was always informed by a residual suspicion about the motives of his fellow monarchs.

The first French war also entangled Henry in the affairs of the House of Stuart. In 1513 James IV suddenly invaded England in order to honour his alliance with Louis XII. The unexpected disaster at Flodden left Scotland with an infant King, to whom Henry was the nearest blood relative. To support his 'right' to determine the regency for the young James V Henry revived the old claim of feudal suzerainty over Scotland. His nominee as regent was his sister, James's mother, but the Scottish Parliament appointed John Stewart, Duke of Albany, instead. Policy towards Scotland and France thus became closely intertwined. Peace was made with France in the Treaty of London, negotiated by Cardinal Wolsey in 1517–18. This treaty, upon which much of Wolsey's later reputation as a tough and able diplomat rested, was deceptively easy, for Francis wished to win Henry away from the future Charles V and the substantive issue was the return of Tournai, for which Francis was prepared—at least on paper—to pay handsomely. No less important was the tacit agreement to withdraw Albany from Scotland, making possible Queen Margaret's regency. Unfortunately, Charles's election as Emperor in 1519 rendered this treaty irrelevant. The issue was now the inevitable struggle between Charles and Francis. Given that Charles's dominions were potentially the greater it was in Francis's interest to strike before the still-adolescent Emperor was fully in control of his inheritance. The revolt of the Communeros in 1520 was too good an opportunity to miss, and hostilities began in 1521.

Henry's response to this war has been among the most debated episodes of his reign. June 1520 saw his famous interview with Francis I at the Field of the Cloth of Gold, an apparent celebration of the new Anglo-French amity. However, the Cloth of Gold was only a spectacle, for Henry's real foreign policy was forged in meetings with Charles V immediately before and after. Charles, who was desperate for an ally, proposed his marriage to Princess Mary, but Henry took little persuading, for he had already formed a strong avuncular attachment to the young Emperor. It was Henry, on the other hand, who outlined the strategy of the alliance: a combined invasion and then partition of France—soon known as the Great Enterprise—in which he would receive the French crown. He would thus control the war and avoid being exploited again.

Wolsey's ostensible attempt to arbitrate between Charles and Francis at Bruges in 1521 was in reality a device to win time. However, once full hostilities began in 1522 the Anglo-Imperial alliance rapidly unravelled, for like his grandfathers earlier, Charles viewed the Great Enterprise as secondary to the struggle for Italy. Henry's initial generosity turned quickly to distrust as he saw himself employed once again as a diversion. Moreover, he himself became the target of a diversionary campaign, for Francis justifiably considered the agreement over Albany abrogated by Henry's alliance with Charles. The return of Albany to Scotland quickly unseated Margaret,

THESE designs (*facing*) for tents in Tudor green and white (*upper*) and decorated with royal beasts, mottoes, and badges (*lower*) were probably prepared for the meeting of Henry and Francis I of France at the Field of the Cloth of Gold.

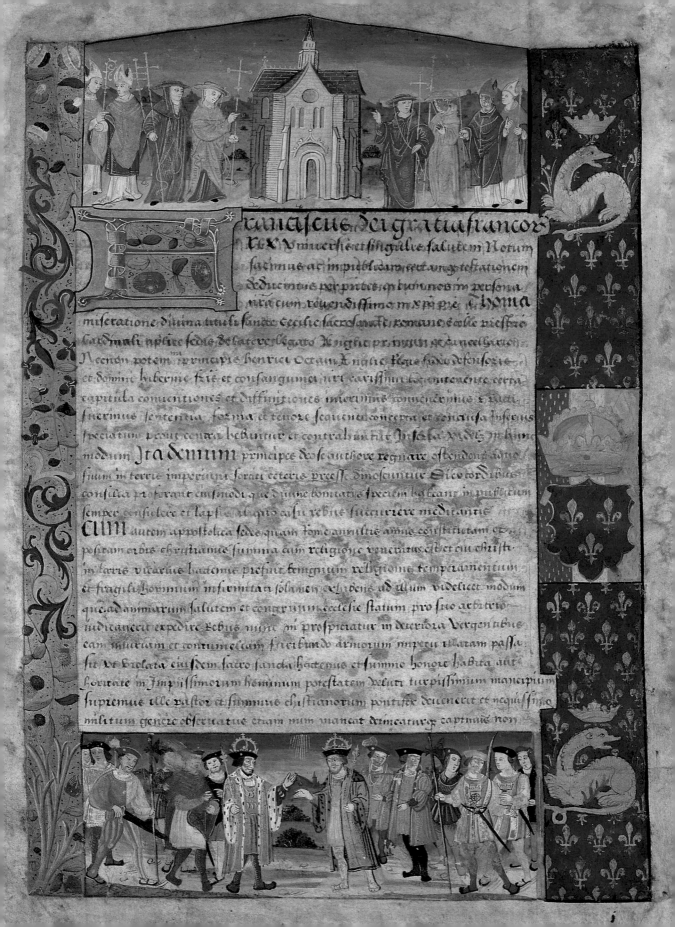

ranaſcus dei gratia francor
Rex Vniuerſis et ſingulis ſalutem Notum
facimus ac in publicam certunq teſtationem
deducimus per prites cp hominos in perſona
noſtra cum reuendiſſimo mxpo prie e Thoma
miſeratione diuina tituli ſancte eccleſie ſacroſancte romane eccle vicebro
Cardinali noſtre ſedis de latere legato Anglie primum cancellario
Neenon totem principe henrici Octaui Anglie regis fidei defenſoris
et domino habeme frie et conſanguineo noſtri cariſſime contrahente certa
capitula conuentiones et diffinitiones inter nos conuenerimus e tacit
fuerimus ſententia forma et tenore ſequente concepta et contracta inferius
ſpeciatim prout contra hebuntur et contrahuntur tie inſeta vides in hunc
modum Ita denium principes deo ſe authore regnare oſtendunt adno
ſuum in terris imperium ſorati ceteris preeſſe dunoſcuntur Dies cordibus
conſilia proferant cuiſmodi que diuine bonitatis ſreceioem hoſian in publicum
ſemper conſulere et lapſis aliquo caſu rebus ſuccurrere meditantis
CUM autem apoſtolica ſedes quam tome omnibus annis conſtitutam ep
poſitam orbis chriſtiane ſumma cum religione veneratus et her cu chuſti
in terris vicarius hactenus preſuit benignum religione temperamentum
et fragili hominum inſirmitati ſolamen exhibens ad illum videlicet modum
que ad animarum ſalutem et contra tuum eccleſie ſtatum pro ſuo arbitrio
iudicauerat expedire rebus nunc in proſpicieur in deteriora Vergentibus
eam iniuriam et contumeliam tribundo armorum impetu illatam paſſa
ſit ut violata eiuſdem ſacro ſancta hactenus et ſumme honore habita aut
horitate in Impiſſimorum hominum poteſtatem veluti turpiſſimum mancipium
ſupremus ille paſtor et ſummus chriſtianorum pontifex deuenerit et nequiſſimo
militum genere obſeruatur etiam num maneat detineaturq captinus non

whose shaky position had been further weakened by her marriage to the Earl of Angus and then her subsequent repudiation of her husband. Although Albany showed little interest in an invasion of England, by 1524 Henry's influence over Scotland had collapsed.

The Anglo-Imperial alliance finally fell victim to Charles's great victory at Pavia in 1525. The result was the reconciliation with France that Wolsey concluded in the Treaty of the More (August 1525), a 'diplomatic revolution' that is no less debated than the events of 1520–1. The new alliance with France remained the corner-stone of Henry's foreign policy until 1529. Its ultimate aim was a vague one of 'humbling' the Emperor by creating an Italian coalition against Charles backed by France and England, though at minimal expense to Henry. Tortuous diplomacy could not, however, disguise the weakness of this coalition and it was in serious difficulty even before its main prop—the papacy—was removed by the sack of Rome in May 1527. If the coalition was to be saved and the Pope freed from captivity there was no alternative to a major French military intervention in Italy. But at the same time the Anglo-French alliance was transformed by the 'leaking' of Henry's desire to have his marriage to Catherine of Aragon annulled. Now Henry had a personal stake in freeing the Pope, and Francis was able in turn to demand more than moral support: specifically, financial assistance for the Italian campaign and, if Charles remained intransigent, an agreement to declare war on the Emperor. War was in fact declared in January 1528, but in the previous month Charles had deprived his enemies of the moral highground by allowing Clement VII to escape.

Nevertheless the 'divorce' initiated a major reshaping of Henry's foreign policy. In 1527 the plan had been for the French to free the Pope from Imperial control by force. However, soon after the Pope regained his freedom Wolsey detected that he was less grateful to his erstwhile liberators than might have been expected. In response he began in 1528 and 1529 to make increasingly explicit threats that unless Henry were gratified he himself would be dismissed and England might even leave the Church. The failure of the French campaign in Italy in 1528 and Francis's decision to seek a settlement with Charles (the Treaty of Cambrai, August 1529) left Henry with only his threats if he wished to persevere. The dismissal of Wolsey in the late summer of 1529, still much debated, may have been simply a demonstration to the Pope that Henry was not bluffing. Yet the fall of Wolsey did not resolve Henry's difficulties. The diplomacy of the divorce continued to be overshadowed by the dilemma encountered in 1528: who was Henry's main opponent, Charles V or Clement VII? This dilemma had its most immediate impact on relations with France. For Francis I the Treaty of Cambrai was merely a truce in his struggle with the Emperor. He encouraged the divorce as a means of keeping Henry and Charles apart, but he would not support Henry in an attack on the papacy. Thus by 1534 England and France were drifting apart, and Henry's only potential allies in his anti-papal campaign were the German Lutheran princes of the Schmalkaldic League. In the long term this new Anglo-German relationship, which led to the Palatine marriage of 1613 and ultimately to the succession of the House of Hanover, was one of the great revolutionary consequences of the Reformation on Britain's foreign relations. In the immediate term the aims of Henry VIII and the Schmalkaldic League were

O NE of a series of treaties (*facing*) signed by Cardinal Wolsey and Francis I of France at Amiens on 18 August 1527: the decoration at the foot shows Henry VIII (*right*) and Francis forming an alliance to free the Pope from the Emperor Charles V and thus make possible the annulment of Henry's marriage to Catherine of Aragon.

A FANCIFUL contemporary view of Henry VIII's arrival at Calais for the Field of the Cloth of Gold in June 1520. Few events illustrate so well the gap between illusion and reality in sixteenth-century diplomacy.

incompatible. The League wanted a religious alliance based on common adhesion to the Confession of Augsburg. Henry simply wanted support for his divorce, the morality of which neither Martin Luther nor the Elector of Saxony was prepared to condone.

Yet despite Henry's provocations the divorce did not lead to intervention by the Catholic powers. In part this was because the papacy did not wish to make an irrevocable breach by fully excommunicating Henry or placing England under an interdict. Charles V had no desire to damage Anglo-Netherlands trade unnecessarily. Lastly, the revival of Franco-Imperial hostilities in Italy in 1535–6, despite papal attempts to mediate in 1537–8, prevented the formation of an effective Catholic alliance. What transformed the situation and initiated the fourth phase of Henry VIII's foreign policy was a sharp deterioration in Anglo-Scottish relations at the end of the 1530s.

The Treaty of the More of 1525 had included another tacit French abstention in Scotland. Yet Henry still faced a crisis there in 1527 when the enemies of the Earl of Angus (who had replaced his ex-wife as regent) proclaimed James V's majority and brought the regency to an end. Only by force could Henry impose an Anglophile government on James and in 1527–8 he was in no position to do so. Angus retired to exile in England, while Henry attempted to win over the new King by kindness. However, not only did Henry's efforts to play the benevolent uncle and persuade James to follow his ecclesiastical policy encounter a truculent independence, but by the later 1530s James was dabbling in English and Irish politics as well. It was not difficult for the ever-suspicious Henry to see the influence of Francis I at work, the more so given James's long visit to France in 1536–7 and his two French brides, the latter of whom—Mary of Guise—Henry had been considering himself. By the end of the decade Henry was coming to see the Franco-Scottish 'alliance' as aimed against him, and deteriorating relations with Scotland led to deteriorating relations with France as well.

The breaking-point was James's refusal to meet Henry at York in 1541. The opportunity to teach him a lesson was provided by the outbreak of a fresh war between Francis I and Charles V in 1541–2. Hostilities on the Anglo-Scottish border in the summer of 1542 led to a mis-

guided Scottish invasion in November which collapsed in the rout of Solway Moss and brought about James's early death. The unexpected accession of the infant Mary gave Henry a fresh chance to control Scotland by assuming the regency himself. Once again, however, he underestimated Scottish independence and was taken by surprise when the Earl of Arran was appointed Governor by the Scottish Parliament. The alternative of accepting this *fait accompli* or challenging it by force was in fact his old dilemma in Scotland resurfacing. Henry chose the first course on the basis of reports that Arran favoured the English policy in religion and was willing to support the marriage of Mary to Prince Edward. The marriage treaty (the Treaty of Greenwich) was signed on 1 July 1543, but Arran proved unwilling to take action against the enemies of the English connection led by Cardinal Beaton and the Queen-Dowager Mary of Guise. Placed in an increasingly difficult position during the autumn of 1543 Arran was eventually won round by Beaton— possibly by an offer to support his own succession to the crown should Mary die. In December 1543 the Treaty of Greenwich was repudiated.

Henry, though breathing fire and smoke over Scottish duplicity, had had his bluff called. Although he mounted an amphibious attack against Edinburgh in the spring of 1544, he was unable to do more because he was trapped by an existing commitment. In the spring of 1543, partly in the belief that Scotland was settled, he had agreed to Imperial proposals for a joint invasion of France in 1544, an apparent return to the early 1520s which involved a mutual agreement to ignore the religious issue. In the summer of 1544 Henry launched the largest of his military expeditions (40,000 men were involved) but craftily limited his ambitions to his long-standing desire, the conquest of Boulogne. Charles responded by making a separate peace (18 September 1544) and abandoning Henry to his own devices. Worries about the financing of a two-front war, expressed as early as the spring of 1544, now were realized as Henry's attempt to fight both France and Scotland in 1545 nearly bankrupted the Crown. His refusal to surrender Boulogne threatened to make a settlement with France impossible, but his Councillors finally persuaded him to accept a compromise (the Treaty of Campe, June 1546) whereby he would retain Boulogne for eight years.

Henry VIII's bequest to his son was thus the temporary possession of Boulogne and a languishing war in Scotland. The Emperor was now concentrating on bringing the Lutherans of the Schmalkaldic League to heel. This might have encouraged a *rapprochement* between England and France, but the Duke of Somerset, for all his Protestantism, displayed little interest in the Lutherans (who were decisively defeated in June 1547) and determined instead to conquer Scotland. His invasion was crowned by a victory at Pinkie (September 1547), but this success inspired him to follow an overly ambitious strategy of forcing Scotland into surrender by the planting of garrisons. These simply became the targets of a military intervention by the new French King, Henry II, in 1548, which was followed by a declaration of war and the besieging of Boulogne in the following year. Owing to frosty relations with Charles V there would be no counter-pressure on France. The cumulative effects of military over-extension and his refusal to abandon the Scottish war led to Somerset's overthrow.

Whatever else they agreed on, Edward's Council were now united on the need for substantial financial retrenchment. In 1550 the decision was taken to surrender Boulogne and to withdraw from Scotland. However, there were limits to possible cuts in expenditure, for while relations with Charles V remained distant, France now controlled Scotland to an extent not previously encountered. In consequence the modernization of the fortress at Berwick was initiated and a perceived threat to Ireland led to subventions from London having to grow substantially. The revival of Habsburg–Valois conflict in 1552 offered a temporary breathing-space, but by the spring of 1553 there were growing fears that the ageing Emperor was dying and that his empire might fragment in the face of the attacks of Henry II. The war did, however, prevent the Continental powers from intervening in the contested succession to Edward VI, though unease at diplomatic isolation may have contributed to Mary's easy victory. Restoration of the Habsburg connection was one of the immediate consequences of her accession, and Charles, seeing divine providence at work in her success, moved quickly to seal the bond by a marriage to Prince Philip, who was forced to abandon with some embarrassment his own negotiations for a Portuguese bride.

The marriage of Philip and Mary caused a political crisis similar to the Scottish reaction to Henry VIII and contemporary Dutch and German unhappiness with the Habsburg Empire. This residual 'nationalist' hostility to dynastic empires—which transcended the religious divide—is one of the most significant international trends of the middle decades of the century. Some opponents of the marriage turned to Henry II, but without success for he was unhappy about aiding heretics against a restored Catholic monarch. Nevertheless the revived Anglo-Habsburg alliance ensured continued tension with France and (ironically) the continuity of the Edwardian policies towards Scotland and Ireland. To placate domestic opinion the marriage treaty was so restrictive that in practice England's utility to Charles and Philip was limited. This became clear in the final Habsburg–Valois war of 1557–8. English participation in the war (ostensibly barred by the marriage treaty and brought about in mysterious circumstances) was minimal and dominated by a possible invasion from Scotland, an issue of little concern to Philip. The dramatic loss of Calais in January 1558 unleashed a storm of mutual recrimination in which the suspicions of both sides came to the fore.

Mary's death thus found the Anglo-Habsburg alliance with few strong supporters on either side, and relations were further exacerbated by the enforced concession of Calais at the Treaty of Cateau-Cambrésis (April 1559), although Elizabeth I bartered it for recognition of her title. English resentment of the marriage to Philip meant that the new Queen was under little pressure to follow her sister's course. If Elizabeth's immediate restoration of the Edwardian Church

PORTRAIT of Sir John Luttrell (1518?–51), commander of two of Somerset's main garrisons in Scotland (Inchcolm in the Firth of Forth, 1547–8, and Broughty Castle, 1548–9), by Hans Eworth. Considered 'one of the strangest of all Tudor pictures' this may be an allegory of the peace of 1550.

ALLEGORY of the abdication of Charles V (1555–6) by Frans Francken. This glorification of the Habsburg Empire at its height explains much of the fear it provoked.

threatened to revive the Edwardian isolation, in Protestant circles fears were assuaged by a confidence in divine providence, a sentiment reinforced by the Protestant rebellion in Scotland in the summer of 1559. A feared Catholic alliance did not materialize and political unrest in France following the death of Henry II (July 1559) and the growth of organized Protestantism enabled English military and naval intervention in Scotland in the spring of 1560 to force the evacuation of the French garrison and to establish an Anglophile and Protestant regency for the absent Mary.

Nevertheless the future of the Anglo-Habsburg relationship remained the major issue of Elizabeth I's foreign policy. The strongest arguments in favour were commercial, both the older Anglo-Netherlands trade and the expanding trade with Spain itself (both domestic products and colonial re-exports). However the dependence of the English Crown on customs revenues had led to attempts in the reign of Edward VI to trade directly with Guinea and Muscovy. As King of

England, Philip had opened the Canaries to English trade, but not the Indies monopoly, thus depriving himself of a powerful lure for his new subjects. In Elizabeth's reign the Edwardian commercial expansionism was revived and justified by a Protestant argument that England was not bound by the papal division of the New World between Spain and Portugal, but it was also encouraged by a number of profitable acts of semi-piracy such as the Reneger incident of 1545 or semi-legality such as the Hawkins Voyages of the 1560s. No less influential were the increased importance of the customs revenues following the revaluation of the customs rates in 1558 and fears that Philip might seek to exploit Elizabeth's dependence on foreign trade. 1563–4 saw the first deliberate attempt by Philip's government (on the advice of Cardinal Granvelle) to employ the commercial weapon by embargoing English trade with the Netherlands and Spain. The English response was to shift the Antwerp Staple to Emden in 1564. Emden was not a satisfactory alternative, but the Netherlands cracked first and public pressure forced Granvelle's resignation and the restoration of the *Intercursus Magnus*. Philip turned to the commercial weapon again in 1569, but the Staple was then transferred to Hamburg and a trade war with Spain continued until 1573–4. The embargoes may have failed, but they further encouraged Elizabeth's government to support wider commercial expansion, and gave England a vested interest in the success of the Dutch Revolt.

Commercial issues were, however, but one consideration in the making of policy; no less important was the religious tension which the events of 1559 had brought to the fore. In 1562 Protestant confidence in divine providence was transformed into fears of an impending religious conflict following the final session of the Council of Trent and the outbreak of a religious civil war in France. France became the scene for a second military intervention, but this time Elizabeth jeopardized her moral position by making the restoration of Calais the price of her assistance. Early in 1563 the French Protestants made a separate peace based on a limited toleration, leaving the English to attempt to retain Le Havre as a pawn for Calais. The affair soured relations between the English and French Protestants for some years, but the French peace settlement did temporarily calm fears of a major religious war, which did not revive until the Duke of Alba arrived in the Netherlands in 1567.

Religious tension also shaped Elizabeth's complex relations with Mary Queen of Scots. Mary's return to Scotland in 1561 threatened to upset the new amity between England and Scotland, and between 1561 and 1565 serious efforts were made to win her friendship and to maintain the Anglophile government. However, Mary's price was recognition of her place as heir apparent to Elizabeth, while retaining the freedom to remarry where she chose. Her sudden decision to marry Lord Darnley in 1565 came close to overturning the amity. Military intervention was seriously discussed in the autumn of 1565, but Elizabeth was saved by Mary's estrangement from Darnley and the murder of David Rizzio in March 1566. The restoration of the Anglophiles and the birth of the future James VI strengthened Mary's position, but in 1567 it was destroyed almost entirely by the murder of Darnley and her marriage to the Earl of Bothwell. Her enforced abdication saw the creation of an Anglophile regency for the young James VI, but Elizabeth refused to recognize her deposition. This in turn may have encouraged Mary to seek to regain her throne by force in 1568 and when that failed to flee to England.

Although she herself had been personally discredited, Mary's position in the English succession was if anything stronger in the summer of 1568 than it had been previously thanks to the

Two of the key figures in the Antwerp nexus of the 1560s: Sir Thomas Gresham (?1519–79), the most influential of the Merchant Adventurers; and Antoine Perrenot, Cardinal of Granvelle (1517–86), who imposed the embargo of 1563. The first portrait is by Antonio Moro and the second by Titian.

death of her main rival (Lady Catherine Grey) at the beginning of the year and the final collapse of the negotiations for the marriage of Elizabeth and the Archduke Charles of Styria in the spring. The autumn of 1568 saw her 'first trial', the examination of the evidence for her complicity in the murder of Darnley, which Elizabeth made the condition for a possible restoration in Scotland. The trial took place against the background of a new civil war in France and William the Silent's attempted revolt in the Netherlands. In December Elizabeth seized bullion being shipped from Spain to the Duke of Alba in the Netherlands. Although this was a clear provocation to Philip II, Alba advised that retaliation be limited to a trade embargo. Elizabeth's motives in seizing the bullion are still debated, for it is not clear whether she was in fact prepared to risk a war with Spain. The upshot was a trade war with Spain and limited assistance to the French Protestants. Mary's fate was left in abeyance, permitting her to become a focus for the internal discontent that resulted in the Northern Rising of November 1569.

The successful defeat of the Northern Rising was, however, followed by the assassination of the Regent of Scotland in January 1570 and the revival of civil conflict there. This in turn led to a fresh attempt to restore Mary to the Scottish throne, but it broke down at the end of 1570 on the refusal of the Scottish Protestants to accept her. The discovery in mid-1571 of the Ridolfi Plot, a conspiracy to depose Elizabeth in favour of Mary, in which both she and Philip II were implicated, brought all discussion of restoration to an end. Although Elizabeth refused demands for Mary's execution in 1572, she had no alternative but to retain her as a semi-prisoner. The Ridolfi Plot owed much of its significance to the fact that it was exposed in a climate shaped by the publication in 1570 of the Papal Bull of excommunication. Yet, as happened regularly in the sixteenth century, the apparent heightening of religious tension was accompanied by a counter trend. In September 1570 the French civil war was resolved by a compromise and the adoption by the French Crown of a more Anglophile policy. This involved the abandoning of Mary, the proposals for a marriage between Elizabeth and the Duke of Anjou, and in 1571–2 discussions of Anglo-French support for a new rebellion in the Netherlands.

The events of 1572 dominated the remainder of Elizabeth's reign. William the Silent's success in the Netherlands now made the Dutch Revolt the focus of European diplomacy in the way the Italian wars had been in the first half of the century, and England's proximity gave her a direct interest in the outcome. Yet the Netherlands also posed a major dilemma: the Anglo-French proposals were for an essentially secular alliance to resist Habsburg imperialism. But this alliance collapsed following the massacre of the French Protestants in Paris on St Bartholomew's Eve 1572, which henceforth would be cited as the prime evidence of Catholic duplicity and the justification for an explicitly religious foreign policy. Elizabeth's response to this dilemma was an idiosyncratic one: the restoration of good relations with Spain in the hope that she might persuade Philip II to agree to a compromise in the Netherlands. In 1574 the trade war was ended and Anglo-Spanish trade underwent a rapid expansion under conditions that allowed English commerce to make its first real penetration of the Mediterranean.

The opportunity for a peaceful solution in the Netherlands came in 1576 when a Spanish financial crisis caused the Army of Flanders to mutiny, and the rebels asked Elizabeth to guarantee the settlement (the Perpetual Edict). Philip's response was deliberately vague but during 1577 it became clear that he would not agree to even the most basic form of religious toleration. Military intervention under the Earl of Leicester was seriously discussed in the winter of 1577–8, but in the end Elizabeth decided to limit herself to financial assistance. A major reason was the revival of French interest in the Netherlands in the form of the younger Duke of Anjou, who offered himself as protector. An opportunity to revive the alliance of 1572 thus suggested itself, particularly to William the Silent, who saw a marriage between Elizabeth and Anjou as the way to secure it. The debate over the Anjou marriage and policy towards the Netherlands between 1578 and 1582 thus became one of the bitterest of the reign. Those most scarred by the events of 1572, Sir Francis Walsingham, Leicester, and their allies, opposed Anjou outright. Elizabeth, whatever her actual views about marriage, Lord Burghley, and the Earl of Sussex were prepared to give the French alliance another try.

Anjou's intervention would only be effective if his brother Henry III supported it, but attempts throughout 1580 and 1581 to discover the King's intentions encountered a wall of obfuscation. Only at the end of 1581 was his unwillingness to assist his brother finally revealed, and it was this

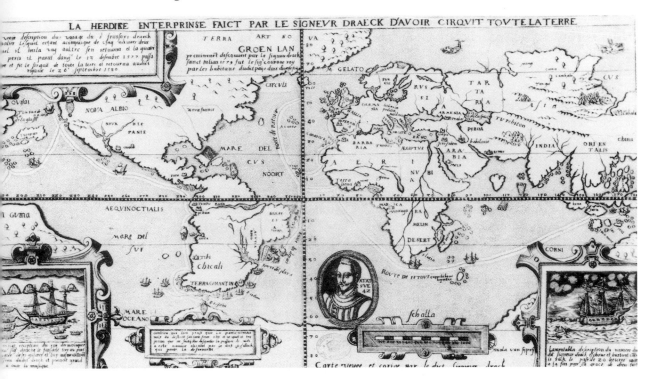

C ONTEMPORARY Dutch engraving of the Circumnavigation Voyage of Sir Francis Drake. The widespread
publicity the voyage received was a testimony to its impact.

discovery that enabled Elizabeth to evade any promise of marriage. Anjou, elected sovereign
lord by the United Provinces, who had declared themselves independent in 1580, was also out-
matched by the able new Spanish Governor-General, the Duke of Parma. Between 1579 and
1584 Parma was able to encourage the defection of the southern provinces and initiate a major
reconquest. The long debate over policy towards the Netherlands was further complicated by
other issues. In 1578–80 the disputed succession to the Portuguese throne led to Spanish intervention to enforce Philip's claim. This inspired equally abortive Anglo-French discussions over
a common response, and Dom Antonío, Philip's rival, was allowed to recruit English privateers.
In September 1580 Sir Francis Drake returned from his Circumnavigation Voyage. He had left
in 1577 under mysterious circumstances (possibly connected to the proposed intervention in the
Netherlands) and his apparent piracy placed yet further strains on Anglo-Spanish relations.
However, his success also appeared to show that the Spanish Empire was extremely vulnerable
to maritime attack and thus inspired the belief that war could be conducted successfully at sea.
Philip II drew the same conclusion and now saw England as a major threat to his empire. Scotland added a further dimension. In 1573 the civil war had ended in the victory of another
Anglophile Regent, the Earl of Morton; by 1578 his enemies had gathered about the young King
and Morton was toppled. In what was almost a repeat performance of the fall of Morton's an-
cestor Angus in 1527–8, Elizabeth was faced with the alternative of restoring Morton by force or
sacrificing him in the interests of good relations with James VI, who, it was feared, might take up

his mother's cause. The debates over Scottish policy were almost as divisive as those over Anjou, and were not resolved until 1584–5 when James was won over by a subsidy and assurances of his succession to the English throne.

The settlement with James VI was overshadowed by greater events. Parma's successful re-conquest in the Netherlands reached its high point in 1584, with the death of Anjou, the assassi-nation of William the Silent, and the siege of Antwerp. In October 1584 the Council agreed that military intervention was unavoidable on the grounds that without English assistance Dutch resistance would probably collapse and, given the history of relations with Philip II, a Spanish victory in the Netherlands would be followed by a direct attack on England. For a final time Elizabeth sought to ally with France, and it was only in the spring of 1585, when it was learned that domestic Catholic pressure had forced Henry III to refuse, that direct negotiations with the Dutch began. These led to the Treaties of Nonsuch in the summer of 1585 under which a small permanent English force was sent to the Netherlands under Leicester. In the meantime, fears that Drake was about to embark on another raid on his empire caused Philip in May 1585 to embargo English shipping. In retaliation privateers were licensed and Drake departed on what became known as the West Indies Voyage.

AN eighteenth-century engraving of the assassination of William the Silent in the Prinsenhof, Delft, 1 July 1584. Fears of the subsequent collapse of the Dutch government led to the English military intervention of 1585.

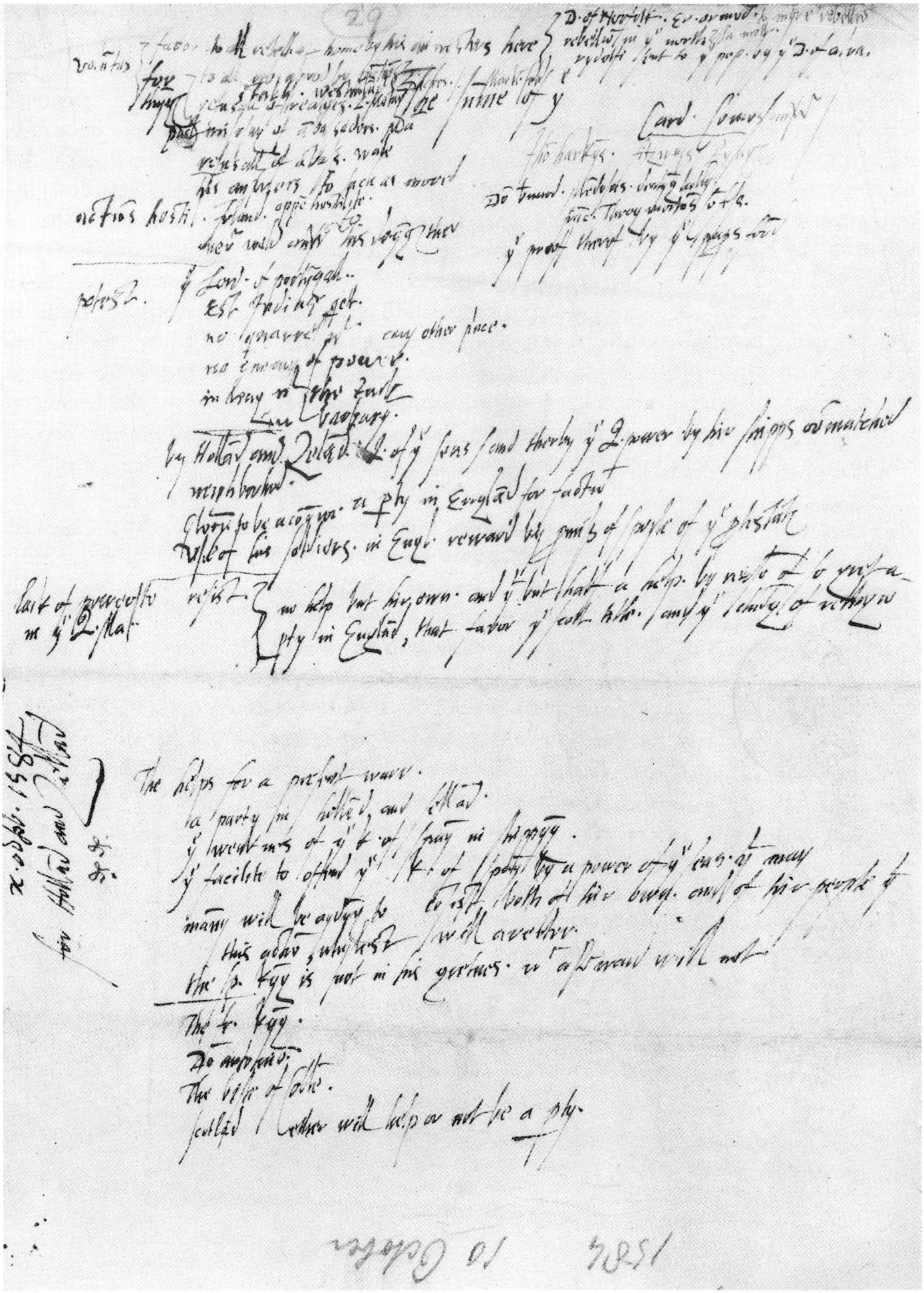
The helps for a perfect warre.

1584 10 October

The outbreak of hostilities on land and sea was not accompanied by a declaration of war, for Elizabeth still hoped that Philip might be prepared to accept a peaceful settlement. Her desire was quickened by the limited success of both Drake and Leicester in 1586. However, Philip could see no alternative to a direct attack on England, and from the beginning of 1586 the preparation of the Gran Armada overshadowed all other considerations. When the Armada arrived in 1588 it was something of an anticlimax, and the failure of the English fleet to do more damage a disappointment. Yet the battle did have two major consequences: thereafter Elizabeth refused to initiate further peace negotiations, and the dispersal of the Spanish fleet revived the English confidence in divine protection.

Nevertheless at the end of 1588 the future conduct of the war remained unclear. In retaliation for the Gran Armada, a major expedition was sent to Portugal in 1589 to incite a rebellion in favour of Dom Antonio, but a brief landing near Lisbon did not disguise its overall failure. No more successful was the effort to cripple Spain economically by converting the privateering campaign into a sustained blockade of the Iberian peninsula. The main achievement of the maritime war was to lessen the economic effects on England by enabling the merchants and shippers previously engaged in Iberian and Mediterranean trade to recoup their losses. On land the military commitment to the Dutch remained paramount, but after 1589 this was overshadowed by a new civil war in France into which both Philip II and Elizabeth were drawn. English support for Henry IV was, however, limited and his ultimate success was the result of his decision to convert to Catholicism in 1594. On the other hand, the French campaigns had taken the pressure off the Dutch, who were no longer in danger of collapse.

By 1595 the 'war' had reached a stalemate, but it was then revived by Henry IV's declaration of war against Spain and the Earl of Essex's success in persuading Elizabeth to return to the offensive. Both were influenced by the claims of the Spanish exile Antonio Pérez that Philip II was a tyrant and that Spain would revolt if military pressure was maintained. In this 'Triple Alliance' (England, France, and the United Provinces) the religious issue was again overshadowed by the old theme of defeating Habsburg imperialism. This phase of the war began with the flamboyant success of the raid on Cadiz in 1596, but the Army of Flanders held its own against a French invasion of the southern Netherlands, and the next English maritime attack (the Islands Voyage of 1597) was a failure. In 1598 Henry yielded to papal requests for a peace, and the war returned to the defence of the United Provinces. The mutiny of the Army of Flanders in 1599 prevented a new Spanish offensive, but a Dutch attempt to exploit it in 1600 was unsuccessful, and both sides then settled down to the long siege of Ostend (1601–4). For England, however, there was now a novel aspect to the war, a major rebellion in Ireland. Prior to 1596 Philip had abstained from direct intervention in Ireland, but Cadiz changed Spanish strategy and in 1601 a small expedition landed at Kinsale. By this point Tyrone's rebellion had become the major focus of English military activity and the major drain on Elizabeth's finances. However, the Spanish landing proved a disaster, for it drew Tyrone out of Ulster and gave Mountjoy, Elizabeth's commander, the chance to shatter his army on 24 December 1601.

Notes made by Lord Burghley during the Privy Council meeting of 10 October 1584 that decided on intervention in the Netherlands. Those at the top of the page outline the deterioration of Anglo-Spanish relations during Elizabeth's reign.

Tyrone finally capitulated at Mellifont just before the news of Elizabeth's death reached Ireland and this cleared the ground for the new King. Since 1585 James's interest in the English succession had kept him allied to Elizabeth though an onlooker on the war. Worries that Spain might attempt to prevent his accession inspired a sustained attempt to win friends among the other Catholic powers, which left a number of hostages to fortune. No foreign challenge in fact materialized, and as a neutral James was able to initiate peace negotiations fairly swiftly. These negotiations were not, however, imposed by the new King, for in 1602 the Council had concluded that the financial burden was such that once Ireland was secured, peace should be sought. In the event the stalemate that had characterized the war also shaped the peace. The Spaniards were forced to compromise on formal concessions to British Catholics, while the English did not obtain freedom of trade with the Indies. The Netherlands issue was left in abeyance.

ENGRAVING of the great siege of Ostend (1601–4). Although the Anglo-Dutch garrison was ultimately forced to surrender, the long duration of the siege reflected the professionalism of both armies and came to symbolize the stalemate of this phase of the war with Spain.

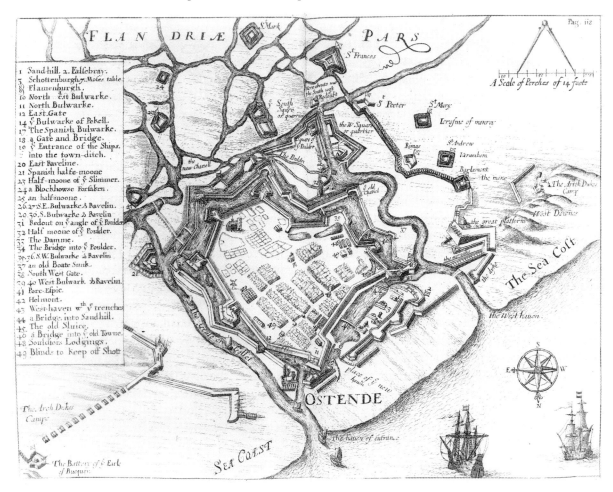

Given that England had entered the war for primarily defensive ends this settlement was no defeat. The war was never intended as a struggle for maritime supremacy or for colonial empires. The one English American colony of the period (Roanoke) was a private venture, which was abandoned in the press of more important matters, and the blockade of Spain had not forced Philip to the conference table. Elizabeth was no altruist, but she possessed neither martial nor dynastic ambitions and her foreign policy was conducted on an unusually intellectual plane. Moreover, thanks largely to the role thrust on her of protectoress of Protestantism, she enjoyed a moral stature in Europe that none of the earlier Tudors had possessed. Henry VIII's foreign policy was essentially one of personal responses, in which a number of the key episodes still defy complete explanation. By contrast, only one episode in Elizabeth's reign—the seizure of the treasure ships in 1568—falls into this category.

A more serious criticism of Elizabethan foreign policy is that it shares the conservatism that inspired her domestic policy. Her diplomatic service did not expand. The main change was the final elimination of the clerical ambassador, although his replacement—the university-educated layman—also frequently possessed a civil law degree. France remained the one permanent resident posting. The embassy in Madrid was terminated in 1568, and only from 1585 was a permanent agent posted to the Netherlands. Accurate intelligence of the Catholic world posed a major problem, though the government was able to gain much from agents in the shadowy world of English Catholic exiles. The career of Sir Francis Walsingham, who became an international figure during his embassy in France in 1570–3, inspired a belief that diplomatic success might lead to high office, but in the event this was not to be realized. Elizabeth played an understandably lesser role than her father in naval and military affairs. The navy was reduced in size to roughly thirty warships, and, whatever the modernization of individual ships, it was not significantly increased during the war with Spain. If adequate to protect the Narrow Seas, it was not large enough to implement the ambitious naval strategy of the 1590s effectively. The modernization of the Crown's military forces, on the other hand, was one of the great under-appreciated achievements of the reign. This was a slow process that began in the wars of Edward VI's reign and was not complete until the 1580s. Its two great successes were the substantial English contingent in the Dutch army after 1585 and the reformed militia. The former were the equals of the best of the Continental professionals, while the latter, however flawed, was—like the Poor Law—a precocious experiment in the creation of a national system quite unparalleled on the Continent.

The key to Elizabethan conservatism remains financial, and it is on the success of its financial policies that Elizabethan government must be judged. Here foreign policy played a central role, for the peculiar circumstances of European politics in the second half of the sixteenth century placed England in a uniquely critical position. Not only were the possibilities for military and naval intervention practically limitless, but over £1 million of Elizabeth's wartime expenditure took the form of loans and subsidies to allies. Moreover, this was a government deeply conscious of the disasters created by military over-extension in Edward VI's reign. That it was able to conduct a reasonably successful foreign policy without bankrupting the Crown, for all the failures in detail, was its great accomplishment. The danger lay in the bequest to Elizabeth's successors of the myth of a glorious foreign policy that they found impossible to live up to.

19 BRITAIN AND THE WORLD UNDER THE STUARTS

1603–1689

JOHN REEVE

1. Rex Pacificus: *James I, 1603–1625*

When the representatives of England, Spain, and the Spanish Netherlands sat and faced each other across a table at Somerset House in London on 10 May 1604, a new era began in British life. Their negotiations brought to an end the long Anglo-Spanish war which had begun almost twenty years before. The costly Elizabethan war gave way to an age of opportunity and conflict. It was an age in which the domestic and foreign affairs of the western European states were deeply intertwined. Powerful international trends worked against isolationist tendencies. Confessional religious conflict was still rife in Europe. Bitter economic rivalries, fuelled by conceptions of the limited wealth of the world, meant that war, trade, and overseas expansion increasingly merged. And in the years to come, the rise of European absolutism at the expense of representative institutions placed parliamentarians on guard against threatening constitutional models in neighbouring states and their influence elsewhere. The Stuart age was one, moreover, in which the provinciality of British culture matured into more cosmopolitan awareness. The propertied classes began the Grand Tour and international trade increased. The winning of great power status also brought new commitments, in Europe and elsewhere. At the beginning of the seventeenth century, the British kingdoms constituted a middle power at best. At the end they had begun a struggle with France for the domination of the oceans and commodities of the world.

The architect of the Treaty of London had been Robert Cecil. But it was King James who allowed the initiative to prosper. James was a sincere pacifist, a reactionary against the violence of his native Scotland, and a lazy man adverse to the demands of conflict and war. His ambition was expressed in the desire for a dynastic union with Habsburg Spain as a mode of entry into the highest circles of European power and prestige. Paradoxically, a canny man with considerable political experience, he succeeded in avoiding the disasters which befell his son and the next

THE wedding suit (*left*) in which the future James II married the Catholic Mary of Modena in 1673—an important moment in the growth of English fears of a Catholic succession, since Charles II, despite his sixteen acknowledged bastards, had no legitimate issue.

THIS dramatic representation of the Great Fire of London, 1666 (*below*), shows the medieval cathedral of St Paul's and most of what was then central London engulfed in flames, in a fire that raged for three days.

An unknown artist depicted the members of the English (right) and Hispano-Flemish (left) delegations at the Somerset House peace conference in 1604. That year the Treaty of London established the framework of Anglo-Spanish relations for the next twenty years.

British generation, but failed in the great enterprises he set himself—a match with Spain and the mediation of peace in Europe. He played a critical role in the conclusion of the Twelve Years' Truce of Antwerp (1609) between Spain and the Dutch, but from then on his important efforts abroad met with little success.

The Treaty of London had been controversial in England, and it had been made with little regard to her Protestant allies the Dutch. Over the next decade pro- and anti-Spanish factions were active at the Jacobean Court. The powerful Howard interest, particularly the Earl of Northampton (d. 1614), were Hispanophile and subject to Spanish bribes. Their fall by 1614–15 was preceded by the arrival in 1612 of the Count of Gondomar as Spanish ambassador. Gondomar was a major influence upon James, turning him against the Dutch, having Sir Walter Raleigh executed in 1618 after his failed expedition to central America, and holding out hopes of a dynastic match. Gondomar aimed to neutralize English leadership of any potential anti-Habsburg bloc. England became a focus of Spanish espionage and intelligence-gathering during these years. These moves were opposed by Protestant nobles such as Ellesmere and Southampton.

ABRAHAM STORCK'S depiction of the Four Days' Battle, 1–4 June 1666 (*facing*), during the second Anglo-Dutch war. Fearing French attack, the English command divided its fleet, enabling the Dutch to inflict significant losses during this engagement off the French and Flemish coasts.

Peace with Spain pleased many London merchants, creating new opportunities for overseas expansion and reopening southern European trade. The export of light English cloth to this area was an increasingly prosperous activity. The Jacobean navy was corrupt and in disrepair, but commerce and colonization still prospered, bringing customs revenues. The Jacobean peace brought the tangible beginnings of the British empire, with settlement in North America and the Caribbean and regular trade with Asia. The English East India Company had actually been chartered in 1600, even before the Dutch Company. Beginning at Surat in 1612 it entered the pepper trade, attacking the local Portuguese. Over time it traded in various spices and drugs and in Indian textiles. The Virginia Company established Jamestown in 1607 and was exporting tobacco within four years. An expedition under its aegis began settlement at Plymouth in the early 1620s. Emigration to the Americas was stimulated by religious dissent and anti-Hispanism, the quest for profit, and agricultural depression at home. British expansion was not planned by government, although government approved of it. Private enterprise made the running, and the Crown quickly found it to be a valuable source of loans. That expansion was also inadvertent in its origins: Dutch control of Indonesia turned the English to India; Spain's defence of her American empire forced British settlers into North America. Like other European powers, the British settled in the Occident but not the Orient. Unlike those powers their settlements were essentially self-directing and self-supporting.

By the early 1620s the long expansion of the European economy had ended in depression, largely caused by war—war which brought about the destruction of James's foreign policy. By 1609 Germany was divided into two armed camps—the Protestant Union and the Catholic League. James worked to defuse the armed Hispano-Dutch truce in Cleves-Jülich in 1614–15. He succeeded then because a major war was not then seen by any one of the major powers as being in its interest. Ironically, his royal marital diplomacy, designed to win him laurels as a great moderator, brought him ever closer to involvement in a great military conflict. In 1613 he had married his daughter Elizabeth to Frederick, the Calvinist Elector Palatine, and he pursued a Spanish match for Charles, Prince of Wales. In 1619, against James's advice, Frederick triggered a religious war

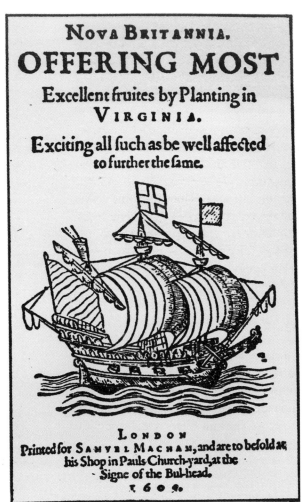

A PAMPHLET advertising Virginia to Englishmen in 1609. This advertisement promised dividends on joint stock investment for seven years, to be followed by subdivision of the lands of the colony.

ELIZABETH OF BOHEMIA, *c.*1620, by Peter Oliver. In 1613 Elizabeth Stuart, daughter of James I, married Frederick, the Elector Palatine. Elizabeth and her family were driven out of central Europe to exile at the Hague by 1621. She returned to live in England after the Restoration and died in 1662.

in Germany by accepting the Crown of Bohemia in an election disputed by the Emperor Ferdinand II. Frederick's forces were defeated outside Prague in 1620. Spanish and Imperial armies overran the Palatinate, gaining control of the Rhine valley: a critical strategic link between Spanish Italy and Flanders. As the German conflict escalated, the impending expiry of the Truce of Antwerp in 1621 threatened to convert it into a general European war. James was trapped between his official Protestant and dynastic commitments and his desire for peace with Spain. He attempted to mediate in the German crisis, seeking to have Frederick and Elizabeth restored, and endeavoured to link this approach to the Spanish marriage scheme. Meanwhile there were calls in England for war in the Palatine and for the Protestant cause. James met Parliament in 1621, probably seeking to build up his credibility with Spain, but he was not really prepared to go to war. Foreign policy became a constitutional issue. The King, influenced by Gondomar, dissolved the Parliament rather than terminate his dealings with Spain. Prince Charles and the Duke of Buckingham complicated the marriage negotiations with a rash trip to Madrid. The match eventually foundered on the religious issue: James's heir could not convert to the Roman Church and the Infanta María had no intention of marrying a heretic, being supported by her brother, Philip IV. Spain had been talking largely to keep England out of the war. Charles and Buckingham, seeking revenge, made common cause with the parliamentary war lobby in 1624, obtaining money for military action. Although he had not declared against Spain when he died in 1625, James could not stop the accelerating drift to war. At a time when the conflict in Europe was deepening, he had been out of step in seeking to keep the peace.

2. *War, Peace, and Parliament: Charles I, 1625–1640*

Charles Stuart was as ill-suited to conduct state diplomacy in a dangerous world as he was to govern effectively at home. While distinctly unsuited to kingship, he took his monarchical duties (including foreign policy) very seriously: a disastrous combination. He was monarch more by accident than by design, entering the direct line of succession on his brother Henry's death in 1612. He lacked the essential political qualities of realism and compromise. In his early years as King he was manipulated by Buckingham and could not work with Parliament—a fatal handicap in seeking to fund a war. Abroad, as at home, he acquired very quickly a reputation for untrustworthiness and inconstancy. In foreign policy he adhered, as he did in constitutional matters and religion, to fixed positions and prejudices. Deeply Hispanophile, he admired Castilian wealth, power, manners, and culture. He hated the French as faithless and the Dutch as power-ful and dangerous republican upstarts. Unlike his father, Charles felt no personal commitment whatsoever to the international Protestant world. This attitude went hand in hand with his im-patience of orthodox Calvinism at home. He was an innovator in foreign (as in domestic reli-gious) policy, against the established and deeply held sentiments of the bulk of his governing classes.

The war with Spain which Charles prosecuted on his accession was a hot-headed act of in-tended revenge. He had wanted the match and when it failed he felt snubbed by those by whom he most wished to be accepted. For Charles the war was also a dynastic crusade, seen as a means of pressuring Spain to act within the Habsburg councils to facilitate his sister Elizabeth's restora-tion. Spain was, however, the greatest power on earth at this time: her diplomats respected and her armies recently victorious and feared. Her wars were underwritten by control of the vast silver reserves of Spanish America. The kingdoms of the British Isles were not in this league. They lacked the capacity to field the large armies of the age of the military revolution. This was not simply a matter of scale, but also of lack of an adequate system of war finance. Britain could still make an impression, however, on the European war. To do so was a matter of selective strat-egy. If Spain were the enemy, the natural allies were the Dutch, and the natural theatre of opera-tions was the sea. In an age of economic warfare, the large quantity of Spanish maritime traffic was vulnerable. The Dutch demonstrated this spectacularly by capturing the silver fleet off Cuba in 1628. Spain also became desperate for relief from English attacks at sea in 1628–9. Sea power was not translated into diplomatic leverage, however, and more than this—in the 1620s Charles's and Buckingham's mismanagement meant that their war-making capacity, and thus their ability to influence European affairs, was largely thrown away.

Parliament, in voting initial supply for the war in 1624, had favoured naval 'war by diversion' against Spain. This strategy was largely inspired by the legend of Elizabethan foreign policy. James had preferred an expedition by land to the Palatinate so as to avoid a wholesale confes-sional war. (The eventual expedition, under the mercenary Count Mansfeld, never even reached Germany.) Charles and Buckingham, acting as Lord High Admiral, fell between two strategic stools. They allied with the Dutch, but also with Denmark, overcommitting themselves finan-cially and associating the English Crown with the military defeat of Christian IV. An attack on the Spanish treasure fleet and on Cadiz failed in 1625. Buckingham had hoped for an Anglo-French alliance but Richelieu outmanœuvred him, engaging England against Spain while France put down the Huguenots. Personal antagonism between the Duke and the Cardinal led to an Anglo-French war in 1627–8. Charles was officially at war with both the great Catholic monarchies of western Europe: a lunatic foreign policy. Buckingham failed to raise the siege of the Huguenot stronghold of La Rochelle, his expedition to the Isle de Rhé in 1627 being a bloody fiasco. The domestic ramifications of the war were dire, with bitter constitutional conflict, oppo-sition to the French war, impending royal bankruptcy, Buckingham's assassination, and, above all, the King's unpopularity and the deep disappointment of hopes raised for the Protestant cause. This last, with the interconnected issue of English church reform, led to the collapse of Charles's third Parliament in 1629.

The business of extricating himself from the European war was, for Charles, a more complex task than getting into it. He was indecisive, there were political divisions at home, and England was being manipulated by France and Spain. A pro-Spanish faction, led by Lord Treasurer Weston, was opposed by the war hawks led by Dorchester, Secretary of State. 1629 brought the Peace of Susa with France which was followed by the Anglo-Spanish Treaty of Madrid in 1630. Charles did not capitalize on the great Swedish victories of the early 1630s, which almost certainly could have brought the Palatines back to Germany, because he could not face the thought of another Parliament. He was unrealistic in dealing with Spain, which wanted English help against the Dutch in return for actual concessions in Germany. Charles never ratified the Cottington Treaty of 1631 for the Anglo-Spanish partition of the Dutch republic. The Count-Duke of Olivares, Philip IV's first minister, had largely achieved his objective of isolating the Dutch by the Treaty of Madrid. Charles had presided over a constitutional breakdown of foreign policy. In a world at war he had lost both the capacity to fight and to conduct effective diplomacy. Worse still, the war years had generated opposing patterns of ideology, fear, and suspicion which would play a role in the coming of civil war.

During the 1630s Charles was essentially a pro-Spanish neutral and war profiteer. Spanish silver was sent via England to pay the Army of Flanders. Charles favoured Spain in British port, shipping, customs, and fishing arrangements, troop levying concessions, and convoy protection —a reversal of traditional policy which had favoured the Dutch. This reflected Charles's preferences, but it was also the further aggravation of new Anglo-Dutch friction attendant on Holland's rise to great commercial power. In a sense Charles was ahead of his time in seeing the republic as a threat and setting the stage for the Anglo-Dutch conflicts of the late seventeenth century. His attitudes suited Hispanophile ministers and Laudian clerics fearful of a fourth Parliament. But they were highly provocative to those such as the Earl of Warwick and John Pym who would eventually lead the Long Parliament. For the moment they institutionalized themselves with others in the Providence Island Company, sketching out alternative foreign and religious policies and awaiting their chance. Charles's regime was also haunted by the spectre of the Palatine reversionary interest. Elizabeth and her children, with impeccable Protestant credentials, were very popular in England.

English trade revived and boomed during the 1630s, the benefits of neutrality increasing when France entered the war against Spain in 1635. Textile exports to both northern and southern Europe were the staple commodity. Trade with the Baltic was particularly important: the region provided grain and naval supplies. Overseas there was marked expansion of the British presence in the

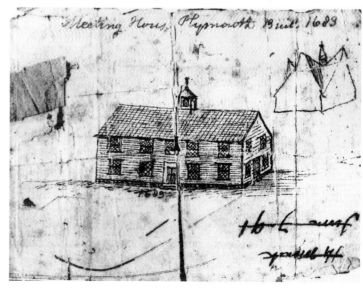

THE meeting house at Plymouth, Massachusetts, erected in the 1680s, which survived into the eighteenth century. Plymouth and Massachusetts Bay were in fact separate colonies until 1692 when the former was absorbed by the latter.

American hemisphere and the new Atlantic economy. Virginia survived and became a Crown Colony, and Charles supported Maryland as a refuge for Roman Catholics. Laud's policies caused a flood of religious emigrants to New England which had 20,000 inhabitants by mid-century. Yet the Caribbean, which appeared as a place of agricultural and piratical opportunity, attracted more migration. The eastern Caribbean was progressively settled, with tobacco-growing using, at this point, British labour.

The navy was expanded in the 1630s by means of Ship Money, but without being used against the Dutch it did not impress the Spaniards sufficiently to allow progress to be made on the German question. A failed English embassy to Vienna and a revival of pro-French sentiments at Charles's Court, in 1636–7, were not enough to persuade him to re-enter the European war. The Scottish revolt made diplomacy a function of a domestic emergency. Various schemes for foreign Catholic aid were materially unproductive but politically inflammatory. The Catalan revolt of 1640 effectively put paid to dealings for monetary assistance from Spain, creating the context for what soon became the Long Parliament. In 1639 the Dutch under Tromp had mauled a Spanish fleet in the Downs, violating neutral English waters while the English fleet looked helplessly on. Charles's personal rule thus ended as it had begun, with diplomatic failure and military humiliation.

3. *Civil War and Great Power, 1640–1660*

Foreign relations were more a part of the coming of the British civil wars than of their outcome. Once the wars had begun both Charles I and the English Parliament developed individual foreign policies. Charles's policy was relatively simple: to obtain help from abroad to suppress rebellion. Parliament's had the more complex aims of achieving recognition, protecting shipping and trade (especially that of London), and preventing any pro-royalist intervention. The great powers of western Europe, France, Spain, and the Dutch republic, were all officially neutral in the conflict but had definite partialities. The Dutch Orangist party, linked to the Stuarts by Mary's marriage in 1641, favoured the King and facilitated a flow of money and arms. Popular sympathies in the republic were with Parliament. The Franco-Spanish war governed the attitudes of the two Catholic monarchies, each striving to combat the other's influence in the British Isles. France eventually aligned itself with Charles but gave him little aid. Cardinal Mazarin in Paris feared an English republic friendly to Spain, but failed to establish a Franco-Scottish alliance to have Charles restored. Cárdenas, the Spanish ambassador in London, cultivated both moderate and radical politicians but his work was destroyed by the advent of Cromwell's resolutely Protestant regime. Yet during the 1640s the Anglo-Spanish axis opposed French diplomacy, and sought to secure trade and the narrow seas against French and royalist attack.

The European reaction to the execution of Charles I was one of universal horror. Despite claiming legitimate succession to the King's government in foreign policy, the new English republic was a virtual pariah state. Spain led the way in granting recognition in 1650, seeking advantage over France. In 1649 Mazarin and the Regent, Anne of Austria, cut all French trade with England and waged an undeclared war against the Commonwealth for another four years. Prince Charles looked to France for support in his restoration and found sympathy there. But amidst the civil strife of the Fronde and the Spanish war she had other concerns, and Mazarin was reluctant to provoke the revolutionary regime. The Commonwealth was thus able to consolidate its security by 1651, pacifying Ireland and Scotland, the latter an obvious base for Franco-royalist operations. Although foreign policy was made by the English Council of State, with Cromwell on campaign, these years encouraged his interest in a French alignment as a form of national security: an attitude which later dovetailed with his religious hostility to Spain.

The first major international test for the Commonwealth came with the Anglo-Dutch war of 1652–4. The breakdown of Anglo-Dutch relations after almost a century had a mixture of causes. Ideas of Christian republicanism flourished in England in the wake of the revolution, embracing the idea of an aggressive Protestant foreign policy. The Council of State sent an ambassador, Oliver St John, to the Hague in 1651 to seek closer alliance and to canvass the idea of political union. The Dutch had different priorities and their response was negative. There was an ideological reaction in England against their supposed materialism and religious corruption. The collusion of the Dutch Orangist faction with the Stuarts was also a sore point. Anglo-Dutch mercantile competition, heightened after the Hispano-Dutch peace of 1648, was also a major factor. The English Navigation Ordinance of 1651 was essentially aimed at excluding Dutch involvement from England's world trade. The enforcement of the Ordinance and the searching of neutral ships for contraband led to war. A clash between Blake and Tromp off Dover in the spring of 1652 precipitated the conflict. In this, as in the later second and third Anglo-Dutch wars, fighting revolved around both sides' efforts to control the waters of the southern North Sea. In all these conflicts the English had a larger combined fleet and better firepower but a shortage of naval stores. They were, however, strong in privateering, taking a thousand ships as prizes in the first war world-wide. The great quantity of Dutch commercial shipping was distinctly vulnerable. The English won major fleet actions in these wars but could not exploit them. The Dutch survived with their seamanship, defensive strategy, and financial resources. England had gained control of the first war by 1653, but it was political changes at home which led to the moderate peace of Westminster in 1654. The Nominated (or Barebones') Parliament of 1653 and the beginning of Cromwell's Protectorate gave power to those sympathetic to Dutch Protestantism. The treaty reflected Cromwell's aims of securing the Commonwealth and opening the way to a Protestant alliance. English royalists were expelled from the Dutch state and the House of Orange excluded from power, although the Dutch would not agree to renew their war with Spain. The boldness of Cromwell's intervention in Dutch politics, depriving the Stuarts of Dutch help, impressed Europe with the power of the Protectorate.

Despite the excellent intelligence-gathering of his *alter ego* John Thurloe, Oliver Cromwell made his own foreign policy. That policy can be and has been criticized by historians. The case against him holds that he was a backwoods amateur, an anachronistic ideologue, who did not understand economic forces or great power politics; that he squandered the victory over the Dutch, was duped by Mazarin, and failed to confront the rising power of France while engaging in a costly war with Spain. There is truth in this but more on the other side. Cromwell had luck and made mistakes but became a statesman of much greater international sophistication and achievement than his critics allow. His confessionalism had its internal logic: he saw Spain in decline as an Antichrist ripe for the kill after thirty years of struggle. His conviction that he was an instrument of the Almighty, moreover, was seasoned with considerable *realpolitik*. He had risen through struggle and bloodshed and thus understood and valued power. He avoided the

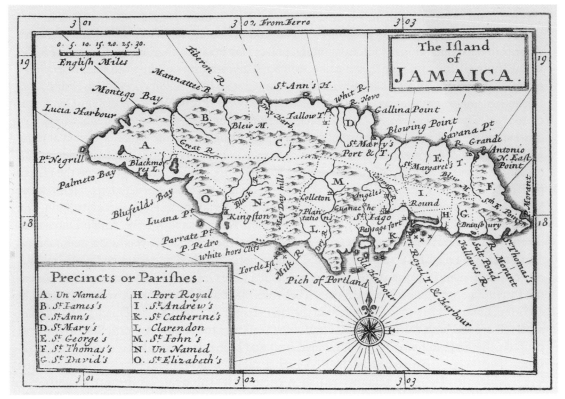

N early map of Jamaica. Mortality amongst its first settlers was high, but the colony developed during the reign of Charles II. Port Royal was an infamous pirate haven and the base of Henry Morgan, the notorious plunderer of the Spanish Caribbean during this period. The town was swallowed up by an earthquake in 1692 in what contemporaries saw as divine retribution.

passivity and impotence which had characterized pre-Civil War foreign policy, and unlike the early Stuarts had a conception of the national interest and of the unity of domestic and foreign affairs. His primary aims for the Commonwealth were security, survival, and respect and while he lived he achieved them. The Restoration would vindicate his view of the Stuarts as a real and residual threat. His pro-French and anti-Spanish policy limited their influence in France, forcing them to ally with a weaker and more distant power in Spain. It also delayed (until after his death) the Franco-Spanish peace which would assist their restoration. His building up of the navy was a major step towards English great power and was balanced by the necessary Continental commitment. Under Cromwell, England (and Britain) achieved European respect as a naval and military power which was second to none.

On becoming Lord Protector Cromwell had two suitors for England's friendship in France and Spain. With the Dutch war ending he also had an army and navy to keep occupied and to justify financially. The Stuart threat was the primary reason for Cromwell's choice of France by August of 1654, when an English expedition against the Spanish Caribbean was authorized. An Anglo-French commercial treaty of 1655 represented the new alignment and a military alliance followed in 1657. The Cromwellian 'Western Design' in the Caribbean in 1654–5 was seen in

England and France as a failure. Directly descended from the Providence Island Company strategy, and conceived of as the beginning of a general attack on Spanish America, it failed to secure Hispaniola, its designated objective, but resulted in the capture of Jamaica instead. Anglo-Spanish maritime conflict resulted in English successes against two treasure fleets and heavy mercantile losses to Spanish action in European waters. An Anglo-French attack on the Spanish Netherlands in 1658 brought a victory at the Battle of the Dunes and English possession of Dunkirk. This eliminated a base for Spanish privateering and possible royalist invasion. The war, however, was unpopular in England. Expensive and damaging to trade, it allowed the Dutch economy to recover. It undermined support for the Protectorate and generated commercial support for the Restoration.

Cromwell was also involved in the Baltic region. In the 1650s he sought to preserve a Baltic balance of power and English access to trade, signing commercial treaties with Denmark and Sweden. An Anglo-Swedish axis balanced the Danish alliance with the Dutch. There was ultimately a conflict of interest between Charles X's regional ambitions for Sweden and Cromwell's desire for a religious crusade against Spain, Austria, and Rome. But the Protector's Baltic policy was basically successful.

The revolutionary and Cromwellian eras saw important developments in overseas expansion.

S UGAR production in the French West Indies *c.*1665, showing the stages of the milling process using slave labour. At the mill the cane is crushed, the juice flows out and is boiled (foreground). The resulting syrup was allowed to cool and crystallize before being purged by water of molasses. This system was pioneered by the Portuguese in Brazil and adopted by the English and French in the Caribbean.

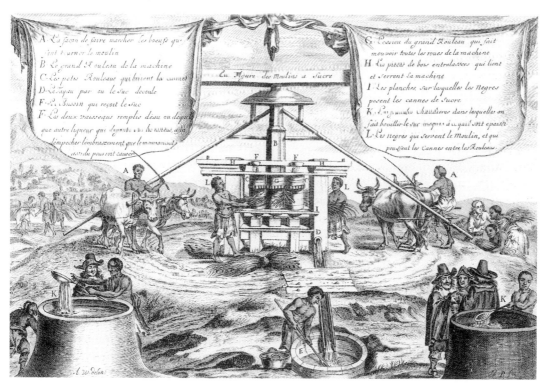

The Commonwealth readily established its authority over the colonies, where many royalists had gone into exile. The civil wars apparently did no enduring damage to Britain's world trade and a Council of Trade was established in 1650. The Navigation Act of 1651 constituted the beginning of a system of regulated imperial commerce. Under Cromwell, a treaty of 1654 gave access to the Portuguese empire (balancing Dutch power in Asia), the East India Company was re-chartered in 1657, and trade with China was begun. But it was in the Americas that British interest and activity were increasing by about 1650. English West Indian plantations began concentrating on sugar cultivation, exploiting the horrors of the African slave trade. Cromwell instituted a policy of aggressive annexation, taking possession of Jamaica (1655) and using force against French and Dutch colonists in North America. In rivalling other European powers in the American hemisphere and giving momentum to imperial expansion his policy pointed the way to the future.

4. *Britain and France, 1660–1685*

Under Charles II Britain was less of a force in international affairs than under Oliver Cromwell. This was also, like the early Stuart era, a time in which foreign policy and domestic politics were intimately related and in which European influences within England were very powerful. Charles was, like his father, a man difficult to fathom and, like his grandfather, a political survivor. From the age of 12 he grew up in a hard school, of civil war, exile, and deprivation, and he seems never to have forgotten the fate which befell his father. His principal political aim was to preserve his throne. An able but indolent man, he was capable of combining principle and pragmatism with a political flexibility which eluded his father and brother. His years of wandering gave him a wide cosmopolitan experience of Europe and a clear leaning towards France, the French model of absolutism, and Roman Catholicism. He seems to have deeply admired the power of his cousin Louis XIV, and his Francophilia extended to a liking for French mistresses. The pro-French policy he developed was a distinct blend of personal preference, politics, and ideology.

The major foreign influence upon later Caroline external relations was the ambition of Louis XIV and the rising power of France. Following his assumption of government in 1661, Louis embarked on a policy of French aggrandizement in Europe. His tools were a highly efficient diplomatic apparatus, an increasingly powerful army and navy, and his own sheer political professionalism. He also had very considerable financial resources. He correctly diagnosed the political weakness of Charles's position in England but was concerned to neutralize her as a factor in his own international schemes. This involved protecting Charles from having a popular anti-French policy forced upon him, as well as playing King and Parliament off against one another. In the end he succeeded in turning Charles into a virtual French pensioner.

The list of domestic issues relevant to Charles's foreign policy is pretty comprehensive: religion, the royal prerogative, royal financial inadequacy, and the succession—issues all heated by European affairs. As under the early Stuarts, an ideological nexus linked religious and constitutional attitudes. For the 'whigs' fear of popery and absolutism focused on the influence of France instead of Spain. Within the new power triangle of Britain, France, and the Dutch republic, Charles deeply feared a Franco-Dutch alliance. He also saw William III of Orange, not Louis

W ILLEM SCHELLINKS, *The Dutch in the Medway*. Dutch warships burst into the Medway on 12 June 1667, burning part of the fleet anchored at Chatham and seizing the flagship *Royal Charles*: a national disaster for England.

XIV, as the threat to European peace. He believed his father and grandfather had made a fatal error in becoming entangled in a parliamentary war policy. He wanted to maximize his domestic political and financial independence. Ultimately his preferred solution was to follow his father's policy of satellite diplomacy with the great power of Europe. And like his father he hoped for personal peace, customs revenues from trade, and foreign aid (in his case from France) in the event of rebellion.

On his restoration in 1660 Charles ended the Cromwellian Spanish war but his Francophile orientation was clear. His childless marriage to the Portuguese Catherine of Braganza and his sale of Dunkirk to the French were widely seen as anti-Spanish moves. Charles was sceptical of the need for the second Anglo-Dutch war (1665–7) but succumbed to a variety of mercantile, ideological, and political pressures. His brother James, Duke of York, Lord High Admiral and connected with the Royal Africa Company, favoured the conflict, as did enemies of Clarendon, who did not. The war, which involved a devastating Dutch attack on the Medway in 1667, was a failure from England's point of view. The compromise peace of Breda that year reflected Anglo-Dutch fear of French ambitions in the Spanish Netherlands. The war also resulted in Clarendon's

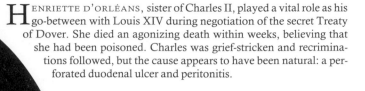

Henriette d'Orléans, sister of Charles II, played a vital role as his go-between with Louis XIV during negotiation of the secret Treaty of Dover. She died an agonizing death within weeks, believing that she had been poisoned. Charles was grief-stricken and recriminations followed, but the cause appears to have been natural: a perforated duodenal ulcer and peritonitis.

fall as a scapegoat and the rise to power of the 'Cabal': a motley collection of politicians who were influential for another seven years.

In the 1660s Anglo-French relations became a pivotal issue in England. There was widespread opposition to French designs and their religious and constitutional implications. France essentially replaced Spain as the national enemy. An anti-French group in government brought about the Triple Alliance (of England, the Dutch republic, and Sweden) in 1667–8. (Louis had effectively broken it up by 1672.) Charles may have regarded it as a bargaining chip with France and a form of insurance. Simultaneously he was seeking a French alignment and secured it by the secret Treaty of Dover in 1670. This was the linchpin of his foreign policy and reflected his views and those of a faction at Court who shared them. He was in fact, of necessity, conducting a covert foreign policy and exposing himself to the risk of French blackmail. Charles committed himself, essentially, to an Anglo-French war on the Dutch to be subsidized by France; he was to receive territorial gains at Dutch expense. He stated his intention of declaring his Catholicism and officially converting to Rome, implying his willingness to countenance toleration for English Catholics and (although this is debatable) to attempt the progressive re-Catholicization of England. Louis was to provide money and troops to help quell any consequent rebellion. The religious article of the treaty was concealed from the Protestant English ministers. Charles's motives were probably a mixture of the religious, the constitutional, the financial, the diplomatic, and the strategic. He never made the personal religious declaration and Parliament would not suffer a suspension of the penal laws, but he did make war on the Dutch.

England's third Dutch war (1672–4) was expensive, politically destructive, and gained virtually nothing. Louis forbade the dissolution of Parliament in 1673 but William of Orange conspired effectively with the English opposition to block supply. Plans in fact existed for an English revolt to be aided by a Dutch fleet: something of a glimpse into the future. At home the legacy of the war was the polarization of English politics and views of foreign policy, with damaged trust between King and Parliament. Abroad, Louis XIV decided England was an unreliable ally and simply sought her passivity.

In the mid-1670s there was tension between the pro- and anti-French policies of Charles and his Lord Treasurer Danby. Parliament, while disliking the King's leaning to France, was reluctant to trust him with an army (which could be used in England) to fight her. William of Orange wanted English support but Louis gave Charles large sums to facilitate his independence from the war lobby. In 1677 and 1678 Charles allowed Danby to pursue anti-French measures (William's marriage to James's daughter Mary, Dutch alliances, and the sending of troops to the Spanish Netherlands), seeking leverage over Louis. The French King was forced to end his Dutch war at Nijmegen (1678) but retaliated by conniving with the opposition to bring about Danby's fall. As the exclusion crisis developed, Louis feared William's taking advantage of Charles's weakness and bailed him out. The 1681 subsidy treaty brought Charles £400,000 over four years and continued his role as a pacified French satellite. This, with a revival of trade and customs, purchased the personal security he desired.

Under Charles II there was significant expansion of the fleet, and dedicated work by Pepys and

A N early depiction of a Portuguese attack on the English at Surat, in north-west India, site of the East India Company's first trading post on the sub continent. The Portuguese were earlier arrivals in the area and resented the English as interlopers.

the Duke of York. Britain achieved a high level of naval self-sufficiency with supplies now coming from North America. The later Stuart period continued the trend towards a permanent national naval force—a force which would soon overtake the French and give Britain her teeth as a great power. The period was also a very significant one for trade and colonial affairs, despite conflicts over authority between London and the colonies. After 1675 the Lords of Trade developed the 'old colonial system'—of closed imperial commerce protected by tariffs and guarded by military and naval power. London began to compete with Amsterdam as a centre of financial and economic activity. There was growth of involvement in Canada and West Africa with the new Hudson's Bay and Royal Africa Companies trading in beaver furs and African slaves and gold respectively. In the 1670s New Amsterdam (renamed New York) was captured from the Dutch and the New England Indian frontier was pacified. In Asia the East India Company grew in prosperity and political power. Calcutta became the effective capital of India with the textile trade and the Company conducted intra-Asian commerce, taking Indian opium to China in exchange for tea, silk, and porcelain. Here were the origins of Britain's Oriental wealth and of her modern greatness.

5. *Britain, Holland, and Europe, 1685–1689*

The rapid collapse of the rule of James II within the British Isles was a spectacular instance of British affairs being basically subject to wider European events. James was of course also a critical factor. Militarily experienced and religiously sincere, he was also politically inept and detached from the feelings of his people and of his Protestant relatives. Detesting weakness, he was like his father in his unwillingness to compromise, and his Catholicizing and strongly monarchical tendencies were plain to see. They were predicated, imperceptively, on a pro-French but pacifist approach abroad, which failed him when the total pragmatism of Louis XIV's attitude towards him became apparent and left him floundering for a policy at home and abroad.

An important event in the background to the crisis of 1688 was the action of Louis XIV against the Huguenots in his revocation of the Edict of Nantes in 1685. This fanned the Catholic issue in England and did much to undermine James. As Europe moved towards general war in 1687–8, Britain became one element in a wider drama in which Louis and William III were the critical players. Both were wary of the future use of British power, which could tip the scales of Europe in favour of the League of Augsburg and against France. William also feared an Anglo-French alliance against him. Louis, willing to help James only to the extent that his own interests were served, sought to neutralize Britain and embroil William in a British civil war. William's aims were to break James's power in his kingdoms, secure the British succession for Mary and himself, and to enlist British resources in his coming struggle with France.

The birth of the Prince of Wales in June 1688 of course threatened William's long-term Anglo-Dutch strategy. Simultaneously, in the context of an escalating international crisis in western Europe, an Anglo-French attack on the Dutch (as in 1672) appeared imminent, and the future of the archbishopric of Cologne seemed likely to ignite a war between France and the German princes. William and the Dutch state took an initiative in deciding to invade England which was bold, well-prepared, and in the end stunningly successful. Secret resolutions of the States of Holland on 19 September placed the republic squarely behind the invasion plan. The combination of

French economic and strategic threats united the Stadtholder and the States party, who had disagreed over the peace of Nijmegen. It was a plan designed to serve Dutch interests above all. Two days earlier Louis had attacked Philippsburg, committing his main army to fight on the Rhine: he was not in a position to help James. William's invasion force of 21,000 men included the best Dutch regiments. He had military superiority over James, loyal troops, English political connections and support, efficient propaganda, and even favourable winds. In the weeks following the Dutch landing on 5 November James could put up no real resistance and his position collapsed. He fled to France three days before Christmas. The Dutch military occupation of London created circumstances favourable to the political outcome which William desired. He and Mary were proclaimed in February 1689. Under the Bill of Rights and the Act of Settlement, the Catholic granddaughters of Charles I through Henriette of Orléans were barred from the English succession.

While the revolution of 1688 brought continuing Dutch political influence in Britain, it increased the standing of William in the Dutch republic and in Europe generally. It also changed totally Britain's relationship with Europe. England entered the war of the League of Augsburg in May 1689 and Scotland soon followed. Under William Britain would emerge as a major and interventionist anti-French power, changing the whole picture of European international relations. Meanwhile across the Atlantic, the revolution of 1688 precipitated the collapse of James II's monarchical Dominion of New England, with armed revolt in defence of colonial self-determination—events whose significance probably lay far in the future.

Further Reading

What follows is essentially a small cross-section of the most accessible and lively published works on each of the major themes of this volume. It begins with some general surveys and with some key collections of primary source material. This is followed by short collections of titles thematically arranged in the same sequence as they appear within the book. Only books (and not articles) have been included. Many titles were nominated by more than one author, and the General Editor has used his discretion where best to locate them. The notes added to some titles are those of the General Editor although often based on suggestions by individual authors.

General Works

(a) General Surveys

Smith, A. G. R., *The Emergence of a Nation State, 1529–1660* (London, 1984). An outstanding 'starter' text-book.

Coward, B., *The Stuart Age: A History of England, 1603–1714* (London, 1980). Another excellent textbook for the latter half of the period.

Stone, L., *The Causes of the English Revolution, 1529–1642* (London, 1972). A short and brilliant but dated essay.

Guy, J., *Tudor England* (Oxford, 1988). An authoritative advanced textbook.

Russell, C., *The Crisis of Parliaments: English History, 1509–1660* (Oxford, 1971). A very well-sustained, long, and fertile interpretative essay on the period.

Patrides, C. A., and Waddington, R. B. (eds.), *The Age of Milton: Backgrounds to Seventeenth-Century Literature* (Manchester, 1980). An excellent guide to all aspects of the political, social, and cultural history of the second half of our period, written to provide 'backgrounds to seventeenth-century literature'.

Worden, A. B. (ed.), *Stuart England* (Oxford, 1986). The best illustrated history to date, covering just the second half of the period of this book.

(b) Collections of Primary Source Material

Elton, G. R. (ed.), *The Tudor Constitution: Documents and Commentary* (2nd edn., Cambridge, 1982).

Kenyon, J. P. (ed.), *The Stuart Constitution, 1603–1688: Documents and Commentary* (2nd edn., Cambridge, 1986).

Dickens, A. G , and Carr, D., *The Reformation in England to the Accession of Elizabeth I* (London, 1967).

Hurstfield, J., and Smith, A. G. R., *Elizabethan People* (London, 1973).

Porter, H. C., *Puritanism in Tudor England* (London, 1970).

Wootton, D., *Divine Right and Democracy: An Anthology of Political Writing in Stuart England* (Harmondsworth, 1986).

Prall, S. E., *The Puritan Revolution, 1649–1660* (London, 1968).

Roots, I., *The Speeches of Oliver Cromwell* (London, 1989).

Browning, A., *English Historical Documents, 1660–1714* (London, 1953).

The Landscape of Britain

(a) Surveys

Reed, M., *The Age of Exuberance, 1550–1700* (London, 1986). The best introduction.
Cantor, L. M., *The Changing English Countryside, 1400–1700* (London, 1987).

(b) The Countryside

Thirsk, J. (ed.), *The Agrarian History of England and Wales*, vol. iv: *1500–1640* (Cambridge, 1976).
——(ed.), *The Agrarian History of England and Wales*, vol. v, part I: *1640–1750* (Cambridge, 1984). Both offer wonderful detail on agrarian regions and changes in practice.
Whyte, I. D., *Agriculture and Society in Seventeenth-Century Scotland* (Edinburgh, 1979).
Parry, M. L., and Slater, T. R. (eds.), *The Making of the Scottish Countryside* (London, 1980).

(c) Town and Countryside

Coleman, D. C., *Industry in Tudor and Stuart England* (London, 1985). Short, authoritative, and with a full bibliographical guide to each major industry.

(d) Towns

Clark, P., and Slack, P., *English Towns in Transition, 1500–1700* (Oxford, 1976). Another short and authoritative guide.
Borsay, P., *The English Urban Renaissance: Culture and Society in the Provincial Town, 1660–1770* (Oxford, 1989). An advanced but entertaining monograph.
Beier, A. L., and Finlay, R. (eds.), *London, 1500–1700: The Making of the Metropolis* (London, 1986). Reprints the most influential essays on this key topic.
Lynch, M. (ed.), *The Early Modern Town in Scotland* (London, 1987). A collection of essays rather than a coherent overview.

The Unification of Britain

(a) The Unification of England

Williams, P., *The Tudor Regime* (Oxford, 1979). Part III is the best introduction to the unification of England.
Smith, R. B., *Land and Politics in the England of Henry VIII: The West Riding of Yorkshire, 1530–1546* (Oxford, 1970). A pioneering but detailed study.
Hassell Smith, A., *County and Court: Government and Politics in Norfolk, 1558–1603* (Oxford, 1974). The classic study of dynamics of a divided country community.
MacCulloch, D., *Suffolk and the Tudors: Politics and Religion in an English County, 1500–1600* (Oxford, 1986). A splendidly nuanced study showing a different pattern from the previous study of Norfolk.
James, M. E., *Family, Lineage and Civil Society: A Study of Society, Politics and Mentality in the Durham Region, 1500–1640* (Oxford, 1974).
—— *Society, Politics and Culture: Studies in Early Modern England* (Cambridge, 1986). Important and detailed studies of the Scottish Border region.

(b) The Formation of Britain

Bradshaw, B., and Morrill, J. (eds.), *The British Problem, 1534–1707: England, Ireland, Scotland, Wales* (London, 1996).
Ellis, S. G., and Barber, S. (eds.), *Conquest and Union: Fashioning a British State, 1485–1725* (London, 1995).
—— *Tudor Frontiers and Noble Power: The Making of the British State* (Oxford, 1995).

(c) The Incorporation of Wales

Williams, G., *Recovery, Reorientation and Reformation: Wales c.1470–1642* (Oxford, 1987). A standard work.

Jenkins, P., *A History of Modern Wales, 1536–1990* (London, 1992). The early chapters offer a refreshingly new interpretation.

(d) England and Scotland

Lynch, M., *Scotland: A New History* (Edinburgh, 1992). The early modern chapters are especially witty and vivid.

Wormald, J., *Court, Kirk and Community: Scotland, 1470–1625* (London, 1981).

Ferguson, W., *Scotland's Relations with England: A Survey to 1707* (Edinburgh, 1977). Waspishly polemical.

Brown, K. M., *Kingdom or Province? Scotland and the Regal Union, 1603–1715* (London, 1992).

Mason, R. A. (ed.), *Scotland and England, 1286–1815* (Edinburgh, 1987).

(e) England and Ireland

Ellis, S. G., *Tudor Ireland: Crown, Community and the Conflict of Cultures, 1470–1603* (London, 1985).

Canny, N. P., *The Elizabethan Conquest of Ireland* (London, 1976).

Brady, C., *The Chief Governors: The Rise and Fall of Reform Government in Tudor Ireland* (Cambridge, 1995).

—— and Gillespie, R. (eds.), *Natives and Newcomers: Essays on the Making of Irish Colonial Society, 1534–1641* (Dublin, 1986).

Canny, N. P., *Kingdom and Colony: Ireland in the Atlantic World, 1560–1800* (London, 1988).

(f) Triple Monarchy

Lee, M., *Great Britain's Solomon: James VI and I in his Three Kingdoms* (Urbana, Ill., 1990). A study of King James VI and I.

Levack, B. P., *The Formation of the British State: England, Scotland and the Union, 1603–1707* (Oxford, 1987).

Russell, C., *The Causes of the English Civil War* (Oxford, 1990). Finds the causes in all three kingdoms.

FAMILY, HOUSEHOLD, AND SOCIAL STRUCTURE

(a) General Works

Wrightson, K., *English Society, 1580–1680* (London, 1982).

Amussen, S. D., *An Ordered Society: Gender and Class in Early Modern England* (Oxford, 1988).

Houston, R. A., *The Population History of Britain and Ireland, 1500–1750* (London, 1992). A brief and lucid guide to a large and difficult field.

Laurence, A., *Women in England, 1500–1760: A Social History* (London, 1994).

(b) More Advanced Works

Pollock, L. A., *Forgotten Children: Parent–Child Relations from 1500–1900* (Cambridge, 1984).

Spufford, M., *Contrasting Communities: English Villagers in the Sixteenth and Seventeenth Centuries* (Cambridge, 1974). Outstanding studies of how land and wealth were redistributed, how children were educated, and how religious belief was expressed in three very different Cambridgeshire villages.

—— *The Great Reclothing of Rural England: Petty Chapmen and their Wares in the Seventeenth Century* (London, 1984).

Wilson, C. A., *Food and Drink in Britain: From the Stone Age to Recent Times* (London, 1973).

Hobby, E., *Virtue of Necessity: English Women's Writing, 1649–1688* (London, 1988).
Houlbrooke, R. A., *English Family Life, 1576–1718: An Anthology from Diaries* (Oxford, 1988). An attractive collection of extracts from contemporary diaries etc.

Social and Cultural Institutions

(*a*) *Education*

O'Day, R., *Education and Society, 1500–1800: The Social Foundations of Education in Early Modern Britain* (London, 1982).
Charlton, K., *Education in Renaissance England* (London, 1965). A discussion of élite ideas about élite and mass education.
Cressy, D., *Literacy and the Social Order: Reading and Writing in Tudor and Stuart England* (Cambridge, 1980). Measures literacy levels by social group and region.
Davies, F., *Teaching Reading in Early England* (London, 1973).
Kearney, H., *Scholars and Gentlemen: Universities and Society in Pre-Industrial Britain, 1500–1700* (London, 1970).
MacConica, J. K., *The History of the University of Oxford*, iii: *The Collegiate University* (Oxford, 1986). For every aspect of 16th-century Oxford.
Cressy, D., *Education in Tudor and Stuart England* (London, 1975). A useful collection of extracts from original documents.

(*b*) *The Law*

Baker, J. H., *An Introduction to English Legal History* (3rd edn., Butterworths, 1990). Vital for this as for all periods.
Prest, W. R., *The Inns of Court under Elizabeth I and the Early Stuarts, 1590–1640* (London, 1972). Far more than a guide to legal education.
Brooks, C. W., *Pettyfoggers and Vipers of the Commonwealth: The 'Lower Branch' of the Legal Profession in Early Modern England* (Cambridge, 1986). A social history of attorneys and solicitors which also charts the increase in legislation.
Sharpe, J. A., *Crime in Early Modern England, 1550–1750* (London, 1984). An excellent survey.
Cockburn, J. S., *A History of English Assizes, 1558–1714* (Cambridge, 1972).
Herrup, C. B., *The Common Peace: Participation and the Criminal Law in Seventeenth-Century England* (Cambridge, 1987).
Ingram, M., *Church Courts, Sex and Marriage in England, 1570–1640* (Cambridge, 1987).
Veall, D., *The Popular Movement for Law Reform, 1640–1660* (Oxford, 1970).

(*c*) *The Theatre*

Bevington, D. M., *From Mankind to Marlowe: Growth and Structure in the Popular Drama of Tudor England* (Cambridge, Mass., 1962).
Walker, G., *Plays of Persuasion: Drama and Politics at the Court of Henry VIII* (Cambridge, 1991).
Ingram, W., *The Business of Playing: The Beginnings of the Adult Professional Theater in Elizabethan London* (Ithaca, NY, 1992).
Bentley, G. E., *The Jacobean and Caroline Stage* (7 vols., Oxford, 1941–68). Still an indispensable port-of-call.
Gurr, A., *Playgoing in Shakespeare's London* (Cambridge, 1987).
Mullaney, S., *The Place of the Stage: License, Play and Power in Renaissance England* (Chicago, 1988).
Maguire, N. K., *Regicide and Restoration: English Tragi Comedy, 1660–1671* (Cambridge, 1992).

THE MENTAL WORLDS OF THE ARISTOCRACY AND THE COMMONS

(a) The Aristocracy

STATUS

Cooper, J. P., *Land, Men and Beliefs: Studies in Early-Modern History* (London, 1983). Especially chs. 2–4, which are the best discussion of what made a gentleman a gentleman.

Heal, F., and Holmes, C., *The Gentry of England and Wales, 1500–1700* (London, 1994).

James, M. E., *Society, Politics and Culture: Studies in Early Modern England* (Cambridge, 1986). Especially the essay entitled 'English Politics and the Concept of Honour'.

Stone, L., and Fawtier Stone, J. C., *An Open Élite? England 1540–1880* (Oxford, 1984).

CULTURE

Ford, B. (ed.), *The Cambridge Guide to the Arts in Britain*, vol. iii: *Renaissance and Reformation* (Cambridge, 1989) and vol. iv: *The Seventeenth Century* (Cambridge, 1989). For the cultural and aesthetic concerns of the gentry.

Girouard, M., *Robert Smythson and the Elizabethan Country House* (New Haven, Conn., 1983). A case study of the political significance of the country house that has more of general value than the more narrowly architectural surveys.

Heal, F., *Hospitality in Early Modern England* (Oxford, 1990).

Young, A., *Tudor and Stuart Tournaments* (London, 1987).

Gittings, C., *Death, Burial and the Individual in Early Modern England* (London, 1984).

(b) The Commons

STATUS

Wrightson, K., and Levine, D., *Poverty and Piety in an English Village: Terling, 1525–1700* (New York, 1979). Establishes the dynamics of change in rural England.

Campbell, M., *The English Yeomen under Elizabeth and the Early Tudors* (London, 1960). A pioneering analysis of the emergence of the rural middling sort.

Houston, R. A., and Whyte, I. D., *Scottish Society, 1500–1800* (Cambridge, 1989).

CULTURE

Thomas, K. V., *Religion and the Decline of Magic: Studies in Popular Beliefs in Sixteenth and Seventeenth Century England* (London, 1971). The classic introduction to the mental world of the period.

—— *Man and the Natural World: Changing Attitudes in England, 1500–1800* (London, 1983).

Macfarlane, A., *Witchcraft in Tudor and Stuart England: A Regional and Comparative Study* (London, 1970). Really a study of its prevalence in Essex, but opening up lots of avenues to an understanding of the fears and tensions of the period.

Larner, C., *Enemies of God: The Witch Hunt in Scotland* (London, 1981). For the strikingly different Scottish pattern.

Capp, B., *Astrology and the Popular Press: English Almanacs, 1500–1800* (London, 1979). This and the next two afford excellent introductions to the print culture of the period.

Spufford, M., *Small Books and Pleasant Histories: Popular Fiction and its Readership in Seventeenth-Century England* (London, 1981).

Watt, T., *Cheap Print and Popular Piety, 1550–1640* (Cambridge, 1991).

Underdown, D., *Revel, Riot and Rebellion: Popular Politics and Culture in England, 1603–1660* (Oxford, 1985). Examines the evidence for cultural conflict before and during the English Revolution.

Crawford, P., *Women and Religion in England, 1500–1720* (London, 1993).

Reay, B. (ed.), *Popular Culture in Seventeenth-Century England* (London, 1985).

Fletcher, A. J., and Stevenson, J. (eds.), *Order and Disorder in Early Modern England* (Cambridge, 1985).

Seaver, P. S., *Wallington's World: A Puritan Artisan in Seventeenth-Century London* (London, 1985). A masterly reconstruction based on the voluminous writings of a Nehemiah Wallington, a London craftsman.

MONARCHS, COURTS, AND POLITICAL CULTURE

(a) The Tudors

Anglo, S., *Images of Tudor Kingship* (London, 1992).

Starkey, D. R. (ed.), *The English Court: From from the Wars of the Roses to the Civil War* (London, 1987). An excellent series of essays looking at the Court reign by reign.

Loades, D. M., *The Tudor Court* (London, 1986).

Thurley, S., *The Royal Palaces of Tudor England: Architecture and Court Life, 1460–1547* (New Haven, Conn., 1993).

Aston, M., *The King's Bedpost: Reformation and Iconography in a Tudor Group Portrait* (Cambridge, 1993). A brilliant analysis of a mid-16th-century allegorical painting.

Yates, F. A., *Astraea: The Imperial Theme in the Sixteenth Century* (London, 1975).

Bates, C., *The Rhetoric of Courtship in Elizabethan Language and Literature* (Cambridge, 1992).

(b) The Stuarts

Strong, R., *Henry, Prince of Wales, and England's Lost Renaissance* (London, 1986). An exciting survey of the might-have-beens of 17th-century history.

Levy Peck, L. (ed.), *The Mental World of the Jacobean Court* (Cambridge, 1991).

Smuts, R. M., *Court Culture and the Origins of a Royalist Tradition in Early Stuart England* (Philadelphia, 1987).

Sharpe, K., and Lake, P. (eds.), *Culture and Politics in Early Stuart England* (London, 1994).

—— *The Personal Rule of Charles I* (New Haven, Conn., 1992). A massive revaluation and statement of the case for a much-maligned king.

Aylmer, G. E., *The State's Servants: The Civil Service of the English Republic, 1649–1660* (London, 1973). A sophisticated group analysis and evaluation.

Zwicker, S. N., *Lines of Authority: Politics and English Literary Culture, 1649–1689* (Ithaca, NY, 1993).

PATTERNS OF REFORMATION

(a) The State Church

PRE-REFORMATION AND EARLY REFORMATION

Duffy, E., *The Stripping of the Altars: Traditional Religion in England, c.1400–c.1580* (New Haven, Conn., 1992). Traces the vibrancy of pre-Reformation Catholicism and argues that the Reformation was imposed slowly and ineffectually from above.

Barron, C., and Harper-Bill, C., *The Church in Pre-Reformation Society: Essays in Honour of F. R. H. Du Boulay* (Woodbridge, 1985).

Dickens, A. G., *Lollards and Protestants in the Diocese of York, 1509–1558* (Oxford, 1959).

—— *The English Reformation* (London, 1964). The classic statement of the view that the Protestant Reformation advanced rapidly with an alliance of state action and popular support.

Scarisbrick, J. J., *The Reformation and the English People* (Oxford, 1984). Doubts the popularity and effectiveness of a Reformation imposed from above and enjoying little popular support.

Haigh, C., *English Reformations: Religion, Politics, and Society under the Tudors* (Oxford, 1993). Note the plural form of 'Reformations', indicating that this is an account of a halting process and not of a clean break.

Youings, J. A., *The Dissolution of the Monasteries* (London, 1971). The most judicious of the many studies.

Loades, D. M., *The Reign of Mary Tudor: Politics, Government and Religion in England, 1553–58* (London, 1979). A moderate account of a doomed reign.

Hughes, P., *The Reformation in England* (3 vols., 1950–4). Vol. ii is a moderate statement of the case for Mary and the way she went about restoring Catholicism.

CONSOLIDATION OF THE REFORMATION

MacCulloch, D., *The Later Reformation in England, 1547–1603* (London, 1990). An excellent short survey.

Collinson, P., *The Religion of Protestants: The Church in English Society, 1559–1625* (Oxford, 1982). The major statement of the development of the Established Church under Elizabeth I and James I.

—— *The Elizabethan Puritan Movement* (London, 1967). The classic study.

THE STUART CHURCH

Fincham, K., *Prelate as Pastor: The Episcopate of James I* (Oxford, 1990). An impressive study of the Jacobean episcopate.

Tyacke, N., *Anti-Calvinists: The Rise of English Arminianism, c.1590–1640* (Oxford, 1987). Discusses the rise of 'Laudianism'.

Fincham, K. (ed.), *The Early Stuart Church, 1603–1642* (London, 1993). A collection of essays by most of those involved in recent debates about the Caroline Church.

Spurr, J., *The Restoration Church of England, 1646–1689* (New Haven, Conn., 1991). Supplants all previous studies of the Restoration Church.

(b) Religious Liberty

ROMAN CATHOLICISM

Bossy, J., *The English Catholic Community, 1570–1850* (London, 1975). Seeks to show that Catholicism was reborn in new forms.

Dures, A., *English Catholicism, 1558–1642: Continuity and Change* (Harlow, 1983). A short and judicious summary of the debate aroused by the foregoing.

Haigh, C., *Reformation and Resistance in Tudor Lancashire* (Cambridge, 1975). Lancashire had more Papists and more Puritans than anywhere else.

PROTESTANT DISSENTERS

Watts, M. R., *The Dissenters*, vol. I: *From the Reformation to the French Revolution* (Oxford, 1978).

MacGregor, J. F., and Reay, B. (eds.), *Radical Religion in the English Revolution* (Oxford, 1984). Essays on each of the major sects.

Hill, C., *The World Turned Upside Down: Radical Ideas during the English Revolution* (London, 1972). Or at least an account of those who may have tried to turn it upside down. A classic.

Davis, J. C., *Fear, Myth and History: The Ranters and the Historians* (Cambridge, 1987).

Hill, C., *A Turbulent, Seditious and Factious People: John Bunyan and his Church, 1628–1688* (Oxford, 1988).

Keeble, N. H., *Richard Baxter: Puritan Man of Letters* (Oxford, 1982). The best of several short biographies.

—— *The Literary Culture of Nonconformity in the Later Seventeenth Century* (Leicester, 1987). A book which gets closer than any other to the experience of those who were the outcasts of the Restoration.

Champion, J. A. I., *The Pillars of Priestcraft Shaken: The Church of England and its Enemies, 1660–1730* (Cambridge, 1992). For the disintegration of Protestant thought.

Grell, O. P., Israel, J. I., and Tyacke, N., *From Persecution to Toleration: The Glorious Revolution and Religion in England* (Oxford, 1991). Essays to commemorate the tercentenary of the passage of the 'Toleration Act' of 1690.

Government and Politics, 1485–1689

(a) The Early Tudors

Lander, J. R., *Government and Community: England, 1450–1509* (London, 1980).

Storey, R. L., *The Reign of Henry VII* (London, 1968).

Chrimes, S. B., *Henry VII* (London, 1972).

Elton, G. R., *Reform and Reformation: England, 1509–58* (London, 1977). Restatement of the interpretation that has dominated the second half of the century.

Gwyn, P., *The King's Cardinal: The Rise and Fall of Thomas Wolsey* (London, 1990). Overstates an interesting case which seeks to rehabilitate Wolsey.

Gunn, S. J., and Lindley, P. J. (eds.), *Cardinal Wolsey: Church, State and Art* (Cambridge, 1991).

Elton, G. R., *The Tudor Revolution in Government* (Cambridge, 1953). A book that has stimulated forty years of debate.

Coleman, C., and Starkey, D. R. (eds.), *Revolution Reassessed: Revisions in the History of Tudor Government and Administration* (Oxford, 1986). The latest instalment of that debate.

Scarisbrick, J. J., *Henry VIII* (London, 1968).

Starkey, D. R., *The Reign of Henry VIII: Personalities and Politics* (London, 1985).

Loach, J., and Tittler, R. (eds.), *The Mid-Tudor Polity c.1540–1560* (London, 1980).

(b) The Reign of Elizabeth I

Haigh, C. (ed.), *The Reign of Elizabeth I* (Basingstoke, 1984).

MacCaffrey, W. T., *The Shaping of the Elizabethan Regime: Elizabethan Politics, 1558–1572* (London, 1969).

Graves, M. A. R., *Elizabethan Parliaments, 1559–1601* (London, 1987). A short summary of much recent rethinking.

Clark, P. (ed.), *The European Crisis of the 1590s* (London, 1985).

Haigh, C., *Elizabeth I* (London, 1988). A harsh modern verdict.

(c) The Early Stuarts

Hirst, D., *Conflict and Authority, 1603–58* (London, 1986). An outstanding advanced textbook, especially good on the second half of the period.

Lockyer, R., *The Early Stuarts, 1603–42* (London, 1989).

Smith, A. G. R. (ed.), *The Reign of King James VI and I* (London, 1973).

Burgess, G., *The Politics of the Ancient Constitution: An Introduction to English Political Thought, 1603–1642* (Basingstoke, 1992). A wonderfully clear exegesis of the political debates of the period.

Russell, C., *Parliaments and English Politics, 1621–1629* (Oxford, 1979). Perhaps the most influential book of recent years.

—— *Unrevolutionary England, 1603–42* (London, 1990). Important essays.

Hughes, A., *The Causes of the English Civil War* (Basingstoke, 1991). A short and effective synthesis.

(d) The Civil Wars

Aylmer, G. E., *Rebellion or Revolution? England, 1640–1660* (Oxford, 1986).

Morrill, J. S., *The Revolt of the Provinces: Conservatives and Radicals in the English Civil War, 1630–1650* (Harlow, 1976).

—— *The Nature of the English Revolution: Essays* (Harlow, 1992). Influential essays.

Kenyon, J. P., *The Civil Wars of England* (London, 1988). The best account integrating military and political affairs.

Morrill, J. S. (ed.), *The Impact of the English Civil Wars* (London, 1991).

(e) The Interregnum

Hutton, R., *The British Republic, 1649–1660* (Basingstoke, 1990).

Morrill, J. S. (ed.), *Revolution and Restoration: England in the 1650s* (London, 1992).

Coward, B., *Cromwell* (Harlow, 1991). A short, effective biography.

Hill, C., *God's Englishman: Oliver Cromwell and the English Revolution* (London, 1970). A lively and polemical biography of Cromwell.

Morrill, J. S. (ed.), *Oliver Cromwell and the English Revolution* (London, 1990). A collection of essays by leading scholars on different aspects of his career.

(f) The Restoration

Jones, J. R., *Country and Court, 1658–1714* (London, 1978).

Hutton, R., *The Restoration: A Political and Religious History of England and Wales, 1658–1667* (Oxford, 1985).

Harris, T., Seaward, P., and Goldie, M. (eds.), *The Politics of Religion in Restoration England* (Oxford, 1990).

—— *Politics under the Later Stuarts: Party Conflict in a Divided Society, 1660–1714* (Harlow, 1993).

Scott, J., *Algernon Sidney and the Restoration Crisis, 1677–1683* (Cambridge, 1991). An important reconceptualization of that crisis.

Kenyon, J. P., *Robert Spencer, Earl of Sunderland, 1641–1702* (Cambridge, 1958). The finest of all early modern biographies.

Marshall, J., *John Locke: Resistance, Religion and Responsibility* (Cambridge, 1994).

Miller, J., *James II: A Study in Tyranny* (London, 1977).

Western, J. R., *Monarchy and Revolution: The English State in the 1680s* (London, 1985).

(g) The Glorious Revolution

Jones, J. R., *The Revolution of 1688 in England* (London, 1972).

Speck, W. A., *Reluctant Revolutionaries: Englishmen and the Revolution of 1688* (Oxford, 1988).

Israel, J. I. (ed.), *The Anglo-Dutch Moment: Essays on the Glorious Revolution and its World Impact* (Cambridge, 1991) Emphasizes the international dimension of the Revolution of 1688.

BRITAIN AND THE WORLD

(a) Sixteenth Century

Wernham, R. B., *Before the Armada: The Growth of English Foreign Policy, 1485–1588* (London, 1966). This remains the standard survey.

Doran, S., *England and Europe, 1485–1603* (London, 1986). A brief but necessary supplement to the foregoing.

Russell, J. G., *Peacemaking in the Renaissance* (London, 1986). A case study of Cambrai but of wider interest.

Ramsay, G. D., *The City of London in International Politics at the Accession of Elizabeth Tudor* (Manchester, 1975).

—— *The Queen's Merchants and the Revolt of the Netherlands: The End of the Antwerp Mart* (Manchester, 1986).

Rodriguez-Salgado, M. J., and Adams, S. (eds.), *England, Spain, and the Gran Armada, 1585–1604: Essays from the Anglo-Spanish Conferences, London and Madrid, 1988* (Edinburgh, 1991).

(*b*) Seventeenth Century

Howat, G. M. D., *Stuart and Cromwellian Foreign Policy* (London, 1974).

Jones, J. R., *Britain and the World, 1649–1815* (Brighton, 1980).

Black, J., *A System of Ambition? British Foreign Policy, 1660–1793* (London, 1991).

Elliott, J. H., *Richelieu and Olivares* (Cambridge, 1984). A masterly introduction to statecraft.

Wilson, C., *Profit and Power* (Cambridge, 1955). A study of the Anglo-Dutch wars of 1651–74.

Parker, G., *The Military Revolution: Military Innovation and the Rise of the West, 1500–1800* (Cambridge, 1988). For essential (though disputed) background.

Kennedy, P. M., *The Rise and Fall of British Naval Mastery* (London, 1983). The early chapters are important for the themes of this book.

Glossary

This glossary consists of short definitions of terms that occur in the course of this book and which readers may find it helpful to have defined. Italics within definitions indicate terms which themselves appear in the Glossary.

Act of Union the Act passed in the English and Scottish Parliaments of 1707 confirming the treaty by which the Parliaments and executive wings of government of the two kingdoms were united and brought together. The treaty also provided for the autonomy of the episcopal Church of England and the *Presbyterian* Church of Scotland and for the maintenance of separate legal processes and substantive law in both kingdoms.

Acts of Uniformity English parliamentary Acts of 1549, 1552, 1559, and 1662 in which forms of worship and religious practice were prescribed, and penalties appointed for those who failed to conform. There is an Irish Act of Uniformity in 1560 which is based on the English Act, but there are no later Acts of Uniformity in Ireland and none at all in Scotland.

Adiaphora theologians distinguished between those beliefs and practices which were necessary for salvation and those which represented custom and practice necessary for good order but which might be changed from time to time and place to place. Their name for these latter was adiaphora or 'things indifferent'.

Advowson the right (usually held by laymen) to choose the clergyman to hold a parish living. Advowsons were a form of property and could be bought, sold, or rented out.

Altar in Catholic and *Laudian* churches, it was the table (usually against the east wall of a church) where Christ's sacrifice on the cross was re-enacted and where bread and wine were transformed into Christ's body and blood. Mainstream Protestants preferred the name 'holy table' or 'communion table' and emphasized that the minister was recalling Christ's sacrifice as 'full, perfect and sufficient' for God's plan of salvation.

Anabaptists a sect originating in the Low Countries and Germany which preached a fundamentalist Protestantism centred on a belief in adult and not infant baptism. 'Anabaptist' became a general term of abuse hurled at radical Puritans.

Antinomianism the belief that those within the covenant of grace (i.e. those called to salvation) were incapable of sin.

Arminians those accused of following the Dutch theologian Arminius, who believed that Christ died for all and that each person had an active part to play in achieving the saving grace made possible by His redeeming sacrifice.

Assize court the twice-yearly visit by royal judges (travelling in pairs) on circuit around England. Increasingly these courts came to deal with most 'felonies', i.e. crimes carrying the death penalty.

Baptist a believer in adult and not infant baptism. The Baptists broke away from the Church of England and preached that only those who were 'born again in the spirit' and incorporated into their Church through adult baptism could be sure of salvation. Probably the best known seventeenth-century Baptist was John Bunyan.

Benefit of clergy a privilege originally granted to all those in holy orders which exempted them from temporal punishments for specified offences. Since the test of those able to claim the privilege was to read a verse of scripture, the privilege came gradually to be extended to cover many literate laymen. It was abolished in 1706.

Black Bartholomew Day the commemoration throughout Protestant Europe of the day in 1572 when several leading *Huguenots* were assassinated, sparking off an orgy of killing, 3,000 being massacred in Paris and 8,000 elsewhere in France.

Bond of Association in 1584 the English Parliament called on all Englishmen to rise up against anyone who made an attempt on the life of Queen Elizabeth, and invited them to swear to seek out and kill anyone involved in such a plot—i.e. it licensed lynch law.

Books of Orders these were published during times of economic crisis between the 1580s and the 1630s and contained lists of crisis-management measures. They were instructions to Justices of the Peace and other local officials, and required them to send reports on their activities to the Privy Council.

Border surnames these were semi-autonomous clans or kinship groups, addicted to reiving (banditry) and robbery, who inhabited the upland regions of the Anglo-Scottish marches. They acted together, collectively sought vengeance for injuries, and often accepted joint responsibility for their misdeeds.

Brehon Law the customary system of law and legal practice in use amongst the Gaelic Irish and increasingly supplanted by English legal custom and practice. It was virtually extinguished by the mid-seventeenth century.

Broadsheet a publication printed on one side of a large sheet of paper; typically a petition or a polemical poem. Very often illustrated with a woodcut.

Calvinist a follower of John Calvin; one with a specially strong belief that the Bible contained all things necessary for salvation and with a deep iconophobia, one who believed that God, with foreknowledge of mankind's Fall, issued an eternal decree predestining some people to salvation and permitting others to endure the penalties of the Fall, i.e. eternal damnation. Only those granted a saving faith were made capable of expressing that faith in good works.

Chantry a place (normally a side chapel or altar in a parish church) where a priest said masses to help to release the soul of a deceased person from *Purgatory*.

Chapbook a small, inexpensive pamphlet of popular tales, ballads, etc., as sold by a pedlar or 'chapman'.

Clarendon Code a name later and inappropriately given to a series of distinct Acts of Parliament in the 1660s aimed at penalizing those who absented themselves from services in their parish churches, or who took part in unauthorized services.

Common Law the coral reef of precedent and custom which formed the substance of English criminal and much civil law. It defined legal procedures and was interpreted by the judges through an exercise of 'artificial reason'. It was subject to modification and change only through parliamentary Acts.

Comprehension the name given to attempts made in the later seventeenth century to soften the terms of the 1662 *Act of Uniformity*. Proponents of 'comprehension' wanted to make the terms of membership of the Church of England easier, for example by making the use of particular rites and ceremonies prescribed in the Prayer Book optional, and by releasing those of 'tender conscience' from taking particular oaths.

Conduct books guides to appropriate behaviour directed at particular groups in society—gentlemen, their wives, middling sorts, etc.

Congregationalists those Protestants who favoured the disestablishment of the Church and the effective autonomy of every parish to choose its own minister, discipline its own members, and devise its own liturgies, with the advice of other Christians but generally without any external coercive force. (Congregationalists were often also called Independents.)

Copyhold a relatively secure form of land tenure in which the tenant held land on stated terms registered in a manorial court roll and in return for (usually small) annual rents. Such holdings were normally transferable within families on payment of an 'entry fine' for recording the transfer on the roll.

Corporation Act the Act of 1662 which empowered commissioners appointed by the Crown to expel those councillors, aldermen, and other town officials they deemed politically or religiously unsound, and to replace them by men loyal to Church and King.

Corpus Christi the Feast, much developed in the two hundred years before the Reformation, which celebrates the real presence of Christ in the bread and wine consecrated at the mass.

Court Baron a manorial court held in the presence of the Lord of the *Manor* or (more usually) his steward, in which *freehold* tenants acted as jurors. The Court Baron could hear pleas of debt and trespass, could regulate agricultural practices within a *manor*, and could make rulings about the 'custom' of the *manor*.

Court Leet held by the steward of the Lord of the *Manor* in the presence of all adult male inhabitants. They elected constables, had jurisdiction over lesser interpersonal offences (such as minor affrays), and oversaw the quality of bread and ale.

Covenant see *National Covenant, Solemn League and Covenant*.

Declarations of Indulgence the attempts made by Charles II (1662, 1672) and James II (1687, 1688) to grant to *Dissenters* relief from the laws requiring them to attend church, and to permit them to hold religious assemblies other than those laid down by law.

Deist someone with a rationalist belief in a creator God or divine clockmaker who set the universe going, but with little or no faith in an immanent or omnipresent Christian God or in the scriptures and the creeds as infallible guides to human behaviour and the divine plan of salvation.

Demesne that part of a manorial lord's land which was reserved for his own use.

Disafforestation the suppression (usually in return for compensation) of the Crown's special powers to exercise jurisdiction within areas designated centuries before as royal forests. Many of these areas had long since lost their trees.

Dissenters those who refused to conform themselves to the practice and discipline of the Church of England. Otherwise known as Nonconformists.

Distraint the legal power to confiscate someone's property usually for failure to pay what is owed to an agency of the state (e.g. for non-payment of taxes or fines, or for breach of bail terms etc.).

Enclosure the practice (also known as engrossing) of taking the great open or common fields of medieval England which were farmed communally and dividing them into individual hedged or ditched holdings; and the practice of hedging and ploughing land that had previously been waste or common.

Endowed schools those schools which received a charter and an endowment of money or property. Most such schools offered a classical curriculum. Many became 'public schools' while others retained the character of town *grammar schools*.

Erastian someone who emphasized the authority of the laity and of the secular state in relation to matters of religion (e.g. in granting powers of excommunication to laymen or bodies dominated by laymen, or in granting to Parliament the right to define doctrine or to determine forms of worship).

Exclusion Crisis the name sometimes given to the political crisis of 1678–81, when one of the aims of those critical of royal policies was to secure the passage of an Act of Parliament debarring Charles II's brother and heir, James Duke of York, from the succession to the throne.

Fifteenths and Tenths a parliamentary grant of taxation, first introduced in 1334. It was a tax on land and other forms of wealth and became increasingly burdensome on smaller landholders. It continued into the seventeenth century, but then fell into disuse.

Five Mile Act an Act of Parliament of 1665 which debarred any minister deprived of his living as a result of the *Act of Uniformity* of 1662 from coming within five miles of any parish in which he had ever served.

Forced Loans all monarchs from the mid-fifteenth century to the 1620s used prerogative powers to require their subjects to lend them money in times of war and national emergency. These loans were then turned into taxes retrospectively by Parliament. Charles I's contentious collection of Forced Loans in 1627 led to the *Petition of Right*.

Franchises grants made by the Crown, to particular individuals or corporate bodies, of privileges, legal exemptions, and private rights (such as the rights to hold markets or fairs, to collect tolls, or to take for themselves what would otherwise be royal revenues, such as treasure-trove, wreck, swans).

Freehold a form of tenure in which a landholder paid little or no rent and generally had complete freedom to sell or use the land as he wished.

Furlong a term used in ploughing to indicate a length of furrow. It was most usually taken to be 220 yards (one eighth of a mile) long, though in some counties the measure is greater or less (e.g. in York-shire it was 440 yards).

Gavelkind in most parts of England, the eldest son inherited by right most of his father's property (= primogeniture). But in Kent and a few other areas, local custom provided for the equal distribution of property between all sons, and this practice was known as gavelkind.

Grammar school an endowed school, usually in a town, in which a classical curriculum was taught.

Heretic someone who denied one or more teaching which the Established Church held to be necessary for salvation. Well over 300 men and women were burnt to death as heretics in the reigns of Henry VIII and Mary I.

Homily a sermon. The Book of Homilies was an official collection of sermons issued by the Church of England from the 1540s onwards that was to be read wherever the parish clergy could not preach (because not licensed to do so) or chose not to preach themselves.

Hornbook a starter-aid in teaching a child to read. It usually consisted of an alphabet and the Lord's Prayer on a single sheet of paper mounted on a tablet of wood and protected by a thin veneer of translucent horn.

Huguenots the name given to members of the French *Calvinist* Churches from the 1560s onwards (see also *Black Bartholomew* and *Revocation of the Edict of Nantes*).

Independent see *Congregationalist*.

Intercursus Magnus commercial treaty between England and Burgundy, signed in November 1496.

Justices of the Peace commissioners appointed by the Crown in every county to administer justice and to enforce an ever-widening body of social and economic legislation. In 1500 there were about 20 Justices in every shire, by 1700 often more than 100.

Ket's Rebellion a rebellion led by Robert Ket in East Anglia in 1549, essentially as a protest against the social and economic policies of the Duke of Somerset, Protector for the young Edward VI, and including a difficult-to-gauge religious dimension.

King's evil kings and queens were thought to have special powers to heal specific diseases, normally of a scrofulous or tubercular kind. These acts of royal healing are known as 'touching for the king's evil'.

Latitudinarians those churchmen in the second half of the seventeenth century who favoured an open, comprehensive Church which insisted on few beliefs and practices as necessary and sought to work with all those of goodwill who wished to find room for themselves within the state Church.

Laudian the practices and beliefs associated with Archbishop William Laud (1573–1645)—with a strong emphasis on ceremonialism, clericalism, and clerical hierarchy, i.e. emphasizing the apostolic and traditional rather than the reformed and *Calvinist* aspects of the Church of England.

Leasehold an agreement by which land was held for a fixed annual rent for a stated period of time or for a number of lives (usually three), thus allowing the lease to be passed from one generation to the next.

Long Parliament the name given at the time and since to the Parliament that assembled in November 1640 and which sat until it was dissolved by armed force in April 1653. See also *Rump Parliament*.

Lords Lieutenant royal appointments (almost all from the peerage) with responsibility for local security matters and control of the local militias. The system began in the mid-sixteenth century and was operating in all counties by the 1570s.

Manor a unit both of jurisdiction and landholding: 'a manor is of lands, woods, meadow, pasture and arable; it is compounded of demesnes and services of long continuance'. See *Court Leet* and *Court Baron*.

Militia Acts the Acts of 1558 and the 1660s which created and regulated the organization, payment, and training of local defence forces in every county.

National Covenant the solemn bond signed and joined by most of the people of Scotland in 1638 to preserve the Church of Scotland in *Presbyterian* and *Calvinist* purity against the innovations of Charles I and his father.

Neoplatonism the adaptation of Plato's philosophy to Christianity, in which God is seen as divine reason, and human reason as divine illumination. Associated especially with the 'Cambridge Platonists' of the Restoration, who emphasized contemplation and 'holy living' over dogma and ritual.

Nonconformists those who refused to conform themselves to the practice and discipline of the Church of England. Otherwise known as Dissenters.

Overbury Affair a political scandal in 1615. Sir Thomas Overbury, who was privy to a scandal surrounding the King's favourite, the Earl of Somerset, was murdered so that he could not betray his secret, and the contract for his killing was traced back to Somerset and his wife.

Pale the area around Dublin which was under the direct control of officials appointed by the King of England up to and beyond the creation of the kingdom of Ireland in 1541.

Petition of Right the parliamentary address accepted (and given statutory force) by Charles I in 1628. By accepting it, he agreed not to attempt again to raise *Forced Loans*, not to imprison his subjects without showing cause known to the law, not to billet soldiers on civilian households, and not to subject civilians to martial law.

Pilgrimage of Grace the general name given to the series of uprisings in 1536 and 1537. The main risings were in Lincolnshire and Yorkshire with subsidiary risings in other northern counties, and the rebels' causes were a mixture of religious and secular concerns.

Poor Law the general name for a body of legislation mainly in the reign of Elizabeth that sought to distinguish the deserving from the undeserving poor and to provide an elaborate network of relief provision for the former and punishment for the latter.

Poynings' Law the law of 1494 by which no bill could be introduced into the Irish Parliament without prior consent of the king confirmed by letters bearing his seal.

Predestinarian one who believed that God, with foreknowledge of mankind's fall, issued an eternal decree predestining some people to salvation and permitting others to endure the penalties of the Fall, i.e. eternal damnation. Only those granted a saving faith were made capable of expressing that faith in good works.

Presbyterians those who believed that all ministers were equal and that for any minister to claim a superiority of orders over others was wrong; those who believed in strong structures of ecclesiastical discipline, but made up of layers formed from the bottom up—parishes nominating to local bodies, who nominate to regional bodies, who nominate to national bodies. Presbyterianism developed strongly in Scotland but not in England.

Pride's Purge the episode on 6 December 1648 in which a detachment of soldiers commanded by Colonel Thomas Pride surrounded the Houses of Parliament and purged out those members who were willing to make a settlement with the King on terms unacceptable to the Army leaders. They arrested 70 MPs and prevented many more from taking their seats. The Purge was a prelude to the trial and execution of the King. (See also *Rump Parliament*.)

Prophesyings meetings of local clergy in Elizabeth's reign to hear one another preach and to promote greater preaching skills. Approved of by the bishops and disapproved of by the Queen, who saw the potential in them for seditious preaching.

Purgatory in Catholic belief, where the souls of the dead go to be purged of their sins before God admits them to heaven (a process helped by the prayers of the living). This was a belief denied by the Protestant Churches.

Puritans those (especially between 1560 and 1650) who wanted to purify the Church of England of the 'dregs of popery' in its government, worship, and doctrine. Also known as 'precisians', as 'the hotter sort of Protestants', as 'the godly', or as the strictest adherents of *Calvinism*.

Purveyance the royal right to purchase supplies for the royal household at fixed (and low) prices. This was a grievance much aired in early Stuart Parliaments. Purveyance and similar special royal rights were replaced by a tax on all hearths in 1662.

Quakers the largest of the Interregnum sects and the most extreme in their opposition to all forms of church government and prescribed forms of worship. They denounced the professional clergy and organized *tithe* strikes and other forms of civil disobedience. In the Restoration they became progressively less militant but remained the most reviled and persecuted of all sects.

Recusants those who deliberately absented themselves from Church of England services (the term applied particularly to Catholics). Those who did so absent themselves (especially heads of households) became liable from the 1580s to heavy fines or other penalties.

Revocation of the Edict of Nantes in 1598 King Henri IV of France granted his Protestant subjects extensive religious and civil liberties in the Edict of Nantes, which he pledged would be irrevocable. His successors whittled away these rights and in 1685 Louis XIV disowned his predecessor's pledge and revoked the Edict entirely. Many of the victims of the ensuing persecution fled to England, to the embarrassment of the Catholic James II. (See also *Huguenots*.)

Rogationtide the three days before the Feast of the Ascension, when solemn prayers were chanted as all members of a parish 'beat the bounds' of the parish. There were secular as well as religious reasons why people needed to know exactly where parish boundaries lay, and these ceremonies survived the general cut-back on processions that took place at the Reformation.

Rump Parliament the name give to the Parliament that survived *Pride's Purge* and sat on from December 1648 to April 1653. Although dissolved by Cromwell in 1653, it was recalled after his death in May 1659 and met fitfully and ineffectually until February 1660. (See also *Long Parliament*.)

St Bartholomew's Eve Massacre see *Black Bartholomew*.

Schmalkaldic League alliance of Protestant (Lutheran) princes and cities, formed in December 1530

Scrivener a legal copyist, especially someone who drew up legal contracts, and a middleman who arranged loans.

Separatists those who withdrew completely from the Established Church and organized themselves into their own religious conventicles or sects. (Those who dutifully attended their local parish church *and* joined in the activities of illegal assemblies are often known as semi-separatists.)

Ship Money money raised on royal writs (without parliamentary consent) to provide ships in times of national emergency (as in the 1590s and 1620s). Until 1635 it was a charge laid on coastal regions, but Charles I then tried to levy it as a regular levy on the whole country. Between 1635 and 1639 it proved a financial success and a political disaster.

Shrievalty the job to be undertaken by sheriffs. Each county had a sheriff appointed annually to collect royal revenues and arrest those who disturbed the King's (or Queen's) peace.

Solemn League and Covenant the agreement between the English and Scottish Parliaments in 1643 by which the Scots sent 20,000 troops to join the parliamentarian armies in England. In return the Long Parliament promised that a single form of church government would be introduced into the kingdoms of England, Scotland, and Ireland and that a federal union of the kingdoms of England and Scotland would be developed.

Star Chamber a court consisting of the king's Privy Councillors and the judges which was responsible for investigating public order offences and alleged perversions of justice for a century up to 1641. It lost popularity in the 1630s following the savage punishments inflicted on Puritan critics of royal policies.

Statute of Uses a controversial Act of Parliament passed in 1536 against the practice by which major landowners avoided death duties by creating bodies of trustees who would own their estates for the benefit ('use') of the heir in the event of the landowner dying young. Such was the resistance to the Act that Henry VIII was forced to replace it with a much more limited measure in 1540.

Subsidy a parliamentary grant of taxation, first introduced in 1523. It was a tax on the profits of land and other forms of wealth and became less efficient with time as the rich became increasingly underassessed. It was replaced by other forms of direct taxation from the civil war years onwards.

Surplice a white linen robe worn by an officiating clergyman before and after the Reformation. When it was insisted on by Elizabeth, it was denounced as a 'popish rag' by the *Puritans* who wanted ministers to wear a black gown, representing the minister's teaching function.

Tabling out the practice of boarding a child in a private home close to a school during term time.

Test Acts two Acts of Parliament in 1673 and 1678 which imposed oaths on those holding public office and also on those serving in either House of Parliament. The oaths were so designed that virtually no Catholic could take them. They were thus expelled from office. James II tried to get the Acts repealed, but they remained in force until 1828.

Things Indifferent see *Adiaphora*.

Tithe one-tenth of the produce of a parish was supposed to be handed over to the vicar or rector and/or to a lay 'impropriator' who possessed the right by virtue of being descended from (or having acquired possession by purchase from) the original builder of the church. Many purchasers of former monastic lands were lay impropriators. Tithe disputes were a constant source of friction throughout the seventeenth century.

Treaty of Greenwich treaty between England and Scotland in July 1543 which proposed a union of the kingdoms through the marriage in due course of Henry's heir, Prince Edward, and the infant Mary Queen of Scots. The treaty was disowned almost immediately by the Scots.

Union of the Crowns the union, in 1603, of the Crowns of England and Scotland, when James VI of Scotland was declared the closest descendant by blood of the deceased Elizabeth: he was the grandson of her father's sister.

Usher under-master at a school.

Vocation Tudor and Stuart men and women believed that everyone was called by God to a particular role in life, as in the Church, a profession, a trade, etc.

Chronology

1485 Battle of Bosworth: death of RICHARD III and accession of HENRY VII

1486 Marriage of Henry VII to Elizabeth of York unites rival royal houses

1486 Battle of Stoke secures Henry's position

1487 Defeat of Lambert Simnel, pretended 'Prince in the Tower'

1489 Rebellion in Yorkshire and north-east England over levels of taxation; Duke of Northumberland murdered

1489 King's eldest son Arthur proclaimed Prince of Wales; Council for Wales and the Marches created at Ludlow (continues in developed form until 1641)

1491 Spasmodic attempts of Perkin Warbeck, pretended 'Prince in the Tower' to gain the throne with support from Kings of France and Scotland; captured and executed 1499

1492 Siege of Boulogne; peace with France at Treaty of Etaples

1493 James IV declares the end of the Macdonald Lordship of the Isles (not fully enforced until 1545)

1494 Poynings' Law lays down that no legislation can be introduced into the Irish Parliament without prior consent of the King

1496 *Intercursus Magnus*, comprehensive commercial treaty with the Netherlands

1497 John Cabot, sailing from Bristol, lands in Newfoundland

1497 Rebellion in Cornwall over taxation

1502 Death of Arthur, Prince of Wales

1502 Treaty of Perpetual Peace between Henry VII and James IV sealed by marriage of James to Henry's elder daughter

1509 Death of HENRY VII and accession of HENRY VIII

1511 Henry VIII joins the Holy League, papal-led alliance against France

1513 English defeat the French at 'Battle of the Spurs'

1513 English troops occupy Tournai (until 1518)

1513 Battle of Flodden: JAMES IV of Scotland and one-third of the Scottish nobility killed

1513 Rise of Thomas Wolsey, initially as war administrator, but soon to be chief minister in Church (Archbishop of York and Cardinal Legate) and State (Lord Chancellor)

1516 Publication of Sir Thomas More's *Utopia*

1518 Treaty of London, settlement of war with France

1520 Field of the Cloth of Gold, formal interviews between Henry VIII, Charles V, and Francis I

1521 Henry VIII publishes *Assertio Septem Sacramentorum* and is given title 'Defender of the Faith' by the Pope

1521 'The Great Enterprise'. Henry VIII and Charles V plan joint operations against Francis I

1521 Third Duke of Buckingham executed for allegedly seeking the Crown (or the succession to the Crown)

1523 Wolsey successfully introduces the parliamentary subsidy

1525 Wolsey fails to introduce the 'Amicable Grant', a non-parliamentary grant intended to fund an invasion of France

1525   Treaty of the More: peace with France

1525   First edition of William Tyndale's New Testament in English published

1527   Henry VIII begins negotiations with Rome for a divorce (annulment)

1529   Treaty of Cambrai: settlement of war between Charles V, Francis I, and Henry VIII

1529   Wolsey dismissed from all his civil offices; he dies. More becomes Lord Chancellor

1529   Reformation Parliament meets (in seven sessions to 1537)

1532   Minor war between England and Scotland (to 1534), fought in the 'Debatable Lands'

1532   Submission of the Clergy recognizes Henry's superiority over matters ecclesiastical if not matters theological

1532   Sir Thomas More resigns as Lord Chancellor

1532   Death of Archbishop Warham removes obstacle to settlement of Henry's divorce proceedings in England

1532   Anne Boleyn becomes pregnant

1532   Thomas Cromwell becomes Henry's chief minister

1533   Thomas Cranmer appointed Archbishop by the King and confirmed by the Pope

1533   Henry marries Anne Boleyn; subsequently, Cranmer annuls Henry's marriage to Catherine of Aragon; Princess Elizabeth born

1533   Parliament passes the Act in Restraint of Appeals which prevented Catherine appealing to Rome and proclaimed that 'this realm of England is an Empire'

1534   Act of Supremacy ends all papal jurisdiction in England

1534   Trial and subsequent (1537) execution of the Earl of Kildare signals major change in English policy in Ireland

1534   Trial of Lord Dacre signals major change in Henrician policy towards Scotland

1535   Henry VIII and Thomas Cromwell order the *Valor Ecclesiasticus*, a survey of the wealth of all religious houses.

1535   Publication of Miles Coverdale's English translation of the Bible

1535   Execution of Sir Thomas More and Bishop John Fisher for refusing to accept Henry's claim to be Supreme Head of the Church

1536   Catherine of Aragon dies; Anne Boleyn executed; Henry marries Jane Seymour

1536   Royal Injunctions order all clergy to instruct youth in the Lord's Prayer; Ten Articles Act brings strong Lutheran influences to bear on religious practice

1536   Dissolution of the smaller monasteries

1536   Pilgrimage of Grace, the greatest of all sixteenth-century rebellions against royal policies; in fact a series of semi-autonomous risings

1536   Franchises Act allows the King to revoke inalienable grants of jurisdiction made by himself and his predecessors

1536   Series of Bills introduced into Parliament (culminating in the Act of Union of 1543) which incorporates Wales into an enlarged English state

1537   Prince Edward born; Jane Seymour dies

1537   Thomas Cranmer publishes *The Institution of a Christian Man*

1538   Passage of Act providing for the registration of all baptisms, marriages, and burials in all parishes

1538   Injunctions lay down that no one unable to read a primer should be admitted to receive holy communion

1539   Act of Six Articles heralds a theological backlash

1539   Dissolution of the Greater Monasteries

1540   Henry marries Anne of Cleves (Jan., annulled July) and Catherine Howard (July)

1540   Thomas Cromwell executed

1540   War with France

1540   Completion of reforms that produced a new-style corporate Privy Council, combining deliberative and executive functions

1541   Act erecting Ireland into a Kingdom annexed to the Crown of England

1541   Catherine Howard executed for adultery

1542   Lord Deputy St Leger announces policy of 'Surrender and Regrant' in Ireland to bring Gaelic Lords into a feudal relationship with the King

1542   Scottish invasion of England; the Scots are heavily defeated at the Battle of Solway Moss; JAMES V of Scotland 'turned his face to the wall and died'

1543   War with France

1543   Treaty of Greenwich (July) to end Anglo-Scottish war; proposed marriage of the Prince of Wales to Mary, infant Queen of Scots; Scots disown the Treaty (Dec.)

1544   Henry VIII plans 'Rough Wooing' of Scotland (campaign of terror to make Scots reconfirm the Treaty of Greenwich); English invasions of Scotland continue until 1550

1544   English occupation of Boulogne (until 1550)

1546   Treaty of Campe: peace with France

1547   Death of HENRY VIII and accession of EDWARD VI; Edward Seymour, Earl of Hertford, becomes Duke of Somerset and Lord Protector

1547   Dissolution of the Chantries; clerical marriage permitted; first *Book of Homilies* published

1547   English victory over the Scots at Battle of Pinkie

1549   Act of Uniformity imposes first Prayer Book of Edward VI which creates a fully vernacular liturgy

1549   Rebellions in South-West and in East Anglia (Ket's Rebellion); fall of Somerset; power passes to John Dudley, Duke of Northumberland

1552   Second Prayer Book of Edward VI draws on radical Continental Protestant models

1553   Death of EDWARD VI; Northumberland fails to place Lady Jane Grey on the throne; accession of MARY I

1553   Restoration of the Mass

1554   Marriage of Mary to Philip II of Spain; reconciliation of England and Rome and restoration of papal jurisdiction

1555   Kentish (or Wyatt's) rebellion against the Spanish match

1555   Public executions of Protestant 'heretics' begin (282 men and women burned for heresy 1555–8); Cranmer deprived of his offices

1556   Archbishop Cranmer executed by burning

1557   Anglo-French War leads to permanent loss of Calais

1558   Marriage of Mary of Scotland to Francis, heir to French throne

1558   Militia Act, the basis of local defence for several centuries

1558   Publication of John Knox's *First Blast of the Trumpet against the Monstrous Regiment of Women*

1558   Death of MARY I and accession of ELIZABETH I; France declares Mary of Scotland Queen of England

1559   Acts of Supremacy and Allegiance once more end papal jurisdiction in England; declare Elizabeth to be Supreme Governor; and establish a Church 'that looked Catholic and sounded Protestant'. Similar provisions approved by the Irish Parliament for the Church of Ireland

1559   Lords of the Congregation rebel against French Catholic domination of Scotland

1559   Treaty of Cateau-Cambrésis: comprehensive peace treaty between Spain, France, and England

1560   Elizabeth sends expeditionary force to Scotland and (by the treaty of Edinburgh) forces French to withdraw all troops; Lords of the Congregation secure power and Scottish Parliament abolishes papal jurisdiction and the Mass

1560   Death of Francis II without impregnating Mary prevents danger of a single claimant to the crowns of France, Scotland, and England

1561   Mary returns to Scotland

1562   Elizabeth nearly dies of smallpox

1563   Convocation approves the Thirty-Nine Articles

1563   First edition of John Foxe's *Actes and Monuments* (or Book of Martyrs), which was more widely read and more influential in creating Protestant attitudes than any book except the Bible

1565   Marriage of Mary of Scotland and the Earl of Darnley

1566   Archbishop Parker's *Advertisements* require all clergy to wear the surplice

1566   Elizabeth under strong parliamentary pressure to marry

1567   Darnley murdered; civil war in Scotland

1568   Mary Queen of Scots escapes to England and is imprisoned (until her execution in 1587)

1569   Northern Rising against Elizabeth I and in favour of Mary Queen of Scots and Catholicism

1570   Pope issues bull of excommunication against Elizabeth ('*Regnans in Excelsis*') calling on her subjects to overthrow her

1570   English Plantation of East Ulster

1570   Roger Ascham's *The Schoolmaster* published

1571   Ridolfi Plot to depose Elizabeth. Mary implicated but Elizabeth refuses to execute her

1571   English Presbyterians publish *The Admonition to the Parliament*

1572   Execution of Thomas Howard, fourth Duke of Norfolk, for conspiring with Mary Queen of Scots against Elizabeth

1572   An Act of Parliament makes the payment of poor relief mandatory on all householders not themselves in receipt of alms

1572   John Field and Thomas Wilcox circulate their *Admonition* calling for the further reform of the Church

1573   Privy Council introduces the 'trained bands' or specialist militia alongside the general militia

1573   Brief English invasion of Scotland to secure the position of the Protestant Regent

1576   Publication of William Lambarde's *Perambulation of Kent*, pioneering county history which inspired many others

1577   Archbishop Grindal suspended for opposing the Queen who wishes prophesyings (training exercises in preaching) to be suppressed

1579   Major rebellion in Munster (the Desmond Rebellion, suppressed 1583)

1579   John Stubbs sentenced to have his hand cut off for criticizing Anglo-French marriage proposals

1580   Jesuit missionaries arrive in England

1580   Francis Drake completes a three-year circumnavigation of the globe and is knighted.

1581   Parliament approves fines of £20 a month for non-attendance at church by 'popish recusants'

1582   Act makes all Catholic clergy found in England liable to execution (more than 100 killed by 1603)

1583   Throckmorton Plot to assassinate Elizabeth

1583   First royal theatre company established

1583   Publication of Sir Thomas Smith's *De Republica Anglorum*, perhaps the best early modern attempt at social analysis

1583   Archbishop Whitgift's *Three Articles* aim to identify and prosecute Presbyterian minority in the Church

1584   Plantation of Munster (completed 1589)

1584   The 'Black Acts' in Scotland halt the advance of strict Presbyterianism

1585   Treaty of Nonsuch pledges English military assistance to the Dutch rebels against Philip II; war with Spain in many theatres continues until 1604

1585   First (failed) attempt to found a colony in North America (Roanoke, Virginia)

1586   Privy Council introduces Books of Orders for regulating the work of local JPs, a policy repeated in crisis years until the 1630s

1586   First engagements involving English troops fighting Spanish troops in the Netherlands

1586   Babbington Plot uncovered; Mary implicated

1587   Execution of Mary Queen of Scots

1587   Cope's 'Bill and Book', the most concerted Elizabethan attempt to persuade Parliament to reform the Church of England along Presbyterian lines

1588   Philip II sends the Gran Armada to invade England: it is dispersed by bad weather and the English Navy

1588   First of Shakespeare's plays staged (last one first staged 1613)

1588   Publication of William Morgan's Welsh translation of the Bible

1590   Publication of early parts of Edmund Spenser's *Faerie Queene* (complete edition 1596)

1590   First of several amphibious expeditions launched by Elizabeth over the decade against Spanish targets in Portugal, the Azores, Cadiz, etc.

1591   English troops sent to assist French Protestants in Brittany

1592   Scottish Parliament passes 'the Golden Acts' strengthening Presbyterianism

1593   Publication of Richard Hooker's *Of the Laws of Ecclesiastical Politie*

1593   Execution of John Greenwood and Henry Barrow, two leading Protestant separatists

1594   Nine Year War in Ireland begins

1596   Privy Council raises Ship Money from the coastal regions for the provision of the Navy (prefigures Charles I's more controversial actions)

1596   Blackfriars Theatre, built for Shakespeare's players, completed

1596   Robert Cecil becomes Secretary of State as his father William, Lord Burghley, moves towards retirement and death (1598)

1597   Those disobeying Books of Orders made liable to Star Chamber prosecution

1597   Major codification of the various acts for the relief of poverty into the systematic 'Old Poor Law'

1598   Publication of King James VI's *Trew Law of Free Monarchies*

1599   Publication of King James VI's *Basilikon Doron*

1600   Foundation of the Dutch East India Company

1601   Spanish invasion of Ireland (3,500 troops land at Kinsale)

1601   Failed *coup d'état* by the Queen's petulant favourite, the Earl of Essex, leads to his execution

1603   Death of Elizabeth I and accession of James VI of Scotland to be James I of England and Ireland

1603   Surrender of Tyrone at Mellifont ends Nine Year War in Ireland

1604   Hampton Court Conference considers reform of the English Church

1604   Treaty of London ends war with Spain

1605   Gunpowder Plot

1605   Publication of Francis Bacon's *Advancement of Learning*

1606   Act of Union of the Kingdoms debated in the Parliaments of England and Scotland but not approved

1606   Judges find for the King in Bate's Case, permitting the King to levy impositions (prerogative surcharges on customs duties)

1607   Flight of the Earls of Tyrone and Tyrconnel prepares way for English and Scottish plantations in Ulster

1607   Midlands Rising against enclosure of the common fields

1607   Foundation of the Virginia Company

1608   Judgment in Calvin's Case naturalizes as Englishmen those Scots born after the Union of the Crowns

1608   First Gaelic Irish translation of the Book of Common Prayer is published; it is half a century too late

1609   James is instrumental in brokering the Truce of Antwerp between Spain and the Dutch

1610   Attempt to rationalize royal finance—the Great Contract—breaks down

1611   Publication of the Authorized Version of the Bible

1612   Death of Robert Cecil, Earl of Salisbury, ends a half-century of political domination by the Cecils

1612   Death of Henry, Prince of Wales, leaving James's less gifted younger son, Charles, as heir to the throne

1613   Marriage of James's daughter Elizabeth to the Elector Palatine

1613   The Earl of Somerset, James's favourite, accuses the Earl of Essex of impotence in order to have Essex's marriage annulled so that he can marry Lady Essex

1615   The Overbury Scandal: Lord and Lady Somerset convicted of murdering Sir Thomas Overbury for threatening to reveal the secrets of the Essex divorce scandal

1615   Emergence of George Villiers, later Duke of Buckingham (1623), as the new royal favourite

1616   Sir Edward Coke, Lord Chief Justice, is sacked as a judge, the first for more than a century; many more sackings follow later in the century

1617   James makes his only return visit to Scotland after becoming King of England

1617   Irish Articles promulgated (they are more unambiguously Calvinist than the English Thirty-Nine Articles of 1563)

1618   Synod of Dort at which British representatives affirm Calvinist teaching and condemn Arminianism

1618   Execution of Sir Walter Raleigh

1618   Outbreak of the Thirty Years War; James's son-in-law quickly ejected from his electorate by Spanish troops; James seeks Anglo-Spanish marriage treaty as part of a settlement of the disputes

1619   Inigo Jones designs the Banqueting House in Whitehall

1621   Parliament revives impeachment so as to prosecute (*a*) monopolists (*b*) Francis Bacon

1623   Prince Charles and the Duke of Buckingham travel to Spain in a vain attempt to win the Infanta's daughter for Charles; they return humiliated and demand war with Spain

1624   James declares war on Spain and pays Danish mercenaries under Count Mansfeld to recapture the Palatinate: the expedition fails

1625 Death of JAMES VI and I and accession of CHARLES I

1625 Charles marries Henrietta Maria of France, but quickly falls out with France over the honouring of the marriage treaty and over Louis XIII's persecution of Protestants

1625 Charles seeks to cancel all the land grants made by his Stewart predecessors so that he can regrant them on terms more favourable to the Crown and the Church (the Act of Revocation)

1626 Buckingham leads failed expedition against Cadiz

1626 York House Conference upholds Arminian teaching, in effect reversing Dort

1626 Charles declares war on France

1626 Attempt by the House of Commons to impeach Buckingham; Charles forced to dissolve Parliament

1627 Buckingham leads failed expedition to Île de Rhé (near the besieged Protestant stronghold of La Rochelle)

1628 Parliament passes the Petition of Right, effectively limiting the Crown's right to imprison at will, to billet soldiers on civilians, and to punish those who refused to pay prerogative taxation or make prerogative loans

1628 Buckingham assassinated

1629 Violent scenes mark ending of Charles's third Parliament; seven MPs charged with sedition and imprisoned, Charles embarks on his 'Eleven Years Personal Rule'

1629 Treaty of Susa marks peace with France

1630 Treaty of Madrid marks peace with Spain

1630 Foundation of the Massachusetts Bay Company

1632 Van Dyck settles in England as Court painter

1633 William Laud enthroned as Archbishop of Canterbury

1633 Charles I visits Scotland, is crowned, and makes mischief

1633 Thomas Wentworth, later Earl of Strafford, takes up appointment as Lord Deputy in Ireland and begins to introduce his policies of 'Thorough'

1633 William Prynne sentenced to lose his ears for libelling the Queen

1634 Ship Money levied on the coastal regions

1635 Ship Money extended to inland counties

1636 New canons for the Scottish Church promulgated

1637 New Scottish Prayer Book promulgated by proclamation

1637 William Prynne sentenced to lose the stumps of his ears and others their ears for libelling the Bishops

1638 Majority of Scottish political nation subscribe to the National Covenant to withstand religious innovations

1638 Judges decide (in the case of *Rex* v. *Hampden*) in favour of the King's right to enforce the payment of Ship Money

1639 King plans to use English, Irish, and Scottish troops to impose his policies on the Scots. Planned invasion collapses

1640 King fails to get support from a Short Parliament to raise troops against the Scots; he attacks Scotland anyway; the Scots defeat him at Newburn and occupy north-east England; King constrained to call the Long Parliament

1641 Constitutional reform: Strafford executed and other ministers and judges impeached or forced into exile, Triennial Act passed, and prerogative courts and prerogative taxation abolished; and ecclesiastical deadlock—Root and Branch Petition

1641 Treaty of Edinburgh leads to Scottish troops being withdrawn

1641 Irish Rebellion against the English Planters leads to widespread massacre of Protestants

1641 The Grand Remonstrance itemizes royal misgovernment, remedies achieved, and remedies to be sought

1642 King attempts to arrest leading parliamentary critics and fails; King withdraws from London; military and political provocations escalate; Civil War breaks out; Battle of Edgehill fails to settle the disputes

1642 Parliament orders the closure of all theatres (ban lasts until 1660)

1643 The English Parliamentarians and the Scottish Covenanters form alliance around the Solemn League and Covenant; the Scots promise to send 20,000 troops into England and the English promise a federal union of the English and Scottish states and a single system of church government and practice

1644 Battle of Marston Moor, the largest of all civil-war battles, won by the Parliamentarians and the Scots

1644 Publication of John Milton's defence of intellectual liberty, *Areopagitica*

1644 Parliamentary trial of Archbishop Laud (culminating in his attainder and public execution in Jan. 1645)

1645 New Model Army created and wins Battle of Naseby

1646 King surrenders and First Civil War ends; rise of the Levellers calling for more accountable government

1647 Failure of many attempts at peace; Army grandees and Levellers debate the fundamentals of the constitution in Putney church

1648 King signs the Engagement with dissident Scottish nobles and launches the Second Civil War which his supporters lose

1649 Public trial and public execution of CHARLES I and abolition of monarchy in England and Ireland; the Scottish Estates proclaim Charles II King of Britain and Ireland

1649 Publication of *Eikon Basilike* begins the cult of Charles I as the martyr-king

1649 The Rump of the Long Parliament acts as interim government of England (until 1653), nominating its own executive Council of State

1649 Cromwell leads army of conquest against the Irish Confederates

1650 Cromwell breaks the back of Irish resistance, and returns home to lead invasion of Scotland; he defeats the army of the Covenanters at the battle of Dunbar

1651 Charles II crowned King of Britain and Ireland at Scone; Scots invade England and are defeated at the battle of Worcester; Charles II flees to the Continent

1651 Failed Anglo-Dutch negotiation for a federal union of the two republics

1651 English Navigation Ordinances aimed at Dutch carrying trade

1651 Publication of Thomas Hobbes's *Leviathan*

1652 First Anglo-Dutch War breaks out (ends 1654)

1652 The Act of Settlement threatens to expropriate most Irish landowners and to confine the Catholic population in the western fastnesses of Connaught between the Shannon and the Atlantic; it is partially realized

1653 Cromwell dissolves the Rump Parliament

1653 The Army Council summonses a constituent assembly of 144 hand-picked men to prepare a longer-term settlement of the nations of Britain and Ireland (July); the Assembly resigns power back into Cromwell's hands (Dec.); he is installed as Lord Protector under *The Instrument of Government*

1655 Failure of a major Royalist attempt to overthrow Cromwell (Penruddock's Rising); Cromwell appoints the Major Generals

1655 Cromwell dispatches army and naval forces to capture Hispaniola: it fails, but captures Jamaica instead

1656 Cromwell declares war on Spain and makes a treaty with France

1656 Persecution of the Quakers peaks with public torture of James Nayler, convicted by Parliament of 'horrid blasphemy'

1657 Cromwell declines a parliamentary invitation to become King but accepts a revised paper constitution—*The Humble Petition and Advice*

1658 Death of Cromwell

1659 Collapse of the Republic; restoration of the Rump; political and military disintegration; the year ends in anarchy

1660 The General in charge of the Army in Scotland, George Monck, marches south, occupies London, and calls free elections; the resulting Parliament (the Convention) initially plans to recall Charles II on terms but after Charles II's Declaration from Breda (which promises to leave all disputed issues to be settled by Parliament) Charles is recalled unconditionally

1660 Restoration of CHARLES II and moderate settlement approved by the Convention

1661 Savoy conference between Anglicans and Presbyterians fails to produce compromise on forms of worship

1661 New Parliament seeks a more partisan Cavalier and Anglican settlement

1662 Act of Uniformity restores Anglican church order and worship 'lock, stock and barrel'; Charles II's attempts to secure liberty for tender consciences by prerogative action stymied

1662 Charles II establishes the Royal Society by royal charter

1664 First Conventicle Act lays penalties on those attending illegal Protestant services other than those established by law in the Act of Uniformity

1664 Second Dutch War (ends 1667)

1665 Great Plague hits London (and Eyam); Five Mile Act bans the clergy who resigned/were ejected in 1662 from living in or even visiting their former parishes

1666 Great Fire of London destroys much of the city

1667 English fleet destroyed (battle of the Medway)

1667 Publication of John Milton's *Paradise Lost*

1667 Lord Chancellor Clarendon goes into exile under threat of impeachment

1670 Secret Treaty of Dover, for Anglo-Dutch alliance to dismantle the Netherlands and for French help to assist Charles remain in power after declaring himself a Catholic

1670 Second Conventicle Act increases penalties on those attending illegal Protestant services other than those established by law in the Act of Uniformity

1671 Publication of Jane Sharp's *The Midwives Book*, the only such book written by a practising midwife in the early modern period

1672 Third Dutch War (ends 1674)

1672 Charles II issues the Declaration of Indulgence permitting Dissenters to hold licences to worship outside the Anglican Church

1673 Parliament pressures the King to withdraw the Declaration and passes the First Test Act, imposing new and stringent oaths designed to prevent Catholics from remaining in public office

1674 Corn Bounties introduced as England enters new era as net exporter of grain

1677 Marriage of James, Duke of York's elder daughter Mary to William of Orange, Stadtholder of the Netherlands

1678 Publication of John Bunyan's *Pilgrim's Progress*

1678 Titus Oates launches the Popish Plot

1679 Danby impeached; the Exclusion Crisis breaks

1681 Charles's opponents overreach themselves; popular concern about the Popish Plot wanes; Charles launches 'the Tory reaction'

1683 The Rye House Plot, an assassination plot, fails and costs the lives of several leading republicans, including Algernon Sidney

1685 Death of CHARLES II and accession of JAMES II (of England and Ireland) and VII (of Scotland); Rebellions of the Duke of Monmouth (south-west England) and Earl of Argyll (south-west Scotland) brutally suppressed

1686 James launches programme to achieve full religious and civil equality for Catholics; Anglicans protest and refuse to co-operate

1687 James attempts to 'woo the Whigs'—appoints them to office, begins campaign to pack Parliament with supporters of religious liberty, issues Declaration of Indulgence

1687 Publication of Isaac Newton's *Philosophiae naturalis principia mathematica*

1688 Seven Bishops tried for claiming the King's Declaration of Indulgence was illegal; they are acquitted of the charge of seditious libel

1688 James and his wife have a son after eleven years of marriage, opening up the prospect of a Catholic dynasty

1688 William of Orange invades England to procure a free Parliament, an Anglo-Dutch military alliance against Louis XIV, and a public inquiry into the legitimacy of the Prince of Wales; James flees to France

1689 The Convention declares that James's flight is an act of abdication, that the throne is vacant, and invites WILLIAM and MARY to be joint rulers; the Scottish Parliament deposes James for tyranny

1689 The Convention Parliament passes the Bill of Rights to prevent William III from governing like James II; it does not stop him governing like William III

1689 Toleration Act grants pusillanimous rights of free religious assembly but no civil equality to Protestant Dissenters

1689 John Locke's influential *Letter Concerning Toleration* published

Maps and Family Tree

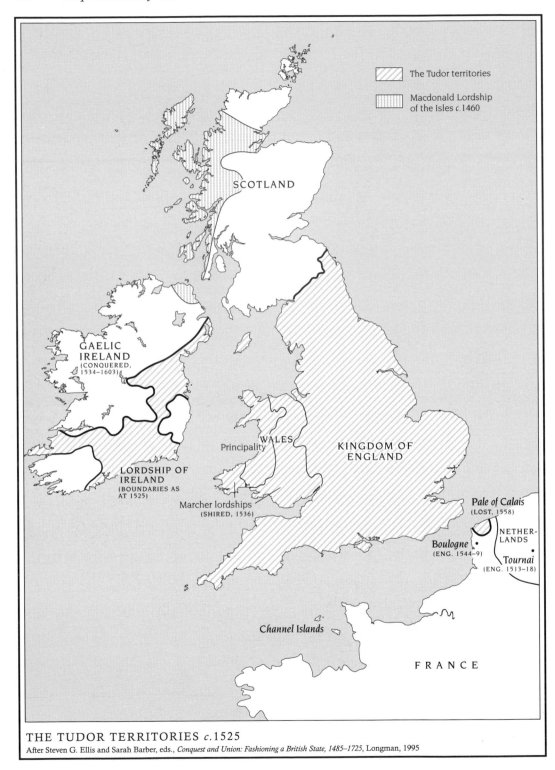

SCOTLAND

GAELIC
IRELAND
(CONQUERED,
1534–1603)

LORDSHIP OF
IRELAND
(BOUNDARIES AS
AT 1525)

WALES
Principality

KINGDOM OF
ENGLAND

Marcher lordships
(SHIRED, 1536)

Pale of Calais
(LOST, 1558)

NETHER-
LANDS

Boulogne
(ENG. 1544–9)

Tournai
(ENG. 1513–18)

Channel Islands

FRANCE

The Tudor territories

Macdonald Lordship
of the Isles *c.* 1460

THE TUDOR TERRITORIES *c.*1525

After Steven G. Ellis and Sarah Barber, eds., *Conquest and Union: Fashioning a British State, 1485–1725*, Longman, 1995

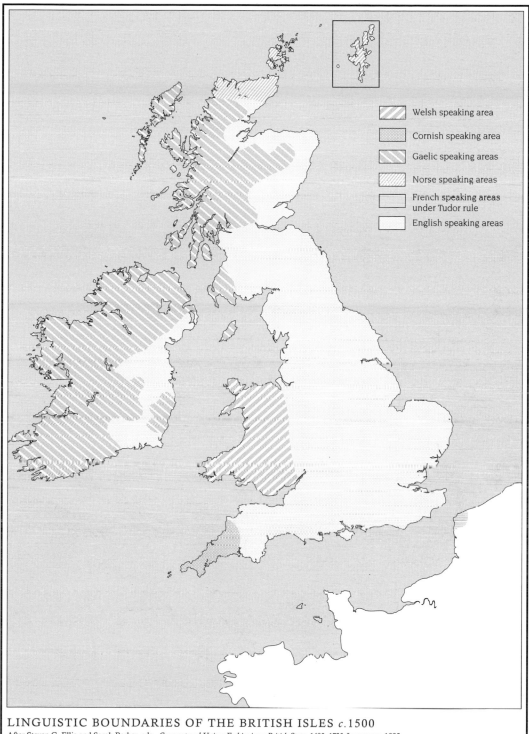

LINGUISTIC BOUNDARIES OF THE BRITISH ISLES *c*.1500

After Steven G. Ellis and Sarah Barber, eds., *Conquest and Union: Fashioning a British State, 1485–1725*, Longman, 1995

The legend of the map reads:

- Welsh speaking area
- Cornish speaking area
- Gaelic speaking areas
- Norse speaking areas
- French speaking areas under Tudor rule
- English speaking areas

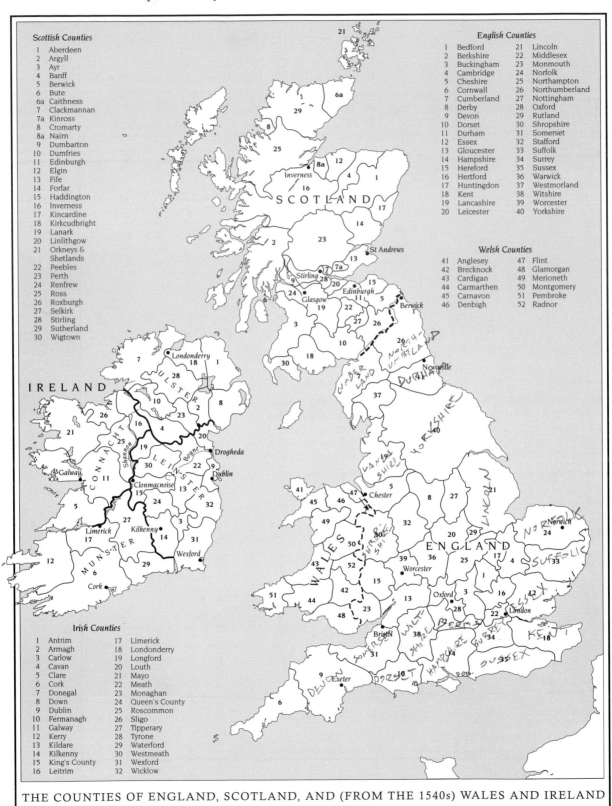

Scottish Counties

1 Aberdeen
2 Argyll
3 Ayr
4 Banff
5 Berwick
6 Bute
6a Caithness
7 Clackmannan
7a Kinross
8 Cromarty
8a Nairn
9 Dumbarton
10 Dumfries
11 Edinburgh
12 Elgin
13 Fife
14 Forfar
15 Haddington
16 Inverness
17 Kincardine
18 Kirkcudbright
19 Lanark
20 Linlithgow
21 Orkneys & Shetlands
22 Peebles
23 Perth
24 Renfrew
25 Ross
26 Roxburgh
27 Selkirk
28 Stirling
29 Sutherland
30 Wigtown

English Counties

1 Bedford
2 Berkshire
3 Buckingham
4 Cambridge
5 Cheshire
6 Cornwall
7 Cumberland
8 Derby
9 Devon
10 Dorset
11 Durham
12 Essex
13 Gloucester
14 Hampshire
15 Hereford
16 Hertford
17 Huntingdon
18 Kent
19 Lancashire
20 Leicester
21 Lincoln
22 Middlesex
23 Monmouth
24 Norfolk
25 Northampton
26 Northumberland
27 Nottingham
28 Oxford
29 Rutland
30 Shropshire
31 Somerset
32 Stafford
33 Suffolk
34 Surrey
35 Sussex
36 Warwick
37 Westmorland
38 Wiltshire
39 Worcester
40 Yorkshire

Welsh Counties

41 Anglesey
42 Brecknock
43 Cardigan
44 Carmarthen
45 Carnavon
46 Denbigh
47 Flint
48 Glamorgan
49 Merioneth
50 Montgomery
51 Pembroke
52 Radnor

Irish Counties

1 Antrim
2 Armagh
3 Carlow
4 Cavan
5 Clare
6 Cork
7 Donegal
8 Down
9 Dublin
10 Fermanagh
11 Galway
12 Kerry
13 Kildare
14 Kilkenny
15 King's County
16 Leitrim
17 Limerick
18 Londonderry
19 Longford
20 Louth
21 Mayo
22 Meath
23 Monaghan
24 Queen's County
25 Roscommon
26 Sligo
27 Tipperary
28 Tyrone
29 Waterford
30 Westmeath
31 Wexford
32 Wicklow

THE COUNTIES OF ENGLAND, SCOTLAND, AND (FROM THE 1540s) WALES AND IRELAND

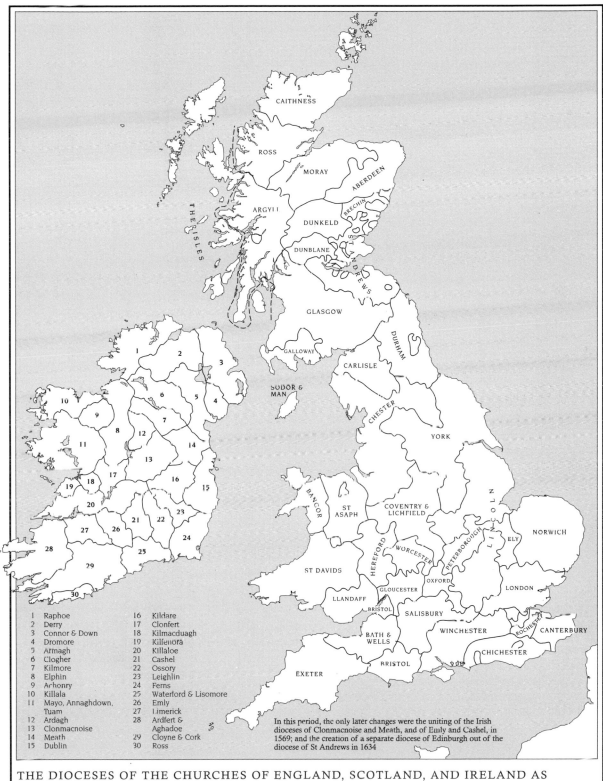

1	Raphoe	16	Kildare
2	Derry	17	Clonfert
3	Connor & Down	18	Kilmacduagh
4	Dromore	19	Kilfenora
5	Armagh	20	Killaloe
6	Clogher	21	Cashel
7	Kilmore	22	Ossory
8	Elphin	23	Leighlin
9	Achonry	24	Ferns
10	Killala	25	Waterford & Lisomore
11	Mayo, Annaghdown, Tuam	26	Emly
12	Ardagh	27	Limerick
13	Clonmacnoise	28	Ardfert & Aghadoe
14	Meath	29	Cloyne & Cork
15	Dublin	30	Ross

In this period, the only later changes were the uniting of the Irish dioceses of Clonmacnoise and Meath, and of Emly and Cashel, in 1569; and the creation of a separate diocese of Edinburgh out of the diocese of St Andrews in 1634

THE DIOCESES OF THE CHURCHES OF ENGLAND, SCOTLAND, AND IRELAND AS CONFIRMED IN 1559/60

The Royal Houses of England (1485–1603), Scotland (1473–1603), and Great Britain (1603–1727)

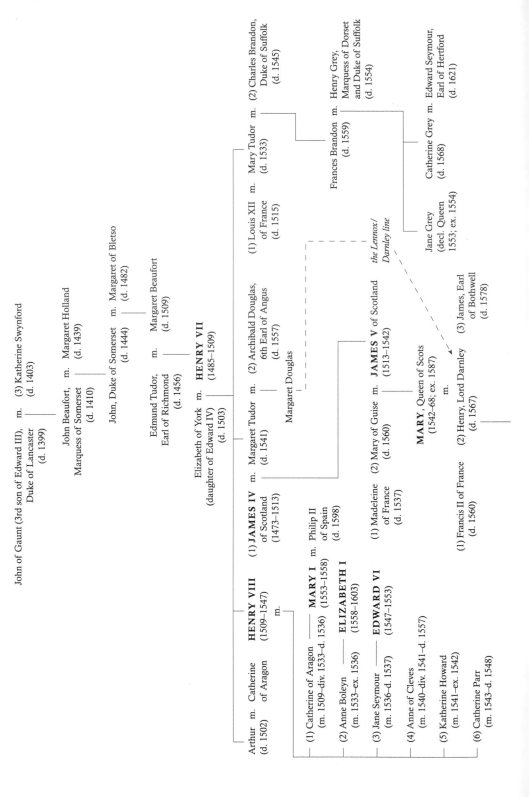

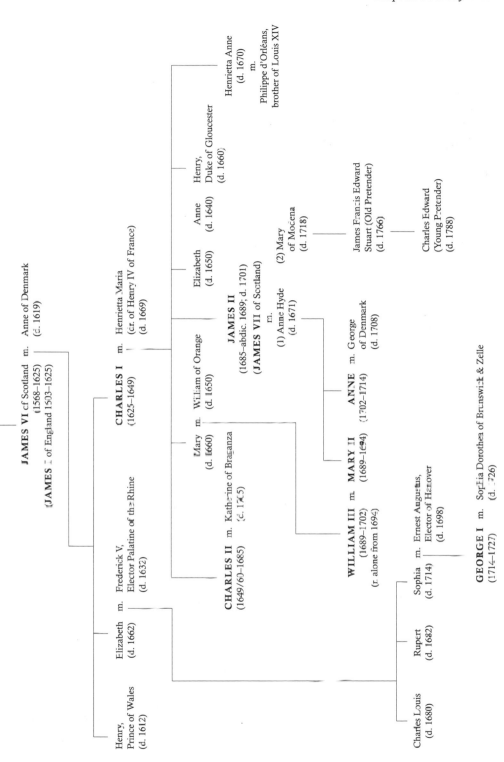

LIST OF PICTURE SOURCES

The editor and publishers wish to thank the following who have kindly given permission to reproduce the illustrations on the following pages:

British Library 532 a 1; **220** British Museum; **222–3** Museum of London; **223** (*bottom*) British Library G7884 fii–12; **227** Royal Collection Enterprises; **228** British Library C18 d. 2; **230** National Portrait Gallery, London; **233** Pinacoteca Nazionale, Siena (photo: Scala); **235** British Library MS Roy 18AXLV111; **237** Staatliche Museen, Kassel; **239** Fotomas Index; **242** British Library c. 175 ff21; **245** British Library C700h2; **246** (*top*) A. F. Kersting, (*bottom*) John Bethell/Bridgeman Art Library; **248** Gemaldegalerie, Dresden (photo: AKG Berlin); **250** Mansell Collection; **251** Mansell Collection; **252** British Museum; **254–5** © Museum of London (photo: Bridgeman Art Library); **256** National Portrait Gallery, London; **259** Robert Harding Picture Library; **260** A. F. Kersting; **261** © Sonia Halliday Photographs; **263** Cambridge University Library; **265** British Library; **268** Frick Collection, New York (photo: Bridgeman Art Library); **269** National Portrait Gallery, London; **270** Thyssen-Bornemisza Collection (photo: Bridgeman Art Library); **272** Bodleian Library MS. Douce 363. fol. 71; **273** National Portrait Gallery, London; **274** Collection of the Earl of Pembroke, Wilton House (photo: Bridgeman Art Library); **276** Arthur Fryer, Almonry Museum, Evesham; **278** Fotomas Index; **281** Thomas Photos, Oxford; **282** A. F. Kersting; **285** Victoria & Albert Museum, London; **287** © Ashmolean Museum, Hope Collection; **291** British Library BL 768877; **294** A. F. Kersting; **299** British Library 852g 10–0opp; **301** Mary Evans Picture Library; **302** Mansell Collection; **304** (*and inset*) National Trust Photographic Library/P. Lacey; **306** British Library; **307** Mansell Collection; **311** National Portrait Gallery, London; **313** Angelo Hornak Library; **315** Fitzwilliam Museum, Cambridge (photo: Bridgeman Art Library); **316** Fotomas Index; **319** National Portrait Gallery, London; **321** Christie's Colour Library; **322** National Portrait Gallery, London; **323** National Portrait Gallery, Edinburgh (photo: Bridgeman Art Library); **326** (*left and right*) National Portrait Gallery, London; **328–9** Fotomas Index; **331** National Portrait Gallery, Edinburgh; **334** Public Record Office; **335** British Library 523 a 2; **336** National Portrait Gallery, London; **339** British Library; **340** National Maritime Museum, Greenwich; **343** Woodmansterne; **344** National Gallery of Art, Washington; **347** © Marquess of Salisbury; **348** National Library of Scotland; **349** British Tourist Authority; **350** © Marquess of Salisbury (photo: Courtauld Institute); **352** National Portrait Gallery, London; **353** Society of Antiquaries, London; **354** National Maritime Museum, Greenwich; **356** The Folger Shakespeare Library, Washington; **358** Royal Collection Enterprises; **363** National Maritime Museum, Greenwich; **364** A. F. Kersting; **366** A. F. Kersting; **368** British Library E1533; **369** British Museum BMC 220; **370** British Library E1175 (3); **371** British Museum 305950; **374–5** British Library C107 K9; **375** (*bottom*) Fotomas Index; **376** British Library 669 f 16 (32); **378** British Library E833/14; **380** British Museum 50561; **383** National Portrait Gallery, London; **386** National Portrait Gallery, London; **389** British Museum 82542/2/5; **391** British Museum 50361/2; **392** By courtesy of Oxford City Council; **394** (*top*) British Museum, (*bottom*) Mansell Collection; **395** British Museum 1688–1186/2215; **398** British Library MS Cotton Aug. I ii 57; **399** Royal Collection Enterprises; **402–3** Royal Collection Enterprises; **405** Courtauld Institute; **406** Rijksmuseum Stichting, Amsterdam; **408** (*left*) Rijksmuseum Stichting, Amsterdam, (*right*) Nelson-Atkins Museum of Art; **410** Fotomas Index; **411** Public Record Office; **414** Fotomas Index; **417** National Portrait Gallery, London; **418** Range/Bettmann; **419** Victoria & Albert Musuem, London (photo: Bridgeman Art Library); **421** Range/Bettmann; **424** Fotomas Index; **425** Fotomas Index; **427** Maidstone Museum & Art Gallery, Kent (photo: Bridgeman Art Library); **428** National Portrait Gallery, London.

In a few instances we have been unable to trace the copyright-holder prior to publication. If notified, the publishers will be pleased to amend the acknowledgements in any future edition.

Picture research by Gill Metcalfe.

INDEX

In this index, numbers in *italics* indicate references to the black and white illustrations and their captions; an asterisk indicates references to colour illustrations *facing* the page number given; and numbers contained in angled brackets < > indicate items defined on that page as part of the glossary. Life dates of individuals, including English and Scottish monarchs, are given wherever possible (in parentheses). However, regnal years—without parentheses—are given in the case of continental European rulers (including popes), in the hope that readers will find these more useful. The regnal years of British rulers can be found in the Family Tree on pp. 466–7. There are no index references to the Chronology, Family Tree, or Maps.